THE INTERNATIONAL CITY MANAGERS' ASSOCIATION

Municipal Management Series

THE TECHNIQUE OF
MUNICIPAL ADMINISTRATION

MUNICIPAL MANAGEMENT SERIES

THE TECHNIQUE OF
MUNICIPAL ADMINISTRATION

Fourth Edition, 1958

Published for the Institute for Training
in Municipal Administration by
THE INTERNATIONAL CITY MANAGERS' ASSOCIATION
1313 EAST 60 STREET
CHICAGO, ILLINOIS

FOREWORD

The Technique of Municipal Administration is one of a series of ten volumes on municipal administration published by the International City Managers' Association. With the exception of this volume and the two new texts, Supervisory Methods in Municipal Administration and Management Practices for Smaller Cities, each volume deals with one field of municipal administration. The exceptions are texts designed to serve more than one departmental area. Each of the ten books is a complete and separate treatise.

The nature and approach of this series can best be explained by a brief review of its origin and development. In 1934 the International City Managers' Association received the first of several special grants from the Spelman Fund of New York for the preparation and administration of in-service training courses for municipal officials at the administrative or management level. This training program has been developed by the Association through its Institute for Training in Municipal Administration.

In its early years the Institute confined its training activities solely to training by the correspondence course method. This of course required the preparation of study materials. It was soon discovered that the published texts available were not suitable for the kind of training for which the Institute was established. It was necessary, therefore, for the Institute to prepare its own training texts, and by 1941 eight texts had been published; all eight have been revised several times.

Some of these volumes were prepared under the direction of a single editor or compiler; others are the product of many contributors. All, however, have drawn heavily from the experiences of practical administrators, and all have been subjected to the tempering fire of many critics selected from among outstanding administrators, consultants, and students of municipal administration.

During the first seven years after the Institute was established the texts were made available only in connection with enrollment in its correspondence courses. It soon became apparent, however, that this restrictive policy required modification to meet two new demands. First, there was a demand for these texts for use in connection with group training projects, including both in-service training for public officials and pre-entry training provided by colleges and universities. Second, there was an increasingly insistent demand that these texts be made available as reference volumes for public officials and students of local government. Early in 1941 this demand was acknowledged by a lifting of the ban on the sale of these unique training texts and they were made available for purchase through the International City Managers' Association.

Prior to the present year the Association offered eight training courses. In 1958 a new course was made available, Management Practices for Smaller Cities, for in-service training of mayors, managers, city clerks, public service directors, and other administrative officials. The course in Supervisory Methods in Municipal Administration, also offered for the first time in 1958, represented a change in policy of the Institute — a change designed to meet a long-felt need. The supervisory training is aimed not at improving the work of the administrator but at refining the ability of supervisory personnel to work effectively toward organizational goals while serving with understanding in the task of directing employees. The course for supervisors includes several innovations: two sound film strips, supplementary printed material, and case studies.

The two distinguishing features of the volumes in this series are traceable directly to their origin. First, they approach municipal problems from the point of view of top-level administrators — city managers, department heads, and their principal aides. Supervisory Methods in Municipal Administration is of special interest to the top echelon of city administrators in their capacity as supervisors, although it is designed primarily to aid the lower echelons of leadership. Second, because they were prepared as the basis for training courses, the emphasis in these volumes is on the "how" rather than the "what" of municipal administration. They are not intended as detailed manuals or as expositions of model systems of administration, but their objective is to help the administrator analyze his duties and responsibilities and to suggest approaches and methods that other administrators have proved by actual experience.

These texts during the past 24 years have established their value both as training manuals and as reference manuals. They are widely used by universities and colleges in courses in municipal administration, particularly at the graduate level. They also are used as the basic texts in group in-service training classes for city hall administrative personnel. Finally, the chief administrators and department heads of many local governments use the ten books in the series as guides in solving local problems.

Orin F. Nolting, Director
International City Managers' Association

Chicago
March, 1958

PREFACE

In every local government there is a management job to be done. If public services are to be administered both democratically and efficiently, someone must assume responsibility for planning, organizing, coordinating, and controlling the administrative machinery. In most municipalities there is a chief administrative official — mayor, city manager, city clerk, or whatever his title may be — who is charged with the responsibility for managing the city's administrative services. In some cities management powers and responsibilities are shared by several officials. But regardless of the form of government or the distribution of responsibility, the functions of management are being performed — either well or poorly. The purpose of this volume is to define the job of management in municipal administration and to suggest techniques and practices which will help municipal officials in management positions to carry out their duties effectively.

There may be some who contend that management is an art too subtle to be defined and too personal to lend itself to instruction. But difficult as the task is, it is not impossible. Beneath the superficial differences in the positions and the apparent nonconformity in techniques, careful analysis reveals that "over-all administration" or management, has certain common characteristics wherever it is found, and that although the techniques of management may vary in detail, they are based upon common approaches to administrative problems.

No attempt has been made in this volume to define in detail the duties and responsibilities of a "model" municipal administrator or to prescribe an assortment of guaranteed techniques which will work wonders in any city under all circumstances. What has been attempted is an analysis of the functions of management, an indication of the scope of management in municipal administration, and suggestions, by way of illustration, of some of the techniques that the experience of successful administrators has proved to be most useful.

This is a book for the chief administrator, but it is more than that. Many of the principles and practices set forth are relevant to the task of managing a single department, and department heads may profit from a familiarity with them. In addition, students of public administration will find here a local-level reflection of current theory and practice in the broader field of general public administration. Previous editions have been widely used by colleges and universities.

The first edition published in 1940 pioneered in defining the management job in municipal administration. At that time there were no standard duties and responsibilities assigned to the chief administrator, but in the intervening years the rise of the appointed executive and the strong mayor have resulted in some standardization of the role of the chief administrative officer. In later editions published in 1945 and 1947 the suggested role and techniques of the chief administrative officer were modified to incorporate lessons learned from the use of the text in training municipal administrators. In the present edition there is a new chapter on administrative research and planning, the function of city planning has been set out in a chapter of its own, discussion of the theory of organization has been revised toward a more flexible approach to "principles" of organization, several chapters have been consolidated or expanded, and the entire volume revised to incorporate new developments since 1947 when the third edition was issued.

For preparation or revision of one or more chapters grateful acknowledgement is made to: Robert L. Funk, Assistant Director, Municipal Finance Officers Association, for sections on finance and programming of municipal services; Professor A. M. Hillhouse, Graduate School of Business and Public Administration, Cornell University, for the chapter on administrative measurement; Selden G. Kent and John M. Urie, Division of Research and Budget, City of Phoenix, Arizona, for material on administrative research and planning; G. M. Morris, Associate Director, Public Administration Service, for the chapter on organization; Keith Ocheltree, Senior Staff Assistant, Public Personnel Association, for the chapter on personnel administration; Dennis O'Harrow, Executive Director, American Society of Planning Officials, for the chapter on city planning; Charles S. Rhyne, General Counsel, National Institute of Municipal Law Officers, for the chapter on legal services and regulatory procedures; Peter P. Schauffler, Assistant Director, Department of Commerce, City of Philadelphia, for the chapter on the techniques of direction; Ralph L. Snyder, Village Manager, Highland Park, Illinois, for the chapter on the relation of the administrator to council and other agencies; and Donald C. Wagner, Managing Director, City of Philadelphia, for the chapter on the role of the administrator. We are also indebted to several well-known authorities in the field of public administration for significant contributions they made in writing or revising one or more chapters in the earlier editions. Among these authorities are Louis Bronwlow, the late Clarence A. Dykstra, Herbert Emmerich, C. A. Harrell, the late Lyman S. Moore, Clarence E. Ridley, Herbert A. Simon, and Donald C. Stone. The editing of this edition was the responsibility of Jeptha J. Carrell, Director of Training of the International City Managers' Association.

Unpublished material and correspondence was used in the preparation of this volume, as well as materials in many published reports and pamphlets for which credit has been given in the text. For all statements of fact and opinion the Institute, of course, assumes full responsibility.

Chicago   Institute For Training In
March, 1958   Municipal Administration

TABLE OF CONTENTS

LIST OF FIGURES AND TABLES

Chapter 1

THE ROLE OF THE ADMINISTRATOR

The role of the chief administrative officer of a city is that of marshalling the resources of the city government to carry out in an efficient manner the program determined upon by the city's elected officials, both legislative and executive. This job of "administering" is present whenever a group of human beings get together to accomplish a task. It is not limited to any particular historical period, nor to any special place, nor to any single type of governmental organization. The emphasis placed on administration varies, however, in different settings, and recent years have seen administration become an increasingly important part of the governmental process.

The Emergence of Administration

The importance of administration in city government today, and the highly technical and complex nature of the administrator's job, are a reflection of the changes that have taken place in cities in the past century: notably the growth in number of services provided by the city government and changes in city life.

Growth of City Services

It is a far cry from the night watch, which at the turn of the 19th century patrolled the streets of Boston and halted every hour to inform the citizenry that all was well, to the city police department of the 20th century; from the pump and well beside each village house to the farflung water system of the modern metropolis; from no organization for public health purposes to the many activities of a city health department today.

Even a brief listing of some of the new functions of city government for the last two decades alone serves to indicate the striking degree of growth and change: development of industrial districts; urban renewal plans; preventive mental health programs; alcoholism counseling programs; performance budgeting; electronic traffic controls; machine processing of criminal records; radio control of emergency vehicles; inspection of swimming pools; infant welfare services; dental health programs; clinics for pre-natal care; homemakers services; installation of safety zones; community centers; playgrounds; golf courses; skating rinks; swimming pools; airports; heliports; incineration of rubbish; snow removal; fluoridation; mercury vapor street lighting; expressways; microfilming of vital records; machine accounting; air pollution control; rodent and insect control; sewage treatment.

Changes in City Life

Municipal functions have not only increased but have also changed in character. Modern science has made community services — sewage treatment, criminal identification and the treatment of mental disease for example, increasingly more technical and less intelligible to the public. Consequently, there has been a greater reliance on specialized services and this has accentuated the importance of administration. These significant changes in the extent and character of municipal functions may be ascribed to a number of factors which are more or less interrelated:

1. The proportion of urban population in the total United States population has increased from 28.6 per cent in 1880 to approximately 64 per cent in 1956. This transition from rural to urban living requires the performance of many functions on a community basis. Such services as supplying water, disposing of waste and providing police and fire protection are no longer individual responsibilities.

2. In the past several decades there has not only been a steady movement of population from rural areas to cities but also a counter movement of people from the central core of cities to the suburbs. These movements of population have resulted in the creation of densely populated metropolitan areas which in 1955 contained approximately 76 per cent of the total urban population. This concentration of population in metropolitan areas has created many challenging problems, such as traffic control and air pollution control.

3. The rapid formation of many small governmental units has made the task of providing adequate services by each of these jurisdictions more challenging. In order to provide required services in an efficient , economic manner many of these jurisdictions have entered into intergovernment agreements. These agreements have taken many forms: authorities; consolidation; special districts; agreement by a community to service an adjoining community; and, in a few instances, the creation of an over-all metropolitan government.

4. There has also been a movement of industry from the cities to the less populated areas. To counteract this movement, cities have initiated programs of industrial redevelopment. These programs are aimed at attracting only those industries which would strengthen the economic base of the community.

5. Modern science has made possible the performance of many functions that are clearly of community interest but could not formerly be performed because of lack of knowledge. One example is in the field of public health where many large cities have already recognized the need for a preventive mental health program.

In the midst of these developments there has risen a concept in municipal government in which emphasis has shifted from a "police" to a "service" and "regulatory" concept. Where government was once asked to do little more than protect the life and property of each individual, it is now expected to render a multitude of services which the individual would be unable to procure for himself. In addition, municipal government is called upon to regulate many private activities in the interest of public welfare and safety. These include not only zoning, licensing, and inspection activities, but also land development and urban renewal to benefit the entire community.

Increased Importance of Administration

The end result of this development of municipal functions has been to increase the importance and technical character of administration in municipal government. Legislative problems are of no less magnitude than in an earlier period — a city council must be prepared to deal with weighty questions of public safety and welfare when it determines a city policy for housing, health services, policing and the like. Nevertheless, these basic policy questions are interwoven with technical issues that require the attention of specially trained persons for their satisfactory solution.

The central questions of city government in a modern democracy have come to be: how can the actual administration of the city's complex services be delegated to persons who are competent for the job without sacrificing control by the public over the policies followed by its "servants"; how can the legislative body, in laying down the general lines of policy, secure the technical assistance and advice it needs in order to make wise decisions; and how can municipal administrators assure themselves of obtaining and keeping the technical personnel to properly meet the demands of the service?

The "bridge" which is needed between the policy forming and administrative activities of government is provided in the structure of most American city governments by the office of "chief administrator" — the mayor or the chief administrator under the mayor in mayor-council cities, or the city manager in council-manager cities. His is the task of making certain that the administrative work of government is carried on at a high level of competence, that the democratic controls over policy imposed by the city council and the mayor are transmitted to administrative employees, and that the city council and the mayor receive adequate advice on the technical implications of their decisions. It is the purpose of the present volume to discuss these tasks of the chief administrator in city government and to suggest techniques which will be helpful to him in performing successfully his highly difficult and complex job.

But why *one* man? Why insist that there should be a single bridge between policy formation and administration, a bridge at which all the numerous administrative activities of the city find a common meeting place? No better answer has been given than the one offered some years ago by a man who himself had spent 20 years in the chief executive position of an American city. His answer, though directed specifically to city managers, applies with equal force to the mayor and chief administrative officer in mayor-council cities:

"Why, then, do we have city managers? The answer is that a governmental organization (or any other organization for that matter) isn't just a lot of people who are busy doing different jobs. Nor is it just a collection of different programs — health programs, police programs, public works programs — each designed to meet some public need. Rather, an organization is a group of people who are working *together* on a number of different programs, all of which are related to each other. But cooperative effort isn't produced by spontaneous combustion. People don't just work together. They have to be brought together and kept together. That is why we have managers — to fit people, and agencies, and programs together so that each supports the other. And this means private persons, and agencies, and programs as well as public. The city administration is only one part of the broader community organization, and it is the manager's job to achieve effective cooperation among all of the organizations and programs within the community."[1]

Scope of the Administrator's Job

The administrative officials of a city do not pave the city's streets, put out the city's fires, or capture the city's criminals — laborers, firemen, and policemen are hired to do that. Nevertheless, the reason why there is a chief administrative officer is to make

---

[1] Frank L. Cloud, "Management Through Cooperation," Public Management, November, 1942 (Chicago: International City Managers' Association), p. 324.

certain that the persons who are responsible for performing these very tangible and definite services do their work well — better than it would be done without him. His job is one of influencing other people, and his time is largely taken up with personal contacts — either face-to-face contacts or written communications. When 21 city managers kept for a week a daily record of time spent on different activities, they reported an average work week of 54 hours. On the basis of a six-day week, their average nine-hour day was distributed as follows:

> Talking with citizens in office and over telephone — 2 hours
> Conferences with department heads — $1\frac{1}{2}$ hours
> Planning current activities and future work — 1 hour
> Handling correspondence — 1 hour
> Formal and informal meetings with city council — 50 minutes
> Inspecting municipal activities — 50 minutes
> Attending meetings and talking before various groups — 40 minutes
> Preparing official reports — 30 minutes
> Interviewing candidates for positions — 20 minutes
> Miscellaneous — 20 minutes

More important, however, than the number of hours the executive spends telephoning, conferring, writing, and reading , is the question of what he says and hears on the telephone and in conferences and what he writes and reads in letters and memoranda. The core of the manager's job lies in the guidance and direction which he gives to the works of the city government.

It may be desirable to define the chief administrator's job by marking out a boundary line between the administrator and the legislative body. However, in practice this is one of the most difficult tasks facing the administrator. On the other hand, the boundary between the administrator and the departments which he controls can be more readily defined. These two boundaries form the subject of discussion in the next two sections of this chapter.

Policy and Administration

Early theorists held that the legislative body should make "policy" decisions, while the executive should make "administrative" decisions. This distinction between policy and administration was based on the fact that two strikingly different elements enter into any practical decision. One of these is the "why judgment," in which are reflected the *ends* (or they may be called objectives, aims, or values) at which the decision is directed. "Why" judgments are concerned with the goals to be accomplished.

The second element of decision is the "how judgment," which is concerned with the *means* to be used in attaining the desired ends. "How" judgments are based on research, experience, and expert knowledge which make it possible to predict the probable results and effectiveness of the procedures used in reaching these goals.

Governmental organizations frequently have been designed with the idea of having one agency, the legislature (city council), make the decisions as to ends upon the basis of "why judgments" and another, the administration, make the decisions as to means upon the basis of "how judgments." The implication behind this theory of organization is that there are two kinds of decisions each involving only one of two factors. Actually, this is not the case. There are not two kinds of decisions each involving one factor — but one kind of decision involving two factors, although to varying degrees in particular cases.

It is impossible to classify any but extremely minute decisions as purely subjective "why judgments" or purely objective "how judgments." Therefore, while any decision involves these elements of "why" and "how," it is not ordinarily possible to break the decision into separate determinations of "ends" and "means" which will correspond with the "why" and "how" elements respectively. In order to understand more clearly the intimate relationships in any practical governmental problem between judgments of "why" and "how," it will be helpful to analyze the issues that arise in the construction of a new street. It is necessary to determine: (1) is a new street needed? (2) how does it fit into the city plan? (3) what kind of pavement should it have, what should its width be, etc.? (4) should the project be financed by operating revenue, assessments, a bond issue or a combination of all three? (5) should the project be let on contract or done by the city's own working force?

First, these decisions must be made in terms of the aims of the street construction program: the transportation system is intended to conserve the time of the city's inhabitants in transporting themselves and their goods from place to place; in doing so it must keep accident hazards at a minimum; it must provide smooth pavements for riding comfort and reduce wear and tear on motor vehicles; these advantages must be balanced against the cost to taxpayers of providing them; and finally, the principles of equity to be used in distributing tax burdens must be agreed upon. Each of these items is a part of the larger question: why should the street be built?

Second, these decisions must be made in the light of scientific and practical knowledge as to the effect which particular measures will have in realizing these objectives: possible routes will be studied to determine their cost and their time savings for commercial and passenger traffic; the relative smoothness, permanence, and cost of various types of pavement will be investigated; the total cost and distribution of cost will be computed for alternative means of financing (sinking fund, special assessment, etc.). Each of these items is part of the broad question: how can the street be built?

Of course, when a city sets about to build a street the decisions are not always chopped up into their parts in the exact fashion illustrated above. Regardless of whether these individual items are expressly considered or not, every one of them is at least implicitly involved in the construction project — and it might well be argued that if they are not always made explicit, they usually should be. The final decision about such a project depends, then, upon the relative weight which is given to the different aims of the project, and on knowledge as to the extent to which any proposed plan will attain these aims.

Should Authority Be Divided?

If it were possible to separate legislative from administrative action at the point where the "why" leaves off and the "how" begins, how could this be accomplished? It has sometimes been thought that this specialization could be brought about by a "separation of powers" — by dividing authority between legislative and administrative agencies — giving the former authority to determine "why" judgments, the latter authority to determine "how" judgments. "Authority" means the right, in case of a disagreement, to have the last word. If two agencies disagree, then the one with "authority" makes the final decision.

Division of authority, however, has not proved a workable basis for distinguishing the administrative from the legislative role. One reason for its failure has already been seen. In a practical situation, the "why" and the "how" elements are intermingled. Thus, returning to the illustration of a street construction project, it will be seen that the actual questions which must be decided, e.g., the design of the street, the means of financing, etc., involve both "why" and "how" elements. To separate these elements so that they could be decided by different agencies would require an elaborate and generally impracticable logical analysis of each such question. Therefore, if the legislature is to make all "why" judgments, it will of necessity make many "how" judgments as well. On the other hand, since even the most minute administrative action may involve "why" elements, the administrator must of necessity make many "why" decisions. The line of separation of the tasks of the legislator and administrator will not, and cannot, coincide exactly with the line that has been drawn between "why" and "how." Furthermore, the division must be put on some other basis than authority.

The primary reason for providing for legislative rather than administrative decision of important matters is to assure democratic control over the activities of government. Unlike questions of execution, policy questions cannot be decided by only finding "what the facts are." The democratic determinant of the "why" judgment is to find out "what the people want" by having them elect their representatives. The initiative, referendum, and recall have been devised to supplement these periodic procedures for assuring popular control.

In a democratic society there is reserved to the legislative body the right to review the work of the administrative officers carrying out its wishes, in order to make sure that the job is being satisfactorily done. Authority (i.e., "the last word"), therefore, must always lie with popularly elected officials, and these cannot surrender their final authority without abrogating the democratic rights of the people.

For two reasons, then, to divide final authority between legislature and an appointed administrator is impossible. First, granting ultimate authority to decide any question to the administrator is a renunciation of democratic principles. Of course, a very great number of decisions will actually be made by the administrator, but the legislative body always must retain the right to review, when it wishes, any one of these decisions. Second, in practical situations, the "why" and "how" elements of problems cannot usually be allocated to separate agencies for formal decision.

The Division of Work

If "division of authority" does not afford a satisfactory basis for distinguishing the work of legislature and administrator, then this distinction must be found in a "division of work." The legislature can delegate to the administrator, subject to final control and review, those matters which it feels that the administrator will decide in accordance with the legislature's judgments of value.

To understand under what conditions "why" judgments may be entrusted to the appointed administrator, it is necessary to understand what factors, other than legislative direction, are influential in molding the administrator's decisions. The administrator himself is a member of the community. The customs, beliefs, values, ideals of the community will be in large measure identical with his own. In many spheres of action this pattern of community values can be relied upon to supplement legislative enactments. His professional training, too, will be important in molding the administrator's judgments. The physician can usually be relied upon to make those decisions which will benefit the health of his patient. The engineer will design structures which will accomplish their purpose efficiently. It is only rarely that it is necessary to question the judgments of the doctor or engineer, in his technical work, but it is frequently necessary to make certain that his values coincide with those of the community at large.

Many questions which the legislature will not feel justified in delegating to the administrator will involve in their solution numerous considerations of technical fact and administrative workability. On such questions the administrator will be expected to advise the legislature as to the implications of proposed legislation, in order that the measures which are adopted will, in fact, attain the desired goals. *The importance of such advisory functions to the legislature cannot be overemphasized.*

Under this conception of the relationship between administration and legislation there is established, not a division of authority and a system of checks and balances, but rather a division of work in which the administrator makes many decisions involving both "how" and "why," subject to the review of the legislature, and the legislature likewise makes many mixed decisions influenced by the expert advice of the administrator. The aim must be to establish a working partnership between legislature and administrator, and a major task of the chief executive is to present problems for decision in such a way that these principles will be preserved. How he may do this, particularly within the framework of council-manager government, will be discussed more fully in Chapter 2.

Translating Decisions Into Action

Having reviewed in broad outline the relationships between policy and administration, the next step is to examine in more detail the way in which decisions reached by the legislative body and the chief administrator are carried into action. Simple situations are conceivable where the administrator would carry out his own decisions — or even where the legislative body might execute its own policies. As soon as governmental services grow to the point where the effort of several persons is required to maintain them, this is no longer possible. Then it becomes necessary to develop processes whereby legislative and administrative decisions can be translated into action through organized effort. To bring this organized effort into being and to sustain it is a prime responsibility of the chief administrator.

Delegation of Decision Making

It should be observed, first of all, that it is possible not only to delegate the actual performance of services to the various parts of the organization but also to divide the task of making decisions. Within the framework of broad policy laid down by the legislature the chief administrator may make decisions dealing with execution. In turn, the persons who are given the task of carrying out these decisions may in the process of execution need to make further decisions.

The simple function of paving a street will again serve as an example. The council will determine whether or not it shall be paved, how the cost shall be met, and perhaps the general type of construction. An engineer and the purchasing agent will propose the specifications for the materials, decide what concerns will furnish them, etc. An engineer will in all likelihood determine the grade of the pavement. The director of public works will determine how the job can best be done and will select equipment, a superintendent or foremen to supervise the work, etc. Finally, to the superintendent and foremen will be left the responsibility of deciding on details of construction and convenience to adjoining property owners during the actual progress of the work. The task of making correct decisions becomes thereby a larger or smaller part of the job of each member of the organization.

Specialization and Coordination

The organization which is established to make and execute decisions is almost always characterized by specialization — particular tasks are delegated to particular parts of the organization. Such specialization increases the effectiveness of the organization in many ways, but it also creates a need for coordination, which is achieved partly by arranging the staff in a hierarchy or pyramid of responsibility and authority.

Within this hierarchy there is specialization so that one division of the organization is responsible for, and thus has authority over, a particular portion of the task. The work of the official at any given point in the hierarchy and the types of decisions he must make and execute are relative to the particular task that has been assigned him. Thus decisions on "broader" issues tend to be concentrated toward the top of the hierarchy.

Management

Since the administrator is trying to accomplish things not alone through his own efforts but also through those of a group, a part of his decisions and activities will be directed toward leading his subordinates toward effective action. These directive and coordinating activities, which increase in importance as we progress toward the top of the hierarchy, are properly called "management activities." It may be seen that management activities and the principles which underlie their successful performance are relatively independent of the exact nature of the agency which is being administered or the services which it performs. They are activities and principles which are common to all organizations where men try to achieve purposes through group effort.

An administrator, to do a successful job, must know more than "management." He must know not only how to manage but how to manage the particular kind of organization for which he is responsible — a fire chief must understand not only management, but also the science of preventing and fighting fires; a police chief must understand management, but also the techniques of preventing and solving crime. It goes without saying that the chief administrator of a city needs to understand management but he also needs to understand what a city is, what kind of people live in it, what services they need and expect from their city government, and how their city government can give them those services. The question, for example, whether fire engines should answer alarms outside the city limits is not a "management" question, but it is one which the chief administrator and his council are frequently called on to answer.

It is true that the administrator at the top needs to know more about management, but can get along with less knowledge about the technical aspects of the job, than the man further down in the ranks. The police chief will usually know more about techniques for combatting crime than will the chief administrator — and the captain of detectives may know more about crime detection than the police chief. Not to make a virtue of necessity, it should be emphasized that the chief administrator is able to do a satisfactory job not *because* he knows less about certain things than do his subordinates, but *in spite* of that fact. He does not have as frequent use for this technical knowledge as do his subordinates, and he can usually delegate technical decisions to them. Nevertheless, the more he knows about the work of his departments, and the more he knows about cities as a whole, the more effective he can be as a chief administrator. The ideal chief administrator for a city is the man who is a jack-of-all-trades, but master of two — he understands thoroughly the art of management, and he is well versed in the broad problems of city government.

Most of the points discussed in this volume are applicable, though on a reduced scale, to the management of a single city department, as well as to the management of an entire city government.

Administrators and Operatives

The officials and employees at different levels of the administrative pyramid may generally be distinguished by the type of work they do. The terms "administrator" and "supervisor" are usually used to refer to the levels of the hierarchy above the first — the lowest level being designated as "operative." The breadth of issues involved in decision will decrease toward the lower levels of the hierarchy. Top administrators will be concerned with decisions of broad scope and with the coordination of the structure below them; at the lower level subordinate administrators will make decisions on somewhat narrower issues and will direct and coordinate by direct oversight.

At a still lower level, "operatives" will decide and execute, but will not be responsible for the work of any subordinates. Thus the hierarchy will be characterized by "vertical" as well as "horizontal" specialization. At a risk of gross oversimplification, it might be said that work at the top levels is characterized by management and policy decisions, at the middle levels by technical and management decisions, at the operative level primarily by "doing," secondarily by "deciding," and not at all by "managing."

However, it is not often possible to pair off neatly the functions delineated here with persons who perform them. Generally speaking the larger the organization the easier it is to make such a pairing. In an organization like the federal government or a large city there are persons who are concerned almost exclusively with making long-range decisions, others who directly supervise subordinate personnel and of course there are thousands who are almost entirely "operatives." In a small city, on the other hand, the chief administrator decides, supervises, and operates, and in this case "specialization" refers primarily to the distribution of his own time and the organization of his own thinking rather than to any assignment of employees in a complex organization.

Even in the larger organizations it should not be thought that all functions of decision take place at the very top, and those of operation at the bottom. The broader functions of administration filter down through the organization from the chief administrator to the foreman of the road gang and even in a sense to the members of the gang themselves. The passerby who stops to watch two laborers synchronize the blows of their sledgehammers sees coordination in its most rudimentary form. Of course at the top these functions take up the largest proportion of the employee's time and this proportion diminishes steadily down through the organization.

Elements of the Management Process

The chief administrator's management responsibility, then, is to take a group of human beings and to mold them into a smoothly functioning administrative organization capable of accomplishing efficiently the aims which are set for it. To do this successfully he must make use of a wide range of administrative techniques and processes, which for convenience may be classified under four major heads: *he must plan*; *he must organize*; *he must direct*; and *he must act as chief representative of his organization*. In carrying out these management tasks he uses personnel, financial, and legal resources. Each of these terms deserves something in the way of a preliminary explanation.

Planning

To plan is to explore, to anticipate, and to evaluate — to explore all the possible alternative courses of action, to anticipate their consequences, and to develop and evaluate them in detail before reaching a final decision. Planning means that each of the thousands of decisions which are made in the course of day-to-day administration are not independent of and isolated from each other, but are reached as the logical consequences of a broad over-all scheme. Not a brick is to be laid for a new fire station until the location of that station has been considered in relation to the probable location of future population of the city, the street plan, the need for other physical improvements, and so forth. Not a dollar is to be spent on a new playground until its effect on the operating budget of the recreation department has been fully considered. The salary for an individual policeman is to be determined as a part of a comprehensive classification and pay plan for all city employees.

Planning involves the collection and examination of information and ideas, and the casting of programs or policies to guide future actions. Plans may be of large, or of small scope; may provide for a period of years, or for an hour; may anticipate the inevitable, or the uncertain. An official map showing all street lines in the city, and a blueprint for a culvert are both plans; a six-year program of municipal improvements, and an agenda for tomorrow's council meeting are plans; a scheme of organization for property tax collection, and an organization scheme for handling a disaster which may never occur are both plans.

Everyone in the administrative organization takes part in the planning process, even down to the individual police officer patrolling his beat or to the filing clerk in the city clerk's office. At the management level, however, the chief administrator must review the plans of his department heads to make certain that they are consistent with each other and with the broad policies prescribed by the council, and he must formulate those broad plans or programs which embrace the administration as a whole. In Chapters 9 and 10 this important subject of planning will be considered in greater detail. Elsewhere in this volume planning will also be discussed frequently because it enters as a vital element in all administrative action.

Organization

To organize is to define the specialized tasks of individual officers and employees, to establish the broad outlines of interrelationship, and to determine the lines of authority. But organization is more than a mere splitting of the group into subgroups. There must be transmitted to all members of the organization an understanding of the unifying purpose of the whole group, and of the contribution of each subgroup to it. A clerk in the police department must be brought to realize that he is part of a city government which is concerned with nothing less than the welfare of all its citizens; that his particular department is responsible for protecting those citizens and their property from violence or theft; that to do so, criminals must be arrested, and that his own particular task is to help keep the records which make those arrests possible.

Since work may be divided in many different ways, the effectiveness of the organization will depend upon the skill with which the work division is arranged. The major principles and problems of organization will be considered in Chapter 3, while particular organization problems and techniques will receive special treatment in the chapters dealing with personnel, finance, research and planning, and legal services.

Direction

The third management function is to direct the administrative organization. Direction can be thought of as requiring command, coordination, and control.

Command. To command is to issue the orders necessary for the execution of plans, policies, and assignments. The tools of command include rules and regulations and the work order.

At the level of the chief administrator, command has tended to be exercised not so much by issuing day-to-day orders covering the details of the organization's work, as through persuasion and the use of tools: setting over-all objectives for organization units, assigning responsibility for these objectives to capable subordinates, allotting these subordinates budget resources to carry out their assignments, and intervening in their work only to establish broad policies and procedures.

Coordination. To coordinate is to fuse the various segments of the organization into going machinery, keeping principal objectives foremost and reducing to a minimum conflicts of purpose and activity. It insures that the right hand knows what the left hand is doing and that both work together and not at cross purposes. One might say that coordination is the active modification of organization in the day-to-day work of administration.

No matter how skillfully the organization is designed, there are bound to be many situations in which there is a conflict of authority, where responsibility is not clear, or where in some other way the boundary between two organization units is indefinite. It is the task of the chief administrator to see that organization units maintain a liaison at these points of contacts, that conflicts are peacefully resolved, and that, where necessary the organization is modified to prevent their repetition. New and expanded services performed by local governments have tended to fall between the traditional departmental concepts and therefore coordination has become more important and more complex.

Control. To control is to ascertain that the tasks which have been assigned are being carried out in an efficient and intelligent manner. Control is a continuous function of administration and implies an audit (not merely in the strictly financial sense) of all operations. Control depends upon an adequate flow of information upward through the organization to the chief administrator, and to the auxiliary agencies which administer control devices. Its most common medium is a system of "internal" reports — a series of daily, weekly, monthly, quarterly, and annual reports which inform the administrator whether or not revenues are meeting expectations and insure that expenditures are made according to plan or that the plan is being changed to fit the changing situation.

Satisfactory techniques of issuing orders, achieving coordination, and controlling operations are essential to, but do not guarantee, effective direction of the administrative organization. The effective administrator is one who carries out all these functions of direction in a spirit of leadership. He conceives of direction as a two-way process involving not merely his own authority but the esprit de corps and cooperative enthusiasm of the entire organization. After all, the chief administrator is only one man, yet he is responsible for the direction of the efforts of dozens, hundreds, or even thousands of members of the organization. If he attempts to supply the motive power for the whole organization he will inevitably fail, for it does not require the inertia of many persons to swallow up the energy of even the most vigorous executive. The chief administrator must think of himself as a "starting mechanism" which releases the energy of his subordinates, and applies it to the tasks of the organization. His whole aim must be to free the energy of others through the development of their initiative so that he may conserve his own energy and make it felt throughout the entire organization.

Some of the principal techniques of direction will be described in Chapter 4, but other devices and policies contributing to effective command, coordination, and control will receive attention in almost every chapter of this volume.

Administrative Representation

The administrative organization has many contacts and relationships with other organizations, groups, and individuals — with the council; with other governmental agencies, federal, state, and local; and with the public. The logical representative of the city administration in these many contacts and relationships is the chief administrator. This does not mean, of course, that subordinate officers and employees will have no external contacts. It means simply that there is a need for some central point of contact on matters affecting the administration as a whole.

If the council had to deal individually with each administrative department or agency, its task would be hopelessly complex and confused. Therefore, the chief administrator, particularly in a council-manager city, serves as the principal representative of the administrative organization. He takes the policies and programs decided upon by the council and puts them into effect by assigning particular tasks to the appropriate administrative units. Likewise the needs and recommendations of individual administrative units are transmitted through him to the council. He is also the focal point of control by the council over the administration. Reports prepared by individual departments are consolidated and interrelated by him and are then transmitted to the council for review, criticism, and action.

In the relations of the administrative organization with external agencies and individuals, the chief administrator plays a similar role. Many direct contacts with other agencies or with the public will be made by subordinates, but his office remains the principal point of contact for those whose interests cut across departmental or agency lines. He is therefore responsible for establishing the basic standards and policies governing public relations in the broadest sense of the term.

Personnel, Financial, and Legal Procedures

Cutting across this classification of the tasks of management into activities of planning, organization, direction, and representation is a second set of categories of almost equal importance: personnel, finance and law. Every organization, regardless of the nature of its work, is made up of people; every organization requires funds to pay salaries and buy supplies; every organization — particularly if it is a governmental agency — works within a legal framework. Since these elements are common to all organizations management techniques of wide application have grown up for the handling of these particular procedures.

Personnel Management. Organization has no meaning apart from the persons whose tasks and relationships it defines. In a sense, an organization is simply a mosaic of human individuals, and to blend them into a harmonious picture requires not only a skillful arrangement of the pieces, but that the pieces themselves — the organization members — be correctly chosen.

Personnel management is more than merely an aspect of organization, for it is an instrument through which the administrator plans and directs as well as organizes. To give a man the title of chief administrator and vest in him the responsibilities of adminis-trative management is only an empty gesture unless this responsibility is accompanied by broad powers to select, direct, and discipline the personnel of the organization. The tech-nical processes of recruiting, examining, record-keeping, and other details of personnel administration may be delegated to specially trained persons, but determination of policies for "staffing" (the selection of personnel) and the over-all control of personnel are essen-tial parts of administrative management.

Fiscal Management. The act of organizing is not complete when individual depart-ments and divisions have been designated and their tasks assigned. What each depart-ment can do will depend on the funds it has available. In the budget, which is an annual plan of administrative activities, all activities are reduced to dollars of proposed expendi-ture, and these are balanced by recommendations as to how these dollars are to be ob-tained from the taxpayers. Thus, the several departments are assigned certain activities to perform, and are given corresponding appropriations or allotments.

It will be seen that fiscal management, like personnel management, comprehends planning and directing as well as organizing. The budget, for example, is an instrument of fundamental importance for formulating plans and translating them into definite organ-ization tasks. In recent years, the concept of "performance budgeting" has been increas-ingly applied to give the administrator a more useful fiscal tool. When the emphasis is on a performance-type budget, the administrator can both better understand and better explain the plans and accomplishments of the activities under his jurisdiction. A work program, indicating the number of units of work to be accomplished, accompanied by a periodic reporting system showing the completion of these work units are very effective tools in the field of fiscal management.

Fiscal management must provide also for controls in the execution of plans. Any departure from the plan of action will dislocate the financial arrangements, and will re-quire alterations of the work program. Fiscal management is therefore an inseparable element of administrative management.

Here again, however, a distinction must be made between broad policies and basic controls, on the one hand, and the technical procedures and details, on the other. The collecting of taxes, the keeping of books and ledgers, and similar tasks can be delegated — the fiscal machinery can be operated by technicians, but control of this machinery is a function of administrative management.

Legal Administration. A city government can exercise only those powers granted it by charter or state law. Further it carries out many of these powers by enacting addi-tional legislation in the form of ordinances and resolutions. Its plans are frequently em-bodied in law (a zoning ordinance, for example), the major outlines of departmental organ-ization are often specified in charter or ordinance, and direction often takes the form of law (the budget ordinance, an ordinance authorizing condemnation proceedings for street-widening, and the like).

The technical legal activities — bill drafting, prosecution, and similar tasks — are matters which the chief administrator will delegate to his legal specialists, but the basic policy decisions with respect to the content of laws and the policies and procedures of enforcement are matters of concern to the administrator himself.

Public and Business Administration

It was pointed out previously that management is found in any type of group activity, and that certain problems and principles pertain to all types of administration. If this is so, the manager of a private business will employ many of the same techniques as the manager of a city — and to a very considerable extent this is true. As a matter of fact from the time of the first development of management theory, there has been a continual interchange of ideas between students of business administration and students of public administration. However, there are certain differences between administration in private industry and in government due to inherent differences in the nature of the two types of enterprises. These differences will suggest the proper limit to the transfer of principles and procedures from the one field to the other, and emphasize the need for special study of the techniques of city management. Some of the main differences between public and private business are:

1. Public administration must work in the white glare of publicity. In the forefront of every public administrator's mind is the question: What will be the public reaction to this or that activity or procedure? To the public administrator's own sensitivity to public opinion is added the even greater concern of his council over the immediate popular reaction. The average industrial administrator meets this problem on a vastly reduced scale because he is dealing with only a small segment of the public, and because an atmosphere of secrecy and privacy in private industry is traditional.

2. The public administrator (assuming his honesty and integrity) has the interest of the public paramount in all his acts. The private administrator is expected to keep the interest of his organization foremost and the public interest secondary. This roughly is the distinction between service and profit.

3. Government is not controlled by a profit and loss statement. It is necessary, therefore, to develop different incentives for efficiency and different modes of measuring results. "Profit" to the administrator should be making the most of the available resources regardless of economic conditions, through the use of skills and techniques to provide the greatest amount of service.

4. The public administrator works within a network of legal and regulatory restrictions to which he must conform and which often can be changed only by a formal process involving sometimes the specific consent of the people. The private administrator is often bound by regulation and sometimes by law but to a much lesser extent, and the process of change in private industry is more flexible.

5. The relationships of the public administrator are far wider and more complex than those of the private administrator. The public administrator is concerned not only with the general public and special groups but also with several levels of government and with a large number of public agencies with whose programs his own must coordinate.

To list these principal differences between public and private administration is to reveal that under modern conditions the differences are steadily diminishing. Not only are more and more businesses being treated as public utilities, but practically all are now considered (in fact, if not in law) as being to a greater or lesser extent "affected with the public interest." This means that private administrative acts are being subjected more and more to public review and control, and that they can no longer be considered exclusively "private."

This development has been hastened by (1) the rise of large-scale business which makes monopoly closer to "normal" than free, untrammeled competition and which makes large-scale business a legitimate subject of public concern; (2) the wide extension of the corporate form of business organization whereby ownership has been divorced from management and as a result of which it is no longer possible to assume that the interests of management will always coincide with the interest of either owners or the public. This last factor is of particular importance because it points to the need for professionalization of private as well as public administrators. A professional sense of responsibility to the community which they serve must be developed in both groups of administrators if community interest is to prevail over individual advantage.

While private industry has come more to resemble government in its scale and the public implications of its operations, government has come more to resemble private industry in methods and organization. Numerous developments of private industry have been used in the improvement of government. Among these are centralized personnel management, cost accounting, and efficiency movements in shop and office. Conversely, government agencies have pioneered many administrative methods which were later adopted by private industry: punched-card tabulating machines, personnel testing in recruitment, staff assistance to administrators (first extensively developed in military administration), and many others. Similarities in all problems of administration — public or private — indicate that the exploration of the possibilities of exchange of techniques between government and industry has just begun.

The Art of Administration

The preceding pages will indicate the general scope and approach of this volume to problems of management. The treatment will be as concrete and specific as it can be made within the limits of our present knowledge of what makes good administration. No person who has had any experience whatever in actual management needs to be told, however, that the manager's art cannot be reduced to a simple set of rules to be kept on the blotter pad and referred to as occasion requires.

Administration is not merely *knowledge,* it is *skill.* Reading and study alone cannot make a man an administrator any more than they can make him a tennis player or a typist; for the "muscles" used in management, like the muscles used in tennis, will develop the necessary coordination only with exercise. But mere practice without instruction does not greatly improve performance. Experience, like athletic training, needs careful coaching to be effective in developing skill. This coaching the administrator can give himself if he combines a study of the administrative techniques which have generally been found effective in practice with a self-consciousness and awareness of the methods he follows in his own management work.

There is one other limit which must be frankly recognized in stating "principles" of administration. Administration is concerned with human beings — and with some of their most intangible qualities — their morale, initiative, and loyalty. The great administrator is one who is able to deal with human beings in all their individuality: who has a thorough mastery of management tools, but who is able to adapt these tools and subordinate them to the necessity of maintaining effective interpersonal relations.

Man's behavior is determined by so many intangibles and imponderables that it is rarely possible to formulate answers to the problem of directing a group of men in the accomplishment of an administrative task. Because every administrative situation varies, the application of set principles of administration is not as effective as a sense and a feel for what a particular situation requires.

Much of the administrator's task involves the skillful handling of negotiations. This is a particularly critical activity in the early stages of policy making. But there are few, if any, rules of conduct for negotiation. This is, rather, a problem in the appropriate expression of ideas. Countless complexities of personality assume a position of importance in such circumstances, and these are never the same for two individuals.

Another area in which principles of administration are of only limited usefulness is the important field of policy and program formulation arrived at in such a way as to uncover not only important areas of agreement, but also the serious differences. As one author has put it, "In watching responses of the staff, the administrator must have an appreciation for subtlety and innuendo and possess keenness in recognizing 'straws in the wind.' The 'unofficial' together with the 'official' reactions and relations between topside and staff influence importantly negotiations which are undertaken within the organization, and they affect critically the efficacy of the whole system of communication."[2]

The administrator must be capable of seeing beyond the present skirmish or current triumph, focusing on the "grand strategy," and adjusting his plans and expectations so as to achieve the ultimate end. Here again is an element which is more of art than it is of principle. Flexibility, and a combination of the philosophical with the practical are significant needs of the good administrator.

Principles, structure and other excellencies of technical arrangements in administration are not unimportant, but they give their greatest service when, "under competent men they are employed creatively and skillfully to realize the purposes for which an organization has been established."[3]

Yet, within this limitation, there remains a body of techniques, principles, maxims — call them what you will — which are of the highest usefulness to the administrator who uses them discriminately; which are distilled from the accumulated experience of administrators in thousands of organizations over several generations; and which no single administrator is likely to acquire unaided in a single lifetime of management.

---

[2] See Milton E. Muelder, "The Art of Administrative Leadership," Public Management, February, 1951, p. 28.
[3] Ibid., p. 29.

Chapter 2

RELATIONSHIPS WITH COUNCIL AND OTHER AGENCIES

One of the functions of the chief administrator is to act as the chief representative of the administrative organization in its relations with the council, with other governments, and with the public. The subject of "public relations and public reporting" is discussed in Chapter 13. It is the purpose of this chapter not only to suggest means by which these relations may be made productive and cooperative, but also by a further exploration of the relationship between legislation and administration to clarify the definition of administration offered in Chapter 1.

Although this text has been designed and prepared primarily for the city's chief administrator, regardless of his title or form of government, this one chapter departs somewhat from the general approach in that the relationships discussed are those in a council-manager city. This is done primarily because any attempts to discuss the relationships between the council and the chief administrator in terms that would apply equally well to all forms of government would require such broad generalizations and so many qualifications that it would be more confusing than helpful. It also facilitates the clear discernment of the relationship between legislation and administration.

The specific application of this chapter to the council-manager form does not mean that it has no application to other forms of government. To the extent that a mayor or commissioner is chief administrator as well as a legislative and ceremonial leader, many of the observations and suggestions in this chapter can be applied to mayor-council and commission-governed cities. However, anyone reading through this chapter for information on the relationships of the mayor to the council must recognize the significant differences between the council-manager and the mayor-council posts of chief administrator. The city manager is appointed by the council and holds office at its pleasure. This is a substantially different "power relationship" from the position of the mayor, who may be either directly elected by the people or elected to the council and then selected by his fellow members as the chief administrative officer. In either case, the mayor leads from political strength, and this inevitably colors the relations which he enjoys with the council.

Relations With the Council

Mutual Understanding

Of all the relationships existing throughout council-manager government, none is more important than that of the council and the manager. The success or failure of the council-manager plan depends in a large measure upon the working relationship that exists between the representative council and the professional manager.

There are subtle matters of tact and good sense which if understood and honored by the manager will make for a smooth relationship between the manager and the council. One experienced manager has put it this way:

"1. Never forget that the council, to the best of its ability, expresses the will of the people. There will be times when you will not understand why the council takes certain actions but you will find that the council is generally right and that the members express public opinion as they see it and as they learn it from their constituents.

"2. Formal acts of the council become public policy, and you as city manager must always do your best to translate these policies into action. You should do this in a manner to best realize the intent of the council. In some cases you may not agree with the policy, but it is your duty as city manager to carry out the policy to the best of your ability unless it is illegal or fraudulent."

"6. Lead those whom you contact — members of the council, subordinate employees, and citizens — into the proper channel by tactful suggestion rather than by too persuasive argument."

"10. Give credit where credit belongs and always give the council members all the credit you can.

"12. Work hard to gain and keep the full confidence of the council . . . . . . and your job will be easier."[1]

<u>What the Council Expects From the Manager.</u> The most important aspect of local government is policy making and this duty rests exclusively with the council when it operates under the council-manager plan. While the chief duty of the city manager is the "administration of policy," this is a phrase which needs explanation. Further, it is quite impossible to make an absolute delineation between policy-making and administration. Under normal circumstances, however, the city council will expect the city manager to:

Be the chief administrative officer of the city and be responsible to the city council for the proper administration of all affairs of the city.

Appoint, and when necessary for the good of the service, suspend or remove officers and employees of the city except as otherwise provided by the city charter or law, and to direct and supervise their work.

Prepare the budget annually, and submit it to the council annually together with a message describing the important features, and be responsible for its administration after adoption.

Prepare and submit to the council as of the end of the fiscal year a complete report on the finances and administrative activities of the city for the preceeding year.

Keep the council advised of the financial condition and future needs of the city and make such recommendation as he may deem desirable.

Recommend to the governing body a standard schedule of pay for each appointed office and position in the city service, including minimum, intermediate, and maximum rates.

Recommend to the governing body (from time to time) adoption of such policies as he may deem necessary or expedient for the health, safety, or welfare of the community, or for the improvement of the administrative services.

Consolidate or combine offices, positions, or departments, or units under his jurisdiction, with the approval of the city council.

---

[1] L. P. Cookingham, "Some Guideposts for City Managers," <u>Public Management,</u> April, 1956, pp. 77-79.

Attend all meetings of the city council unless excused therefrom and take part in the discussion of all matters coming before the council.

Supervise the purchase of materials, supplies, and equipment for which funds are provided in the budget.

See that all laws and ordinances are properly enforced.

Investigate the affairs of the city or of any department or division. Investigate all complaints in regard to matters concerning the administration of the government of the city and in regard to service maintained by the public utilities in the city, and see that all franchises, permits, and privileges granted by the city are faithfully observed.

Devote his entire time to the discharge of his official duties.

Perform such other duties as may be required by the council, not inconsistent with the city charter, state law, or ordinances.

These are the expectations of the council in their dealings with the manager, but this is only one side of the problem.

What the Manager Expects From the Council. The manager hopes to deal with a council which:

Gives the manager the tools he needs for the jobs assigned to him.

When assignments are given to the manager, makes clear what is to be done and when work is to be completed.

Criticizes the work of the city manager when it is deserved, but gives the criticism in private so that the issue can be objectively analyzed in an atmosphere of harmony and mutual understanding.

Assures the manager of a fair hearing in controversial situations, and does not question the manager's motives until he has had a chance to tell his side of the story.

Acts in an understanding and sympathetic manner.

Gives the manager a respectable hearing on his recommendations and proposals.

Keeps public meetings on a high plane by avoiding ridicule and sarcasm in relations with fellow councilmen or the city manager.

Deals with administrative officers or employees who are under the jurisdiction of the city manager solely through the manager in any matters of importance.

Issues directives only as a body to the manager.

Division of Work

Both the council and the city manager deal with municipal policy. This is not to say that the council deals only with policy making and the city manager only with administration of policy — a distinction which is unrealistic. No one can divide the subject matter of municipal government into two categories, policy and administration, in order to assign them as exclusive provinces to the council and city manager respectively.

In solving the more important problems of municipal government, the city manager and the council must work together on the same subject matter, each making his own contribution. For example, perhaps the most important problem facing a city government each year is its budget. The city manager prepares the budget; the council studies it and revises it if it wishes, then adopts it; the city manager then puts the budget into effect. Another example is the question of regulatory ordinances. The city manager may recommend such ordinances or furnish the council the information on which such ordinances may be based; members of the council may individually propose ordinances, discuss those introduced by other members, whether or not at the suggestion of administrative officials, and by majority vote adopt those that are satisfactory; after adoption the ordinances are enforced by the city manager and his subordinates. As another example, there is the problem of garbage collection. The city manager may plan and propose a system of garbage collection, and he may manage the system that has been adopted, but the council must approve any general scheme that is adopted, and its members may propose, modify, reject, or adopt any system they wish.

Because the work of the council is so intimately connected with the work of the city manager, it is impossible to make generally applicable rules specifying what subjects shall be left entirely to the discretion of the city manager by the council. A rule, for example, that says that purchases amounting to more than a certain sum must be awarded by contract by the council, while smaller purchases may be made by the manager on his own authority, may determine the formal routine by which purchases are made, but it will have very little to do with the fundamental relationship between the council and city manager. One council may follow the city manager's recommendations in awarding large contracts and give him a free hand in his minor purchases, while — under exactly the same rule — another council may ignore the manager in awarding contracts and insist that he consult with the council before making even petty purchases.

It is even more difficult to devise a rule suitable to cities of all sizes. In a very small city, the extension of a sewer or the purchase of a fire truck may involve important questions of municipal policy that deserve careful attention by the council. In a very large city, such work is merely routine business to be handled by the city manager or his administrative subordinates.

There is, however, a clear and fundamental difference between the function of the council and the function of the city manager. To determine policy, the council must consider and make decisions on the main problems of the municipality, regardless of whether solutions are proposed by its own members, by administrative officials, or by private citizens. In doing so, it may take into consideration any facts that it considers pertinent, and give the city manager, by collective action, orders setting forth the general objectives that it wishes to attain. It is not the function of its members to attempt to administer personally the policies that it determines, or to influence the administrative officials charged with the execution of those policies.

To administer policy, the city manager serves the council by providing it with advice and information on the conduct of municipal affairs, and by putting into effect its decisions through the use of municipal funds and personnel. As the servant of the council, he should not attempt to guide or control the selection of council members by the voters, or to bring political influence in any form to bear on the decisions of the council.

Informing and Advising the Council

To aid in the intelligent and democratic determination of policy by giving adequate information and disinterested expert advice to the governing body is perhaps the most difficult and important task of the administrative official. A governing body of laymen needs technical advice and information on which to base its decisions of policy, and technical assistance in the preparation of those formal orders by which it controls its expert personnel. The expert administrator does not detract from democracy; on the contrary, he makes the democratic ideal attainable.

One of the principal effects of the council-manager plan is to make every action of the administrator subject to instant control by the governing body, the council. The service that the manager can provide the community depends upon his ability to explain to laymen the advantages of policies that he proposes and the administrative methods that he follows. There is real value in this. It forces the expert administrator to consider his proposals in the light of general interests of the community, rather than in the light of his own specialized interests or technical preoccupation; and it gives the administrator a chance to have his proposal considered and supported by a group of men who are interested in all aspects of city government, thus protecting the manager from pressure groups, whose demands may cancel each other when brought before the council as a general court of appeals. The expert in government must never forget his dependence on public support or underestimate the contribution of the political leaders who are his superiors.

The position of the city manager subjects him entirely to the wishes of the elected representatives, but at the same time it gives him an opportunity to exercise the broadest and most far-reaching influence on the conduct of city government. In such a position he must not take opposition to his suggestions as a personal affront, or ask for support for his ideas as a personal favor. He must meet hostility and suspicion with a willingness to provide information and unbiased advice. He must assume the function of lessening the bitterness of partisan disputes over policy by furnishing facts that speak for themselves. The effectiveness of the city manager's leadership is increased by patience and impartiality.

No manager could administer his city satisfactorily if he were not free to initiate recommendations for legislative action. But he should make it clear, both to the council and to the public, that the ultimate decision, however arrived at, is the council's policy rather than his own. He should be prepared to give the council his advice and recommendations on every important issue. The fact that an issue may be controversial does not warrant the avoidance of his responsibility. It is his obligation to see that the council makes up its mind in the light of all the available facts, those that weigh against his recommendations as well as those that favor them. If the manager supplies the council with all pertinent facts he has a right to expect the public to hold the council, and not himself, responsible for the council's decisions.

Periodic and Special Reports. In order to keep both the council and the public informed on municipal affairs, the city manager usually goes beyond his oral reports at council meetings by making periodic financial and statistical reports on municipal activities, special reports on matters referred to him by the council, and annual reports which are sometimes published for distribution to citizens.

A regular monthly or quarterly report containing a financial statement showing expenditures and unexpended balances of all the budget accounts is prepared by many city managers, and enough copies are duplicated to permit distribution to all the councilmen. The financial material may be supplemented with statistical information on the activities of the city departments, the principal accomplishments of the month, and progress in special projects. These reports may also be useful for limited public distribution to interested individuals and civic organizations. As this kind of report should be designed to give the council members continuing, routine information about month-to-month operations, it is advisable to bring up to date in each report the same financial statements and tables. The inclusion of comparable data for previous years will also facilitate interpretation. Most of the material included will lend itself readily to graphic presentation — an excellent way of giving a continuous picture of operations. In many cases, graphs can be prepared by simply adding to the line of the graph used in the previous report. These reports should be carefully prepared to make it easy for the layman to use the data correctly and to draw valid conclusions from them.

Another means used by managers is a complete, current file of detailed administrative reports, made available to the councilmen and the public in the manager's office. This file should be merely an orderly arrangement of the material submitted by department heads which the manager uses in his regular administrative work. Such a file, because of its greater detail, will serve to supplement the regularly prepared reports.

A city manager may prepare a special report to supply the council with the details of a particular problem which has arisen or to cover matters referred to him previously by the council. No general rule can be made as to the uses for which a written report is better than an oral one. The written report is more satisfactory for the presentation of statistics, charts, and pictures; it serves as a permanent record; and copies may be released to the press if the council desires. The oral report, on the other hand, may often serve better in making an explanation to the council; it permits a more personalized relationship, and it usually requires less effort in preparation. Frequently, of course, both types of reports may be used in covering one subject.

Written reports on subjects on which council action is pending are naturally most valuable if the council members are able to obtain them in advance of the council meeting. Some managers mail special reports to the councilmen or attach them to the agenda when it is issued in advance of meetings. Other managers, however, are reluctant to release a report before a meeting, fearing that the councilmen may form an opinion on the basis of the report before having heard the manager's oral supplementation. If an advance report is issued, care should be taken to see that it does not reach the press either from the manager or a councilman unless all the councilmen have an understanding that it is to be released.

The Conduct of Council Meetings

Procedures followed by the council and the administrator in preparing for council meetings are important both in facilitating the administration of municipal affairs and establishing the basis for dealing with the general public. The council must be prepared not only to consider the information supplied by the chief administrator from the point of view of its own members, but to weigh the effect of its decision on the general public and to consider the point of view of those petitioners who appear at the public meetings.

To facilitate action in council meetings it is desirable to prepare an agenda as a program for discussion and action. The city manager, being in the best position to know the relative urgency of the various items to be discussed, and being the responsible agent and advisor of the council, should prepare the agenda. In some cities the city clerk retains the job of transmitting the agenda to the council members, with more or less control over its contents. While it is unimportant which officer performs the secretarial work of sending the agenda to councilmen or of assembling the list of routine details which require formal action by the council, it is an essential part of the function of the city manager to select, in order of priority, a list of the more important matters to be discussed.

Responsibility to a Collective Body. Since the manager is the administrative officer for the council as a whole, it is desirable for him to maintain the confidence of all its members rather than depend on the support of any group or faction. For this reason, it is generally best for a city manager not to discuss with individual councilmen matters which may be on the agenda or may come before the council at some early date. There are occasions, of course, when discussions of this nature are unavoidable but the manager is most likely to avoid giving an impression of partiality or favoritism if he gives the same information and opinions to all council members that he gives to any one of them.

One city manager, who in general refuses to discuss with individual members of the council items of business which have not been considered by the council as a whole, reports that he makes an exception of the mayor, and "on rare occasions" discusses matters with individual members of the council prior to discussion at a full meeting "when that individual, through his special knowledge, can advise me or where some member of the council because of his special interest in certain matters might become pre-committed to a certain position without a complete picture of all facts."

To give the council an opportunity to ask informally for information and to discuss municipal affairs without the restrictions of procedural regulations, many city councils hold informal preliminary meetings prior to their formal public meetings. Since no official record is kept of such a meeting, the councilmen are less on their dignity, less inclined to oratory, and more likely to come to a complete understanding and decision in a short time. However, there are dangers in the informal meeting.

In some states it is illegal to take official action of any kind in a meeting which is not open to the public, and which is not a formal meeting of the city council. Unless wisely used, the informal meeting may easily develop into a meeting of greater importance than the one open to the public. In a case of this sort the public meeting becomes stilted, discussion is short and unrevealing, and the public is deprived of the information and interest which comes out of the normal give and take of discussion in council meetings. Some councils, finding a popular prejudice against any private meeting of the governing body, have invited the public and the press to their preliminary meetings.

There are certain circumstances in which most councils favor a private meeting, excluding the public and perhaps the press. Closed meetings of this nature are sometimes essential when public purchase of property and city hall personnel matters of a personal nature are under discussion. In some cases the press will be interested in attending such a meeting for the purpose of getting background information, and will agree not to publish an account of the meeting.

As an aid to conducting council meetings as orderly sessions for the prompt transaction of legislative matters, it is the manager's responsibility to keep the council adequately informed, taking into the consideration the needs of all the city departments. For this reason it is undesirable for the council to rely for information on subordinates of the city manager, without first hearing the city manager's opinion and summary of the pertinent data.

It is impossible and undesirable for the city manager to control the questions asked by the councilmen or to forbid his subordinates to answer direct questions. By several methods, however, he may induce the council to avoid the embarrassing and confusing situations that might arise from public disagreement among administrative officials. First, the manager should attempt to anticipate the questions of the councilmen and should discuss them in advance with his immediate subordinates. Second, those subordinates should be informed of the considerations and point of view which shape the city manager's policy on important issues, so that they may keep that policy in mind when making recommendations on important questions. Third, the manager may sometimes tactfully intercede to answer a question directed to a subordinate. Fourth, the manager may request the council to permit him to bring in a complete answer after further investigation and study. And finally, the implications of this procedure should be talked over with the council, which should in general understand the desirability of permitting the manager to coordinate proposals of policy from his administrative subordinates.

Use of Council Committees. The two common types of council committees are the standing (permanent committee) and the special (temporary) committee. Whether or not there should be standing committees in the council under the council-manager plan depends somewhat on local circumstances. The typical small council has made the standing committee system generally superfluous, but in some cities with somewhat larger councils it has been found that standing committees are favored by local tradition and are not necessarily a handicap to centralized administration.

Advocates of the committee system usually base their arguments on the greater effectiveness and speed with which council committees can discharge the duties incident to policy formation. A city manager in a large city with a council of seven members is of the opinion that "It is much easier to sit down in the office with two or three men and thrash out very thoroughly a proposition which they can support in the council as a whole than it is to sell the council on some new technical controversial matter without support from within the body itself. I find it advisable at all times to discuss with standing committees major administrative policies when these policies may have an unfavorable repercussion." In some cities, furthermore, members of standing committees have carried on valuable work in keeping the public informed of activities of the departments with which they are most closely in touch.

Advocates of council committees claim that they serve three other purposes as well: (1) developing a degree of specialization for councilmen; (2) granting the council as a whole some relief from detail on a variety of matters; and (3) facilitating the conduct of hearings by committees which, because of limited time, could not be conducted properly by the council as a whole.[2]

On the other hand, standing committees have tended to interfere with the manager's control over administration and to slow up the work of the city government. If there is any disposition on the part of the council to follow uncritically the advice and recommendations of its committees, or if the standing committee members try to see personally that the departments with which they deal are well administered, the committee system is likely to conflict with the principle that the city manager's responsibility is to the council as a body, and not to various members and groups within the council.

There is less danger in the creation of special committees to deal with particular problems. The members of such committees are less likely to interfere with the administrative control of the city manager and more likely to restrict themselves to discussions of important temporary problems.

Use of Advisory Citizens' Committees. Many cities during recent years have created special citizens' committees to advise the city council or chief administrator on specific problems or to develop public understanding and support for proposed projects such as public improvements or charter amendments. Normally they are appointed for a single purpose and are automatically discharged when their work is completed. In addition to being temporary, they are generally "semi-official" in that they are not provided for by charter or ordinance and have none of the powers or responsibilities which permanent boards and commissions possess. They are created by resolution or informal agreement between the council and the administrator.

---

[2] J. W. Ferguson, City Council Organization and Procedures in Los Angeles County (Los Angeles: Bureau of Governmental Research, University of California, 1955).

In their role as a weathervane of public opinion, the reactions of committee members may indicate to municipal officials the political acceptability of a program felt to be in the best interest of the city. The citizens' committee can also be useful in the promotion of such programs by the conduct of a publicity campaign and through personal contacts with individual citizens. Citizens' committees have been used to supplement technical knowledge of municipal officials in specific areas. Appointment of technicians and professionals frequently provides the city with specialized advice, experience and training at no cost.

The use of citizens' advisory committees, however, has not met with uniform success and in some cities committees have failed to fulfill the purpose for which they were created. Many failures can be traced to indiscriminate use of committees, poor appointments, failure to provide proper staff assistance or failure to define committee responsibilities and the problem with which it is to deal.

One of the pitfalls in the use of the citizens' committee is the tendency to rely on the citizens' committee when committee service is not called for. An administrator or a council may attempt to shirk the responsibility of making decisions on controversial issues by appointing a committee which can bear the political pressures and repercussions. Again, a committee may be appointed with the expectation that it will study a problem and arrive at a conclusion already determined by the appointing authority. Citizens serving on committees do so at no compensation and often at considerable inconvenience to themselves. Attempts to use committees in these two ways may thwart the purpose of the committees in general and alienate a group of influential citizens.

Another serious shortcoming in the use of advisory committees is that the appointing authority will frequently find it difficult to reject a committee report with which it does not agree since this may result in unfavorable reactions from committee members and the community.

The citizen advisory committee should be used sparingly, restricting it to those instances when the regular officials require technical advice or desire to obtain or promote "grassroots" sentiment.

Administering the Council's Policies

A municipal council may work most effectively if it concentrates its attention and deliberation on major aspects of municipal policy. It can get its policies administered most effectively if it entrusts that administration to the city manager, without interfering with his work. These two ideas are fundamental assumptions of the council-manager plan.

Legislation and Administrative Action.
Nevertheless, most councils legislate on a great many details that are not questions of public policy. Thus they waste their attention on trivial decisions that should be made as a part of the routine of administration. Partly by state legislation and charter provisions and partly by custom, councils are required to approve in detail a great many actions that they have already ordered in principle.

For example, in many cities the council is repeatedly called on to authorize various actions that they have already approved in the budget or in some ordinance by which public policy was first determined. Thus the city manager cannot act to carry out the policy that the council determined without coming back to the council a number of times for approval of his administrative decisions. The council may have to act more than half a dozen times on a single street or sewer improvement: it may first refer the matter to the city manager and order him to prepare plans, then make an appropriation and ask for bids, then receive them and ask that they be tabulated, then accept one of the bids, then authorize progress on the work, and finally accept the completed work. If the improvement is to be paid for by special assessment, more actions of the council are necessary, and each formal ordinance usually requires several readings. To open bids, to refund taxes erroneously collected, to receive and file requests for petitions from citizens or organizations, to approve ordinances to pay bills, to grant permission for department heads or the mayor to leave town for the day — these actions and hundreds of others may require resolutions or ordinances by the council.

To enact such detailed legislation makes it impossible for the council to devote adequate attention to public policies and thus detracts from its general control over the city government. Furthermore, it handicaps the work of the city manager to force him to obtain legislative approval for minor administrative action, and unless the council supports him unanimously, it may expose the administration of the government to political attack at every point. Aside from these administrative considerations, the necessity of dealing with minute details has been found to discourage men of ability and public spirit from accepting nomination for councilmanic office.

The council and the city manager may together apply four remedies to this trouble: first, they may seek legislative or charter amendments to remove the necessity for detailed legislation; second, they may seek the help of the city attorney in avoiding any legislative action that is not absolutely necessary; third, they may delegate rule-making powers to the city manager whenever such delegation is legally possible; and fourth, they may handle whatever routine legislation remains necessary by the expeditious enactment of ordinances and resolutions compiled and presented under the direction of the city manager.

When state laws or charters provide too detailed an outline of municipal action, it may make a great deal of difference whether the city attorney, in interpreting their application to particular municipal actions, is sympathetic with the administrative point of view. The interpretation of laws and the drafting of ordinances are ordinarily functions of the city attorney, and therefore his attitude has an important influence on council procedures and accordingly on council-manager relations. His attitude may determine whether numerous repetitive actions by the council must precede administrative action, or whether the council need only lay down the lines of general policy and entrust its administration to the city manager.

If the city attorney is not familiar with administrative law, and if he knows no more of public administration in general, and council-manager government in particular, than he has learned from reading the charter of the city, he is apt to lean toward unworkable legalistic interpretation. For this reason the selection of a city attorney is a critical decision. If the city manager appoints the attorney, he should look for a man with some knowledge of administrative law, public administration, and council-manager government, or at least with a sympathy with administrative objectives. If the council selects the city attorney, the city manager should explain to the council the considerations that should govern its choice. The city manager should do his best to encourage any attorney who is appointed to recognize the differences between public and private law, not only as related to actions of the city *versus* outside persons, but also as to actions wholly within the government. He may be able to help the attorney by providing him with books and periodicals which provide such information.

The problem of reducing unnecessary action by the council may be further simplified by proper delegation of rule-making powers to the administrator. In order to carry on city services it is necessary from time to time to issue instructions, rules, and regulations governing situations in which citizens come into contact with the administration. Details of the relationship between municipal departments and the public must be standardized and formalized to some extent to make possible the administration of certain functions, of which the best examples are building inspection, public health work, refuse collection, and public utilities. Administration would be a difficult problem if applicants for building permits, for example, did not have to fill out a prescribed form, or if each citizen prepared his refuse for collection in a different way, or if any plumber could make an unsupervised connection to the city water mains.

It is impossible for the council to pass ordinances covering such minute regulations, and accordingly most councils give the manager the responsibility for issuing such regulations. They do so either (1) formally, by attaching to ordinances a clause such as "the city manager shall prescribe such rules and regulations as are necessary for carrying out the provisions of this ordinance," in which case the rules will presumably have the force of law, or (2) informally, by failing to pass any detailed regulations when such regulations will obviously be necessary to administer the law, leaving the city manager free to prepare them. Failure to comply with administrative rules issued with a specific grant of power is ordinarily not punishable by law, and such rules are usually enforced by the withholding of some privilege or service.

The delegation to the city manager of power to make rules having the force of law is increasing. The older and more conservative view is that, since the law-making power has been delegated to the council by the state, it cannot be delegated further to an administrative officer. However, the modification of this rule to fit modern conditions has been gradually accepted. But not every state is willing to admit such a practice yet, and the administrator, through the law department, should be certain of just what powers the council can delegate to him. Even when delegation is permitted in principle, there are certain standards to be followed in the legislation to insure legality. A study of the court's attitude toward this subject indicates three standards to observe:[3]

1. A legislative body or agency cannot delegate its powers of a legislative character. It can provide for the performance of administrative and ministerial functions and can delegate such powers.

2. The administrative details must of necessity be left, in part, to administrative officers or employees or to those acting in an administrative capacity.

3. Administrative regulations must be based on legislative standards sufficiently definite to direct and control administrative decisions; thus (a) the fee to be charged must be definite, (b) the term of any license, privilege, or permit must be fixed with sufficient definiteness in the ordinance or by reference to qualifications definitely determined by some other agency or regulation, and (c) standards should not permit the exercise of an arbitrary or uncontrolled administrative discretion.

Rules which managers issue in many cases cannot readily be distinguished in the minds of the average citizen from the council's ordinances. Therefore, all such rules should be quite clearly designated as being issued by the manager, with a statement as to the specific source of authority for their issuance whenever such a specific source exists. The content and wording of rules should avoid going any further than necessary to make ordinance provisions workable.

Some city managers have been so careful to avoid infringement upon the legislative function that they have had council enact as ordinances virtually all those rules and

---

[3] Ambrose Fuller, "Limits on Administrative Discretion," Public Management, August, 1939, pp. 234-35.

regulations directly affecting private citizens. Just as in the case of rules governing subordinate employees, this practice seems undesirable (except in those cases where legal enforcement of the rules requires that they be ordinances of the council), because it results in overformalization and loss of flexibility.

In supervising the issuance of these rules, the manager should ordinarily insist on clearance through his office in order to assure consistency throughout his administration. Some of the criteria which he may desire to follow are reasonableness, clarity, brevity, consistency in style with good public relations, and possibly uniform typography. Some cities have issued copies of ordinances with interpretations and rules inserted in the appropriate spots in the text. This practice has the two advantages of combining all related information in one publication and of making clear the reason for the existence of administrative rules which supply details omitted in the ordinance.

To the observer who expects the council to act only on questions of policy after careful deliberation, the reading of many ordinances by titles in rapid fire order and the perfunctory voting of them may seem to indicate carelessness and lack of interest. But it may mean only that the council is clearing red tape out of the way for consideration of more important matters. Some councils have been able to cut a great deal of legislative red tape by giving instructions to administrative officials either informally or by legislation on general principles, and then enacting without a great deal of deliberation or discussion the routine legislation required to put these instructions into effect.

In short, the legal distinction between legislation and its execution is quite different from the administrative distinction between the determination and the administration of policy. Therefore, when the council has once made up its mind on a policy, it is useless and unwise for it to take that matter up for deliberation every time a technicality requires legislative action. A logical corollary to this principle is the principle that the city manager should keep the council informed of any action that he has the legal power to take but that involves a question of policy.

Dealings with Subordinates. The council that wants to hold its city manager responsible for the administration of its policies must give him adequate authority to take administrative action. To do this the council must not only avoid detailed legislation which interferes with the manager's ability to carry out its previously expressed policy, but it must not — either through its individual members or as a body — interfere with the manager's control of his subordinates.

The city manager must make it clear to the council that he can accept full responsibility for administrative action only if there is no interference with his authority. The first fundamental aspect of this authority, of course, is the right of choosing his appointees. The second is that all relations between the council and the administrative organization should be carried on through the city manager's office. Third, the city manager should ask the council to refer to him for advice all petitions dealing with matters that he is administering.

1. The right to make appointments is one of the essentials of administrative authority. The council that wishes its city manager to act as a chief administrator must understand this principle. Every city manager should make sure that it does so before accepting appointment, and should make every effort to preserve this understanding thereafter. This does not preclude the manager from informing the council in advance of important personnel selections, nor even in some cases seeking the advice from the council as to desirable qualifications to be sought in candidates for a key position.

2. So that all relations between the council and administrative organization may be

carried on through the city manager, he should request the council not to give directions
to subordinates either formally or informally and to secure its information about all but
strictly routine aspects of the administration from the manager. No attempt should be
made to restrain free, informal contacts between councilmen and administrative officials,
but the city manager should instruct his subordinates. Subordinates should either refer
inquiring councilmen to him or report promptly to him whenever it has been necessary to
give information to a member of the governing body. (These general rules, of course, do
not refer to the giving of routine facts and figures, which may be furnished councilmen as
well as private citizens without any trace of formality or need of a report to the chief administrator). This requirement is not merely to preserve the manager's appearance of
authority, but it is necessary if a councilman is not to be misled by getting information
on a subject from one department that is not balanced with information on related subjects
from another department.

3. The council frequently has to handle petitions from citizens dealing with administrative matters. Very few citizens have any idea whether their petition calls for administrative action, and therefore might be presented to the city manager or some employee,
or whether it requires a decision of policy which only the council can make. One cannot
expect every citizen to make up his mind whether to route his petition through the administrative or the legislative side of the government. The council, therefore, must take the
responsibility for the proper routing of petitions. The council should be encouraged to
refer immediately to the manager by formal action all those petitions dealing with matters
under his control. He, in turn, should report back to the council on the ultimate disposition of each petition, and then the council may consider the petition itself if the petitioner
is not satisfied.

Similarly, the council should refer to the manager those citizens who desire to
enter a public complaint in council meetings on any matter properly subject to administrative decision. In most cities, citizen delegations and even individuals are permitted
to appear at council meetings and to present requests directly to the councilmen. This
practice is usually in keeping with local tradition, even though the complaint may be one
which the manager has never had an opportunity to remedy. The council may use two
methods to avoid such cases. It may establish a rule which requires that complainants
must arrange with the manager or clerk in advance to have their complaints on the agenda.
This rule will give the manager an opportunity to learn the nature of the complaint and
perhaps remedy the situation before it reaches the floor of the council meeting. Or, if
the citizen insists on being heard publicly, the council may courteously listen to the complaint, then without discussion formally refer it to the manager and set a definite date for
his report to be returned.

The council should hesitate to give a detailed hearing to a person who has not made
a reasonable effort to exhaust the administrative remedies. If he has honestly failed in
his attempt to get satisfaction from the manager, the council should then be willing to
listen patiently. The solution of this problem, as well as to many other problems of relations between the council and the administrator, must be worked out on a basis of mutual
understanding. Many councilmen are not familiar with the principles of administrative
responsibility and do not realize the effects on the administration of certain of their actions. In many cases, merely to explain the problem and to illustrate it with examples
from mutual experiences will get the desired cooperation from the councilmen. Certainly
no coercion may be used by the administrator; he therefore must be willing to make every
use of diplomacy.

The manager should not desire to stop the receiving of complaints by councilmen so long as the councilmen follow proper administrative lines in seeking their remedy, but he should do everything in his power to make such a system unnecessary. First of all, he should have an adequate complaint bureau and encourage its use by citizens. In handling complaints, no discrimination should be made with respect to persons, in order to impress upon the citizen the fact that he needs no especial influence to get results. Second, each complaint received through a councilman should be dealt with as efficiently as any other, but the employee dealing with the complainant should never give the impression that the complainant is getting anything more than the consideration he would have obtained if he himself had notified the complaint bureau or operating department.

Whenever a councilman is willing to refer the complainant instead of the complaint to the manager, it is good practice for the manager to call the councilman by telephone at a later date and advise him of the action taken. This follow-up service keeps the councilman informed as to the manager's methods of handling matters and thus serves to increase the councilman's confidence in the management, if the matter is properly handled. It is also good practice to keep individual councilmen well informed on administrative matters, not in order to ask their advice on how to do a thing or what action should be taken but to advise them of the action taken and reasons therefor. This information often serves to enable councilmen to make the proper reply to a complaining citizen, which he could not make if he were not informed, and it also leaves the impression with the citizen that he has an alert councilman as his representative.

The manager should set up a simple but formal system for insuring that matters referred to him by the council are promptly handled by the department heads so that requested actions are carried out and reports prepared without delay. Any council appreciates the prompt meeting of its requests which such a formal system evidences.

The system employed need not be complicated. If council minutes are printed or typewritten, the city manager may cut up and distribute a copy to the proper officials, or use a rubber stamp to indicate the point of reference. In many cities the manager uses a simple form for reporting council action to department heads. The form provides space for description of the council action and for the manager's instructions for disposition. If the matter is one requiring follow-up, a copy is kept in the manager's office for that purpose.

Representing the City Government to the Public

The city manager holds a key position in his community and this gives him an unusual opportunity to function as a leader. The potential value of community leadership, however, carries with it the necessity for the manager to give special attention to his relations with the council. He must take pains to make it entirely clear that he considers himself the subordinate of the council, and he must observe certain restrictions on his conduct.

First, the city manager must be particularly careful not to come into conflict with his council on important controversial issues. He should not publicly criticize any actions that the council has taken and should not make talks on undecided controversial issues if such talks are likely to embarrass the council members. Whenever he speaks on matters of municipal policy, he should not express decided opinions unless he is sure that his remarks will not embarrass members of the council. If he wishes to make it clear that his personal inclination had been toward some point of view rejected by the council, he may do so if he maintains an impartial attitude by analyzing facts and presenting both sides of the question at issue.

Second, it is best for the city manager not to discuss any question on a personal or political basis; even if he is stating a conclusion reached by all members of the council, he should state it from an administrative point of view, disregarding factional questions and refraining from personal references to the opposition.

Third, the city manager should make clear his subordination to the council and should not compete with its members for public attention. He should urge the mayor and councilmen to assume publicly the responsibility for controversial decisions and when he himself speaks, he should make it clear to the audience the ultimate decision is to be made by the council — not by himself.

The city manager should take care that due credit is given the council in reports released to the newspapers on matters of public policy. He should avoid releasing news stories that should properly come from councilmen or from the clerk of the council. In order to educate the public to the understanding that the council determines municipal policy, it may be desirable to have initial news stories on municipal accomplishments such as street paving work or park programs reported to the public through the council rather than directly by the manager. If a special committee of the council, together with the city manager and one or two other administrative officers, is engaged in a study of some municipal problem, statements to the papers should be given out by the ranking council member of the committee, unless the councilmen prefer to have the city manager issue the statement.

A manager need not hesitate to discuss matters on which the council has made a decision with which he agrees. If, for example, the council has voted a bond issue which requires approval in a public referendum, the city manager may publicly advocate the passing of the issue. He should feel free to explain the reasons for the bond issue and the entire background on which the council made its decision. Participation by the city manager in an electoral campaign of this character is entirely different from his participation in a campaign for the election of members of the council or for other political office. An electoral contest for a public office is a political contest, but an electoral contest for the approval or disapproval of a bond issue is merely the use of the electoral device to refer a legislative matter from the representatives of the people to the people themselves. If the manager properly can advise the council of impending matters, it is also proper for him to advise the people of impending legislative matters that the council has referred directly to the people.

The city manager is free to act as a community leader in the great majority of municipal policies which do not involve political controversies. To administer the policies determined by the council he must persuade those citizens affected as well as give orders to his subordinates. Many city managers have rendered their most valuable service to their communities by inducing their councils and electorates to approve of new services which had formerly been entirely unknown to them. As long as the city manager makes clear his willingness to carry out any policies that the council determines, it is a part of his function to explain in an impartial and factual manner the various policies which it would be possible for the government to follow.

Complications and Compromises. The relationship between the council and the city manager is a delicate equilibrium, and can be easily upset. For example, there is the not-uncommon situation in which the city manager is under political attack by a minority of the council members. In circumstances of this nature the city manager, although unable to maintain a cordial relationship, should be careful to maintain an attitude of personal neutrality toward those who are attacking him, for to enter actively into political disagreements will only make him more vulnerable to political attack.

If a majority of the members of the council will not defend him, he is in an untenable position. It is unwise for him to meet privately with majority members, both because it makes more difficult a reconciliation with a minority, and because it gives the minority further excuse for attacking the city manager as a political enemy. The city manager is then reduced to one of two courses: he may deal with the mayor on legislative matters and depend on him to further the policies of administration with the council, or he can maintain a purely formal relationship with the council, protecting himself by getting the council to approve as many as possible of the decisions that may lead to controversy.

The city manager is in nearly as difficult a position when group leaders outside the council choose to attack him or his relationship with the council. The council itself is in the best position to overcome this difficulty, which often stems from a lack of understanding that it is the city manager's normal function to make recommendations to the council and that this function does not represent an unwarranted assumption of the legislative responsibility of the council. While giving the city manager discretion in the work of administration, the council should not leave the impression that the manager has become personally responsible to the public for his actions, and it should take the trouble of explaining to the public the reasons for the city manager's actions and the fact that those actions were taken at the wish and with the support of the elected governing body.

A manager can often serve effectively as a community leader without heading a committee or taking direct leadership in civic programs. By searching out and discovering the many real leaders existing in the community, interesting them in new improvements for the community, and keeping them supplied with new ideas and encouraging them to work together, he can achieve far more than by direct leadership of his own.

Relations with Independent Boards and Officers

The problem of coordinating the many municipal activities in a community is greatly complicated in those cities which still have a number of boards and commissions operating certain municipal services. The independent status of these agencies is normally due to selection of membership by the mayor or council or by direct election. Although they operate in about the same geographical area as a municipality they are either separate administrative divisions of the city or an independent unit of government. Common examples of such boards are school boards, park or recreation boards, utility boards and library boards.

In addition, there may be officers who are either elected by the people or appointed by the mayor or city council, such as the city clerk, city attorney, and perhaps a finance officer, and who are therefore more or less independent of the control of the city manager. The task of coordinating the activities of these independent boards and officers with the work of the municipal government requires tact and patience, since in most instances coordination must be achieved by common agreement, not by legislative authority. Long-run coordination is, of course, generally more readily achieved when the council exercises the appointing power and some control over the finances of the independent body or office.

When the City Manager is a Member of Independent Board

Coordination is often best achieved when the manager is a member or ex officio member of the independent board. This gives him an excellent opportunity to gain an understanding of the problems and needs of a particular service administered by the board. As a member he can inform other members about the whole municipal government and encourage them to see how their particular service fits in with municipal services as a whole. If the manager disagrees with other members of the board on a particular problem and is frank in letting the board know about it, he may find it easier to present his point of view on matters presented by the board to the council.

Most administrators find that membership on a board is a distinct advantage in securing coordination, but in those instances where the manager must advise the council with respect to recommendations made by a board, he may be at a disadvantage if he disagrees with the board and at the same time is a member of it. For this reason some administrators feel that to serve as a member of the board might involve too great an overlapping of the legislative and administrative functions. Where there is a clear-cut difference of opinion in the membership of the board it often falls to the administrator to make the final decision, and he may be in a better position to make a decision if he is not a member of the board.

When the Manager is Not a Member of Independent Agency

If a manager does not have official status on the governing body of an independent agency, he may want to take one or more of the following steps:

1. Let the members of the independent agency know that their work is important, that he wants to work with them, and in no way intends to take advantage of his office for the purpose of dictating agency policies. If the agency is not satisfied with any decision he must make, he should let it be understood that he would have no objection if the agency goes directly to the council.

2. Invite independent officers and members of boards to attend periodic meetings at which matters of interest to such agencies will be discussed, or at which general municipal policies affecting their special interest are discussed. Some city councils make a practice of holding a joint meeting at least once a year with each independent board to talk over the work of that agency.

3. Whenever possible, deal with independent agencies in an informal manner rather than by formal letters or regulations as the best means of developing mutual understanding. A visit to the office of the independent agency or a luncheon meeting is preferable to indirect contact.

4. Place at the disposal of the several independent agencies any service or advice that the regular city departments can provide. This may take the form of auxiliary services, such as personnel, accounting and purchasing. It may take the form of information supplied by copies of orders and regulations, newsletters, and the oral presentation of facts and ideas. The work which the city does for the independent board or officer should be handled with the same dispatch and promptness as a matter which comes under the direct supervision of the chief administrator.

5. Give full credit to the independent agency for favorable results. The manager should not shirk any criticism that may come to him in connection with his part in carrying out matters jointly agreed upon.

Key Officials

The manager must make a special effort to obtain the cooperation of city attorneys, clerks, treasurers or auditors who are appointed by the city council, or elected directly.

They must be assured of the manager's need for their help. Good relations are aided by special mention in the manager's monthly or annual reports, or in his public talks when he refers to the value of cooperative assistance provided by these officials. Every person likes to feel needed and valued, and if the manager will cultivate the assistance and guidance of these officials it will not be long before they are asking for and taking suggestions from the manager.

Relations with Other Governmental Units

Other Local Units

There are over 100,000 local government units in the United States. The county or township, the city or town, and the school district are to be found in almost every urban area, and in many parts of the country these units are supplemented by sanitary districts, mosquito abatement districts, and a host of other special units. In metropolitan areas there is a particularly complicated pattern of local governments with overlapping or contiguous boundaries. In such a setting the task of administering a city government includes the establishment and maintenance of cordial relations with the city's governmental neighbors.

Cooperation to improve services to the citizen can be secured by either informal or formal means. The informal methods are substantially those discussed under the previous heading, "Relations With Independent Boards and Officers." Conferences, luncheon meetings, telephone conversations and other forms of personal contact make up the informal methods. Formal actions may include exchange of general services, temporary loans and joint use of equipment and personnel, performance of a service by one governmental unit for another, joint performance of a service, and cooperative administration through state leagues.

In order to establish or perform selected services on a cooperative basis, the municipality must have, either in the city charter or state legislation, the authority to perform the service and the authority to sell, buy, or jointly perform such services. Many states in recent years have given cities greater power to enter into such arrangements. In some states municipalities may exercise territorial powers of a specified nature beyond their legal limits, but within their spheres of influence.

It is becoming more common for states to give cities power either to transfer certain services to another unit or to authorize the county or other units to perform for the city certain municipal services. Finally, cities are authorized in many states to enter into arrangements with other units for the joint administration of services either by contractual or administrative arrangements. Municipal officials are making increasing use of these various devices for the integration of certain services.

Formal arrangements between communities normally should be contained in a written agreement. A written agreement has the advantage of delineating for each party its respective responsibilities, and offers some protection from misunderstanding from arbitrary interpretation when elections change the personnel of a council or a board.

Exchange of General Services. Arrangements under this heading may vary from an exchange of advisory facilities to joint planning for the use of office space and scheduling of a proper sequence or operation of the activities of the city to fit into the activities of other local units. In between are such exchanges of service as cooperation between city and county officials in locating and securing a proper description and determining the ownership of tax delinquent property, or the purchase by one unit from another at approximate cost of such items as gravel, sand, and gasoline. In this type of arrangement it may be desirable to have written contracts to provide for a plan of handling the work and reaching proper charges and credits.

Temporary Loans and Joint Use of Equipment and Personnel. Some of the common examples of this kind of arrangement are the joint use of police radio, joint use of central garage facilities, and even the occasional transfer of personnel between cities to meet peak loads. A city department may keep a list of all city-owned equipment as well as the equipment owned by other units, and arrangements may be made in advance for joint use or temporary transfer of equipment from one unit to another, either to meet peak loads or to avoid the necessity of having to provide duplicate equipment. Such arrangements should be planned for in advance, and plans for financing and administration should be agreed upon. The cooperative use of personnel is found in joint inspection services such as milk inspection, for example, or in the appointing or deputizing of an agent of one unit to represent another governmental unit.

Performance of a Service by One Governmental Unit for Another. There are probably few municipalities that do not provide one or more services to suburban villages or rural areas. Fire fighting services on a contract or special charge basis, the provision of municipal utility services and similar arrangements are common.

Some cities have found it advantageous to act under state laws permitting the county to contract for the performance of certain functions which can be more efficiently and effectively administered on a county rather than on a city basis. Welfare, health and assessment administration are the services most commonly delegated to the county.

Joint Performance of a Service. The area of administration may be enlarged through voluntary cooperation and mutual agreement between two or more adjacent governmental units for the joint administration of certain services by contractual or administrative agreement. In some cases a special district is created. Some of the municipal functions commonly covered by joint agreements are sewage disposal, trunk line sewers, education, and libraries.

Cooperative Administration Through State Leagues. The exchange of services and information between cities has been aided by state leagues of municipalities, many of which provide field services on technical problems such as ordinance revision and codification, accounting installations, and audit work. Through the leagues, municipalities in a few states have developed joint purchasing services, joint personnel services, joint financing activities, joint pension schemes, and a variety of other cooperative measures. The Michigan Municipal League, for example, has been of great help to many Michigan cities in purchasing fire hose, chemicals, traffic paints, water meters, street name signs, centrifugal pumps, and fire alarm equipment on a joint basis. Many state municipal leagues have established in-service training programs for various groups of municipal officials.

Advantages of Written Agreements. A written agreement between two or more units for a certain service enables each party to know just what its responsibilities are, how the respective services of all parties can be brought together, and how the cost of the service is to be shared. The success of the joint program is better assured under such an agreement than under an informal arrangement which may result in misunderstanding. The formal agreement or written contract between two or more units may be necessary in some instances in order to overcome certain legal difficulties or to meet legal requirements, or it may be desirable merely to clarify various aspects of the joint program. But in all cases it is quite important that agreements be based on a clear and thorough understanding evolved from a well thought out plan.

A written agreement between two or more units generally includes the legal author-ity for action, states the reason for the agreement and the objectives sought, provides for placing responsibility and allocation of work between the several units, specifies the date on which the agreement becomes effective and ends, and provides for a method of making changes. There is little that can be done under an informal agreement when one unit is unwilling or unable to continue with the arrangement. In a written agreement, however, if one of the units involved wishes to drop out, certain steps as specified in the agreement must be followed. Changes in a written agreement can become effective only after ap-proval by all parties to the contract.

State Governments

State Legislation. Since cities are legally creatures of the state, their administra-tive functions and procedures as well as their broad policies and programs bear the im-print of state legislation. For this reason, it is essential that the city manager give close attention to the development of state legislation as it affects the municipality. What can and should the administrator do to influence state legislation affecting the city? How and by whom should the city's interest be presented?

The primary role of the manager should be that of expert advisor. He, more than any other individual, is in a position to know how proposed legislation will affect the op-erations of his city government or what new legislation may be needed. He must there-fore accept the responsibility for studying proposed legislation and for analyzing its prob-able effects on the city government.

The next step is to take some definite action favoring or opposing the proposed leg-islation. The manager's first concern will be to secure the approval of his council before taking any further action. Unless the council agrees with his interpretation and recom-mendations he should not feel free to take any direct action himself. After the manager and the council have reached an agreement as to the city's interest in specific state leg-islation, the next step is to see that this interest is represented before the state legisla-ture. Here again the administrator usually prefers an inconspicuous role providing the facts and arguments for others to present to the public and to the legislature. While there may be exceptions, in most cases the burden of argument may be left to elected officials of the city, to local representatives in the state legislature or to interested citi-zen organizations.

A particularly valuable aid to administrators in legislative matters in most states will be the state league of municipalities. Many of these leagues are doing outstanding work in representing the interests of cities in state legislatures. Through their secre-tariats they keep city officials informed of proposed legislation affecting cities, analyze the probable effects of such legislation, and bring the pressure of united municipal opin-ion to bear upon the legislative bodies. More and more municipal officials are directing their contacts with state legislatures through this effective channel. Individual adminis-trators are, of course, still responsible for passing on the findings of the league secre-tariat to their own councils and citizens and for representing local attitudes and interests in the league. The league is a supplement, not a substitute for local analysis and repre-sentation.

Nonlegislative Matters. The city manager will be the focal point of contact with officials of the state government in nonlegislative matters. State influence in these matters takes various forms: grants-in-aid, advisory services, direct services, and various types of administrative supervision and control.

Most states offer grants to cities for education and for highways, and many states give similar aid for libraries, health work, and other activities. The manager must assume the responsibility for seeing that the city receives its fair share of grants-in-aid, and that appropriate action is taken to secure any necessary improvements in grant legislation.

Most cities fail to take full advantage of the advice and information available to them through state agencies. In many cases this is due to the failure of otherwise excellent state offices to publicize their services adequately, but if this is the situation the city manager should go out of his way to find out what is offered. The most common services include publication of numerous manuals and bulletins, giving of individual financial and technical advice, and holding of periodic conferences in many fields.

Typical of the numerous free direct services available to cities in some states are the installation of new methods and procedures for certain city departments, the maintenance of a central state criminal identification office, and the lending of personnel and equipment in times of special municipal need.

The administrative supervision and control of local municipalities by the state government includes such activities as financial audit; the requirement of periodic reports on various activities; state review and approval of certain acts (e.g., approval of bond issues); state certification of local officials; and state adoption of rules and regulations in specific fields (e.g., public health regulations). The city manager must acquaint himself with all such requirements established by the state and the procedures to be followed.

Federal Government

The federal constitution contains no mention of cities. Traditionally, the national government and the cities have both dealt with the state but not with each other. However, this relationship began to change in 1930's and has now reached the point where some voices are being raised for the creation of a "Department of Urbiculture," for special federal action to aid in the solution of the complex problems of metropolitan areas, and for many other forms of direct federal-city relations.

The present interest areas common to municipalities and the federal government can be grouped into three categories: the provision of information, advice, and services by the federal government to the municipalities; the provision of financial aid by the federal government to the local unit; and the requirement of municipal compliance with certain federal controls and regulations (e.g., compliance with airport regulations).

The municipality's role, and therefore the role of the city manager in influencing federal legislation is much more tenuous than in the field of state legislation. In general, however, the same principles apply to the administrator's role in influencing federal legislation. The main artery for expressing municipal opinion on federal legislation is now the American Municipal Association. The city manager can usually best express the local unit's feelings with reference to specific legislation through the American Municipal Association and through personal contacts with representatives from the local area. Many legislators value the opinion of specific persons found to be reliable and objective sources of information.

Conclusion

Government exists to serve the needs and wants of the people. In fulfilling these wants on the municipal level the relationship between the council and the city manager — between the legislature and its chief administrator — is the keystone of effective democratic government. Fruitful relationships are based on mutual confidence and understanding, the same ingredients that leaven all cooperative human endeavor. It is a responsibility of the chief administrator to make every effort to establish and maintain a good working relationship with the council by recognizing his responsibility to a collective body, by avoiding factional disputes, and by intelligent leadership. The administrator must also create an atmosphere of cooperation between the municipality and other governmental organizations in order to obtain optimum services at minimum cost for the people of the community.

Chapter 3

THE ORGANIZATION PROBLEM

The typical city government provides police and fire protection, maintains a safe water supply, disposes of waste and refuse, constructs and maintains streets and other public ways, fosters the good health of its residents, builds and operates leisure time facilities, and in a variety of other ways contributes to the well-being of the community. The manifold services which a community receives from its local government require the full time work and attention of many individuals in almost as many separate occupations. They involve the use of myriad items of equipment and the operation and maintenance of a physical plant which normally represents the largest single investment in the community.

Individual human accomplishment demands an orderly application of the resources available to the individual. To an infinitely greater degree, the orderly and effective conduct of a municipal government requires sound organization — sound in respect to identification of component parts, assignment of functions, definition of authority and responsibility, facilitation and coordination of individual accomplishments, provision of support where needed, and creation of lines of communication.

Ideally an organization should be fluid and adapted, as necessary and without undue formality, to meet the requirements of any particular situation or time. Moreover, organizational relationships should encourage individuals to exercise imagination and initiative and yet produce a controlled quality of work or service. However, if a chief executive is to be accountable for the level and kind of performance by all organizational components, the organizational structure must take on a certain formality or rigidity to provide the continuity and orderliness required for the management function.

Organization is one of the elementary aspects of administration. As it is in large part a matter of structure and lends itself to being charted, it becomes a useful means of identifying or depicting other aspects of administration. For example, the organization chart may define the "chain of command" or indicate the points of control or review of administrative actions.

Aside from its utility as a pedagogic or illustrative device, the intrinsic relationship which organization bears to administration is subject to many different views. One extreme position was stated in 1733 by Alexander Pope in his famous couplet: "For forms of government let fools contest; whatever is best administered is best." The other extreme is represented by various organizational theorists who have formalized and defined organizational principles to the point that organization is on a par with administration or comprehends all aspects. The common view of public administrators is somewhere in between these two extremes.

Nature of the Problem

What do we mean by "organization"? Mooney defines it as "the form of every human association for the attainment of a common purpose."[1] Thus, any motive calling for associated human action must express itself in organization. Since this definition identifies organization as a pure process, a dual relation is indicated: on one hand, to the people who create and use the process, and on the other, to the aim or object of the process. The process itself, the internal structure, represents "organization" and is the subject of his analysis.

Urwick notes three aspects of organization.[2] The static or structural aspect, he compares to designing an automobile. The other two are dynamic or operating aspects. When the design is completed, there follows the selection and training of individuals to discharge the various groups of responsibilities involved in the design; the automobile has to be built. When that is done, the individuals must be directed, in constant coordination, toward the objective for which the undertaking was set up; the automobile is driven toward its destination.

Urwick confines his analysis to the static or structural aspect of organization which he defines as "determining what activities are necessary to any purpose and arranging them in groups that may be assigned to individuals." He argues that mechanic and dynamic concepts of organization be kept distinct and be dealt with in order. The structure comes first and without reference to the individuals available to man individual positions. This he emphasizes, is not to say that there should never be any adaptation of organization to the strengths and weaknesses of a particular individual. Such adjustment may be desirable and convenient. But if it is carried out after a correct distribution of functions has been established, it can be treated as an exception incurred to meet a personal situation, to be restored to the "normal pattern" as soon as an opportunity presents itself.

Mooney, Urwick and other early organizational theorists regarded organization, *per se*, as a separate field of inquiry. They stressed the common aspects of all organizations and minimized the distinction between public and private. People were viewed as fundamentally rational and thus there were "principles" to which their behavior within group efforts conformed.

Many recent writers reject the traditional theory that structural concepts of organization can be created separately from the actual characteristics and peculiarities of the persons who happen to inhabit the organization at a particular time.[3] Organization is viewed as a human institution which rests not only on formal arrangements, skill, and numbers, but even more on attitudes, enthusiasms, and loyalties. To these writers, the central problem of organization is fitting together organization structure and human nature, recognizing the dimensions of personality or the variables involved in personality. Thus, organizational behavior becomes an important and, to an extent, controlling aspect.

The older organizational theory tended to emphasize the power of human reason to master the facts of human relationships and arrange the relationships logically to achieve predetermined goals. The newer theory gives increased recognition of nonrational

---

[1] James D. Mooney, Principles of Organization (New York: Harper and Brothers, 1947). 225 pp.
[2] Lyndall F. Urwick, Scientific Principles and Organization (New York: American Management Association, 1938). 16 pp.
[3] Dwight Waldo, Ideas and Issues in Public Administration (New York: McGraw-Hill, 1953). 462 pp.

factors in human nature. It stresses the emotional and even subconscious as well as social factors which cause organizations of human components to be what they are.

In attempting to bring the nonrational and irrational within its scope and control, the new theory aims at more perfect management control of an organization but, at the same time, becomes less authority-oriented. Direction is achieved indirectly through use of and emphasis upon the data and concepts of psychology and sociology. There is an increasing interest in the massive emotional substructure of organization and the structures of informal organization. Identifying and analyzing the variety of informal patterns of influence to which members of an organization respond is thus held to be one of the main answers to the organizational problem.

Can a conceptual separation be made between organizational mechanics and the human personalities within the organization? The practical answer to this question is a dual one. Certainly, some of the precepts of traditional organizational theory have a demonstrated validity, at least to the extent of being useful criteria for analysis of organizational strengths or defects. "Specialization," for example, is one of those precepts; its undisputed advantages in manufacturing processes have been clearly recognized ever since the industrial revolution, and there is some carry-over of those advantages in present-day municipal organization. At the same time the problem of morale and personnel cannot be shunted aside by concern with logic and structural qualities.

The main purpose of organization is fitting together individuals and their tasks as productively as possible and this chapter recognizes organization as both a technical or structural problem and a human problem. The administrator must seek to find the best, most rational ways to achieve multiperson group action to attain enumerated goals; this is a technical problem. Also, he must be concerned with the nonrational factors, human and other, which force amendment to the rational plan. It has been suggested that there is merit in a system of organization analysis at the practitioner level that begins with the rational, then adjusts in terms of human and social necessities.

Urwick, while still maintaining the structural nature of the organizational problem, makes a not-too-different observation. With a going concern where there are people and habits and customs to deal with, he suggests that the administrator imagine a "clean sheet" and draw up an "ideal" organization for an undertaking of that particular size and circumstance. Then "lock it in your desk — but make two resolutions:

"1. Whenever a position falls vacant or any organization change is desirable, you should pull it out and have a look at it."
"2. As far as is humanly possible, you will never make a change in organization in the wrong direction, that is away from the 'ideal,' always toward it." [4]

The reference to a "going concern" brings into focus another consideration in organization analysis, a consideration which is particularly magnified in municipal administration. When a manager moves into a city administration, he will inevitably find a fixed structural pattern and established intra-personal relationships. A municipal organizational structure reflects past and current environment within which were shaped the policies not only of the local government itself but also of the state of which the city is legally a creation. The establishment of policy frequently involves a selection, arbitration, or reconciliation of the interests and points of view of conflicting elements of the

[4] Lyndall F. Urwick, The Theory of Organization (New York: American Management Association, 1952), p. 14.

body politic. Organizational patterns created or set in motion within one context carry on and become accepted even though the context within which they were created is completely changed. Federal and state legislation affect the organization pattern.

Intelligent decision as to the type of administrative organization best suited to the needs of a city depends not upon application of a formula or set of principles but upon the studied consideration of a multitude of factors.

Approach to Organization Analysis

The traditional approach to a study of organization has been in terms of requirements of "specialization." It is assumed that individuals are recruited on the basis of possession of particular skills involved in the performance of particular jobs. Further, activities are assigned to departments on the basis of their close relationships and to permit specialized supervisors or department heads. Specialization may be vertical as well as horizontal — special tasks are assigned not only to different departments in the organization, but different tasks are also assigned to workers, foremen, and on up the supervisory line. There are decisions which only the chief executive is permitted to make, others are made by department heads, others by subordinates subject to departmental approval, and so forth.

Many writers have treated individual positions as the "building blocks" with which departments and the city government are constructed. The basic question in constructing an organization thus becomes, "Which blocks are so similar that they can be put together to form a unit?" Much has been written about the basis for determining similarity, e.g., process, purpose, clientele served, or other measures. The question of the basis for division of work is of course pertinent to the problem of organization but it is not synonymous.

At any one time that the chief executive turns his attention to the organization problem apart from other aspects of management, two facts become evident:

1. There are a variety of functions and services being performed through a maze of organizational units in which a number of individuals participate.

2. The organizational pattern does not conform to any established theory of organization and the mere "charting" will require arbitrary amendments in order to make it "fit" the dimensions available. Certain parts of the "organization" may be so disjointed that they may escape attention completely.

The executive is unlikely to know why the organization is what it is, and it is probable that determining why would be an extremely difficult project. To approach the question of organization solely in terms of grouping or re-grouping "blocks" to achieve a rational division of work is clearly unrealistic.

Developing an organization which meets complex and complicated needs of a city government is a task involving consideration of many questions. The questions cannot be easily categorized, but at least for purposes of discussion they may be grouped as follows:

1. What are the objectives of the organization? Or, what is expected to be accomplished by various elements of the city government?

2. What is the environment, legal and political and other, within which the organization must operate? What are some of the deterrents to achieving a rational organization?

3. How should functions be assigned to departments? What are the considerations and criteria in the departmentalization of the city government?

4. What coordinative mechanisms are needed and will best serve the purpose of making parts of the organization into something responsive to the chief executive?

5. How can the services and tasks to be performed be fitted together most productively with the people available to perform them?

6. What are the human problems? To what extent is an organization determined by the people within it?

The next several paragraphs discuss how one goes about attempting to find the answers to these questions.

Organization Objectives

The measure of the effectiveness of an organization should be on the basis of the results accomplished in relation to its objectives. This implies that the objectives be defined in such a way that the results not only can be expressed in terms of the objectives but also may be accurately measured.

In most private industry, objectives and results can be defined and identified relatively easily. In the first place, a private company has the basic objective of making a profit for its owners; the extent to which it accomplishes this is not difficult to ascertain and measure, although, of course, the nature of the particular company organizational pattern may have less bearing on the profit level than environmental and other factors such as the state of the national economy. The functional objective may be to produce automobiles which are competitive in all particulars in the automotive market. Again, organization performance can be related to, and to a considerable extent, measured in terms of the objective.

On the other hand, most public organizations do not have ends which are concrete enough to permit application of ready-made criteria. A municipal government, for example, exists to provide services and facilities required by law or otherwise determined to be its responsibility. How does one measure the effectiveness of a political institution in providing facilities and services?

Responsiveness to Public Interests

A municipal organization should be responsive to public interest and demands. This is probably the basic objective of a democratic government, but it is a vague one by which to relate or measure or even identify the criteria of measurement. Public interests and demands not only change and express themselves in different ways, but are subject to conflicting interpretations. Moreover, needs and demands must be met within available financial resources or other limitations which make the organizational effort only one of the factors in the organization's total effectiveness.

Obviously, some individual components of the total organization may be isolated and criteria for analyzing their effectiveness developed with some precision. For example, by identifying and classifying incidents requiring police attention by type, time, and location, it is possible to deploy the men and equipment of the patrol division of a police department on a reasonably sound and accurate basis with respect to actual and projected need and the "objective" of responding promptly to incidents occurring.

The effectiveness of the municipal government with respect to protection of people and property, however, is measurable only in the incalculable sense of the number of crimes, accidents, and fires which do not occur because of preventive measures taken. Many different units operating within many different contexts all contribute to the objective of making a community a safe place to live. Moreover, it is probable that many of the activities or programs which should contribute to this objective are not included in the organizational structure.

The first consideration in organization analysis is with objectives, but it must be concerned with needs and programs, rather than with subordinate units and powers and duties of departments and commissions. It involves much more than how a police department can best be organized to accomplish specified departmental assignments — even more than the question of how police and related public safety activities of the city government can be organized. The fundamental consideration, and the starting point of organization analysis and construction, is "What are the needs, met and unmet, of the community in the public safety area and to what extent are existing functional and organizational arrangements directed toward meeting those needs."

"Efficiency and Economy"

Reference has been made to measuring the effectiveness of an organization in terms of its objectives. As matter of fact, "effectiveness" in itself becomes an objective of municipal government. The terms "efficiency and economy" have, of course, become shibboleths in almost every consideration of organization revision. To many persons who believe the less money spent by government the more retained by the taxpayer, "efficiency and economy" mean less expenditure without respect to social needs and objectives. Most practitioners and writers in public administration use this term, not in any miserly sense, but to express the fundamental goal of most human effort — to accomplish the work at hand with the least expenditure of human and material resources.

The expression, "efficiency and economy" is frequently used in a still larger sense to express the objective of justice or fairness to the "consumers" of governmental services. This connotes more than the best ratio between effort and resources expended to work achieved. It relates to the whole problem of husbanding the resources of the community for maximum use and enjoyment by present and future "consumers." A vague and general "objective," yes, but certainly one which must be reflected in organizational considerations if the organization is to survive. Neither efficient dictatorships nor well-intentioned but poorly guided bureaucracies are apt to be long-lived organizations.

Relating Results to Objectives

The difficulty in defining and clearly articulating goals and objectives of municipal government in terms which can be counted or expressed on a profit and loss statement has been partly responsible for two erroneous approaches to the organizational problem which have characterized the efforts of some practitioners and students of organization. One is to impute objectives to an organizational unit to which identifiable accomplishments are related. This can be an interesting exercise but is likely to contribute little to helping the organizational unit accomplish the social purposes for which it was created.

The other approach is to begin with existing established structure and be concerned with detaching and adding parts, divisions, or consolidating departments, and so on, i.e., a "block" shifting process. In the latter instance, the organization skips over the identification of basic social objectives and their relations to the principal public service areas for which the government is responsible or within which it has significant responsibilities.

The organizational problem must be approached in terms of what functions the city is performing, why they are being performed, what units have responsibility for what segments, what the needs are, and what the relation is between needs and the provision of facilities to meet them. In other words, with the existence of modern communication and other facilities, with vastly improved police and firefighting techniques, and in view of the cost of separate police and fire departments, does a city need both police and fire departments? In view of the expanded role played by schools in community affairs, should the city's cultural and recreational and library and other programs develop without relation to schools? Should expanding medical and social service programs be integrated with existing departments? Can a city organize for good traffic engineering and street development without being concerned with mass transportation or parking?

Organizational Environment

There is general agreement that a municipal organization should possess certain properties which are implicit in the integration of authority and responsibility. Among these "properties" are:

1. Rational departmental grouping along functional lines.

2. Absence of independent administrative agencies and boards.

3. Adequate staff services and other managerial aids to the chief administrator.

4. Absence of "restraints" such as excessive legislative definition of structure.

5. Possession by the chief executive of the means, in terms of tenure, appointive power, and administrative discretion, to exercise executive power and to be held accountable for the direction of city affairs.

6. A good social environment for development of a good working force.

Why, in view of the common agreement on the need for an integrated, systematic, and rational arrangement of administrative agencies, do so many public organizations fall short of these attributes?

Political Influences

Principally, it is because it is a political organization and is established and controlled by laws, statutes, and ordinances which originated in a variety of ways. Citizens view the purposes or objectives of government in different ways. This brings into play many forces and pressures for dispersion and compartmentalization of administrative activities.

The alternative to a single focus of the governmental process is control over administrative programs through the diverse and complex paths of influence which can be exerted on administrative agencies through direct contacts, group associations, pressures of special opinion channels, and the countless interrelationships which connect people at specific jobs with the persons whom these jobs interest and affect. External pressures and forces contribute to making an organization what it is and have to be taken into consideration in any attempts at rationalizing the organizational structure.

Inertia and Preservation of *Status Quo*

Another characteristic of a public organization, or perhaps for that matter any large organization, is that of inertia. Preservation of the status quo sometimes appears to be the overriding objective within some organizations. The fact that an organization resists changes must be recognized and considered in any attempt to analyze it or change it. Such an attempt automatically disturbs the habit pattern of the individuals who make up the organization, and these individuals will be uneasy to the point of resistance to any disturbance of their work pattern.

Thus these pressures, both external and internal, act to shape the municipal organization and, to a considerable extent, tend to "stabilize" it.

"Nonrational" Influences on Organization

Pressures and forces express themselves in the legal framework within which a city government must operate. This includes the state constitution and general and special statutes applying to the city, the city charter, and court decisions affecting municipalities. These legal provisions often establish and require organizational features which are incompatible with the recognized attributes of a "good" organizational structure.

When the organizational problems of a going concern are being given attention, the many statutory provisions in effect preserve the status quo and thus represent inhibitions to establishing an effective organization. Nevertheless, if and when these inhibitions to effective organization are overcome, the features of "good" organization are, in turn, almost certain to be given legal status.

Viewed within a larger context, what a municipal organization does — how it is organized to perform its functions — is essentially outside the organization's own control. Many new programs and functions undertaken by cities in recent years — housing, redevelopment, welfare, social service, and venereal disease control, for example — have had their origin and received their impetus outside municipal government. As a new program is created and becomes a city function, a new agency to administer it often follows. Experience shows that sometimes this is the only way a new program can get a real start. Older agencies into which, from the point of view of purpose or process, the new program might be fitted would have failed to provide the drive and emphasis intended by the legislative body.

An institution as complex and as subject to as many forces and pressures as a city government cannot be reshaped radically or suddenly to conform to any rigid concepts of effective organization. Many forces and pressures work actively for the continuation of administrative dispersion and other features of "poor" organization.

Historical Concepts of "Democracy"

In most states, original constitutional and statutory provisions relating to the structure of city government were written during the period when the prevailing theory sought to insure responsiveness to popular wishes through popular elections. The number of elective administrative posts in city government have been steadily declining in favor of "integrated" organizations. Nevertheless, it is difficult to change an elective office into an appointive one, or even more difficult to amalgamate the functions and activities performed by a former elective officer with related functions and activities for redistribution and assignment on a rational basis.

Voters become accustomed to voting for an office and have a tendency to feel that it is appropriately elective. Moreover, there is a tendency to identify the functions historically assigned to an elective officer as having some special "political" significance which should remain intact even if the method of selection of the head is changed. For example, the "functions" of an elective city treasurer have many times been transferred intact to an appointive officer — perhaps a part-time officer. It is more than likely of course that these "functions" when analyzed will be found to consist of cashiering, clerical, and ministerial tasks which can be integrated with the tasks of various units of the finance department.

From the practical standpoint, of course, any move to "lower" an agency head from elective to appointive status must face up to the fact that the incumbent of an elective post has, by definition, a political following, which gives him a status of some strength and independence.

Special Reform Movements

The political process has not always been spotless. As a result, reform movements for special functions have characterized development of municipal government. Personnel and finance, including purchasing, are the outstanding examples of functions whose organization has been determined, to a considerable extent, by reform governments. The establishment of early civil service agencies had to a considerable extent the objective of removing personnel administration from the chief administrative officer or officers of the governmental organization. Even when the need for such inhibitions to "effective," i.e., integrated, administrative organization disappears, efforts to bring personnel administration into the administrative family are apt to be resisted. The extent to which it can be integrated depends in large measure on the factors unrelated to the question of how the function can be best administered.

Special Interests

American society is largely a pluralistic one. Residents of a city have stronger loyalties to particular groups of which they are members than the community as a whole, or, at least, these special loyalties are much more discernible. The Parent-Teachers Association feels that the Education Department should be sacrosanct, for example. Each interest group identifies the public interest as its own and feels that it can best assure that its affairs are properly considered by keeping the agency "independent" — meaning, of course, independent of everyone but the particular interest concerned.

Professionalization

One of the most significant developments in the public service has been the "professionalization" or the binding together of the occupational specialists within the municipal government. Teachers, engineers, assessors, welfare workers, policemen, and firemen have developed close group ties and associations. This has been an important asset to public administration. It has promoted respect for technical expertness, facilitated communication and spread of new developments, and produced a degree of group loyalty and discipline. At the same time, professionalization produces strong tendencies toward separatism. For some, intra-group loyalties may become stronger than loyalty to administrative superiors.

Isolation of Special Programs

There have been widespread and frequently influential beliefs that special kinds of governmental programs should be kept apart from the administrative hierarchy. Such agencies have most frequently been headed by boards and commissions and they generally have legal guarantees against central administrative control.

Planning and zoning administration and tax equalization, for example, are believed by many to be too "controversial" or "political" to be assigned to regular administrative organization. Related are activities considered to be experimental in character or in need of strong public support as pioneering projects.

Departmentalization of City Functions

The term "department" as used here means the largest parts or subdivisions of the city government. The concepts of organization that are used, namely, (1) purpose or function, (2) work process, (3) area, and (4) clientele, were brought into widespread use in the nineteen-thirties by Luther Gulick. These concepts have been widely used in studying and analyzing the composition of organizational structure. They have been useful as an aid to understanding arrangement of structures and in determining what should have priority in creation of departments. They do not, however, furnish ready-made answers which can be applied automatically. Nor are the four alternative methods of grouping mutually exclusive. For example, some departments may be organized by purpose and also decentralized on an area basis.

The fundamental character of these several modes of organization may appear self-evident but this is far from the case. Organization by purpose means grouping together in a departmental organization those positions with subordinate units which are dedicated to the same or similar purposes — the solution of the same or similar problems. The trouble with this definition is that it does little more than indicate the dominant characteristic of the concept, and leaves the exact boundaries to be delineated. For example, several public safety units concerned with traffic, uniform patrol, and criminal investigation are commonly grouped together in a police department. Those concerned with other aspects of public safety are included in a fire department. Is this proper grouping by purpose or should they be integrated into a single department of public safety?

Still another aspect of the definition which gives rise to uncertainty is the difficulty of determining the purpose to which the several administrative units are actually dedicated. What, for example, is the purpose of a city housing authority? It may be possible to determine this exactly only by analysis of legislative intent.

Aside from the inadequacy of the definition is the difficulty — under certain circumstances at least — of differentiating some of the organizational concepts from others. Superficially the distinction is clear. A department of public works is generally characterized as being organized on the basis of work process, i.e., engineering. Cannot such a department also be characterized as functionally organized for the purpose of constructing and maintaining public works? A fire department represents a specialization by work process, i.e., firefighting, as well as purpose. A bureau of old age assistance, for example, can be characterized as organized on the basis of clientele, i.e., recipients of the assistance. But it also reflects the public purpose or function of providing special care and assistance to part of the citizenry.

In view of the shadowy lines delineating these concepts in the abstract, can they be useful criteria in departmentalizing activities? The answer is that while no categorical answer can be given to the question of which type of grouping is better, these concepts represent useful criteria to be weighed in the construction of a department. Here are some of the important considerations:

"Under what conditions should emphasis be laid upon one of these considerations rather than another? In what circumstances should similarity of purpose or function dominate in the development of departmental structure? When are the services rendered to a particular segment of the body politic of paramount importance? What weight, if any, should be given to factors of professional advantage or technical efficiency? How significant is the mere matter of place or territory? These are weighty matters in the creation of a department structure and as such deserve extended consideration." [5]

The construction of departments does not rest solely upon one basis or another, but these concepts enter into the construction and operation of all departments. The problem concerns the emphasis which should be laid upon one basis or the other within a given social context in order to fit together people and forces as productively as possible.

Thus, in various ways agencies can be held out of the main administrative structure and in various degrees can be made independent. These pressures and road-blocks to rationalization of an organization are considerable. Agencies want to be independent, interest groups are concerned with performance of certain functions and want to keep them walled-off; occupational groups want to keep their activities undiluted; and other factors operate to hinder any over-all approach to organization.

To the practitioner concerned with administrative structure, these factors have to be known and considered to much the same degree as the criteria and "principles" of a rational organization.

Organization by Purpose

The grouping at the higher levels of organization is usually on the basis of purpose. This is especially true in a city government, where many diverse services are being administered. In city administration, the principal "line" departments almost always correspond to the major purposes of the city government.

Organization by major purpose encourages the department head to make decisions in terms of defined departmental objectives. Furthermore, if the purposes of the department are made known to its personnel, they will operate more effectively for they will understand the reasons for what they do. This is what Gulick calls "organization by ideas." The greatest advantage which this basis of departmentalization possesses is that it expedites the performance of a given task or the solution of a given problem. If personnel and administrative units concerned with a particular job are under the direction of one administrator, departmental frictions and the necessity of working out agreements with other units are kept to a minimum. Priorities can be established with respect to the needs of the situation rather than departmental requirements. Unity of action is best insured under this form and it is likely that a more completely rounded consideration of all related aspects of a problem will be possible.

From the standpoint of the public, integration according to function has the advantage of conforming to the objectives of government as they are recognized and understood. The public is interested in the end result rather than the methodology. Grouping by

---

[5]Schuyler C. Wallace, "Considerations Which Enter Into the Construction of a Department," in Dwight Waldo, op. cit., p. 119.

purpose fixes responsibility, to some extent at least, for performance and thus focuses public attention on the responsible officials. The opportunity for "buck passing" is reduced.

Despite the advantages inherent in the principle of purpose as the basis for departmentalization, a number of defects are apparent. Some of the disadvantages have been pointed out by Gulick.

"The statement of these strong points of organization by major purpose points the way to its dangers. These are found, first, in the impossibility of cleanly dividing all of the work of any government into a few such major purposes which do not overlap extensively. For example, education overlaps immediately with health and with recreation, as does public works with law enforcement.....

"Second, there is danger that an organization erected on the basis of purpose will fail to make use of the most up-to-date technical devices and specialists because the dominance of purpose generally tends to obscure the element of process, and because there may not be enough work of a given technical sort to permit efficient subdivision.

"Third, there is also danger in such an organization that subordinate parts of the work will be unduly suppressed or lost sight of because of the singleness of purpose, enthusiasm, and drive of the head of the department. For example, medical work with children when established under the department of education as a division is likely to receive less encouragement than it would if independently established in the health department, because after all the department of education is primarily interested in schools and has its own great needs and problems."[6]

The city administrator must frequently face up to the question of the relative advantages and disadvantages of functionalism. Should commercial activities connected with selling water and collecting from customers be assigned to the water department or finance department? Should each department manage its own automotive equipment or should equipment management be centralized? Questions of economy may dictate use of other bases of integration.

Organization by Process

Organization by process is used to obtain the fullest advantages of technical and specialized skills and knowledge, to secure competent professional supervision of technical activities, and to make fullest use of specialized equipment and facilities. Organization by process is used most often in connection with the central service activities of city government — accounting, mechanical equipment pools, and purchasing, for example. Gulick lists the advantages of organization by major process:

"First, it guarantees the maximum utilization of up-to-date technical skill and by bringing together in a single office a large amount of each kind of work (technologically measured), makes it possible in each case to make use of the most effective divisions of work and specialization.

"Second, it makes possible also the economies of the maximum use of labor-saving machinery and mass production. These economies arise not from the total mass of the work to be performed, not from the fact that the work performed serves the same general purpose, but from the fact that the work is performed with the same machine, with the same technique, with the same motions. For example, economy in printing comes from

⁶Luther Gulick, "Notes on the Theory of Organization," in Papers on the Science of Administration, edited by Gulick and L. Urwick (New York: Institute of Public Administration, 1937) p. 22.

skill in typesetting, printing, and binding and the use of modern equipment. It makes no difference to the printer whether he is printing a pamphlet for the schools, a report for the police department, or a form for the comptroller. Unit costs — efficiency in the doing of the job — rest upon the process, not the purpose.

"Third, organization by process encourages coordination in all of the technical and skilled work of the enterprise, because all of those engaged in any field are brought together under the same supervision instead of being scattered in several departments as is the case when organization is based upon some other principle.

"Fourth, it furnishes an excellent approach to the development of central coordination and control when certain of the services, such as budgeting, accounting, purchasing, and planning are set up on a process basis and used as instruments of integration even where other activities are set up on some other basis.

"Fifth, organization by process is best adapted to the development of career service, and the stimulation of professional standards and pride." [7]

But organization by major process like organization by major purpose has its disadvantages as well as its advantages. Chief among these disadvantages is the danger that departments organized by process will be more interested in how a thing is done than in what is done. Many are the accounting reports, for example, which are efficiently and accurately prepared but which serve no useful purpose in administration of a city service. The process may become the end-all and the be-all of administration. With organization by process, too, coordination becomes both more necessary and more difficult than when the agency is organized by purpose.

If the principle of departmentalization by process was applied generally, it is probable that the burden of coordination imposed upon the chief executive would be intolerable. Process departments must be coordinated not only to prevent conflicts, but to guarantee positive cooperation. A failure in one process affects the whole enterprise, and a failure to coordinate one process division with another may destroy the effectiveness of the work being done.

Central Service Agencies. It is common to combine certain stenographic processes, purchasing processes, maintenance of motor equipment, and accounting, for example. In many cases, these processes are withdrawn from the line departments and placed in central service agencies.

The procurement of materials and supplies for all departments is now entrusted in many cities to a purchasing office or agent. Building maintenance and repair, stenographic services, record keeping, and printing or reproduction of office forms are among the other services which lend themselves to performance by specialized agencies. Agencies which are primarily concerned with providing such services to other agencies are referred to here as central service agencies.

From the standpoint of securing effective organization, the principal reason for establishing central service agencies is to secure the benefits of economy and efficiency that result from process specialization. Their function is to provide certain specialized services to the major purpose, or operating departments. Because of the fact that these auxiliary services cut across the several purposes of the operating departments, however, they are often useful to the chief administrator as channels or media for planning, coordination, control, and other management functions. For example, the accounting

---

[7] Gulick, op. cit., pp. 23-24.

office may apply certain mechanical controls over the expenditures of all departments. The personnel agency may require the operating departments to conform to standards or procedures prescribed by the chief administrator. The purchasing agent may refuse to issue a purchase order unless the auditor certifies that the operating department has a sufficient unencumbered balance in its account. Moreover, these agencies may well have been established and given legal status originally for the definite purpose of restricting the authority of departmental administrators.

The combination of service and control functions may cause confusion with respect to the status of such agencies and their relationships to the operating departments and to the chief administrator. It is a common error to assume that, because they are "over-all" agencies cutting across the major operating department lines, they are therefore on a higher level of authority than the operating department. A related error is to assume that service agencies, because their contacts are service-wide and because they sometimes apply controls over operating departments, have an especially intimate relationship to the office of the chief administrator and should be under his direct and detailed supervision.

If, for example, there is no central purchasing office, each department or agency purchases its own supplies. Under such an arrangement, purchasing is revealed in its proper light as a subordinate activity essential to the accomplishment of the major purposes of the department. The important point to be remembered is that the pooling together of the purchasing activities of individual departments through the establishment of a central purchasing office in no way changes the essential character of the service. Purchasing is still only an essential service required by all operating departments. Centralization makes possible the economies of large-scale buying and the efficiency resulting from a staff of full-time, trained personnel, but it does not alter the character of the service. This example could be supported by similar analyses of accounting, property management, and so forth.

These services require no more detailed supervision by the chief administrator than the operating departments. Some services, in fact, may well be performed by one of the operating departments and be subject to direction by the chief administrator only through the operating department head. For example, a bureau of public buildings may be located in the public works department. In other cases, several services may be grouped together in a single agency, as in the case of a "service department" combining stenographic, printing, mimeographing, mailing, and other related services.

Since central service agencies exist primarily to provide specialized services to the operating department, the establishment of separate agencies is justified only to the extent that these agencies contribute to the accomplishment of the major purposes of the operating departments. In other words, there is no point in setting up a host of specialized process agencies unless their establishment furthers the efficiency of the operating departments. To use an exaggerated example, it would be possible to have all stenographic and clerical work assigned to a central auxiliary agency, but the effects of such action on the work of the operating departments would be disastrous. Minor inconveniences to the operating departments resulting from the establishment of auxiliary agencies may be more than offset by the benefits of specialization, but it is both inefficient and uneconomical to carry organization by process to such extremes that the organization cannot effectively serve the public.

Generally speaking, the smaller the city, the greater the advantage of these process specializations. In the very large city, individual departments may be of sufficient size to employ technically competent persons to administer their accounts; in the smaller city, centralization of accounts is almost essential if they are to be adequately handled. The same applies to the other functions. In the large city, it will usually prove advantageous to group in an auxiliary agency certain housekeeping functions for which the individual departments could not maintain an adequate technical staff (e.g., recruitment and examining procedures), at the same time permitting a considerable degree of decentralization of housekeeping functions of a less technical nature.

Thus the large city might have a central personnel agency to administer recruitment processes, to formulate personnel policies for approval of the chief executive (a managerial function), and to advise the individual departments on personnel matters. Each of the larger departments, in turn, would have one or more personnel men to carry on in-service training and similar personnel activities within the department. Merely because a central personnel department or finance department is set up to take care of certain personnel or financial processes does not require that all personnel or finance tasks be taken away from the individual departments and assigned to the central agency.

Organization by Area

In all except the smallest cities, organization on an area basis is likely to be found in at least some of the departments. District fire stations are commonly found even in some smaller cities. Police departments have fewer precinct stations now that motorization of the patrol force has increased its mobility, but in the larger cities there is still a need for some district headquarters. Public works departments, health and welfare services, and park and recreation departments are among the other municipal agencies that have been organized on an area basis in some cities.

In some cases geographical decentralization is essential to the satisfactory performance of a government service: fire fighting forces, for example, are of little value unless they can reach fires in any part of the city within a few minutes after the alarm has been turned in. In other cases, district headquarters have been established for the convenience of the public. In a large city it would be unreasonable, for example, to require welfare clients to come to a central office in order to receive public assistance. Savings in time in the movement of men and equipment, as in the case of the public works department, is another reason for decentralization. Still another justification for organization by area may be the need for employees with an intimate knowledge of a local area; within certain limits, the police department, for example, may profit from having certain of its officers intimately acquainted with the geography and residents of particular neighborhoods.

Whatever the underlying reason for geographical decentralization may be, organization by area raises several difficult problems of administration. First, there is the problem of relationships between the district office and the central office. Unless the district office is given a fair measure of discretion and freedom of action, the "red tape" of overhead supervision stifles initiative and results in serious delays and excess paper work. On the other hand, to allow district offices to operate as more or less independent units is likely to result in confusion of policy, variation in performance standards, overlapping of duties, and extravagant duplication of special equipment and supplies.

Then, there is the problem of lines or channels of authority and responsibility. Shall all orders from above be transmitted through the district supervisor or administrator, or should the several purpose or process agencies of the central office deal directly with their counterparts in the district offices?

Another difficult problem is the coordination of activities of the district offices of one major purpose department with those of another. For example, what relationships should be established between a district fire station, police station, welfare office, and health center? Should they be housed in the same building? Should district administrators assume responsibility for coordinating district services, or should coordination be provided by the central office?

Except in the very large cities there can be no question of replacing the present departmentalization along lines of purpose and process with a specialization by area. However, even cities of moderate size might benefit by using common district boundaries for all departments, and housing the municipal facilities in each principal area in a district "town hall" with central information service. This district office might well be staffed with an interdepartmental liaison officer, responsible to the city's chief executive but having no authority over the line officers in his district. To give this liaison officer any authority to supervise the administration of services in his district would weaken the authority of department heads over their subordinates in the districts.

Organization by Clientele

A fourth possible method of departmental organization is specialization by clientele. An example of such specialization is a bureau of aid to the aged in a welfare department. A major advantage of specialization by clientele is to simplify the administration from the "customer's" point of view. If child health activities are administered by the school department rather than the health department, the child has only one, instead of two, separate contacts with the city government.

In many cases, this seeming advantage is imaginary rather than real, for if different personnel handle the two services within the department, there may be almost as little coordination from the client's point of view as if the services were rendered by two different departments. If a family on relief, a member of which is also eligible for medical care, is visited by a family case worker and also by a medical social worker, the family will probably not be impressed by the fact that all dependent persons in the city are cared for by a single welfare department.

Unquestionably the grouping of subordinate administrative units into a departmental structure on the basis of clientele makes possible a coordination of the activities of the government with regard to particular segments of the public to a degree not attainable under any other form of organization. Most of the services of a municipal government, however, are available to all citizens and seldom are the basic program objectives related to particular segments of the citizenry. To say that recipients of water and health services or police and fire protection constitute the clientele of those departments is a mere juggling of words. The principle of integration on the basis of clientele possesses validity only when the problems peculiar to a particular segment of the population are so closely interrelated that their solution is more easily achieved through this device.

Nevertheless, the clientele considerations are almost always reflected in organization, whether it be centered on clientele, area, process or purpose. Reception desks, information counters, and complaint bureaus are examples found in most departments.

Coordinating Organizational Components

With the departmentalization of program administration within a municipal organization, responsibility for administration of specific programs rests directly with the designated department heads. Achieving proper balance among the various programs and activities and coordinating related programs within financial resources available and established policies and objectives is essentially the responsibility of the chief administrative officer. It is probably a natural corollary of the specialization, whatever the basis, for the various units of an organization to seek autonomy, independence, and security. To achieve these ends, departments or other organizational units tend to resist control by the individual responsible for direction as a whole.

The time and effort of the general administrator is largely devoted to holding the organization together and keeping all parts moving in the same general direction. This is done through various devices and processes of coordination and control. The most popular and widely used device is provision of staff assistance through various management or staff agencies and aids.

Agencies such as those concerned with accounting, budgeting, supply, planning, and personnel are essentially in the category of "overhead." They furnish little direct service to the people and their work is effective only as it paves the way for better over-all administration and more effective performance by the operating — or line — agencies. There are two aspects to the work of these so-called staff agencies; one is that of facilitative service, the other is that of control. These aspects are generally interwoven, and it becomes difficult to identify certain activities of a staff agency in one or the other category.

The total effectiveness of a municipal organization depends much on the way that staff services are set up and carried out. Too much control exercised by or through staff agencies has a stultifying effect on the organization. Too little control results in parts of the organization going in their own uncoordinated ways.

A "good" organization has both elements of separateness and elements of cohesion. Separateness is dictated by the need to fix responsibility for various parts of the total municipal program, and by the fact that the several departments are characterized by differences in clientele, activities, and administrative problems. While organizational units may be characterized by separateness in their respective activities, they are held together by compliance with established policies, standards, and administrative practices. Cohesiveness and unity in an organization must come principally from proper attitudes and actions of members. Administration of the staff services has important bearing on those attitudes and actions.

The manager's problem with respect to organization of staff services is two-edged. With insufficient staff agencies, he will become hopelessly enmeshed in the detail of day-to-day coordination of actions and resolution of conflicts among operating agencies. With staff agencies which attempt to over-emphasize cohesiveness to the point of infringement upon operating departments, he will be continuously concerned with jurisdictional questions between staff and line agencies.

A brief review of the managerial functions and responsibilities of the chief administrator will reveal his need for assistance and point to the kinds of assistance needed. In the discussion of administrative management in Chapter 1, it was pointed out that the principal functions of the manager are to plan, to organize, to direct (to command, coordinate, and control), and to represent the administrative organization in its contacts with the council, with other agencies, and with the public. It was also recognized that some aspects of fiscal and personnel management are so essential to the performance of these basic functions that they may for practical purposes be classified among the principal management functions. These are the essential elements of administrative management, the functions and responsibilities that the chief administrator cannot completely delegate to the individual departments without at the same time renouncing, in part at least, his claim to the title of chief administrator.

To urge that the chief administrator be given assistance in the performance of his management functions and then to insist that managerial functions cannot be delegated may seem inconsistent. The explanation is that, although the authority and responsibility cannot be delegated, some of the work can be done by assistants.

There are two kinds of "staff" or "managerial" assistants. One is the functional specialist with defined or prescribed responsibilities with respect to such things as finance, personnel and supply. The other is the nonspecialist assistant for coordination. The latter, commonly known as an administrative assistant, has no functional responsibility but is an extension of the chief executive's personality.

What are the duties that can be assigned to managerial aides or agencies? Any complete listing of the possible uses of managerial aides is out of the question, but some of the most common may be suggested by way of illustration.

1. Planning. Before programs of future action can be mapped out, information must be collected and studied, differing views must be weighed, costs must be calculated, and personnel requirements must be forecast. Much of this preliminary research can be assigned to managerial aides. This research, it should be emphasized, need not be confined to the mere collection or compilation of statistics or documents. The raw material of planning needs to be arranged and summarized so that the administrator can review it easily and with a minimum expenditure of time. Subordinates will in many cases develop tentative plans or recommendations for final revision and approval by the chief administrator.

2. Organization. As new plans are put into effect or new circumstances arise which affect the application of original plans, corresponding changes must be made in the distribution of tasks and responsibilities among administrative personnel. Minor adjustments within departments can be left to the discretion of department heads, but changes that embrace the reassignment of work among departments are the responsibility of the chief administrator. Here again the administrator can rely heavily upon his managerial aides to keep him informed of difficulties encountered under the existing organization, to collect necessary information, and to help him draft new organizational plans.

3. Direction. As the term is used in this volume, direction includes command, coordination, and control. In each of these phases of direction the administrator has need for assistance.

Orders, directions, rules, and regulations are among the most common tools of command, for after plans have been made they must be translated into action through the issuance of commands in one form or another. No one can command for the administrator, but assistants can put these commands into clear and unambiguous language and see that they are communicated to the proper persons.

Among the devices of control are records, reports, and inspections. No one can relieve the chief administrator entirely of the task of reviewing records and reports and making inspections, but assistants can do much to help him. Subordinates can, for example, operate follow-up files to make certain that orders have been executed, examine for completeness reports submitted by department heads, call the attention of the administrator to items of special importance in reports, and make routine inspections of departmental activities. In other words, managerial aides can supply the chief administrator with extra eyes and ears.

4. Representation. The chief administrator is also the chief representative of the administration, the one man who can represent the entire organization. He must therefore handle countless contacts with the council, with officials of other governments, and with the public. No one can relieve him of this responsibility, but others can help him in collecting information and preparing drafts of letters, statements or proposals for his use.

5. Fiscal Management. The dollar sign is so closely woven into the fabric of administrative management that it appears in each of the principal functions of the chief administrator. Some of the mechanics of fiscal administration — assessing, tax collection, accounting, deposit and disbursement of funds, and the like — do not require the close personal supervision of the chief administrator. Other phases of fiscal administration are definitely managerial in character.

The preparation and administration of the budget, the drafting of fiscal plans to accompany capital improvement programs; the determination of policies governing debt administration or the enforcement of tax collection provisions; the drafting of recommendations for new sources of revenue — these and related matters are of immediate concern to the chief administrator. Here again the administrator needs help. The preparation of the budget is one of his most important tasks, but he can assign some of the work to others. Assistants can compile and arrange departmental requests, see that supporting data are attached to requests, and handle some of the preliminary negotiations or discussions with department heads. In the administration of the budget, the tasks of day-to-day operation of controls over appropriations or allotments can be accomplished by the accounting system.

6. Personnel Management. No administrator can truly manage unless he retains final authority over personnel, including the determination of basic standards of qualification and performance, the authority to administer disciplinary measures, the formulation of employee relations policies, and the responsibility for maintaining the morale of the administrative personnel. In very small cities, he may require little or no assistance in the management of personnel. As the organization becomes more complex, however, he needs assistance. He needs a person or an agency to implement the general standards of qualification with specific requirements, to administer the machinery of discipline and to report the effectiveness of disciplinary action applied, to collect information and conduct preliminary negotiations as the basis for the formulation of employee relations policies, or to advise the administrator as to the status of administrative morale and make suggestions for its improvement.

7. Other Assistance. It has already been pointed out that an administrative assistant can be, in smaller cities, a general utility man to help the chief administrator with any or all of his managerial tasks. It must not be inferred, however, that in cities where the chief administrator has a number of special aides and agencies there is no need for an administrative assistant. There are many tasks which call for the assistance of a "handy man" in the chief administrator's office. Such an assistant can collect information from various departments, draft orders for the administrator's signature, handle interviews with some of the citizens who come daily to the administrator's office, collect information to be released to the press, conduct research on miscellaneous problems, and in scores of other ways relieve the chief administrator of many onerous tasks.

Aside from these specific tasks which can be delegated to an assistant, the chief administrator needs someone in the city hall to whom he can talk freely and frankly about city problems. Not only is it usually impossible for the executive to maintain confidential relations with one department head without antagonizing the others, but further, an administrative assistant is in a better position to consider problems from an over-all management point of view than is any department head. Department heads, too, may wish to discuss problems with someone who will approach them with a fresh viewpoint, and may be reluctant to burden the manager with their troubles but perfectly willing to talk them over with an administrative assistant.

The administrative assistant, having a less exalted status than a department head, will have many contacts among subordinate city hall employees, and can be an invaluable source of information to the executive on employee morale and problems of employee relations — problems which might never come to his attention if this channel did not exist. Finally, the administrative assistant performs a valuable function on those numerous occasions when the chief administrator must be in "two places at once."

All these are functions which the administrative assistant can perform in cities of any size. In cities of moderate or small size the job of assistant may be combined with that of budget officer, and perhaps also personnel officer and even planning officer. As the city grows — if it does — these functions can be split off and assigned to special agencies as suggested above.

The value of a really good private secretary needs no reaffirmation here. Executives in all lines of endeavor, in large and small organizations, have found such an aide invaluable. In many cases the secretary is competent to perform many of the duties that have been suggested for other aides, as well as to take care of the administrator's correspondence, filing, and appointments. In fact, it may be suggested that the administrator who is fortunate enough to have an exceptionally competent secretary might profitably relieve her of much of the routine stenography and give her more responsible assignments.

Committees in Administration

To many persons, the term "coordination" immediately suggests "committee." Since of all devices used in administration, committees are perhaps the most misunderstood, a brief discussion of the role of committees is in order here. The board or commission is essentially a committee form, and the characteristics, both favorable and unfavorable, ascribed here to committees could equally well be applied to boards and commissions.

The committee may be used in three roles: first, as a sort of multiple executive at a point directly within the line organization; second, as a coordinating agency at some point of interrelationship between several agencies; third, as a public relations device.

Executive Committees. The use of the committee as a multiple executive may be dismissed with a few words. It is justified only when the function of the agency is of a quasi-judicial or quasi-legislative nature demanding deliberation as well as action. In such a capacity a committee may be very useful, but it should never be expected to exhibit the energy of administration which is characteristic of a single executive. If the committee is expected to carry on administrative activities in addition to its deliberate functions, the organization should provide for a single administrator directly responsible to the committee, and all administrative matters should be referred to this administrative officer without interference from committee members.

Coordinating Committees. The committee as coordinating agency has more to commend it. It is usually composed of members of the departments or bureaus whose activities are to be coordinated. Committees of this sort have been used effectively in cities to deal with such problems as juvenile delinquency where the police department, the courts, and social agencies all are involved, and where coordination is primarily a matter of program-planning. They are less suitable for the task of day-to-day coordination for the reason that the committee members are usually preoccupied with their regular administrative duties and can devote only a small part of their time to committee work. Coordination requiring immediate decision cannot be achieved through occasional committee meetings.

Citizen Committees. The weaknesses and strengths of committees within the city government are also characteristic of citizen committees. There are two general types of citizen committees common in municipal affairs. There may be special investigating or survey committees to study particular city problems and report to the council; or there may be committees appointed by the administrator, or occasionally the council, to serve as advisory groups for the administrator, either on special major problems arising from time to time or on continuing problems arising in the administration of a regular function.

The functions of such committees must be strictly advisory in character, and it should be made clear to the members at the time of appointment that the administrator wants advice and will give careful consideration to the committee's recommendations, but that he is responsible for administrative decisions and cannot delegate this authority to an outside group, however capable and interested it may be.

What, then, can an advisory committee do? It may furnish technical advice through its membership and it may transmit ideas of the public to the administrator and ideas of the administrator to the public. Committees appointed to give technical advice may be useful to the administrator to guide him in the management of special major projects. In many cases, such an arrangement may be an excellent device for obtaining consulting service from some of the community's best minds. Most cities have citizens who are willing and able to advise on various major problems of administration, although they may know little of the details of municipal management.

Under most circumstances, an advisory committee's duties should be limited at the outset to a definite period of time. This action indicates to the committee that they are expected to make a real contribution while their advice is needed. It removes the very awkward situation so often arising when the administrator and the committee cannot agree, and neither knows just how to wind up the relations. If the advisory committee resigns, the move is subject to various unfriendly interpretations; if it stays on, embarassing questions constantly come up. If a definite period of time has been set, this situation is automatically taken care of, while it is an easy matter to extend the period if everything is running smoothly.

Authority and Responsibility

The discussion thus far of facets of the organization problem has dealt with the broad picture in terms of objectives, forces and influences, construction of departments, and developing organizational cohesiveness. The concern has been with the over-all pattern of the organization. Since organizations are formed to carry definite jobs and purposes, it is essential that the tasks be parceled out to individuals in order that they will fit into the over-all pattern. It is of no use for persons in the higher echelons of an organization to make decisions, no matter how well based, unless these decisions are translated into action by the operating employees at the lowest echelon.

The amount of attention devoted to directing the activities of parts of an organization will depend a good deal on the way in which the work has been divided. Where the work of the whole organization can be divided into fairly distinct and separate sub-purposes, the attention required is less than when the main subdivisions of the organization are process subdivisions, and where consequently almost all work done in the organization must pass through the hands of several of the major departments. One test of whether the work of an organization has been correctly divided is whether the need for coordination and direction has been kept at a minimum.

Certain concepts, or "principles" about how objectives of an organization are translated into action have received wide currency. Whether or not these principles have scientific validity, they have a wide degree of acceptance as, at least, diagnostic criteria.

The Pyramid of Authority

A fundamental concept in organization is that of a pyramid of authority. Each small group of employees is subject to the orders of a supervisor, and this supervisor is subject to the orders of a higher administrative officer, and so forth. The employees are grouped for supervision and direction as described in the earlier discussion of the division of work. When this structure of authority is added to it, the division of work can be translated into an ordinary organization pattern showing the clear lines of authority in the organization.

Experience in establishing systems of authority has led to the enumeration of certain rules, which are often referred to as "principles of administration." Although these rules need to be applied with some caution, they certainly cannot be disregarded in erecting an organization structure. Among them are:

1. Unity of command should be preserved — each member of the organization should have one, and only one, immediate superior.

2. The span of control of each administrative officer should be carefully limited — no person should be expected to supervise directly the work of more than a few subordinates.

3. The total number of levels in the organization should be few — if it is necessary for a matter in dispute to pass through more than two or three levels of superiors before a person is found who has authority over both parties to the dispute, the coordinating mechanism will prove impossibly cumbersome.

4. Authority should be commensurate with responsibility — an administrator must have authority over all the persons who are below him in the pyramid; and the administrator must be given resources which, if efficiently used, are sufficient to complete the task assigned him.

5. Each subordinate should be placed under the superior who is most competent to direct his work — authority is worse than useless if the person in authority is less competent to make the coordinating decisions or less well informed (with respect to possession of the knowledge and information necessary for a correct decision) than the person whom he directs.

Any attempt to apply all these rules in constructing an organization meets with serious difficulties. The five rules just enumerated sometimes conflict with each other, so that in following one of the rules, it may be necessary to violate another. Particularly, there is often a conflict between rules (1) and (5); and, if rule (1) is observed, a conflict between rules (2) and (3).

Unity of Command and its Limits

The argument for unity of command has been well stated by Luther Gulick:

"From the earliest times, it has been recognized that nothing but confusion arises under multiple command. 'A man cannot serve two masters' was adduced as a theological argument because it was already accepted as a principle of human relation in everyday life. In administration this is known as the principle of 'unity of command.' The principle may be stated as follows: A workman subject to orders from several superiors will be confused, inefficient, and irresponsible; a workman subject to orders from but one superior may be methodical, efficient, and responsible. Unity of command thus refers to those who are commanded, not to those who issue the commands." [8]

Nevertheless, insistence on complete unity of command leads to serious difficulties, and as experienced an analyst of organizations as Frederick Taylor deliberately violated this rule in his system of "functional foremen." The reason for the violation is found in rule (5). Particularly in the case of "purpose" and "area" departments, the superiors of an employee may not be in a position to supervise the technical aspects of his work. Suppose that school health work is handled by the education department. The superintendent of education is not competent to decide whether proper medical methods are being used by the physicians in his department. Similar problems arise in the case of an accountant in a police department, an equipment maintenance division in a fire department, a detective unit that is responsible to a district police captain, and in numerous other situations of the same kind. Taylor's solution of such problems was to place the subordinate under the authority of both a "line" supervisor and one or more "functional" supervisors. There has been considerable criticism of Taylor's theory on the ground that it would be impossible to define distinct zones of authority for each of the functional supervisors, and that consequently the subordinate would receive conflicting orders which he would be unable to obey.

The difficulties that result from adhering slavishly to the rule of unity of command, and the difficulties that result from ignoring the rule appear to create a dilemma. The correct answer probably lies between the two extremes that have been described. Military organizations particularly seem to have reconciled the demands of unity of command with the demands of functional supervision, and the solution they have found appears applicable with slight modification to city administration. [9]

There would appear to be no harm in subjecting a single employee to the authority of two or more superiors provided that, (1) separate and distinct zones of authority are defined for the various superiors so that conflicts of authority are as few and far between as possible; and (2) when a conflict does occur, there is one and only one superior whose instructions the employee is bound to follow until the conflict has been straightened out. Suppose, for example, that an officer in the police department is placed in charge of in-service training. His immediate superior in the "line" would be the chief, or an assistant chief, of police; but he would also be under the technical supervision of the training officer in the personnel department. In case he received conflicting orders from his two "bosses," he would follow the direction of the chief of police; and if the chief of police and the personnel officer were unable to resolve their difference, it would be referred upward to the chief executive.

Under such an arrangement, there would really be two sets of "lines of authority"

---

[8] Gulick, op. cit., p. 9.
[9] See L. Urwick, op. cit., pp. 63-69, for an excellent analysis of functional supervision in the British Army.

— one set to be used in the day-to-day work of administration, the other set (the only one usually shown on the organization chart) to be used in case of a conflict of authority. Only the second set would completely observe the rule of unity of command. No confusion need result, and no employee could "pass the buck" nor could he be penalized for failing to carry out conflicting orders. This device, carefully and sparingly used, would seem to offer many advantages over strict adherence to unity of command — providing the members of the organization thoroughly understand the arrangement. It is widely and successfully used in military organization, and almost as widely (though not consciously and deliberately) even in those civilian organizations which are on paper committed to the rule of unity of command. Not to make a virtue of necessity, it should be stressed that where unity of command can be preserved, the administrator should not go out of his way to destroy it.

The Span of Control and the Number of Supervisory Levels

Rules (2) and (3) state that the span of control should be small, and that the number of supervisory levels should be small. In an organization of any considerable size, both of these requirements cannot be satisfied. Consider for example a city government with 500 employees. If no supervisor or administrator were permitted to direct more than five subordinates, then there would have to be about 100 supervisors at the first level, 20 at the second level, and 4 at the third level — or a total of five levels of employees including the operative employees and the chief executive. If an operative employee (A) had a complaint involving an operative employee in another department (B), the complaint would have to pass upward through all these levels to the chief executive, and an order passed downward along a chain of equal length to the other operative employee.

In order to eliminate one level from this organization of 500 employees, it would be necessary to increase the span of control to eight. Then there would be 63 supervisors at the first level, and 8 at the second level. These two schemes of organization — five levels with a span of control of five, and four levels with a span of control of eight — are illustrated in Fig. 1. It can be seen that in the five-level plan, supervisory employees comprise one-fifth of the entire staff, while in the four-level plan they comprise only one-eighth of the total.

Urwick recommends five or six as the largest number of subordinates who should be supervised by a single person, but other authorities have suggested lower or higher limits. Some say three, some five, some twelve, and some set still higher limits. In any case, it is impossible to fix a number that will apply under all circumstances, for variations in the nature of the work performed and the personal capacities of the supervisor must be considered. A single supervisor might direct 20 comptometer operators in routine work, while a director of planning and research might have his hands full with only three or four men directly responsible to him.

Not only the number and type of subordinates, but also the frequency of contacts with superiors and with persons outside the organization affect the size of the work load. A large part of the typical city manager's or mayor's time is taken up with these external contacts with citizens and others, and the number of subordinates he can effectively supervise is correspondingly reduced. Hence, each case must be separately considered if the proper span of control is to be determined.

In a city of less than 100,000 population, a reduction of the chief administrator's span of control to reasonable proportions would not create an excessive number of levels in the organization, hence no serious objection can be raised from that standpoint.

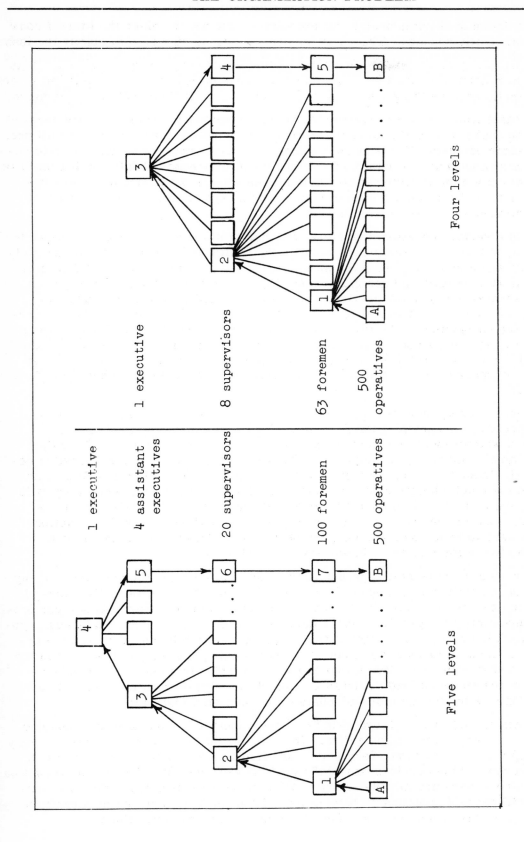

Fig. 1 — Span of Control

Nevertheless, there does not appear to be any very simple way in which the span of control can be materially reduced. The following considerations may help to clarify the issue:

1. A city government carries on a large collection of very diverse services. This is the inherent reason why the chief administrator's span of control is ordinarily so large; to reduce it would require the grouping of services that have little or nothing in common.

At the same time, the very diversity of the city's services means that they have less to do with each other, and less need for close coordination, than if they were all dealing with the same problem. There is only a limited range of matters where action to coordinate the health department with the fire department is needed. It follows that the task of a municipal chief administrator in coordinating the work of 10 subordinates is somewhat less than would be a similar span of control in an organization where the work of the 10 subordinates was more closely intertwined.

There is a serious question, therefore, whether creating a comprehensive Department of Public Welfare, for example, (to include the health, library, recreation, and welfare services) would materially help the situation. In the first place, unless a Director of Public Welfare took over and centralized many decisions which had previously been made by the several functional supervisors (and which should continue to be made by them to preserve their initiative and reduce red tape), he would probably not have a full-time job. In the second place, the few questions of coordination which do arise between such different departments usually involve policy questions of such a fundamental nature, that they would have to be referred upward to the chief administrator in any event, and the Director interposed between him and the department head would do nothing to reduce his work load.

A stronger reason for combination exists in the case of very small departments (building inspection, for example) which cannot afford a well-paid administrator at their head, and which should therefore be generally placed in a department where they can receive some administrative supervision from a fully competent and responsible department chief. In such a case, attaching the small department to a larger one may actually relieve the chief administrator of some of his load and the small department will probably receive more attention than if it reports directly to an administrator who is burdened with more important or at least more pressing matters. Even then, caution must be exercised to avoid making an orphan of the small department by giving it a stepfather who has neither interest in nor sympathy with its work.

2. Perhaps a more helpful approach to the chief administrator's problem than any attempt to reduce arbitrarily his span of control is to increase the managerial aides at his disposal to deal with his work load. Some of the chief administrator's tasks, particularly his responsibility for providing the organization with vital personal leadership, cannot be delegated, but many of his other duties can be performed by subordinates in his office. To this extent the executive is not so much a single person as a "position" in the organization, and it is the executive's whole office — of which he is only one member — that really carries his work load. A later section of this chapter will be devoted to a discussion of means of staffing more adequately the chief administrator's office.

In summary, only in very large cities is there a danger of excessive red tape due to the number of levels in the organization. This would seem to imply that there is every reason to keep the span of control very small, say five or six. Nevertheless, the great range and diversity of the services provided by city government do not make the reduction of span of control a very practicable solution of the managerial problem. The chief administrator will probably continue to have at least 10 subordinates reporting directly to him, and therefore his office must be amply provided with managerial aides.

Other Methods of Direction

Thus far coordination has been discussed as though it were to be accomplished almost entirely by the use of administrative authority — by placing the activities to be coordinated under common direction in the organization. While the lines of authority in an organization are undoubtedly chiefly responsible for giving form to the organization, and system and order to its operations, authority by itself is insufficient to create a smoothly-operating, efficient organization to carry out any complex task. Formal relationships, pretty much restricted by the necessity of maintaining unity of command, must be supplemented by a rich network of informal relations. An engine needs lubrication as well as fuel, and if authority provides the driving force for an organization, other means must be found to supply the oil to lubricate it in its day-to-day operations.

This lubrication is provided by permitting the free flow of information and advice, not only up and down along lines of authority, but across them as well; by instituting training programs to increase the competence of individual employees to make their own decisions without detailed direction from above; and by instilling in employees attitudes toward their jobs and their place in the city organization that will make "self-starters" of them.

Fully as important in achieving this "lubrication" as formal mechanisms are the informal attitudes behind them. In an organization where each staff member is sincerely interested in providing service, where he is aware of and aiming at the organization's objectives, he will himself recognize the need for coordinating his work with that of other organization members and will seek the contacts which will make such coordination possible. To facilitate informal coordination of this kind it is necessary (a) to show each employee how his particular job fits into the larger task of the organization and how it is related to the jobs of others, (b) to create a friendly atmosphere among organization members — particularly between different units — which will encourage consultation, and (c) to provide opportunities for contact between employees in an atmosphere which will encourage discussion.

Nature of Advisory Relationships. To say that A exercises authority over B means that B is expected to carry out the decisions reached for him by A. To say that A advises B means that A makes suggestions to B which B is free to accept or reject. Yet in practice there is not the sharp distinction between command and advisory relationships which these definitions would seem to imply. Unless an administrator is able to convince his subordinates that his decisions are usually correct, he will be able in the long run to exercise very little authority. Even in an army, where outright disobedience is unthinkable, a commander who does not possess an "authority of ideas" — who is not able to carry conviction with his commands — soon finds that his formal authority is sapped by his subordinates' low morale, inertia, and deliberate misunderstanding. Conversely a technical expert whose advice is sought and respected may possess an "authority of ideas" which is accepted as fully and readily as formal authority.

For a complete description of the role of authority in an administrative organization it would be necessary to distinguish: line authority (the right to obedience from a subordinate even in case of a disagreement), functional authority (the right to obedience from a subordinate except in case of disagreement with that subordinate's superior in the line), and the "authority of ideas" (the right to advise).

Organizing Advisory and Informational Functions. Advisory and informational processes in an organization are perhaps most realistically viewed as a form of "internal public relations," for there is nothing to guarantee that advice or information produced at one point in an organization will have an effect at another point in the organization, unless there are means for communicating the advice, and unless it is transmitted in a persuasive manner. It is a common misconception among persons in a staff capacity that to "advise" means only to prepare precisely worded explanatory bulletins or manuals, and to make certain that the proper number of copies of these are prepared, and that they are properly routed. It is not enough that the book of instructions reach every employee's desk — steps must be taken to see that he finds out what is between the covers of the book (and what is not).

In setting up positions of an advisory nature, it is necessary, therefore, to consider at the same time the methods whereby this advice will be communicated and made effective. These difficulties of communication apply, of course, to commands as well as to advice and information. As a matter of fact, the administrator who is serving in an advisory capacity is apt to be at some advantage in solving problems of communication, because he is likely to be conscious of the necessity of transmitting and "selling" his ideas, while the administrator who possesses authority may not be aware of his public relations job.

Training Processes in Organization. Training an employee is really an alternative to "organizing" him — for if he is given preparation which enables him to reach satisfactory decisions himself, it becomes less important constantly to exercise authority over him or to advise him. The more competent the individual employees, the less is the need for a highly centralized organization which permits subordinate employees little discretion, and the less serious are the consequences of any defects in the organization structure.

Training procedures will be discussed at length in Chapter 7. The point to be emphasized here is that the education and training of employees is an important factor to be taken into consideration in designing the administrative organization. It may be possible to minimize or often dispense with certain review processes by giving the subordinates training which enables them to perform their work with less supervision.

Employee training has its greatest value in those situations in which the exercise of formal authority through direction and command proves difficult. The difficulty may lie in the need for prompt action, in geographical decentralization of the organization, or in the complexity of the subject matter of decision, which defies summary in rules and regulations.

Choosing the Proper Method of Coordination

It can be seen that there are a number of distinct ways in which the work of the individual employee can be coordinated with that of other employees: he may be placed under the authority of another, he may be given advice or information to assist him, or he may be trained so that he will be "self-coordinated." It is a major task of organization to determine the extent to which and the manner in which each of these procedures will be employed.

To a very great extent, these various forms are interchangeable, a fact which is far more often appreciated in small than in large organizations. The simplest example of this is the gradual increase in discretion which can be permitted an employee as he becomes familiar with his job. A secretary learns to draft routine correspondence; a statistical clerk learns to lay out his own calculations. In each case training has taken the place of authority in guiding the employee's decisions. To the extent that these other forms of influence supplement, or are substituted for authority, the problem of influence becomes one of education and public relations, as has already been explained.

Administrators have increasingly recognized in recent years that authority, unless buttressed by other forms of influence, is relatively impotent to control subordinates in any but a negative way. The elements entering into all but the most routine decisions are so numerous and so complex that it is impossible to control more than a few so that unless the subordinate is largely "self-controlled" the task of supervision becomes hopelessly burdensome. To cite an extreme illustration: no amount of supervision or direction, and no quantity of orders, directives, or commands would be sufficient to enable a completely untrained person to prepare a legal brief for a lawsuit. In such a case, the problem is definitely not one of direction, but one of selection of a properly trained person.

Likewise, when an organizational unit is large enough so that it can retain within its own boundaries the specialists required for some of its decisions, the need for functional supervision from other portions of the organization becomes correspondingly less. When a department can secure its own legal, medical, or other expert assistance, the problems of functional organization become correspondingly simpler, and the lines of direct authority over the department need less supplementation by advisory and informational services. Hence, the specifications of the employees who are to fill the positions established by the organization are in themselves important factors in determining the final pattern of the organization.

The different forms of organizational influence must be balanced against each other in terms of advantages and costs. A training program involves a large initial investment in each employee, but low "maintenance" costs because of less need for supervision. Orders and commands require no initial "investment," but high and continuing costs of "production" and communication. If pre-trained employees are recruited, salaries may need to be higher, but less training and supervision will be required, and so forth.

Human Problems in Organization

Earlier in the chapter the question was raised — Can a conceptual separation be made between organizational mechanics and the human personalities within an organization? It was stated that the answer was a dual one. For analysis and descriptive purposes, a separation can, and is, commonly made. Otherwise the study of organization would be unmanageable. At the same time, however, there is no denying that a point does exist where the technical processes of organization and human factors must be meshed. As suggested earlier, it would seem to be the essence of management leadership to impose the restriction of large scale rational cooperation as individuals and at the same time encourage their initiative and desire to do a good job.

With respect to the practitioners' concern with the subject of organization, human problems constitute a major inseparable part of the entire organizational problem. To a chief administrator, an organization does not mean very much apart from the people who comprise it. This fact does not negate the validity and utility of the concepts and criteria of rational organizational structure. Most of the so-called principles of organization have their roots in the fact that people are not all-knowing, are limited in their skills, and have different goals and circumstances.

The relationships of the behavior of individuals to the question of organization can be categorized, for discussion, three ways:

1. From the standpoint of the administrator, the organizational structure is a tool

or facility which he uses to accomplish organizational ends. It is thus a personal thing which is affected and shaped according to the personality of the administrator.

2. People who inhabit many of the parts of an organizational structure have skills and abilities and relationships with other inhabitants of the structure. These personal qualifications and relations may or may not coincide with the "ideal" rational pattern, but they shape the actual organization.

3. An organization has objectives but, as a matter of fact, individuals in many work situations have little interest in attainment of organizational goals *per se*. They are associated with the organization as a necessity to gain money or prestige. It has been assumed that personal objectives, if they do not coincide, will be subjugated to organizational objectives. This is not always true in practice, however. In addition, there are obstacles to organizational adaptations designed to meet changing needs. The human appears to be addicted to habit with a predilection for opposing change.

Executive Personality

A city government organization because of its legal bases, need for balancing opposing forces and pressures, and provision of a variety of services is perhaps more "stable" than a more singly-oriented private company. It is quite common for complete changes in the structure of a business enterprise to accompany a change in executive leadership. It is obvious that the impact of personality on organization needs to be recognized and considered. There are a number of characteristics about an administrator which have a vital and proper influence on the organizational structure. They include his basic beliefs, his administrative philosophy, his particular training and management experience, his work methods and habits, the decision-making type he represents, and so forth.

In city government the personal characteristics of the chief administrator himself influence the organization for staff services. Whether some activities are grouped functionally and assigned to subject matter specialists, or are performed by personal assistants, or by the administrator himself are largely questions of personality. How the manager deals with his department heads is influenced by personal factors. Aside from the influences of his own predispositions and practices, the chief administrator must take into account the organizational behavior of his department heads. In this connection the psychologist, Fromm, has developed classifications of major types of personalities in the decision-making process:

1. The *receptive character* is one who believes that his satisfaction comes from an outside source, which he passively accepts — not from his own efforts. Such a person leans on authority for knowledge and help. He is likely to make decisions within the framework of what his superiors expect of him and have told him to do.

2. The *exploitative character* attempts to take things from other people by force or cunning. His decisions are made in the spirit of opposition. He will attempt to make decisions which will enable him to manipulate others for his own ends.

3. People of the *hoarding character* have little faith in anything new they can get from outside. Their decisions are made with a view to security and saving, and they attempt to follow strictly what they are supposed to do.

4. The *marketing character* tends to feel that people can be bought and sold like merchandise. His decisions are made with the aim of adapting himself to whatever may be approved of. No basic conviction is adhered to, and hence the decisions of such men may be quite unpredictable.

5. The *productive character* is found in those who have 'the ability to use their powers and to realize the potentialities inherent in themselves.' This is an ideal type who concerns himself with the welfare of others, who understands others and helps them with the aim of integrating successfully divergent objectives, who likes what he does and in general finds life good. [10]

Aside from personality types are matters of personal preference and competence which influence the pattern of departmental relations. In organizing for public works administration, for example, this factor frequently arises. Some public works engineers prefer to work, and are most productive, outside the office giving direct supervision to engineering and public works operations. Others prefer to work with the slide rule and charts and reports inside the office. In large measure, the organization of public works will be determined by which type is present in any instance.

The Individual and the Job

In the structural sense, the smallest component of an organization is a "position." The standard definition of a position is: "a group of current duties and responsibilities assigned or delegated by competent authority and requiring the full-time or part-time services of an employee." Within this context, the employee, as a personality, serves merely the purposes of delimiting the duties and responsibilities and providing a means of identification. From the position classification standpoint, this approach is necessary and proper. Any good plan of position classification, however, recognizes that changes in duties and responsibilities are regularly occurring and provision is normally made to amend the classification of positions when the changes are observed.

Persons recruited to fill a position will bring a combination of skills and knowledge which differ in some degree from the preceding incumbents. An employee acquires knowledge and special skills with the performance of his assigned work. A new supervisor may review the work of his subordinates more or less frequently than the predecessor. An employee with strong personal or technical qualities may assume leadership without formal designation. Through these and many other ways an organization is shaped in its details. True, the formal structure ordinarily fixes the limits within which the personal and spontaneous forces operate, but, they nevertheless modify the actual flow of relationships.

In this respect, the need for frequent review of the classification of positions is two-fold. One is to serve the personnel administration purpose of reflecting currently the duties performed by each employee. The other is to provide an effective review of the ways in which the organization has shifted and changed within its formally established lines.

Some writers have identified two types of organization, the formal one and the informal one as influenced by human elements. The "informal" organization is based on the responsiveness of employees to their immediate work groups which thus become important channels of organization influence. Moreover a wide range of influences, past and present, lying outside the organization accounts for much of its actual behavior. The management institution in which the main outlines of the "formal" and "informal" coincide is probably the healthy and happy one.

---

[10] Quoted in American Management Association, Organization Planning and Management Development (New York: The Association, 1951), in a paper by Ernest Dale, "Dynamics and Mechanics of Organization," p. 6.

Non-Organizational Objectives

That the human elements are significant influences on formal organization is obvious. In recent years, many writers have been concerned extensively with the behavior characteristics of individuals within an organization. Much attention has been given to the question of how to bring about a closer agreement between the personal objections of the individuals which contribute services to an organization and the organizational objectives themselves. Some writers of this school do not take for granted, as does this volume, the status hierarchy and relations of superior and subordinate as fundamental organizational concepts.

Some recent writers view the attitude survey and motivational studies as the tools of organization research. It is certainly important to the manager to know what the people in the organization think, what motivates them, what their personal needs are which the organization can meet, and to attempt to develop an environment in which personal need satisfaction can be gained out of the activities associated within the organization. But these efforts need to be within the framework of basic purposes and objectives of the city government.

Research in Human Behavior

Organization of group effort is rooted in assumptions about individual and group behavior. In recent years increased efforts have been made to understand human motivations on which social behavior is based. It is too early yet for municipal administrators to make practical application of the research findings which are only tentative and hedged about with qualification. Nevertheless, enough productive work has been done to indicate that highly useful conclusions may one day be available.

"The main problems of organizational structure, organizational policy and effective operation can be solved only if human behavior is understood. How should an organization be set up to accomplish its own objectives? How can the needs and purposes of many individuals be integrated with the needs and purposes of the organization? How can an organization adapt itself to change with a minimum of loss and stress?"[11]

While behavioral research covers a broad range, one or two examples of the type of findings will serve to indicate the possible utility of these research efforts. Likert, for example, states that there are established principles of leadership, and that among those principles are these:

1. Employees are likely to be more productive and to have higher morale under general supervision than under close supervision.
2. Employee-centered supervision is likely to result in higher productivity than is production-centered supervision.[12]

However, the tentative nature of these conclusions is indicated by Likert's reply of "Yes" and "No" to the question, "Do such principles work in practice?" There is need for further study of the specific "conditions which permit a principle to be effective or not ---."

---

[11] Rensis Likert and Samuel P. Hayes, Jr., editors, Some Applications of Behavioral Research, paper by Likert on "Behavioral Research: A Guide For Effective Action" (Paris, France: United Nations Educational, Scientific and Cultural Organization, 1957), p. 11.

[12] Ibid., p. 63.

Continuous Reorganization

Thus far, organization has been described as the structure or framework for the activities of an agency, but it must not be thought that drawing up an organization chart or issuing a set of administrative orders will automatically effect the desired organization. "Lines of authority and command," "responsibility," "coordination," are all general terms which are used to describe the tasks of members of an organization and their inter-relationships. To effect an organization means more than to apply the appropriate titles to its personnel. It means training those personnel in their everyday working habits in the relationships and behaviors which are described in the hypothetical organizational structure. Each member of the group is assigned his role, and the organization is not effected until he learns to play that role in proper relationship with the other members.

Many of the difficulties which arise in agencies are not due to any fault of the organizational structure but to a failure of the personnel to understand or to enact the roles which are assigned them. "Insubordination," "buck passing," "officiousness," and "pull" are abuses commonly found in organization when employees fail to play the roles assigned them. People often speak of "real," as opposed to "paper" authority to indicate the difference between the actual and the theoretical organizational pattern.

The organizational pattern, then, is not a framework which can be arbitrarily imposed upon a group of people working for a given purpose. It is rather an integral and organic element in their existence as a group. The executive who understands this will probably not fall into the error of creating paper organizations which have no existence in reality.

Diagnosing Organizational Ills

How is the executive to decide when his organization is failing in effectiveness and when there is need of reorganization? The problem of evaluating administrative effectiveness is presented in the chapters on direction and administrative measurement. The administrative statistics which the executive receives through regular reports should provide him with a barometer upon which the general level of effectiveness is registered. Unexpectedly high or low readings of the barometer are a cause for further investigation.

In analyzing further the work of particular parts of his organization the executive will gain much from a study of particular cases. This may involve an analysis of complaints received by the administration, or, in such an agency as a welfare department, a sampling of the written case records. Through such studies of the day-to-day activities of his organization the executive will be enabled to diagnose its ills and discover its weak spots. Is there excessive delay in dealing with complaints of crime? Have conflicts in authority arisen between a purchasing agent and a department head? Does a public works department show excessive independence on the part of subordinates and ineffective control at the center? Is there indication that maintenance activities are neglected by a recreation department which is oriented toward the social aspects of its work? Incidents of these types may reveal the need for reorganization.

Before he makes changes in his organization, the chief administrator must be sure that he has evaluated all the possible lines of action and compared their respective advantages and disadvantages. When a trouble spot develops in the organization — when, for example, a series of faulty decisions has been made — the executive may raise these points:

1. Is responsibility for these decisions correctly located?

(a) Could this responsibility be transferred to some other unit?

For example, the public works department may be doing a poor job of designing playgrounds because the design engineer is too far removed from operating and maintenance problems. A possible solution would be to establish a design section in the recreation department.

(b) Should there be greater centralization of this responsibility?

For example, excessive consumption of office supplies in a particular department might, under some circumstances, be remedied by requiring approval by the department head of all purchase requisitions.

(c) Should there be greater decentralization of the responsibility?

For example, in a small city where the building inspector, for sake of convenience, has been placed under the direction of the city engineer, the latter may insist on reviewing in great detail all the decisions of the former, even though the building inspector may be better equipped to make these decisions.

2. Can the quality of decisions be improved without any transfer of responsibility? Perhaps all that is needed is to give the employee who is making the decision the instructions, information, supervision, advice, or training which will permit him to make correct decisions. To refer again to the playground problem, this might be satisfactorily solved by requiring clearance of all plans with the recreation department before approval, and by giving the design engineer an opportunity to study the experience of the recreation department in its use of the poorly designed grounds. The possibilities of strengthening coordinating mechanisms have already been explored earlier in this chapter.

There is perhaps a tendency on the part of administrators, when trouble develops, to think only of the first alternative — transferring responsibility for the decision — and to pay too little attention to the possibility of increasing the competence of the employee who was responsible for the faulty decision by strengthening the coordinating mechanisms. In most cases, the latter method is apt to bring about an improvement more fundamental and lasting than the former.

Limits of Reorganization

When it is realized that organization can be effected only when it becomes part and parcel of the behavior of the personnel, the executive will recognize the need for care and caution in reorganization. A new and complicated plan of organization cannot be imposed upon an agency overnight. The capacity of personnel to work in and through organization develops with training and experience. Simplicity should be stressed during the first steps of organization; further refinements may be introduced later, when the agency shows possibilities of assimilating the more involved structure.

A second essential in reorganization is that every member of the staff understand not only his own part in the administrative structure, but the role of others as well. It is just as impossible for a staff to carry out an organizational pattern which they do not understand as it is for the cast of a play to act effectively unless they not only have a full command of their own lines but also are acquainted with the roles of other members of the cast.

The executive who wishes to build an effective organization must concern himself, too, with questions of method and timing. Where organizational defects are serious, and the need for improvement pressing, a comprehensive survey of the organization, perhaps conducted by consultants called in for that purpose, and a sweeping reorganization may be in order. Such a reorganization will have lasting effects, however, only to the extent that it wins the understanding, acceptance, and approval of the responsible administrative officers in the organization. In the long run, the most fundamental and lasting improvements in organization are usually achieved through the efforts of the chief executive to gradually and skillfully educate his department heads in the principles of sound organization, and to encourage and influence them to bring about the improvement of their own departments.

A final caution to the executive is that he should not expect reorganization to be a road to an administrative Utopia. A complex group of persons working toward a common goal can never have the administrative simplicity of the activities of a single man. The price which must be paid for the advantages of group effort and specialization is the burdensome task of coordination, and even under the most perfect organizational structure that task cannot be eliminated. It must be emphasized again that many of the elements of good organization are mutually incompatible, and hence reorganization must not be thought of as a search for perfection in form but as a weighing and balancing of the relative advantages and disadvantages of the several organizational devices which may be utilized. The executive who has this realistic and organic insight into organization will not be likely to stray far in attempting to improve the procedures of his agency.

Chapter 4

TECHNIQUES OF DIRECTION

The previous chapter dealt with techniques of constructing a piece of human machinery — an administrative organization. But with the construction of the organization the executive's work is hardly begun, for he must take this machinery, put it into operation, apply its power to useful public services, and make in it the numerous day-to-day adjustments which are needed to keep it in first-rate operating condition. This does not mean that the direction of such an organization is purely a mechanical routine. On the contrary, effective direction calls for the highest qualities of human leadership; and the present chapter will attempt to analyze these qualities.

It will prove useful to distinguish three aspects of the job of directing an administrative organization: (1) command — planning the work program of the organization and issuing the orders necessary to initiate it; (2) coordination — articulating and adapting the administrative organization to eliminate obstacles and facilitate progress, and (3) control — making certain that members of the organization are following the pattern set down for them, and that the work program is being carried out. These three tasks make up the central core of the executives job.

This three-fold definition should emphasize, however, the underlying unity of the chief administrator's job, and the role he must play in the organization. Essentially, the chief administrator is a leader, persuading his followers to contribute their best efforts to the work of the organization and combining these efforts into a single coherent pattern. It will be well, therefore, to preface any discussion of specific techniques with a consideration of the executive's role of leadership.

I. The Chief Administrator as a Leader

In the chapter on organization, the chief administrator was described as the man at the top of the pyramid of authority. It is easy, however, to place too much emphasis on this pyramid — to assume that the use of formal authority is the principal means through which the administrator carries out his leadership function. Such is far from the case. Successful administrators know that the use of legal authority is only one of the ways in which they influence their subordinates[1] — that they must *guide* more than *command* and that the emphasis must be on development of morale and on proper training.

Building Organization Morale

The importance of the human relationships in management cannot be overemphasized.

---

[1]See Carl J. Friedrich's Chapter on "Responsible Government Service" in his Constitutional Government and Democracy (Boston: Ginn & Co., 1950), pp. 383-413.

The formal lines of an organization which determine the flow of authority and responsibility are but a shell or framework of the whole network of social relationships which make that organization a living and growing organism. In the long run, the only kind of direction that can make an effective working unit of an agency is self-direction. The administrator must be first and foremost a leader, making the greatest possible use of the capabilities and potentialities of his staff and commanding their loyalty and enthusiasm to the task at hand.

Leadership is involved in every aspect of the administrator's job — in the manner in which he issues orders and gives directions, in the training opportunities he affords his personnel, in the way he offers corrections and reproof for mistakes, and in the encouragement he gives to staff participation in formulating the objectives and the procedures of the group. In an organization characterized by effective leadership, decision and direction are two-way processes, flowing upward from below as well as downward from above. Only through such a process can the detailed knowledge of the man on the job be properly combined with the over-all viewpoint of the executive.

Management thus conceived as positive leadership is primarily a matter of human relations rather than techniques and procedures, and it seems almost self-contradictory to speak of principles of leadership. Yet there are certain general characteristics which distinguish the leader from the mere boss and which help to explain the loyalty and enthusiasm of his organization and the high quality of its performance.

These are some of the principles which the effective leader must understand:

Use of authority and the threat of discipline is one of the weakest tools of leadership.
An inexperienced executive may feel that because he possesses formal authority he can count on the unquestioning obedience of his subordinates no matter what orders he issues. If he attempts to manage his organization according to this notion, he soon discovers the "poverty of power." He sees the morale of his staff disintegrate when they are forced to execute commands which they believe incorrect, or about which they have not been consulted. He sees initiative disappear as they wait for his orders before carrying out the simplest tasks. Even if dissatisfaction does not go so far as to express itself in sabotage, there is all the world of difference between obedience and active cooperation, and it is the latter which makes for an effective organization.

Even military organizations, which can punish disobedience by death, have found that positive morale rather than the negative threat of punishment is the most important basis for discipline and efficiency.

Organization members must understand and approve of the common organization goals. The motives which lead a man to join an administrative organization as an employee are largely personal: the pay is good, the job is steady, his superiors and associates will be persons worth working for or with, or the work seems interesting to him. Before the employee can become an effective member of the organization, however, he must be given a picture of the organization's aims and purposes, he must be convinced of their value and importance, and he must be shown how they are consistent with his own personal goals and ambitions. He must feel that his own future is bound up in the future of the organization. Organizations can sometimes operate without this feeling of unity in the lower ranks — though not without damage to their efficiency — but it is absolutely essential that key administrators, the department heads and their principal subordinates, be deeply imbued with this loyalty. In this regard, the public service benefits greatly from the fact that its objectives are broadly constructive and, if well defined, can command strong support from the inside and respect from the outside.

The executive must permit his subordinates the widest possible participation in the formulation of plans and policies. One of the most effective methods for persuading human beings to adopt goals as their own and to work enthusiastically toward those goals is to give them a feeling that they themselves have helped to determine the goals. The chief executive cannot, of course, abdicate the final responsibility which he and the city council possess for the determination of policy, but the enthusiasm of his organization for that policy is established largely by a sense of having shared in its shaping.

Praise is generally a more effective stimulus than reproof. The effective leader does not underestimate the power of intangible rewards. He knows that praise for work well done may give an employee as great a boost as money.

If it is necessary for the leader to offer reproof to his followers he will be careful that he has all the facts of the case. He will offer the reproof in private and will not use anger to enforce corrective measures. With this done, he will regard the incident as completely closed unless there is a recurrence.

When the loyalty of members of the group is not in question, there should be few occasions for reproof; but when insubordination arises from lack of loyalty to group objectives, it should be treated firmly and promptly. The need for reproof can be minimized by adopting a schedule of regulations that are simple, clear, and carefully publicized throughout the group. If the group participates in the formulation of the regulations — so much the better.

If criticism is necessary of a particular part of a job which is in general well executed, the leader will not fail to make clear his appreciation of the good work as well as his suggestions for improvements of the poor.

Praise for a job well done may encourage a subordinate to exercise initiative; reproof for a job poorly done will only teach him to avoid errors. The administrator who wishes to encourage initiative and vigorous administration in his organization must avoid penalizing too severely those errors which a subordinate makes in good faith and while exercising his discretion. Employees soon sense when they are working in an organization where trouble is most easily avoided by not doing anything which they have not been specifically ordered to do.

Subordinates must be delegated the broadest possible authority to use their initiative and discretion in managing their departments. The technique of delegation is one which most men find extremely difficult to acquire when they assume administrative responsibility. It is not enough that the executive permit his subordinates to participate in his decisions; it is equally important that he permit them to make their own decisions for the management of their departments, within the widest possible limits. Accountability must be two-directional — reaching both downward from the top as authority and upward from the bottom as responsibility.

If final authority to make decisions is delegated to department heads, they may sometimes make mistakes that will embarrass the administrator. But the administrator will sometimes make mistakes in his own decisions, so the possibility of error is no argument against delegation. Any administrator who assumes that his job is to correct the errors made by his subordinates imposes on himself an impossible administrative burden, and encourages in his subordinates an entirely negative error-avoiding attitude toward their work. The risk that a delegated task will be improperly performed is simply one of the inevitable risks of administration. The risk can be minimized by selecting competent subordinates to perform the delegated tasks, and by setting up control procedures to determine how the tasks have been performed, but the risk is only increased if the manager gives insufficient attention to the important policy decisions of the organization in order to spend all his time reviewing details that might better be left to subordinates.

Two particular aspects of delegation will be given more thorough discussion in later sections of this chapter. In the section on command, the types of decisions which the chief administrator should keep in his own hands will be enumerated and discussed. In the section on review, suggestions will be made as to how the executive may effectively review the work of subordinates without centralizing all decision-making functions in himself.

In the last analysis, the basic aim of leadership is to make each member of the group a "self-starter," sincerely devoted to the group aims and resourceful and reliable in furthering them. The desired result is a state of high group morale based on what Friedrich has called the "spirit of craftsmanship."[2] Employees who are sincerely interested in the group objectives and loyal to their leader will develop desirable working habits with a minimum of supervision. Such employees can help to set up their own regulations, participate in dealing with offenders and share in deciding how they shall be treated. The role of the leader is primarily one of guiding the group into broader understanding of its present and future objectives. The broader view of operations which his position gives him provides him an opportunity to see these objectives clearly and to coordinate the group in its striving toward its goal. The leader should regard his position of authority as an opportunity to serve the group, not to command it.

Selecting Department Heads

The success of the chief administrator's leadership will be determined in very large measure by the quality of his principal subordinates. If a department head is incompetent the department will not function as required or the manager himself will have to assume part of the heavy burden of administering it. If a department head is unable to work with others and is constantly embroiled with his colleagues, the awkward consequences can be widespread. There is no sure-fire test for competence and executive ability in the choice of department heads, but an intelligent procedure of selection will go a long way to prevent serious mistakes in judgment. Although the selection of a new department head is an infrequent event it is always an important one; and no act of the chief administrator should receive more careful attention.

The concern of the chief administrator with appointments will extend not only to his own chief subordinates — the department heads — but to their principal subordinates as well. Primary responsibility for the selection of the top men in a department will, of course, rest with the head of that department; but the chief administrator can insist that he be consulted and give final approval when a top position in any department is to be filled. This is justified because these positions are the most likely source for future department heads when vacancies occur, because incompetent persons in a position of such importance could seriously impede and perhaps embarrass the city administration. The power of review should be used sparingly, however, so as to preserve the department head's responsibility and authority within his own department.

The first question to be decided is whether the vacancy will be filled by promotion within the organization, by appointment of some local person outside the city hall, or by appointment of someone from outside the city with waiver of residence requirements.

---

[2]Op. cit., p. 402.

The answer depends in part upon the quality of the men available locally, and the effect either step would have on the morale of the other employees. A city which is large enough to carry on a regular program of in-service training at the administrative level should not find it too difficult to identify and develop within most of its own departments subordinates who are competent to assume the position of department head. Executives who have provided for such understudies or assistant department heads are justified in giving preference to these candidates before seeking a man from outside the city hall. On the other hand, a city should not accept a second-rate department head to avoid appointing an outsider. Even if the immediate reaction of employees to an outside appointment is resentment, this initial liability is not as serious as the continuing consequences of incompetent departmental leadership.

The executives of some cities find that it is very difficult, because of local sentiment, to go outside the city for department heads. In such instances, various local professional groups may be called upon for their advice and opinions regarding the relative qualifications of the two or three best local candidates. Such local agencies may include engineering groups, medical societies, welfare organizations, and so on. Extreme care must be exercised to avoid the cross-fire between factional elements and to assure that the recommendation is based on general merit rather than a formal professional identification.

If no qualified local men are available, then the administrator may logically insist that local residence should not be a qualification. There are a number of ways in which the administrator can seek to convince councilmen, when such is the case, that it is desirable to look outside the city for candidates. One way of accomplishing this is to outline the desirable minimum qualifications and to compare these with the qualifications of the local candidates who have presented themselves. The recommendation of a professional panel as described above may be very helpful here. Full discussion of this question in advance of appointment tends to forestall opposition or criticism of the appointment of an out-of-town man; and such criticism as may be evident will generally subside as soon as the appointee has demonstrated his ability and has become known to the local people.

Duties and Qualifications

If the position is to be filled by outside appointment, a careful job specification will be needed; and this should enumerate the duties of the position and state desirable qualifications (see Fig. 14, Chapter 6). A department head should have organizing ability, knowledge of the job or field of activity he is to head, ability to secure the cooperation of subordinates, energy and drive to do the job, and loyalty to the chief administrator and to the municipal government. But comparatively few of these qualifications can be ascertained through objective test methods, and psychological tests have so far not proved entirely dependable in the selection of executives.

The preparation of specifications for each position before vacancies occur has several definite advantages. It prevents false hopes on the part of subordinates and indicates requirements they must work toward for future advancement. It also tends to forestall the suggestion of unqualified candidates by councilmen for specific department head positions when a vacancy occurs.

If knowledge of the local community is a qualification for a particular department head position, that requirement should be included in the written specifications. The failure of out-of-town applicants to meet that qualification may then be weighed against the possible failure of local applicants to meet other qualifications. It should be clear that knowledge of the "local situation" is usually not as important as knowledge of the operation of the particular department. Within a few months after appointment, an out-of-town appointee with appropriate municipal experience usually will have a greater combined knowledge of both departmental operations and the "local situation" than will a local resident who lacks the broader experience. In some situations a very strong local identification may actually be a handicap.

The task of preparing specifications for department heads can be greatly simplified by adapting for local use the typical specifications prepared by national professional organizations such as the Public Personnel Association, American Society of Planning Officials, National Association of Assessing Officers, and National Association of Housing Officials (all at 1313 East 60th Street, Chicago); the National Recreation Association (8 West Eighth Street, New York); the American Public Health Association (1790 Broadway, New York); and the American Library Association (50 East Huron Street, Chicago).

Other organizations which have not prepared definite specifications but which on request will supply useful information (including salary ranges) are the Municipal Finance Officers Association, American Public Welfare Association, and American Public Works Association (all at 1313 East 60th Street, Chicago); the American Water Works Association (2 Park Avenue, New York); the International Association of Fire Chiefs (232 Madison Avenue, New York); the National Institute of Governmental Purchasing (1001 Connecticut Avenue, N. W., Washington 6, D. C.); the National Institute of Municipal Law Officers (839 17th Street, N. W., Washington 6, D. C.); and the American Institute of Park Executives (Oglebay Park, Wheeling, W. Virginia).

Salary data for many chief municipal officials is contained in The Municipal Year Book, published by the International City Managers' Association.[3] The basic problem in salary determination is how to achieve compatibility with the general level of salaries paid other department heads and still realize the amount necessary to get a man with the desired qualifications.

Canvassing for the Best Candidates

The first step in canvassing is to make known to qualified men that there is a vacancy and that applications are being received. In addition to the methods discussed in Chapter 6 for discovering suitable candidates, it may be advisable to request the personnel exchange service of the American Society for Public Administration (6042 S. Kimbark Ave., Chicago 37) for brief experience statements of men whose records indicate that they have the desired qualifications and perhaps to carry paid advertisements in journals that reach large groups of possible candidates.

The best qualified candidates usually are already employed, and may not actively seek a new position. Therefore the city manager will not want to depend entirely upon voluntary applications but will conduct a wide search and attempt to interest qualified people in the position. He will write directly to the qualified men whose names have been suggested by professional societies and agencies such as those listed above.

---

[3] See pamphlet Trends in Salaries of City Managers (Chicago: International City Managers' Association, 1957), p. 18, for information on the average ratio of various department head salaries to that of the city manager for 782 cities.

Examination and Rating of Candidates

Written examinations may be useful in sampling skills and knowledge for positions where technical knowledge and experience are more important than administrative ability. Technical knowledge can be measured easily by objective written examinations, although it is difficult to avoid an emphasis upon writing ability which may be unrelated to the duties of the job. Candidates for technical positions are examined and certified in some states by various state agencies.

When the chief administrator believes a written test should be part of the selection procedure, the necessary test materials can be obtained from the Public Personnel Association if the city's personnel agency is a member of that organization. The questions used are generally of the broad free-answer type, such as, "Discuss how you would organize and staff a police department in a city of _____ population." It is difficult to grade answers to questions of this type but more objective types of assembled tests have not yet been developed for administrative positions. A candidate who resides at some distance might take the written test under supervision of the personnel agency in his own city.

The use of a procedure generally referred to as an "unassembled" examination permits an objective selection without the use of formal written tests. The selection is made on the basis of education, training, and experience, by systematically comparing definite qualifications of the applicants, as distinguished from merely looking over their records and seeking a few persons' recommendations. The design of the application form is very important in assuring full and readily comparable information on which to base ratings. In evaluating the training and experience of the qualified candidates, the ratings should reflect the quality as well as quantity of training and experience. To assist him in reviewing the qualifications of the candidates being considered the chief administrator may select a small committee of outstanding men in the profession who live in the city or in nearby cities. If such a special examining committee is set up, this fact should be announced in the original notice of the vacancy because of the added prestige this may give the position to be filled.

The written examination and the rating of training and experience may result in eliminating all but a handful of candidates. A further investigation of these candidates embraces letters to references, including previous employers, for their opinion on the ability of the candidate to administer successfully the position in question. Information supplied by references named by the candidate has only a limited value; it may be desirable to check with previous employers and others acquainted with the candidate concerning his qualifications and work. Character investigation is usually best done personally, but confidential mail inquiries have been used successfully. The work involved in checking references and verifying statements may sometimes be assigned to the personnel agency, although there is much to be gained if the chief administrator can himself interview references.

The Personal Interview

It is impossible to make an objective selection by interview alone. Although an important part of the examination, the personal interview should be reserved only for those significant factors which cannot be otherwise determined. It will permit the executive to see the highest ranking candidates for the purpose of checking personality, appearance, ability to converse, and so on. The executive wants to know whether the candidate will fit into the organization, how he impresses those with whom he comes in contact, and how he does things; and he can ask questions designed to ascertain the candidate's attitudes, ideals, and interests. An interview thus enables the executive to test many factors of personal suitability; but technical or administrative ability, initiative, perseverance, honesty, and intelligence cannot be tested or measured through an interview.

The questions to be asked and topics to be discussed in the oral interview depend upon the factors rated. Such questions should therefore be determined in advance in order that similar evidence will be secured on all important points from all candidates. The chief administrator and his personnel officer or other advisers may sit around the table with the candidate. The purpose of the examination is to develop evidence of the possession or absence of certain qualities or traits. This interview is designed to indicate the candidate's personality characteristics and attitude toward his particular job rather than present an encyclopedia of his formal qualifications. The latter is better obtained and analyzed from the written application.

The Final Selection

The responsibility for the final selection of a department head belongs to the chief administrator. The administrator will have before him in writing (1) a comparative review of the training and experience pertinent to the position, (2) statements of previous employers and others who know the candidates, and (3) a record of the personal interviews. After studying carefully all of the information secured about the two or three best candidates and seeking the advice of his personnel and other administrative officers, as well as any local professional organizations in that field of interest, he informs the successful candidate that he is appointed for a probationary period of six months or some other specified time. The administrator has a definite obligation not only to the city and the subordinate employees in the department, but also to the appointee, to make certain during this probationary period that the appointee is properly qualified.

Removal of Department Heads

Although it is not usually possible — or desirable — for the chief administrator to solve his administrative problems by wholesale removals of department heads, nevertheless an incompetent man should not be retained simply because retaining him is the path of least resistance. There are two occasions when this problem of removals takes on special importance: when the chief administrator has just assumed his position, and when a new department head has been appointed and has served his probationary period.

On these occasions it is an important responsibility of the chief administrator to evaluate the work of his department head carefully and to reach a definite decision whether he shows sufficient ability and capacity for development to be retained in his position. The administrator should make a definite evaluation of the man, reach a definite decision, and inform him of that decision. And once the decision that he is incompetent has been reached orderly arrangements should be made for him to find another position. It is no favor either to the man or to the city to postpone the day of reckoning. This same policy applies, of course, not only to department heads but to subordinate employees of the city as well, and the chief administrator bears a responsibility to see that the policy is understood and followed throughout the city.

Developing Department Heads

The general principle that must govern the administrator in his relations with department heads is that in the long run progress cannot be any more rapid than the development of the department heads. The first task must be to encourage in them the same interest in management problems and the same critical attitude toward the work of their departments that characterize his own work.

The administrator must be extremely cautious, however, in imposing upon department heads his own ideas as to proper organization and administration of their departments. Unless he can convince them that the changes he suggests are desirable, they will be given only a haphazard trial. If the initiative can be left to department heads, and if the administrator's suggestions are sufficiently subtle so that department heads can be led to believe that the ideas for change are their own, satisfactory results are more likely to be achieved. One of the best ways of increasing initiative is to make it clear to the subordinate that he has responsibility for his own department and that the chief executive will support his decisions.

Among the methods used by executives to develop department heads and to get them to exercise greater initiative are the following:

1. Urge department heads to affiliate with their respective professional groups; to attend conferences of municipal officials in their field of activity; to read newsletters and technical magazines dealing with activities covered by their departments; and occasionally to study at first hand the practices used in other well-managed cities — all with the idea of keeping abreast of the best developments.

2. Send department heads the articles, reports, and other literature that pass the desk of the chief administrator and that may contain ideas that can be applied locally. Later ask department heads for their opinions concerning the adaptability of methods outlined in the material referred to them.

3. Encourage department heads to offer suggestions for improving procedures or practices in their own and other departments. Suggestions or ideas of the chief administrator can often be made informally in such a way that the department head thinks the ideas are his own. Department heads may be encouraged to attend meetings of civic groups and luncheon clubs in order to get the stimulus of the criticism that comes from citizens.

4. Analyze the periodic and special reports of department heads for information that may provide a basis for discussing problems and methods.

5. Review the annual operating and capital budget submissions and other program statements of the department heads in detail; and give strong and continuing support to all elements in these departmental programs that deserve favorable action.

6. Give department heads full credit for improved administrative methods and commend them for unusually good work.

7. Establish with department heads a working relationship that assures them of a sympathetic hearing no matter what the nature of the problem. At the same time department heads must be encouraged to take the initiative as much as possible and avoid coming to the administrator for advice and suggestions on details.

8. Support or defend department heads in their decisions so far as is possible without jeopardizing municipal policy or doing injustice to citizens. The administrator in many instances may take the blame for mistakes made by department heads and later discuss the matter with them in a constructive way. Harsh criticism by the administrator would serve only to make department heads reluctant to assume responsibility in similar situations later.

9. Encourage department heads to delegate their own work to their assistants. Occasionally have a department head analyze at a staff meeting a specific situation in which he successfully delegated work to subordinates.

10. Hold staff meetings of department heads occasionally to discuss administrative problems of common concern, to sell a new administrative policy or new procedure to department heads, and to make constructive suggestions to the entire group.

11. Conduct a conference-method training course in administrative techniques with department heads. A series of training conferences on administrative management gives the department heads an opportunity to discuss common problems with each other and with the manager, to find out why things are organized as they are and where the organization can be improved, and to obtain a more detached and objective view of their administrative activities than is possible in the daily press of business. In a number of cities this has proved a valuable device for building the department heads into a working team with each of whom understanding his place in the whole picture, and his relations with the others.

12. Learn more about the work of each department so that the department head can be intelligently questioned about his work. The chief administrator need not and cannot be expected to know as much about each department as the department head, but over over a period of years he can gradually acquaint himself with at least the administrative aspects of the work of each department. His knowledge will make discussion with the department head more fruitful, and this in turn will deepen his knowledge. The administrator may fear that this will lead to interference with decisions which properly belong to the department head, but such interference is more likely to result when the executive has an intimate knowledge of just one or two departments (when he has had experience as a city engineer, for example, or as a finance officer) than when he has a well-rounded understanding of the whole city government.

The skillful chief administrator knows the limitations of every department head and the extent to which he must supervise his work. No two department heads will respond to responsibility and to the chief administrator in the same way. Some will be quicker and more intelligent than others. Some will be eager to experiment with methods and procedures while others will be opposed to change. Some may be reluctant to assume responsibility while others are overly independent. Some may have technical ability but very poor technique in public contacts while others may be just the reverse.

A tactful administrator can do much to help his department heads do better work by identifying the weak and strong points of each and by assisting them to correct weakness. The department heads will be receptive to his suggestions and his training efforts if he exhibits in himself the same desire he expects of them. The chief administrator cannot feel embarrassed in asking his police chief to attend training conferences in administrative techniques if the administrator himself is participating in the same course of training. Subordinates will not be resentful of suggestions from the chief administrator if they find that he is receptive to suggestions from them.

II. Command: Translating Policy into Action

From the previous discussion of leadership, one can realize how narrow are the limits of influence that the chief administrator can exercise over his organization. For better or worse, the actual supervision of operative employees will be almost entirely a responsibility of the executive's subordinates, and he must learn to delegate such responsibilities broadly and wisely so that he can concentrate his own efforts on the really important and essential work of command.

What are the responsibilities of command which belong peculiarly to the chief administrator and which he cannot entirely delegate to his subordinates without sacrificing his control over the organization? (1) The chief administrator with his council must assume responsibility for the decisions which determine the basic pattern of governmental services in the city and for the allocation of available funds among these various services. (2) The chief administrator must have responsibility for seeing that each city department is placed under the direction of a competent, forceful department head, and that this department head is stimulated to a continuous and active concern with the efficiency of his department's operations. (3) The chief administrator must retain control of decisions affecting public relations including press contacts, contacts with citizen groups, and employee relations.

How does the chief administrator carry out these responsibilities?

Managerial Planning

Planning of the work to be done is the foundation of effective command. Planning mechanisms are particularly important in carrying out the first of the managerial responsibilities listed above — determining the pattern of city services and allocating resources among the departments.

Managerial planning assures that a connected and consistent program of activities will be carried out throughout the period; it permits a proper balance to be reached between the work of constituent agencies; and it provides the organization with a comprehensive guide to action which relieves the executive of a great part of the burden of day-to-day direction and simplifies his task of coordination and control.

The formulation of the plan depends on detailed information regarding the needs being served by the organization and the cost of service. The plan is embodied primarily in a long-term city plan and in a budget and work program which lay out the task of the individual organization units on a year-to-year basis. Control is secured through records and reports which indicate the adherence of the organization units to the work program that has been laid out.

The less that administrative planning leaves to the day-to-day work of the executives, the better. There always remains the task of providing continuous stimulation, of adapting the program to changing needs and circumstances, of directing the execution of tasks which could not be foreseen in advance, of expediting important parts of the program which have fallen behind the rest, and in general of keeping the plan continuously alive. Systematic procedures must also be developed in order to carry out these subsidiary commands of the executive.

The City Plan

When the city plan is spoken of as a tool of management and command, it is obvious that something more is meant by "city plan" than an attractively printed, highly illustrated report written by a planning consultant and showing where the city might locate some parks and a civic center and how it might widen its main thoroughfare. A modern city plan is a comprehensive, specific program for the future land-use pattern of the city and for all the public services (not merely streets and buildings) needed for that city.

This comprehensive plan likewise includes a rough time schedule showing approximately when major projects are to be undertaken.

To make a city plan of this kind is to make the basic decisions about the long-term development of city services. That is why planning is a managerial responsibility which cannot be entirely delegated to an independent planning agency or an outside planning consultant. Once this basic pattern has been laid down, the work of day-to-day direction consists mainly in determining the conformity of what is being done to the pattern laid down in the plan, and in diagnosing problems which call for revision of the plan (but not for haphazard on-the-spot exceptions to the plan).

The Budget and Work Program

In a city which has a comprehensive long-range plan, the budget is simply a one-year slice of that plan. It is the bridge which carries the plan into action by appropriating and controlling the funds for the coming year's operations.

How are budget priorities to be determined? How does the administrator decide, for example, whether to recommend an increase or a decrease in the police department budget? First, the objectives of each governmental service must be set forth. Then the cost of each particular activity must be measured. Next, the effectiveness of the activity in attaining its objectives must be appraised. Finally, results must be balanced against costs. Activities which have a high cost per unit of accomplishment may be displaced by new activities of equal or greater social value and lower unit cost.

The budget, then, is more than a list of proposed expenditures. It includes (1) a work program showing quantitatively what activities the expenditures will make possible; and (2) estimates of the unit costs of these activities. Effective budget-making requires that periodic studies be made to re-evaluate all activities and their contribution to governmental service so that the marginal value of the last budget dollar in one activity may be weighed against the assignment of that dollar to other activities. This is the essence of budgeting; and it depends on effective work measurement.

Work measurement has been most highly developed and widely applied in the field of public works. The method of developing a work program for street cleaning may be briefly described. A measure of results in street cleaning is the average cleanliness of the street. A measure of performance, called a "work unit," is the number of miles of streets that receive a cleaning treatment. The data needed for the preparation of a street cleaning budget are: (1) data from cost accounts on the cost of street cleaning per unit of performance; (2) data on the amount of dirt removed per unit length of street cleaned; and (3) data on the number of miles of streets to be cleaned. Items (1) and (3) will allow an estimate of the cost of cleaning streets at any desired frequency. Item (2) will indicate the rate at which dirt accumulates on the street and will show how frequently they need to be cleaned so as to be kept at any desired level of cleanliness. The end product for budgeting purposes is a table of costs for various possible levels of cleanliness.

Although work measurement has been most widely applied in the public works department, it is becoming more and more common in fire fighting, recreation, police, welfare, and other city activities. In some fields of municipal service, quantitative measurements and unit costs have not yet been developed, but there is reason to hope that the sphere of measurement will be further extended in the near future. Here is one of the most fertile and useful fields for pioneering by progressive administrators.

Orders

In any organization the executive must issue orders from time to time, but the more effective the organization scheme, and the more effective the planning procedures, the fewer will be the number of specific orders required. Orders issued by the chief executive will relate not only to the specific procedures which should govern the activities of departments but to the general procedures governing contacts between different departments. A number of cities have found it desirable to codify the more permanent administrative orders governing procedures and issue them as administrative codes or manuals. Administrative codes and manuals are more fully discussed later in this chapter.

Of a somewhat different nature are orders issued in response to emergency needs for action. Such orders may secure the removal of a dead animal or may bring the report of a burglary to the attention of the proper police officer. Similar orders may be needed to deal with more serious emergencies, a windstorm, a flood, or a conflagration.

Though the individual occasion when such orders will be needed cannot be anticipated, general procedures should be as carefully planned and thought out in advance as is the case with the comprehensive budget and work program. Whenever a situation requiring official attention occurs with a sufficient degree of frequency, regular methods can be worked out for meeting it with a minimum of executive consideration when each individual case occurs. Thus the handling of the most common types of citizen complaints and reports of criminal acts can be regularized so as to require little or no attention of the chief executive.

The Art of Issuing Orders

An order should not be simply a wish. Its purpose and function is to bring about or to confirm some change in the activity of the operating personnel of the organization. Unless it positively accomplishes this, it is useless.

Order issuing should be sharply distinguished from wishful thinking. Perhaps the chief administrator, while on an inspection tour of the city hall, is impressed by the dinginess of departmental offices. When he returns to his office, he dictates the following "order" to his secretary:

"To all departments: The physical appearance of offices in the city hall is such as to create a decidedly unfavorable impression on citizens who transact business in city offices. Each department is hereby explicitly instructed that its offices must be kept at all times in good order, that desks must be neat, floors well swept and varnished, walls and ceilings clean and painted. All departments will henceforth be held strictly accountable for the appearance and condition of their offices."

This "order" expresses a very laudable aim: the city hall should be kept in a neat and attractive condition. But is the order the method best calculated to bring about the desired result? Do the departments have budget authorizations adequate to keep floors swept and varnished, and walls and ceilings painted? Is this matter within their jurisdiction at all, or is there a separate maintenance department which must at least share the responsibility? For how long a period of time will this order produce any visible effect on the behavior of the staffs of city departments?

This above example might seem exaggerated if it were not taken from an actual occurrence in an administrative organization. It well illustrates the impracticalities of executive wishful thinking. If the chief administrator keeps the following principles in mind when issuing orders, this difficulty can be minimized:

1. No order should be issued until it has been determined that the recipient of the order has authority, and the means at his disposal, to carry it out without neglecting other duties which have been imposed on him.

2. Every order should be written in the language best calculated to impress it on the minds (and habits!) of its recipients — and it should be stated in the simplest possible terms.

3. Every order should be communicated to the persons who are expected to obey it in some fashion which will bring it forcibly to their attention. A bulletin board may be a satisfactory place for certain orders if the persons affected read that board regularly. Orders should not be expected to trickle down through department heads to their subordinates. If they are intended for all employees, all should generally be supplied with copies.

4. There is a limit (and a very low limit) to the rate at which employees can absorb new orders. Case workers in welfare departments have often been swamped with piles of eligibility rules and "interpretations" of rules, which have remained unread on their desks. An unread order will not be followed.

5. If an order is expected to have more than temporary effect, it must be incorporated in some kind of permanent manual available to the persons affected by it, and must be made the subject of periodic in-service training procedures.

6. An order is a "last resort." Before issuing an order, the executive should explore all other possible means of bringing about the desired change — particularly through in-service training procedures.

7. An order should be thought of as a product to be "sold;" and full use should be made of modern advertising techniques. An attractive poster with a three word caption may prove more effective than a precisely worded "directive." The language of soap ads may lack legal precision, but it sells soap.

Evidence of the validity of these principles is provided by the development during the past generation of accident prevention methods. Experts in the field of industrial safety learned by experience that the order: "You are forbidden to operate this machine without first placing the guard in position" is an ineffectual way of bringing about the desired result. Hence, they now concentrate their efforts on training programs and advertising programs in place of orders. Military administrators, too, have long been aware of the limits of order giving. Military field orders specify *what* the subordinate is to do: he is expected to know *how* to do it. The "how to" is imparted to him in the training he receives before he is placed in the field.

Another point which must be kept constantly in mind when issuing orders has been referred to previously — the executive must not lean too heavily on his authority to put his orders across. Some writers suggest that an order should be obeyed not because of the authority of the order-giver, but because the order is recognized as correct by the persons to whom it is issued. This acceptance of "correctness" may stem from general agreement on the best course of action or from a recognition that any form of clearly requested action (in the face of an uncertain choice between alternatives) is better than inaction.

While this conception of order-giving may reflect an ideal of friendly, cooperative, intelligent administration which cannot always be attained fully in practice, still it sets a goal at which the administrator may well aim. Subordinate status creates in most men a certain amount of resentment — often in direct proportion to the subordinate's intelligence and initiative — and this resentment is minimized when the superior and his subordinate focus their attention on applying the best solution to a joint task instead of concerning themselves with questions of authority and status. The effect on the superior is equally favorable, for under these circumstances he is not likely to issue a hasty or ill-advised order merely to "show who's boss."

Assigning Work

The handling of routine matters by departments requires no special instructions from the chief administrator. Questions brought up by department heads and special instructions of the administrator may be handled over the telephone or by conference and where necessary confirmed in writing. Many routine matters can be covered in rules or in administrative regulations that apply to all departments and are issued by the chief administrator's office.

Before work is started on a nonroutine project, the chief administrator, having determined that the council has authorized the work and that funds are available should give a general outline of the work to be undertaken to the department heads concerned. These department heads, and perhaps other staff members such as the city attorney, finance officer, and city engineer, may hold one or more meetings in the administrator's office to discuss the problems involved, methods of procedure, type of construction, sequence of various parts, etc. The resulting work order issued by the administrator is usually addressed to the department head in charge of the work, with carbon copies going to the heads of other departments concerned. Each department head then knows at what points in the procedure his department may be affected.

The chief administrator places special emphasis in such orders on results to be achieved since detailed instructions leave too little discretion to the department heads. If possible, the order should relate to work or policies the department head already understands or has carried out.

Oral directions are to be preferred: (1) when a subordinate may need to discuss the order with his superior; (2) when an order is in the nature of a rebuke (not to be aired before the public or other city employees); (3) in the case of minor orders which establish no precedent for future use. Some administrators confirm in writing the decisions reached in conference or by telephone for purposes of record and follow-up.

Written orders are usually desirable: (1) when major nonroutine matters are involved; (2) when the order is a step in a formal process; (3) when a record of the order is desirable; (4) when a systematic follow-up is to be made of a citizen's complaint; (5) when special authority is delegated to a subordinate; (6) when the order is intended to instruct as well as direct; (7) when the order serves to announce the administrator's decision on a disputed issue; and (8) when the same order goes to several subordinates.

Many city administrators have developed a routine method of handling orders: standard forms are issued on colored paper stock; forms are numbered consecutively and a carbon copy is retained in the chief administrator's office; each order shows date issued, date it becomes effective, and date on which the job should be completed; and a regular procedure is followed for distributing and posting orders.

Administrative Codes, Rules, and Regulations

Many orders, even those issued in written form, are only of temporary significance. There are others, however, dealing with general matters of organization and procedure which will have effect over an indefinite period; and these should be assembled systematically. Many details of organization and administrative practice are determined by the day-to-day interrelationships of the chief administrator and his subordinates, but these practices may well be recorded in a manual, especially in a large organization. Even small cities will find it desirable to bring much of this material together for the information of all employees and as a source of reference for everyone in the organization.

No standard terminology has yet been developed in this field, and some municipal officials do not clearly distinguish between written regulations that relate to detailed internal administration and those that concern citizens. The former generally are issued by the chief administrator without approval by the council. The latter usually are approved by the council and carry penalties for citizens who fail to comply. The written orders which affect citizens may be called "ordinance rules and regulations."

An *administrative code* is a compilation of administrative regulations that are embodied in the city charter, in statutory law, or in ordinances. An *administrative manual* is a compilation of administrative regulations that have been issued by the chief administrative officer.

The Administrative Code

An administrative code is found in relatively few cities — including such council-manager cities as Cincinnati, Kansas City, Miami Beach, Saginaw, and Wheeling. In most cities the subject matter of a code is contained in the city charter, in statutory law, in a series of ordinances, or in all three. There is a distinct advantage, however, in bringing certain materials together in an administrative code or ordinance, prepared under the direction of the chief executive for adoption by the council. The code should set forth the major features of the administrative organization, outline the functions of the departments and the duties and responsibilities of chief officials, and establish the essentials of certain more important procedures such as personnel management, budget making, purchasing and contracting. Details of organization such as subdivisions within departments and duties of subordinate officials should not be included in the administrative code.

The Administrative Manual

The code should authorize the chief executive to issue and enforce such administrative regulations as are necessary for the effective functioning of all departments. Many administrative matters are constantly changing and subject to frequent adjustment, and to include such details in the code would tend to freeze organization and procedures. These regulations should be compiled into administrative manuals which are comprehensive guides for administrative action and contain considerably more detail than is found in administrative codes. Such manuals are intended especially for employees, and emphasis is on how various tasks are to be carried out. They are useful in training new employees, preparing employees for promotional opportunities, enabling employees to broaden themselves in their general knowledge of the municipal government, and providing a basis for a common understanding among employees as to the meaning of the code and their own responsibilities and duties. Manuals must be written in the light of what is administratively feasible. The amount of detail included varies with the subjects covered, the particular desires of the chief administrator and department heads, the size of the city, and the content of the charter and ordinances.

Administrative manuals may be prepared under the direction of the chief administrator to cover details common to all departments or by a department head to cover the operations of his department. The subjects most commonly covered by separate manuals are detailed personnel, purchasing, and budget procedures. For example, personnel rules may first be drafted by the personnel office and submitted to the personnel advisory commission (if any) and the chief executive for review and approval. If a comprehensive personnel manual is to be developed, the rules will cover such matters as applications for positions; preparation and conduct of examinations; certification and probationary appointment; preparation and administration of position classification and salary plans; maintenance of employment lists; personnel records; arrangement of transfers; promotions and demotions; control of working conditions; service ratings; and administration of discipline. These rules elaborate upon the standards laid down in a personnel ordinance or in the administrative code.

Not all manuals need to be prepared under the direction of the chief executive. Authority and responsibility for the operation of a department should be delegated to the department head, who should also be expected to develop procedure and practice manuals which may amplify and supplement general manuals and set forth practices peculiar to that department. Departmental manuals set forth specific office procedures and routines as well as a detailed delineation of the organization. The responsibilities of each organization unit are related to each function; and the successive steps to be followed in processing work are outlined. A description of the control, preparation, and routing of each report and form used in that particular department is usually included.

In medium-size and small cities the administrator may decide upon one general manual of administrative practice. A manual of this nature could include such headings as objectives of municipal government; form of government; general information; duties and responsibilities of department heads; matters for special attention of designated departments; the city manager's office; general office practice; field practice; purchasing procedure; the budget and expenditure control; personnel regulations; the administrative department; the general organization chart; and a plan of disaster preparedness. Administrators who do not want to issue such a complete manual may find in this list some items which may be handled in the form of memorandums.

Compiling Codes and Manuals

To say that most cities will benefit by compiling an administrative code and an administrative manual does not in any sense imply that these cities need more rules and regulations than they have now. Every city executive issues a substantial number of orders that he expects to have permanent effect. It is unfair to expect employees to obey this mass of regulations unless they know what the regulations are, and the simplest way to make them available to employees is to embody them in a systematically arranged manual.

The first step in preparing a manual (or a code) is to compile all regulations that are in effect. The next step is to weed out contradictory and obsolete regulations. The executive must realize that the usefulness of the manual will be in inverse proportion to its bulk. Furthermore, there is always a temptation for the executive, particularly when he is compiling a systematic manual, to decide for his employees things that they are perfectly competent to decide for themselves. Excessive rules, in addition to destroying resourcefulness, cause needless irritation to city employees and reduce the speed and effectiveness of governmental action. Uniformity in certain matters is essential; but in other cases uniformity has no practical value whatsoever, and such cases should not be covered by manual rules just to make the manual "complete."

A third step in manual preparation is to rewrite any regulations that are not stated in simple, clear, and understandable English. There is no need for complicated legalisms in a manual of instructions for city employees. The final step is to add any regulations on important points that are not covered by existing rules. The inclusion of each new rule should be very carefully considered for justification.

The preparation of the manual, however, is only the first step in seeing that the regulations it embodies are carried out. The manual should be a central tool in the pre-service and in-service training of employees. As a matter of fact, administrative manuals may well be developed through training conferences between municipal employees and their supervisors. Employees in any case should be requested to offer constructive suggestions on manual contents, for this will result in a more practical and complete document and in better acceptance of the result.

Because an employee has once been exposed to training in manual regulations does not mean that he will remain trained permanently. Procedures should be set up for periodic retraining and testing, to determine that employees retain and keep up to date their understanding of the regulations that govern them.

The greatest possible leeway should be allowed department heads in determining the rules of procedure for their own departments. Although rules for the operation of a single service should be cleared with the chief executive, they are ordinarily prepared by the head of that service. If departmental rules are limited to matters peculiar to the department and city-wide rules are left to the executive, there should rarely be any conflict as a result of departmental rules. The desire to avoid rigidity in any of these administrative manuals should be made quite clear. Uniformity does not mean permanence. The administrator will make changes from time to time as new methods and ideas develop and as new conditions arise.

The chief administrator should provide for a regular method of numbering, indexing, and filing regulations in the manual. The decimal system of numbering commonly used in compiling statutes is the most satisfactory because it permits the insertion of new material between existing regulations. If a loose-leaf binder is used, amended sections can be replaced immediately, the index can be revised periodically, and the manual will always be up to date. Each regulation should specify by titles and dates any previous documents which it amends and restate them fully as amended, indicating by underlining or italics the new provisions. Every regulation should indicate the effective date, and a complete file of all types of written regulations should be kept in the chief administrator's office and in the city clerk's office. Finally, routine arrangements should be made for keeping the manual up to date — discarding and amending outmoded rules and adding new ones (with the same process of careful review) to keep up with the changing needs of government.

Council Adoption of Rules

This chapter is not concerned with rules and regulations prepared by an administrator for the control and regulation of private citizens. It is often necessary under the provisions of ordinances, charter, or law, to have such rules ratified by the council.

The rules discussed in this chapter are those promulgated for purposes of control of personnel within the administrative framework, usually in accordance with a general grant of power to the chief executive in the charter or administrative code; and such rules rarely require enactment by the council. Some administrators, because they deemed it legally necessary, because they thought it made the rules more binding, or because the council felt it desirable, have had numerous administrative rules and regulations enacted by the council after preparation by administrative officers; but such enactment constitutes a legislative infringement on administration and robs administrative rules of their flexibility. In a proper organization it would appear to serve no useful purpose.

Decisions the Chief Administrator Should Make

The heart of the task of directing an administrative organization consists in making certain fundamental decisions for that organization — and in refusing to make other decisions which should properly be made by subordinates. Which decisions should the executive make and which should he delegate? The problem of council-manager relations and the proper line of demarcation between the legislative body and the chief administrative officer has already been discussed in Chapter 2, and the present analysis will be confined to the division of work between the chief administrator and his administrative staff.

What are the criteria or standards, applicable to the small city and the large city alike, which should guide the executive in dividing the decision-making job between himself and his city council on the one hand, and his department heads on the other?

1. *Any decision to increase or decrease appreciably a service which the city provides its citizens should come to the executive for approval, either for his decision or so that he may present the matter to the city council for determination.* If, for example, a group of citizens makes it known that they would like a more complete program of snow removal than has been carried on in the past, their request should be neither approved nor denied by the public works director without clearance with the chief administrator.

2. *Any essential variation in the budget should receive the chief executive's approval.* The budget sets up a program of work for the year either in terms of work units or in terms of dollars-and-cents of expenditures. The chief administrator spends a good many weeks of discussion and thought each year on his budget; and after the program has once been formulated by the administrator and adopted by the council, any variation from that program should be cleared with the administrator. For instance, if a large amount of money is allotted for street widening on a partial assessment basis and because of litigation the program is not as extensive as expected, a transfer of funds from this program to some other service where requirements have increased should not be permitted without the administrator's approval.

3. *Any change in policy with respect to the enforcement of municipal ordinances or regulations affecting citizens should clear over the executive's desk.* Even though the enforcement of regulatory ordinances is usually entrusted to individual departments, the chief administrator has an over-all responsibility for all such regulations. Although good administrative practice requires a periodic weeding out and codification of ordinances, most cities have a body of legislation that for one reason or another has fallen into disuse and is not enforced. No department concerned should be permitted to alter its enforcement policy with respect to such legislation without the approval of the chief administrator. No decisions have more serious consequences for the public relations of the city government than those involving law-enforcement policy.

4. *Any matter which is to be presented to the city council should first be brought to the attention of the chief administrator.* A troublesome problem for any city executive is that of knowing in advance what is going to be presented to the council. Matters for council consideration originate chiefly from: (1) the executive himself, (2) department heads, (3) citizens who present their suggestions to the executive or in person to council members, and (4) councilmen. It is desirable that the executive know all these matters in advance, though it is probably impossible completely to eliminate by-passing except perhaps in the case of department heads.

How can the executive deal with this problem? It is obviously neither possible nor desirable that he stand as a censor between the council and the public and administrative departments. He must have information on these matters, not to keep them from the council but so that when they are presented he will have the information necessary to assist the council in reaching an intelligent and well-considered decision. If the executive has an "open door" policy, making it easy for his employees, the public, and councilmen to discuss matters with him, it will usually seem to them the most natural and simplest procedure to come to him first, before raising matters for council consideration.

5. *Whenever a citizen is dissatisfied with some aspect of city operations and is unable to receive satisfaction from the department head concerned, the executive must evidence his willingness to hear the request or complaint.* His main aim will be to satisfy himself, and his complainant, that the department head gave careful, courteous attention to the complaint and acted within his discretion in disposing of it. Unless the department head's action has been arbitrary, the chief administrator will ordinarily support his decision and explain its reasonableness to the complainant. If he attempts to re-decide the issue on its merits, he will seriously undermine the authority and morale of the department head, and overload himself as well.

Appeals of this kind take a great deal of the executive's time, but he must be ready to deal with them. Complaints come from citizens, from councilmen themselves, and from employees, and unless the executive handles them, they will be handled by the council, over his head.

6. *The executive must resolve all conflicts which arise out of inter-departmental relations.* Frequent inter-department feuds may be a symptom of faulty organization or of the incompetence of one of the administrators involved, but in the best of organizations the exact division of work between two departments will sometimes be in doubt and a disagreement will result. It is a primary function of the chief administrator to step in and straighten out such disagreements before they reach the "feudin'" stage.

7. *Decisions involving relationships with other governmental units are a direct responsibility of the executive.* Citizens come to the executive's office with complaints and grievances about agencies over which the executive has no control. State or county officials having some local problem take it up with the city executive because he is the man closest to the problem. The executive can, of course, refuse to deal with questions outside the scope of his formal authority, but in doing so he will not improve the attitude of citizens toward their city government, and he will unwittingly teach them to by-pass him in their dealings with the city.

Similarly when the city is requesting funds or legal authority or some service from a state or federal agency, the city's request will carry more weight if it is presented by the chief administrator than if some subordinate makes the contact. In these situations the subordinate seldom has sufficient over-all knowledge of the city's administration or authority to conclude an agreement.

8. *When an emergency arises in the city for which no procedure has been worked out, the handling of the emergency should be under the executive's direction — or he should designate the official who is to be responsible for handling it.* The reasons why the executive is concerned with emergencies are clear. First, even if his subordinates are fully capable of coping with the problem and have adequate authority, citizens will come to the executive with their problems and will expect him to be informed and on the job. Second, although the fire chief has sufficient authority to deal with an ordinary fire, the control of a conflagration requires close cooperation with the police department, the water department, and other agencies of city government.

The executive must be on the job if for no other reason than to make certain that this cooperation is instantaneous and complete. The executive's administrative skill will be exhibited in serious emergencies by his ability to intervene just far enough and no farther than is necessary to make certain that his subordinates have sufficient authority to cope with the situation. If he refuses to go far enough he will be tempting chaos and disaster. If he goes farther he will undermine the self-confidence and self-reliance of his subordinates.

9. *The executive should give final approval to appointments by his department heads of their chief subordinates.* As indicated earlier in this chapter, high level deputies and assistants in the departments can have a very important effect upon the city's present and future performance; and the chief executive should be satisfied as to their qualifications.

These nine points cover the principal classes of decisions that should be cleared by the chief administrator. But the executive is faced not only with the question of what decisions he should make, but also how he should make them. Confusion on this score may lead to serious overloading of his schedule. To say that an executive should approve a particular decision does not mean that he must personally perform all the footwork leading up to the decision. In many of the cases listed above, for instance, the chief executive should not act at all until he has received the findings and recommendations of his subordinates; and then his action should be confined to a mere approval or disapproval of the plan suggested to him.

Another question of very great importance is where the problems originate that come to the executive for decision. The average executive's time is taken up largely with matters that are brought to his attention by others. He has very little opportunity either to get a detached, over-all view of his city's problems or to act as a sparkplug initiating improvements in the city government. There is a serious need therefore for devices and procedures that will periodically call up for re-examination the basic decisions that guide city activities. As far as possible, foresight and prevention should take the place of cure.

The planning procedure will give the executive this initiative and permit him to exercise leadership in the development of the city's major programs. Without a strong planning organization, the executive's role in the city government will be confined to answering questions raised by others; and making decisions for the city on a hand-to-mouth basis without reference to long-term needs or possibilities.

Not only does the city's service program need to be planned, but the chief executive has a particular responsibility to give his city a periodic "management audit" — an examination of the efficiency of its administrative procedures as thorough and as revealing as the fiscal audit which the financial records undergo regularly. Large cities can and should hire management experts to conduct such an audit and subject the procedures of each department to a careful examination. Since small cities usually cannot or will not do this, in these communities the task of carrying on a continuous management audit becomes an important part of the executive's job.

Safeguarding Managerial Time

The busy executive will say: "It is all very well to talk about the necessity of the administrator exercising initiative, instead of merely answering questions posed to him by others; but how does he escape from the constant stream of letters, interviews, phone calls? How does he find time to take this long-run view?"

Interviews with Citizens

The typical city manager spends nearly one-fourth of his work day in talking with citizens and other callers who visit his office or who telephone. Most city managers prefer the "open door" policy (no formal office hours) even though it means more hours at the office. The "open door" policy does not mean that the executive will see any visitor at any time and for any purpose, but rather that he will arrange to see any citizen whose business cannot be satisfactorily handled by someone else or who insists on seeing him in person. In other words, no one who insists on it will be denied an interview. Several methods by which the time devoted to interviews may be reduced are simple and obvious.

1. An assistant to the administrator may interview the caller and handle the matter in question, or he may escort the caller to the appropriate departmental office. Some larger cities have had success with service or complaints offices with a staff specializing in this work.

2. The secretary may advise a caller that the executive is busy but will be free later if he cares to wait. She may suggest that she would like to save him the waiting time if he can tell her his request or problem. Often the matter is settled immediately, or the caller is referred to an administrative assistant or to the appropriate departmental office. In any event the caller has the satisfaction of knowing that he could have seen the executive had he waited.

3. If it appears that the caller will not be satisfied without seeing the chief administrator, the secretary may take from the files any material the administrator will need to see in connection with the call. After looking this over, the administrator can come to the outer office where, with both executive and caller standing, the subject of the visit generally is settled within two or three minutes.

4. When the administrator takes the caller into his office, he may keep his door open so that the caller can see others waiting outside in the reception room. The administrator's secretary may bring in the name of the next caller even though the administrator is still engaged.

5. If the interview appears to be unusually long, the administrator's secretary may telephone him (if his door is closed) and inquire if he desires to be interrupted. If so, the secretary finds an excuse to remind him of other pressing business.

6. When a citizen telephones the administrator's office for an appointment, the secretary may switch the call to the administrator, who in many instances can transact the necessary business over the phone.

Contacts with Department Heads

The next largest part of the typical city executive's nine-hour day is spent in conferences with department heads, including the heads of independent boards and commissions and other governmental units. While most executives do not want to devote less time to this important function, it is possible to make such conferences more effective and also to secure a better distribution or balance of time spent.

There is no best practice in contacting department heads because much depends upon such factors as the number of department heads reporting to the executive, the characteristics of the departments, and the temperaments and personalities of the executive and the department heads. Here are some of the methods used by individual city administrators to economize time in these contacts:

1. Department heads are given full authority to proceed in all matters other than those discussed in the previous section.

2. Department heads do the preliminary thinking and planning on important departmental matters and on problems referred to them by the administrator, and they submit their recommendations, either in writing or orally, for the administrator's approval.

3. Numbered orders are sent to department heads in connection with specific work to be done or problems to be solved, the department head noting the disposition of the matter on the form and returning it to the administrator.

4. When the proper handling of a routine matter has been determined by an assistant or by department heads and approved by the administrator, the procedure is standardized and put into the form of a manual provision, instruction or record form, for repeated application in the future — and the administrator is relieved of the need for repeated review.

But the chief administrator must do more than merely delegate work and responsibility to department heads. He needs their advice and assistance in solving numerous problems. Conferences with department heads often save time because all the facts and alternative procedures can be considered prior to making a decision on a matter that affects two or more departments or agencies. Conferences are most valuable and time-saving when the executive knows definitely the questions to which he wants answers, has in mind the best answers that he can possibly develop, and comes out of the conference with better answers than he had when he entered it. To avoid any misunderstanding, it is often desirable to put into the form of a memorandum to all interested department heads the conclusions reached at such a conference.

The experience of executives with conferences may be summarized as follows:

1. Most city executives find that after they have been in office several months and major policies have been settled, regularly scheduled meetings of all department heads are not worth the time spent. Such meetings are useful only when broad policies or matters which concern all departments are to be considered, or when the executive wants to inform all department heads concerning important changes in administrative policy.

2. Special conferences with two or more department heads and with the heads of other governmental units that may be concerned with a particular problem usually are preferable to meetings attended by all department heads.

3. Holding conferences with individual department heads is the practice followed by most city managers. Some managers prefer to call at their own convenience at the

office of the department head, while other managers set a regular time of the day for certain department heads to come to the city manager's office.

Many executives subject themselves to unnecessary interruptions by people within their own organization when a telephone call or memo would suffice. The executive does not want to adopt any procedures that would tend to stifle the free interchange of ideas, but subordinates do not need to walk into the chief administrator's office at any time on any and all matters.

The executive's secretary and his administrative assistant will have free run of his office, and some city managers have found they can safely extend the same privilege to the city hall reporters of local newspapers.

To reduce interruptions, some executives request department heads to write memos on matters that are not urgent and can be settled by an instant "O.K." or rejection by the executive. If the matter calls for further thought, the executive can consider it calmly and then inform the department head of his reaction. Stating simple questions or facts in written form requires careful and thorough thinking on the part of subordinates, and the task of the executive in giving his answer is made correspondingly easier. Where the question appears to lead to a long exchange of memoranda, however, it may be easier and quicker to thrash it out in one session by phone or in person.

Perhaps the most important single step the chief administrator can take to safeguard his time is to make certain that the structure of his organization is sound. The problems of organization have been discussed at length in Chapter 3, but two aspects of organization which have special significance for the manager's time budget deserve mention here:

1. Reduction in span of control is usually an effective means of reducing work load, and particularly in reducing the number of contacts with subordinates that are required. For reasons stated in Chapter 3, however, this method is less effective in the case of municipal executives than in many other situations.

2. Administrative assistants can relieve the executive of much of the time-consuming portion of his load by performing the tasks enumerated in Chapter 3. The executive will find it very helpful to keep a detailed record of the way in which he spends his time for a few days or weeks. Upon careful analysis of this record, he will undoubtedly find that he has performed a number of detailed tasks which in the future he can turn over to his secretary or to his administrative assistant. By making such a survey periodically, he can determine how much secretarial and executive assistance is required in his office, and how that assistance can be employed most efficiently to relieve him of routine duties.

III. Coordination

To a certain extent, coordination is brought about by the organization itself. But mechanisms can never eliminate the very important task of adapting the organization to changing problems and facilitating its activity.

Lack of coordination appears in a number of forms: Subordinates may indulge in "jurisdictional disputes" each claiming authority to make a particular decision; or they may indulge in buck-passing, each disclaiming authority to make a particular decision; or decisions may be reached on insufficient information because the requisite information is possessed by some other unit than the one reaching the decision.

One point that has already been made in Chapter 3 will bear re-emphasis here. The manager must always keep clearly in mind the distinction between deciding what is to be done and deciding who is to decide — between selecting a particular grade of paper for departmental correspondence, and designating the purchasing agent as the person who will have authority to make that decision. Except for the major policy questions which must reflect the executive's own final judgment, most of his decisions should be of the second sort. Failure to recognize this distinction leads to an over-centralization of decision-making in the organization, burdening the chief executive with a mass of detail and destroying the lines of authority that have been carefully set up in the organization plan.

The executive, if he misunderstands his role in jurisdictional disputes among subordinates, can be the worst enemy of coordination in his own organization. He can lead his subordinates to believe that they need pay no attention to the plan of organization, and that if they encroach on the area of other members of the organization there is a good chance the executive will support them. What is urged here is that the executive must really delegate authority, and must respect the judgment of the subordinate to whom he has delegated it.

Assuming that the administrator learns of jurisdictional disputes or buck-passing when they arise, what measures can he take to secure coordination? First of all, permanent remedial measures should be based not so much on individual instances as upon a review of the whole administrative picture over a period of time. Faulty coordination may indicate the need for one or more of the following steps:

1. Reinstruction of the officers concerned as to their duties. If lack of coordination results from failure of subordinates to understand the division of work or lines of authority, they need instruction as to why the lines are drawn as they are.

2. Modification of the division of work and lines of authority. Frequent jurisdictional disputes may indicate the need for revamping the organization to reduce inter-agency points of contact. When "shuffling bureaus" for this reason, the executive must be careful he does not substitute new friction points for the ones eliminated, or lose other advantages of the previous form of specialization. Moving a playground maintenance division from the public works department to the recreation department may eliminate certain disputes between those two divisions but may lead to lower efficiency in maintenance operations, or to new disputes between the divisions responsible for playground construction and playground maintenance, respectively.

The executive must also satisfy himself that in the reorganization he is not merely moving the dispute from the inter-departmental level to the inter-divisional level. Putting two agencies under the same "heading" in the organization chart is not an automatic guarantee they will "coordinate." The agencies can be just as aloof within one department as in two. The main advantage of grouping the agencies to be coordinated is that this reduces the number of levels of authority through which jurisdictional disputes must pass, and hence reduces the chief administrator's work-load. It does not necessarily eliminate the disputes.

Perhaps the most constructive approach to those problems of coordination which arise when decisions are made upon insufficient information is to strengthen the processes of communication within the agency itself. This can be done in a variety of ways.

A central file of information accessible to all departments concerned is often a solution. A comprehensive city plan is just such a file, indicating to each department the plans and programs of the others. As another example, all the social welfare agencies in the city (public and private) may maintain a joint file of all families in the city with which they have contact.

Another method of exchanging information is by requiring "clearance." This does not necessarily mean "approval." The "clearing" agency may or may not be given authority to veto the original decision. It may simply be given notice that action has been taken; it may be given a period to review the proposed decision and offer comments; it may be given authority to disapprove the decision; or it may participate in the planning and discussions leading up to the decision — with or without the appointment of a formal committee. No clearance requirement should be established unless the need for it has been clearly established, and the "milder" forms of clearance should generally be preferred to the more severe. Prompt action should be encouraged in every way.

There is an unfortunate tendency, however, for clearance requirements to accumulate, and to persist after the need for them has passed. They require, therefore, periodic review to determine their continued usefulness as compared with their cost in time and money. It should be a definite policy throughout the organization to make a periodic audit of all documents and procedures to determine whether the number of information copies can be reduced or perhaps an entire form eliminated.

The clearance procedure and the central file may be combined. For example, the budget officer or the planning officer may be given authority to pass on construction projects to ascertain that they conform with the city plan. An effective procedure for formulating and administering a comprehensive city plan thus affords a most important coordinating device.

Responsibility for Coordination

The chief administrator can take no more important step to secure coordination than to place upon each member of the organization a definite responsibility to integrate his work with that of other organization members. The fundamental conditions which make this possible have already been stated in Chapter 3: each employee must know where he fits into the organization, the atmosphere among employees must be friendly, and contact among employees must be frequent.

Of the weaknesses of employees that may lead to failure on one or more of these three points, ignorance is the most easily cured, and training is usually the most effective remedy. All new employees need to be given information about the organization of the city government and particularly that part of it in which they are located — and old employees need to be brought up to date from time to time on these same matters. In training all employees for their jobs, special attention needs to be given to those points where the employee's work affects other divisions and departments.

More serious human failings, frequently encountered, are misplaced ambition and loyalty. Many employees take the attitude that they are working for the X division of the Y department, rather than for the citizens of their city. Any action which threatens the jurisdiction of their bureau, its budget, or its independence is treated as a declaration of war. This attachment to one's "own" organization is a very natural thing. It often leads to a commendably high morale within the unit which commands this loyalty, but it can have disastrous results for coordination of that unit with other units. Usually it has its origin in the attachment which most persons form for any group of which they are a part; occasionally it results from the ambition of a department head or other administrator who thinks his salary, prestige, and power depend on the size of his department.

In dealing with jurisdictional disputes which come before him, the chief administrator has an excellent opportunity to re-educate his department heads toward a broader loyalty to the city government as a whole. He should demand that his subordinates consider jurisdictional problems not in terms of the limited aims of their particular departments but in terms of the comprehensive aims of the city.

It is at the departmental level that the chief administrator's influence must first take effect; but the sense of city-wide loyalty, to be effective, must penetrate far beyond the department heads. In the long run the real responsibility for coordination must rest with the employees. When confronted with an inter-departmental conflict of any sort, they must take the initiative in an attempt to resolve that difficulty in a mutually satisfactory manner before they bring it to the department heads and then to the chief administrator for solution. The latter should not tolerate subordinates who insist on "standing on their rights" in every petty matter and who treat the city organization as a court system with himself as the highest court of appeal.

No matter how carefully the chief administrator defines jurisdictional lines, or clarifies them in settling disputes, there will always be important areas of overlap. Subordinates must become reconciled to this fact, and to the absolute necessity of approaching problems of conflicting authority with attitudes of cooperation and conciliation.

IV. Control

Control is usually defined as the process of determining that orders have been faithfully and carefully carried out; but this definition gives control a rather negative meaning. The present section will attempt to adopt a more positive viewpoint in keeping with the emphasis earlier in the chapter on leadership as contrasted with authority. From this viewpoint, the major use of control techniques is to enable the executive to determine whether his leadership is maintaining an effectively functioning organization, or to what extent failures occur in its operation. This definition emphasizes that the purpose of control is not so much to check on the executive's subordinates as it is to permit the executive to check on his own leadership.

A city executive casually inspecting a fire station, for instance, discovers that the motor equipment is dirty and poorly maintained. Further investigation leads him to conclude that this is not an isolated instance. What action should he take? Should he issue a general order that all fire department equipment be cleaned at once? Should he insist that the fire chief issue such an order? Should he reprimand the fire chief? He will probably do at least the latter, but there is an even more important step he should take in addition: he must ask himself what missing element in fire department morale, what deficiency in the fire chief, or what fault in the organization of equipment maintenance could have led to the necessity of his personal intervention in a matter of this sort. He must translate the immediate problem of fire truck maintenance into a broader question of organization, procedure, and leadership.

Successful leadership is leadership which calls into the service of the organization the enthusiasm and initiative of subordinates. If control were employed to destroy that initiative it would defeat the purpose of leadership. Control procedures must be concerned not only with things the subordinate has been commanded to do or not to do, but almost equally with the way in which he has used his own discretion where not limited by orders.

The Review of Work

The basis for control is information. Perhaps the most difficult task of the executive, a task which becomes more difficult as the organization grows larger is to learn what is actually going on in the organization. One thinks of the executive's position as a vantage point from which he can get a bird's eye view of the administrative structure. It can be such a vantage point, but unless the executive sets up machinery to collect systematically data about the administrative activities of his subordinates he will find that his vantage point affords him only a very indistinct and tardy view of what is actually going on. A discussion of control must begin therefore with review processes.

Types of Information

Review may extend to the results of the subordinate's activities measured in terms of their objectives; to the tangible products of his activities, if there are such; or to the methods of their performance.

When a department is working toward a clearly defined objective, then a primary method of review is to ascertain the degree to which this objective is attained — the results of the activity in negative or positive, long-range or immediate terms. A city manager, for instance, may evaluate the fire department in terms of fire losses, the police department in terms of the crime and accident rates, the public works department in terms of the condition of streets, the recreation department in terms of services provided.

A simpler method of review is to watch the employee at work. In this case the review extends to procedures and techniques rather than to the product or result. It is a prevalent form of review at the foremanship level but not one which is of much general use to the executive.

Work can be reviewed then by evaluating the degree to which objectives are attained or by actually observing it in the course of performance. In Chapter 12 methods of evaluating work will be discussed at some length; the task of the present chapter is to show how work measurements and other information about the organization are used in executive control.

Use of Information Obtained Through Review Processes

There are two major functions which a review process may perform: testing the quality of decisions being made by subordinates (to improve subsequent decisions or correct bad decisions which have already been made); and holding subordinates responsible for following orders and policies in making their own decisions.

In the first case, review is the means whereby the executive learns whether decisions are being made correctly or incorrectly, whether work is being done well or badly by his subordinates. It is a fundamental source of information which may be used to influence subsequent decisions (issuing orders or laying down new policies covering points on which incorrect decisions have been made or retraining employees in those aspects of their work which review has shown to be faulty). It is also a helpful appeal mechanism (permitting individual decisions with grave consequences to be systematically studied by a higher authority).

In the second instance, review is often essential to be sure that policy decisions reached by the chief executive and the council are carried out. Authority depends to a certain extent on the availability of sanctions to give it force, and sanctions can be applied only if there are some means of ascertaining when a policy has been respected and when it has been ignored. Review supplies the person in authority with this information.

Review Processes and Centralization

It has been emphasized that if an organization is to be successful the initiative of subordinates must be encouraged. There is a very close relationship between the manner in which the executive reviews the work of his subordinates and the degree of centralization or decentralization that results. Well-conceived review methods can be an effective means of preserving the executive's final responsibility for the work of his subordinates and at the same time leaving to the subordinate wide discretion in carrying out the work. Poorly constructed review procedures will result in a rapidly increasing centralization of authority in the chief administrator's office — with the result that he will be severely overburdened and his subordinates will move only when pushed.

Review is sometimes conceived as a means of detecting wrong decisions and correcting them, and this concept may be very useful as applied to those very important decisions where an appeal procedure is necessary to conserve individual rights or democratic responsibility. But under ordinary circumstances, the function of correcting the decisional processes of the subordinate is more important than the function of correcting decisions.

Review, in other words, can have three consequences: (1) if it is used to correct individual decisions, it leads to centralization by actual transfer of the decision-making function; (2) if it is used to discover whether the subordinate needs additional guidance, it leads to centralization through the issuance of more complete rules and regulations limiting his discretion; (3) if it is used to discover where the subordinate's own resources need to be strengthened, it leads to decentralization.

Tools of Executive Control

Effective direction of a city government by the executive requires standard practices for gathering and compiling the information used in control, together with certain routine procedures based on this information. The principal sources of information are written reports, inspection, conferences, and surveys. The two most significant routine procedures based on these sources of information are budget control, and follow-up control.

Reports

What periodic reports should the chief administrator require from his department heads? How often should these be submitted? How should the form and content be determined? It is impossible to provide specific and detailed answers to these questions that will fit the needs of every city, but it is possible to suggest some approaches to these problems that may be profitably applied in any city.

The first step is to ascertain the uses to which periodic reports may be put. Reporting needs will vary from city to city, but they may be classified roughly according to their principal objectives.

1. Periodic departmental reports provide the chief administrator with a check on

the progress of plans and programs. This is best illustrated with respect to the annual budget. The administrator must have periodic reports throughout the budget period indicating how much each department has spent to date out of its appropriation and how much work it has done with the money spent. Such reports need to be supported by a breakdown of the annual budget into monthly or quarterly work and spending schedules which give the administrator a reliable basis for determining whether progress to date is consistent with his program for the whole year.

2. The administrator needs periodic reports on the "results" obtained from money and effort expended by the various departments. It is not enough for the administrator to know that a given amount of work was done; he also needs to know what effect that work had in accomplishing certain objectives. Appraisal of results is at present a hazardous undertaking, because the objectives of municipal government are oftentimes poorly defined and because available measurement techniques are far from satisfactory; but consciously or unconsciously every administrator anticipates and measures results. It is only by careful comparison of actual with anticipated results that the administrator can improve his budget-making ability.

3. The administrator needs periodic reports as a basis for altering his plans or programs to meet changing circumstances. Changes are necessitated either by unforeseen developments in the need for certain services or by a disparity between estimated and actual revenues. With respect to service needs, the administrator must rely on certain indexes, either scientific or rule of thumb, to provide him with "storm warnings." If traffic fatalities rise sharply, he may need to approve a transfer of more police officers to traffic duty. If playground attendance greatly exceeds estimates, more supervisors may have to be added. He needs to explore each field of municipal activity to discover what indexes are most reliable and then make sure that these indexes are reported to him periodically. On the revenue side, the administrator needs at least monthly reports comparing actual and estimated receipts classified by sources, and periodically revised forecasts of cash position.

4. The administrator needs records and reports to help him appraise the efficiency of administrative operations. "Efficiency" is a term that is often misused in the field of municipal administration; and popular measures of efficiency may in reality measure only economy or gross output. Actually, "the efficiency of administration is measured by the ratio of the effects actually obtained with the available resources to the maximum effects possible with the available resources."[4] The administrator must therefore be continually asking whether a better job could have been done with the same personnel, time and money or as good a job could have been done with less expense or in a shorter time.

Results and expenditures may be compared from year to year and from city to city. In those activities to which cost accounting is applicable, "unit cost standards" may be established for specific units of work. "Work and cost statements" are commonly used to report such information to the chief administrator. Less exact measurements of efficiency may be made from reports covering amount of work done, cost of the work, and results obtained. In those fields in which intercity statistics are compiled by some reliable agency, a broader base for efficiency analysis is possible.

5. Finally, the administrator needs reports to provide him with the information necessary for further reports to be issued by himself. The administrator is expected to

---

[4]C. E. Ridley and H. A. Simon, Measuring Municipal Activities (Chicago: International City Managers' Association, 1943), p. 3.

know what is going on in the various departments and to digest, relate, and interpret these happenings in terms that have meaning for the entire body of city employees and for the public at large. If the administrator is to be the focal point of administrative information, he must be supplied with a steady stream of information from the several departments; and all of the various kinds of information suggested in connection with other uses of reports are also useful to the administrator for this purpose.

With these general objectives or uses in mind, the administrator may prepare reporting specifications to fit his own needs. The frequency and content of these reports should be determined by the administrator himself, after consulting with department heads; and the reports should contain what the administrator wants to know, rather than what the department head would like to publicize. There is a difference of opinion, however, as to how far the administrator should go in prescribing the departmental records upon which period reports are based. Some executives study departmental records and make detailed recommendations for their improvement; others leave this problem to the judgment of their department heads, believing that satisfactory reports will automatically require the keeping of adequate basic records. Furthermore, departmental records have uses other than supplying information to the chief administrator. The department head usually wants additional information recorded for his own use. Persons and agencies outside the city hall — state and federal agencies, professional associations, and taxpayers' groups — may also require or request the recording of administrative data.

Much useful advice about records can be obtained from outside the city government. Records may be periodically reviewed by consultants and auditing firms — especially for suggestions for improving financial records and reports. The record experiences of other cities constitute very helpful guides.

Furthermore, in almost every field of municipal administration there is a professional organization or technical society that can be consulted for advice with respect to records and reports, and there are a growing number of "model" records and report systems sponsored by such agencies. For instance: the International Association of Chiefs of Police and the Federal Bureau of Investigation sponsor a Police Department Consolidated Monthly Report (copies available from the FBI); a Fire Department Consolidated Monthly Report form has been developed by the National Fire Protection Association; and the National Committee on Governmental Accounting has published an entire volume, *Municipal Accounting and Auditing*, which gives recommended forms and procedures for fiscal reporting (released through the Municipal Finance Officers Association, 1313 East 60 Street, Chicago). These recommended records and report forms can be modified or adapted to local needs, and their use has the advantage of facilitating comparisons with other cities and the collection of comparable data on a nation-wide basis.[5]

It has been pointed out that the total value of a system of departmental reports is greater than the sum of its parts. The correlation of these reports by the executive adds to their individual values; and various devices can be used to facilitate the integration and interpretation of information yielded by periodic departmental reports.

In one city the executive maintains in his office a master loose-leaf ledger book with sections for each department. Each section contains at the end of the year 26 individual sheets, 13 for financial and 13 for activity control; for each group of 13, one sheet shows annual estimates and the other 12 the monthly figures. When the final figures for the year are tabulated it is possible not only to compare the actual expenditures and work

---

[5]A set of suggested monthly departmental report forms are published in Monthly Administrative Reports For Cities (Chicago: International City Managers' Association, 1950), 32 pp.

completed with the estimates at the beginning of the year, but also to analyze and compare the trend month by month. Two ledgers of this nature are open for inspection by the public in the city hall. At the close of the second year the older ledger is filed permanently to be made available for historical and reporting purposes. A single summary sheet showing the main budget items and providing an index to the detailed budget expenditures is more frequently used by the council and the public than any other part of the ledger, and only when detailed information is requested by the council is it necessary to refer to the other sections. The more detailed sheets are used mainly by the chief administrator for control and comparison purposes.

In a number of cities some of the data from departmental reports are kept in ledger form (with monthly detail sheets for each department) or translated into charts and graphs. These sheets and charts are also useful to the administrator in reporting administrative developments in council meetings or in conferences with department heads.

Inspections

Inspection of work in progress and completed is a follow-up device widely used by all administrators. Most city managers visit department offices in the city hall two or three times a week, and also make periodic tours of construction work and other municipal activities outside the city hall. These inspections are frequently not scheduled; the administrator merely drops in or passes by to see how things are going. Some administrators visit outside work on the way to the office in the morning; others, except in the largest cities, spend an hour or more each afternoon visiting offices or making outside inspections.

These outside tours are often made at the request and in the company of the department head. In any case there should be no suggestion of snooping in the executive's inspectional activities. A critical test of the executive's skill in leadership and the effectiveness of his relationships with his department heads is his ability to carry on inspectional activities without embarrassment or strain on either side. Any changes or alterations he wishes to suggest should, of course, be made through the department head.

Many inspectional activities can be carried on simply by visiting department heads in their own offices instead of calling them to the executive's office when there is something to discuss with them. Department heads in familiar surroundings are more apt to unburden themselves of their administrative troubles, and to ask the executive for advice and assistance. By accustoming employees to his frequent visits, the executive will be more likely to get an accurate picture of normal working conditions than if each inspection is a "dress review." Through these personal contacts, too, employees will feel his direct interest in their work, and morale will be given a lift.

There are certain things which the executive can learn by inspection, but many things he must learn in other ways. He cannot tell by inspection whether fire losses are being kept down — but he can tell something about the maintenance of fire equipment and the way in which his firemen perform in action. In inspecting, he should use his eyes chiefly for three things: (1) to evaluate the public impression of his departments — that is, to judge how a private citizen might react toward the city government when he comes into contact with it, (2) to appraise the morale of employees in each department; and (3) to obtain a basis for intelligent questioning of and discussion with his subordinates. It might be stated as a general rule that the executive can exercise more effective leadership by asking questions than by giving answers.

Conferences

Staff conferences provide a useful information-gathering device particularly where problems of coordination are involved. When more than one department is concerned, the executive will of course abstain from taking action when he has heard only one side of the story, and the staff conference is often a very useful way of getting all sides. The conference group, however, should be confined to those actually involved or possessing some necessary information on the matter.

Group training sessions should be mentioned again here as an important conference method. Group training is not usually thought of as a control device, but a manager may find a conference-method group training course in administrative technique a valuable method of learning more about his subordinates and about the departments they are administering.

Surveys

Periodic reports and inspections need to be supplemented, from time to time by a thorough survey of the operations of each department. This may be conducted either by an administrative analyst on the executive's staff or by an outside agency. The function of an administrative survey is to assist those responsible for administration of the department to rethink their problems systematically — not to impose a prefabricated blueprint showing how they should operate. The survey takes the administrative officials out of the rut in which any person tends to fall under the press of day-to-day duties and gives them an over-all view of the department which they might not otherwise get. The survey, then, must emphasize its information-gathering phase as strongly as its recommendations and reorganization phase.

Budgetary Control

The budget has already been mentioned as a means of laying out the work of departments. Equally important is its function as a control procedure to determine whether operations have been carried out in accordance with plans. For this purpose periodic financial statements are required which compare actual expenditures with budgetary estimates. Also required are periodic work statements which compare actual performance with the work program.

The procedures used in budgetary control are discussed in Chapter 8. The essential feature of the system of control is that each expenditure be distributed to individual accounts as set up in the budget statements and that expenditures be limited to the unencumbered balances of those accounts and to the purposes for which they were scheduled. The officer who is entrusted with the task of budget supervision will refuse to validate any expenditures beyond the allotted amount. If adjustments are required in any of the allottments by changed circumstances, these adjustments must receive the approval of the city administrator. If adjustments required affect the major purposes of appropriation, the approval of the council may be needed. Department heads must be held strictly to the plan that has been decided upon.

Parallel controls must be set up to determine whether the program of work is being carried out on schedule. The system of monthly administrative reports already described in this chapter should provide the needed information on "number of work units completed." Not only must accomplishments be measured, but these accomplishments must be considered in relation to cost, so that unit costs which are out of line with past experience or expectations may be quickly detected and their causes investigated. Failure of the work program to progress as anticipated may require a reconsideration of the original budgetary allotments.

Follow-up Techniques

Orders cannot be left to themselves to be executed. The executive is responsible for their execution, and he must make certain that they have been carried through. Indispensable checks on the performance of subordinates and on matters requiring further attention are obtained by various types of follow-through or follow-up control.

Although varying widely in application from one department to another, the follow-up principle is always the same. It consists of keeping a pending file or check-list of all current duties to be performed and of all matters to be completed and inspecting it periodically to determine what business is still unfinished.

Daily follow-up controls should be maintained on all matters calling for future action for which the administrator's office is responsible or which it might overlook. Use of such a system will avoid the otherwise frequent occasions when a department head or other official fails to take an agreed-upon action on schedule.

All such matters may be filed by the date checked for the receipt of a reply or the completion of the work; and if the routine check upon the follow-up material for the day shows that the information requested or the completion of work is overdue, appropriate action is taken. Complaints require particularly careful follow-through to insure proper disposition and the notification of affected people.

Reports, inspections, conferences, surveys, and budgetary controls are in fact all follow-through devices in the execution of work. All of these tools of executive control are aimed at assuring that the programs of the city government are carried out on time and as planned.

Summary

In this chapter techniques have been discussed which will assist the administrator in the task of directing his organization. It has been emphasized that underlying these techniques are certain basic principles of leadership which involve the leader's personality and character. Fundamentally the leader's task is one of stimulating, educating and developing his subordinates rather than commanding them. A single man cannot supply the energy to operate a large administrative organization — if he tries, he will fail. But he can supply that all-important element of directive energy which organizes, directs and coordinates the vastly more powerful combined energies of his staff.

The administrator exercises three principal directing functions: (1) command, (2) coordination, and (3) control. For effective direction, his command functions should be exercised as much as possible through long-term planning, careful budgeting, and in-service training rather than through a continuous flow of on-the-spot orders. Coordination should be used to settle the day-to-day problems of internal friction and misunderstanding that afflict even the best organized administration. Control is necessary not to correct past mistakes but to prevent future mistakes by providing adequate channels of information through the organization to points of decision and by assuring that the government's work is proceeding. The aim in all three functions is to give life and purpose to the city government, making it a vigorous, responsive and effective agency for community service rather than a leaden bureaucracy.

Chapter 5

PROGRAMMING MUNICIPAL SERVICES

A city government exists to give services to the people of the city and to regulate certain of their activities for the common good. No decisions are more important in the city government than those that determine what services shall be provided and what activities shall be regulated. Unfortunately, the attention given to these decisions is not always proportionate to their importance. It is easy to accept without question a pattern of day-to-day operations and to take for granted the over-all program of city services. On the other hand, the task of making a really basic and thorough study of the service program is difficult.

Estimates must be made of the future prospects of the city in terms of population, economic situation, and physical development. All sorts of intangibles need to be weighed, and comparisons made of the relative worth of highly dissimilar activities — fire protection and playgrounds, streets and policing, library service and snow removal. It is no wonder that the administrations of many cities have never attempted to evaluate systematically their program of services, but have simply accepted the existing pattern as it has developed through a succession of historical accidents.

This failure to make long-term decisions is often reflected in the budget procedure. In many cities departmental budget estimates are based primarily upon the amount spent during the previous year. In some cases "justifications" are required only for the proposed increases in expenditures — it is apparently assumed that the current level of expenditure has already been "justified." As a result of this, the basic assumptions determining the current expenditures — the level of city services — are never examined at budget time. One city may have heavy expenditures for the fire department because years previously indignant citizens demanded that all possible measures be taken to prevent the recurrence of a serious conflagration. Another city may not have a crime prevention bureau in the police department simply because there has never been one. Still another city may have an exceptionally large building inspection staff because ten years earlier it had a period of very rapid growth.

In comparing local governmental services performed by various cities, one cannot help being impressed by the wide diversity of patterns. Of course, these variations may be explained in part by differences in the types of services needed by different communities, and by differences in their ability to pay for services — but that is by no means the whole story. A large part of the reason lies simply in the failure of most cities to undertake comprehensive programming and evaluation of their services.

A lack of long-term programming shows up particularly in the matter of capital expenditures. These generally fall into two classes: (1) acquisition of land and rights-of-way and (2) construction of major public works, such as public buildings, bridges, grade separations, tunnels, viaducts, major traffic thoroughfares, sewer systems, off-street parking, and public utilities. In addition, the provision of housing for low-income families and the acquisition and preparation of land for redevelopment are now recognized in many cities as a justifiable and necessary public enterprise. Ordinarily, a city provides what it needs of the foregoing items singly, when the need in the particular case has become sufficiently acute to dramatize the extraordinary expenditure which is usually required. Thus, the city's financial resources, including bonding capacity, may be exhausted by provision for a few capital items, while other needs are neglected.

In contrast to this haphazard method a comprehensive plan will indicate what things are needed, the relative importance of the various items, and the location, character, and scale of what is to be done to satisfy these needs. The long-term service program will schedule these items over a period of years, so that they can be provided as needed, within the limits of the financial resources of the community.

Responsibility for Programming

To determine what services a city should provide is basically a policy matter. It is up to the citizens through their elected representatives and through such devices as referendums, opinion polls, citizen committees, and public hearings, to determine what the municipal "standard of living" shall be. If they decide that they can get along with a poor grade of fire protection, or that they cannot afford a better grade, it is not for the chief administrator or the department head to substitute his judgment for theirs.

The role of the chief administrator or of other administrative experts in advising the people of a city what services they ought to have is exactly like the role of an expert on family expenditures advising how to live within the family income. He can tell a family what the consequences will be of spending their money in various ways: that if they don't spend at least a certain amount for wholesome foods they will be likely to contract nutritional diseases of one sort or another; or that unless they spend a certain amount for insurance, they will not be economically prepared should accident or death befall the breadwinner. But in the last analysis, if the family weighs these consequences and decides that it would rather skimp on its food budget in order to have money to buy books, or that it would rather save more at the expense of its clothing budget, the expert has no right to object. These, after all, are matters of taste and relative values on which individuals have a perfect right to differ.

Similarly, the fire chief may point out that certain expenditures will be required if the fire insurance rate is not to be raised; and the police chief may submit his expert judgment that the robbery problem will become serious unless he can put five more patrolmen on the street; but it is still up to the people of the city to decide, after they have heard their experts, whether such services are worth their cost, and whether the expenditure for fire protection is more important or less important than the expenditure for police protection.

What, then, are the responsibilities of the chief administrator and his staff for the programming of city services? They have these responsibilities:

1. It is up to the chief administrator to see that the pattern of city services is periodically and systematically reviewed by the people of the city through their legislative body; and that the various alternatives are presented to them for increases and decreases in particular services, for the discontinuing of services, and for the initiation of new services.

2. It is up to the chief administrator and his staff to see that estimates, as accurate

as possible, are made available to the policy-determining agencies for predicting the consequences of increasing or decreasing the expenditures for particular services. That this is an extremely difficult task may be admitted — but this in no way excuses the administrative staff from carrying it out as completely as possible.

3. It is up to the chief administrator and his staff to conduct continuing studies of each individual service performed by the city to assure that their performance, at the accepted level, is done effectively and economically.

What has been said here about services applies equally to the city's regulatory activities: food inspection, zoning, building regulations, and so on.

The City Plan

The major steps involved in establishing a long-term program for the city are the development of a city plan and the construction of long-term service programs and capital budgets based on the plan. Complementing the service program will be a program of regulatory action to carry out those parts of the plan which require control of the activities of citizens.

Content of the Plan

The content of a comprehensive city plan and the way in which such a plan is drawn up will be considered at length in Chapter 10. As a basis for the present discussion, however, it will be helpful to enumerate the principal elements that make up the plan. The foundations of the plan rest upon data about the social and economic characteristics of the city, and estimates as to how these characteristics will change with time. To plan intelligently for a city requires a clear understanding of its inhabitants, their age, income, nationality, and racial characteristics; and the economic base of the city — the types of business and industry on which it rests, their stability in the face of business fluctuations, and their future prospects.

The plan itself, developed out of these data, contains two main elements. These are (1) a plan for the pattern of land uses; and (2) a plan and program for community services. These two elements are usually coordinated by the development of a comprehensive "Master Plan."

Land Use. This part of the plan forecasts where people will live, where they will work, where they will shop, and where they will take their recreation. It also deals with the general character of the various residential, commercial and industrial districts of the city.

Community Services. The other part of the master plan deals with the facilities provided the inhabitants of the city by the municipal government, by other governmental agencies, and by public utilities. This includes a thoroughfare plan, a transportation plan, a transit plan, a plan for utilities (private and public), a plan for market sites, a plan for public buildings, a plan for recreation areas, a school site plan, and a plan for such community amenities as street tree-planting, architectural supervision of commercial buildings, preservation of areas of historical significance, and regulation of outdoor advertising.

The Plan as "Prediction" and "Proposal"

A city plan has two sides — it is both a prediction and a proposal. On the one hand, the city plan seeks to estimate or predict how large the population of the city will be at various dates in the future, how the people will earn a living, where they will live and where they will work, how many automobiles they will have and how much they will use them. On the other hand, the city plan contains recommendations to guide the future development of the city — proposals for city services, proposals to be implemented through the zoning law and other regulations, and proposals to be implemented through public education.

Both as a prediction and as a proposal the city plan is an essential basis for the program of services. In predicting the changes that will take place in the city, the plan forecasts the kinds, magnitude, and distribution of the various services that will be needed. In proposing that the development take certain directions, the plan forecasts the kinds of services and regulations that will be required to implement it.

It should be emphasized that the plan is not a static conception of an ideal future city, but the description of a series of future cities, to be attained in five, ten, fifteen years, and so on. Only if the plan includes a time schedule for its various projects will it provide an adequate basis for the service program and for the capital budget. Allowances must of course be made for amendments to the plan as circumstances require it.

Implementation of the Plan

There are three principal ways in which the city plan is carried out:

Regulatory Action. The use of property by private owners is controlled by the zoning law, building regulations, and subdivision controls. Public utilities, if privately owned, are regulated by franchise and ordinance.

Public Services. The execution of the street transportation plan, the park and recreation plan, and plans for schools and other public buildings is largely a matter of providing public funds for the construction, maintenance, and operation of the necessary facilities.

Education of the Public. Many of the recommendations of the city plan may require nothing more than the "enlightened self-interest" of the people of the city to carry them out — but extensive campaigns of public education may be needed to "enlighten" the self-interest. A city free from street litter is a goal that can be reached only with citizen cooperation.

The Service Program

Although there is no one best way to prepare and administer the program of public services, the following are the principal steps that have to be taken:

1. Enumerate carefully the objective or objectives of each department of the city government.

2. Estimate how the need for each municipal service is expected to increase or decrease over a period of time due to change in population, and other factors.

3. Identify the key factors that determine the cost of each municipal service.

4. Set tentative standards of quality or adequacy for each service.

5. Having taken steps 2, 3, and 4, determine the approximate annual cost of

providing each particular service. Subdivide this into (a) annual operating and maintenance costs, and (b) cost of needed capital improvements and major equipment purchases.

6. Estimate the revenues that would be derived at existing tax rates, and at lower and higher tax rates, together with revenues from sources other than taxation.

7. Combine the expenditure estimates for the several city departments and balance them against the estimated revenues — adjusting the several items to achieve a balance.

8. Draw up a capital budget, scheduling by years the capital items needed by each department to carry out the service program. A general program can be drawn up for 15 or 20 years, with a more specific year-by-year schedule for the first five or six years.[1]

9. Draw up the annual budget, basing it directly on the long-term service plan and the first year's installment of the capital budget.

The long-term program, once established, is not a static thing. It needs to be reviewed periodically so that it will meet the changing needs of the city. The changes made in it from time to time will reflect modified estimates by the city planning agency of the city's future development, decisions of the city council to alter the emphasis on various city services, changes in methods, organization, efficiency and price levels that affect the cost of providing particular services, and changes in the city's financial prospects.

Developing a program of this kind is not an overwhelming task if the steps are taken one by one. Almost every city is already carrying out a large part of the above procedure, but many cities are losing the principal advantages of long-term planning through failure to program in a systematic and integrated fashion, rather than to deal with the steps piecemeal. In many cities that have comprehensive city plans, the plan remains merely a design upon paper because there is not an adequate bridge — in the form of the capital budget, long-term operating budget and the annual budget procedure — between the long-term plan and the every-day administrative activity in the city hall. In other cities an elaborate annual budget procedure becomes an almost useless routine of paper-work because the annual budget is not properly related to a long-term service program and a city plan.

In the following sections the specific steps involved in developing the long-term service program will be studied in greater detail. First, however, there needs to be an explanation of some of the assumptions underlying the procedure.

Assumptions Underlying the Programming Procedure

It is assumed, first of all, that final control over public policy — and particularly over standards of public service — should rest with the public and its elected representatives. Hence the procedure should provide that these standards shall be established by a legislative process with adequate provision for expert assistance to the legislative body.

The second assumption is not so much an assumption as a fact — that substantial changes in current rates of spending can usually be made only as a result of corresponding changes in service. Once it is admitted, for example, that the fire department needs five engine companies and two ladder companies, and that the companies should be manned with an average strength of ten men, the budget of the fire department is practically determined. It can be reduced substantially only by reducing the number of companies or

---

[1] For a good discussion of the relation of long-term planning and capital budgeting see Planning for Public Works (Washington, D. C.: Government Printing Office, 1957). 25 pp.

by reducing the average manpower per company; that is, by lowering the level of the service provided.

A third assumption is that the city must have long-term plans for its operating budget as well as its capital budget, and that these two parts of the expenditure plan must be properly related to each other. Although there has been a great deal of progress among cities in the last few years in the adoption of capital budget programs, too often the capital budget has been developed with insufficient attention to the effects it would have on the operating budget. One city, for example, carried out a comprehensive playground construction program that gave the city 54 new playgrounds but no plans had been made for financing the large expenditure necessary to staff and operate the playgrounds. New schools, new fire stations or the addition of a new service will require added personnel and will increase operating budgets.

In other cases, the capital budget has been constructed by projecting into the future current revenues and current operating expenditures, and assuming that the difference between revenues and expenditures was the amount available for capital expenditures. No consideration was given to possibilities of increasing or decreasing revenues or operating expenditures, or to the fact that capital expenditures must bear a proper relation to operating expenditures. Often allowance has not been made for fluctuations in revenues and costs resulting from changes in business conditions and in price levels.

A final assumption of this procedure is that many expenditure items that are relatively fixed in the short run — it is impossible to decrease them materially — become highly variable when they are looked at from the long-run standpoint. A building, once constructed, or a piece of equipment, once purchased, becomes a "sunk cost" and it is usually wasteful not to maintain and operate it as long as it lasts. In the short run, nothing can be done about the buildings and equipment already on hand; in the long run these can be programmed as easily as operating costs. Even personnel costs are relatively rigid in the short run. It is much easier from every standpoint to decrease the size of the department gradually by not making personnel replacements, than it is to decrease it overnight by discharging employees.

Measurement of Objectives and Needs

As previously stated the first two steps in programming municipal services are to identify the objectives of each municipal department and to measure how the need for services in each of these categories can be expected to vary as the city grows and develops.

In the process of formulating the program, each municipal department would be required to set forth in a comprehensive manner a list of its aims and purposes. Not only is this an essential step in programming, but it is a valuable stimulant to the thinking of department heads about their organizations. The department head who knows he will be expected to justify his program of activities in terms of definite objectives will be alert to prune activities that have lost their usefulness, or that are out of balance with the overall goals of the organization. (Some discussion of the objectives, and methods of measuring their attainment, of particular municipal departments will be found in Chapter 12.)

In the case of some departments objectives are specific and concrete, and it is easy to relate the activities of the department to the objectives. In other cases, municipal departments have objectives that are relatively intangible and their relation to the program of activities may be rather difficult to assess. An example of a unit with a concrete objective is the snow removal division of the public works department; an example of a department whose objectives are difficult to state in specific terms is the municipal recreation department. Moreover, it is easier, but far less meaningful, to state the objectives of an organization in terms of immediate aims than it is to state the ultimate goals of the program of activity. It is easy, for example, to state the objectives of a municipal recreation department in terms of participant-hours of recreational activity provided, but this tells little of what these publicly provided recreational activities are intended to do for their participants. The closer the statement of objectives comes to the real goals of the administrative program in terms of basic human values, the more valuable it is for intelligent programming of municipal services.

Relating the program of activities to objectives requires not only a clear and comprehensive statement of these objectives but also a careful measurement of the magnitude of the problem to be faced in reaching the stated goals. A municipal library might state as its objective the circulation of 30 books per year for each 100 people in the community. (This is intended merely as a simplified example, and it is not implied that library objectives can be stated purely in terms of number of books circulated.) In this case the per-capita circulation would be a statement of the objective, but the magnitude of the administrative service problem would depend also upon the population of the community.

The magnitude of need for city services to meet each objective will depend upon the population of the city and its characteristics, the economic base of the community, the land use pattern, and other factors. The need for fire protection will vary with the extent and location of various types of built-up areas. The need for schools will depend upon the distribution of children of school age. Similar measures of "service need" can be constructed for each municipal service, basing the estimates of population, land use, and the like upon the city plan. Population estimates may show, for example, that the high school population ten years hence will be 400 greater than at present, and that two square miles of new residential area will require fire protection at that time.

Setting the Standard of Adequacy

The fourth step in programming listed above is determining the level of adequacy at which service is to be provided — the standard of living to be maintained, so to speak. Almost every municipal objective permits various degrees of attainment. It is not a question of whether there will, or will not, be fire protection; the question is how intensive the fire protection will be — how far the city should go in trying to reduce fire losses. Even when the city government has decided what its goals are, and what the magnitude of needs is, it still must decide to what degree the needs will be met. This is a very crucial question for long-term programming, because the level of adequacy of the services is just as important in determining operating and capital costs as is the range of objectives and the magnitude of need. A city of 10,000 that wishes to provide an acre of park land for each 100 inhabitants is faced with just as large an administrative problem and just as large an expenditure as a city of 25,000 that proposes to provide an acre of park for each 250 inhabitants.

It cannot be repeated too often that there is no such thing as the "proper" standard of service or "minimum adequate" standard of service that a city ought to maintain, any more than there is a standard for the number of neckties a man ought to have in his wardrobe. By the same token, it is impossible to determine by the application of any scientific yardstick, that a city is spending too much for a particular service — maintaining too high a standard. The question is, what does the city want? What standard of municipal services do the citizens desire, and what are they willing to pay for?

One reason for insisting on this point is that in a number of cases persons or organizations interested in particular municipal functions have set forth recommendations which purport to fix the minimum amounts that cities should spend for these functions. The National Recreation Association, The American Library Association, The National Board of Fire Underwriters, and others, have in some cases taken the position that experts in particular municipal functions are competent to set expenditure standards for cities in their respective fields. On the contrary, however, the analysis in this chapter shows that expenditure standards involve not only technical questions, but also value judgments and decisions on financing.

On the other hand, there are certain common sense methods that the city can use to determine whether or not a particular expenditure is worth while. Particular programs conducted by the recreation department might be analyzed, for example, to determine the cost per participant-hour, of carrying on the program. If it were discovered that some activity was costing $15 per participant-hour, the question would arise as to whether this money could not be spent more productively in other directions.

Citizen demand for services is another relevant criterion. This applies particularly to services such as recreation and library facilities provided to citizens as consumers. Of course, the response to citizen demands does not need to be too literal. A city librarian may justifiably decide that it is more important to supply the library with a copy of a standard technical work to be used by persons in local industrial plants, than it is to get another copy of a best-selling novel. Also in recognizing demands for services, the distribution of the demand must be distinguished from its intensity. The wishes, however strongly expressed, of a small pressure group that wants special consideration do not necessarily merit the same consideration as the less coherent desires of the wider body of citizens.

In some cases, the point of diminishing returns for municipal services can be determined roughly by estimating their money value. Suppose the question arises of installing a system of storm sewers. From past experience estimates can be made of the frequency of rains of flood proportions, the amount of damage caused by them, and increased storm water flow resulting from increased building density, and these estimates can be compared, at least in rough terms, with the cost of installing and maintaining the sewers. It is sometimes possible to evaluate the savings in time to motorists attainable by widening a thoroughfare. Even where accurate money estimates of value are not possible, or where other factors than money value must be taken into account, estimates of the order of magnitude of the prospective savings will help the city avoid expenditures that are ridiculously disproportionate to the service they provide.

The programming of municipal services requires, then, that the objectives of the program of activities be set forth; that the magnitude of the need to be served be estimated; and that there be determined the level of adequacy at which each service is to be provided. These three items correspond to the first, second, and fourth steps of the programming process. The discussion turns next to the identification of key cost factors (step three).

Identification of Key Cost Factors

Because the objectives of a municipal activity are sometimes highly intangible, it is often not possible to measure the unit cost of providing service directly in terms of the level of adequacy with which objectives are realized. Somewhat more tangible and concrete units must be found for estimating the cost of the program. It will be found that in the case of almost every municipal service there are two or three critical factors on which the cost of the entire service hinges. An important step in programming is to identify these key factors and to express the service program in terms of them.

In the fire department, for example, the key factors are the number of fire companies of various kinds, the standard complement of men for each type of company, and the average salary of firemen. The land-use map of the community provides the basis for the measurement of need for fire protection, and the standard of adequacy can be expressed in terms of the average distance apart of fire companies in areas of different types, and the number of men per company. Combining the land-use data with the standard of adequacy, the number of companies and number of men required can be estimated, and from this, annual operating and capital costs can be determined within relatively narrow margins.

Let us illustrate this for a hypothetical city. It might be decided that the city should be prepared to mobilize nine engine companies for a single large fire; that there should be an engine within three-quarters of a mile of every point in high value districts, within one and one-half miles in closely built residential districts, and within three miles in sparsely built residential districts; and that a ladder truck should be within one mile in high value districts, two miles in closely built residential districts, and three miles in sparsely built residential districts. Manpower requirements might be established at 14 men for each engine company in high value districts, and 10 in other districts; 16 men for each ladder company in high value districts, and 12 in other districts. The average salary expenditure might be assumed at $4,500 per employee, and the average non-salary expenditure as 25 per cent of the salary expenditure. Application of this standard to the land-use map of the city might show the need, either at present or at some specified future time, for 11 engine companies and two ladder companies, having a total manpower of 163; and a total budget of about $917,000.

In the case of the police department, data on the geographical distribution of police "incidents" and "hazards" provide the basic measurement of need for police service. The standard of adequacy can be phrased in terms of the average "work load" of a policeman expressed in the number of police incidents. From an analysis of this sort the number of policemen needed and the cost can be estimated.

The identification of key factors in the public works department is relatively simple. In the case of street cleaning, for example, the number of miles of various sorts of streets to be cleaned provides the basic measurement of need. The frequency of cleaning is the standard of adequacy. These two together determine the number of miles to be cleaned per week, and experience as to the average cost of cleaning per mile permits this figure to be translated into a cost estimate.

These illustrations will serve to show how the estimated expenditures can be related to service standards in the case of some of the major city departments. Similar methods of analysis can be used for the other departments.[2]

For purposes of long-term estimation, because there are so many variables and unpredictables involved, it is not usually worth while to go too far in refining the measurement methods. For many purposes, if it is decided that a given standard of service should

[2] See Herbert A. Simon, Fiscal Aspects of Metropolitan Consolidation (Berkeley: University of California, Bureau of Public Administration, 1943), Chapter III. Also see case studies in performance budgeting published by the Municipal Finance Officers Association, Chicago: An Administrative Case Study of Performance Budgeting in the City of Los Angeles (1954); Performance Budgeting and Unit Cost Accounting for Governmental Units (1954); Performance Budgeting for Libraries (1954); Performance Budgeting for Hospitals and Health Departments (1956); and "Some Non-Cost Accounting Approaches to Performance Budgeting," by Frank P. Sherwood, Public Management, January, 1954.

be maintained, this standard can be translated into terms of per capita cost or an estimated standard unit by the methods suggested here, and these cost figures projected into the future.

The Revenue Program

An important purpose of the long-term expenditure plan is to prevent the city's expenditures from exceeding its income — to balance its budget. A balanced budget, from the standpoint of long-term planning, means not only that income each year equals outgo but, just as important, that the city is not accumulating a bonded debt which it cannot carry without sacrificing operating services.

Estimating Revenues

A first step in developing the revenue side of the long-term plan is to estimate the revenues that will be obtained if the city's existing fiscal policies are retained. In estimating future revenues the following information must be secured: trends in assessed valuations; property tax yields; trends in municipal taxes other than property taxes; trends in miscellaneous sources of revenue such as licenses, special assessment levies, property and investment earnings, reserves or surpluses carried over from a period, earnings of revenue-producing utilities available for general purposes; probable shares in state-collected, locally shared taxes; and probable state and federal aids.

The second step is to explore alternative fiscal policies. How much would the revenue derived from the property tax be increased or decreased by specified changes in the tax rate or as the result of a reassessment program? How much revenue might be obtained from a municipal income tax, sales tax, or from business license taxes? What would be the effect on available revenues of various borrowing policies?

The final step is the selection of a general fiscal policy from among the alternatives that have been explored. As has already been pointed out, the revenue policy should be determined at the same time that the expenditure policy is fixed. The two go hand-in-hand and it is not a sound procedure to settle one of them, and then adjust the other to fit the first.

Determining a Revenue Policy

Decisions must be reached as to what sources of revenue shall be used to finance city services, how much of each source, and what the relation shall be between current financing from taxes and other revenues on the one hand, and borrowing on the other. A full discussion of these points is impossible here, for the problem involves the whole subject of public finance, but a few of the major issues can be pointed out.

In selecting revenue sources the factors that must be considered include legal authority of the city to use the source in question; distribution of the tax burden among various classes of taxpayers; ease and cost of administration; the possibility of avoidance through mobility; and sensitivity of the source to changes in business conditions.

Legal Authority. A municipality's power to raise revenue by taxation is derived from the state constitution, state statutes, and the city charter. In most states the cities are rather severely limited both as to which revenue sources they may legally tap and as to how high the rates may be on these various sources. Any proposals for new levies must be given legal scrutiny to determine whether they come within the authorization of state law.

A Fair Tax System. The question of what is a "fair" local tax is a particularly troublesome one. Two of the possible criteria for distribution of the tax burden are (a) benefits received, and (b) ability to pay. It is a reasonable policy to impose taxes in proportion to benefits received in the case of services of a commercial nature, and services to property. Under the same circumstances there is often good justification for financing the service by means of direct charges to users.

There are many other municipal services, however, particularly those of a welfare nature, or relating to health, recreation, and education, that are conducted for the benefit of the community as a whole, and that are most appropriately financed on the basis of ability to pay. Unfortunately, there are almost no taxes that a municipality can impose which are true measures of taxpaying ability. The only tax that really meets this test is a personal income tax with progressive rates, and it is neither legally nor economically possible for a city to impose such a levy. The local tax which comes closest to being an "ability" tax is the general property tax. Sales taxes do not meet the test because they are regressive — proportionately, they weigh more heavily on low-income groups than upon high-income groups. A similar objection can be raised against gross income taxes.

A further complication in the problem of tax justice is that certain taxes — and this applies with particular force to the general property tax — are "capitalized." That is, the tax is taken into consideration by buyers and sellers of property and is reflected in a decrease in property values. At the time such a tax is imposed, property values tend to be reduced and present owners of the property tend to pay the whole future tax in the form of the reduced value of the property; while subsequent purchasers take the property "free" from tax because they allow for the tax in the price they are willing to pay for the property. In the case of taxes which are largely capitalized the only policy to be followed from the standpoint of justice among taxpayers is to keep the levy at a relatively stable rate so that changes in capitalization will not take place.

Because of limitations and restrictions on the types of taxes municipalities can adopt, the question of "fairness" may need to be considered in view of the entire tax system — federal, state, and local — rather than in terms of a particular tax to be imposed by the municipality itself.

Ease and Cost of Administration. No tax collects itself, but taxes vary widely in the percentage of the levy that must be spent for their administration. No new levy should be imposed by a city until an estimate has been made of the administrative cost and until this cost has been determined to be reasonable or an alternative study has been made of the feasibility of the tax being collected jointly for several cities by a county or by the state.

Avoidance Through Mobility. City officials are sometimes inclined to believe that their revenue troubles would be over if the states gave them broader authorization to tap new tax sources. Nothing could be further from the truth. There are very few kinds of taxes that adapt themselves to administration by small local units. Practically all local taxes, if sufficiently high, encourage avoidance by moving activities outside the city limits. It would be an exaggeration to claim that the pronounced movement of industries to the suburban sections of metropolitan areas is solely for the purpose of tax avoidance, but high taxes in the central cities have certainly had a part in producing the movement. What is true of large metropolitan centers is doubly true of smaller communities. A city as large as Philadelphia may be able to impose an income tax without substantial avoidance or reduction in property values, at least in the short run, but in smaller communities such a tax might result in a serious migration.

Sensitivity to Business Fluctuations. From the standpoint of the city government's finances, it is highly undesirable that tax revenues should fluctuate widely with changes in business conditions. From the standpoint of taxpayers, this same flexibility is eminently desirable. Individual cities cannot solve the problems of business depression within their boundaries, but it will be increasingly necessary for cities to fit their financial programs into the plans of the state and federal governments for combating booms and depressions. This point will be discussed further in connection with borrowing policies later in this chapter.

The Municipal Revenue Picture

The real property tax traditionally has been, and still is, the principal source of municipal revenue. In recent years it has been increasingly supplemented by other sources — notably grants, shared taxes, nonproperty taxes, and license fees. As already pointed out, reasons of equity among taxpayers urge that the property tax rate remain relatively stable. On the other hand, if assessments are accurate and are adjusted promptly to changing economic conditions, the tax will exhibit large fluctuations in yield between boom and depression, and will usually present a serious delinquent tax problem during hard times. Several of the nonproperty taxes such as income and sales taxes being adopted by municipalities are subject to the vagaries of the business cycle.

License fees, while increasingly used as an easily-tapped revenue source, usually lead to a patchwork tax pattern in which there is no particular rhyme or reason to the way different classes of taxpayers are burdened. Looking at the revenue picture as a whole, cities must look forward to a somewhat inflexible revenue situation — except for the possible increase in shared taxes and grants. Moreover, in most cases radical changes in the local revenue pattern would involve more objectionable features than advantages.

Service Charges

It was stated earlier that service charges might be justified in the case of services of a commercial nature. This statement needs to be enlarged and qualified. It is seldom desirable to charge more than the out-of-pocket cost of providing it. Higher charges discourage the use of the service, and from the standpoint of the general welfare, the use of a service should be encouraged up to the point where the value derived from an additional unit of service is just balanced by the cost of providing that additional unit of service — i.e., the out-of-pocket cost.

Suppose, for example, that a toll bridge is constructed. The principal items of annual cost — interest, depreciation, maintenance of the structure and operation — are either independent of the amount of use the bridge gets, or only slightly affected by it (maintenance of the road surface would be the major exception). Hence, regardless of the overall cost, it would be desirable to encourage additional use of the bridge so long as the new users paid enough to cover any resulting increase in maintenance cost. Since it is not possible to charge the "marginal" user a different toll from that charged the individual who would still use the bridge even if the tolls were higher, the optimum toll — that which would derive the most social utility from the bridge — might very likely be insufficient to cover all the capital charges and other fixed costs.

Where service charges are imposed, the amount of the charge should be related to the total cost of providing the service, but it is not essential in all cases for the service to be entirely financed by the service charge. This argument can be extended to the case of municipally owned utilities. From the standpoint of economics and the general welfare it is generally undesirable for the city to raise money for the general fund by imposing unnecessarily high utility rates; and there may be good reason in some instances to partially subsidize a municipal utility (as in the toll bridge example) from local taxes. High rates may restrict use of the utility and decrease the benefit the community could derive from the large fixed investment.[3]

Borrowing Policies

From a long-term viewpoint borrowing is not really a source of revenue, for the loans must be repaid with interest. Nevertheless, the long-term financial plan may need to provide for the financing of certain large expenditures from borrowing, to be repaid from subsequently collected revenues.

The power to borrow is one of the most useful and important assets of a municipality, but it must be used with a critical and intelligent regard for its justifiable purposes and within safe and reasonable limits. Strong credit — the ability to borrow when necessary on the most favorable terms afforded by the market for municipal securities — is an objective that no municipality can afford to ignore. Hence a sound borrowing policy for any community is one which seeks the conservation rather than the exhaustion of credit. This involves, in general, borrowing as sparingly as possible and repaying as rapidly as possible.

Limits as to purpose, conditions, and amount of municipal borrowing are set variously by law, but within most of these legal limits there is wide range for the application of sound judgment, or the contrary, by local administrative authorities. Many such laws fall far short of providing dependable borrowing standards, and the best of them afford an inadequate substitute for the responsibility of municipal officials.

Purposes for Borrowing

A city may resort to borrowing for any number of reasons. It is, therefore, pertinent to ask to what extent borrowing for these various purposes represents sound public policy, and to what extent it is a dangerous and undesirable practice.

Certain types of capital expenses may be financed safely and reasonably by long-term loans. The capital costs of self-supporting enterprises, such as water and power systems, may justifiably be met by borrowing, provided the amortization of the debt is sufficiently rapid to keep ahead of the depreciation and obsolescence of the structures financed by the loan. The debt should be paid off sufficiently rapidly so that the enterprise will be virtually free from debt by the time it is necessary to replace the facilities.

Bond issues are also a legitimate means of financing projects that are large and costly in relation to the municipality's current financial resources, that have long utility,

---

[3] This point of view has general acceptance among economists concerned with the problems of welfare economics. The argument has no bearing on the question of whether municipal operation of utilities is "cheaper" than private operation. In making utility cost comparisons, all costs, including those financed by hidden or direct subsidies, should be taken into account.

and that are not of a frequently recurrent type. Where capital expenditures in a particular year will, because of the construction of a project of this nature, be substantially higher than in an average year, it may be preferable to finance the project with a loan rather than to attempt to collect the extra amount in taxes by a large increase in the tax rate for this particular year.

Where the principal purpose of the borrowing is to smooth out wide fluctuations in the annual budget, the loan need be made only for a period sufficient to achieve this smoothing out. There is no particular logic in spreading the amortization of the loan over the whole life of the structure that is built. For example, a city may wish to spread the cost of a new school building over five or ten years to avoid a sizeable "bulge" in the annual budget, but there might be no need to contract a twenty-five or thirty-year debt for this purpose.

Moreover, the amount of borrowing necessary to eliminate budget fluctuations can be kept at a minimum if the city carries out the kind of long-term programming and capital budgeting that has been described in the first part of this chapter. Perhaps the city expects to build only one school building in the next ten years, but in the intervening years it may construct a new city hall, or a series of playgrounds, or carry out a street widening project. If all these projects are scheduled in relation to each other over the period, the annual fluctuations in capital expenditures will be greatly reduced — and the need for long-term loans correspondingly eliminated.

A third legitimate reason for borrowing is to help finance the extension of municipal facilities in a growing city which antitipates a substantial increase in its assessment rolls. It would be unfair to the present taxpayers of such a community to expect them to pay in cash for improvements constructed in large part for individuals who will come in to the community subsequently. When street improvements are made on vacant property in outlying sections of the community, they are often financed by loans to be repaid from special assessments. Where the improvements are of a more general nature, they may be partially financed by loans to be repaid from general taxes over the useful life of the improvements. Subdividers should, of course, pay their fair share of the cost of extending municipal facilities.

In spite of the undoubted legitimacy of financing expenditures of this kind by borrowing, extreme caution must be urged upon cities in their estimates of probable growth. A large part of the financial difficulties that encumbered many cities during the depression resulted from over-optimism with respect to population increase. If the expected population fails to materialize, then of course, the present taxpayers are saddled with the repayment of loans for facilities that the community could very well do without. A very strong argument for financing at least a substantial part of new improvements, even in a growing city, out of current revenue, lies in the sobering effect such a policy has upon estimates of the scale of the facilities needed.

Extensive emergency expenditures may be financed, in part at least, by borrowing. Catastrophes of nature, such as flood, fire, or earthquake, may give rise to immediate and large financial needs for which the taxing power is not sufficiently responsive or has been temporarily too weakened to meet. A genuine emergency arises with the advent of a serious business depression and its accompanying demands for the relief of the unemployed. The utilization of borrowing for this purpose has special justification in view of the decline of taxpaying capacity in a depression and the threat that higher taxes may handicap recovery. Such a borrowing program may be undertaken with impunity, however, only when a municipality's borrowing traditions have been sound. If a credit reserve has been built up in times of prosperity by holding debt well below capacity to pay, a city can issue bonds for emergency purposes without dangerously mortgaging its future. If a city's past borrowing policy has been improvident, however, an emergency may find it without a market for its bonds. This is a strong argument in favor of a partial pay-as-you-go policy of capital financing in periods of good business.

Authorities are emphatic that a municipality should never resort to long-term borrowing to finance its ordinary current expenses. Borrowings do not represent actual revenue, since they create an equivalent liability which must be met from future taxes. This clear-cut stricture on current expense borrowing does not apply, of course, to short-term loans in anticipation of the receipt of taxes, although there are limitations and objections to this practice.

The Pay-as-You-Go Plan

Some cities, warned by their own experience with debt or that of neighboring communities, attempt to follow a pay-as-you-go plan of financing all capital outlays from current revenues. A city may seek to avoid borrowing entirely, or to finance at least a substantial part of its capital improvements out of the current budget.

Feasibility. The feasibility of partial or a complete pay-as-you-go plan depends upon the type of community, the character of its expenditures, and its existing debt structure. As already pointed out, old established communities are in a better position to avoid borrowing than new and growing communities. Pay-as-you-go financing is more feasible in a large city, where capital expenditures are rather uniformly recurrent, than in a small community. The transition to a pay-as-you-go policy is far easier for a city that has only a small debt than for a city that must make heavy payments for the amortization of existing debt at the same time it is financing new improvements out of current revenue. To put the matter another way — the closer a city is to a pay-as-you-go policy, the easier it is to go the rest of the way. The first mile is the hardest.

Advantages and Disadvantages. To ask whether a pay-as-you-go policy is desirable for a community is really the same as asking whether there are any circumstances under which the city is justified in borrowing. This question has already been discussed above.

The principal advantages that may be claimed for the pay-as-you-go scheme — and they are very real and substantial advantages — are that it encourages conservatism in the construction of capital improvements; that it prevents the city from committing too large a proportion of its resources to the amortization of debt — with the consequent neglect of operating services; and that it conserves the credit of a city for a time of extreme emergency when good credit may be a vital necessity.

Another claim made for the pay-as-you-go policy is that it is far cheaper than the policy of borrowing to finance improvements. In one sense this is true — current financing relieves the city of the burden of interest payments. This may be of considerable importance, particularly if there are over-all taxing limits in the state law or the city charter. In another sense, it is not true that financing on a cash basis is cheaper. By borrowing money, and incurring interest charges, the city relieves its taxpayers of part of their immediate tax burden in favor of future payments. Any taxpayer who is able to invest his tax "savings" at an interest rate at least as high as that which the city pays on its bonds can more than afford to pay taxes later for the amortization of the city debt. Any taxpayer could "hedge" against his future liability for debt amortization by purchasing a sufficient amount of city bonds, and the interest and principal payments he would receive on these bonds would just balance his additional future tax liability. For this reason, the "savings" argument is not as sound as the other arguments that have been advanced for a pay-as-you-go policy.[4]

While there are many important reasons for avoiding debt, there are two sides to the argument. Money spent for municipal improvements is not being wasted. It provides the community with services and facilities of wide public benefit. A city which proposes to adopt a pay-as-you-go policy must consider whether such a policy will require it to forego a high community standard of services and, as a result, to handicap its industries, its commerce, and its citizens.

Transition Procedures. The procedures for shifting to a partial or to a complete pay-as-you-go basis are several. One is to shorten gradually the life of all new bond issues; each new issue being given a somewhat shorter life than the preceding one. Declaration of a construction holiday for a few years, until a substantial portion of the outstanding debt is reduced, is a more heroic, but also more difficult, approach which cannot be recommended under most circumstances. Another plan is to increase gradually the proportion of capital outlays to be met from current revenues, slowly arriving at the desired goal. Requirement of a "down payment" out of the current budget the first year of the improvement can be stepped up year by year. This procedure is required by New York statutes and is being followed as a matter of policy by Philadelphia. It is easier in good times than in bad to initiate such a program. A long-term capital budget is an essential tool in shifting to the pay-as-you-go basis.

Other Borrowing Policies

The practice which some cities pursue of financing practically all capital improvements out of borrowed money — the all-loan policy — can hardly be dignified as long-term financial planning. The arguments offered to support such a practice are untenable for all except the smallest municipalities.

Debt Equalization. Under a debt equalization plan maturities of peak years are levelled by refunding so that, roughly, an equal annual debt service load over a period of 15 or 20 years is attained. Such a plan ignores the possible future need for additional borrowing, and is very likely to lead to a pyramiding of debt. This plan cannot be recommended.

Gross Bonding Plan. The so-called "gross bonding plan" likewise cannot be recommended, because of its overemphasis upon bonds as a means for financing capital improvements. Under this plan a city authorizes at one time a large bond issue to cover a planned program over a long period. The bonds are not issued, however, until needed.

The sole advantage of the gross bonding plan is that it forces the city into over-all planning of all its capital needs, rather than meeting these needs in piecemeal fashion. Hence it may encourage long-term planning.

Cyclical Borrowing. Another long-term plan is to alternate a pay-as-you-go policy with an all-loan policy, depending upon the stage of the business cycle. This plan will be discussed more fully in the next section of this chapter.

---

[4] Some of the history of the pay-as-you-go plan is traced in Frank A. Neff, Municipal Finance (Wichita, Kansas: The McGuin Publishing Company, 1939), pp. 127-46. A good pay-as-you-go report of recent years is Mabel L. Walker, "Pay-as-you-Go," Real Estate Reporter and Building News, October, 1945. Also see W. E. Willman, "City Hall Built Without Bond Issue," The American City, October, 1955, and A Program for Partial Pay-as-You-Go Financing (Baltimore: Maryland State Planning Commission, November, 1954), 3 pp. plus appendix.

Measuring Capacity to Pay

In general, debt-paying capacity must be gauged by the amount and quality of a community's resources and by its legal and practical ability to draw upon these resources for payment. There is no precise method of determining how much debt a municipality can carry and eventually repay, but there is ample evidence that no large proportion of any municipality's resources can be pledged to the payment of debt obligations without weakening it financially, undermining its operating efficiency, and narrowing its prospects for advancement.

It is an objective of sound borrowing policy, moreover, not to attempt to skirt the margin of insolvency but to keep debt within a range proved to be conservative. This can be done by the application of a few simple principles.

First, the legal borrowing limit established by most states is not a safe standard to follow. At best it constitutes a maximum limit; and usually it is either so high, or permits so many exceptions, or is so vitiated by the overlapping of local borrowing units, as to be quite ineffective. Thus, the only sound policy is to determine a realistic limit, somewhere within the legal limit, which fits the community.

Preliminary to determining safe borrowing limits is the need for computing a community's actual debt. Immediately our unstandardized system of local government intrudes itself as a complicating factor. Anywhere from one to a half-dozen or more local governing units may be doing the borrowing for the same community. While a city administration can control directly only its own debt, it cannot afford to ignore overlapping school, county, and special district debt. Occasionally, overlapping governmental units have cooperated to time the issuance of debt and limit its amount in relation to the general responsibility of each. Thus, governmental units in San Diego County, California, have held meetings to decide which of the overlapping units was to issue bonds at a particular time. It is the actual local public debt that the taxpayers of any community are called upon to support, irrespective of whether it is handled through one agency or a number of agencies.

The most commonly used methods of measuring municipal debt are by population and by the valuation of taxable property, i.e., by expressing it in per capita figures or as a ratio of assessed valuation adjusted to estimated full value. Per capita figures have a reasonable degree of utility for comparative purposes if allowances are made for the fact that per capita resources vary from city to city. The ratio to taxable valuation is a more useful figure, for it endeavors to show a relationship of debt to resources for payment. It falls short of precision, however, because of the varying composition of tax bases and because of the difficulty of exactly determining full value. The two measures are nevertheless fairly dependable guides in gauging debt load if they are considered in conjunction with other available data on community resources.

On the basis of experience in the depression, which was a genuine test of debt-paying capacity, it may be said that very few cities with debt ratios falling below 10 per cent of full taxable value encountered any serious difficulty in meeting their obligations. The range between 10 and 15 per cent was in the doubtful zone, with both good management and unusually stable and substantial resources required to avoid trouble. Practically all cities with debts above 15 per cent of the taxable value of property of the municipality met with financial disaster and are carrying a lasting financial handicap. In general, therefore, a ratio of 10 per cent would seem to mark the upper limit of safety.

There are conditions, however, under which modifications should be made. The 10 per cent ratio is too high for cities that are approaching economic obsolescence, whose main support is upon some exhaustible natural resource, or whose economic background is highly unstable. Allowance must be made, moreover, when chronic tax delinquency shows a substantial portion of the base to be undependable. Per capita debt figures serve as a means of checking — if per capita debt rises above the median, justification must be sought in actual local resources that are correspondingly above the average.

In appraising the direct debt of a municipality it is often stated that the margin of safety rests in annual principal and interest requirements which do not rise above 25 per cent of the budget. Such a standard would encourage false security if applied to a city which had deferred the bulk of its debt service requirements far into the future. A sounder rule is that retirement of 5 per cent of principal plus the total interest requirement for the year should not exceed 25 per cent of a normal budget.

This discussion on paying capacity has thus far dealt with cities which have the power to levy taxes without legal limitation for the payment of debt. For those under an over-all tax rate limit, or handicapped by any unduly restrictive form of tax limitation, there appears to be little option except to make the best of an irrational situation and hope that the untenable conditions that arise will force the granting of relief. Any tax rate limitation which deprives a city of adequate current revenues inevitably forces resort to borrowing as the alternative and tends to prevent the maintenance of sound debt policy.

Duration of Loans

It is an axiom of public finance that loans for public improvements should be retired within the period of useful life of the physical facilities which they have financed. This should not be construed too literally in the case, for example, of undepreciable items such as land. A theoretical period of usefulness, furthermore, may be curtailed by other forms of obsolescence than actual wear and tear, and maintenance costs tend to increase as the improvement advances in age.

It is only for exceptional purposes that bonds should run for more than twenty years. Borrowing for a longer term may prove justifiable, for example, for the more permanent facilities of a water system designed with a large excess capacity for the future. Improvements of rather temporary utility, such as some types of street paving, call for ten-year bond issues, thus reducing the justifiable average life of a city's debt. As a practical general rule, a city should keep its debt retirement so scheduled that at least 25 per cent of the principal is always due for amortization within a five-year period.

The issuance of bonds for non-capital purposes, such as unemployment relief and the funding of operating deficits, is merely an expedient for tiding over an emergency period when taxpaying capacity is below normal. Such loans should be of short duration, not exceeding a ten-year period and preferably five years or even less. When the funding of a deficit is the result of retarded realization of tax revenues, repayment should not be postponed beyond the period of reasonably anticipated collections.

Other Factors Influencing Debt Policy

Periods of low money rates provide the most economical time for the financing of necessary improvements. Cheap money should not be permitted to encourage extravagance, but it may well dictate the time for putting through major improvements which, while they can be further postponed, will have to be constructed in the not-distant future. This is particularly true in the financing of revenue-producing enterprises. Not only will low interest affect the level of service rates which must be charged, but it may be the factor that will make a project self-supporting.

Finally, borrowing policy should be related to the stability of a community. Stability can be measured by such factors as population trends and the type and diversification of a city's economic resources. If, for example, dependence is mainly upon one industry, and particularly one that is subject to wide fluctuations, or upon an exhaustible natural resource, there is a distinct need for pay-as-you-go financing to keep debt at a minimum.

Form of Debt

When a debt policy has been formulated, it remains to decide what forms of bonds shall be issued, how they shall be marketed, and other procedural steps. These questions are more closely related to financial administration than to the problems of over-all programming, and their discussion will be postponed until Chapter 8.

Financial Policies and Business Cycles

Reference has been made several times to the necessity of correlating a city's financial policies with the changing phases of the business cycle. The business cycle must be taken into consideration in programming public works projects, in choosing between borrowing and financing out of current revenues, and in establishing a policy with respect to reserves for capital outlays.

Modern theories of public finance stress the importance of governmental fiscal policy as a counterweight to the contraction of private business activities during a depression. Under the so-called "Full Employment Bill" the federal government is loosely committed to a policy of compensatory spending to combat business depressions. It is to be hoped and expected that state and local governments will adopt fiscal policies that will dovetail — or at the very least, will not conflict — with those of the federal government.

One way in which the cities can cooperate in such a program is by scheduling future public works in a sufficiently flexible manner so that the program can be accelerated during periods of business recession, when public expenditures are desirable, and slowed down during boom times, when public expenditures add to the inflationary pressure. The purpose of the public works reserve project, which received considerable attention in postwar planning activities, was to accumulate a reserve of public works projects that could be undertaken at the end of the inflationary period. Presumably the federal government will give cities some incentive to adapt their public works programs to the needs of the business cycle by making loan funds available to them on favorable terms during periods when public spending is desired. Such help will be indispensable if cities are to follow a sound cyclical financing policy. [5]

A second contribution cities can make to such a fiscal program is to follow flexible revenue policies, increasing taxes during periods of great business activity, and cutting taxes as sharply as possible during times of recession. Public spending will have a

---

[5] But see Eugene C. McKean and Harold C. Taylor, Public Works and Employment from the Local Government Point of View. (Chicago: Public Administration Service, 1955). Data presented in this study would indicate that local public works have little influence on the business cycle and further that local public works are more likely to be related to up-swings in the cycle since demand, both consumer and industrial, generated at that level of the cycle may necessitate local public works such as schools and public utilities.

"pump-priming" effect only if the public expenditures are not counter-balanced by heavier taxes. A flexible revenue policy of this kind is consistent with a balanced budget only if the city is willing to finance some of its capital outlays during depression times with bonds, to be paid off during a more prosperous period; or if the city is willing to accumulate reserves during prosperous times to be used for capital expenditures during a time of depression; or some combination of these two policies. From what has already been said about borrowing policies, it is obvious that the accumulation of reserves is generally the safer policy, so far as it is possible.

Reserve Funds

Financing capital improvements out of an accumulated reserve fund (sometimes called "capital reserve") is the opposite of borrowing. The time table is reversed for the taxpayer. This plan can be recommended for small municipalities where the pay-as-you-go plan is not feasible. A combination of reserve fund and bond plan can be used. If a new school building will be needed five years hence, the small community can tax ahead over the five-year period for part of the capital funds, then finance the remainder from bonds, spreading the cost also toward the future.

Some method has to be provided to protect accumulated reserve funds, to insure that the tax money will go for the planned capital improvements. Such funds, for example, might be deposited by municipalities with the state treasurer in a municipal credit reserve fund, to be invested and held until time for construction of the improvement provided that state statutes permit this procedure. This plan could be of great service to small units of government in particular. Large cities may also find in such reserve funds a satisfactory means of effecting the transition to a pay-as-you-go policy.

Administrative Procedure for Long-Term Programming

Having considered the basic policy issues involved in laying out a long-term program of municipal services and a long-term capital budget, consideration must be given next to the specific administrative procedures that may be used to formulate the plan.

Initial Formulation of the Program

As has already been pointed out, the long-term service program must be formulated in close relationship to the city plan, and the plan must look forward over a considerable period of years. It is not necessary, however, to project an actual schedule of proposed capital improvements for more than a five- or six-year period. On the basis of the service program, a capital budget should be prepared, therefore, outlining capital improvements and the methods for financing them over a five- or six-year period.

The first year's program in the capital budget becomes the authorized capital budget for the year of adoption. The remaining five years represent a tentative program. By an annual revision there is available at all times a carefully thought-out plan for six years ahead — a six-year "moving schedule." The capital budget, even if formally authorized, is a tentative program only, subject to periodic revision. Implementation of the capital budget year by year comes through the current budget. Every year as the current budget is prepared, a year of the capital budget is incorporated in it.

It is highly desirable to apply the principle of comprehensiveness to service programming and capital budgeting — to include all functions, even though some of them, schools for example, are not directly controlled by the city council. Revenue-producing as well as completely self-supporting utilities should also be included, regardless of means of financing. The objective is to embrace in the planned program all improvements for the city at large, whether to be paid for by the property tax, utility rates, or other revenue sources.

In the initial stages, formulation of the expenditure side of the service program and capital budget is a primary responsibility of the city planning or budgeting agency working in close conjunction with the department heads, and under the general supervision of the chief administrator. The initial revenue plans should be prepared by the budget officer and the finance department, also working closely with the chief executive. Preparatory to presenting the tentative proposals, with their principal alternatives, to the city council, these two parts of the plan have to be brought together by collaboration of all the interested parties, and particularly the chief executive, the planning director, the finance director, and the budget officer.

Hearings and Approval

The service program and capital budget should not receive official approval until there has been opportunity for broad citizen participation in their consideration. In the last analysis, it is the people of the city who should say whether the standard of living and the financial plans proposed for them are what they want. After the program has been formulated, therefore, and has been given preliminary consideration by the council, it should be printed and distributed to local business, civic, and taxpayers' groups, labor organizations, and other community organizations that might be, or should be, interested. This publicity is particularly important if taxpayers subsequently are called upon to authorize bond issues for parts of the capital budget, or to vote special tax levies for certain of the capital projects, but it is essential in any event. The aid of a citizens' advisory committee is particularly valuable in securing public reactions, suggestions, support, and approval.

Financial presentation of the plan to the council is the duty of the chief administrator. In the process of council consideration, there should be provision for public hearings. It is not essential, though probably desirable, that the entire capital budget over the five- or six-year period be officially adopted. The usual procedure is to adopt with modifications the first year of the capital budget as a part of the current budget, and then tentatively to authorize the remainder of the program, subject to annual revision and reauthorization. These tentative authorizations are not binding, however, on future councils.

The long-term service program, in so far as it is not embodied in the capital budget, should receive the same kind of hearings and authorization as the city's master plan, prior to or simultaneously with the adoption of the capital budget.

The advantage of presenting the entire service program and capital budget to the council is that an opportunity for a public hearing is afforded, thereby arousing greater citizen interest, and if tentatively approved, the long-term plan has official status.

Each capital appropriation ordinance should specify that a fixed percentage of the funds shall go to the proper division or bureau in the engineering department, or department of public works, for surveys and preparation of plans and specifications. Such a provision enables the maintenance of a satisfactory staff for efficient supervision or execution of the capital improvement program.

Execution of the Capital Budget

Putting the capital budget into actual operation is a year-by-year process. Each year when the current budget is formulated, one year of the capital budget is incorporated. No accurate accounting records, therefore, are kept on the capital budget as such; it becomes a matter of record only when the capital items appear in the current budget.

A capital budget commission, or citizens' advisory committee, should take part in the formulation and periodic revision, but not in the execution, of the budget. The latter is the function of the chief administrator and his department heads. The commission or committee may, however, take part in discussing with the council the advisability of adopting the one year's capital program as revised.

The charter should stipulate whether amendments can be made during the year and by what authority, and whether capital outlays can exceed the authorizations in the current budget. If an improvement is not undertaken during the year authorized, the authorization should lapse, and new action should be required if it is to be included within the next year's program.

The Annual Budget

If the procedure that has been outlined here is followed, the making of the annual budget becomes a relatively simple matter, since it is merely a question of authorizing a one-year segment of the long-term plan and capital budget. Much of the time and trouble that now goes into the making, justification, and consideration of the annual budget estimates could be more profitably spent in formulating the long-term plan.

Even when planning has been comprehensive and thorough, however, the budget is an important document, for it provides the legal authorization for actually carrying out a portion of the plan, as well as means for controlling the execution and seeing that it conforms to the plan. In the city that has not made long-term plans, the annual budget is even more important, for it represents the only organized "thinking ahead" that the city has done about its problems.

Prerequisites to Effective Budgeting

A number of basic prerequisites are essential to effective budgetary procedure:

1. An adequate budget law to establish the legal basis for the budget.

2. A comprehensive budget document that includes all expenditures and all receipts of the city government including those from special funds as well as public service enterprises of the city government.

3. A complete inventory of all municipal functions and activities, including a system of records and reports to provide information on volume of work required to maintain specified levels of service.

4. Adequate forms and procedures for the compilation, review and adoption of the budget.

5. Adequate machinery for the implementing of the budget, including an adequate system of executive allotments, adequate accounting records including cost accounting records, adequate budgetary control accounts, and an adequate system of progress

reporting on the execution of the budget in terms of both dollars of expenditure and work accomplished.

6. A continuous and comprehensive program for operations analysis and management research directed toward the end of determining the most effective organizational structure and best operating procedures.

7. Qualified personnel capable of evaluating municipal activities and formulating financial plans, and in sympathy with the policies of the municipal administration and the spirit of the budget law.

The last point is, of course, as vitally important for programming as for budgeting. The best budget law and planning procedure will not bring effective budgeting without the proper attitude on the part of the officials charged with the formulation and execution of the plan and budget. If these are looked upon as a barrier rather than a tool for effective exercise of the managerial functions; if the letter of the budget law is observed but the spirit of the law is violated; if budgeting is considered a necessary annual responsibility rather than a year-round method of channeling and controlling municipal operations — in short, if budgeting is not looked upon as a method of attaining the fullest return for each dollar of public funds spent, if it does not become a day-by-day way of administrative thought, the best-formulated set of forms and regulations will not attain the desired objective.

The essentials of a sound budget system include a plan of operation culminating in a formal budget document, together with the machinery and procedures necessary to formulate that plan and then to execute it once it has been approved. Under an approved budget approach emphasis is placed on the service program and the estimated dollar cost of achieving that program. The discussion to follow will briefly cover the essential attributes of a sound budget system, the procedure and forms necessary in its formulation, and the pitfalls which should be avoided. The accounting procedures to be followed in executing the budget will be explained in Chapter 8.

Legal Basis for the Budget

The ideal situation is for the legal basis of the budget to be established in the city charter, supplemented by administrative rules and regulations which outline the procedure in greater detail. It is generally desirable that the broader, more important aspects of these administrative regulations, which should be designed to carry out the provisions of the charter, be approved as a municipal ordinance. The charter should merely outline the broad budgetary system for the city, leaving to the local officials the formulation of forms and procedures. For example, it is undesirable that the form of budget estimates be prescribed by charter or by ordinance — this should be left to administrative officials — but the charter should provide for the preparation of detailed estimates of receipts and expenditures.

Model Budget Law. The model budget law drafted by the National Municipal League, after providing that the law is applicable to all units of the local government and setting the date of the city's fiscal year, defines the general nature and scope of the budget. The model law requires that the budget be a complete financial plan for the next fiscal year and that it set forth all proposed expenditure for all agencies of the city, including municipally owned and operated utilities. It would also include the actual or estimated deficits for prior years, debt service charges, expenditures for outlays, and projects financed by special assessments. Under provisions of the model law, the budget would also set forth the means of financing the proposed expenditure program. The latter is a highly important part of the budget plan to which adequate consideration is frequently not given.[6]

Responsibility for Budgeting

Budgeting is a managerial function and, although detailed operations with respect to this function may be delegated, responsibility for the budget report to the council should rest with the chief administrator. In cities where there is no single chief executive, or where a board, the legislative body, or a committee of that legislative body is charged with responsibility for the budget, it is desirable that the legislative body delegate to a single individual responsibility for the actual preparation of the budget and its execution.

The Budget Calendar

A budget calendar should be prepared showing the dates when necessary actions must be taken or completed with respect to various phases of the budget program. Frequently these dates are established by charter or ordinance. This calendar, together with pertinent excerpts from state statutes, charter provisions, ordinances, and administrative rules which govern the formulation or execution of the budget, should be compiled in such form as to be available for ready and convenient reference.

It is important that the fiscal year and budget year coincide, and it is highly desirable that the tax calendar be correlated with the fiscal year so as to either eliminate temporary borrowing entirely or reduce it to a minimum. Having the first tax installment fall due on the first day of the fiscal year will usually accomplish this objective.

Preparation of Expenditure Estimates

Approximately three months prior to the close of the fiscal year all spending agencies of the city government should be requested to submit to the budget-making authority their proposed work programs and estimates of their expenditure requirements for the next fiscal year. In order that adequate time will be available for review and consideration of budget requests and evaluation of service programs, the estimate sheets should be filled out and returned by a specified date — perhaps 60 days prior to the close of the fiscal year.

The foregoing time stipulations are approximations and will vary somewhat with the size of the city and with other local conditions. In the case of very large cities, the time allowed may need to be extended; in the case of small cities, shortening the period may be possible. A city with a long-term plan will need less time for budget preparation than one without such a plan. The important thing is to time the schedule in such a manner as to allow sufficient time for adequate consideration of the budget and its adoption by the council before the beginning of the fiscal year. It is also important that the budget be prepared as near as possible to the close of the current year, so as to permit the fullest possible appraisal of the year's experience with respect to budget operations and also to permit better visualization of conditions as they will exist during the year for which the budget is being prepared. Where dates are established by law, such dates will of course govern.

Standardized budget request forms, accompanied by instructions regarding policies to be followed in making estimates and instructions for filling out the forms, should be furnished the spending agencies by the budget authority. The instructions, which should

[6] National Municipal League, Model Accrual Budget Law, 1946, or Model Cash Basis Budget Law, 1948.

go out under the signature of the chief administrator, should outline to the various departments the general over-all plans of the chief administrator and the policy which he proposes to pursue with respect to fiscal operation during the next year. In addition to written instructions the chief administrator should hold a conference with his department heads in which he outlines and discusses with them the over-all policy proposed for the coming year. This is essential in order that the operating departments may have an idea as to the extent to which they can make equipment purchases, increase services, etc. The most recent revision of the long-term program forms the basis for the departmental estimates.

Separate estimates should be required for each organizational unit within the department and all expenditures should be included, even if financed by special funds. The detailed listing of expenditures — actual and estimated — should conform to the account classification of the finance department. The account classification should be such and the request forms should be so designed, as to show the expenses of each activity for each organizational unit, for each major governmental function, and for each fund. Expenses should be detailed by object of expenditure i.e., personal services, materials and supplies, etc. — which, in turn, will automatically permit classification by character — ordinary recurring expenses, capital outlays and debt redemption. Objects of expenditure should be related to activity or function to be performed. Use of the standard classification by function and activity set forth by the National Committee on Governmental Accounting is recommended.[7] Before a municipality can prepare a budget on a performance basis in which activities or programs are to be presented it must inventory and classify its functions and activities. This can best be accomplished using a standard accounts classification.

1. Work Program Forms   (Figs. 2, 3, 4 and 5). All spending agencies should support their budget requests with proposed work programs based on the long-term service program. The content of work programs will depend upon the completeness of the cost accounting system or other work measurement approaches in use and also upon the degree of refinement to which work programming has been developed in the particular municipality. In some instances unit cost data are available in great detail. This should be the case particularly in public works and similar departments. In other cases the proposed work program merely consists of a narrative explanation which outlines in general the work to be performed, or the program may be related to the man-hours of work required to accomplish it.

The man-hour approach has considerable merit since personnel costs comprise the major portion of the cost involved in performing many municipal services. Furthermore, this approach is useful when cost accounting systems may call for more expenditure than merited by the additional information that could be provided by such a system. Where a product is involved, such as the construction of a street or the production of water, cost accounting is the preferable method.

The work program is an essential — perhaps the most essential — part of the budget procedure, regardless of whether the city has prepared a long-term program, for it insures that each bureau or division head plans the major activities of his unit for the year ahead. He will list the major types of work carried on and estimate the volume or burden of such work for each month. As far as possible the volume should be calculated in some measurable work units, such as patient-days for a hospital, number of examinations for a

---

[7] A Standard Classification of Municipal Accounts (Chicago: National Committee on Governmental Accounting, 1953).

PARKS
BUREAU

RECREATION AND PARKS
DEPARTMENT, BOARD, COMMISSION OR AGENCY

PROGRAM AND PERFORMANCE

Active Cemeteries, Maintenance and Operation
(Acct. #300204.)

This program provides for the operation, maintenance and perpetual care of 7 city-owned cemeteries with a total area of 395 acres. The following table presents the principal factors in the work load:

	Actual 1955-56	Estimate 1956-57	Budget 1957-58
Stones and Monuments, Total	23,255	23,955	24,700
Interments	1,108	1,100	1,100
Lots	18,382	18,562	18,742
Single Graves	5,790	5,905	6,020
Walks & Roadways (Sq. Ft.) Total	3,309,357	3,309,357	3,316,337

Perpetual Care Maintenance

Lots	8,390	8,570	8,750
Single Graves	1,218	1,323	1,428
Single Graves Limited Care	332	422	512

Volume of Service

Adult Interments	1,039	1,020	1,020
Child Interments	67	50	50
Disinterments	27	25	25
Reinterments	12	12	12
Lot Sales	27,944 sq.ft.	20,000 sq.ft.	20,000 sq.ft.
Lots Placed in Perpetual Care	27,683 sq.ft.	18,000 sq.ft.	18,000 sq.ft.

Unit Cost

Cemetery Acres Maintained	395	395	395
Cost per Acre	$ 418	$ 448	$ 461

Fig. 2 — Work Program Information, Richmond, Virginia

FOLIO

DEPARTMENT **BUILDING AND SAFETY** 21.1
TITLE AND CODE NO.
FUNCTION **Protection of Persons and Property** 20
TITLE AND CODE NO.
SUB-FUNCTION **Structural Regulations** 21
TITLE AND CODE NO.

WORK PROGRAM

CITY OF LOS ANGELES
BUDGET ESTIMATES
FISCAL YEAR 1956-57

1	2	3	4	5	6	7	8	9	10	11	12	13	14	15	16	17	
	ACTIVITY AND SUBACTIVITY		LAST COMPLETED FISCAL YEAR (ACTUAL)				CURRENT FISCAL YEAR (EST.)				FISCAL YEAR 1956-57 (EST.)						
LINE	CODE NO.	DESCRIPTION	WORK UNIT	WORK UNITS	PER-SON-NEL	TOTAL MAN-HOURS	MAN-HOURS PER UNIT	WORK UNITS	PER-SON-NEL	TOTAL MAN-HOURS	MAN-HOURS PER UNIT	WORK UNITS	MAN-HOURS PER UNIT	TOTAL MAN-HOURS	OVER-TIME MAN-HOURS	REGU-LAR MAN-HOURS	PER-SON-NEL	LINE NO.
1	21.17	Heating & Refrigeration																1
2		Inspection																2
3	.170	Division Admin.	B	--	2	4176	--	--	2	4176	--	--	--	4176	--	4176	2	3
4	.171	General Inspection	Insp.	80221	16.6	34661	0.43	82500	14.6	30485	.37	104650	.40	41860	100	41760	20	4
5	.172	Clerical Services	Permit	39150	2.9	6055	0.15	34000	2.8	5846	.17	46400	.18	8352	--	8352	4	5
6	.173	Eq. Lic. & Inv.	Inv.	3462	1	2088	.60	3200	1	2088	.65	3200	.65	2088	--	2088	1	6
7	.174	Inv. & Pros.	Inv.	597	1	2088	3.50	600	1	2088	3.48	600	3.48	2088	--	2088	1	7
8		Totals-H & R Insp.			23.5	49068			21.4	44683				58564	100	58464	28	8
9																		

Fig. 3 — Work Program Information, Los Angeles, California

SECTION 2 — OPERATING BUDGET — CURRENT LEVEL

The following instructions pertain to the preparation of the current level portion of the operating budget estimate.

2.1 — Preparation and Use of Work Program — Form CAO-9

Use this form to record information pertinent to the current level work program. In the blank spaces at the top of the form, enter the titles and code numbers of the department, function, and sub-function. Activities and sub-activities should be listed in numerical sequence on one or more sheets. (See Exhibit No. 1) Do not list the activity partly on one sheet and partly on another. If the space remaining at the bottom of the sheet is insufficient to completely list the activity, the listing should begin on the top of the next sheet.

Activity Number and Title (Columns 1 and 2)

List and underscore the code numbers and names of the activities assigned your department. Sub-activities are a further breakdown of activities. Sub-activities should be indented and listed in code number sequence and name immediately below the activity to which they pertain. Leave a blank space between each activity listing. Use the sub-activity list developed in cooperation with the City Administrative Officer for this purpose. (See Section 5 — Appendix) See Exhibit 1-A for listing Compensated Time Off and Turnover Requirements if your Monthly Utilization Report is on a net man-hour basis.

Work Unit (Column 3)

Insert the applicable work unit for measurable work and the code letter for unmeasurable work.

Measurable Work

Each department head should select the work unit which is most indicative of the sub-activity being performed so that the work involved can be converted into total man-hours. As a guide to the selection of department work units, each must meet the following criteria:

1. The work unit must be countable;
2. The work unit must express output;
3. The work unit must reflect work effort;
4. The work unit must have consistency;
5. The work unit must be expressed in familiar terminology.

Unmeasurable Work — There are many sub-activities, the personnel for which must be provided regardless of the actual number of work units performed. Those sub-activities include positions required by Charter or ordinance, organization structure, and "fixed" assignments. In order that such personnel will be accounted for in the work program, the following code letters should be used to designate such unmeasurable work:

Code Letter	Category	Examples
A	Charter or Ordinance Provisions	Commission, General Manager, etc.
B	Organization Structure	Bureau or Division Heads
C	"Fixed" Assignments (Day Shift Only)	Elevator Operators (Day)
D	"Fixed" Assignments (Night Shift Only)	Guard (Night)
E	"Fixed" Assignments (Day & Night Shifts)	Library Telephone Operators
F	"Fixed" Assignments (3 Shifts — 7-day week)	Desk Sergeants, Diesel Plant Operators
G	Fixed Units on Two-Platoon System	Fire Companies
H	Not classified above	

Since each department head is more familiar with his own operations than anyone else, he will be expected to make the determination as to what work units most adequately describe the work performed by his department. The staff of the City Administrative Officer will be glad to advise and make suggestions for your guidance, but it is your responsibility to prepare your own work program consistent with these general instructions.

Fig. 4 — Directions For Completing Los Angeles Work Program Form

Last Completed Fiscal Year (Columns 4 through 7)

The data shown in the following columns are derived from the departmental Personnel Utilization Report (Form CAO-26).

Work Units (Column 4) — In Column 4, show the actual number of work units performed as reported in Column 9 of the June Personnel Utilization Report (CAO-26).

Personnel (Column 5) — In Column 5 enter the number of personnel shown for each sub-activity and activity in Column 9 of the previous June's Personnel Utilization Report. See Exhibit 1 for preparing a gross man-hour work program and Exhibit 1-A for preparing a net man-hour work program containing provisions for compensated time off.

Total Man-Hours (Column 6) — In Column 6 enter the man-hours shown for each sub-activity and activity in Column 9 of the previous June's Personnel Utilization Report.

See Exhibit 1 for preparing a gross man-hour work program and Exhibit 1-A for preparing a net man-hour work program containing provisions for compensated time off.

Man-Hours Per Unit (Column 7) — Use the figures shown in the previous June's Personnel Utilization Report.

Current Fiscal Year (Columns 8 through 11)

Based on a projection of the actual figures reported in Column 9 of the most recent Personnel Utilization Report (CAO-26) available, and after giving consideration to seasonal variations, provide figures for the full year. See Exhibit 1 and 1-A for the procedure to be followed for a gross or net man-hour basis.

Next Fiscal Year (Columns 12 through 17)

After reviewing the actual number of work units performed in the last completed year and the estimate for the current year, enter in Column 12 your best estimate of the total number of units to be performed in the next year. The reasons for any significant increases or decreases must be fully explained in a written statement accompanying your work program.

In Column 13, show your best estimate of the man-hours per work unit after due consideration is given to the figures shown in Column 7 and 11 and after considering the possible effect of new methods installed in the current year or to be installed in the next year.

The total number of man-hours required is obtained by multiplying the estimated number of work units shown in Column 12 by the estimated man-hours per unit shown in Column 13. The total will be recorded in Column 14.

The total man-hours required as shown in Column 14 should be segregated into those which will be performed during regular working hours and those which will be performed on overtime. Show the estimate for overtime man-hours in Column 15 and the estimate for regular man-hours in Column 16.

The estimated number of personnel required for each sub-activity is derived by dividing the estimated total number of regular man-hours required as shown in Column 16 by 2,088 man-hours. The result is to be shown in Column 17.

For unmeasurable work, the total man-hours required should be shown in Column 14. Regular man-hours should be computed on the basis of 2,088 man-hours for each full time employee. Overtime and regular hours are to be shown in Columns 15 and 16 as for measurable work. The number of personnel required, the entry in Column 17, is obtained by dividing the regular man-hours in Column 16 by 2,088.

Where the work program is being presented on a net man-hour basis, the figures shown in Column 17 as a result of following the above instructions, should be shown in parentheses. The figure thus shown in Column 17 for compensated time off and turnover requirements must be redistributed to each sub-activity on an appropriate basis. The sum of this amount to be distributed to a sub-activity plus the net personnel figure already shown in parentheses for each sub-activity should be typed in above each parenthesized figure in the manner indicated in Exhibit 1-A.

Activity Totals

When all information has been entered for all sub-activities included in a particular activity, totals should be shown for Columns 5, 6, 9, 10, 14, 15, 16, and 17. The departmental total for all activities will also be shown in those columns immediately following the last activity total.

Fig. 4 — (Concluded)

MUNICIPALITY OF _____ Work Program 1958				Fund: General Function: Sanitation Department: Public Works Submitted by: A. S. Stone Date: October 10 1957			
		Actual and Estimated 1957			Estimated 1958		
Operation	Work Unit	No. of Units	Unit Cost	Total	No. of Units	Unit Cost	Total
1	2	3	4	5	6	7	8
Refuse Removal	Tons	7,165.8	$3.41	$24,435.38	7,432.7	$3.35	$24,899.55
Refuse Disposal	Tons	8,376.4	.89	7,455.00	8,620.3	.92	7,930.68
Street and Alley: Flushing	Cleaning Mile	805.4	1.31	1,055.07	875.2	1.23	1,076.50
Sweeping	Cleaning Mile	1,750.3	2.10	3,675.63	1,762.5	2.06	3,630.75

Fig. 5 — Work Program Sheet

health laboratory, tons of refuse to be handled by a refuse disposal plant, etc. After the volume of work has been estimated, the work must be translated into estimated costs. In some fields this can be done by applying unit cost estimates to the number of work units. In other departments unit cost figures may not be available or useful for this purpose; in such a case the department head will calculate monthly expenditures for payrolls, supplies, and so forth, necessary to carry out his program.

It is unfortunate that many municipalities carry on their budgeting without use of work programs, or at best, with highly inadequate work programming. Under such conditions it is impossible for the chief administrator to know what services are being rendered for the expenditures made. It is impossible for him to evaluate the adequacy of those services, and it is impossible for him to properly justify, before the legislative body, the expenditure program which he recommends.

Work programming is the only logical and sound approach to the problem of preparing budget requests. It eliminates a large portion of the guessing from budgetary processes and it permits a more adequate evaluation of the need for proposed expenditures. Finally, by the use of work programs, responsibility for reductions in the chief administrator's recommended appropriations can be placed where it belongs — upon the legislative body. If, for example, the recommended appropriation of the public works department is reduced, the council should be asked to designate which activity or item in the annual or long-term service program it desires reduced. If the reduced appropriation makes possible only one garbage collection per week instead of the proposed two, or if it reduces the amount of paving which may be performed from ten miles to eight, the council should make the specific determination. Although the final decision in such matters rests with the council, the administrative staff has a responsibility, of course, to make recommendations as to where appropriation cuts can be made with the least harm to municipal services.

Figure 2 illustrates one method for presenting work program information in narrative and statistical form. Such a presentation is adaptable to inclusion in the budget document. Figure 3 and its accompanying instructions present a more detailed approach where measurable units are present. Man-hour columns could be used where measurable units cannot be found. Figure 4 is another variation for presenting work program information.

2. Detailed Expenditure Request (Figure 6). The work program indicates the estimated work program of the department. The expenditure request form used by many

APPROVED:
DEPARTMENT HEAD _____
DIVISION HEAD _____

CITY OF SAN ANTONIO
DETAIL OF BUDGET REQUEST
DETAILED EXPENDITURE CLASSIFICATION

PREPARED BY: _____
DATE : _____

DEPARTMENT		DIVISION			ACTIVITY			ACCOUNT NUMBER	

1. OBJECT NUMBER	2. EXPENDITURE CLASSIFICATION	3. ACTUAL EXPENDITURE 1955 - 56	EXPENDITURES CURRENT FISCAL YEAR			7. PROPOSED BUDGET 1957 - 58	8. WORK COLUMN
			4. ACTUAL 7 MONTHS	5. ESTIMATED 5 MONTHS	6. TOTAL 1956 — 57		
1-00	PERSONAL SERVICES						
1-10	Regular Salaries						
1-14	Fee Basis Salaries						
	TOTAL PERSONAL SERVICES						
2-00	CONTRACTUAL SERVICES						
2-01	Communications						
2-06	Postage						
2-08							
2-80	Injury Medical Expenses						
2-96	Expense Allowance						
2-97	Unclassified						
	TOTAL CONTRACTUAL SERVICES						
3-00	COMMODITIES						
3-01	Office Supplies						
3-05	Janitor Supplies						
3-97	Unclassified						
	TOTAL COMMODITIES						
4-00	FIXED CHARGES						
4-01	Retirement Costs						
4-03							
4-20	Payment of Bonds and Notes						
4-21	Interest and Exchange						
	TOTAL FIXED CHARGES						
5-00	CAPITAL OUTLAY						
5-04	Land						
5-08	Buildings						
5-12	Improvements Other Than Buildings						
5-16	Automotive Equipment						
5-20	Machinery and Equipment Other Than Automotive						
5-24	Library Books						
	TOTAL CAPITAL OUTLAY						
	GRAND TOTAL						

Fig. 6 — Detailed Expenditure Request

APPROVED:
DEPARTMENT HEAD: _____
DIVISION HEAD: _____

PREPARED BY: _____
DATE: _____

CITY OF SAN ANTONIO

BUDGET REQUEST FORM

DETAILED SALARY CALCULATION

DEPARTMENT		DIVISION			ACTIVITY			ACCOUNT NUMBER						
1. JOB CLASSIFICATION	2. NAME	3. PAY RANGE & STEP	4. DATE EMPLOYED CURRENT JOB CLAS'FICAT'N	5. PAY INCREASES			6. SALARY CALCULATIONS – BUDGET YEAR							
				NO. IN CURRENT CLAS'FICAT'N	DATE OF MOST RECENT	DATE(S) PROPOSED	FIRST RATE		SECOND RATE		TOTAL SALARY			
							MONTHS	RATE	MONTHS	RATE				

1. Instructions for Column 1, Job Classification, specify the cutoff date for the inclusion of positions, provide that positions would be ranked from the highest to the lowest salary range, and specify that only the official job titles used in the pay plan are entered.

2. Instructions for Column 2, Name, outline how to handle positions authorized yet still vacant, and specify that subtotals should be entered for employees holding the same position.

3. Instructions for Column 3, Pay Range and Step, refer the employee completing the form to the pay range schedule included in the budget instructions.

4. Instructions for Column 4, Date Employed Current Job Classification, are self-explanatory.

5. Instructions for Column 5, Pay Increases, explains what should be done in case that an employee has not received a pay increase since employment or if a pay increase is due before a certain date.

6. Instructions for Column 6, Salary Calculations — Budget Year, indicate pay rates and service before a cutoff date, explain the handling of longevity pay and hourly wages, and further directions are given for the estimation of overtime pay.

Fig. 7 – Detailed Salary Estimate

cities relates objects of expenditure required to accomplish the work programs. Actual expenditure data is filled in by the department of finance and estimated expenditures to the close of the fiscal year immediately preceding the budget year are jointly compiled by the department of finance and the budget division. Amounts requested for the coming fiscal year are then inserted by the department preparing the request form. Data on fixed charges such as debt retirement, interest, judgments and costs, sinking fund requirements and similar items of fixed and unavoidable costs are completely filled in by the department of finance.

3. Detailed Salary Estimates (Figure 7). This schedule is supplementary to the detailed expenditure request. It fully details proposed salary increases, additional positions and the proposed salary schedules for such positions. This form normally also indicates temporary positions, estimated overtime that may be required during the year and indicates step increases in salary that will occur for some of the personnel during the fiscal period. Frequently this form is accompanied with a form which summarizes the personnel data.

4. Detailed Budget Request Forms for Expenditures Other Than Personnel. To the extent deemed necessary, detailed request forms may be required for other object classifications of expenditure. Figure 8 illustrates such a request form for outlays. Detailed request forms may be required for memberships and subscriptions, travel and travel allowances for privately owned motor vehicles used for public business, and for new construction. This information is summarized and brought forward to the detailed expenditure request form such as illustrated in Figure 6.

5. Supplemental Budget Requests (Figure 9). Budget forms 2 through 8 provide information compiled on a basis consonant with policies established by the city manager or other chief executive of a city. These are presented as part of the information upon which department heads are to compile their budget estimates. They cover costs of providing normal, recurring services at predetermined levels. If new or expanded services are believed to be desirable by the departments, this information is assembled on the supplemental budget form and includes justifications by the department for expanding or adding new services. Dividing the budget in this fashion makes it easier for management, the city council and the general public to review budget requests and to determine future work programs of a new or nonrecurring nature.

Revenue Estimates

Revenue estimate forms showing actual revenues for the last two completed fiscal years should be prepared for each collecting agency. The collection agency in cooperation with the chief finance officer or the budget director should estimate the receipts for the current year and the estimated revenues for the succeeding year. Included in the revenue estimates should be estimated receipts from a tax levy at a tentative rate set by the chief administrator in accordance with his plans for the coming year. The same revenue classification should be used as that followed in the city's accounting and reporting system. The standard terminology and classification adopted by the National Committee on Governmental Accounting is recommended.

The chief finance officer in cooperation with the budget director should also estimate the surplus at the close of the current year, the amount of which should be the first item in the proposed means of financing the new budget.

All departments should be required to estimate and show all revenues collected.

INSTRUCTIONS:
(1) PREPARE IN TRIPLICATE
(2) SEND TWO TO BUDGET OFFICE
(3) RETAIN ONE FOR FILE

CITY OF SAN DIEGO
DEPARTMENTAL BUDGET REQUEST - OUTLAY

1.DEPARTMENT	2.ACTIVITY	3.DEPT.& ACT. NO.	4.REF. NO.

5.DISTRIBUTION OF OUTLAY ITEMS TO FACILITIES.

A.FACILITY OR LOCATION	B.NO.	C.BUD.O.	D.FACILITY OR LOCATION	E.NO.	F.BUD.O

6.EQUIPMENT OR OTHER OBJECT OF OUTLAY EXPENDITURE

A.QUAN	B.DESCRIPTION

7.SIMILAR EQUIPMENT AT SAME LOCATIONS		8.AVERAGE DAILY USE (HOURS, MILES, ETC.)	
A.QUAN	B.DESCRIPTION	A.PRESENT EQUIP.	B.REQUESTED EQUIP.

9.EXPLAIN NECESSITY FOR, OR BENEFITS TO BE EXPECTED FROM THIS EXPENDITURE

10.IS REQUEST CONTINGENT UPON INCREASE OR PERSONNEL? (IF 'YES', EXPLAIN)

☐ YES
☐ NO

11.LIST EQUIPMENT TO BE DISPLACED

A.INV. NO.	B.DESCRIPTION	C.RECOMMENDED DISPOSAL

12.ESTIMATED COST		UNIT COST	TOTAL COST	FOR USE BY BUDGET OFFICE STAFF
IN SPACE (B) THRU (E) SHOW ADDITIONAL COSTS NECESSARY TO PLACE ITEM IN SERVICE	A.PURCHASE PRICE			
	B.LABOR			
	C.MATERIAL			
	D.			
	E.			
TOTAL COST (ITEMS A THRU E)				

13.EXPLAIN ADDITIONAL COSTS (B THRU E OF 12 ABOVE)	14.SIGNATURE OF REQUESTOR

RESERVED FOR USE OF BUDGET OFFICE

15.COMMENTS OF BUDGET ANALYST	16.PRIORTY
	17.APPROVED

FORM 336 (REV.11/29/50)

Fig. 8 — Detailed Budget Request — Non-Personnel Outlay

It is highly desirable that all receipts be deposited with the city treasurer; however, even in those instances where the practice is to have the collecting agency retain and spend certain revenues — and this is a practice that is never justifiable — such revenues should be estimated and shown on the budget sheets. Any estimated surplus in such departmental funds should also be estimated and included in the means of financing the new budget. In some instances it may be desirable to indicate individual department collections as a memorandum entry on detailed summary departmental expenditure forms. This can be helpful in evaluating departmental service charges in relation to policies for establishing such changes to partially or fully cover costs of performing the service.

Revision of Estimates by Chief Administrator

In the consideration of individual departmental and bureau requests the chief administrator relates the request to the long-term program, giving consideration (with varying weights) to such factors as: (1) the work programs together with their unit costs; (2) the amount expended in the preceding year by each department and the results obtained; (3) the relative importance of the department's work compared with the functions of the municipality as a whole; (4) possible economies through improved operating methods; and (5) the relative need for the services that the particular department provides for the community.

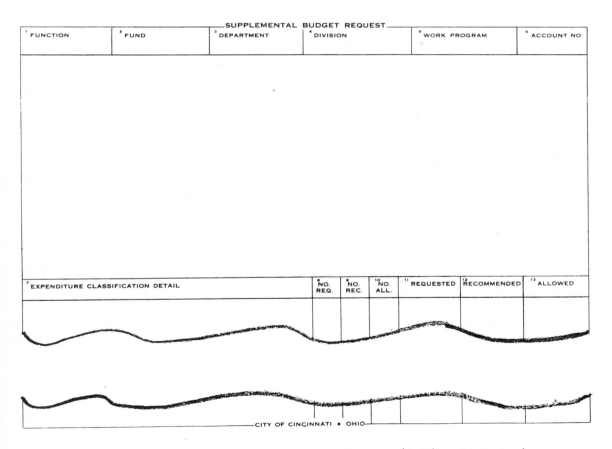

Fig. 9 — Supplemental Budget Request (8-1/2 x 11 inches)

After the chief administrator has received and analyzed all the budget estimates and tabulations, including the relationship between proposed revenues and expenditures, he should discuss each departmental request with the proper department head. This gives the department head an opportunity to lay his needs and requests before the administrator in person; at the same time the chief administrator has a chance to explain to the department head the relationship of his request to the total budget and the financial problems which the municipality faces.

After the budget conferences have taken place, the chief administrator makes the necessary decisions regarding his recommendations to the city council. In deciding upon the budget as a whole he must give consideration to estimated revenues and the tax rate which he wishes to propose, his policy and legal limitations with respect to possible borrowing, and the total amount of expenditures which he is willing to recommend for appropriation. It is necessary to weigh the public value of the proposed work program and balance the cost of that which should be done against ability to pay the bill.

The Budget Document

Since the budget document is the means by which the budget is presented to the legislative body for its consideration, it is essential that the document include information that will aid in determination of the appropriation and revenue policies. This means that the budget document must necessarily contain more than just the bare estimates of expenditures.

It need not, however, include all of the mass of detail required of departments in submitting their budget requests. This should be available to answer questions that may be raised by the city council or the public. Properly designed departmental budgetary request forms, however, greatly facilitate preparation of the budget document. If headings and detail of departmental forms are properly worded and scheduled they can serve as headings for similar presentation in the budget document in summary form.

The budget document should be duplicated for distribution to the council and interested groups and individuals among the public. While the amount and type of information to be included depends upon the comprehensiveness of long-term plans, and to some extent upon local conditions, nevertheless, it should contain at least the following items:

Part I — Summaries

1. A budget message, in which the principal budget items are explained, the municipality's experience during the past year and its financial status at the present time are outlined and recommendations regarding the financial policy for the coming year are made

2. A budget summary showing all estimated revenues and expenditures on a single page. Revenues are here generally classified by main sources, and expenditures by major function. If the municipality operates several funds, revenue summaries should indicate source and distribution of each source to the various funds. The expenditure summary should indicate major functions and activities to be performed and the funds used in accounting for them. (Such expenditure summaries not only indicate the total cost of performing a certain function but may also indicate a need to change the fund structure of the city.)

3. A budget summary, showing resources and expenditures for the current year, each of two preceding years, and estimates for the coming year.

Part II — Detailed Revenue Estimates

4. A schedule showing in detail revenues from each source for the current expenditures for the coming year.

Part III — Detailed Expenditure Estimates

5. A schedule or schedules showing the fixed and uncontrollable expenditures for the coming year.

6. Departmental schedules showing for each department its expenditures for the past two years; estimated expenditures for the current year; departmental requests; and the amount recommended by the chief administrator. This information should be classified by fund, function, activity, character, and object.

7. Departmental work programs. (Departmental work programs might well be shown with departmental expenditure schedules. See Figs. 10 and 11 for illustrations of the approach used in Hartford, Connecticut, and Cincinnati, Ohio).

PERSONNEL DATA	ACTUAL 1955-56	ESTIMATED 1956-57	BUDGET 1957-58
REGULAR POSITIONS			
Clerk Typist 2	1	1	1
Clerk Stenographer 2	1	1	1
Semi-Skilled Laborer	1	1	1
Sidewalk Const. & Rep. Frmn.	1	1	1
Cement Finisher	1	1	1
Street Inspector	6	6	6
Street Inspector-Supervisor	1	1	1
TOTAL REGULAR POSITIONS	12	12	12
MAN YEARS PAID	11.8	11.8	11.9
OVERTIME HOURS PAID	564	528	528

EXPENDITURE RECAP	ACTUAL 1955-56	ESTIMATED 1956-57	BUDGET 1957-58
PERSONAL SERVICES			
Regular Payroll	44,988	47,475	48,098
Overtime Payments	1,078	1,075	1,075
TOTAL PERSONAL SERVICES	46,066	48,550	49,173
NON-PERSONAL EXPENSE			
Inspectors Bus Tickets	750	750	750
Materials Used by Repair Crew	287	845	800
Maintenance City Property	35,623	43,425	46,350
Sidewalk Assessment Work	14,030	23,000	20,000
TOTAL NON-PERSONAL EXPENSE	50,690	68,020	67,900
OUTLAY			
Major Installation	5,958	-	5,700
TOTAL DIVISION	102,714	116,570	122,773

CITY OF HARTFORD
ANNUAL BUDGET

PUBLIC WORKS
CURBS AND WALKS   31-11

All activity of the Sidewalk Division has been combined in code 31-11 including the office staff previously reflected in 31-01, the repair crew formerly in 31-12, and sidewalk assessment work once charged to 31-17. However, curb and walk work included in paving projects is absorbed in the street maintenance account.

This division inspects the condition of all sidewalks, curbs, driveways, ramps, house numbers, street signs, parking meters, and water and gas gates along 215 miles of city streets. Orders are sent to property owners to repair walks and drives. In the event of non-compliance, the city may order the work done and the bill charged against the owner. Revenue code 7316 reflects the amount of reimbursement.

Installation of sidewalk and drive on the north side of Allen Place along the cemetery, $2,700, and replacement of walk at South Green, $3,000, are included in outlay. The maintenance program is outlined below:

CITY RESPONSIBILITY	ACTUAL 1955-56	ESTIMATED 1956-57	BUDGET 1957-58
WORK MEASUREMENT			
Curbs - lin. ft.	13,351	21,363	22,000
City-owned walk - sq. ft.	4,394	5,500	5,500
City-accepted walks-sq. ft.	3,995	5,000	5,000
COST			
Curbs	$30,913	$37,395	$39,600
City-owned walks	2,460	3,445	3,500
City-accepted walks	2,250	2,585	3,250
TOTAL	$35,623	$43,425	$46,350
PRIVATE RESPONSIBILITY			
Walks and drives - sq. ft.	20,844	33,424	30,770
Cost	$14,030	$23,000	$20,000

Fig. 10 — Work Program Data, Hartford Budget

————————————WORK PROGRAM BUDGET SUMMARY————————————

MAPPING - 05

Included in this Work Program are such essential mapping projects as the House Numbering Map Record, the Paving Record Maps, the Topographic Survey Records, the newly developed City Map, and the Sewer Tap Record Maps.

In addition to these are the Underground Records Maps which locate existing sewers, water lines and other utilities throughout the city.

[1] FUNCTION PUBLIC WORKS SERVICES	[2] FUND GENERAL BOND FUNDS	[3] DEPARTMENT PUBLIC WORKS	[4] DIVISION ENGINEERING	[5] WORK PROGRAM MAPPING	ACCOUNT NO. 23-03-05-00
[7] EXPENDITURE CLASSIFICATION	[8] EXPENDITURE FOR 1955	FOR 1956	[9] CURRENT APPROPRIATION 1957	[10] REQUESTED FOR 1958	[11] RECOMMENDED FOR 1958	[12] ALLOWED FOR 1958	[13] INC. OR DEC.* OVER CURRENT APPROPRIATION
PERSONAL SERVICES		39,295	47,497	53,363	53,363		5,866
CONTRACTUAL SERVICES		3,404	1,300	600	600		700 *
COMMODITIES		225	100	200	200		100
CURRENT CHARGES		---	---	---	---		---
FIXED CHARGES		---	---	---	---		---
PROPERTIES		56	363	S U P P L E M E N T A L B U D G E T			---
DEBT SERVICE		---	---	---	---		---
TOTAL		42,980	49,260	54,163	54,163		5,266

[14] PERSONNEL COMPLEMENT	[15] 1955 AUTH.	ACTUAL	1956 AUTH.	ACTUAL	[16] 1957 AUTH.	ACTUAL	[17] 1958 REQUESTED	[18] 1958 RECOMMENDED	[19] 1958 ALLOWED	[20] INC. OR DEC.* OVER 1957
REGULAR			9	10	14	10	14	14		---
PART-TIME			3	3	--	--	---	--		---
TOTAL			12	13	14	10	14	14		---

[21] PERSONNEL COMPLEMENT BY POSITION TITLE	[22] 1957 AUTH.	ACTUAL	[23] 1958 REQ.	REC.	ALL.	[24] 1958 REQUESTED	[25] 1958 RECOMMENDED	[26] 1958 ALLOWED
REGULAR PERSONNEL								
Prof Engineer I (Civil)	2	2	2	2		12,006	12,006	
Draftsman II	2	1	2	2		9,135	9,135	
Draftsman I	6	4	6	6		20,100	20,100	
Engineering Technician I	3	2	3	3		11,424	11,424	
Draftsman III	1	1	1	1		4,698	4,698	
TOTAL REGULAR PERSONNEL	14	10	14	14		57,363	57,363	
PART-TIME PERSONNEL	N O N E		N O N E			---	---	
OVERTIME	N O N E		N O N E			---	---	
TOTAL GROSS PERSONAL SERVICES	14	10	14	14		57,363	57,363	
LESS ESTIMATED SALARY SAVINGS	-	-	-	-		4,000	4,000	
TOTAL NET PERSONAL SERVICES	14	10	14	14		53,363	53,363	

[27] PROGRAM PERFORMANCE DATA	Unit	[28] 1955 ACTUAL	[29] 1956 ACTUAL	[30] 1957 ESTIMATED	[31] 1958 ESTIMATED
Underground Record Maps	Map Sheet	43	8	8	15
City of Cincinnati Map	Map	.4	.5	1	.5
Topographic Survey Maps	Map Sheet	27	45	70	50
Paving Record Maps	Mi. of Street	10	0	10	150
Street Dedication Maps	Mi. of Street	0	59	75	75
Sewer Tap Record Maps	Map Sheet	10	32	10	50
Civil Defense Maps	Map	12	15	20	20

————————CITY OF CINCINNATI · OHIO————————

FORM 52

Fig. 11 — Work Program Budget Summary

Part IV — General Information

8. Fund balance sheets showing estimated assets, liabilities, reserves and surpluses or deficits as of the close of the current fiscal year.

9. A statement for each fund showing for the two preceding years actual cash balance at the beginning of the year, receipts and disbursements during that year, and the actual cash balance at the end of the year, as well as estimates of the same items for the current year and the coming year.

10. A debt statement comparing outstanding debt with the debt limit.

11. A debt schedule showing principal and interest requirements by years for existing debt, and for new bonds to be issued under the terms of the proposed budget.

12. An analysis of tax delinquency and special assessment delinquency.

13. A schedule of short-term borrowing transactions during the past two years, the current year, and the proposal for the coming year.

Part V — Tax Levy

14. A schedule calculating the tax rate required to finance the budget.

Part VI — Drafts of Ordinances

15. A borrowing ordinance.

16. An appropriation ordinance and tax levying ordinance to give legislative effect to the budget.

17. A schedule of salary and wage rates applicable to each class of position. (Necessary only if the salary scale is fixed by ordinance.)

The Budget Message. The value of the budget message needs to be stressed. In too many cases this message is nothing but a formal letter of transmittal; but it can and should be much more. Here is an opportunity for the chief administrator to explain to the legislature and to the public the principal budgetary problems and the reasons for his recommendations. Because of the many hours he has spent digesting the great mass of information, estimates, and requests, he is in a position to discuss with authority not only the needs of the government but also the successes and weaknesses of the several administrative units. In this message he can also relate the current budget to long-term problems and policies, to basic assumptions on which budget estimates, particularly revenue estimates, were predicated, and can direct special attention to the major issues involved. Through this medium he can give meaning and purpose to what may otherwise appear to be a confusing compendium of details. A one-page formal letter of transmittal is not sufficient; what is needed is a brief (from two to six pages, perhaps) summary of the salient features of the program represented by the budget document, together with an analysis of the general fiscal picture. A well prepared budget message will serve the dual purpose of summarizing fiscal policy and interpreting figures for use by governing bodies, citizens, and newspapers.

Coverage. A good budget document takes into consideration all the funds of a municipality. Often the general and special revenue funds constitute the main body of the document, while utility, working capital, and special assessment funds may be included in an "annexed" or "auxiliary" budget printed in the back of the budget document.

Distribution. Although the only budget document to be duplicated in the past frequently has been the chief administrator's recommendation to the legislative body, there is a growing movement for a second budget document to be prepared and printed each year. The second document is published after the legislative body has acted upon the executive's proposals, and shows the budget as it was adopted. Since the original document is only tentative and is subject to change by the council, publication of the adopted budget is even more important and more valuable than the publication of the administrator's original plan.

Consideration of Budget by Council

With the completion of the budget document, the chief administrator formally presents it to the legislative body on or before the date set by the municipal charter, ordinance, or his budget calendar. He should allow the legislative body sufficient time to give the budget a thorough and exhaustive examination well in advance of the date upon which the appropriation and tax ordinance must be passed.

After receipt of the document, the council may either consider it in a committee of the whole, or it may refer the budget to a standing finance committee or a special committee of that body. In a small council (nine or fewer members), the budget should be considered by the entire body rather than by a smaller committee. There should be an announcement to the public and to interested groups of the dates of the budget hearings and the availability of copies of the proposed budget. In reviewing the budget, the council or its committee will usually set aside time for three things: first, consultation with the chief administrator, with the budget officer, and (particularly in the large cities) with department officials, for explanations and questions; second, public hearings wherein citizens may express their sentiments; and third, an opportunity for the council or committee itself to discuss the budget in executive session.

After the consultation and hearings have been concluded, the finance committee or the committee of the whole must decide what its recommendations shall be. These are then reported back to the council itself, which has further opportunity to debate and consider the budget.

When the council has completed its consideration of the budget, it is necessary to give the document formal approval in the form of ordinances. Most municipalities are required by law to pass only an appropriation ordinance and a tax levy ordinance. No official recognition is given to the other revenue estimates in many cities, since the ordinary municipal procedure requires that revenue measures be passed only when they take effect, instead of annually. In some municipalities, however, the revenue estimates are officially written into the city ordinances, even though the estimates have no effect upon collections.

The form of the appropriation ordinance is very important. If the ordinance appropriates to departments by totals, the details shown in the budget document are not binding and may be modified by the chief administrator. If, on the other hand, the ordinance is written around a detailed budget in such a way as to make the detailed statements of the budget document a part of the ordinance, each item shown becomes a control item, unchangeable except by subsequent council action.

The most generally accepted practice is to require that the budget document show the detail, but that the appropriation ordinance assign the monies to activities by totals This permits the chief administrator to set up control accounts in detail, but leaves him free to transfer from one type of expenditure to another within the limits of the council's lump sum appropriations. In some cases, however, state legislation or the city charter requires the appropriation ordinance to contain greater detail.

Some Defects of Budgets

Incompleteness. Since the budget is a financial plan for a municipality over a definite period of time, it should contain a complete statement of all the anticipated revenues and receipts and of all the anticipated expenditures of the municipality during that period. It should show nonrevenue receipts from borrowing as well as revenue receipts from all municipal taxes, municipal enterprises, and intergovernmental receipts. It should show capital expenditures. All funds ought to be included and unless they are, the budget may present a distorted and misleading picture of the financial transactions of the city.

Obscurity and Confusion. Some municipal budgets tend to hide a part of the salary expenses of the city departments. For example, it is sometimes customary to charge part of the salary of the city engineering forces to construction jobs that are financed from bond funds. If, in the budget of the general fund where the engineering department's ordinary expenses are located, only a portion of the salaries of the engineering department are shown without further explanation, the engineering expense of the city is grossly understated, and the omitted salaries are not exposed to legislative or public scrutiny. The complete expense of operating the departments should be shown in the budget and a sufficient offsetting item included, to show the amount to be financed from borrowed funds. Similarly, salaries or costs met from other funds should be noted and cross-referenced.

Another defect of some municipal budgets is that they do not always accurately reflect the administrator's work plan. Department heads may make up budget estimates without giving consideration to their work program for the succeeding year. As the program gets under way, it then becomes necessary for the department heads to request contingent appropriations, special transfers of funds, and other devices to finance the items that were not adequately forecast in the beginning. In some cities, the budget is deliberately understated for certain items, such as snow removal, with the understanding that an emergency appropriation will be given each year to finance the cost. This is a very misleading practice, since under these circumstances the budget never represents the real financial estimates of the city for the ensuing period.

Misleading Figures. Debatable items are occasionally buried in a maze of budget figures. This is especially true when there are changes tending to increase the total appropriations. It would probably be an improvement if the budget-makers were required to set up the budget proposal in such a way that all changes tending to increase the total appropriations would stand out clearly for special legislative and public consideration. In some cases this is accomplished by placing separate columns in the budget for the changes or increases from the preceding year's appropriations. In other budgets, this is accomplished by placing the current expenses carried over from the preceding year in one place and the current expenses appearing in the budget for the first time in a separate section or classification. This arrangement focuses the attention of both the council and the public upon the proposed increases, thus greatly simplifying budget consideration.

Continuing Appropriations. The practice of making continuing appropriations is another hindrance to good budgeting. In some cities certain receipts are reappropriated to a given department or activity by a standing law. This system tends to give the department a proprietary interest in those receipts, removes the activity from periodic council review and control, makes the budget difficult to complete, and may give an activity either more or less money than it needs, since the reappropriation is not based upon an annual review of actual financial needs.

Budget Execution

The annual budget procedure is by no means completed with the adoption of the budget ordinances by the council. There remains the task of making certain that expenditures are actually carried out in accordance with the budget plan. Budget control is primarily an accounting process, carried out in the first instance by the finance department; and discussion of the procedures for accomplishing such control will be deferred to Chapter 8.

Organization for Programming and Budgeting

Comment has been made from time to time in this chapter on the various departments of the city government that play a role in long-term programming, capital budgeting, and preparation of the annual budget. It should be clear that all these activities represent one of the central responsibilities of the chief administrator that must be discharge either by the administrator himself, or by an officer or agency directly responsible to him

Existing organizational arrangements in most cities place responsibility for budget formulation either in a budget officer responsible to the chief executive or, more commonly, in a budget division of the finance department. In small cities of course it may be a personal responsibility of the chief administrator or the finance director. Long-term programming, when it is done at all, is sometimes a responsibility of the planning agency, sometimes of the finance department.

Where a thoroughgoing budget process has been developed, and where budgeting is properly related to long-term programming, there would seem to be strong reasons for coordinating these two functions closely and for organizing both as a managerial responsibility. In those cities where the city planning agency is directly responsible to the chief administrator, and is headed by a director appointed by him, there is much to be said for a combined budgeting and long-term programming division within the planning department.

In cities where the city planning agency is headed by a board or commission, or is otherwise independent of the chief administrator, responsibility for programming and budgeting should be placed in a budget officer, who will act in a managerial capacity as advisor to the chief administrator. The precise form of organization will depend of course on the size of the city. In the small city a part-time budget officer who performs other functions in the chief administrator's office may be sufficient, while a large city will need a competent staff working under the direction of a full-time budget officer. In some small cities it may be desirable to vest responsibility for budget preparation in the finance officer, but this should not be done unless he is appointed by and directly responsible to the chief administrator. Where the budget agency is not combined with the planning department, a careful division of work will need to be worked out between these two so that there will not be conflict or a duplication of effort.

Chapter 6

PERSONNEL ADMINISTRATION

Throughout this volume it has been often repeated that administration is concerned with people. In a very real sense then all management is personnel management; nevertheless, there are certain special management activities which are usually referred to as "personnel administration." Although there is no universally accepted definition of personnel administration in municipal administration, the term is usually applied to those techniques which are directed toward recruiting employees; placing workers in positions where their efforts will result in the greatest possible yield; classifying their positions and determining their compensation; training them; caring for their health and welfare; transferring and promoting them; enforcing fair and uniform disciplinary measures; and providing fair policies relating to retirement and layoff.

Even with this restricted definition, which excludes all of the day-to-day activities of directing and supervising employees, it is easy to see that personnel administration must be a major concern of the whole administrative staff, from the chief administrator all the way down to the first-line supervisor. All of these are concerned to a greater or lesser extent with recruitment, placement, and separation.

It has been found best in most organizations of any size, however, to assign certain aspects of personnel administration to a central personnel agency, which then becomes one of the important auxiliary agencies of the organization. This centralization not only makes possible more effective administration, but assures uniformity of treatment. There are, of course, many aspects of personnel administration that are so intimately connected with the task of day-to-day management that they remain the responsibility of line officials even when a central personnel agency exists.

The central personnel agency is useful not only for the performance of auxiliary functions but also as an advisor on matters of personnel policy to the chief administrator. However, the chief administrator, like the line supervisor, cannot divorce himself completely from personnel activities by the establishment of a personnel agency; he retains final responsibility for all personnel functions, or at least those which have not been formally removed from his control by law. Personnel administration is an integral part of over-all management, and the chief administrator is vitally concerned with it in many ways.

1. The chief administrator must see that the city government is properly organized to handle its problems of personnel administration, and that personnel functions are properly divided between the central personnel agency and the line departments.

2. The chief administrator must see that long-term plans are laid out for the development and replacement of personnel, so that the city government will continue over a period of years to be staffed by competent and effective employees at all levels.

3. The chief administrator has a particular responsibility for the development of

administrative personnel, and for providing replacements for key administrative positions.

4. The chief administrator must see that the work of the auxiliary personnel agency is coordinated with that of the line departments in their day-to-day work.

5. The chief administrator must see that adequate training programs are developed for employees throughout the city service.

6. The chief administrator must establish and maintain positive and constructive employee-relations policies that will secure a high level of employee morale and loyalty.

This chapter, and the following one, will deal with the responsibilities of the chief administrator in personnel administration and the ways in which a personnel agency can assist him in discharging these responsibilities. The internal operations of the central personnel agency will be described and discussed only so far as is necessary for understanding their relation to the job of the chief administrator.

Long-Term Planning for Administrative Staff

The history of an organization is the history of the persons who join it, who work in it and are promoted through it, and who finally leave it through death, resignation, retirement, or dismissal. Since it is normal for the top positions in any organization to be filled largely by promotion from below, the competence of the men who can be appointed to these top positions will depend on the kind of people who were recruited to the organization 20 years previously, and the way in which they developed in it. Hence, the chief administrator who is interested in more than immediate results — who is concerned with what is going to happen five, ten, or more years from now — will want to do some thinking about his long-term problems of personnel replacement and development. There are a number of things he can do, with the assistance of his personnel agency, to analyze his long-term needs.

Devices for Analyzing the Flow of Personnel

The administrator can begin by drawing up an organization chart, because in general the flow of personnel to positions of greater responsibility follows organizational lines. Next, he can determine whether there is a man at a lower level of the organization who would be competent to step into each key administrative position. For each spot where a competent replacement is lacking, there is an immediate job of training one or more prospective understudies — and the equally important job of determining why present personnel practices have not provided replacements. Some possible reasons for a lack of qualified candidates will be discussed later in this section.

After preparing and studying his organization chart the administrator should record on the chart the age of the individual who occupies each administrative position. This will show in what parts of the organization promotion opportunities are likely to be few and far between, and in what parts numerous opportunities for advancement will likely occur within the next few years. Again, this information is simply a preliminary to devising a plan of action for replacements and promotions.

A third step is to indicate on a copy of the organization chart the normal personnel "flows." The items of information to include are:

1. The regular promotional channels, (for example, perhaps senior clerk-typist positions are normally filled from the ranks of junior clerk-typists);

2. The points in the organization at which individuals are usually recruited from the outside. These may occur at all levels of the organization chart: for example, in some organizations junior engineers would normally be appointed from among recent college graduates rather than from the ranks of draftsmen or other sub-professional employees already in the organization;

3. Promotional ceilings — that is, positions in the organization from which there is no normal promotional outlet. Whether a position has such a ceiling may depend, of course, on the educational preparation of the person occupying it.

Studies of this kind can be carried out in small cities or in large ones. In the larger cities the chief administrator will be concerned only with the higher levels of the organization chart. He would see to it, however, that similar studies were made by his department heads in their respective departments. These studies will be extremely useful in discovering problem areas. Some possible uses are suggested in the following section.

Providing for Advancement of Personnel

The chief administrator is particularly concerned with the staffing of administrative positions. Although specialized skill and experience are necessary for some administrative jobs, in many such positions the needed skills are of a general nature requiring a knowledge of management and a broad understanding of city government. In most cities, promotional opportunities for administrators are restricted much more closely to organizational lines than is either necessary or desirable. This is particularly true of junior administrative positions, where there is every argument for giving the men who will at some later date be the key administrators of the whole organization the broadest possible experience.

A second area of particular concern for the chief administrator is that of recruitment policy. He must examine the chart of personnel flows to determine whether these flows will normally bring to the higher levels of the organization individuals who will be competent by training, experience, and ability, to fill these positions. The situation must be studied from the top of the organization downward — that is, each executive position must be traced downward to determine where the persons who eventually fill these positions are normally recruited into the organization. In addition to the flow chart, the organizational biography of individuals now holding such positions will help answer this question.

Suppose a position normally requires a college graduate who has certain administrative experience and is not too old. A serious discrepancy is revealed if a study of the promotion chart shows that individuals promoted to these positions normally enter the organization as high school graduates, work on the average 35 years before they receive this particular promotion, and ordinarily have no prior administrative experience of the desired kind. Where situations of this kind occur the personnel flows and the personnel rules and procedures upon which they depend must be revised.

A third area of concern to the administrator, closely related to the one just discussed, is the relationship of the personnel rules and procedures to the normal flows in the organization. For example, the experience qualifications required for a particular position in the classification plan may make transfers across departmental lines impossible. Age requirements for a particular position will have an important effect on the ages at which individuals will normally reach certain levels of the organization. Salary levels will have an important bearing on the kinds of individuals who can be attracted to certain positions. The relative weight given to merit and seniority in promotions will largely determine whether the ablest men can be brought rapidly to positions of responsibility.

Some Special Problems in Personnel Planning

Special personnel problems, often very severe ones, are found in organizations that are expanding rapidly in size; that are being reduced in size; or that are being "upgraded," that is, in which new personnel are being brought in with higher entrance qualifications than the present staff.

Of these three, the expanding organization presents the fewest problems. Because of the large number of promotional opportunities, employee morale will generally be high, and it will be possible to promote the ablest men rapidly without serious damage to the attitudes of other individuals with greater seniority. On the other hand there is danger that this process of rapid promotion will bring into the higher ranks of the organization individuals who have had insufficient background and experience. For this reason the expanding organization has more reason to bring in individuals from outside, even into its higher ranks, than an organization that is stable. Where one city department is expanding rapidly it may be possible to supply a part of its staff from other city departments whose personnel have fewer opportunities for advancement.

The problems of the organization that is being reduced in size are exactly opposite to those of the expanding organization. Again, their solution requires the freest possible use of channels of sidewise transfer, so that the abler individuals in the organization can be transferred to positions of equivalent responsibility in other parts of the city hall. If it is possible to carry out the weeding process largely on the basis of competence rather than seniority, the declining organization offers some opportunity to build up the average competence of its staff. In practice, however, the more competent members of the organization, seeing the lack of promotional opportunities, are the first to leave, and in practice also it is usually impossible to disregard seniority completely in making reductions in force.

There may also be special morale problems when a long-time employee has risen to a key post and is due to retire in the foreseeable future. In order to prepare for his retirement, steps must be taken well in advance to have someone ready to step into his post. This may call for a gradual delegation of administrative responsibilities to an understudy, while at the same time utilizing the older employee in such a manner as to be able to take advantage of his knowledge and experience. Getting the employee to accept such a plan may post a rather delicate human relations problem.

Another important management decision is whether those who are recruited and developed for key posts are to be specialists or generalists. There is always a tendency to specialize, and in general, the larger the organization, the greater this tendency. It is a management responsibility to cultivate an administrative staff having broad and diversified experience. This requires a program of carefully planned work assignments for potential key administrators.

At times the chief administrator may want to upgrade an organization by a deliberate process of bringing into it new staff possessing high qualifications. Here there is the obvious morale problem of bringing an adjustment between the old and new staff, and reconciling "old timers" to the change. If the new employees can be brought in mostly at the lower levels, and if the normal rates of retirement, death, and resignation can be counted on to clear a sufficient number of promotional channels for them, then the prospective difficulties may not materialize; otherwise upgrading is a piece of major organization surgery.

Guideposts in the Development of Staff

The specific procedures outlined here for the development of personnel do not tell the whole story. More important than specific procedures is the understanding and application by the chief administrator of a few underlying principles:

1. A top-notch administrative staff cannot be created overnight. It can only be developed over a period of years.

2. Such a staff can be built by: (a) recruiting high-grade men; (b) developing these men through instructive, varied experience and progressive responsibility in the administrative organization; (c) reappraising constantly the available talent to discover strengths and weaknesses, and to remedy the latter; and (d) providing the promotional opportunities and responsible, creative tasks that will hold the best men in the organization and keep them working with all their effort and ability.

3. The chief administrator must himself retain responsibility for and participate actively in the program of staff development. A personnel agency can help by expertly advising him on personnel matters and by relieving him and his organization of the burden of routine, technical personnel functions. The task of developing key staff, however, must remain primarily in the hands of the chief administrator.

More than any other single factor, the chief administrator's own qualities of leadership and managerial skill will determine how much success he will have in retaining and developing competent subordinates. Loyalty to him, and to the goals he establishes for the city administration can become the strongest driving force in the self-development of his assistants.

Organization for Personnel Management

Legal Authorization for the Personnel Program

The enactment of sound personnel legislation does not insure effective personnel administration, but intelligently conceived legislation will provide a defensive bulwark against bad personnel practices. Experience has clearly shown that a sound, long-range personnel program will best succeed if given some legal status. Otherwise an entire program may be junked by new officers unsympathetic to the merit principle.

The chief reason for putting personnel provisions into law is to insure some continuity to the merit system. Within any one individual's administration, however, an excellent personnel program may be developed despite the absence of any personnel provisions in the state law or the city charter. The administrator will be handicapped only by the fact that he cannot assure employees of the permanence of the merit system.

Basic personnel legislation may be found in the state laws or constitution, in charter provisions adopted by direct vote of the people, or in less stable, but therefore more flexible, provisions made by city ordinance. There are, as yet, no categorical answers as to what will work and will not work in personnel management. Hence, it is impossible to write into the basic law statements that would be certain to cover all future needs. Probably the best solution, therefore, rests in using a broad constitutional or charter provision which clearly defines major policies and objectives and authorizes a further definition of the program by act of the legislative body. Stability is thus given to the program; yet sufficient flexibility is provided to meet changing and special conditions. Personnel legislation, in common with other legislation, may thus be saved from freezing detailed administrative procedures into the organic law.

Structure of the Personnel Agency

Specialized personnel services are among the services most commonly assigned to central auxiliary agencies. Although each department might do its own examining, job classifying, personnel record keeping, and so forth, best results can be expected from a central agency serving all departments.

Sometimes, but not always, the chief administrative officer has considerable freedom in deciding how the personnel function is to be integrated with other municipal services. It is necessary to recognize, however, that there are many municipalities where a very formal civil service law dating back many years is the major controlling influence in determining how the total personnel job is to be carried out. Furthermore, in some states, the organization and operations of local civil service commissions are based on blanket state statutes which allow little or no leeway for changes in the structure or functions of the personnel agency. The adjustment of such state requirements to local operating needs can be a major problem.

There are three general patterns of organization for personnel administration:

1. The independent civil service commission. This type of organization may be established by state statute, charter provision, or local ordinance. It is usually a multi-member body having a secretary or other administrative officer and such other technical and clerical staff as may be required. Such commissions usually possess legal authority to examine, classify positions, develop policies and rules relating to conditions of employment and administration of the system, and to perform a variety of other functions. Often they have broad power to serve as trial boards or appeal bodies in cases of removal for disciplinary reasons. The degree to which such commissions are empowered to set aside or modify disciplinary action varies from complete authority to nullify administrative acts to advisory powers only.

2. The personnel department. Under this type of organization, the personnel department is considered to be an important arm of over-all management. The head of the department is a member of the chief administrative officer's management team and personnel functions are fully integrated with all other municipal services and functions. The personnel officer is the chief administrative officer's principal advisor on day-to-day matters of personnel policy and operation.

3. The personnel function as one duty assignment of a general administrative assistant. This kind of organization is usually found in smaller jurisdictions. Here again, the individual having this assignment serves as the administrator's representative for personnel matters, but he also has other management responsibilities.

In the final analysis, it becomes the responsibility of the chief administrative officer to develop his own personnel policies and objectives within the framework of the particular governmental structure in which he operates. On occasion this may require positive and continuing effort by the chief administrative officer to develop close cooperative working relationships by (a) formulating clear-cut personnel policies and objectives consistent with his management philosophy, (b) communicating those policies and objectives to those officials who have varying degrees of independent legal authority in the personnel realm, and (c) being aware of legal considerations and receptive to points of view which may necessitate compromise or recourse to alternate courses of action.

The Division of Responsibility for Personnel Work

It should not be thought that a central personnel agency can single-handedly produce a sound personnel program. Every individual in the government shares in the success or failure of the program. Personnel administration is not something that can be isolated completely — its problems permeate virtually every day-to-day administrative problem. It is the responsibility of the chief administrator to make his employees "personnel-conscious." The responsibilities of the several divisions of the government in the personnel program may be reviewed briefly:

The Council. The basic decisions affecting the personnel program, within the framework of charter provisions, are made by the legislative body, the council. In most cases the council must adopt ordinances establishing the personnel agency and defining the general policies of the city relative to methods of recruitment, salaries and wages, conditions of employment, retirement plans, and so forth. Furthermore, its power to make appropriations gives the council a continuous control over the number and caliber of employees, as well as power to determine in broad outline what the work of employees will be. Although a wise council will not attempt to legislate in detail on all personnel matters, the final power of decision on personnel policy matters rests with the legislative body.

Management. The chief administrator is, or should be, the chief personnel officer of the city. To the heads of the various departments and agencies he may delegate much of his authority to provide specific direction and control over employees, and to the central personnel agency he may assign much of the specialized personnel work common to all agencies. He must retain, however, the final authority and responsibility for the formulation of the standards that will govern personnel administration throughout the entire organization.

The Personnel Agency. This agency is responsible for the application of the broad policies and standards outlined by the council and the chief administrator. It provides certain personnel services (examining, classification, etc.) to the other departments and agencies, and it is expected to keep abreast of the newest and best techniques available in the field of personnel administration.

In addition to these auxiliary services, the personnel agency, or at least certain of its officers, has managerial functions to perform. The head of the personnel agency should not only direct the technical work of the agency but he should serve as an aide to the chief administrator in personnel matters, advising his superior on questions of personnel policy and translating the administrator's policies into specific regulations, procedures, and the like. This can only be done if the personnel officer is a full-fledged member of the management team and participates in the formulation of major decisions.

Department Heads. A great deal of the personnel work in any organization must be done by the heads of the several departments and agencies. They formulate the plans and policies for their particular agencies — subject to the guidance and approval of the chief administrator and the council — and they issue the orders necessary to put these plans and policies into effect. They are closer to the employees and more familiar with operating problems than the chief administrator or the personnel agency and are therefore in the best position to make decisions on training needs, placement problems, salary increase awards, and a host of other problems provided, of course, that they cooperate closely with the personnel agency and obtain its advice on these decisions.

Supervisors. Most of the specific commands or orders, training, and appraisal of employee performance must be provided by the various supervisory officials in the several departments, whatever their rank or title. The immediate superior of an employee is not only the channel through which order and control from above are applied, but he is also the source of much detailed direction. No discussion of personnel administration is complete that fails to recognize the important role of the supervisor, foreman, and straw-boss. More specific recognition of the role of supervisory officials will be given later in this chapter, in the section dealing with in-service personnel activities, and also in the following chapter on training.

Employees. Personnel administration is applied not only from top to bottom in an organization. Every employee in the organization plays a part — active or passive — in the formulation and execution of personnel programs. If he does nothing else, he receives direction and instruction, and his responsiveness or lack of responsiveness to direction and training affect the morale of the organization, as well as the quality of its perform-ance. Employees, either as individuals or acting in organized groups, contribute actively to the formulation of personnel policies and standards, especially with respect to such problems as salaries, hours, working conditions, and separations from the service. The role of employees in personnel administration will be further emphasized in a later sec-tion of this chapter dealing with employee relations, and also in the following chapter on training.

Elements of Personnel Administration

Personnel operations involve the following phases:

First, there is the process of getting people on the job; the hiring or recruiting stage. It includes letting qualified people know about employment opportunities, deter-mining which of those who seek employment are qualified, and placing them in positions where they will probably make good.

The second phase deals with all personnel processes that have to do with the em-ployee after he is on the payroll. This will be called the in-service phase. Included in this second category are such matters as transfer, promotion, and demotion; measuring performance on the job through service ratings; training programs; employee-employer relationships; discipline; health, safety, and welfare programs; and keeping necessary personnel records to produce prompt significant information about the employment situa-tion within the service.

The third stage may be termed the separation phase of personnel administration. Inevitably there comes a time when an employee must be separated from the payroll. This may come about through a voluntary resignation; through a dismissal because of in-competence; through a reduction in work forces because of lack of work or funds; or through retirement because of disability or age. Included in this category also are the temporary separations known as leaves of absence for various purposes such as military service or education.

Two very important techniques of personnel administration will be singled out for special treatment: position classification and salary standardization, because these have a bearing on all personnel matters from recruiting to separations.

Although an effort has been made to simplify personnel administration by reducing it to a few phases, personnel problems are highly complex. It is a commonplace to say that human relations offer difficult problems for solution. Human beings are of many patterns. They differ widely in their temperament, intelligence, interests, skills, work habits, and attitudes. They differ in basic inheritances and environment. These differ-ences lead to conflicts which are difficult to adjust under any circumstances and which become more of a problem when people are brought together in a work situation. It is the role of personnel administration to take into account human characteristics and behavior in order to make an effective working unit out of people with mixed interests and abilities. This is no small task, and the techniques are far from perfect for achieving this end. However, it is possible to bring about considerable improvement in dealing with employment situations by combining common sense with certain personnel techniques that have proved their worth.

Position-classification is the basic management tool in the field of personnel administration. It is the process of, first, identifying jobs and ascertaining the nature of their duties, responsibilities and qualification requirements; and second, grouping these jobs into "classes" on the basis of their similarity in these respects. This process makes it possible to provide like treatment to similar positions in matters of recruitment, examination, pay, training and all other aspects of personnel administration.

The basic unit of a classification plan is the class, into which are grouped all positions substantially similar in kind and level of work and qualifications requirements. In a typical classification plan, for example, the Junior Stenographer class would contain all positions involving, as a major part of the duties, taking routine dictation and transcribing the notes. It would be the class of work to which a beginning stenographer in an office would ordinarily be assigned. The Senior Stenographer class would contain positions where the dictation is difficult and technical and where the employees may be required to answer some correspondence without dictation, or supervise other stenographers.

The principal tool used in securing information for the classification plan is the classification questionnaire. An example of this kind of questionnaire, together with instructions, is shown in Figs. 12 and 13. Information obtained from classification questionnaires should be supplemented by direct observation of employees at work, and by questioning them on points which are not clear in the questionnaire. Not only does this give the classification man first-hand information about the jobs, but it makes the employees feel that their work has been carefully studied and that those doing the classification work have sufficient facts to classify their positions correctly.

When complete and accurate information has been obtained about every position in the service, positions are then grouped by major occupations: engineers, accountants, clerks, and so on. The engineers' group is then subdivided into electrical, sanitary, civil, and so on. Then each subgroup is studied to separate positions involving different levels of difficulty and responsibility. These final subdivisions are the basic classification units called classes: Junior Civil Engineer, Senior Civil Engineer, and the like. This procedure is followed for every occupation.

The assignment of an official title to a class does not preclude the use of informal office titles where these may be more appropriate. A position which is officially classified as a Senior Clerk may be very appropriately referred to, for office purposes, as a Stock Records Clerk, Inventory Clerk, or some other designation which describes the work of the particular position. Official class titles would be used, however, for all personnel action, and for budgetary and payroll purposes.

After the structure of the classification plan has been determined, specifications are prepared describing each class of positions in the service. The class specification usually contains a statement of duties and responsibilities, type of supervision received and exercised, desirable or minimum qualifications for the position, and examples of duties. An example of a class specification is shown in Fig. 14.

The position-classification plan is a basic tool for the personnel agency and the administration in carrying out its other personnel functions, particularly in recruiting,

POSITION CLASSIFICATION
QUESTIONNAIRE

1. Mr. Mrs. Miss	Last Name	First	Middle Initial	4. Commission, Board, or Department
2. Official Title of Position				5. Division or Institution
Usual Working Title of Position				6. Section or Other Unit of Division or Institution

3. Regular Schedule of Hours of Work

	From	To
Mon.		
Tues.		
Wed.		
Thur.		
Fri.		
Sat.		
Sun.		

Length of Lunch Period _____

Total Hrs. per Wk. _____
Explain rotation of shifts, if any:

Hrs. of "On-Call" Time per Wk. _____

7. Place of Work or Headquarters

8. Is your work ☐ Full-Time? ☐ Part-Time? ☐ Year-round? ☐ Seasonal? ☐ Temporary?

If work is *seasonal, temporary, or part-time*, indicate part of year or proportion of full-time: _____

9. Do you receive any maintenance (room, meals, laundry, etc.) in addition to your cash salary? ☐ Yes ☐ No

10. Describe below in detail the work you do. Use your own words, and make your description so clear that persons unfamiliar with your work can understand exactly what you do. Attach additional sheets if necessary.

TIME	WORK PERFORMED	LEAVE BLANK

11. Name and Title of Your Immediate Supervisor:

12. Give the names and payroll titles of employees you supervise, if five or fewer. If you supervise more than five employees, give the number under each title. If you supervise no employees, write "*none.*" _____

Fig. 12 — Classification Questionnaire

13. Machines or equipment used regularly in your work. Give per cent of time spent in operation of each:

	%		%
	%		%
	%		%

14. What are the nature and extent of instructions you receive regarding your work?

15. What are nature and extent of the check or review of your work?

16. Describe your contacts with departments other than your own, with outside organizations, and with the general public.

CERTIFICATION: I certify that the above answers are my own and are accurate and complete.

Date_____   Employee's Signature_____

STATEMENT OF IMMEDIATE SUPERVISOR

17. Comment on statements of employee. Indicate any exceptions or additions.

18. What do you consider the most important duties of this position?

19. Does this position involve typing?

☐ No

☐ Yes — Give % of time spent in typing   %

20. Does this position involve shorthand?

☐ No

☐ Yes — Give % of time spent in taking shorthand.   %

21. Indicate the qualifications which you think should be required in filling a future vacancy in this position. Keep the position itself in mind rather than the qualifications of the individual who now occupies it.

	Basic Qualifications	Additional Desirable Qualifications
Education, general:		
Education, special or professional:		
Experience, length in years and kind:		
Licenses, certificates, or registration:		
Special knowledges, abilities, and skills:		
Age, sex, physical requirements, or other factors:		

Date_____   Immediate Supervisor's Signature_____

STATEMENT OF DEPARTMENT HEAD OR OTHER ADMINISTRATIVE OFFICER

22. Comment on the above statements of the employee and the supervisor. Indicate any inaccuracies or statement with which you disagree. Please comment on the qualifications suggested by the supervisor _____

Date_____   Department Head's Signature_____

Fig. 12 — (Reverse side)

INSTRUCTIONS AND SUGGESTIONS FOR
FILLING OUT POSITION CLASSIFICATION QUESTIONNAIRE

*Do Not Attempt To Fill Out Questionnaire Until You
Have Read These Instructions*

WHAT THE CLASSIFICATION SURVEY IS

This is a job inventory. It is not concerned with your ability on the job or with your qualifications. The kind of work you do and the responsibilities of your position are the things to be shown on the classification questionnaire.

This survey is simply an analysis of the duties and responsibilities of positions in order to develop a classification plan. This plan will consist of a grouping together of all positions having substantially similar duties and responsibilities and requiring like abilities and skills for successful performance.

The classification plan is used as the basis for sound practices in selection, promotion, and transfer, and for uniform and equitable compensation standards. It is essential that the plan be accurate and fair. Therefore, detailed and exact information about the duties and responsibilities of each position is necessary.

You are the best person to provide complete information about your job. You know the exact duties you perform and your responsibilities. Consequently, you are asked to fill in the classification questionnaire. Use great care in doing this, so that a clear and complete understanding of your job can be obtained from your answers. The information provided through questionnaires will be supplemented by information obtained by discussions of the work of individual positions with supervisors and the employees themselves in a number of cases. However, the information provided by you on your classification questionnaire will be very important in determining in what class your position belongs. Your statements will not be changed by your supervisor.

Do not copy other people's answers even though their work is the same as your own. We want your own statement of your work—not the ideas of others about your work. Ask your supervisor to explain questions you do not understand, but use your own words in answering all questions. If you are new on your job, ask your supervisor what duties you will have in addition to those with which you have already become familiar.

PART I — TO THE EMPLOYEE

Read these instructions carefully. Write your answers on one copy of the questionnaire. See that they are correct and complete. Then type your answers on the other two sheets. Sign and return the two typewritten forms to your supervisor within five days. Keep your work copy of the questionnaire.

If you cannot type yourself, write your answers on one sheet and return the forms to your supervisor for copying within five days. He will return the forms to you for review, dating, and signature. Then return the typewritten copies to him and keep the sheet which you filled out originally.

The following explanation will help you to understand just what information is wanted. Read the explanation for each item just before answering each question.

ITEM 1 — Give your last name first, then your first name, then your middle initial. Indicate whether Mr., Mrs., or Miss by crossing out the two designations which do *not* apply.

ITEM 2 — Give your present official title as carried on the payroll. If you do not know, ask your supervisor. Under "Usual Working Title of Position," write the title you and your fellow workers customarily use for your job.

ITEM 3 — Indicate your regularly established work schedule, showing your regular starting and stopping times for each day, the length of your regularly established lunch period, and the total number of hours in your regularly established work week. If your official work schedule varies from week to week, show the average number of hours you work in the space for "Total Hrs. per Wk." If you are subject to rotating shifts, explain the system of rotation as it affects you, indicating whether you change shifts at weekly or monthly intervals and what shifts you rotate through. If your job requires that you be available at a specified location a fixed period each week for emergency service as required, in addition to your regular work time, indicate the average number of hours per week involved in this "on-call" or "stand-by" time.

ITEM 4 — Enter the name of the major branch of the jurisdiction in which you are employed, giving the name of the department, board, or commission in which you work.

ITEM 5 — Enter the name of that division or other principal subdivision of the department in which you work.

ITEM 6 — Enter the name of that section or other unit of the division or institution in which you are employed.

Fig. 13 — Instructions for Completing Classification Questionnaire

EXAMPLE IN THE ENGINEERING FIELD

6 months: I lay out and trace plan-profile sheets for street improvements. I reduce survey notes, balance traverses, and plot maps from the field books brought in by the field survey parties, also plot cross-sections and planimeter for cut and fill areas.

2 months: Etc.   I draft . . . etc.

EXAMPLE IN THE ACCOUNTING FIELD

10%:   I supervise three clerks assigned to the cost accounting system for road construction and maintenance.

10%:   I assemble job record reports, post to summary sheets, and do other routine work.

5%:   I tabulate and prove material for weekly, monthly, and annual reports.

2%: Etc.   I compile . . . etc.

EXAMPLE IN THE CUSTODIAL FIELD

1/2 day: Washing floors, walls, windows, and woodwork by hand.

1/3 day: Polishing metal; waxing and polishing floors with a polishing machine.

ITEM 11 — Give the name and title of your immediate supervisor—the person to whom you look for orders, advice, or decisions.

ITEM 12 — If you have five or fewer persons under your supervision, give their names and payroll titles. If more than five, give their payroll titles and give the number of employees under each title. If you supervise no employees, write "none."

ITEM 13 — List here any major items of equipment, machines, or office appliances which you use in your work and the approximate percentage of your working time which you spend in the operation of each.

ITEM 14 — What instructions or directions does your supervisor give you in relation to the work you do? How detailed are his instructions about what you are to do and how you are to do it? You may have had instructions only when you were new on the job. You may get special instructions with each new task. Describe the nature and extent of the instructions you receive.

ITEM 15 — Describe the check or review that is made of your work. Are there any automatic checks by other offices, or are there procedures which would catch any errors you might make? How final are the decisions you make about your work? Describe such features as these.

ITEM 16 — Explain the nature and purpose of important contacts you have with people other than your fellow workers. Is the purpose to obtain or give information, to persuade others, or to obtain cooperation? What problems and difficulties are involved?

PART II — INSTRUCTIONS TO SUPERVISORS AND DEPARTMENTAL OFFICIALS
Method of Distributing and Reviewing the Classification Questionnaires

You will be supplied with a complete set of three Classification Questionnaires and a copy of these Instructions for each employee under your supervision.

Give each employee a set of Classification Questionnaires and Instructions. Ask employees who have access to typewriters to work out their answers on one copy, and then type them on the other two copies, and return the two signed typewritten copies to you within five days.

Ask those employees who cannot type their own questionnaires to write their answers on one sheet and return the complete set to you within five days, for typing. When typed, return all three copies to the employees. Have the two typewritten copies reviewed, dated, signed, and returned to you.

Go over each employee's questionnaire carefully to see that it is accurate and complete. Then fill out Items 17 to 21, inclusive. The immediate supervisor should fill out Items 17 to 21 on the questionnaire forms of only those employees whom he directly supervises. A department head should not fill in these items for employees whom he directs through a sub-executive but only for those to whom he assigns work directly. In all instances, the director or other administrative officer, or a representative designated by him, should look over both the employees' and their supervisors' statements and indicate under Item 22 any inaccuracies found. Neither the immediate supervisor nor the administrative officer, however, should make any alteration or change in the statements made by a subordinate.

If there is a regular position under you which is temporarily vacant, or if an employee is not available to fill out the questionnaire, please supply a form for that position, made out as accurately as is possible. The fact that an employee did not fill out the form and the reason should be clearly indicated. If the employee returns, he should fill out and submit his own questionnaire.

Fig. 13 — (Continued)

ITEM 7 — Enter the room number, building name or street location of building, and name of the city in which you work, as Room 182, Memorial Hospital, Capital City. If you work out of doors or on projects at different locations, as in a highway district or on institutional premises, give the room number, building name, or street location of building, and city in which your headquarters are located—that is, the place where you report for instructions, etc.

ITEM 8 — Indicate by checking the appropriate box whether your job is full-time or part-time, and whether it is of a year-round character or whether you are employed only, for example, for the summer months or for some other limited period. If you work part-time, indicate whether you work half-time, three-quarters time, five hours a week, or otherwise show what proportion of full-time employment is involved in your job. If you work seasonally or on a temporary basis, indicate for how long a period your employment is expected to continue during the year.

ITEM 9 — If you receive maintenance in the form of meals, lodging, laundry, or the like, either for yourself or for both yourself and your family, *in addition to your cash salary*, check the "Yes" box. Maintenance, as used here, does *not* refer to reimbursement for travel and transportation expenses incurred in the course of official travel.

ITEM 10 — This, the most important question on the form, is where you tell in detail exactly what you do. Each kind of work that you do should be carefully explained. The task which you consider most important should be given first, followed by the less important work, until the least important is described. If your work varies from season to season or at specific times, duties should be grouped together according to such periods. Give your complete work assignments over a long enough period of time to picture your job as a whole. If one kind of work takes one-half your time, say so. If another kind takes one day a month, say that. You may prefer to show the time spent on different duties as percentages or fractions, as 75% of your time, or one-third of the year. Use whatever method you think will give a clear understanding of how you spend your working time, but be sure to show how much time is used for each type of work. Do not state it is impossible to estimate the time spent on various tasks; it may be difficult, but you are in a better position to do this than anyone else.

If you are performing duties other than those of your usual position, describe both. In describing the temporary position, you should give the name of the person you are replacing, how long you have been filling in for him, how long you expect to continue doing so, and the reason, such as vacation, sick leave, etc.

If necessary for a full explanation of your job, attach copies of forms used, being careful to explain how each is used and what entries you make, but do not attach copies unless you feel they are needed to describe your work.

Make your description so clear that anyone who reads your answer, even if he knows nothing about your job, will understand exactly what you do. Be specific; do not use general phrases.

Examples of work in different fields are given below as a guide to the kind of statements wanted. Do not copy *these* examples—use your own words. Ordinarily it will take all the space provided on the questionnaire to tell what you do. *If you do not have enough space, attach additional sheets.*

EXAMPLES IN THE LABOR FIELD (Skilled and Unskilled)

2 months:	I dig trenches with pick and shovel. Mr. Brown, my boss, tells me where to dig and when to stop.
1 month:	I fill wheel barrows with sand or gravel and take it to the concrete mixer. I tamp concrete after it is poured into forms.
1 month: Etc.	I ride a ten-ton flat-bed truck and help load and unload bags of cement, heavy rock, reinforcing steel........etc. We generally haul from the warehouse yards to maintenance or construction jobs. I wash the truck . . . etc.

---

3 months:	I operate a tractor on construction work as follows:...
1 month:	Hoisting work with a two- or three-drum hoist. (Vacation relief.)
2 months:	Pile driving for retaining walls, excavations, and foundations. Sometimes I . . . etc.

EXAMPLES IN THE CLERICAL AND RELATED FIELDS

Average 4 hrs. per day:	I type vouchers in duplicate to accompany invoices, after they have been approved by Mr. Jones and extensions checked by Miss Smith.
2 hrs.:	I type reports from rough pencil copy.
1 hr.: Etc.	I also . . . etc.

---

2 days:	I file purchase orders chronologically and by department and vendor.
1 day: Etc.	I sort and distribute letters.

10%:	I take dictation from Mr. Brown, including letters, memoranda, and drafts of speeches, but Miss White takes all his engineering dictation.
5%: Etc.	I file . . . etc.

Fig. 13 — (Continued)

Suggestions for Filling Out Items 17 to 21

ITEM 17 — Do not change the employee's statement. Read them through and then give your opinion of their accuracy and completeness. Is it a good description of the position? Has he neglected to give a full picture of his duties and responsibilities? Has he overstated or understated them? Has he put emphasis on the wrong points? Either comment generally on his statements or refer to specific items.

If you have a number of positions under you which are practically identical, it will be sufficient to answer Items 18 to 21 fully for one such position only, and then refer to such answers on the other questionnaires. You can merely state, "Same as John Doe."

ITEM 18 — Sum up what you consider to be the distinguishing aspects of the employee's job. What are the most important functions carried on in this position? What operations in the job contribute most to your organization? Is the position a beginning or an advanced one?

ITEMS 19 and 20 — If the job involves any typing or shorthand, even if merely incidental, answer these items completely. If not, check "No."

ITEM 21 — With full consideration of the duties and responsibilities of this position, tell what are the basic qualifications of a person you would choose for the position if it were to become vacant. What must he know? Of what basic subjects, procedures, principles, laws, or regulations must he have a knowledge? Must the knowledge be thorough or is a general knowledge or familiarity sufficient?

What abilities or skills must a successful employee possess? How much formal education is necessary? What course or subjects are required? Which are desirable but not essential? Is previous experience necessary? If so, how much experience, and in what type of work? What degree of physical strength, agility, or endurance is necessary? For what purpose is it used, e.g., for walking, lifting, etc.? Please be as specific and complete as you can in answering these questions.

Indicate, wherever possible, both the basic qualifications required to fill the position and the desirable qualifications which you would like to have in a new employee.

Instructions to Department Head or Other Administrative Officer

Either you or your authorized representative should review the information on the form, complete Item 22 indicating any additions, omissions, or inaccuracies and offering any pertinent comments, and then sign the original of the typewritten copies in the designated place.

Return of Completed Questionnaires

One copy of the questionnaire signed by employee, supervisor, and administrative officer—the original of the typewritten copies—should be submitted for each employee in the department within no more than two weeks of the date of distribution of the questionnaires to employees. The carbon copy of the completed typewritten form is for departmental files.

Fig. 13 — (Concluded)

determining pay schedules, promoting and transferring employees, and developing training programs.

1. An intelligent recruitment program is impossible unless there is enough information about positions to indicate the type of person and qualifications needed to fill them. The information about the duties of the position and its level of difficulty given by the class specification is used to establish the proper qualifying requirements and the testing measures to be used in determining which candidates best meet these requirements.

2. The classification inventory is essential so that a salary may be attached to each position which reflects its relative worth when compared to other positions.

3. A classification of positions is useful in transferring employees, because it helps appraise the extent to which an employee's previous work qualifies him for the duties of the position to which he is being transferred.

4. The inventory is needed in selecting employees for promotion. Each promotion raises the question of who should be eligible for it on the basis of merit and fitness, and the question of compensating the employee at a higher rate for assuming more responsible work.

5. The position-classification inventory also furnishes valuable suggestions for developing training courses. It indicates the types of jobs for which training may be desirable, and the job duties in which employees may need to be trained.

The classification plan must be continuously modified to keep it up to date. When the city undertakes new activities, new classes of positions may be created; when services are discontinued, some classes may be dropped. What is more, the work of individual employees changes from time to time as a result of the addition or deletion of functions, departmental reorganizations or procedural changes. Means must be established for keeping abreast of these changes so that the classification plan will at all times reflect the actual situation of the service. As a continuing matter, both supervisors and employees should be invited to report changes in duties of individual positions, so that positions may be reallocated when necessary. Provision should also be made for periodic review of positions in the service so that any changes which may not have been reported will be observed and the necessary steps taken to correct faulty allocations. Many jurisdictions have established a policy of regularly reviewing a specified portion — usually 20 or 25 per cent of all positions each year.

The question has often been raised as to how many positions are necessary before a classification study should be made. The answer to this can be given categorically. The need for a classification study arises as soon as there are two positions within the same agency. It is necessary to know if those positions embrace identical duties and, therefore, should be compensated at the same salary level. It is necessary to know the relative level of difficulty, so that if there is a difference the higher position will command a higher salary range. The positions must be compared to determine if they can be filled by persons of the same qualifications or if they require individuals of different qualifications.

The Pay Plan

The salaries a city is able to pay its employees will probably be the most important single factor in determining the kind of employees that can be attracted to the city service. Good salaries will not guarantee good employees — if recruitment and selection techniques are inadequate — but low salaries will prevent the city from obtaining very many employees of high caliber.

ACCOUNTANT I

DEFINITION

This is beginning level professional accounting work.

Employees in this class are responsible for the maintenance of a set of accounts in the office of the director of finance or for assisting in a departmental accounting office on assigned phases of the accounting work. Limited independent judgment is exercised in applying standard accounting techniques according to established procedures and regulations. Some employees supervise a limited number of clerical personnel. Close supervision is received by employees assigned to the central accounting unit and the work of all employees is reviewed through regular audits of books and periodic reports.

EXAMPLES OF WORK PERFORMED

Maintains general books of accounts according to established account classifications, including general ledgers and journals; makes adjusting entries and prepares periodic financial statements.

Maintains cost account records by allocating cost items to a variety of accounts, according to prescribed classifications.

Supervises clerical employees in the preparation of payroll time sheets, vouchers for payment of invoices, and summary data for the budgets.

Supervises and reviews the accounting and record keeping work of subordinate units.

Assists in reconciling expenditure control figures with supporting data.

Assists in the preparation of periodic financial reports.

Supervises preparation and processing of requisitions for materials, supplies, and equipment.

Records and balances daily receipts.

Performs related work as required.

REQUIRED KNOWLEDGES, SKILLS AND ABILITIES

Knowledge of accounting principles and procedures.
Some knowledge of municipal accounting principles.
Some knowledge of office methods and procedures.
Ability to maintain general ledgers and journals.
Ability to prepare periodic financial statements.
Ability to supervise and direct the work of clerical employees.

DESIRABLE EXPERIENCE AND TRAINING

Graduation from a four year college or university with major course work in accounting; or any equivalent combination of experience and training.

Fig. 14 — Example of Class Specifications

By and large, salaries are fixed competitively — by the competition of employees seeking jobs of certain kinds, and by the competition of employers seeking employees of certain kinds. If the city wishes to recruit high school graduates for a particular job, it must offer a salary at the same general level that high school graduates are able to obtain elsewhere. Moreover, if it wishes to employ the best graduates for the job, it must offer a somewhat higher-than-average salary, and must be sure that the job is one that affords opportunities for advancement.

For some types of employees — particularly the skilled trades and clerical workers — the city is in direct competition with private employers who use people in the same occupations. In this case, the city must meet the going rates of pay, or must offer compensating advantages such as greater security of employment, or must accept an inferior quality of employee.

In other employments — the police and fire services, teaching, and library work — public agencies may be almost the sole employers. In this case the competitive element is no less present, for salaries must be set that will attract competent people to the occupation, and that will put on the city's payroll the best of those who are in the occupation.

It is a more difficult task to fix salaries for supervisory and administrative positions in city government. Governmental agencies do not pretend to compete with private industry in the compensation of executive personnel. On the other hand, some individuals are attracted to public employment by its security, and because they would rather work for the public interest than for the profit of a private employer. Moreover, the individual who has risen in the ranks of city employees, no matter how able he is, will not usually find it easy to transfer from public to private employment, particularly if his experience is in an occupation peculiar to governmental employment. Hence, competitive forces are not as sharp in determining salary levels for executives as they are at lower levels of the administrative pyramid. Nevertheless, it must be admitted that current salary scales for executives in most cities are not sufficient to attract a fair share of the able and ambitious young men of the country to the municipal service.

Within any one occupation, salaries exhibit a range that depends on the degree of difficulty and responsibility of the employee's work. In fixing the salaries for individual positions, a very important consideration is to get a proper relation between the salaries of the various individuals who work in positions of varying difficulty and responsibility within a single occupational group. Consistency of the salary scale within the city hall is equally important with consistency of the city's scale with that of other employers in the community.

The position-classification plan is the basic tool used to secure this internal consistency. When positions have been grouped into classes, each containing all the positions substantially similar in duties and responsibilities, it is possible to establish salary rates for each class which will be fair and equitable for all positions found in it. It is also possible to compare the various classes of positions within each occupational group so that properly related pay differentials may be established between the several classes. Finally, by making studies of salaries in private employment for positions comparable to particular classes in the municipal service, the pay plan can be related to established wage and salary levels in the community.

For each class of positions there is established a minimum salary, to be paid to employees on entrance to the class, and a maximum salary, beyond which no employee occupying a position of that class can be advanced. In most jurisdictions, at present, pay ranges provide a maximum which represents an increase of 25 per cent to 30 per cent over the minimum salary. Between the minimum and maximum salary are a number of steps to provide for salary advancement as a reward for meritorious service and increased usefulness. In the lower brackets, these salary steps are small, perhaps $10 per month; in the higher salary brackets, the steps may be as large as $50 per month. This is logical, since a very small increase could not be regarded as an adequate reward for increased usefulness in more responsible positions. Increases should bear a percentage relationship to base pay if they are to be meaningful at all levels of employment.

The advantages of a salary range for each class of position are apparent. The minimum salary is judged to be the lowest salary that might reasonably be paid considering the level of difficulty of the work and the kind of person who will be qualified to hold the position. As time goes on, the employee increases in usefulness because he knows more about his work. Therefore, a series of salary steps is provided so that this increased usefulness may be recognized and so that there will be an incentive for the employee to learn more about his work and to improve his performance. The maximum salary is the top salary that may reasonably and economically be paid to any employee performing work of that class. His opportunities to obtain a larger salary than this must lie in being promoted to more responsible work where a new and higher salary range will be opened up to him.

There is great value in having a well-conceived pay plan. In recruiting it provides the basis for letting prospective candidates for employment know what they may expect in the way of compensation for their services. So far as in-service activities are concerned, it has a general "toning up" effect on the morale of the service. It does away with those rankling jealousies which occur when employees are paid at unequal salary rates. It provides for increased incentive to do better work and reap the rewards of salary advancements. So far as the separation phase of personnel administration is concerned, a properly conceived pay plan provides the basis for determining retirement contributions and benefits and for an equitable separation wage.

Recruitment

Getting qualified persons into the service cannot be accomplished in a hit-or-miss fashion. The essential elements of a recruiting program are these: (1) advertising employment opportunities; (2) encouraging qualified people to apply for vacancies as they occur; (3) determining the relative order of fitness of those who apply for particular kinds of work, either through a written test or some other suitable means; and (4) placing candidates in positions for which they are apparently qualified. The methods for accomplishing these objectives may be simple or complex, depending upon the size and character of the city and the state of the employment market.

Advertising Employment Opportunities

It pays to advertise employment opportunities in the public service just as it pays to advertise or to promote any product. The challenge of the public service cannot be met by supinely sitting by, expecting the "best brains and the stoutest hearts" to apply for positions in the public service. The type of employee needed in the public service is one who is a "going individual" and has a high professional regard for his present work. He must be won from his present occupation or attracted to public service at the outset of his professional career.

There are certain techniques which have proved helpful in keeping the citizenry informed about their public service in general and of employment opportunities specifically. If these techniques are properly used, they will encourage qualified people to seek public employment when vacancies do occur.

1. Several public jurisdictions have had very good success with a series of radio talks given by public officers and employees along the lines of a "Know Your Government" program.

2. Many jurisdictions have been successful in encouraging their local newspapers to run a column on government affairs.

3. Talks may be given by various government employees before service clubs, schools, and other public gatherings.

4. Some jurisdictions follow the practice of binding the class specifications together in a volume and making it available to those who want information about the various jobs in the public service. As a modification of this practice, some jurisdictions publish a list of the titles of positions and their salary rates.

This task of "selling the public service" is of a general character and does not attempt to tell about specific job vacancies. Now let us see briefly how specific employment opportunities in the public service are made known to the general citizen.

1. Class specifications are prepared describing the various classes of positions in the service (see Fig. 14), as part of the position-classification plan.

When a vacancy occurs, the class specification is used in announcing the vacancy, so that qualified people may see the kind of position involved and the qualifications required of those who seek employment in that position. These notices are posted conspicuously in schools, libraries, post offices, and other places where the public is likely to see them. In addition to making the notice attractive and having it give a clear picture of the position involved, it is essential that it be brought to the attention of qualified people. Its usefulness will be largely destroyed if this is not done.

2. News stories carried in the local papers are a very effective means of advertising specific employment opportunities in the public service.

3. Radio and television have proved to be excellent media for announcing vacancies in municipal service. Several agencies have had good results with the use of "spot" announcements of examinations.

4. Maintenance of a card file or list for each position, showing the names of individuals and organizations to whom are mailed announcements of future examinations in the particular position and similar positions, is another helpful device. When someone applies for a position in which there is no vacancy, he is told that his name will be placed on the mailing list for that particular position. Some agencies publish a periodic bulletin carrying announcements of all examinations and maintain a mailing list for its distribution.

5. Present employees can be encouraged to carry news of vacancies by word of mouth to their friends who might be interested in the public service. An enthusiastic employee can frequently do a first-class face-to-face "selling job."

Any agency may readily appraise the relative value of the several devices suggested by simply asking the applicant on the application blank where he first heard of the vacancy. Regardless of the method used, the important point to bear in mind is that good people have to be sought out and encouraged to seek public employment. This is done in two ways: first, by arousing community interest generally in the government and describing the challenge that public service offers; and second, by telling citizens about specific vacancies as they occur in the public service.

Attracting Qualified Applicants. In the previous section general and specific techniques for telling about employment opportunities in the public service have been discussed. The need for telling the story in an interesting and arresting fashion so that truly qualified persons might be induced to apply has also been suggested. Next comes the consideration of how qualified persons may be actively encouraged to seek public employment. The basic principle is to get "under their skin" — to make them see the challenge of public employment. This is all the more necessary in higher bracket positions because, generally speaking, government cannot compete successfully with business on the basis of salary alone. It is observed that government as compared to private industry pays generally at a higher rate for lower-level positions and at a much lower rate for higher-level positions. It is in competition for the higher bracket positions that the public service is at a disadvantage in so far as salaries are concerned. Therefore, it must offer other inducements and must make a real effort to secure the best persons possible.

Here are some of the methods that have been used successfully in securing qualified people for public employment.

1. Personal invitations and letters (or even telegrams, in some instances) inviting the person to participate in an examination have proved quite effective.

2. Personnel letters have produced good results when addressed to business firms, professional societies, and professional firms asking them to circulate the notice of the vacancy and the description of it among members of their organization who might be interested.

3. Educational institutions have been "scouted" by some personnel agencies for people with a high potential for doing outstanding work once they are on the job. This is a technique employed quite commonly in private business. It has been used to a limited extent by public service agencies, but not nearly to the degree which its usefulness would justify.

4. Making application relatively easy is one of the best ways to attract qualified personnel. Busy people often do not like to go through the drudgery of filling out an elaborate application form. In public jurisdictions operating under formal civil service systems, it is necessary to impose certain requirements to safeguard the integrity of the system, but care should be taken that these safeguards do not become so cumbersome as to defeat the end of the merit system, which is to secure well-qualified people for the public service.

5. Assurance that their qualifications will be reviewed by their professional equals is one effective means for getting qualified people to apply, particularly in top-ranking professional, technical, and administrative positions. Many jurisdictions follow the policy, in filling this type of position of having outstanding men in the profession to which the position belongs serve as a special examining committee to pass on the qualifications of applicants.

In this section and the one immediately preceding it, great stress has been placed on advertising employment opportunities in the public service and in seeking qualified persons. Along with this, however, care should be exercised to see that every citizen has a fair opportunity to present his qualifications for positions for which he believes himself suited. The public announcement procedure, through bulletin board notices and newspaper stories, gives wide circulation to employment opportunities. However, if public jurisdictions assume a passive role in so far as recruiting employees is concerned, and many of them do, they will not avail themselves of the best possible talent. For this reason, particular emphasis has been placed on the need for seeking out qualified people.

Measuring Candidates for Public Employment

Individuals differ markedly in their basic abilities and skills. These basic traits are further conditioned by the environment in which the individual has been raised. The range of individual differences as they relate to any class of positions in skills and knowledge is tremendous. The recruiting phase of personnel administration has as one of its principal objectives the measurement of these individual differences and the establishment of some order of merit so that those who possess the requisite skills and knowledge to a considerable degree will be placed ahead of those who possess lesser amounts.

The measurement process may be viewed as a series of screens through which those seeking employment must pass in order to prove that they have the necessary qualifications to do the particular job. Each screen is designed to measure a particular attribute that will be needed for successful job performance. These screens must be varied in accordance with the particular position to be filled. The same set of screens obviously cannot be used to sift out the unfit for the position of Junior Stenographer and the position of Junior Civil Engineer.

The screening process for filling any position will be successful only if it is designed with a realistic understanding of the necessary qualifications and with a due regard for the promotional channels open to employees who occupy the position in question. Measurement methods have often been defective in the past particularly because of two factors: (1) failure to recognize that aptitude — or potential for growth — may be more important to many jobs than the present state of the applicant's abilities; and (2) failure to consider promotional channels and the long-term needs of the service. These two factors are very closely related.

1. Aptitudes and Abilities. Many skills can be learned rapidly on the job, with or without formal training. The performance of employees in such positions, after they have been on the job for several weeks, will depend not so much on their knowledge of the job on the day they were selected as on their aptitudes — their knack for learning the particular skills that are required for job performance. A "manual dexterity" test, for example, may be a more valid basis for selecting individuals who are expected to become speedy typists, then a highly competitive speed typing test. The reason for this is that typing speed will vary greatly depending on the opportunities the individual has had for practice immediately before the test, while a good manual dexterity test will be a much better indication of the individual's typing speed "ceiling" if she is placed in a typist's job. Of course, the manual dexterity test would not be used alone but in connection with a typing test requiring a minimum qualifying speed, and certain other tests as well.

To use another example, universities have found that the grades of an entering student can be predicted better from a general college aptitude test, than from tests of his information on particular subjects. In the past, civil service testing has been too much of the specific information or specific experience or ability variety. The trend in progressive agencies is toward examining for aptitudes rather than for specific information in entrance tests.

2. Promotional Channels and Long-Term Needs. There are few Junior Engineer

positions that could not be filled by individuals who lack engineering college training. Nevertheless, engineering graduates are commonly recruited to these positions as a source of promotional material for higher engineering positions. This same principle needs to be applied more broadly in the city service. In recruiting, it must be assumed that the majority of those employed who remain any length of time in the service will be promoted at least once and probably several times. If that is so, then individuals must be recruited who will have training and aptitudes that will later fit them for the higher positions. No one should be recruited to the police force whose education and intelligence will not later make him a likely candidate for sergeant or even lieutenant. This can be overdone, of course. The morale of an army all of whose privates were would-be generals would not be high. Errors have been more often committed in the opposite direction, however.

The principal steps in the screening process are: (1) evaluation of minimum qualifications, (2) evaluation of training and experience, (3) written examinations, and (4) oral interview. These are not always used in exactly the order in which they are taken up here.

Evaluation of Minimum Qualifications. The second screening process occurs in connection with submitting a formal application for the position. It must be determined early in the measurement process which candidates are to be admitted to other tests. If this is not done, the other measurement devices become tremendously lengthy and costly because of the large numbers who must be tested.

When the applications are received, they are studied to see if the individual meets announced requirements as to age, height, and weight, and other more-or-less stereotyped requirements. Some candidates are eliminated on the basis of this preliminary review.

Evaluation of Training and Experience. The training and experience of each competitor should be carefully studied so that a proper rank order may be established of the relative appropriateness of the backgrounds of the candidates. The best practice is to rate training and experience on a combined qualitative and quantitative basis, with greater weight given to recent and especially applicable experience. This may be illustrated by the following example. The training and experience of a group of competitors for the position of Principal Stenographer is being rated. One competitor has had 20 years of stenographic experience, none of which, however, has included more than routine dictation and simple related clerical work.

Another competitor has had five years of stenographic experience, three of which have been as secretarial assistant to the head of a large business organization. On a purely quantitative basis, the competitor with 20 years' stenographic experience would be rated higher than the one with five years of experience. However, for the position to be filled, the competitor with five years of experience has had a much higher grade or quality of experience and should probably be ranked ahead of the competitor with 20 years of experience.

Written Examinations. The written examination may be designed to measure aptitude or acquired knowledge in a particular field. Its basic purpose is to obtain in a reasonably short time a sampling of the knowledge and ability of the candidates. It is impossible to test every ability and all knowledge which the candidate may possess. However, this sampling process follows the same principle as the taking of core borings in a concrete highway to determine if it comes up to specifications. The assumption is made that a sufficient sampling of core borings will show if the road meets specifications and will stand the traffic for which it has been planned. These samplings may not yield absolutely perfect results — the highways may still have some bad spots which were skipped when the sample core borings were taken. The same is true of written tests. Some persons judged to be qualified on the basis of the samplings may later prove to be unsatisfactory on the job because of other deficiencies. However, the assumption may fairly be made that the results of the samplings are reasonably accurate for most individuals.

Oral Interviews. Another very important measurement device is the oral interview. There are two types of oral interviews. One may be called the oral examination where the competitor is actually tested orally with reference to his occupational information in a certain field. This may be done for some positions where it is believed that the type of competitor sought would not participate in a lengthy written examination. It may be conducted for low-grade positions where language inadequacy might be an unnecessary handicap in a written examination.

The oral interview is used more often, however, as a means for determining if the candidate possesses and can demonstrate those personal traits or characteristics which are essential to the position to be filled. Knowledge, skills, abilities, aptitudes, the appropriateness of education and previous experience, and physical condition are best measured by more objective devices. It is best not to attempt to assess any of these during the interview, which is more aptly used for a systematic evaluation of the intangibles of personality and attitude which are important to long-range job success.

The interview should be used to evaluate candidates on such attributes as (a) appearance and voice, (b) facility of oral expression, (c) mental alertness and perceptivity, and (d) attitude. Interviewers must recognize at the outset that absolute "objectivity" is impossible, and in some circumstances may not even be wholly desirable. It is essential, however, to use a systematic procedure and to evaluate all candidates on the same factors in order to arrive at valid conclusions.

This kind of interview is a part of the testing process, and the estimate of the candidate's suitability becomes a part of his final score.

Oral Interviewing Technique. In the small city the oral interview is likely to be a particularly important part of the selection process, because of the cost of conducting formal written examinations where only one or two positions are to be filled. Where this is the case, particular care must be taken with the interview so that it will be a valid selection device. All-too-many administrators possess the dangerous illusion that they can judge a man's personality, character, and ability in a five-minute informal chat. The wise administrator — reflecting on the many occasions when closer acquaintance and association has completely reversed his judgment of a man — is modest of his ability to appraise others. He realizes that if the interview is to have any value it must be conducted according to a carefully-thought-out plan, and that he must guard against snap judgments based on surface appearances. He keeps in mind too that the object of the interview is to evaluate each candidate for the position in comparison with the established standard and with the other candidates. Some of the common-sense rules for successful interviews are these:

1. Plan the interview. A written list should be prepared of the items on which each candidate is to be questioned. If this is not done, the information obtained from several candidates will not permit comparison among them, and important items will be forgotten in some interviews. Preparation of the list will usually show that a part of the desired information can be more easily obtained from the candidate on an application form prior to the interview. The application form can then provide the starting point for additional questions.

2. <u>Put the candidate at ease.</u> The interviewer will be better able to judge the candidate's every-day personality if he conducts the interview with casualness, interest, and sympathy than if he adopts the technique of a cross-examining lawyer.

The interview should be conducted in privacy and without interruptions. The interviewer should greet the candidate in a courteous and friendly manner, and should give him his full attention during the entire interview. By showing interest the interviewer will be able to draw the candidate out. It is usually most effective in the first part of the interview to let the candidate tell his story in his own way, bringing him back to the point if he wanders. His own statement can then be supplemented by further questions on points he has not covered.

Unless the interviewer himself keeps to the point, he will encourage the candidate to waste time with irrelevant matters. Any tendency of the interviewer to talk about himself or his troubles will cast doubt on his interest in the candidate, and will tend to make the candidate ill at ease. The interviewer must make certain his questions are understood. Sometimes apparently false statements by the candidate are due to misunderstood questions. Leading questions that suggest the proper answer to the candidate should be avoided.

3. <u>Discount surface indications.</u> For example, the nervousness, or lack of it, of a candidate is no criterion of his ability, or even (within limits) of his personality. One candidate may be nervous because he is very much interested in the job and anxious to get it; another because he knows he really does not possess the qualifications; a third because he has an introverted personality. Contrariwise, a candidate may be at ease because he is confident of his ability and preparation, because he is indifferent as to whether he gets the job, because he is lacking in ambition, or because he enjoys dealing with people.

Personal appearance is another factor that the interviewer may unconsciously overvalue. Of course, personal appearance, and even handsomeness, may be relevant if the job is one involving numerous contacts with the public or with other people, but in most positions it is a matter of distinctly secondary importance. Other qualities that have no bearing on the job to be filled should also be discounted. In interviewing for jobs which require basically manual skills, undue weight obviously should not be placed on vocabulary and grammar.

The interviewer must make allowance for personalities that happen to differ from his own in non-essentials. If the interviewer is careful of personal appearance he may react unfavorably to the candidate who is presentably but casually dressed; if the interviewer himself is indifferent to such matters, he may react unfavorably to the candidate who is too carefully dressed.

It should be remembered that certain specific characteristics that appear in the interview do not necessarily correspond to analogous characteristics on the job. Neatness in dress is not a reliable indication of orderliness in work habits; much less is the speed or apparent alertness with which the candidate answers questions a measure of intelligence, or even of the speed of his mental processes.

There are a large number of important traits that cannot be reliably measured by the candidate's behavior in the interview itself, such as honesty, cooperation, leadership, and initiative — although evidence on some of these points can be gathered from his employment history.

Above all the interviewer must guard against being taken in by his own pet prejudices or by quack "character analysis" schemes. Scientific research has shown that schemes based on such factors as head shape, handwriting, hair color, and the like are absolutely useless as selection devices. It will help the interviewer to discount irrelevancies if, after the interview, he will make an honest attempt to analyze in detail the bases for his over-all favorable or unfavorable reaction to the candidate. This immediate reaction will be modified by later review of the interview record, but it may subconsciously influence the interviewer's subsequent decision.

4. Check the candidate's statements by getting specific facts. Most candidates will naturally picture themselves in the best light possible, but some individuals are considerably more modest than others. It is in the interest of both the interviewer and the candidate to direct the discussion towards specifics in terms of previous pertinent experience and training. This needs to be done skillfully by the interviewer without obvious effort to deflate or inflate the candidate's own estimate of his suitability for the job.

5. Keep a careful record of the interview. Usually, factual information supplied by the candidate should be recorded while the interview is in progress. If done unobstrusively, the candidate will not be disturbed by this. Immediately after the interview, the interviewer should complete the written record and analysis, following the points of the interview outline. The record should close with a general statement of the interviewer's appraisal of the candidate. If the interviewer permits himself to be interrupted before he makes his record, he will find his impressions fading at an alarming rate, and a record made even an hour later may be practically worthless.

In making the record, the interviewer should attempt, so far as possible, to separate facts from inferences and conclusions drawn from facts. Doing this will increase the objectivity of his judgment and will assist him in analyzing the interview evidence. "The candidate's hair was unkempt" is a much more useful statement in the record than "The candidate's appearance was untidy." "The candidate described four occasions on which he had suggested significant improvements in procedure in a previous job" is to be preferred to "The candidate has great initiative."

6. Give the candidate information about the job. The most important function of the interview is to secure information about the candidate. The interview should also be used to give the candidate an accurate picture of the job to be filled. This will help the candidate decide what kind of information would be relevant, and will often lead him to reveal his own enthusiasm, or indifference to a job of this particular kind.

The interviewer will want to point out to the candidate the opportunities which this job, and employment with the city, will afford him, but he must be careful to avoid overselling the job for this can only lead to dissatisfaction, if the candidate is hired, and rapid personnel turnover. It is best to give the candidate the facts — good and bad — so that he can decide for himself whether or not he would be happy in the job.

The foregoing are the principal screens used in the measurement of candidates for employment. They may be used in various combinations. Ideally all of them should be used. However, there are situations where time and funds will not permit an extensive measurement program, in which case one or more of the screens can be eliminated and still yield better results than the random trial-and-error method for selecting employees.

In addition to these major screens there are others which are often used. These will now be discussed briefly.

Performance Tests. In the performance test the candidate is required to demonstrate his ability by doing a piece of work closely resembling a job situation. Candidates for bricklayer may be required to demonstrate their skill by actually laying bricks. There are many varieties of performance tests that may be used. Since a performance test is an actual sampling of a job situation, it makes a very practical appeal. However, there are a number of disadvantages to its use. In the first place, it takes time for each competitor to execute his assignment, and where large numbers are to be measured it is difficult to do so within a reasonable length of time. It also may mean a considerable outlay for equipment. Moreover, it may place too much emphasis on skill, and too little on aptitudes. However, this testing device has its uses and should not be overlooked.

Medical and Physical Tests. Another screening device is the medical or physical test. Many public jurisdictions require a medical examination before an applicant may be placed on the payroll. Not only is this intended to safeguard the health of present workers but it is also a safeguard to the individual so that he will not be assigned to duties which he is physically unable to undertake. It has a more selfish purpose, too, in that it is a safeguard against specious claims for workman's compensation. The medical examination will reveal any disabling physical defects at the time of employment so that the employee may not later claim a work-connected disability for which the government must pay him compensation. The foregoing refers to the more general type of medical examination which may be given to all employees; but there are other types.

For many occupations it is necessary to have employees who are nearly perfect physical specimens and who have the necessary agility to perform their duties. This is the case with respect to policemen and fire fighters, for example. The physical requirements of these two occupations call for considerable physical endurance and above average agility. Where an occupation is hazardous or the physical requirements are stringent, it is common practice to give a rigorous medical and physical examination. In the medical examination candidates are eliminated who have any serious organic defect which may impair their usefulness in the service or may render them prone to accident. The physical test is designed primarily as a measure of the candidates' athletic ability. It may consist of a battery of exercises including high jump, standing broad jump, rope climbing, and so forth. Usually in such examinations there are minimum and maximum height and weight requirements.

In setting up physical and medical standards, it is essential to avoid going overboard in the direction of imposing unnecessarily high requirements. This is particularly true in a tight labor market. It is also important to recognize that the presence of a physical handicap is not, in itself, sufficient grounds for ignoring the other potentialities of a candidate. Many forward-looking organizations have made notable progress in adjusting their personnel policies to make full utilization of physically-handicapped persons. From the management viewpoint, a highly significant result of such a program has been the discovery that such handicapped persons, when properly placed, are able to hold their own and sometimes excel their able-bodied fellow workers.

Character Investigations. Except in the federal government the character investigation as a selection device is used to only a limited extent in the public service. After all measurements have been applied, there remains the question of the candidate's character and standing in his community. He may be excellent professionally and technically, yet his reputation may show a series of black marks. Attempts to get information about the character of the candidates by letter of reference have produced decidedly indifferent results. In order to get truly reliable character references, it is almost necessary to assign the function to an investigator who goes out into the community and investigates the reputation of the candidate. Such character investigations attempt not only to determine the standing of the candidate in his community but also to determine previous work habits and attitudes as indicated by former employers.

The Original Placement of Personnel

This is the final stage in the recruiting process. Following the administration of the selection measures, it is common practice to rank these competitors according to their performance in the several selection measures. This rank order is determined by combining and weighting their performance in the several tests. It is now assumed that those appearing on such a register are qualified for the particular position for which they have been measured. This is the source of supply to fill those vacancies which are not to be filled by promotion or transfer.

Certification Procedure. The usual procedure for the final selection from among the qualified candidates has been formalized in those cities having a central personnel agency: (1) The appointing administrative officer notifies the agency of the specific vacancy. (2) The names of several eligible applicants are submitted to the appointing officer — the top three, in most cities. (3) The appointing officer interviews those certified and notifies the personnel agency which one he is hiring. All hiring techniques are aimed, however, at helping the appointing administrator find a competent employee, and no system should so operate as to force the appointing officer, either through law or tradition, to hire someone whom he believes will not properly fit into the position.

Probationary Period. The last step in the recruiting process is the probationary or working test period. Most public jurisdictions, and almost without exception those operating under a formal merit system, require that the employee serve for several months on trial to determine if he can do the work satisfactorily, prior to his receiving the status and full privileges of a civil service employee. This working test is highly important, for it is the final measure of the employee's ability to do the work. He should be observed carefully to determine if his performance is satisfactory. Every aid should be given to the employee so that he may become properly adjusted to his new work environment. Too frequently an employee is put to work without receiving proper instructions about his job. This may result in mistakes for which he is not really to blame.

It should be remembered, too, that it is not only the employee but also the organization that is on trial. If the employee is not properly trained in his work during the probationary period, he may feel that the organization he has joined is a second-rate one. Many public jurisdictions are conducting probationary training courses. These are of two general types. One is orientation training designed to acquaint the employees with the general features of the organization for which he works, its functions, the general flow of work through the organization, and the special need for courtesy when his work involves public contacts. The other type is specific job training to enable him to learn the job more quickly and systematically.

There is one problem that should be mentioned in connection with the probationary period. Most jurisdictions provide for a fixed probationary period for all classes of positions. There has been some objection to this procedure, for it is reasoned that a Junior Stenographer may be adequately tried out in her work in three or four months, whereas a Highway Inspector may not definitely prove his worth until he has been on the job for eight or twelve months. There is much to be said for this point of view. The most logical arrangement would be to have a varying probationary period for different classes which would be sufficiently long to permit trying out the employee in all duties that he might reasonably be expected to perform in that position. A street maintenance foreman may be quite satisfactory on summer assignments but later prove unsatisfactory on winter maintenance work. In such cases, the probationary period should be of sufficient length to have permitted the trial of that employee during both seasons and on all types of work to which he might be assigned.

In-Service Activities

Department heads and supervisors are, of course, interested in seeing that qualified people are selected for their working forces. With few exceptions, however, they have no particular person in mind for the job which they have to fill. They may have definite views as to the qualifications of the person whom they are seeking, but in only a few cases have they actually decided on any particular person whom they would like to employ. With in-service personnel matters, however, relationships have been built up between employees and their supervisors. The supervisors have become personally acquainted with the work habits and attitudes of employees and have developed likes and dislikes for employees. These prejudices are also shared by rank and file employees for and against supervisors. Therefore, any personnel process affecting the status of an employee when he is in the service must, of necessity, take into consideration those relationships which have been built up out of the fact that employees and supervisors have been brought together in a work situation.

What personnel processes are involved in the in-service phase of personnel administration? These may be listed: adjustment of the employee to work where his services may be utilized to the best advantage by transfer, promotion, and demotion; measurement of employee performance on the job (service ratings); installation of employee training programs; development of an employee relations policy; establishment of policies and working arrangements with respect to employee unions and other organized groups; establishment of proper policies with reference to hours of work, leaves, and attendance; payroll check and certification; development of health, safety, and welfare programs; establishment of effective machinery for handling employee grievances; and discipline.

Transfers

Employment is not a static affair. Frequently it becomes necessary to transfer an employee from one position to another. Where such a movement from one position to another does not involve a material increase or decrease in the duties and level of responsibilities, it is termed a transfer. Transfers are essential to a proper mobilization and utilization of working forces. They serve a number of purposes, the principal ones being; (1) to effect the proper placement of the employee in a position which will make the greatest use of his skills and knowledge; (2) to train employees in different kinds of work by assigning them to a variety of positions, so that they may later be advanced to more responsible work in higher classes; (3) to bring about maximum productivity in the working forces by moving employees about to take care of peak loads as they occur in various parts of the organization; (4) to alleviate situations where there is a fundamental personality clash between an employee and his supervisor which would be corrected by assignment to another supervisor; (5) to utilize valuable employees whose services might otherwise be lost as the result of organizational changes or discontinuance of functions.

Promotions

Promotion may be defined as the assignment of an employee to a position involving more difficult duties and a higher level of responsibility than the position he previously held. Promotions constitute one of the most important and yet one of the most troublesome problems in personnel administration. A promotion policy that follows the principle of filling more responsible positions only by advancing those already in the service may, in time, lead to a situation in which mediocre persons occupy key positions in the service. On the other hand, a policy that regularly provides for opening higher positions to those outside the service may tend to lower morale, since those in the service feel they do not have a chance for advancement to higher positions.

What the promotion policy should be cannot be categorically stated. The policy should be sufficiently flexible to be adjusted to the particular situation. If there are employees in the lower positions whose qualifications suit them for advancement to the higher positions in question, then it is highly desirable to promote from within the service. If there is any doubt about the qualifications of those in the service to fill the higher position, then those outside the service as well as those in the service should be given consideration.

There is also the problem of opening promotions on a service-wide basis or limiting them to those in the division or department in which the vacancy occurs. The same reasons are advanced for the latter policy as are advanced for not permitting "outsiders" to compete for higher positions. The best solution to this problem is to administer promotions on a service-wide basis. When a promotional list containing the names of qualified people from several departments is established, it is normally desirable to fill promotional vacancies from that list without reference to whether the employee is presently in the department or division where the vacancy exists. There may be special circumstances, however, under which the duties of a promotional vacancy require intimate familiarity with the operations of the unit, which in turn may necessitate limiting the promotion to employees in that department.

An element in connection with promotion recruitment which does not occur in original recruitment is the frequent provision for giving some weight and consideration in the final ranking of competitors to their performance on the job. This is done through service ratings, which will be discussed later in this section. Some argue against using service ratings of the employees on the theory that they are rated on their performance in the positions they now hold and not on their potentialities for advancement to more responsible work. Whether or not service ratings should be used, and the relative weight which should be given to them in the final ranking of competitors, will depend upon the degree to which the higher position possesses characteristics found in the lower positions. If there is a high correlation, it is a fair assumption that successful performance in the lower class provides a valid and reliable basis on which to predict success in the higher class.

Demotions

Demotion may be defined as the assignment of an employee from a position bearing higher duties and responsibilities to a position of lesser duties and responsibilities. It may be used where an employee has failed to make good in a position of a higher class but would be a productive worker in a lower class. It is sometimes used as a substitute for a layoff: instead of laying off experienced workers in the higher ranks, a policy may be adopted whereby employees are reduced in rank to lower classes. They are thus retained in the service so that they may be advanced again should available funds and work create higher positions to which they might be reappointed.

Under this plan, employees are demoted down the line, and the actual layoffs or separations from the payroll occur in the lower-rank positions. Demotion may also be used as a disciplinary measure where an employee is capable of doing the work of a position but is inclined to "take it easy." Sometimes such a demotion may stimulate the employee to produce the work of which he is capable. For the most part, however, demotion as a disciplinary measure does not accomplish the desired results.

Since demotions involve some loss of prestige and usually a loss in salary, means should be taken to insure that supervisors do not use this device capriciously and for reasons other than the good of the service. For this reason, it is quite common to provide that where an employee is demoted, he may appeal the demotion to an impartial agency.

Service Ratings

Service rating may be defined as the measure of worth of the employee in the performance of his duties. Many plans have been devised for rating and evaluating employee performance. Each plan has its followers and its critics. In general, they all have as their primary purpose the provision of some means whereby the supervisor may report on the performance of the employee as he sees it, so that these reports may be of value in showing the relative performance of the employees in any given working force. Regardless of the arguments against service ratings, the fact remains that employees are continually being judged on the performance of their work. It seems logical, therefore, that some means should be devised whereby these judgments can be rendered in a consistent manner which will truly reflect the worth of the employee to the organization. This information is essential if proper decisions are to be made regarding employees who merit consideration for promotion, employees who should be retained if it becomes necessary to lay off workers, and employees who should be advanced in salary as a reward for meritorious service. Almost every decision affecting the status of an employee once he is on the payroll comes back ultimately to his performance on the job. Therefore, it is highly essential that some means be provided for evaluating his present performance.

A service rating may be viewed as the accomplishment profile of the employee. It shows in what characteristics the employee is strong, where he is weak, and where he is average when compared to other employees who are doing similar work. Such a profile is invaluable when making decisions which affect the status of the employee. If the rating shows the employee possesses a thorny disposition, he should not be transferred or promoted to a position involving many public contacts. If the rating indicates he is careless he should not be assigned to a position where accuracy is of considerable importance. Not only do the ratings serve as danger signals to point out deficiencies, but they have a positive value as well. By studying the profile carefully it may be possible to institute corrective treatment whereby the employee may be trained to overcome deficiencies and weak spots in his performance. Service ratings may also show up faulty supervision and point the way for corrective treatment directed toward the supervisor rather than toward the rank-and-file employee. These latter uses of the service rating may, over the long run, prove to be the most productive.

The problem of rating employee performance is still in the experimental stage, as is evidenced by the number of different rating plans now in use. In spite of disagreement among the experts as to the proper rating system to use, there is general agreement about certain fundamental concepts: (1) the supervisor must be carefully trained in the technique of making ratings; (2) the employee should be rated on the work he is doing, in comparison with others doing similar work; (3) the supervisor should be able to justify his judgment by direct evidence indicating how he arrived at the rating; and (4) the employee should have an opportunity to discuss his ratings with his supervisor.

The fourth point in the foregoing paragraph merits special mention. There is a growing conviction that the process of informing the employee of his strong and weak points is one of the most crucial factors determining the over-all effectiveness of the evaluation process. The use of the periodic rating as an occasion for the supervisor to have adequate and informal discussion of his characteristics with each employee, and to make remedial suggestions is an effective means of improving employee morale, attitudes, and productivity. If this vital step is omitted or de-emphasized, the rating process may fail to produce the results which management hopes to achieve.

Employee Training

One of the most important in-service activities is the training of personnel. The growing acceptance of the importance of training and the increasing realization of the administrator's responsibility for establishing and supporting training programs give special emphasis to this activity as a technique of progressive administration. For these reasons the subject of training has been singled out for special treatment in the following chapter and will not be discussed further at this point.

Development of an Employee-Relations Policy

For years it was not recognized that employees should have any part in the formulation and administration of a personnel program. It was thought that the determination of policies affecting the recruitment, placement, and separation of employees was strictly management's prerogative. More recently, however, there has been a growing appreciation of the contributions which employees can make toward adoption and acceptance of modern methods of personnel management.

So long as major personnel policies are decided by management alone, employees will tend to regard them with distrust. A rather general human characteristic is to like and accept the familiar and to resent and resist innovations. Understanding does not readily take place through the media of instruction forms and special bulletins, although they help. True understanding takes place when we work with a problem and follow it through as it unfolds. Thus more effective personnel administration will be obtained as employees are invited to participate in the solution of personnel problems as the answers are being sought. To hand them the answers gives them no appreciation of the problem and results in their feeling that there surely must be a sly trick somewhere.

Management has traditionally been organized through its councils, "kitchen cabinets," and conferences. It has thus been able to offer a united front and to express coherently its views on administrative policy. Until recently employees, on the other hand, have been loosely knit, with diversified and sometimes opposing interests, which often left them a prey to the playing-off of one interest group against another. Without organization there was no opportunity for employees to focus their attention on a common problem, to weigh the interests of the various employees, and to come out with a solution which represented the greatest good for the greatest number. There are strong forces at work now in both public and private enterprises leading to a more effective organization of employees so that their views may be coherently and intelligently presented through spokesmen of their own choosing.

Nothing seems more in keeping with the traditions of our democratic form of government than granting employees the right to organize into associations which have for their purpose the betterment of employment conditions. Not only are there real gains to be effected through helpful suggestions made by spokesmen representing the employees, but there are intangible benefits to be derived from permitting employees to share in the credit for a good personnel program which is well administered and accepted. It is far simpler for management to formulate personnel policies without the delays occasioned by consulting and negotiating with representatives of employees. Of what avail is it, however, to decide on a policy and then have it disregarded or its effectiveness seriously diluted because it is not acceptable to employees? In nine cases out of ten the same policy determination would have resulted through consultation with employees. The important point is that if the employees have shared in the formulation of that policy they will see to it that it works.

Employee Unions

Associations of municipal employees have more and more been taking the form of unions, affiliated in many cases with the American Federation of State, County, and Municipal Employees, the International Association of Fire Fighters, or the Fraternal Order of Police. "Blue collar" workers in municipal government are also frequently affiliated with local trades and craft unions. Municipal governments have by no means settled the question of what the attitude of the city should be toward such unions of municipal employees.

From one standpoint the problem of unionization of public employees is inseparable from the attitude of the public and employees toward unions in general. In an industrial city whose private industry is largely unionized, attitudes favorable to unionization of public employees, and a desire of the employees themselves for organization will generally prevail. In a commercial city, located in a predominantly rural area, or a residential suburb, apathy or even hostility toward organization will more likely be encountered. For this reason, the chief administrator must realize that many of the questions involved are rather basic and difficult policy questions, and that primary responsibility for formulation of the union policy should rest with the community and the city council, rather than with the administrative staff. The chief administrator retains the important responsibility, of course, of advising the council on the probable effects of alternative policies upon employee relations and morale.

The carry-over of the philosophy and techniques of the labor union movement into public employment creates special problems. The city, though an employer, is still a representative of the public interest, and policies that might be appropriate in the relations between employees of a private business and their employer might not be suited to the relations of city employees to the city government.

Strikes. It is widely, though by no means universally, felt that the strike is not an appropriate weapon against a governmental employer. Events of recent years have made clear, however, that the problem is not really one of public employment, but of the interruption of services that are essential to the public health and safety, or to the economy. Many public functions fall into this category, but so do many private industries (coal mining, and transportation, for example). An answer to this problem in municipal government can be framed only against the background of general public attitudes and laws concerning strikes in essential industries.

Closed Shop. The introduction of the closed shop into municipal government would violate both the laws of public employment and the principle of the merit system. Unions of governmental employees have not advocated the closed shop, although in actual practice the closed shop has been (extra-legally) obtained for employees in the skilled trades in many cities.

Union Recognition. "Recognition" means simply the willingness of the city government to negotiate with the unions as representative of its employees. There are certainly no legal obstacles to recognition. The demand of some unions for a written contract with the city raises more difficult questions, and the extent to which personnel officers can go in binding a city to a contract, as well as the subject matter of such contracts raise broad legal questions.

Hours of Work, Attendance, and Leave

A well-conceived personnel program will establish policies with regard to uniform hours of work for employees, vacation leave, sick leave, and other leaves of absence. Not only are the stockholders in the public enterprise interested in seeing that employees are paid a salary commensurate with their work, but they want assurance that the employees are performing their work according to a reasonable and uniform work day. Wide variation in hours of work and in the various leave privileges will only result in employee unrest and dissatisfaction. The careful work of salary standardization may be destroyed or seriously impaired by failure to establish uniform regulations in hours of work, attendance, and leave. For example, a clerk receiving $300 a month for a 44-hour week is receiving less than a clerk doing the same work at the same salary for a 38-hour week. Although he takes home the same pay each month, he is presumably producing more and thus is receiving less for each unit of work, as well as for each hour worked.

Health, Safety, and Welfare Programs

It is difficult to appraise the dollars and cents value of health, safety, and welfare programs. Such a value must be considerable, however, for most of the large industries operating under the profit motive have elaborate programs running into great expense. Probably in no other phase is the public personnel program so deficient as it is in respect to these activities. For the most part safety is left to the building superintendent, who is usually not qualified in this particular field. The health of employees, if it receives any consideration at all, is usually in the hands of untrained rest room attendants. Adequate nursing and medical care is offered in only a few public jurisdictions. Posture furniture to prevent excessive fatigue is seldom found in public offices.

Perhaps the principal retarding factor has been that these programs are regarded as frills that cannot be undertaken at public expense. Actually, such programs have a legitimate place in public personnel administration. Those public jurisdictions which have incorporated these programs are able after a few years to offer evidence of their value in improved employee morale and efficiency. The same has been true in forward-looking private industry where management has given major emphasis to work environment factors affecting the health and safety of employees.

Pay Roll Checking and Certification

The certification of payrolls before salaries are paid is essential to secure reliable information with regard to employment conditions in the various departmental organizations and to provide a means of enforcing compliance with rules and regulations governing personnel transactions. The purpose of this certification is not to penalize appointing authorities who are acting in good faith for minor irregularities but to enforce compliance with required procedure and legal requirements. Payroll certification makes possible a uniform system of personnel accounting and thereby insures uniformity in hours of work, in leaves granted, in the use of descriptive class titles and compliance with salary schedules.

Grievance Procedures

As an organization grows larger and more complex, definite policies for channeling and disposing of employee grievances are imperative. In the final analysis, grievance procedures must fit the size and nature of the organization and the degree of geographical centralization or decentralization. Experience shows that effective grievance machinery rests on certain tested principles, including the following:

1. Management effort should be directed toward detecting and eliminating potential causes of grievances before they arise.

2. Grievances should be settled as close as possible to the point of origin.

3. When settlement cannot be achieved at the immediate supervisory level, appeal to the higher management echelons should be simple, direct and final. An overly elaborate grievance procedure involving time-consuming appeals through several levels to the top is not only ineffective but can also become a major grievance in itself.

Discipline

Closely related to the employee-relations policy are questions of discipline. Discipline, in this connection, simply means orderliness. In any organization, even of moderate size, certain rules and regulations must be established to insure that all employees will devote their efforts to the organization goal, and will not neglect their duties. If the organization is adequate in other respects — if it is receiving constructive, positive leadership from the top administrators; if it has an adequate employee relations policy; and if, as a consequence, employee morale is high — discipline will not be a serious problem. Even in this case some attention needs to be given to the exceptional employee who will abuse his privileges, take advantage of the leniency of his superiors, and whose laxness will demoralize his fellow employees unless it is kept in check.

The topic of leadership has already been discussed at length in Chapter 4, and the topic of employees relations in the previous sections of the present chapter. Little needs to be added except a few comments on how discipline can be maintained in a manner consistent with the principles that have already been laid down for developing cooperative relationships between employees and the administrative staff.

Disciplinary policies need to be designed on the assumption that disciplinary measures will have to be applied only to the exceptional employee. Self-discipline, based upon morale, leadership, and employee participation, should be the general rule. Rigid, legalistic tardiness rules, for example, may do more harm to the attitudes and efforts of the vast majority of employees than they will accomplish in gaining an additional twenty minutes attendance, per week, of an offender. Whenever it becomes apparent that rigid discipline is necessary to enforce attendance during working hours of most employees, there is conclusive evidence of a serious failure in leadership.

There may be exceptional situations where elaborate systems of points and penalties — merits for superior performance, and demerits for breach of the rules — may be useful for securing discipline. In most cases, however, such a system turns the whole matter of rules observance into a game, with the employees playing on the opposing team to the management. A more constructive approach is, first, to define clearly the employees' obligations and duties in a comprehensive employee-relations policy, and second, to see that the policy is reasonably and impartially enforced by the supervisory staff.

"The need for disciplinary action arises under a great variety of circumstances. The ordinary causes include: (1) inattention to duty — tardiness, laziness, carelessness, breakage or loss of property, etc.; (2) inefficiency; (3) insubordination, violation of law or regulation, including the rules against political activity; (4) intoxication; (5) immorality;

(6) lack of integrity, including violation of a recognized code of ethics, failure to pay debts, soliciting or accepting a bribe, or deliberately neglecting to enforce the law. A common formula which is elastic enough to cover a multitude of sins is 'conduct unbecoming an officer.'"[1]

In any event, and especially when an employee may be likely to appeal, the reasons for the action should be reduced to writing in as specific and concrete terms as possible. By doing this at the outset, management narrows the issues and helps to focus attention on the specific grounds for taking action, rather than leaving opportunity for allegations of discrimination or personal prejudice.

Among the formal disciplinary methods that are available for dealing with situations calling for such action are oral or written reprimands, overtime work, demerits, withholding salary increases, loss of seniority rights, fines, suspension without pay, demotion, and removal.

The selection of the proper disciplinary method is a difficult one which does not lend itself to any simple formula. Several general suggestions can be made, however. First, the principal object of discipline is to improve the performance or behavior of the offender rather than to punish him. In some cases, punishment may be the best corrective for his faults, but in other cases severe discipline may destroy the employee's spirit and diminish his future value to the service.

Second, certainty and promptness in disciplinary action are usually more effective than severity. Particularly to be avoided are periodic "drives" for enforcement of tardiness, safety, and other rules, with periods of lax enforcement between them.

Third, before taking disciplinary action, every effort should be made to determine why the employee failed to observe the rule. Not only will unfairness be avoided in this way, but situations may be revealed where the employee, by reason of conditions at home, of health, or the like, is prevented from doing his best work, and where it may be possible to assist him in solving his problems.

Fourth, the punishment should "fit the crime." The severity of disciplinary action should be related to the offense. It would hardly be wise or just to discharge an employee for being tardy once. Repeated minor offenses, however, can become serious as suggested below.

Fifth, penalties for repetition of offenses should be of increasing severity, and should lead after several offenses to dismissal. Retention in the service of an employee who persists in violating the rules will only demoralize the other employees.

Disciplinary action will normally be initiated by the immediate superior of the employee who is to be disciplined. Where the penalty imposed is severe (suspension, demotion, or removal), final approval should be vested in a higher official.

Separations

Every employee entering the public service will some day leave it for one reason or another. The problems of separation are equally as baffling and complex as those encountered in dealing with employees in the service. Work relationships — good, bad, or

---

[1]Leonard D. White, Introduction to the Study of Public Administration (New York: The Macmillan Company, 1955), pp. 394, 395.

indifferent — have been established between the employee and his department head, and each has developed a definite opinion of the other. Employees have developed a proprietary attitude toward their positions. The sum of these problems makes the question of developing an adequate separation program one of the greatest challenges facing public personnel administration today.

Four of the important types of separations may be recognized readily: (1) layoffs due to lack of work or funds; (2) temporary suspensions for disciplinary purposes; (3) dismissals for incompetence, insubordination, or conduct unbecoming a public employee; and (4) retirements.

Layoffs

Layoffs are not to be confused with disciplinary separations, for they occur only as the result of the need to reduce forces because of lack of work or funds. Practices in effecting layoffs vary considerably. Usually, the order of layoff is based upon seniority or a combination of seniority and service rating. The weight attached to the service rating usually depends upon the adequacy of the service rating system or the degree of faith in its objectivity. Customarily the names of employees laid off are placed on re-employment lists with preferred status for appointment when vacancies occur in the class for which they have been found qualified.

When reductions in force are necessary it is reasonable to expect that appointing authorities should give primary consideration to the good of the service. This means that consideration should be given first to the activities to be curtailed and the classes of positions which will be affected. Any arbitrary reduction without regard to the needs of the service may do irreparable harm and may result in a penny-wise and pound-foolish policy. The second consideration involved in a layoff is the determination of which individual employees should be released. In deciding this question primary consideration should be given to merit and fitness, although some weight should also be accorded to seniority. The employee's merit and fitness will be reflected in the periodic rating reports covering his performance. There is little consistency in a personnel program which religiously adheres to the principle of merit and fitness in deciding other personnel questions and then reverts to the exclusive use of a nonmerit factor, such as seniority, in effecting layoffs.

Employee groups as a general rule have favored seniority as the basis for making layoffs. This has resulted from their skepticism or outright distrust concerning service ratings as they are now administered. As previously noted much of the skepticism and distrust has arisen because of lack of participation by employees in developing the rating system. Most of the benefits of improved security and the attempts to establish a career service are lost when layoffs are based solely on seniority.

Suspensions

Suspensions constitute a disciplinary action intermediate between a reprimand and an outright dismissal. Usually a time limit of 15 to 30 days is established on suspensions during which the employee receives no pay. When it is believed that an employee's attitude or work habits are such as to call for a greater penalty, the appointing authorities should be required to use the machinery provided for dismissals. A system of suspensions is desirable to enable the appointing authority to maintain proper control over subordinates.

Dismissals

There is great diversity of opinion concerning the proper method for handling dismissals of employees who fail to measure up to a reasonable standard of efficiency or whose work habits and attitudes constitute an unwholesome influence on their associates. There is general agreement that the employee should be protected against arbitrary and capricious dismissal for religious, political, or personal reasons and that some means should be established to prevent dismissals for these reasons. This is one of the most perplexing problems in public personnel administration today. On the one hand there are many public officials who oppose centralized personnel administration on the grounds that it interferes with their control over their working force. They resent any formal control over their decisions, and more specifically those controls relating to the dismissal of employees.

On the other hand, there are the employees, who almost without exception want a review of dismissal actions with final authority for the dismissal vested in an independent agency. They demand this on the grounds that it is the only protecting bulwark against the prostitution of the public service by prejudicial action of politically-minded appointing authorities. Both sides have probably overstated the problem. Many administrators who complain most bitterly against the unreasonable protection afforded the public employee under certain formal systems have never tried to dismiss an employee and are not in a position to speak authoritatively from first-hand experience.

It seems, therefore, that the solution to the problem lies somewhere between absolute control and no control, to be exercised by an impartial agency. Public personnel administrators have explored this middle ground with a view to developing a procedure that will satisfy both viewpoints. The following appears to be the most effective means for accomplishing this: an employee should have the right to appeal his dismissal to an impartial body. The investigation of this agency would be thorough but any hearings would be conducted informally without the aspect of a court trial.

The agency may then either sustain the action or make other recommendations concerning the disposition of the case. The agency would not, however, be empowered to enforce its recommendations except when the dismissal was made for political, religious, or personal reasons. Under this procedure the employee is protected against dismissal for arbitrary reasons. He is protected against unfounded evidence for it is unlikely that an appointing authority would go through with a dismissal which would not stand a public airing. As noted earlier in this chapter, it is wise management policy to provide a discharged employee with a statement setting forth, on a purely factual basis, the specific grounds for action. This policy can in itself do a great deal to reduce the number of appeals.

Retirement

If a career in municipal service is to be made attractive to city employees, definite provision must be made for their retirement when they reach an age when they can no longer perform their duties with the necessary skill or vigor. A sound retirement policy is equally essential from the standpoint of administrative efficiency. The usual result when a city does not have a formal retirement system is that there grows up a practice of granting disguised pensions — of retaining employees on the payroll when they are no longer competent to do their jobs. It is hardly to be expected that an employee who has given 25 or 30 years' service to the city will be summarily dismissed and left without means of support, but many objections can be raised against the disguised pension as a method of taking care of him.

First of all, the presence in city offices of these employees who are obviously not doing a full day's work, is harmful to the morale of other employees and gives the public an unfortunate impression of the municipal service. Moreover, a scheme that is based, as this one is, on a "charity" concept is not fair to the self-respect of these veteran employees. Finally, the city has no way of knowing what its disguised pensions cost, or whether all superannuated employees are treated on an equitable basis.

To meet these objections every city needs a definite, clear retirement policy, and a formally established retirement system to carry out the policy. It is usually considered desirable to finance the system by joint contributions of employees and the city. The city can justify its contribution because of the retirement system's value for employee morale and because the system relieves the city of its burden of disguised pensioners. Employee participation in the plan encourages in the employee a sense of responsibility for his future financial status and, since the city also contributes, the element of "forced saving" does not often meet strong employee opposition.

However financed, the system should be operated on an actuarial basis, that is, contributions should be set at a level which will provide over the years sufficient funds to pay the benefits which have been promised. Since the total benefits paid are usually deceptively low during the first few years, rising steadily as more employees reach retirement age, a plan cannot be successfully operated on a cash basis. The only way in which proper contribution rates can be fixed, sufficient to produce the funds needed for benefit payments, is by a careful examination by an actuary of the age distribution and life expectancies of city employees in relation to the benefit provisions and retirement ages specified in the proposed retirement act. A system of rates which has worked satisfactorily in one city, or which has been calculated by an actuary for that city, cannot safely be adopted by another city without an independent actuarial examination. Hence, one of the first steps to be taken by a city that contemplates setting up a retirement system is to call in a competent actuary.

Like any insurance scheme, the plan must cover a sufficient number of employees to pool the individual risks — many authorities think there should be several hundred. Consequently, the small city may not be able to set up a sound system of its own. Where a statewide retirement system for municipalities exists, participation in that system is undoubtedly the best solution for the small city. In other cases it may be possible for a number of cities to set up a joint system, although legal difficulties would stand in the way in most states. Still another possibility is for the small city to contract with a private insurance company that underwrites group retirement plans.

A wide range of benefit provisions is to be found in existing retirement systems. It is generally agreed that eligibility for retirement should be based on a combination of age and service factors. It is not good practice, nor is it consistent with the basic aims of a retirement system to permit (as is done in many fire and police pension plans) retirement after 20 or 25 years of service regardless of age. While some arguments might be advanced for setting a lower retirement age, (and correspondingly higher contribution rates) for policemen and firemen than for other city employees, there is certainly no reason why any man who is not disabled should be retired at age 46 simply because he has been 25 years in municipal service. Pensions are intended to take care of employees who are no longer able to render effective service by reason of age or disability — they are not a reward for rendering a stated amount of service.

Benefits, on the other hand, will usually vary with years of service. The contribution rates can be set at such a level that an employee who has served, say 25 years, will receive a retirement allowance of 50 per cent of his average salary for that period, with a correspondingly larger or smaller allowance for longer or shorter service. The specific allowances can be written into the act, but perhaps a more flexible and financially sound plan is to provide that the accumulated contributions of the city and the employee, with interest, will be used when the employee retires to purchase him an annuity. The amount of this annuity, though not absolutely fixed, could be estimated with sufficient accuracy so that the employee would know how large an allowance he might expect.[2]

Most retirement systems make retirement compulsory on the attainment of a certain age. In view of the increasing average age of the population and the increasing number of able-bodied older citizens, many authorities are beginning to question the wisdom of such provisions. The future is likely to see the retirement age made variable, in accordance with the ability and desire of the individual to continue working.

Allowances for prior service — service accumulated before the plan was established — is always a troublesome problem in setting up a new plan. To give full allowance for such service would usually require prohibitive contributions from the older employees, and usually the city is willing and able to foot the bill, prior service usually receives only partial credit in computing allowances. Membership in the retirement system is usually made optional for persons already employed by the city when the plan is established, but compulsory for new employees.

More and more jurisdictions are investigating the advantages of integrating local retirement systems with social security. By taking this approach, the basic provisions of social security coverage become the floor of the total retirement plan, upon which is superimposed the employer-sponsored retirement system of the municipality.

In addition to the importance of retirement plans to the over-all personnel program their effect upon the financial position of the community is also important. Following is a 1957 policy statement of the Municipal Finance Officers Association:

"Many local governments are not financially able to pay the compensation required to attract career employees but offer as an alternative inducement to enter public service superannuation pay or retirement income.

"It is suggested that: (1) public administrators recognize that at present competition exists for qualified personnel and that failure to more nearly meet competitive rates of compensation and provide for meritorious promotions at an accelerated schedule, and to grant reasonable fringe benefits for employees who perform efficiently and competently, can result in inferior technical and administrative staffs to the detriment of public administration generally; (2) governmental units should recognize the merit of providing superannuation, pension or retirement income as a supplement to federal social security benefits. Such provisions are importantly essential in effectuating a policy of economy and efficiency in public administration."[3]

Non-Merit Factors in Personnel Administration

Although many public personnel systems are silent on the positive features of an adequate program, virtually all at some time or another offer special considerations to

---

[2]These suggestions obviously touch on only a few of the most important features in a comprehensive retirement policy and plan. For further discussion of this topic see Retirement Plans for Public Employees (Chicago: Municipal Finance Officers Association, 1958).

[3]Part of a resolution adopted by the Executive Board of the Municipal Finance Officers Association on June 6, 1957.

large or small groups of applicants and employees. Among the most significant non-merit factors — factors which do not bear a direct relationship to merit and fitness — are the following:

Veterans' Preference

The loss to the men and women who serve their country in times of war can never be properly appraised. Many meet death, others are permanently disabled, others are forced to interrupt promising careers and have difficulty in picking up the threads again. Probably the larger part of this debt to the veterans can never be paid. No one will deny the reasonableness of some preferential credit to veterans who are capable and who desire to enter the public service; but thinking veterans themselves are opposed to a system of preference that would in any way injure the public service.

Perhaps the most satisfactory scheme of veterans' preference is one which (a) fixes minimum educational and experience qualifications and a minimum passing grade on the examinations for veterans and non-veterans alike, and (b) allows veterans who meet the qualifications and reach the passing grade a certain number of additional points. Schemes that allow additional points to all veterans without reference to minimum standards and schemes that place all veterans receiving a passing grade at the top of the eligible list are less desirable — certainly from the standpoint of the public service, and often from the standpoint of the veteran who is thereby placed in a job he is not competent to perform.

Where veterans' preference is granted, it behooves the personnel agency to take active steps to interest the best veterans in the public service. Unfavorable experience with veterans' preference after the first World War was due, in part at least, to the fact that many persons who were unsuccessful in private positions were attracted to the public service by veterans' preference allowances. At present the term "veterans" includes the great majority of American men born since 1916. Out of this great reservoir of talent the public service, even if hampered by unreasonably extreme preference laws, can secure by a program of positive recruitment first-rate employees for public positions.

Since the justifiable purpose of preference laws is to aid the veteran to re-establish himself in civilian life, veterans' preference should be granted only in examining for original appointments. In matters of promotion, dismissal, and layoff the veteran should stand on the same footing as other employees, making his own way by meritorious service.

Residence

One of the principal factors contributing to the low prestige of the public service has been the residence barrier which excludes all but "home town boys for home town jobs." Many persons who would be interested in a career in the government are either barred by these personnel "tariff walls" or are discouraged from embarking on a career which is limited to a restricted geographical area. The practice is particularly vicious when it operates to restrict the opportunity of the government as employer in filling technical, professional, skilled and other high posts. Certain parts of the government service have escaped this blight to a large extent. School teachers, city managers, and librarians, for example, are commonly appointed without regard to residence. For the lower grade clerical and unskilled positions, where salaries are relatively low, there is much to be said in favor of recruiting the personnel locally. Transportation and living costs make this necessary in most instances. When the application of a hard and fast residence requirement deprives a community of the opportunity of recruiting qualified people who live within a few miles of its boundaries, however, there is strong argument for dispensing with such restrictions.

Seniority

Seniority is the lazy way out of problems of personnel administration. It is readily reduced to a single formula which employees can understand and, for the most part, endorse. Except for its simplicity, the seniority basis for making personnel adjustments has little to commend it. If it could be fairly assured that increased usefulness and efficiency went hand in hand with length of service, then the problems of personnel administration would be largely solved. This does not prove to be the case, however, and in spite of the difficulties involved in appraising employee performance the answer to making personnel adjustments on the basis of proved merit and fitness must lie in this direction.

Dependency

The concept that those with dependents should be given preferential consideration in appointment, promotion, and retention again stems from the charity concept of the public payroll. When other factors are equal such preferential consideration may be in order, but as a substitute for merit and fitness it has little place in modern personnel administration.

Chapter 7

TRAINING FOR THE MUNICIPAL SERVICE

Modern municipal government as a rapidly changing, increasingly complex service demands skills, knowledge, and attitudes which can be acquired only through training. Experience, a valuable teacher to be sure, has not been adequate to the task of providing familiarity with physical and administrative innovations. As the impact of city government on urban life has grown, the need for training and retraining has become more urgent, calling for better direction of the training function by the chief administrator.

The chief administrator may call on the educational system for help, he may delegate authority for the organization and development of certain parts of a training program to the personnel officer, he may expect supervisors to function as important figures in the program, but the ultimate responsibility for the skill and competence of city employees is his. The educational system shares in the responsibility because training is an educational activity; the personnel officer because training is closely tied in with other personnel functions; and the immediate supervisor because a large portion of the training takes place in the normal day-to-day relationships between the supervisor and those supervised. However, since training in the broad sense can be the most important means of achieving city efficiency and effectiveness and since the chief administrator is responsible for effective and economical direction of city business, the chief administrator must devote a significant portion of his efforts and time to the general field of training.

Few administrators would question the value of training, but many neglect it because of an insufficient knowledge of what should be taught, how instruction should take place, and who should be trained. This chapter is designed to aid the administrator in finding the answers to the "what," "how" and "who" of training.

Some Basic Definitions

What Is Training?

The first requisite of training is that it must aid the employee to increase his skills or knowledge; a second requisite is that the skills and knowledge must be intimately related either to the work in which the employee is engaged or to work to which he may be assigned; a third is that a program designed for this purpose must be planned and organized. Combining these specifications, one may accept the definition proposed by the Committee on Employee Training of the Public Personnel Association: "Training is the process of aiding employees to gain effectiveness in their present or future work through the development of appropriate habits of thought and action, skill, knowledge and attitudes."

Several aspects of this definition are important. Even though the employee may become more effective in his work entirely through his own unaided efforts to improve himself, this is not considered training. Training includes the concept of aid for the employee in the process of increasing his competence — aid which may assume a variety of forms, as suggested later in this chapter.

A second aspect of the definition is the emphasis placed upon the employee. Training is not the imposition of skills and knowledge from above or from the outside; it is a process in which the role played by the employee is of maximum importance. Training must result in a change in the work habits of the employee, in his attitude toward his job, or in the information and knowledge which he applies in his daily work. Without active participation by the employee, it is very unlikely that this change will occur. This concept of training as a process in which both the trainer and the trainee participate is of exceptional importance. It is the basis of several training principles to be discussed later, and it conditions the success of the training program.

A third aspect of the definition concerns the phrase, "effectiveness in their present and future work." A training program is intimately related to specific practical jobs. The employee may participate in a variety of educational programs which are not termed training because their relationship to the present assignment of the employee or to tasks to which he may be assigned in the future is remote or nonexistent. This emphasis is the basis for the distinctions which follow in the next section concerning the various forms of education and training.

Terminology of Training

"Training" and "employee education" are used interchangeably by some but are considered by others to be mutually exclusive. The definitions which follow are intended only to clarify relationships among various forms of education and training and do not, of course, state fully the content of any one of the terms. They also serve to distinguish between (a) educational opportunities made available to the employee for self-improvement along lines of his choice and as a stimulus to morale and (b) educational preparation aimed directly at raising the level of occupational performance. In the former, government takes an interest; for the latter, it assumes responsibility. A city government does not have the time, money, or resources to identify training with education and assume responsibility for providing all the educational opportunities demanded and required by employees. On the other hand, the city government should not go to the other extreme and say, as some public service trainers urge, that training is not education but something completely divorced from the educational process. What, then, are the various forms of education and training as they relate to the public service?

1. Pre-entry education — the sum of all educational experience acquired by the individual before he is accepted as an employee.

2. Pre-entry training — that portion of pre-entry education which may be given an individual in contemplation of his entering a specific occupation but prior to his acceptance as an employee.

3. Post-entry education — the sum of all education experience acquired by the individual after he is accepted as an employee.

4. In-service training (or post-entry training) — that portion of post-entry education which is designed to improve performance in, or to prepare for, a specific employment.

5. Vestibule training — that portion of in-service training which prepares an individual for a specific occupation or employment after he is accepted as an employee but before he actually goes on the job.

These definitions will be useful only to the extent that they are not permitted to create hard and fast lines. To illustrate, a course in Spanish might legitimately be considered in-service training for a policeman in a Texas border town or for a file clerk in a New Mexico recorder's office, but it would be considered post-entry education for these same employees in other cities where Spanish has only a cultural value. The distinction between in-service training and other forms of post-entry education is not a line but a shadowland. There will be differences of opinion as to where particular programs fall — whether in the realm of in-service training or among other forms of post-entry education. But if the basic test — the relationship of the program to the work of government — is kept constant, many current conflicts will disappear.

Training as a Philosophy

There is some danger that training may, in the process of definition, be reduced to mere mechanics. It has already been suggested that training is a process implying an interacting relationship between trainer and trainee. Training is also an administrative way of thought. A group of top executives in industry are reported as having estimated that nine out of every ten management functions can be classified as education and training. This is because the basic task of management is to get work done economically and effectively, and wherever there is work to be done employees must be trained to perform this work with economy and effectiveness.

If training is incorporated in the administrator's thinking about his job; if training is considered an integral part of the administrator's method of getting work done; in short, if training is part of the administrator's working philosophy, then training will assume a variety of constructive forms which will condition the attitudes and work-habits of employees from top to bottom of the administrative organization.

Wholehearted acceptance by the administrator of the training idea will enable him to visualize training opportunities in his day-to-day relationships with his subordinates, will facilitate the use of staff conferences for training purposes, will lead to the planning of employee experience in terms of training, will facilitate a continuous administrative search for training opportunities wherever they exist or can be made to exist. Only by such wholehearted acceptance will training become a live, creative method of making government work.

Pre-Entry Training

While pre-entry training is not a matter in which the city is primarily concerned, the administrator will want to be certain that his personnel policies — and particularly his recruitment policies — are designed to take best advantage of the great stream of educated men and women that is produced by colleges and universities.

Securing a fair share of the top-flight college graduates for municipal employment is not merely a matter of active recruitment. The public service must be prepared to receive them, to give them constructive practical experience to supplement their academic training, and to make possible careers for them that can compete in attractiveness with the careers offered by private industry. On three points, particularly, city recruitment policies need to be reviewed: (1) residence requirements, (2) opportunities for employment of scientific and professional students, and (3) opportunities for employment of students trained in the social sciences and business. On the first point only a word is necessary. As long as residence restrictions prevent professional and administrative employees from moving freely from city to city, cities will be at a grave disadvantage with other organizations in recruiting such persons.

Except for the residence problem just mentioned, cities are generally quite well prepared to receive and employ the graduates of engineering, law, and medical schools. In this area perhaps more adjustment is needed in the schools than in the cities. While the professional school does a satisfactory job of technical training, it often does nothing to prepare its students to deal with the legal, fiscal, or administrative problems of city government. Yet from this group of engineers, doctors, and lawyers, the city customarily recruits many of its department heads and other responsible administrative employees. Public officials could perhaps take the initiative here to urge upon professional schools a broadening of their curricula which would permit students to be introduced, at least, to the problems of government and administration.

In the field of the social sciences, employment opportunities are less satisfactory, yet training in business, economics, public administration, and sociology would appear to be the most appropriate background for those officials who will be concerned with the city's fiscal, personnel, and planning problems. Career lines need to be opened in the city government which will lead from college graduation, through subordinate posts where the employee can gain constructive experience, and finally — for those persons who have proved themselves — to the top policy-making jobs.

There is general agreement that training in municipal administration should be at the graduate level and that the training should be either preceded or accompanied by public employment. The full cooperation of city governments will be needed to make this possible. They must provide interneship opportunities for new graduates who have not had previous work experience, and they must give every encouragement to educational leaves for their own junior administrators so that they can take advantage of the graduate programs offered by the universities.

These are the principal areas, then, in which the city administrator needs to concern himself with pre-service training in colleges and universities. He must provide opportunities to college graduates for careers in the municipal service; he must encourage some broadening of professional training to include an introduction to governmental and administrative problems; and he must cooperate with the universities in developing training programs at the graduate level which combine training in public administration with actual work experience.

Establishing a Training Program

Organization for Training

Problems of organization for training are not serious. The primary responsibility of the chief administrator has already been established. The responsibility flows down through the organization, each supervisor in the line assuming responsibility for the development of his subordinates. This responsibility may be most easily fixed by calling to account the supervisor whenever an employee is demonstrably weak or incompetent in the performance of his job. No employee should be discharged without a full accounting by the supervisor of methods used to train him.

While an employee may often be personally at fault when it is necessary to discharge him, the fault more often than not lies (a) with the recruitment process by which he was originally selected, (b) with the work conditions which cause him to become mal-adjusted, or (c) with the supervisor who has not taken sufficient time and pains to tell him what his job is and to teach him how to do it. The training of supervisors is an important aspect of any training program and will be discussed more in detail later in this chapter.

Even though training is a responsibility of the operating departments, certain auxiliary services are necessary in order to make it effective. Information should be collected on training opportunities outside the city government — in the public schools, in institutions of higher education, in zone classes conducted cooperatively by several cities, in correspondence courses conducted by professional organizations, in institutes conducted by state and federal agencies, etc. Supervisors need not only constant stimulation but organized assistance both in training on the job and in arranging formal classes with teachers and course materials. In addition, some training programs will be called for which cut across bureau or departmental lines — e.g., a course in public relations for reception clerks and other employees in constant contact with the public.

Auxiliary training functions are of sufficient importance as an aid to operating departments to make it imperative that at least one individual in every city government, large or small, be given definite responsibility for the stimulation and development of training. In the smallest city governments, for lack of personnel and resources, the chief administrator will find it impossible to delegate this responsibility and will have to assume it himself. In the medium-sized and larger cities, where authority can be delegated, the question arises as to where the auxiliary training should be delegated. Wherever the personnel agency is an integral part of the administrative organization, where it is doing a positive personnel job as a service to the operating departments, there are several reasons why auxiliary training activities should be provided by the personnel agency.

1. Training is supplementary to the recruitment process. The nature of experience and education made a prerequisite to employment determines in large degree the training job to be done. In-service training and prerequisites to employment must be harmonized and integrated to produce fully competent employees.

2. The classification plan will, to a very large extent, furnish the basis for training content in terms of class duties. A future development of the class specification may very profitably include a statement of the in-service training required if the employee is selected in accordance with the qualifications set forth in the specification.

3. Service ratings disclose employees whose training is weak and, if carefully analyzed, reveal training requirements which are common to many employees.

4. If the personnel agency reviews disciplinary cases, it should be assured that supervisory responsibility for training has been fully exercised. A situation apparently requiring disciplinary action may, as already suggested, be caused by supervisory laxity.

5. The promotional system often provides credits for the completion of training courses. If promotions are carefully controlled by the personnel agency, some discretion needs to be exercised as to courses for which credits will be allowed. This discretion can perhaps best be exercised if the personnel agency is also in charge of the development of training.

Enough has been said to demonstrate the desirability, always in theory, often in practice, of associating training with other personnel activities. There are still many city governments, however, where the personnel agency, because it is primarily a "control" rather than a "service" agency, is remote from the operating organization. Under no circumstances can training be permitted to become remote from the daily administrative routine. It is successful only when it becomes part and parcel of that routine. Administrators cannot successfully be compelled to accept a training program; rather they should be persuaded to accept it as a positive aid to administrative performance. Rather than assign auxiliary training functions to a "remote" or "negative" personnel agency, the administrator should seek an alternative. He may either make the training supervisor directly responsible to himself or attach the training supervisor to some other agency, such as the budget office.

The first alternative is usually to be preferred, as training is not intimately related to the other managerial or auxiliary functions of government.

In order to assure departmental control of training activities and to keep the training supervisor working and thinking in terms of departmental requirements, it will usually be found desirable to establish a steering committee representing department heads and employee organizations. It is particularly important that employee groups be consulted continuously in the development of the training program inasmuch as employee interest is an essential ingredient of the training bill of fare.

Incentives for Training

Without active employee participation in planning for training, the program is apt to run into the insurmountable barrier of employee apathy and lack of interest. This failure to secure initial planning has caused the downfall of more than one apparently well-conceived training program. Mere representation on the steering committee which plans the program is not in itself a sufficient stimulus to employee interest. Active administrative interest in the provision of training opportunities will do much to assure employees that their efforts to increase competence are appreciated in administrative quarters. But the administrator should go even further to assure himself that every trained employee has an opportunity to apply his training on the job and that no employee is hampered by an unsympathetic or incompetent supervisor. Lack of opportunity to apply training to the job can be disastrous to morale and may destroy all employee interest in training.

Suggestions have been made for other incentives such as giving credit for the completion of training courses in service ratings and promotional examinations. The fact that an employee has completed satisfactorily a given course should certainly be spread on his personnel record for the information of any appointing officer who is considering him for promotion. It is highly doubtful if he should be given fixed credits for the completion of a course. There are several reasons:

1. The increased competence of the employee should be reflected on the job, and the service rating should measure competence in terms of job performance rather than in terms of courses completed. The same can be said of promotional examinations.

2. Giving fixed credits for the completion of courses may fix in public service training the curse of the academic curriculum — taking courses merely for the credit attached.

3. Courses which may increase an employee's qualifications for promotion to one position may have no bearing on his qualifications for promotion to another position.

4. Awarding of credits will involve the personnel agency in the difficult if not impossible task of discriminating between courses which qualify and those which do not.

The best incentives are active administrative interest in the training program, the satisfactions that come from better performance of the job and the better rendering of service to the community, and the knowledge that increased competence on the job will be measured by service ratings and promotional examinations. These are to be preferred to fixed credits of any kind.

The Training Survey

In the initial stages of a training program a thoroughgoing analysis of the training situation is required. Such an analysis should be based on the following data:

1. Number of employees
2. Occupational classifications
3. Previous education of employees
4. Previous experience of employees
5. Age distribution of employees
6. Need for training opportunities
   a. Expressed by supervisors
   b. Expressed by employees
   c. Revealed by service ratings

This preliminary analysis should be followed by a conference with the steering committee in order to develop:

1. An appreciation of the philosophy and significance of in-service training

2. An appreciation of the fact that training goes on in some manner and that it might as well be done in the best way

3. Review of current training techniques — both those used within the government itself and those used elsewhere

4. Identification of major training requirements

5. Determination of what is needed to meet these requirements by way of:

   a. Development of training opportunities within the government
   b. Use of local public schools
   c. Use of local or near-by colleges and universities
   d. Use of services provided by state agencies
   e. Use of services provided by federal agencies
   f. Use of services and materials provided by national professional organizations

Similar conferences may be needed with bureau chiefs and supervisors who are unrepresented on the steering committee. In any event the conferences should result in a determination of training priorities, a determination of specific training programs to be developed within the government, and a determination of outside resources to be tapped. Such a training analysis will usually disclose at least the following large groups of employees who require training:

1. Fire and police officers
2. Employees who meet the public
3. Professional and scientific employees
4. Administrative personnel
5. Supervisors
6. Clerical employees
7. Employees who write letters

These large groups are, of course, subject to further breakdown. A large police force, for example, will require individual training programs for:

1. New recruits
2. Experienced patrolmen
3. Command officers
4. Record clerks
5. Communications officers
6. Detectives
7. Crime prevention officers
8. Identification experts

Any thoroughgoing survey of training needs will usually not stop short of including every city employee. Even the chief administrator should not overlook the possibility that he himself might profit by participation in an organized training program.

Training Within the City Government

The smallest city cannot avoid the necessity of conducting some of its own training, but even the largest city will profit by taking advantage of cooperative facilities available outside the city government. A comprehensive municipal training program will therefore always partake both of intramural training activities and of outside resources. This section will deal with the development of training opportunities within the government, and the next section will present some of the cooperative facilities that are available.

There are certain simple questions which need to be answered in the development of the training program. What are its objectives? What methods are best adapted to fulfill these objectives? What shall be the content of the training program? Who shall train? Who shall be trained? When shall the training program be given? Where shall the training program be given? One additional question will be discussed later in this chapter: how can the training program best be evaluated?

Definition of Objectives

It is axiomatic that the objectives of any training program should be carefully and specifically defined. Without a clear concept of purpose at the outset, it is impossible to develop a constructive program, employees will probably be disappointed, and the training movement in the city government may receive a serious setback.

Objectives will usually be found in one or more broad groups:

1. To provide the employee with specific skills which he does not now possess or to develop specific skills in which he is not adequately trained. These skills may be manipulative (how to shoot a revolver with speed and accuracy) or non-manipulative (how to interview a relief client in order to obtain complete and accurate information). In either case the objective is to equip the employee to perform a specific operation.

2. To provide the employee with information which he needs in order to perform his daily tasks competently. As an illustration, a fireman needs basic information about the chemistry of fire in order to "size up" a fire intelligently and to take adequate precautions against common hazards in firefighting.

3. To provide the employee with the proper attitude or approach towards his job. For example, the command officers of the police department should understand, appreciate,

and accept the proper concept of the role of the city government in labor disputes. Similarly, the traffic officer should appreciate and accept the proper approach toward a traffic law violator, the building inspector should accept the proper approach to the citizen in order to secure cooperation in observance of the building code, and the reception clerk should adopt the proper attitude toward the inquiring citizen. Training objectives which fall in this class are often the most difficult to achieve because they involve replacing deep-seated prejudices and habits with new ways of thought and action. Some of the most subtle successes in training are won in this field.

4. To prepare the employee for promotion to a higher post or transfer to another job. This objective usually partakes of one or all of the first three but is mentioned separately because it sometimes raises special problems, particularly if there is no opportunity for the employee to apply his training immediately to the job.

5. To provide the employee with a basic understanding of the objectives and operations of the whole organization for which he works. It is often desirable for the employee, particularly the routine worker, to get a glimpse of the major objectives of his department or city government and to understand the functions of the major agencies. Even though this insight may not impinge directly on his work, it stimulates his morale and makes him a better representative of the government in the community. Courses designed to fulfill this objective are often called orientation courses and must be planned with care and ingenuity in order to maintain interest at a high pitch.

6. To provide the employee with a thorough understanding of all work being done in the city government or in the community to which his own work is related. In the case of the routine worker filing documents day after day, it may stimulate morale to see how the filing process contributes to order and dispatch in government business. In the case of the relief investigator it is absolutely essential that he understand the functions of other welfare agencies, public and private, with respect to his clients.

Objectives must be carefully defined, because in many cases they will determine the methods to be used.

Methods of Training

Methods available to accomplish the objectives just enumerated are many. They range all the way from informal attempts of a professional employee to improve the work habits of his secretary to formalized classes for groups of employees taught by instructors.

Thumbnail sketches of a few available methods may aid in decisions as to which method or methods to select for a given purpose.

Demonstration. Whenever it is desired to develop manipulative skill, the demonstration is called for. The principles of the four-step method, which is a tradition in vocational education, are particularly applicable to this training device, although they are applicable elsewhere also. The four steps are:

1. Preparation. The mind of the learner is prepared to receive the training by the teacher, who relates the new skill to skills already learned and states some of the uses of the new skill, thereby creating a desire in the learner to acquire it.

2. Presentation. The teacher demonstrates the new skill.

3. Application. The learner then practices the new skill under supervision until he acquires some "doing" ability.

4. Testing. The instructor devises situations where the learner can utilize the new skill, and not until he can use the skill to the satisfaction of the teacher and without help is the lesson complete.

These four steps are designed to take the learner along a process which may be diagrammed as follows:

Expert "doing ability" level

Amateur "doing ability" level

Appreciation level

Information level

Uninformed

The top level is often attained only by extensive experience in the use of a skill. A fire officer may be trained to the point of amateur ability in sizing up a fire, but he will become an expert only by experience in sizing up a variety of types of fires.

While these educational principles are easy to recognize in the transmission of a manipulative skill, it is more difficult to devise situations where they can be applied when a non-manipulative skill is involved. To put it another way, it is more difficult to reproduce actual working conditions under which a trainee can, for example, practice and be tested in the art of interviewing. Yet training is most successful when carried on under actual working conditions.

Conference Method. The conference method, which is widely used in vocational education and which is just beginning to find its place in public service training, is just another name for organized group discussion, in which a small number of persons seek by group thinking to advance the thinking of each member of the group. The conference method has been found particularly valuable for:

1. Enabling a group of experienced workers to profit by sharing their individual experiences.

2. Reaching solutions to difficult problems for which there are no generally accepted solutions.

3. Persuading an experienced group to accept voluntarily principles and solutions which could not be imposed upon them.

4. Leading a group to recognize a need for further training by the identification of pressing problems in their work which they are unable to solve for themselves.

5. Securing an analysis of particular jobs to which all members of the group contribute or on which they all agree.

The conference method is just a variant of the scientific method generally accepted by modern scientists, philosophers, and psychologists. Generally, the several steps of a conference discussion are: (a) identification of a problem, (b) assembly of facts, (c) selection of those facts which are relevant to the solution of the problem, (d) evaluation of the facts, (e) formulation of a decision. The extension of the scientific method beyond the conference would involve the application and testing of the decision or solution in actual practice.

The "pure" conference is one in which the leader gives no instruction and imparts no information, functioning only to draw out the members of the group and to organize their thinking for them. As such it is the most democratic method of training because content is contributed entirely by the trainee group. In practice the "pure" conference is rarely if ever achieved. By his selection of ideas and his organization of them, the conference leader necessarily contributes to conference content.

Experienced conference leaders have evolved techniques with which anyone who utilizes this training method should be familiar. Space permits only a brief summary here of some of the special applications of the conference method:

1. The staff conference, which is a familiar administrative device in any organization, may very well be given a frequent training objective by the intelligent use of the conference method. The chief executive who trains himself as a conference leader will find unusual opportunities to convert the staff conference into a training device for the enrichment of his department heads.

2. The training of department heads as conference leaders enables the use of this training device throughout the organization.

3. The most frequent application of the conference method has been in training of foremen and supervisors. The wise administrator recognizes the need for improving the quality of supervision in almost any organization, in view of the importance of the intimate relationship which exists between superior and subordinate. The way in which this supervision is developed is perhaps the most important single factor in determining the morale and effective performance of the employee. Unfortunately supervision is still an art and not a science, and supervisors and foremen are notoriously "set" in their ways. The conference method is a means of securing voluntary acceptance of best principles and practice by a democratic sharing of information and experience. The successful use of the method depends on a leader skilled in drawing out discussion and in helping the group to organize and evaluate its own thought.

The Lecture Method. The lecture method, although still in wide use in both the educational system and public service training, is often looked upon as an outmoded educational tool. The lecture has undeniable weaknesses. Only the most inspired and able lecturers can maintain the attention of an audience at a high pitch over any appreciable period of time, and then the audience is often held more by the speaker's voice, tone, manners, and appearance than by the content of the speech. Some, if not most, of every lecture is lost by each member of the audience due to the rise and fall of his attention. These weaknesses are, of course, intensified whenever the lecturer is neither inspired nor particularly able.

But the lecture, despite its weaknesses, is the best method for accomplishing certain purposes. Because of its inspirational possibilities, it is sometimes a method of stimulating a group to further study. If printed materials are unavailable, the lecture becomes the quickest and surest way of imparting factual information. It is also a method of orienting a group in the objectives of either the training program or the governmental organization for which they work. Finally, the lecture gives the training group a personal contact with outstanding leaders which they sometimes cannot secure in any other way.

There are a number of devices which can be used to supplement the lecture and which compensate for some of its weaknesses. A mimeographed outline placed in the hands of the audience prior to the lecture enables trainees to follow the lecturer's thought more closely. It also has the merit of compelling the lecturer to organize his own presentation. Mimeographed summaries of the lecture enable trainees to recall significant points which are made. Trainees can be instructed in methods of taking notes. Visual aids such as charts, film strips, and even sound films may enable the lecturer to put his idea across more effectively.

If an open forum follows the lecture, trainees are enabled to participate actively, the speaker discovers obscurities that need to be cleared up, and the speaker is compelled to test his presentation against the observations and criticisms of the group. Wherever possible the speaker should be persuaded to define the objectives of his lecture as precisely as he can, realizing always that a limited number of precise objectives is more apt to be realized than a large number of objectives vaguely defined. By such means as these the weaknesses of the lecture method may be minimized.

Planned Experience. Whenever it is desired to give an employee some versatility, carefully planned rotation of assignments may be the best training device. This is the method used to train medical internes, who specialize for a few days, weeks, or months at a time in obstetrical cases, first-aid accident cases, contagious diseases, and so forth. It is equally useful to give well-rounded experience to a police detective in various classes of felonies and misdemeanors, to a personnel assistant in the various functions of the personnel agency, or to an administrative assistant in the various activities of the administrator's office.

Thus an administrative assistant may spend a month accumulating material for the annual report, a second month making initial reviews of budget estimates, a third month on a classification survey, and a fourth month making recommendations to the manager on all matters pertaining to two or more departments. As this process continues he will acquire some understanding and skill in public relations, finance, personnel, and coordination. If the experience is to have real training value, it must be planned with a training objective and should be supplemented by reports from the trainee and conferences with his superior based on these reports. Carefully planned experience of this type often has rich training values. Some of those who have utilized it successfully are city managers in training their assistants, the TVA in training junior personnel workers, and the New York City health department in training professional public health doctors and nurses.

Other examples of planned experience with a training objective are attendance at conventions and visits to other cities. National, regional, and state conferences of public officials are no longer the junket trips of a bygone day. State leagues of municipalities and national professional organizations have developed programs designed primarily to aid the public employee to solve his problems on the basis of the experience, information, and insight of his colleagues. Periodic attendance at a convention lifts the employee out of his rut and gives him a sense of belonging to a larger group which is striving with him for similar ends. Carefully planned visits to other cities, near or far, enable the employee to become acquainted with new techniques by seeing them in actual operation. A city government will progress very slowly if it learns only from its own experience.

Still another type of planned experience is the temporary exchange of personnel. This device is used very rarely, but it has rich possibilities despite the obvious administrative difficulties involved. A six-month exchange of able, alert police lieutenants would benefit both the men and the police departments they serve. An exchange of employees between a state and a municipal government would broaden the point of view of both the supervisory government and the supervised government. Because of lack of experience, considerable experimentation with this device is needed.

Any of these types of planned experience — convention attendance, inspection trips, and exchange of personnel — should be controlled by the requirement of a full report from the employee involved if the training values are to be fully preserved.

Educational Leave. Many employees seek educational leave for the purpose of completing work for a degree or to secure training at some outside institution which is unavailable elsewhere. Whenever this leave is requested without pay, it should be freely granted. Few employees will be found indispensable, and the administrator should make every effort to encourage the educational ambitions of employees.

Occasionally the leave sought by the employee will serve the interests of the government to the point where leave with pay may be granted. This has been the case, for example, where policemen have been sent to the FBI National Police Academy for training which would not otherwise be available to the city.

There are some who would encourage in the public service the university practice of granting sabbatical leaves to be used by the employee for any desired purpose with the intent of stimulating the freshness of viewpoint which comes from new experiences and change of scene. Sabbatical leaves would have undoubted values for selected employees, but the value for all employees would be questionable, and the difficulty of drawing the line would be great. At present no governmental agency grants regular sabbatical leaves, but many governments grant educational leaves with pay under close control to insure that the governmental interest will be served.

Visual Aids. It is well known that many people are visually minded — they learn more from charts, diagrams, pictures, and moving pictures than they do from the spoken or written word. Visual aids are therefore a valuable supplement to teaching methods. However, visual methods rarely function as an independent method and must be tied in with other methods such as the conference and the lecture.

Experiment is required before the training values of the film are fully known. The administrator who seeks to develop a film for training purposes should consult a film technician before he proceeds. The film technician and the trainer must be brought together before a good film with maximum training value can be produced. The average city government will rarely find it economical to produce a film for the training of its own employees because of the expense involved.[1]

Circulation of Reading Materials. A flow of literature comes in to every city hall which can be utilized for training purposes if it is classified and routed to employees according to their specialized interests. From time to time employees may be required to read and report on books which bear significantly on their jobs. One outstanding police department requires its command officers to report every two months on one book from a prepared list of references not only in police work but in public and business administration generally. This is a training device which any city, no matter how small, can put into effect at once. The brief report required from the employee should, of course, show how his reading reflects on his job. It is often possible to secure the cooperation of the public librarian of the city in the development of this training device.

What Shall Be Taught?

How can the content of a training program best be determined and developed? The basis of an in-service training program designed to improve performance on the job is an analysis of the job itself to discover the manipulative operations, the non-manipulative skills, the related information required to perform the job with maximum competence and effectiveness. Job analysis is a fundamental technique in vocational education. It should be at the command of every instructor who seeks to do a thorough job of teaching.

---

[1] A relatively new development is the "filmed case study." The Division of Audio Visual Education, Graduate School of Business Administration, Harvard University, has compiled a library of such studies.

Job analysis has, however, been developed most extensively for trade and industrial occupations where manipulative skills are paramount. It remains to be seen whether job analysis can be applied successfully along traditional lines to occupations such as those found in the public service where non-manipulative skills, a sense of relationships, and an understanding of basic objectives are the heart of the job. It is significant that the only widespread application of job analysis to a public service occupation comes in the work of the fireman, which has a distinct trade and industrial character.

However, the fundamental objective of job analysis — to give instruction "functioning content" (i.e., to tie the instruction to the job) — is sound, and it is to be hoped that analyses will continue to be made of occupations in city government. In order to be useful, however, these analyses must be based on something more than a "time and motion" study of the job involved. The analyst must have a clear concept of relationships and attitudes which are necessary to give the analysis significance.

The use of job analysis as a basis for course content assumes the availability of several exceptionally skilled workmen in the occupation whose knowledge and experience can be tapped to develop job content. Outstanding workers in the occupation are always a principal source of information as to what should be taught in order to improve job performance. But other sources should be utilized wherever available. State and local training programs should be tied in with standard systems of procedure and with accepted principles at every opportunity.

A program for training municipal accountants not only should train in the operation of a municipal accounting system in accordance with law and practice within the state but should also equip the accountant with an understanding of municipal accounting principles which will enable him to be a constructive critic of local practices. Standards are being developed along national lines in many functional fields — fire, police, finance, health, recreation, personnel — which must find their way into local training programs if they are to be effective.

It should be remembered also that many advances within a field of activity come from outside as well as from inside the field. A civic organization, the National Fire Protection Association, has been responsible for many improvements in fire department administration. The uniform crime reporting system which is the basis of police records systems in this country was formulated not by policemen or police chiefs, but by men trained in the field of general administration.

Training content will develop from the experience of skilled workers in the field, and content should always have the approval of these workers, but every available source should be utilized. Job analysis should be recognized both as a source of training content and as a means of developing an interest in training by those for whom the training program is designed.

Who Shall Train?

It has already been suggested that every employee responsible for the work of others is a trainer. What is said below about the selection and training of instructors applies equally well to the training of supervisors as trainers.

In some local training programs it becomes necessary to select an instructor. Every such instructor should be experienced and skilled in the work in which the trainees are engaged and should be known by the trainees to be so. In other words, the instructor should have occupational experience, skill, and prestige. In addition the instructor must have the ability to teach, to "put over" what he knows. In a few cases this ability may come naturally, but in most cases it is developed by means of teacher-training. Within certain limits, teacher-training services are available from the state board for vocational education in every state and should be requested by any city official concerned with a training program. A teacher-training program gives the potential instructor an appreciation of the difficulties encountered by the beginner or learner, a basic understanding of the psychology of learning, a knowledge of teaching techniques available, skill in the organization of teaching materials, and some practice teaching under supervision.

These are the primary factors to be considered in the selection of an instructor— occupational skill, experience, prestige, and teaching ability. Consideration may also be given to such factors as speaking ability, writing ability, cooperativeness, diversity of experience, and a variety of personal traits such as initiative, persistence, patience, tact, intellectual integrity, and leadership ability. A word may be said about diversity of experience and intellectual integrity. Other things being equal, the teacher with experience in more than one governmental organization has an advantage over the teacher whose experience is limited to a single jurisdiction. The wider experience is apt to induce a breadth of viewpoint which prevents a man from saying, "This is the way it should be done because this is the way we do it in this city." He is more apt to think along sounder lines: "This method is right because it is tested by experience in many places and is superior to other methods which have also been tested and found wanting." The last viewpoint is a hallmark of an able teacher and leads to the second trait mentioned — intellectual integrity.

The teacher who possesses intellectual integrity has the courage to say, "I don't know, but let's find out" when such is the case. The teacher without intellectual integrity attempts to bluff his way through when his knowledge and experience fail him. Bluffing is a serious defect in the teaching of children because it is unfair to the children. In the training of adult workers it is not only unfair to the workers, but the teacher himself can rarely avoid being found out. In any case the teacher who will bluff has no business being a teacher.

When and Where?

These questions are of minor importance but are included because they must be answered in planning a program. The basic question of time is whether the training program should be conducted on government time, employee time, or both. If a training program is designed to improve proficiency on the job, there is every justification for its being conducted on government time. At the same time it must be recognized that in a number of municipal activities the absolute necessity of having employees at fixed posts and the lack of an adequate supply of "relief" workers requires that employees sacrifice their own time for the sake of the training program. Many governments have run successful "after-hours" training programs. A useful compromise, often adopted, is to split the program between government and employee time. In the city of Eau Claire, Wisconsin police officers have responded well to a program providing payment for training after hours, with training pay deferred throughout the year until shortly before Christmas.

The most convenient location for a formal training class is, of course, the city hall. If suitable classrooms and conference rooms are not available in the city hall, however, facilities of the public schools or a near-by college may be secured.

Should Training Be Continuous?

The complaint is sometimes made by department heads and supervisors that employees spend so much time in training that they don't have sufficient time to do the government's work. The solution to this difficulty is simple. The process of improving employee competence is a continuous one. It is involved in most of the contacts between a supervisor and his subordinates. Formal training programs where employees must be taken from their jobs are only one segment of the training program and should never be permitted to become so frequent that governmental work suffers rather than gains.

Formulating the Training Program

This chapter has discussed the various elements of a comprehensive training program: how to determine what employees are in need of training and what types of training are needed by each group; how to select the proper training methods; and how to organize the necessary training facilities. If the city government is to have an adequate training program these elements must be fitted together into a definite administrative plan for training. Formulation of this plan is the responsibility of the training officer, subject to the approval of the chief administrator. If there is no training officer, direct responsibility for drawing up the program and seeing that it is carried out falls upon the chief administrator himself.

The training plan can best be formulated in three parts: vestibule training for positions filled by outside recruitment, vestibule training for positions filled by promotion, and other in-service training. The two "vestibule" programs should explicitly provide for the training of every single employee, in every single classification, who is new to his job. The third program divides again into two parts: a temporary program for present employees who should have, but didn't, receive vestibule training; and a long-run program of periodic re-training for all employees.

In developing the plan, a complete schedule should be prepared for each position class in the service showing, for each of the programs listed above, exactly what training is needed and how it will be carried out. Among the items to be included in this schedule are: the agency or agencies responsible for each part of the training program (will the training be done by regular line supervisors, by a departmental training officer, or by a training officer in the central personnel agency?); the frequency with which re-training should be given (how often should a series of management conferences be offered for command officers in the fire department?); the time required to carry out the training; and the best instructional methods for each portion of the program.

On the basis of these schedules for individual position classes the training officer can work out his program of "courses." In many cases employees from several position classes can be handled together — in a public relations training course, for example. The training officer will need to determine for each course of training what facilities — rooms and materials — will be needed, the number and length of sessions required, where instructors are to be secured and how trained, what instructional methods are to be used, and how the expenses are to be financed.

It is obvious that a plan as comprehensive as this cannot be developed overnight. Emphasis in the early stages will naturally center on vestibule training, but may gradually shift to the re-training program. At every stage the active cooperation of the individual departments must be secured. On them will rest the primary responsibility for determining training needs and for developing their supervisory staff for training functions. If the departments show themselves sympathetic to the idea of training, a great deal of decentralization may be permitted, and is highly desirable, in carrying out the program. If the departments are not convinced of the importance of training, greater pressure — and salesmanship — from the chief administrator's office will be required, and the departments will need more help in analyzing training needs and developing programs.

Regardless of the degree of decentralization that is permitted, the training officer should have full information about the training being carried on in each department, so that the chief administrator can judge the adequacy of the program. After the comprehensive plan has been drawn up, the periodic reports of the training officer to the chief executive should indicate to what extent the plan is actually being carried out, and should measure, so far as that is possible, the effect which the training program is having in improving the work of city departments.

During the initial stages of the training program, special attention needs to be given to the training of instructors, a prime responsibility of the training officer; the training in management of department heads, a personal responsibility of the chief administrator; and the training of supervisors, a joint responsibility of the training officer and the departments. The department head who has seen the values of training as applied to his own job will usually be an enthusiastic proponent of training within his department. The chief administrator is the only one in a position to start his department heads off on their personal training programs, both by setting them an example in his own case, and by organizing conferences for them.

Training Department Heads

This matter of training department heads has already received some discussion, in Chapter 4, as one aspect of the job of direction. There are three principal areas in which such training is needed: (1) technical training in the departmental field of specialization, (2) training in techniques of management, and (3) an introduction to the broad problems of municipal government. Training under the first heading will usually have to be left to the department head himself, although the possibilities of group training among the top personnel in each department have hardly been touched in most organizations.

As far as training in management and in local government problems are concerned, the responsibility rests clearly with the chief administrator. The conference method is usually the most effective for training of this type and level, but something is probably to be gained by bringing in a qualified outsider, perhaps a professor at a local college, to organize and lead the discussion. Such a conference leader can keep the discussion on an objective level, help the group formulate abstractly their everyday problems, and draw out the broader implications of their very practical and concrete experiences.

In the case of training in local government, full use should be made of expert talent outside the city hall. Joint conferences with state and federal officials might prove a highly valuable part of such a program. A professor of public finance might be called in to discuss federal-state-local fiscal relations. Several of the department heads, too, would be able to contribute in the fields of their specialties; the city attorney, for example, in the field of municipal law.

Training Supervisors

Experience with training in industry has shown that the first-line supervisors are a key group in the training program. Their attitudes toward training, like those of the departmental administrators, will do much to determine the success or failure of the training program. Moreover, no matter how extensive the formal training program is, a large part of all of the training that goes on in the organization will continue to be the informal day-to-day training of employees by their immediate supervisors.

Supervisor training is usually most effectively conducted by the conference method. A very effective program of such training was developed during World War II by the War Manpower Commission, and was widely applied in industry and in the federal government. This Training Within Industry program consisted of three separate courses: (1) the job-instruction program which was designed to teach supervisors how to instruct employees; (2) the job-methods program which was designed to help supervisors raise employee output by making the best use of personnel and facilities at hand; and (3) the job-relations program which was designed to guide supervisors in their relationships with subordinates. In addition, there was a course in program development which was designed to tell management how to go about establishing and carrying out a training program.

The job-instruction course would be applicable to almost every city department. The War Department gave the course to all administrative personnel, including civilians. The first part of the program teaches the supervisor how to get ready to instruct: constructing a time table; breaking down the job into its important steps; preparing the right equipment, materials, and supplies; and having the work place properly arranged. The program then teaches how to instruct: preparing the worker — putting him at ease; finding out what he already knows; getting him interested; presenting the operations one at a time, stressing key points; trying out the worker, having him do the job, correcting errors, having him explain key points; following up — putting the worker on his own, checking frequently, and encouraging questions.

The job-methods program is designed to develop in supervisors a constructively critical attitude toward their work. The four steps involved are: (1) analyzing the job; (2) questioning every step — why it is done, where it should be done, how it should be done, who should do it, when it should be done; (3) developing the new method — eliminating unnecessary details, combining steps, rearranging the sequence, simplifying the steps, writing up the new method; (4) applying the new method — selling it to the boss and the operators, getting final approval, putting the new method to work, giving credit where credit is due.

The job-relations program proceeds on the premise that people must be treated as individuals. In dealing with personnel problems, the supervisor is instructed to: (1) get the facts — making sure he has the whole story; (2) weigh alternatives and decide; (3) take action — determining who should handle the problem, and the proper timing; (4) check results — following up on the action, watching for changes in output, attitudes, and relationships.

The programs where built up on the premise that all supervisors have five needs; knowledge of the work, knowledge of responsibilities and organization procedures, skill in instructing, skill in improving methods, and skill in leading. Experience shows that the skills acquired through this training become a part of day-to-day operations. They develop supervisory confidence and resourcefulness in how to proceed. They are simple, down-to-earth, understandable, and usable by the man on the job. They should have wide applicability, with a little adaption, to the city hall.

It can be seen from this brief outline of the training program for general employees, for department heads, and for supervisors, that the potentialities of such programs are limited only by the amount of time which can be made available for training purposes. The chief administrator who understands the part that training can play in building a competent staff will not be penny-wise and pound-foolish in begrudging the time and effort needed for this activity.

Cooperative Training Facilities

One theme which has run consistently throughout this chapter has been administrative responsibility for training. This is not to say, however, that the administrator may not be assisted by auxiliary aids within the organization, as suggested in the section on organization, or by educational aids from outside the government. The administrator should make a careful survey of such outside aids as are available and utilize them to maximum advantage. This section will comprise thumbnail sketches of such outside aids as are normally available to any local government.

Local Public Schools

In addition to providing physical facilities for training, the local public schools may offer adult vocational classes of value to city employees in such subjects as stenography and typing, blueprint reading, drafting, and accounting. These courses will seldom be aimed at the peculiar requirements of the city government but will be offered generally for employed workers. The city government should appraise these courses fully and organize courses of its own only when certain that the local schools do not or cannot meet its objectives. In any event the technical advice of local school people should be sought in the organization of instruction and course materials. The local schools may also be helpful in the training of teachers.

The Near-By College or University

It is a rare city that is more than a few miles from an institution of higher education. These institutions vary greatly in their capacity to contribute to an in-service training program. Some institutions not only recognize a responsibility to assist in the training of public employees but have recruited faculty members especially qualified for this purpose. Recognition of training courses for college credit will often meet the expressed need of city employees for an opportunity to earn degrees while continuing to work. The city government needs to be assured that training courses continue to meet government needs and are not altered for the purpose of fitting into a college degree sequence. In other words, from the standpoint of the government the fulfillment of training needs is more important than the fulfillment of degree requirements. Where these two can be harmonized there are many advantages which accrue from university participation in the government's training program. It tends to broaden the training by bringing in an outside viewpoint. Cooperation between university and government is healthful for the community which both serve.

State Boards for Vocational Education

Each state has a board for vocational education which cooperates with the federal government in the administration of a federal-aid system of vocational education. The last vocational education act, the George-Barden Act, makes money available to the states to pay the salaries and expenses of directors, supervisors, and teachers of agricultural subjects, home economics subjects, trade and industrial subjects, and commercial subjects, and for the training of such teachers.

State vocational boards have been in the business of training employed workers for more than 30 years. Their aid should be welcomed by public service trainers. In addition to financial assistance when it is necessary to compensate teachers, the state boards are generally well equipped to give technical service in the training of teachers and in the organization of training materials and courses of instruction.

State boards for vocational education have been particularly successful in the organization of training for firemen, and fire training programs have been organized in more than half the states under these auspices. Public service trainers have much to learn from methods that have been tested and found successful in other areas of vocational education, even though these methods may require adaptation to public service requirements.

The financial resources of state boards for vocational education have been particularly helpful where a cooperative training program for several cities is required. This is generally the case when the number of employees in a given group in a single city is too small to justify the organization of a training program for the government of that city alone. A number of state boards have employed itinerant instructors in such fields as fire, police, waterworks, and sanitary inspection to meet the needs of the small city, while others have financed zone classes for employees of a number of cities.

State Leagues of Municipalities

A few state leagues have taken the initiative in providing training opportunities for city employees through regional schools, short courses, and institutes. The state league should be expected to take the lead in stimulating training in its member cities and in arranging for cooperative training activity by the small cities. The more progressive cities may well assume some responsibility for stimulating training-mindedness in other cities.

Professional Organizations of Public Officials

One of the major functions of a professional organization is to stimulate the personal growth and training of its members. For this reason the professional organization is rare which is not concerned with the establishment of training opportunities for its members. Services of professional organizations in the determination of training content have already been referred to. In addition some organizations have initiated training programs of their own. The National Recreation Association has conducted a national training program in New York City for recreation administrators and a traveling institute for recreation workers; some local sections of the American Water Works Association conduct short courses for water works officials; and the International City Managers' Association sponsors a correspondence course series for municipal administrators. State organizations of public officials also can be useful in eliciting an interest in training on the part of their members.

Civic Organizations

Civic organizations, such as local chambers of commerce and service clubs and the National League of Women Voters, enter the training picture mainly by giving recognition, support, and prestige to the efforts of the local government to raise the level of performance of its employees. Many cities have given impetus to training by arranging for the public award of certificates at a meeting arranged by a local service club. Civic organizations may also lend a hand by seeing that the budget provides adequate funds for training.

State and Federal Agencies

State-local and federal-local relations provide a means for participation in local training programs by agencies of the state and federal governments. Thus, a state department of health will often aid a local program for the training of food inspectors; the Federal Bureau of Investigation sponsors a National Police Academy for the training of highly selected policemen; the Bureau of Standards has counseled continuously in the organization of training for weights and measures inspectors in Virginia. These are but three illustrations of aid that can be secured from a state or federal agency in almost any training program for city employees.

One federal agency, the Office of Education, requires special mention. The Office of Education administers the federally aided system of vocational education in cooperation with the states. Because of the authorization for public service training in the George-Barden Act previously referred to, the Office has assumed a responsibility for guiding public service training along sound lines and for clearing information on experience with particular techniques and materials. As this experience grows, city governments will be able to initiate training from the point at which other cities leave off instead of having in most instances to start from scratch as in the past.

This brief description of cooperative facilities is admittedly incomplete. It suggests only that the alert administrator will do well to look around him for all the help he can secure before he launches a training program.

Evaluating the Training Program

One of the most troublesome questions now arising in the development of training is, "How can it be determined whether the training program is a success or failure?" Unfortunately the intensive development of educational measurement in the school system is not very helpful in the appraisal of training programs for adult workers, because it has relied almost exclusively on testing procedures which measure only whether the child has learned what the school aimed to teach him and do not measure his use of this knowledge. An in-service training program is successful to the extent to which the trainee applies his new-found skills, knowledge, and attitudes on the job and to the extent to which this application results in more effective performance of governmental functions.

The evaluation of in-service training has not as yet proceeded far enough to justify any elaborate discussion here. There are several ways of approaching the problem:

1. From the standpoint of *a priori* principles of successful education. The questions to be asked here are: Does the program elicit the interest of the training group? Are approved educational methods used? Is the instructor occupationally experienced? Is the subject matter appropriate and is it well organized and presented? These questions can be partially answered by observation, but they cannot be fully answered without adopting one of the other approaches.

2. From the standpoint of trainees. Trainees themselves are often the best judges of the training offered. In a voluntary course, do trainees tend to stay with a course to completion or do they tend to drop out? If they tend to drop out, the course has probably been found inapplicable on the job or has failed to hold employee interest.

Valuable viewpoints can be secured from trainees at the completion of the course if questions are carefully formulated and if the anonymity of responses is preserved. Questions should be specific rather than general. Trainees should be asked not whether the training program was good or bad but what aspects were particularly helpful, what weaknesses were particularly evident, what particular applications trainees were able to make on the job, what subjects offered were least helpful, what subjects not offered should have been included. By testing trainee opinion in this way the training program can be continuously adapted to meet employee requirements. But even this approach will not be a final test of the value of training.

3. From the standpoint of supervisors of trainees. Supervisors are in the best position to observe the performance of trainees on the job. Supervisors should be asked the same kinds of questions as those suggested for trainees and should always participate actively in the formulation and adaptation of the training program. In the last analysis, supervisory appraisal of job performance is only as valid as the system of service ratings in use. Service ratings will be most valuable to the training program if they produce individual profiles of employees showing strength and weakness. If a large proportion of stenographic employees are rated as strong in typing speed but weak in grammar and punctuation, the suggestion for training is obvious; and the training program should produce some marked change in these profiles at the end of the next training period.

Supervisory opinion also is not the final test of training because it does not test the extent to which final objectives are achieved. The purpose of a training program is to increase the effectiveness of governmental performance. And the improvement of individual job performance is only a means to this end.

4. From the standpoint of the city government. The training objective just stated suggests that the fundamental basis for evaluation lies in the measurement of the extent to which the government is effective in the performance of its line functions. Unfortunately the relation between training and the end product is not always clear, and the existence of training as a cause and governmental performance as a result can seldom be stated with certainty. But a training program which is not reflected in improved performance of the governmental function can seldom be justified.[2] Three examples will serve to illustrate this basic form of appraisal.

A midwestern city which conducted an intensive training program for members of its police department discovered that over a period of years the traffic injury index went down, the proportion of crimes cleared by arrest increased, the proportion of arrests followed by conviction increased, and other indexes of police performance had a favorable trend. A careful survey showed that other factors which affect these indexes had been relatively constant — number of automobiles on the road, ability of the prosecutor, integrity of the courts, and so forth. The two significant changes in the police department during these years seemed to be an improved selection process and the training program. Therefore it was concluded that the training program had made a direct contribution to the improved service to the community rendered by the police department. Note that careful account was taken of other factors which might have accounted for the progress made. Note also the opportunity that measures of this kind afford for isolating specific weaknesses. If all indexes improve except the proportion of arrests followed by conviction, it may suggest the need for improved training in the securing, preservation, and presentation of evidence.

In a state which had conducted a statewide program of fire training for five years,

---

[2]The problem of measurement is covered in Chapter 12.

analysis showed that fire losses in that state had decreased 20 per cent more than national fire losses. Inasmuch as the end purpose of fire training is to reduce the loss of life and property by fire, this seemed to be tangible evidence of the value of the training program.

Occasionally a training program can be given a dollars-and-cents value. In one western city, a safety program, of which employee training was a major element, resulted in a refund to the city of $40,000 from the state compensation commission due to the marked reduction in employee injury claims.

These three cases illustrate a method of evaluation that should become more common as training programs mature. Such measurements can rarely be made with absolute assurance of their validity, but they do serve as a fundamental frame of reference for testing the program. The immediate purpose of a training program is to improve the performance of individual employees, but its end purpose is to improve the performance of government. Evaluation in terms of these end purposes will have more meaning than any other type.

Other Educational Opportunities

Earlier in this chapter a distinction was made between in-service training and other forms of post-entry education. While this distinction is valid as a means of determining whether the expenditure of governmental time and funds is justified, it should not be implied that the government is wholly disinterested in educational opportunities which, while they do not contribute directly to improved job performance, do stimulate employee morale and satisfaction. An employee's opportunity or lack of opportunity to "ride" a personal hobby such as photography, music appreciation, Browning's poems, or electrical engineering may condition his whole attitude toward life — including his job.

A progressive personnel policy will seek, therefore, to acquaint the employee with all educational opportunities in which he may have an interest. And the administration need not be surprised if employee acceptance of some of these "non-training" opportunities makes a contribution to personal growth on the job and therefore has a training value. It is only because funds are limited and because the training value of such education is indirect that the government concentrates its own funds on educational programs that have a clear-cut relation to job performance.

Summary

This chapter may be concluded with a review of training principles, some of which are explicit in this chapter, while others have been implied:

1. Primary responsibility for training rests with the chief administrator, but every department head, bureau chief, and supervisor shares in the responsibility.

2. Successful training is a process in which active participation by the trainee is essential.

3. Trainee participation develops only when the training program elicits the interest of those engaged.

4. Much significant training takes place in the informal day-to-day relationships of superior and subordinate.

5. A large proportion of the training that needs to be undertaken is not susceptible to a high degree of organization.

6. Any employee responsible for the work of others is also responsible for seeing that his subordinates know what their functions are and how to perform them.

7. The most satisfactory evaluation of training lies in some measurement of the governmental activity in which trainees are engaged.

8. Two essential requisites of an instructor are occupational skill and prestige and ability to teach.

9. A training program should be built on priorities.

10. Training should be continuously adapted to the needs of government and society.

11. Training must be more than a mechanism — it must be an integral part of administrative philosophy and method.

Chapter 8

FINANCE ADMINISTRATION

If this chapter were to approach the subject of municipal finance from the finance officer's point of view, or from the point of view of the student seeking a general picture of fiscal problems and operations, the task of selecting and organizing the material would be a relatively simple one. It would then be possible to follow the orthodox classification of municipal finance subjects — budget making and administration, assessment of property, collection and disbursement of funds, general cost accounting, and so forth. The purpose of this chapter, however, is not to present in condensed form the fundamentals of good fiscal practice, but rather to emphasize the role of finance in management and to suggest some of the techniques and policies that may be useful to the chief administrator of a municipality. Just how this approach affects the choice of subject matter and the distribution of emphasis may be indicated by a brief review of the distribution of responsibilities within the broad field of finance administration.

Fiscal Functions and Responsibilities

Legislative Functions

The basic fiscal powers and responsibilities belong to the legislative body, the city council. It is the council that makes the final determinations as to amounts and purposes of expenditure, and it is the council that determines how the burden of paying for municipal services shall be spread through taxation and other sources of municipal revenue. To ensure that its policies and determinations have been faithfully followed by the administration, the council should receive periodic operating reports and exercise fiscal control through an independent post-audit of all fiscal transactions.

Managerial Functions

All of the basic managerial functions — planning, organization, direction, and administrative representation — have their fiscal implications.

Almost every plan affecting municipal services needs to be reduced to dollars and cents of expenditure and to be balanced by corresponding plans for raising the required revenue. We have already seen in Chapter 5 that the administrator needs, as a minimum, an annual plan or program of municipal activities and services, i.e., a budget. In addition to this annual plan there may be long-term plans which also have their fiscal counterparts.[1] These may include long-term operating budgets and capital budgets. To properly anticipate effects of capital improvement additions, such as new fire or police stations, and the

---

[1]Municipal Finance Officers Association, A Newer Concept in Municipal Budgeting, Special Bulletin 1957D, Sept. 16, 1957. 4 pp.

need to redirect the emphasis for certain types of services that will need to be performed, it may be essential to prepare projections of operations some years into the future. Capital improvement plans over a period of years are manifested in capital budgets. Debt planning and a sound borrowing policy are needed to ensure that deferred payments will be related to succeeding budgets and to maintain adequately the credit of the municipality.

Organization was defined in Chapter 1 as the division of work among individuals and groups of employees. The budget implements the "paper plan" of organization by distributing appropriations to different units for specified purposes or activities. The unifying force of organization is also represented by the budget, which not only divides the work but distributes it according to a balanced plan or program.

Through the device of executive allotments of budget appropriations and assignment of work programs, the administrator gives direction to the work of the organization and puts plans into effect. The control features of direction are particularly well implemented by fiscal devices — control accounts, purchasing requisitions and vouchers, and so forth, and a system of administrative departmental reports on work program status and progress.

In his role as chief representative of the administration, the chief administrator also uses fiscal instruments and devices. His budget estimates present to the council a balanced program for the entire administration. His regular and special reports to the council and to the public contain financial data. Many of his negotiations with officials of other governments are centered around the transfer of monies from one government unit to another or from one fund to another fund, or the conduct of activities which have their fiscal counterpart.

Operating Department Functions

The role of the operating departments and agencies in finance administration is an important one, although it is frequently ignored in discussions of fiscal responsibilities. By far the greatest portion of municipal expenditures are made by the major operating departments — police, fire, public works, and the like. These operating departments are not mere disbursing agencies, however. The administrator's budget estimates are based primarily upon the recommendations and requests of his department heads and their subordinates. Action for the incurring of expenditures is initiated by the operating departments. Budget administration likewise is shared by the administrator with his department heads. In some cases — utility departments, for example — the operating agencies are also important sources of revenue through earnings.

Auxiliary Functions

Many fiscal functions and procedures are commonly assigned to specialized auxiliary agencies. Assessment of property for taxation, collection of taxes, establishment and operation of accounting systems, safeguarding and disbursement of funds, and the purchasing of supplies are the most common services provided by auxiliary fiscal agencies for the operating departments. Auxiliary fiscal agencies also assist the administrator by providing procedural aids to budgeting and fiscal control. The accounting system, including cost accounting, provides information to the administrator (and to the council); control accounts and purchasing procedures are useful aids in budget administration; revenue estimates and bookkeeping services are essential in budgeting; and so forth.

This brief sketch of the division of fiscal functions and responsibilities is admittedly incomplete and superficial, but it will serve as a background and point of departure for the limited discussion of fiscal techniques and policies to follow.

Organization of Fiscal Services

For the purposes of this chapter it is not necessary to consider in detail the distribution of fiscal authority and responsibility among officials and agencies. All that will be attempted is a brief discussion of the place of fiscal units within the administrative structure and a few suggestions regarding the internal organization of a finance department.

Place of the Finance Department in the Administrative Organization

A logical organization for fiscal services calls for: (a) a consolidated finance department embracing all fiscal services (except the post-audit), and (b) the integration of fiscal services with the rest of the administrative organization by placing fiscal services under a chief finance officer responsible to the chief administrator.

Consolidation of Fiscal Services. There are many cities which have a number of separate and sometimes independent fiscal units or agencies. The offices of assessor, treasurer, and controller, for example, are sometimes separate offices reporting to no common head other than the chief administrator or the council. This lack of integration not only increases unnecessarily the number of persons whose work must be reviewed by the chief administrator, but it also fails to recognize the interrelationships of the various fiscal services. Furthermore it deprives the administrator of the advantage of having one fiscal officer upon whom he can depend for information and advice on all fiscal problems. Centralization of finance administration facilitates fiscal control and makes possible complete fiscal reporting; where account keeping is decentralized, reports are frequently prepared on different bases by various departments, which makes it difficult to prepare a complete, coherent report, or to obtain an accurate over-all picture on municipal operations.

Relation of Finance Department to Chief Administrator. Once all fiscal services have been consolidated in a single department, the next question is — to whom should the finance director be responsible? In some cities the finance director is elected by the people or is selected by, and responsible to, the council. To be sure, there needs to be some fiscal control over the administration, but this should be provided by an independent post-audit (either continuous or periodic). It is unfair to hold the administrator responsible for fiscal management if he is not given corresponding authority to fulfill this responsibility. Most fiscal activities are auxiliary services, and the administrator therefore needs to have control over agencies that are supposed to serve the operating departments if he is to be responsible for the activities of such operating departments.

The chief finance officer will usually play a dual role. On the one hand he will be the head of an auxiliary agency, and as such he must direct and supervise the various technical activities of his department. On the other hand, he is a managerial aide, advising the administrator on problems of finance and implementing the administrator's plans and policies with appropriate fiscal devices.

Internal Organization of the Finance Department

Fiscal functions or activities of a municipality may be roughly classified as follows: (1) budgeting, (2) accounting, (3) collecting, safeguarding, and disbursing of funds, (4) assessing, (5) purchasing, (6) debt and investment management, and (7) post-auditing. The first — budgeting — has already been defined as essentially a managerial function, while the last — post-auditing — is a legislative control function. The others are all primarily auxiliary services. This classification suggests a logical organization of a finance department. The functions of the finance department proper will be those classed as auxiliary services, and they may be assigned to subordinate bureaus or divisions. In smaller cities some of these divisions may be combined or one or more of the functions may be performed by the finance officer, but in a large city the work of the department may conform to the following pattern based essentially on the Model City Charter prepared by the National Municipal League.

Division of Accounts. The division of accounts keeps the general accounts of the city government; prescribes all subsidiary accounts; exercises pre-audit control over all receipts, commitments and expenditures; prepares all payrolls and issues all checks; furnishes financial data for the preparation of the budget and supplies accounting information required for budget execution; maintains the budgetary allotment system; maintains inventory records of all municipal property; and maintains and supervises the cost accounting system. This division may also do the billing for taxes, special assessments and service charges. If statistical and accounting machines are centralized, as they should be, this division may prepare assessment rolls and various statistical reports and analysis. The exercise of these duties belongs directly to the controller (or comptroller), as chief of the division subject to the general supervision of the director of finance.

Division of Treasury. The division of treasury is responsible for the collection, custody, and disbursing of the funds of the municipal government. It is generally recommended that the treasury functions be centralized in a single division headed by an appointed treasurer responsible to the director of finance. The treasurer should be responsible for the custody of all cash and securities, and for the disbursement of funds on warrants drawn by the division of accounts. He should also be required to maintain current records establishing the accountability for cash and securities in each of the municipality's funds. In small cities, the treasury function may be handled in whole or in part by a local bank.

The collection of all revenues and receipts should be done by representatives of the treasurer's office whenever practicable in order to unify responsibility and permit better control. The not-uncommon practice of having an independent tax collector, apart from the treasurer's office, is not recommended. However, in certain situations — particularly where there are only occasional collections in an isolated office — the actual collection may be made by employees of another department. Where this is done, the procedures and forms should be worked out in cooperation with the division of treasury, and frequent — daily, if possible — payments should be made to the treasury by the collecting department. In small cities, with compactly located offices, all payments by citizens may be easily centralized in the treasurer's office. In a growing number of states property taxes are collected by the county and certain nonproperty taxes, such as sales taxes, are collected by the state thus freeing the city from this task.

The once-common practice of having the treasurer redeem warrants is being supplanted by one under which the treasurer merely countersigns warrants, thereby making them checks, payable at local banks. Generally this practice is preferred. It frees the treasurer's office from a job that banks are much better qualified to perform; it eliminates the need for holding large cash reserves in the treasurer's office; it simplifies the internal procedure of the office; and it permits the personnel of the treasurer's office to devote their major effort to the important task of collecting amounts due the city.

Division of Assessment. The division of assessments is responsible for the assessment of property for taxes, determination of special assessment benefits, and preparation of tax and assessment rolls, unless the latter has been delegated to a central machine section. Some states require that assessments be made by the county, and in most the state exercises some control over the assessment procedure by (1) directly assessing some classes of property, such as utilities, (2) by proffering technical advice and assistance, and (3) by direct supervision over the assessment procedure.

Where assessing is a municipal function, the division of assessment should be headed by a single appointive officer directly responsible to the finance director. The practice of having an independent assessment department, headed by an elective or appointive board of assessors, is not recommended. The board system for assessing property has shown itself to be generally unworkable in practice. Use of the election process to obtain assessors fails to recognize the important technical qualifications required.

Division of Purchases. The division of purchasing buys, inspects and tests the supplies, materials and equipment purchased by the city and occasionally purchases certain contractual services for the various departments and agencies of the city government. It often maintains storehouses for supplies and materials. Central services, such as mailing and duplication for the various city departments are frequently performed. Insurance for all city departments is usually handled by this division.

The Budget Bureau. The budget bureau aids in the preparation and administration of the budget. The proper relationship of this office and its head to the department of finance is a source of some disagreement. If budget preparation is regarded as being the sole responsibility of the chief administrator, a good case can be made to have the budget officer directly responsible to the chief administrator. The budget office may be assigned the responsibility for conducting organization and management studies, which is one reason frequently cited for having the office directly responsible to the chief administrator because of his immediate and direct concern with these studies. On the other hand, the idea of a centralized and integrated finance department might seem logically to place the budget officer in the department of finance. If the department of finance is properly responsible to the chief administrator there need be no conflict between these two lines of reasoning. If, however, the finance department is not responsive to the administrative policies of the chief administrator, the establishment of a separate budget office directly responsible to the chief administrator is justifiable. In small cities the problem is often solved by the chief administrator assuming the duties of the budget bureau, perhaps delegating some of its operation to an administrative assistant. Even when a bureau is established directly responsible to the chief administrator, the office may be located physically adjacent to the department of finance in order to facilitate use of accounting data required in the proper administration and preparation of the municipal budget. Such an arrangement aids in assuring an orderly work flow and in definitely establishing lines of administrative authority.

Miscellaneous Functions. There are other functions that are properly administered by the finance department. Among them are debt management, the handling of special funds such as pension funds, and some specialized personnel activities. Some cities, which have complicated debt structures, set up independent or quasi-independent boards to administer the operation of debt funds. While this may be practical in some instances, control and responsibility for the management of all financial business of the city should be concentrated in one department. Furthermore, appointees to such boards are usually less experienced and less well qualified than the regular staff of the finance department.

While the administration of personnel services properly belongs in a distinct department, the fact that almost two-thirds of the budgets of most cities are devoted to personal service payments leads to the natural desire in a finance department for a degree of control over such expenditures. The finance department may aid the personnel agency in preparing compensation plans. Providing services for employees is a new and rapidly developing function of the finance department in cooperation with the personnel department. Such activities as keeping accounts for employee credit unions, assisting in the management of group insurance plans, and making requested payroll deductions for hospital insurance, are personnel functions that may logically be carried on by the finance department.

County-collected taxes which are distributed to cities, and state-collected, city-shared taxes create a finance department duty of checking their assessment all the way through to the cash receipt by the city treasurer to make certain that the city has received its due share of the revenues. Municipalities which have taken the trouble to thus audit the work of their counties and states have frequently materially increased their revenues.

The several miscellaneous functions may be fitted into the regular divisions of the finance department in accordance with facilities, individual abilities, and available time. Debt management, because of its importance, will usually be supervised by the director of the department in cooperation with the budget bureau. The same may be said of the cooperative work with the personnel department in preparing compensation plans. The minor services for employees are logically fitted into the accounting division. Finally, the suggested audit of shared taxes collected by another unit of government should be carried on by the finance director and will require services from the divisions of assessment and accounts.

The Post-Audit. Since the post-audit is a legislative control function, it should not be performed by administrative personnel or by independent accountants engaged by the administrator. The council may employ a firm of public accountants to make the post-audit or, in some states, it may have an audit made by a state office. In the larger cities there may be need for a full-time auditor to provide a continuous, independent audit, but in most cities an annual post-audit is sufficient for purposes of legislative control.

Budget Administration

Formulation of the budget has already been discussed in Chapter 5. When the legislative body has completed its consideration of the budget and has adopted the appropriation and tax levy ordinances for the ensuing fiscal year, the budget is, in effect, returned to the chief administrator for execution. This is the second half of the budget cycle. All the steps taken in formulating and reviewing the budget are of little consequence if the fiscal plan is not properly administered.

To enforce the budget properly, the chief administrator must set up a system of budgetary control. Such a system should be built around three essential elements: (1) adequate appropriation and encumbrance accounting; (2) frequent and regular reports on receipts and expenditures of each fund, as well as regular reports on status of work programs or work progress; and (3) administrative audits of expenditures and work programs of the operating units. Larger cities may find it valuable to set up an allotment system for all expenditures from appropriations.

The responsibility for budget enforcement lies with the chief administrator. Good administration may allow him to assign certain budgetary duties to the chief fiscal officer, a budget officer, or an administrative assistant, provided they are subject to his supervision. When such assignments are made, it is important that the heads of operating departments recognize that the fiscal officer or budget officer represents the chief administrator in budget matters.

Budgetary Accounting

Adequate budgetary accounting is the first essential in good budgetary control.

Supporting Documents. Good budgetary accounting demands that all encumbrances be evidenced by a written document presented to the finance officer before the obligation is incurred. Purchase orders should be written in advance, not as confirming orders; withdrawals from stores should have prior approval by the finance officer, and rents, utility services, and other contractual obligations should be recorded as encumbrances. Close relations must be maintained between the fiscal departments and the purchasing department. Unless purchase orders and other such documents are presented to the finance officer for fund approval prior to their issuance, budgetary control is lacking.

A word of explanation is desirable with respect to the encumbering of obligations for personal services. Practice in this connection varies widely. The more general practice is not to make encumbrances for this item but to enter the actual payroll when it is submitted. Where separate appropriations are made for salaries, such a practice may not entail particular danger. Even here, however, particularly toward the close of the year, or with respect to special expenditure programs, there is the danger of exceeding appropriation balances. Moreover, where a separate appropriation is not made for personal services, there is the danger of purchases consuming a portion of the appropriation which was intended for personal services. Some cities solve this problem by encumbering the estimated payroll for a month or quarter in advance. The most dependable and logical solution to the problem is to have separate appropriations for personal services and, in addition, as payrolls are submitted for payment, to have the department involved accompany it with an estimate of the departmental payroll for the succeeding pay period. The amount of this estimate can then be shown as an encumbrance. A number of governmental agencies have found this procedure to work successfully.

The Expenditure Ledger. The keystone of a budgetary accounting system is an appropriation-and-expenditure ledger (see Fig. 15) or an allotments-and-expenditure ledger (see Fig. 16). The appropriation-and-expenditure ledger is more commonly used, because it is simpler, but it does not provide the same control as a ledger based upon allotments.

The principal steps involved in budgetary accounting include:

1. Opening a ledger sheet for each appropriation with the amount of the appropriation and the monthly or quarterly allotments appropriately shown thereon.

2. As obligations are incurred — purchase orders issued, contracts entered, or personnel hired — the amount of this obligation is entered as an encumbrance on the ledger sheet against which it is chargeable, and the unencumbered balance of the allotment is correspondingly decreased.

3. When the items purchased have been delivered or other services rendered, the corresponding encumbrance is canceled, the amount of the actual expenditure is entered, and the available balance is adjusted for any difference between the original encumbrance and the actual expenditure.

Under the foregoing procedure, it is possible to know with respect to each appropriation, the amount of encumbrance outstanding, the total expenditures, and the balance available for expenditures. The procedure assures adequate control over the incurring of obligations under the adopted budget.

APPROPRIATION LEDGER

Department _____
Fiscal Year _____
Sheet No. _____

Account No. _____ FUNCTION _____ CHARACTER & OBJECT _____
Fund _____ NAME _____ NO. _____

DESCRIPTION	DATE	PURCHASE ORDER NUMBER	WARRANT NUMBER	ACCOUNT NUMBER	ENCUMBRANCES		EXPENDITURES	APPROPRIATION	BALANCES TO DATE		
					RESERVED	CANCELLED			APPROPRIATION	ENCUMBRANCES	EXPENDITURES	AVAILABLE

Fig. 15 — Appropriation Ledger Card, Beverly Hills, California

MUNICIPALITY OF _____
Appropriation Ledger
Department: Public Works-Director's Office
Account: Contractual Services

Account No. 2120
Approp. $2000 _____
Rev. Approp. _____
Rev. Approp. _____
Year 1957

Budget Allotment

Month	Original	Revised	Month	Original	Revised
Jan.	$200		July	$100	
Feb.	150		Aug.	100	
Mar.	450		Sep.	150	
Apr.	75		Oct.	150	
May	75		Nov.	250	
June	150		Dec.	150	

Date	Items	Encumbrances				Expenditures			Allotments		Unencumbered Balance of Allotment
		Order No.	Amount of Purchase Order	Orders Liquidated	Total Unpaid Orders	Warrant No.	Amount	Total	Amount	Total	
1	2	3	4	5	6	7	8	9	10	11.	12
Jan. 1	Allotment	--	--	--	--	--	--	--	$200	$200	$200
Jan. 15	A. B. Power Co.	--	--	--	--	103	$50	$50	--	200	150
Jan. 15	Bell Telephone Co.	--	--	--	--	105	25	75	--	200	125

Fig. 16 — Appropriation Expenditure Ledger Sheet (Allotment System)

Revenue Estimates. Revenue estimates are also an important factor in budget execution. Estimated revenues and realized revenues should be set up on the books of the finance department for each source of income, and attention given to the progress of income received throughout the year. In some municipalities, revenue estimates are split into quarterly periods or monthly periods and revenue accounted for in a way similar to the allotment system for expenditures.

Revenue estimates and expenditure allotments should be considered together in making periodic forecasts of cash position. Such forecasts should be made to reflect the probable cash condition of the treasury from month to month and should be corrected and adjusted in the light of actual experience.

If receipts lag behind the estimates, borrowing may become necessary or a little tightening of expenditure control may avoid an impending deficit. Revenue estimates and actual revenues should be compared frequently and the comparisons should be used as a basis for action.

Periodic Reports

A second essential in budgetary control is prompt and adequate reporting, at frequent intervals, on the condition of the appropriations and funds. The finance office should prepare reports not less frequently than monthly for each operating department and a complete report for the chief administrator. The reports should show the total allotments (if used) to date from each appropriation and the total of expenditures and encumbrances against such allotments (see Fig. 17). Reports should also be made on

CITY OF _____

REPORT ON ALLOTMENTS AND ENCUMBRANCES

(Last month of 1st quarter)

Department, Activity & Account	Code No.	Expended to Date			Allotments To Date	Unencumbered Allotment Balance	Total Appropriation	Appropriation Balance
		Disbursements To Date	Encumbrances Outstanding	Total				
POLICE DEPARTMENT	15							
Administrative	15.1							
Personal Services	A	$1,300	$260	$1,560	$1,580	$20	$6,550	$4,990
Contractual Service	B	57	30	87	93	6	375	288
Commodities	C	61	14	75	85	10	325	250
Outlay	D	-	96	96	100	4	150	54
Sub Total:		1,418	400	1,818	1,858	40	7,400	5,582

Fig. 17 — Monthly Report on Allotments and Encumbrances

work progress and related performance (see Fig. 18). One point should be stressed — reports must appear promptly, within a day or two after the close of the period covered; reports lose value very rapidly with delay.

Administrative Audits

Good budget administration is more than a matter of allotting appropriations, keeping encumbrance accounts, and preparing reports. A third necessary element is that of administrative audits, investigations, or examinations by a budget examiner or examiners responsible to the administrator. Such audits are important to the chief administrator and his budget officer both as a source of information by which to be guided in the preparation of subsequent budgets, and as a means of enforcement of the current budget.

		Form CAO-26		MONTHLY PERSONNEL UTILIZATION REPORT - CITY OF LOS ANGELES

Form CAO-26

MONTHLY PERSONNEL UTILIZATION REPORT - CITY OF LOS ANGELES
Month of   October 195_2_
Code No.
Function: Protection of Persons & Property   20
Subfunction: Structural Regulations   21

Department: Building and Safety   Code No. 21.1
Activity: Building Permits & Inspections   21.11

(1)	(2)	(3)	(4)	(5)	(6)	(7)	(8)	(9)	(10)	(11)	(12)	(13)	(14)	(15)
Subactivities		Personnel Utilized			Man-Hours Utilized				Work Performed				Man-Hours per Unit	
Code No.	Description	Est.	Equi-valent	Per Cent	Est.	Gross Man-Hours	Per Cent	Net Man-Hrs.	Work Unit	Est. Units	Actual Units	Per Cent	Gross	Net
.110	Administration	5.0	5.0	100.0	920	920	100.0		B					
.111	Plan Checking	46.2	45.3	98.0	8500	8334	98.0		Building Plans Checked	1800	1694	94.0	4.90	
.112	Public Counter	17.9	20.0	111.0	3300	3670½	111.0		Building Permits Issued	6000	6185	103.0	.59	
.113	Zoning Enforcement	11.7	11.0	94.0	2160	2024	94.0		Building Permits Issued	6000	6185	103.0	.33	
.114	Board Reports	3.7	4.0	110.0	680	736	110.0		Reports	800	763	95.0	.96	
.115	Inspections													
.1150	Administration	4.0	4.0	100.0	736	736	100.0		B					
.1151	Inspections	63.6	69.0	108.0	11700	12683	108.0		Inspections	31000	30251	98.0	.42	
.1152	Masonry Inspections	7.3	7.0	96.0	1350	1288	96.0		Inspections	1500	1468	98.0	.87	
.1153	Relocation	4.2	5.0	120.0	780	920	120.0		Applications	100	92	92.0	10.	
.1154	Maintenance & Occupancy	22.0	20.0	91.0	4050	3680	91.0		Surveys	4500	3712	82.0	1.	
.1155	Parapet Walls	2.8	3.0	107.0	522	552	107.0		Surveys	60	50	83.0	11.	
.1156	Slum Clearance and Rehabilitation	12.0	12.0	100.0	2208	2208	100.0		H					
.116	Clerical	45.6	48.2	106.0	8395.	8876	106.0		Documents	11500	10090	90.00	.88	
.117	Investigations & Pros.	4.0	4.0	100.0	736	736	100.0		Cases	35	51	146.0	14.40	
	TOTALS	250.0	257.5	103.0	46037	47363½	103.0							

(Note: Original form planographed. Size 13" x 8½")

Fig. 18 — Report on Monthly Personnel Utilization and Work Performed, Los Angeles

One of the most fruitful types of audits for purposes of budget preparation and administration is the analytical investigation of a department, bureau, or function. Such an examination may include the assembling and study of comparative receipts and expenditures over a period of years, an inquiry into departmental organization, and the study of particular managerial problems in departments. Sometimes a budget office makes a cross-section analysis of expenditures for a particular object in all departments; for example, a study of all expenditures during a year for automobile operation, or for printing, or for some other specific object.

A work audit is also useful to budgetary control. If the process of budget-making is to be closely related to work programs and unit costs, it is equally necessary that in the supervision of budget execution there be frequent reference to work being accomplished and the cost. The chief administrator or his budget officer needs the information which is developed in an administrative audit of departmental work programs during the year. A work audit might have the same function for the executive as a legislative inquiry has for the legislative body: to furnish information on the amount and character of work performed by a given bureau or division, the degree of efficiency with which assignments were carried out, the extent to which the original work program was followed, and the magnitude of the work still confronting that particular bureau. Just as a financial audit is an examination of financial affairs, so should there be a work audit or examination of the work program as it is carried out.

Allotment System

Cities with tight budgets and larger cities in general will be aided by an allotment system as a means of budgetary control. Under this system expenditure estimates for the fiscal year are translated into a time schedule of work and expenditures.

Purposes of Allotment System. Use of the allotment system for controlling expenditures may have several purposes: (1) to make sure that departments plan their spending so as to have sufficient funds to carry on their programs throughout the year, avoiding year-end deficiencies and special appropriations; (2) to keep expenditures within the limits of revenues that are actually realized; (3) to give the chief administrator control over departmental expenditures commensurate with his administrative responsibilities, allowing him to effect economies in particular activities at his discretion.

Allotment Procedure. As soon as the appropriation ordinance is adopted, department heads should revise their departmental work programs for the ensuing year in light of the changes which have been made in their original "requests." Work to be performed should be scheduled by months or quarters of the year. When the work schedules are complete, each department head should prepare a proposed spending schedule, likewise on the same monthly or quarterly basis, showing the fiscal implications of the work programs. Departmental spending schedules should be prepared within the framework of the appropriation ordinance, with a separate schedule or group of schedules corresponding to each appropriation item. Expenditures should be detailed according to the standard account classification used in the city's accounting system.

Allotment requests should be made up in detail, but allotment approvals and controls are preferably made by function and activity and in total for each major object of expenditure (salaries, supplies and materials, contractual services, etc.) to be made from any given appropriation. Allotments should be made for uniform periods such as months or quarters, but the amount allotted to each period should vary with needs and experience. A quarterly allotment system is generally more practical than a monthly system, although there are many valid exceptions.

In addition to allotment requests from the spending agencies, statements showing estimated receipts by months or quarters should be prepared by the finance officer. The administrator can then compare the total allotments requested for any given period with the estimated receipts for the same period. He will naturally try to keep expenditures within the actual resources available for the period, but should not be so concerned with balancing his books that he undermines the logical work program of any department. In most cases the necessary adjustments can be made by scheduling for late in the fiscal year those items of expenditure — such as new office furniture, equipment, etc. — that are not affected by seasonal demand and are not essential during the early part of the year. He may also want to revise the allotments so as to set up certain unallotted reserves in each department, to be kept for emergencies. During the year the administrator may find it desirable to reduce allotments for expenditure either because receipts are below anticipations or in order to achieve certain economies.

Modifications in Budget

In the administration of the budget there occur situations in which a change from the original plan is desirable owing to changes in work programs or in available revenues. If the change involves an alteration in figures contained in the appropriation ordinance, it is a matter for legislation action. Otherwise, it should be in the hands of the administrator. Generally, the chief administrator may change allotments but only the council may change appropriations.

Three types of modifications are possible: reductions in appropriations, transfers of appropriations, and increases in appropriations.

Reductions. Reductions are usually made in the working out of the allotment system and are carried out under direction of the chief administrator.

Transfers. Appropriation transfers are sometimes desirable, especially within a department. Such transfers should be possible, within limitations, with the approval of the chief administrator. Sometimes, however, the council may want to prohibit certain types of transfers from being made, without its express approval, such as transfers between a salaries appropriation and a materials-and-supplies appropriation, or between ordinary recurring expenses and capital outlays.

Increases. Some emergencies necessitating unforeseen expenditures may occur during the year. Such emergencies may be provided for by the inclusion of contingent funds in the budget document. Such funds should not be allocated in advance, but should remain in the control of the chief administrator or of the council. Where an increase in an appropriation becomes necessary, an allocation can be made from the general contingent fund. Where revenues overrun estimates, the resulting surplus should be available only by council appropriation. Emergency expenditures may also be met from current funds in some cases and subsequent allotments curtailed. If none of the foregoing methods is available, emergency expenditures must be met from borrowed funds upon council authorization, a procedure which is less desirable than other methods.

Practices Impairing Budgetary Control

Budgetary control may be impaired in several ways:

1. Certain funds may be entirely omitted from the budgetary process, inviting manipulations. There is no valid reason to omit any municipal funds from the budgetary process. When such funds are omitted from budgetary control, there is an invitation for municipal officers to charge items to them wrongly.

2. A small contingent fund to meet emergencies is desirable in any municipal budget, but such funds have sometimes been so abused in practice that municipalities have been deprived of them by law or state regulation. Good practice requires inclusion in the budget of only one contingent fund, under control of the chief administrator, with expenditures made only in cases of established emergencies and with detailed accounts of the expenditures recorded and reported. It is often well to disburse the contingent fund only by transfer to other appropriations, the spending of which is properly charged to the departments for which the appropriations are made.

3. Overspending of appropriations is not possible under adequate budgetary control. But by the use of confirming purchase orders, by the failure to prepare encumbrance documents for contractual services until bills are ready for payment, and by similar devices, departments may avoid the control of budgetary accounting and overspending may occur.

4. Supplementary appropriations may be made too frequently. They are a concomitant of overspending. Sometimes such supplemental appropriations are actually planned in advance. A municipal council may make cuts in departmental requests when the budget is adopted with the understanding that additional funds will be provided later in the year on the certification of the department head that an emergency exists because of lack of funds. Such procedure completely nullifies budgetary control, and the budget is of little or no value, being neither observed by the administration nor trusted by the people.

5. Payment of bills may be deliberately deferred, sometimes with the consent of the firms or persons from whom the goods are purchased. In a few cities the accounts are not encumbered when obligations are incurred but are kept on a strictly cash basis. Near the close of the fiscal year laxity in paying bills may result in the incurring of obligations considerably in excess of appropriations, the bills being held until the appropriation for the following year is available. Where this practice is permitted, the amount of bills carried over from year to year tends to grow larger and larger as the overspending of appropriations continues. Lax payment of bills cannot affect budgetary control where satisfactory accrual accounting and administrative controls are in use.

Municipal Accounting

Need for Accounting

The purpose of municipal accounting is to provide the recording of financial information so that it can be utilized (1) as a basis for managing the municipality's affairs, (2) in determining the fidelity of persons administering municipal funds, and (3) as a means of informing interested parties of the municipality's financial condition and operations.

General Accounting Principles

The following general principles, which are recommended by the National Committee on Governmental Accounting, should form the foundation upon which the municipality's accounting system is built:

1. All accounting activities should be centralized under the direction of a single officer, who should supervise the keeping of all accounts and the preparation and issuance of all financial reports.

2. If legal and sound accounting provisions conflict, legal provisions must take precedence, but in such event every effort should be made to seek changes in such legal provisions so as to bring applicable law and sound accounting principles in harmony.

3. The general accounting system should be on a double-entry basis, with a general ledger in which all financial transactions are recorded in detail or in summary. Additional subsidiary records should be kept where necessary. Cost accounting systems should be established wherever costs can be measured.

4. A common terminology and classification should be used consistently throughout the budget, the accounts, and the financial reports.

5. The accounts should be classified in balanced fund groups. The group for each fund should include all accounts necessary to set forth its operation and condition. All financial statements should follow this classification.

6. Every municipality should establish funds called for either by law or sound financial administration. However, since funds introduce an element of inflexibility in the financial system, as few funds as possible, consistent with legal requirements, should be established. The following classifications of funds is recommended: (a) General, (b) Special Revenue, (c) Working Capital, (d) Special Assessment, (e) Bond, (f) Sinking, (g) Trust and Agency, and (h) Utility or other Enterprise.

7. A clear segregation should be made between the accounts relating to current assets and liabilities and those relating to fixed assets and liabilities. With the exception of Working Capital, Utility or Other Enterprise, or Trust Funds, fixed assets should not be carried in the same fund with the current assets but should be set up in a separate self-balancing group of accounts known as the General Fixed Assets Group of Accounts. Similarly, except in Special Assessment and Utility funds, long-term liabilities should not be carried with the current liabilities of any fund but should be shown in a separate self-balancing group of accounts. Revenues should be classified by fund and source; and expenditures by fund, function, department, activity, character, and by main classes of objects, in accordance with standard classifications.

8. The accounting system should provide budgetary control for both revenues and expenditures, and the financial statements should reflect, among other things, budgetary information.

9. As soon as purchase orders or contracts are signed, the resulting obligations should be entered at once as encumbrances of the funds and appropriations affected.

10. The use of the accrual basis in accounting for revenues and expenditures is recommended as far as practical. Revenues, partially offset by provisions for estimated losses, should be taken into consideration when earned, even though not received in cash. Expenditures should be recorded as soon as liabilities are incurred.

11. Inventories of both consumable and permanent property should be kept in subsidiary records controlled by accounts in the general accounting system. Physical inventories of both consumable and permanent property should be taken at least annually and the accounts and records should be made to agree with such inventories.

12. Depreciation on general fixed assets should not be computed unless cash for replacements can legally be set aside. Depreciation on such assets may be computed for unit cost purposes even if cash for replacements cannot be legally set aside providing these depreciation charges are used for memorandum purposes only and are not reflected in the accounts.

13. The accounting for municipal business enterprises should follow the standard classifications employed by similar private enterprises. Each college, hospital, library, and other public institution should follow the standard classification employed by similar private institutions.

14. There should be a periodic audit by independent accountants.

15. Financial reports should be prepared monthly or oftener, to show the current condition of the budgetary accounts and other essential information necessary to control operations. At least once each year a general financial report should be prepared and published.

16. There should be general uniformity in the financial reports of all municipalities of similar size and type.

Cash vs. Accrual Method of Accounting

There are two principal bases of accounting, cash and accrual, although in practice some combination of the two is frequently found. Under a strict cash basis, revenues are accounted for only when received in cash, and expenditures are accounted for only when paid. Under a strict accrual basis, revenues are accounted for when earned, or in the case of taxes and similar levies, when bills are rendered, and expenditures are accounted for as soon as liabilities are incurred. The accrual basis lays emphasis on the period in which the transaction occurs, while the cash basis emphasizes the period in which cash is received. Of the two bases, the accrual is the better, since it makes possible a more accurate accounting by successive periods. The true financial operations and the results thereof for a period cannot be obtained without a proper allocation of all the revenues and expenditures to such period and a comparison of revenues with expenditures.

While the accrual basis is the more accurate, cash must also be taken into consideration. First, an allowance should be set up for the unreceivable or unallotted balance. Second, only those taxes and other receivables should be considered as revenue which will be converted into cash within a reasonable time. Third, in planning the city's expenditures, it is not only important to consider revenues but cash receipts as well, if short-term borrowing is to be avoided.

General Accounting Records and Procedure

The general accounting records and procedure described here are based on the assumption that the double-entry system, which underlies all modern accounting, is used. Under this system each account is divided into at least two parts, respectively known as the debit and credit sides. For every entry made to the debit side of an account or accounts, an entry for a corresponding amount or amounts must be made to the credit side of another account or accounts. Thus, the total of the debit balances must equal the total of the credit balances at all times, thereby assuring the greatest possible degree of accuracy.

The steps in recording a financial transaction consist of (1) journalizing, i.e., analyzing the transaction to determine the accounts to which it is to be posted, and (2) actual posting. The records involved in the first process are the original documents evidencing the transaction and books of original entry, while those containing the accounts to which postings are to be made are known as ledgers.

Original Documents. The recording of an accounting transaction really begins at the time the transaction takes place, for some written evidence is created at that time on the basis of which the transactions will be recorded. For example, payroll sheets form the basis for entries indicating the cost of labor. The basis for the entry setting up accounts receivable is the invoices. Entries for accounts payable are based on purchase orders, vendors' invoices, and vouchers. Such documents or summaries based thereon usually indicate the date of transaction, authority therefor in case such authority is required, and the amount involved. From the original documents, the accounts to which postings must be made are also determined.

Books of Original Entry. The first step in the accounting procedure is to enter information contained in the original documents chronologically on the books of original entry. It is difficult to state the kinds of specialized books of original entry which a municipality should utilize. The determining factors in each case are the volume of transactions and the extent to which summarization is possible. A municipality with a population of about 25,000 will find the following books useful:

1. General Journal. This book assembles accounting information not recorded in any other book (see Fig. 19).

2. Cash Receipts Book. In this book are recorded all transactions relating to cash receipts (see Fig. 20).

3. Voucher Register. In this record are entered all amounts approved for payment. Such approval is evidenced by a voucher, and this document forms the basis for the entry in the voucher register (see Fig. 21).

The Voucher Register can also serve as a Check Register if columns are provided for the purpose of showing dates of payment and the check numbers. In many municipalities the voucher and the check are the same document. If a relatively long period of time elapses between approval of claims and their payment, a separate Check Register should be used.

4. Payroll Register. These records are used to compile the earnings of all persons employed (see Fig. 22).

5. Bond and Interest Register. (See Fig. 23).

6. Other Books of Original Entry. Other books of original entry to be used as needed include Contract and Purchase registers and Insurance register.

Ledgers. The next step in the accounting procedure is posting the figures from the various books of original entry to the proper accounts in the ledgers. Accounts may be classified as to whether they are principal or subsidiary, and the corresponding name is assigned to the ledgers. There is thus a principal or general ledger and subsidiary ledgers.

The General Ledger is the core about which the municipal accounting system revolves. It is the heart of the accounting system, as it carries all the principal accounts which form the basis for the balance sheet and contains the control totals for revenues and expenditures. These accounts are in turn supported by subsidiary accounts which give fuller information. The accounts supporting a particular account are usually grouped together and contained in a separate subsidiary ledger. The total of the balances of the accounts in the subsidiary ledger must agree with the balance of the controlling account in the general ledger.

The number of the subsidiary ledgers to be employed will depend on the number of accounts in the general ledger about which further information is desired. The following is a list of some essential subsidiary ledgers:

1. Revenue Ledger. This ledger contains an account for each revenue source, which is debited with the amount of estimated revenue to be received from the particular source and credited with amounts received.

2. Appropriation or Allotment Expenditure Ledger.[2] This ledger contains an individual account for each appropriation made. These accounts are credited with the amount of the appropriation. As encumbrances are made or expenditures are incurred, the respective appropriations are charged (see Figs. 15 and 16).

3. Tax Rolls. The tax rolls show the amount and kind of taxes (e.g., real, personal property, etc.) due from each taxpayer.

---

[2]For a more detailed explanation of these ledgers, see the discussion in the previous section on budget administration.

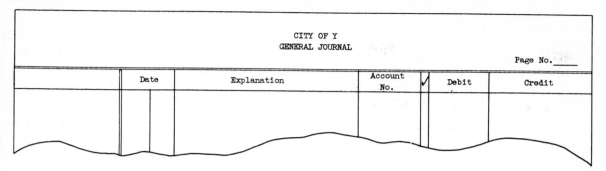

CITY OF Y
GENERAL JOURNAL

Page No. _____

	Date	Explanation	Account No.	✓	Debit	Credit

Fig. 19 — General Journal

CITY OF Y
CASH RECEIPTS BOOK

Page No. _____

Date	Name	Explanation	Fund	Total	Taxes		Miscellaneous Accounts Receivable	Other Receipts	
					Current	Delinquent		Account	Amount

Fig. 20 — Cash Receipts Book

CITY OF Y
VOUCHER REGISTER

Page No. _____

	Date	Name	Explanation	Voucher No.	Total	General Fund	Special Revenue Fund	Working Capital Fund	Other Funds	
									Fund	Amount

Fig. 21 — Voucher Register

CITY OF Y
PAYROLL REGISTER
Week Ending _____ 19__

Name	Occupation	Weekly Time							Total Days or Hours	Rate per Day or Hour	Total Amount Earned	Deductions for	Amount of Check	Check Number
		S	M	T	W	T	F	S						

Fig. 22 — Payroll Register

4. Special Assessment Ledger. A separate account should be established for each installment of a special assessment levy. This account will show: (a) collections, disbursements, and balance of cash available for payment of principal and interest on special assessment bonds; (b) assessments levied, collections, and balance of assessments receivable; (c) interest on deferred assessments set up, collected, and balance; (d) special assessment bonds issued, redeemed, and balance outstanding; (e) interest becoming due, amount paid, and balance outstanding.

CITY OF Y
BOND AND INTEREST REGISTER

Title _____   Amount of Issue _____
Authorized By _____   Purpose _____
Sold to _____   Coupon Rate _____ Payable _____
Price _____   Payable at _____
Bonds Dated _____   Bonds Payable at _____

| Date of Maturity | | | Interest Due | | | Principal Due* | | Principal and Interest Due | Remarks |
Month	Day	Yr.	Coupon Nos.	Bond Nos.	Amount	Bond Nos.	Amount		

*In the case of sinking funds, these two columns would be replaced by a column entitled, "Sinking Fund Contribution."

Fig. 23 — Bond and Interest Ledger

5. Bonded Debt and Interest Payable Ledgers. An individual account is provided for each bond issue in each of these ledgers (see Figs. 24 and 25).

6. Property Ledger. In this ledger are kept individual accounts for each type of fixed property owned by the municipality.

7. Other Subsidiary Ledgers. Other subsidiary ledgers to be used as needed include a Bank Ledger, containing an account for each depository; a Stores Ledger, containing accounts for each type of material or supply used; an Investment Ledger, having an account for each type of investment; and a Contract Ledger, in which an account is provided for each contract.

All financial statements are prepared from the general and subsidiary ledgers. It is accordingly important that the accounts in these ledgers be grouped so that the preparation of financial statements is facilitated. The accounts should be arranged by funds within each ledger. Within each fund the accounts should be classified by groups according to whether they are assets, liabilities, reserves, surplus, revenues, or expenditures. Assets and liabilities are in turn usually grouped in the order in which they are normally expected to be realized. Revenues are ordinarily grouped by source, while expenditures are grouped by functions and organization units.

Municipal Funds

As has previously been indicated, the National Committee on Governmental

Accounting has recommended the use of the following funds: General, Special Revenue, Working Capital, Special Assessment, Bond, Sinking, Trust and Agency, and Utility.

The funds enumerated are the maximum number a municipality should employ. These funds can take care of practically all activities carried on by a municipality. Many cities carry on fewer activities and may be able to use a smaller number of funds. The above recommendations are based on the assumption that there are no legal restrictions as to the number and kinds of funds to be employed. Where the law specifies the funds to be used, legal provisions will of course govern.

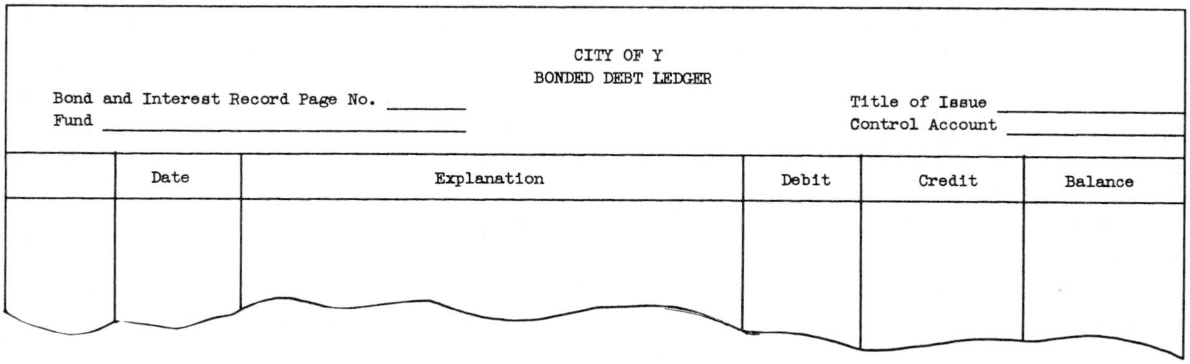
CITY OF Y
BONDED DEBT LEDGER

Bond and Interest Record Page No. ________ Title of Issue ________
Fund ________ Control Account ________

	Date	Explanation	Debit	Credit	Balance

Fig. 24 — Bonded Debt Ledger

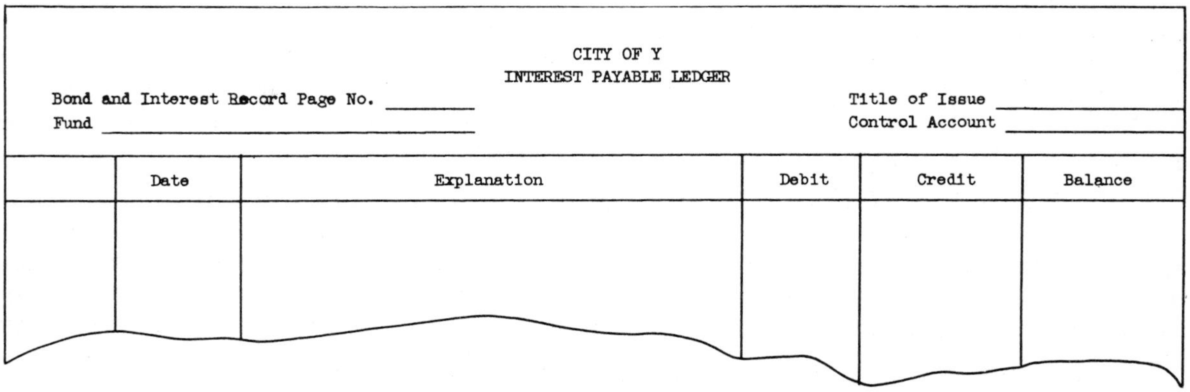
CITY OF Y
INTEREST PAYABLE LEDGER

Bond and Interest Record Page No. ________ Title of Issue ________
Fund ________ Control Account ________

	Date	Explanation	Debit	Credit	Balance

Fig. 25 — Interest Payable Ledger

Each fund should be considered an independent entity. For each fund the total balances of the asset and expenditure accounts must equal the total of the balances of the liability, reserve, surplus, and revenue accounts. The assets, liabilities, reserves, and surpluses of different funds should not be combined except in special cases and with proper identifying records maintained. It is poor policy to permit inter-fund transfers unless legal authorization is given. When authorization is given, such loans should be carried as an asset of the fund lending the money, and a corresponding liability should be set up in the accounts of the borrowing fund.

Accounting for Revenues

In studying municipal finances, it is important not only to note the municipality's financial condition but to analyze as well the factors which brought about the change in condition over a period of time. Such changes are shown by revenue and expenditure statements.

An accounting system must therefore provide for the recording of information regarding revenues and expenditures in such a manner that statements will show the source and amount of revenue accrued and the purpose and amount of expenditures, as well as the organizational unit by which the latter were incurred. Moreover, the system must make possible the preparation of estimates and the comparison of actual revenues with estimated revenues, and appropriations with the expenditures and encumbrances.

Classification of Revenues. It is important that an individual account be set up for each revenue source and that such revenue sources be classified. The National Committee on Governmental Accounting has proposed the following main classifications of revenues: (1) general property taxes, (2) other local taxes, (3) licenses and permits, (4) fines, forfeits, and penalties, (5) revenue from use of money and property, (6) revenue from other agencies, and (7) charges for current services. All of these would be further subdivided. For example, "other local taxes" might be classified into (a) property taxes on publicly or privately owned utilities (when not exempt), (b) business taxes on publicly or privately owned utilities, (c) sales and service taxes, and (d) poll taxes.

Accounting Procedure. The first step in accounting for revenues is to set up the amount of revenue estimated to be available for financing the budget. As estimates are converted into actual revenues these sums will be reduced thus giving the balance to be collected. If this procedure is followed, it will be possible to prepare statements at any time showing for each revenue source the estimated revenue, actual revenue, and excess of estimated over actual, or vice versa. The statement is significant for two reasons. In the first place, it provides the basis for comparing actual revenues with expenditures shown in the expenditure statement. Secondly, it makes possible a comparison between actual and estimated revenue. The latter comparison is important in connection with the preparation of the succeeding year's budget.

Under the accrual basis of accounting there is no relationship between revenues and receipts. Usually it is expected that a great part of the revenue will be realized in cash within the fiscal year, but revenues and receipts for the year will not be the same. For one thing, the city may resort to borrowing, and the proceeds therefrom are not revenues even under the cash basis. Accounting for receipts therefore merits some attention.

Intelligent finance administration necessitates complete information regarding receipts. Such knowledge is necessary in the formulation of financial plans. Expenditures should be timed with expected revenue collections; otherwise temporary borrowing may be required. If collections are smaller than anticipated, it may indicate that the municipality's collection policy has been lax, and it suggests the possibility of enforcing collections.

Collections are reflected in receipts statements. Usually one statement is prepared for the cash account, showing the cash balance at the beginning of the year, receipts and disbursements during the year, and the cash balance at the end of the year. How detailed this report should be will depend on whether the cash or accrual basis is followed. If the cash basis is used, it is important to distinguish between revenue and nonrevenue receipts. Revenue receipts should be classified in the same manner as revenues are classified on a revenue statement where the accrual basis is followed. Similarly a distinction must be made between expenditure disbursements and other payments; the former should be classified in the same manner as expenditures are classified in a statement of expenditures prepared under the accrual basis.

Where the accrual basis is employed, the receipts and disbursements statements would be prepared in summary form. Even here, however, it is important to analyze collections of certain important items. For example, a statement or statistical table should be prepared showing tax levies, collections, and the amount of each tax levy remaining uncollected at the end of each year for a period of years.

Accounting for Expenditures

The accounting procedure of a municipality must be such as to insure that expenditures are incurred in accordance with legal provisions, that adequate values are received in connection therewith, and that they are authorized by the proper authorities. The exact procedure will vary somewhat with the objects for which the expenditures are made. Expenditures may be classified under two principal headings: (1) payrolls (personal services), and (2) purchases (contractual services, materials and supplies, capital outlays).

Payrolls. The steps involved in the preparation of and accounting for payrolls are as follows: (1) keeping attendance records, (2) preparing the payroll, (3) approving the payroll, (4) making payment, and (5) entering payrolls in accounting records.

Attendance records should be kept in the department in which employees work. Standard forms should be devised by the chief finance officer for this purpose. These should be accompanied by written instructions indicating how time reports are to be prepared and certified and when they are to be transmitted to the central office.

Attendance records should be certified not only by the employee keeping them, but also by the head of the department concerned.

The payroll should be prepared in the department of finance. Frequently the time reports and payroll are combined in one sheet, thereby obviating the necessity of copying names and time worked. Fig. 22 shows a sample payroll form designed primarily for employees working by the day or hour; with slight modifications this form can be adapted to use for employees on a weekly or monthly basis.

Payrolls should be scrutinized to determine the authority for each employee's name and salary on the payroll, and also to assure compliance with budget provisions and the adequacy of unencumbered appropriations. Usually certification regarding propriety of employment is made by the civil service agency for civil service employees and by the hiring authority for others. Approval to assure compliance with budgetary provisions may be made by a budget officer, if there is such a budget officer, or by the chief finance officer.

Purchases. The major steps in accounting for purchase expenditures are: (1) examination and approval of purchase orders for adequacy of unencumbered balance in the appropriation chargeable and the encumbering of the appropriation for the amount of the order; (2) pre-audit of the vendor's invoice after the purchased item has been received, and adjustment of the appropriation charge for the difference between the estimated cost as reflected in the purchase order and the actual cost as reflected in the invoice. The procedural steps involved in purchasing are discussed more fully in a later section of this chapter.

A voucher is made out containing all the information necessary to record the transaction. This document also bears the chief finance officer's signature, as evidence of his approval of the voucher. The information contained in the voucher is entered in a voucher register and from there posted to the individual appropriation expenditure accounts in a subsidiary ledger. Total expenditures for the month as shown by the register are entered in the general journal and from there posted to the expenditure control account and the control account for appropriations.

The subsidiary expenditure accounts should be so set up as to make possible the classification of expenditures by funds, function, organization unit, character, and object. Based on the data contained in these accounts, statements should be prepared showing (1) amount appropriated, (2) expenditures, (3) encumbrances, and (4) unencumbered balance. This information should be shown horizontally while functions and organization units will be exhibited vertically. This statement is particularly useful in budgetary control. Statements should also be prepared classifying expenditures by character and object.

Use of Machine Accounting Methods

There has been a rapid development in the use of machine methods in accounting in recent years. Administrators and finance officers are beginning to recognize the advantages to be obtained from the use of accounting machines. The chief advantages of mechanical accounting equipment are: (1) it reduces account-keeping cost, (2) it saves time, and (3) it minimizes the possibility of error.

Machine methods can be used for all branches of municipal accounting, whether it be general accounting, real estate tax billing and accounting, personal property tax billing and accounting, cost accounting, utility accounting, or the preparation of and accounting for payrolls. Many can also be used for statistical compilations and analyses.

Whether or not a municipality should employ accounting machines will depend on whether the equipment can be utilized to its full capacity. It would be uneconomical to install equipment that would remain idle most of the time. However, machines are now being built which can be used successfully for several purposes. By transferring the machines to other departments, or by establishing a central machine-records unit in the finance department, even a small municipality may be in a position to use mechanical equipment. Before installing any type of accounting machines a municipality should make an investigation to determine which machine is best suited for its purpose.

Reports [3]

One of the purposes of good accounting records is to provide the basis of reports which may be used for action by administrative or legislative officials and by citizens in measuring municipal operations and in appraising municipal activities. Financial reports are but one type of municipal report, although a good financial report frequently is the basis for considerable information of a nonfinancial nature. The financial reports of a city are based on the detailed records of the accounting department and on the informal records of the individual departments and agencies. Financial reports should be formed and developed in accordance with the use to which they are going to be put. Thus the same detailed information necessary for an administrative official may not meet the

---

[3]See National Committee on Governmental Accounting, Municipal Accounting and Auditing (Chicago: The Committee, 1951), for the best statement of principles underlying a municipal report and for the actual forms for financial statements and statistical tables.

needs of a legislative group, or of the public. While the same data may be used as the basis for several reports, the method of presentation and the amount of detail may vary for each.

The Complete Annual Financial Report. Every municipality should prepare a complete financial report at least once a year. It is highly desirable that there should be only one report instead of separate reports issued by the chief accounting officer and the independent auditor.[4] This duplication, which is still the practice in some municipalities, involves a loss of effort and money. Moreover, variations in methods of presentation and failure to present reconciliations of variations between statements of the two reports leads to confusion and misinterpretations. It is suggested that either the finance department prepare the annual financial report and include a certificate by the independent auditor that the statements exhibited therein reflect the true financial condition at the end of the fiscal period and the results of operations for the period, or else that the independent auditor's report be used to compile the financial section of the city's report, with the finance director supplying the statistical section and a letter of transmittal. Under this latter proposal the director of finance would prepare the financial section of the municipality's general annual report, which would be based upon and tie in with the auditor's detailed report. Regardless of the plan followed, the report should be issued as soon after the close of the fiscal year as possible and in no event later than three months after the close of the year.

Other Financial Reports. Other financial reports will for the most part be modifications of the general financial report.[5] Those issued for the public vary considerably, although the trend is to reduce figures to graphic illustrations and more readily comprehensible comparisons, while still including basic financial data. Where such popular or abbreviated reports are prepared which use comparative data, an explanation of the fund character of municipal accounting should be included.

The reports to the legislative body are comparatively few and considerably more condensed than are the reports submitted to department heads or to the chief administrator. The types of such reports, and their contents, will depend largely upon the financial reporting policies of the individual officer responsible for such matters and the desires of the legislative body. Whether prepared for administrative or legislative officials, all such reports should be issued at regular intervals and cover definite periods. In all cases, reports should be routed to the council via the chief administrator's office. The data presented should usually be interpreted in accompanying memorandums which should carry the approval of the chief administrator. The reports should be prepared well in advance of any action that is contemplated on the basis of the information given. Reports to the chief administrator should be made not less often than monthly or quarterly, and should contain much the same information as is used in the annual report, but covering only the period concerned plus, in some instances, forecasts for succeeding months.

Cost Accounting

Nature and Uses of Cost Accounting

Cost accounting is the process of searching out and recording all of the elements

---

[4]See National Committee on Governmental Accounting, op. cit., for a statement of general principles of post-audit procedure, as well as a generally applicable specific procedure.

[5]See Clarence E. Ridley and Herbert A. Simon, Specifications for the Annual Municipal Report (Chicago: International City Managers' Association, 1948) and the suggested monthly report forms in the International City Managers' Association, Monthly Administrative Reports for Cities (Chicago: The Association, 1950).

of expense incurred to attain a purpose, to carry on an activity or operation, to complete a unit of work, or to do a specific job. The growing use of cost accounting as a basis for budgeting, planning, and expenditure control is one of the significant developments of recent years in governmental financial administration. Because cost accounting may be profitably applied to most municipal activities, cost-finding procedures often constitute an important part of the financial accounting system of a municipality.

Cost accounting provides a definite means of measuring municipal operations. Casual observations are informative to the administrator, but at best they give only an incomplete picture of conditions and results; they provide no analysis of costs, and they force reliance on memory alone for knowledge of past operations. Only with definite recorded measurements of each kind of work done, and the cost thereof, does the administrator have the complete factual data that is necessary for sound conclusions and for wise decisions.

Value in Management

The value of cost accounting depends upon the extent to which the cost data are put to practical use by the administrator. Cost accounting as a tool of the administrator has worked well in private industries; it has a similar potential value in all branches of public administration. Six main purposes and values of governmental cost accounting can be set forth: (1) it is useful as a form of protection against loss, waste, and inefficiency; (2) it provides data for use in policy determination; (3) it helps in the determination of prices and rates; (4) it aids in establishing sound budgetary control over municipal expenditures, provides information for the establishment of work programs and for estimating probable future costs of various activities, and it approaches the job of budget preparation from the viewpoint of the amounts really needed to carry on government services and activities rather than upon past expenditures alone; (5) since cost accounts assist in fixing responsibility for both good and poor performance, the information procured therefrom may be used in motivating employees, combining personnel into efficient crews, and even in making service ratings; (6) it furnishes the data for relating performance to expense, and for giving the taxpayer accurate information on accomplishments and the unit costs of each activity maintained at public expense.

Applications of Cost Accounting

The test of practicability of "costing" an operation will necessarily vary from department to department. Not all activities can be measured in such detailed units as tons, cubic yards, or linear miles, and occasionally there are some activities, though measurable, for which the figures obtained are of questionable value. There are other types of measurement, however, besides quantity of work; these include effort, as measured by man-hours and machine-hours spent on the job; effectiveness and adequacy, as related to the magnitude of the problem; and efficiency, as expressed in the cost per unit.[6] Cost accounting is particularly concerned with the measurement of efficiency in terms of quantity of work performed as related to cost.

Many officials have balked at the original cost of installing a cost accounting system. However, the cost of the system must be judged against the results produced to determine whether it is as prohibitive in cost as may first appear. The time and effort required to install and maintain it is very frequently more than compensated for by the help which cost figures provide in securing more adequately controlled administration.

---

[6]See Chapter 12, Administrative Measurement.

In devising any cost accounting system, effort must be made to ensure that all elements entering into the cost of a service or material are considered. These elements include labor, materials and supplies, equipment and depreciation, and overhead. A further distinction must be made between direct and indirect costs. The direct costs are those incurred directly for one particular unit of product or service; indirect costs are incurred for several kinds of services or materials, and if not attributable to any particular one, are charged on an arbitrary basis to overhead. However, the basis of allocation of overhead costs should be such as to insure that each unit is charged as accurately as possible with its proportionate share.

In expressing cost figures, it is most practicable to use terms of unit of service or product. This facilitates the comparison of actual unit costs with unit cost standards. In making such comparisons, however, it is essential that identical elements of cost are included in each case. A unit cost standard as applied to government represents the minimum unit cost that can be expected from good management. Applied to street cleaning or repairing for example, it might refer to the minimum cost the officials believe obtainable for cleaning or repairing a mile of street.[7]

Procedures

In keeping cost records, field reports should be used which show the amount of labor, material, and equipment going into each operation or job. These should be filed daily with the officials charged with keeping cost records. The latter should prepare weekly, monthly, and annual cost statements showing work done, total costs, unit costs, units per man-hour, and per equipment-hours, and other analyses for each job and operation, as requested or desired. Such statements should be submitted to the proper department heads, the chief administrator, and the budget officer.

A Work and Cost Ledger (Fig. 26) should be kept. This ledger is the heart of the cost system. It supplies information as to total costs, the units of work done, and the unit cost for each operation or job. Fig. 27 gives a graphic presentation of the flow of information from the various sources and the procedure followed in compiling cost data. In addition to the Work and Cost Ledger, and the report forms necessary to implement the system, there should also be maintained an individual equipment record in order to determine the cost of operation, maintenance, depreciation, and overhead for each piece of motorized equipment. A definite hourly or mileage rate, based on actual costs, may then be established for charging the various jobs and activities with the cost of equipment.

The cost accounts should be subsidiary to and controlled by the general accounts. However, this does not necessarily lead to the conclusion that cost accounts are kept by the division of accounts in the finance department. They may, for practical reasons, be maintained by someone in the operating department. The question of where the cost records should be kept turns upon the criteria of speed and accuracy. If the central finance office can produce correct cost information promptly, it seems wise to place the responsibility there. If the central office is not equipped for the work, the use of departmental cost accountants may be the best system. No matter where the accounts are kept, however, the chief finance officer should be vested with responsibility for functional supervision of the system, with auditing the cost accounting work, and with maintaining general control accounts for the cost accounting system.

---

[7]See Walter O. Harris, Municipal Public Works Cost Accounting Manual (Chicago: Public Administration Service, 1955).

Purchasing[8]

Purchasing is an auxiliary service which can be delegated to specially trained personnel. Nevertheless, it has managerial significance in at least two respects. First, because a large share of municipal expenditures is for equipment and supplies, the chief administrator is naturally concerned with methods and procedures that will contribute to efficient and economical expenditure of city funds. Second, control over expenditures for items purchased is essential if the administrator is to maintain the integrity of his budget. The administrator's chief concerns with respect to purchasing are with organization and procedural controls. That is, he is interested in delegating purchasing responsibilities so as to achieve the maximum economies without serious inconvenience to operating needs, and he wants to establish procedures that will help him to control expenditures.

WORK AND COST LEDGER

Operation Acct._____

Account Number_____

Work Unit_____

Unit Cost Standard_____ per_____ Control Account _____

Year Ending_____

Date (1)	Labor (2)		Equipment				Materials and Supplies (5)	(6)	(7)	(8)	Overhead (9)	Total Cost (10)	Work Units (11)	Unit Cost (12)	Output	
			Hired (3)		City Owned (4)										Per Man Hr. (13)	Per Equip. Hour (14)
	Hours	$Amount	Hours	$Amount	Hours	$Amount										
Jan.																
Feb.																

Fig. 26 — Work and Cost Ledger

Organization for Purchasing

There is general agreement among those who have studied purchasing problems that best results can be obtained by the establishment of a central purchasing office — preferably in the finance department — to handle the purchasing of material and supplies for all departments of the city government. There are a number of reasons why "centralized purchasing" is so generally recommended.

1. Larger quantities of goods can be purchased at one time through joint purchasing, lower prices per unit are possible, and better delivery service may be obtained.

2. Centralized purchasing expedites payment of claims, thereby making possible the taking of cash discounts.

3. Overhead costs under a decentralized purchasing system are large, particularly in those instances in which a department is a large user of material and supplies. It has been estimated that efficient centralization makes possible savings ranging from 10 to 15 per cent of total material costs.

---

[8]The primary sources of information for this section were Russell Forbes and Others, Purchasing for Small Cities (Chicago: Public Administration Service, 1951); and the International City Managers' Association, Municipal Finance Administration (Chicago: The Association, 5th ed., 1955), Chapter 14.

STEPS IN A PUBLIC WORKS
COST ACCOUNTING SYSTEM

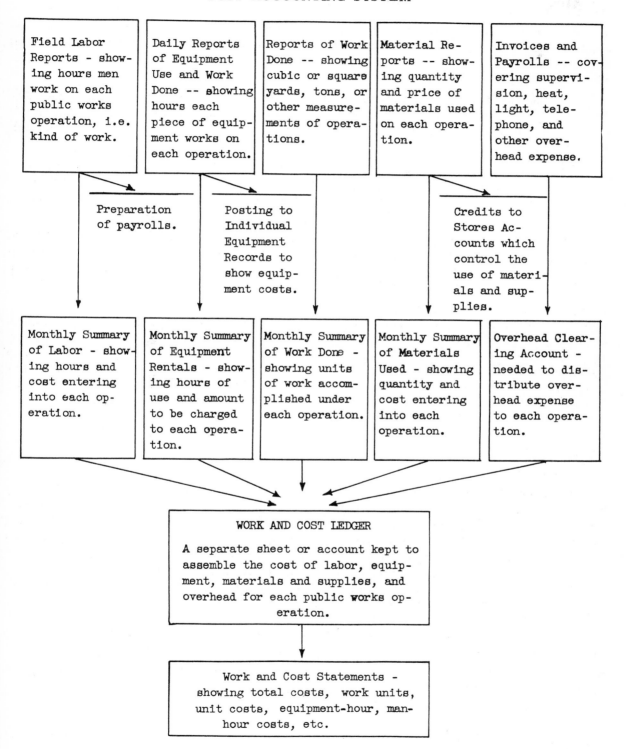

Fig. 27 — Chart Illustrating the Steps in a Public Works Accounting System

4. Centralized purchasing reduces the volume of paper work in conducting purchasing activities. In some cities for example, the actual number of purchase orders issued has been reduced by almost 40 per cent after the adoption of centralized purchasing.

5. A standardization of products purchased and the use of product specifications — both of which are ordinarily associated with centralized purchasing — simplify purchasing, assure uniform quality, reduce the number of different types of articles used, and frequently make possible substantial economies.

6. Centralized purchasing makes possible better supervision and control over materials following their delivery through centralized inspection, testing, and storage services. Inspection and testing also prevent vendors from delivering inferior goods and help in developing specifications.

7. Centralization, except in the case of smaller cities, makes possible the hiring of a full-time, qualified purchasing agent who will be better able to discharge his duties than will a number of part-time agents working in the individual operating departments.

8. Honest, qualified vendors prefer centralized purchasing because it saves time and effort by dealing with only one central department with respect to all the city's needs. Moreover, centralization makes possible the building up of qualified vendors and the control of unreliable vendors who may be unable to make deliveries or who have a record of substituting inferior merchandise.

Purchasing, as other auxiliary services, is essentially a service provided for the operating departments. To carry centralization of purchasing to such an extreme that operating department officials have no authority over or responsibility for purchases for their departments defeats the purpose of specialization. No attempt will be made here to specify just where the line should be drawn between the responsibilities of the purchasing office and those of the using departments; but one of the tasks of the chief administrator is to see that the purchasing office realizes its service role and that it does not assume the right to control or dictate to the using departments with respect to their material needs.

Purchasing Personnel

Purchasing is not a simple task which can be learned overnight. The purchasing agent must be familiar with the hundreds of items used by even the smallest village. He must know sources of supply for each of the commodities — or must know at least how to locate — and the favorable time to purchase each commodity. He must learn the reputation of the suppliers and their ability to serve the needs of the city. He must be aware of the sharp practices sometimes used by vendors. He must be familiar with the state statutes and municipal ordinances regulating purchasing. Expertness in these and other duties of the office comes only with training and experience. For this reason, the purchasing agent should be selected on the basis of merit, he should have no fixed term, and should retain his office as long as he performs his duties in a satisfactory manner.

In the majority of small municipalities under the council-manager form of government, purchasing is a function of the manager. Frequently, the chief finance officer acts as budget officer and purchasing agent, and in some jurisdictions the city engineer or director of public works buys for all departments.

Purchasing Department Records

In most purchasing departments files are kept of requisitions, quotations received from bidders, purchase orders, and general correspondence. In planning future purchases and in carrying on the daily routine, constant reference is made to all these records of past experience. Requisitions are appropriately filed numerically by the requisitioning department. Purchase orders are numbered serially for all purchases and are filed in numerical sequence. The commodity price card record file, on which all purchases are recorded according to commodities, constitutes a record of the price and consumption trends of commodities used, and the sources of supply, and is also useful in tracing purchases. Two other sets of records which should be kept are a specification file and a vendor's catalog file. Commodity specifications are filed according to the name of the commodity. Vendor's catalogs are best filed according to materials.

Standardization and Specifications

Many cities have centralized purchasing in name, but do not obtain the full advantages of such centralization because the purchasing office is merely an order-placing agency. Common failings of such purchasing agencies are: (1) failure to standardize commodities purchased, (2) purchase of commodities by brand name, and (3) purchase of commodities with inadequate specifications.

Before purchases can be consolidated it is necessary to ascertain the types, sizes, and grades of commodities used by the individual departments and reduce them to the minimum actually needed. After this simplification has been achieved, standard specifications describing these commodities should be developed. The process of standardization should begin with those items most commonly used.

The small municipality seeking to establish standard specifications should avail itself of the work already performed by the larger units of government and other agencies. The Federal Specifications Executive Committee, located in the Procurement Division of the United States Treasury Department, has adopted and promulgated specifications for the use of the federal government. Many of these can be adapted to the municipal purposes. "Services of the National Bureau of Standards to Governmental Purchasing Agents," (Letter Circular No. 497), summarized the activities of the Bureau of Standards which are of interest to purchasing agents. The "National Directory of Commodity Specifications," (Miscellaneous Publication No. 178, with supplement), issued by the Bureau of Standards, contains a classified list and brief description of the standards and specifications formulated by national technical societies, trade associations having national recognition, other private organizations, and the federal government, and includes the names and addresses of standardizing agencies and directions for obtaining free copies of the specifications.

Purchasing Procedure

The purchasing procedure consists of the following operations: (1) determination of purchase requirements, (2) conduct of purchase negotiations, (3) award of orders or contracts, (4) handling of emergency orders and purchases on price agreements, (5) receipt, inspection, and testing of deliveries, and (6) approval of invoices. The usual steps required in the purchase of a commodity are graphically illustrated in Fig. 28.

Purchase Requirements. In so far as practicable the purchasing agent should anticipate the future requirements of the individual departments and should consolidate the requirements of the various departments for similar types of items. The fullest advantage of quantity purchases, including lower unit prices, can thereby be obtained. The most effective way of ascertaining such future requirements is by use of the advance requisition, through which the operating departments furnish the purchasing agent with an estimate of

AGENCY	USING AGENCY	PURCHASING AGENT	FINANCE OFFICE	VENDOR
Action Taken	1. Using a requisition form, orders requirements from the Purchasing Agent.	2. Upon receipt of requisition solicits bids from vendor by use of request-for-quotation form or by telephone or advertisement.		3. Upon receipt of request-for-quotation form, supplies best price and returns the form.
		4. Tabulates bids received and makes out purchase order to vendor offering best bid. Distributes copies as shown below	5. Receives copies two and three of purchase order. Encumbers account of requisitioning department. Signs copy of purchase order and returns it to Purchasing Agent as notification of availability of funds.	
		6. After return of signed purchase order, releases original to vendor.		7. On receipt of order delivers commodity to using agency.
	8. Checks delivery; submits report of goods received to Purchasing Agent.	9. Checks report of goods received and sends it to Finance Office.		10. Prepares two copies of invoice and submits to Purchasing Agent.
		11. Compares invoice with purchase order as to unit price and checks against report of goods received and any laboratory test records. Sends one copy to Finance Officer.	12. Checks extensions and footings on invoice, reviews report of goods received, and prepares voucher for payment.	
Forms and Documents Used	Purchase Requisition — File — File — Storage or use — Report of Goods Received	File — Request for Quotation — Reviews and files — Purchase Order — File — Sign File — File — Checks — File	Hold — Furnishes price and returns — Sign File — Reviews when approving invoice — Voucher	Furnishes price and returns — Commodity — Invoice — Converts to cash

Fig. 28 – The Purchasing Process

their requirements for specified commodities over a stated period, such as three months, six months, or one year. Consolidated purchases should be made of all items which can be standardized.

When operating departments desire the purchasing agent to procure a commodity a purchase requisition should be prepared and forwarded to the purchasing agent.

The form illustrated by Fig. 29 is a multiple purpose form that may be used as an advance requisition of departmental needs for a future period, as a requisition for material, supplies, or equipment which are to be ordered from vendors for direct delivery and immediate use, or as a requisition on stores to be filled by the purchasing agent from stocks of goods which he has purchased in advance of actual use. Normally, all requisitions should go immediately to the purchasing agent who will, where necessary, clear them with the chief administrator.

[Name of Municipality]

REQUISITION

Department ....
Deliver to .... Date ....
Required Delivery Date .... Requisition No. ....

Quantity	Unit	Description	Account to be Charged	For use of Purchasing Agency			
				Unit Price	Am't	Vendor	Purchase Order No.

I hereby certify that the articles requested are necessary to conduct properly the activities of this agency.

Signed .... Approved ....
(Head of Department or Authorized Agent) (Chief Executive or Authorized Agent)

Issued from Stores by.................... Received by ....

Fig. 29 — Requisition Form

Purchase Negotiations. As a general rule, wide competition leads to lower prices. Provision for securing competition should be a major element in all purchasing procedures and should be dispensed with only when an emergency requires than an order be placed with the nearest available source of supply, when the amount involved is trivial, or when the commodity or service can be obtained from only one vendor. The responsibility for the development of competition rests with the purchasing agent. He should be continually searching out new sources of supply to meet the needs of the municipality.

Although most laws regulating municipal purchases require that purchases over a minimum amount (usually $500 or $1,000), be advertised in one or more newspapers of general circulation, such advertisements are of little or no value in securing competition for orders of supplies and materials. However, the advertising of large purchases can be justified as a safeguard against limitation of competition and as a protection to the purchasing agent against charges of discrimination or collusion. Even where advertising is used, it should be supplemented by other devices.

Posting notices of pending purchases on bulletin boards in the office of the purchasing agent is a supplementary method of obtaining competition. Bids by telephone are usually acceptable for small purchases or purchases that must be completed quickly. The most satisfactory method of securing competition is to solicit bids by mail through the use of a request-for-quotation form such as is shown in Fig. 30.

Certain municipalities require that quotations be accompanied by a certified check, cash, or bond as guarantee that the bidder will accept the order if it is awarded to him. Except in the case of construction contracts, purchases involving large sums of money, or purchases in which failure to perform would result in loss to the city, the requirement is a needless and expensive safeguard and can be safely dispensed with if the purchasing agent has authority to disqualify vendors who default on their quotations. After bids are opened, the quotations should be tabulated. An ordinary columnar pad, appropriately headed, can be used for this purpose.

Awarding the Order or Contract. The most desirable procedure for the awarding of orders is to require that the award be made on the basis of the bid most advantageous to the city. This provision has the merit of permitting responsible officials to exercise discretion. However, the laws regulating municipal purchases in individual cities frequently require that the award be made to the "lowest bidder." The low bid is not necessarily the best bid; in addition to price, the quality of the commodity and the service reputation of the vendor must be considered. This difficulty is sometimes solved by stating awards will be made to the "lowest responsible" bidder or to the "lowest and best" bidder.

When the award is not given to the lowest bidder, a full and complete statement of the reasons for placing the order elsewhere should be prepared and filed with the other papers relating to the transaction. This explanation and a list of all bids rejected may be entered on the reverse side of the summary of quotations. This record is important. The prices paid by a municipality are of public concern and the purchasing agent may be called upon at any time to justify his action to a disgruntled bidder or an interested taxpayer.

Purchases over a prescribed maximum dollar value should usually be covered by formal contracts. The contract form should be a document prescribed by the city attorney, and he should certify as to the correctness of the contract and the responsibility of the surety. Purchases under the prescribed maximum dollar value are generally made by means of a purchase order which sets forth the general terms and conditions of purchasing, describes the quality and quantity of goods ordered, and states the price quoted in the bid. A sample purchase order form is shown in Fig. 31.

Modern practice requires clearance of the purchase order or contract of purchase with the finance officer to assure that the appropriation balance is sufficient to cover the commitment. The amount of each order or contract is entered as an encumbrance in the appropriation ledger, and a reserve is thus provided for payment of the resulting invoice. This procedure prevents the overspending of appropriations with resultant deficits at the end of the fiscal year. Issues of stores should be cleared in the same way.

Emergency Orders and Purchases on Price Agreements. A number of municipalities permit the using departments to place emergency orders without reference to the purchasing office. This practice is not recommended. As a general rule, emergency purchases should be made by the purchasing office or, if the office is closed, only after communicating with the purchasing agent. Each requisition for emergency purchase should be accompanied by a detailed explanation. Whenever an emergency order is placed by telephone, a confirming order should be sent to the vendor as soon as possible.

[Name of Municipality]

REQUEST FOR QUOTATION

This is NOT an order

To

Date ....
Requisition No. ....
Request for Quotation No. ....

Bids will be received until .... m., ... 19.... at the office of the Purchasing Agent.

Quotations are requested for furnishing the items described below in accordance with terms set forth herein. ALL QUOTATIONS MUST BE F.O.B. DESTINATION and include cost of boxing and cartage to delivery point stated below.

Quantity	Unit	Description	Unit Price			Total
			List	Trade or Govt. Discount	Net	

TOTAL NET BID

TERMS: .... % ....days
or .... % ....days
To be delivered to..................
....
Delivery to be made on or before.....
....
or..........days from receipt of order.

In submitting the above, the vendor agrees that acceptance of any or all quotations by the Purchasing Office within a reasonable period constitutes a contract.

Per ....
Title ....
Date ....

ALL QUOTATIONS MUST BE SIGNED
(over)

Fig. 30 — Request for Quotation

[Name of Municipality]

PURCHASE ORDER

To

Date	Request for Quotation No.	Requisition No.	Purchase Order No.

Deliver to .... Department
Address ....
Via .... on or before..............
(Unless otherwise stated all prices F.O.B. destination)

Quantity	Unit	Description	Account to be Charged	Unit Price	Amount
		Total Amount			

Subject to conditions printed on the reverse side

Do not accept this order unless it is signed below

I hereby certify that this order is authorized by a properly executed and approved requisition.

....
Purchasing Agent

Fig. 31 — Purchase Order

The dangers of emergency purchases may be eliminated by proper use of the price-agreement type of contract under the terms of which a vendor obligates himself to supply all requirements to the municipality for a specified commodity during the period of the agreement, usually at a fixed discount from an ascertainable market price. This procedure is particularly advantageous in small communities in which it is not feasible to invest heavily in stores and in which, although a large number of different items may be used, the volume of consumption of each is relatively low. A request form for deliveries under price-agreement contracts is shown in Fig. 32.

[Name of Municipality]

REQUEST FOR DELIVERY AS PER AGREEMENT

Vendor ....   Request No.......................

Deliver to..   Requisition No......................

Department ....   Date ....

Deliver on or before ....   Purchase Order No................

Quantity	Unit	DESCRIPTION	Acct. to be Charged	Unit Price	Amount

REMARKS: Signed ....

                                          Title ....

Fig. 32 — Request for Delivery Under a Price Agreement

Receipt, Inspection, and Testing of Deliveries. Upon receipt of a delivery, the purchasing office should be notified immediately. A report of goods received, illustrated by Fig. 33, can be filled in by an employee of the receiving department to indicate the quantity, description, and condition of the commodities received. The report of goods received is forwarded to the purchasing agent and by him to the finance officer in order that the vendor's invoice may be audited and approved promptly. This procedure makes it possible to take advantage of all cash discounts offered for prompt payment.

Unless the municipality receives the quantity and quality of the commodities ordered an otherwise sound purchasing procedure is of little value. Adequate inspection of deliveries is an important but often neglected part of the purchasing procedure. Such inspection of deliveries saves the city from losses due to errors or deliberate attempts to defraud. Surface inspection, counting, and weighing of deliveries do not always provide an adequate check on goods received. Physical or chemical tests are sometimes necessary in order to determine actual qualities. The purchasing agent should utilize to the maximum the testing services of the chemists and engineers employed by the municipality. Where these services are not adequate, the agent should have the authority to secure testing services from other agencies. The Bureau of Standards has compiled a "Directory of Commercial Testing and College Research Laboratories," which lists alphabetically the types of commodities which each is prepared to test. State and municipal universities usually afford satisfactory service, and at lower cost than other agencies. Finally, the Bureau of Standards has established a certification plan under which a list of manufacturers have indicated their willingness to supply commodities in accordance with standard federal specifications. These manufacturers are willing to certify, when requested to do so, that their products comply with these specifications. Smaller governmental units, lacking adequate testing facilities, should make fullest possible use of this latter method of assuring the quality of municipal purchases.

Approval of Invoices. Two copies of the invoice should be submitted to the purchasing department by the vendor. There it is checked with the office copy of the purchase order for unit prices, and with the inspection and receiving report for quantity of goods received. One copy of the invoice is filed in the purchasing department; the other is forwarded to the finance office, which checks extensions and footings on the invoice, makes necessary entries in the accounting records, and prepares the voucher or warrant for payment.

Central Stores. All municipalities will find it advantageous to maintain a stock of certain commodities which are in constant or frequent demand. The need for small stocks of stationery and a limited supply of repair parts is obvious. On the other hand, the maintenance of large stocks of a large number of items is becoming less common. Under present-day practices it is possible to buy most articles on long-term contracts or price agreements at quantity prices and obtain delivery in small lots as needed. It is increasingly the practice to let the vendor be the storekeeper with the city keeping on hand only those staple articles which are used currently, in quantities sufficient to prevent shortages and possible crippling of the municipal services. Where stocks of material are kept by the city, they should be subjected to strict stock control, and adequate records should be maintained of the quantities on hand. The responsibility for storeroom management, or for inventory control in the case of a departmental stock room, is usually placed upon the purchasing agent.

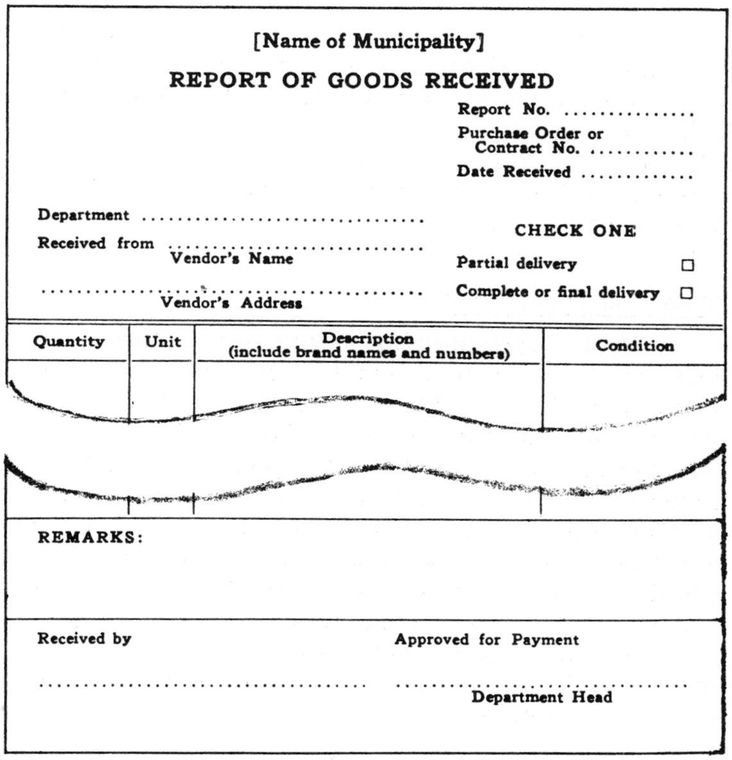
[Name of Municipality]

REPORT OF GOODS RECEIVED

Report No. ....

Purchase Order or Contract No. ....

Date Received ....

Department ....

Received from .... Vendor's Name

.... Vendor's Address

CHECK ONE

Partial delivery ☐

Complete or final delivery ☐

Quantity	Unit	Description (include brand names and numbers)	Condition

REMARKS:

Received by ....

Approved for Payment .... Department Head

Fig. 33 — Report of Goods Received

Cooperative Purchasing. Of particular interest to the chief administrator is the recent trend toward cooperative purchasing by local governments. In several states, notably Michigan, the state leagues of municipalities have inaugurated joint purchasing of such commodities as fire hose, name signs, and paint for their member cities. Local governments in Hamilton County, Ohio, have made outstanding progress in cooperative purchasing. The city (Cincinnati), the county, the library, the school district, and the municipal university purchase jointly such items as coal, oil, soap, paint, and certain pharmaceuticals. Joint purchasing agreements also exist between University City, Mo., and other governmental units functioning within the city.

Such a program may be initiated very simply on an informal basis. All that is required is the agreement of representatives of each jurisdiction to purchase one or more items jointly. Through the pooling of purchases, small municipalities that individually cannot afford a professional purchasing agent may be able to establish a joint purchasing office of high caliber. The prospect of savings under such an arrangement warrants its careful investigation.

Debt Administration

The basic policy questions involved in the use of borrowing to finance municipal expenditures have already been discussed in Chapter 5. After the general borrowing policy has been laid down, however, certain subsidiary questions of debt administration remain that lie largely within the province of finance administration. These include the choice of debt form, special assessment financing, use of revenue bonds, short-term borrowing and the funding of floating debt, marketing of municipal bonds, and debt redemption and interest payment.[9]

Choice of Debt Form

Bonds, according to method of redemption, fall into two general types, sinking fund and serial. An issue of sinking fund bonds becomes due in a lump sum at the end of the term of the loan and is met by annual payments to a sinking fund of amounts which, when invested at compound interest, will produce the amount of the principal by the time it becomes due. An issue of serial bonds, on the other hand, is retired by annual installments directly from appropriations. Serial bonds, in turn, are of two general types. In the case of annuity serials the annual redemption requirement increases gradually to equalize the annual cost of principal and interest over the full period of the issue. Straight serials provide for equal annual payments of principal. Serial bonds have largely replaced sinking fund bonds in municipal borrowing, and in some states the use of the latter by municipalities is no longer legal. Term bonds, however, are sometimes used for revenue producing facilities, particularly new types of enterprises which may not have an established earning period.

Sinking Fund Bonds. Sinking fund bonds have lost favor because of certain disadvantages, among them the complications of sinking fund administration, which requires expert investment of funds and frequent actuarial computations to determine the adequacy of funds and the failure of many city administrations to maintain adequately the necessary payments. For most cities — particularly the smaller ones — and for most purposes, the use of serial bonds is preferable, because of simpler retirement requirements and greater flexibility in marketing and in arranging debt structure.

Straight Serial Bonds. Straight serials have the general advantage of lowering the total borrowing cost and of progressively lowering the annual debt service charge. While service requirements are higher in the early years of the period, the total interest cost is lower because principal is paid off more rapidly. When debt service on a given issue declines progressively year after year, moreover, provision is made for offsetting

---

[9]For a good discussion of debt management see Municipal Finance, Feb. 1957 (Chicago: Municipal Finance Officers Association).

increasing maintenance costs as the improvement deteriorates; and in addition, a margin is steadily developed for new borrowing without increasing the general level of debt service.

The status of money rates may also be an influencing factor in determining which of the two types of serial bonds is to be preferred. If the going rate for short-term maturities is very low and the rate for long-term maturities materially higher, straight serials afford a means of lowering the total cost of the loan by bringing a larger proportion of the principal within the low-rate range. On the other hand, when the demand for short-term money is abnormally heavy, there is no advantage in competing for it in the market. When investors are seeking long-term loans, annuity serials are preferable and sinking fund bonds have special advantages.

Deferred Serial Bonds. There are certain modifications of the serial form of debt retirement which ordinarily should be avoided. This is the case with respect to deferred serial bonds. An exception in favor of the deferred serial may arise, however, when existing debt is scheduled for extremely rapid retirement and deferment for a few years of the first payment on the new borrowing fits better into the city's general retirement schedule and does not retard unduly the rate of liquidation.

When bonds are issued for self-liquidating projects, deferment of the first annual payment becomes justifiable. Normally it should come due after the first year of operations when the bonds are full faith and credit obligations.

Irregular Serial Bonds. Irregular serials are also to be avoided. These include bond issues which are ostensibly serial but call for an abnormally large final maturity. Either a sinking fund must be accumulated, which raises unnecessary complications; or the arrangement indicates a deliberate intention of evasion of payment according to schedule, with ultimate refunding or default.

Relation of Debt Structure to Choice of Debt Form. Fundamentally important in the planning of borrowing is the debt structure. The totality of a municipality's borrowing for tax-supported purposes should be so arranged, (1) that there will be no pronounced irregularities in debt service from year to year to cause erratic gyrations in the tax levy, and (2) that there will be a progressively downward trend in annual requirements which will make room for new borrowings without pyramiding debt service costs. When new borrowing is undertaken it should be so fitted into the existing structure that no irregularities, actual or potential, will result. The use of straight serials normally will tend to facilitate such a program, but no general rule can be laid down as the planning of debt structure often has years of no planning at all as a background. An irregular structure is likely to take some years to correct, may involve some unconventional scheduling of a new borrowing, and sometimes necessitates the judicious refunding of some maturities before past mistakes can be rectified.

In the planning or correction of debt structure, however, any scheme of so-called "debt equalization" is to be avoided as shortsighted and hazardous. This notion contemplates readjustment of debt to spread out annual principal and interest requirements on an even level over a long period of years. Related only to existing debt, such an arrangement is thrown further out of alignment with each succeeding new bond issue. It makes progressively increasing debt service unavoidable and develops vulnerability to the next business depression.

Use of Callable Bonds. Municipal bonds are sometimes issued with the provision that they can be called for payment at the option of the debtor in advance of the maturity date. Such bonds are known as "callable" or "optional" bonds. The call provision may be used with serial as well as with term bonds. It takes a wide variety of forms.

At some times and under some conditions the call feature has definite advantages. When the interest rate at which the optional bonds are issued is normal or high, there is always the possibility that the bonds can be called and refunded at a lower interest rate at some time during the term for which they are to run. This may be because of a period of low interest rates or because a municipality has been able to improve its credit standing. In considering the desirability of making bonds callable, however, it must be borne in mind that this feature ordinarily makes bonds less attractive to investors and tends to increase the original rate at which they can be sold. For this reason there is likely to be little financial advantage and possibly a financial loss, in making bonds callable when sold in periods of low interest rates. Some of the objection can be removed, however, if the time when bonds become callable is set several years from the date of issue and a reasonable premium is required for calling. The call feature also may have a proper place in a revenue bond issue since earning estimates at the time of issuance may have been ultra-conservative.

Special Assessment Financing

Special assessment bonds offer, in theory, an admirable means of assessing the cost of improvements of localized benefit upon the direct recipients, and of permitting the property owners of a limited area to secure and pay for a type or quality of improvement superior to that which the city generally can afford. In actual practice, however, special assessment bonds have often been used to dodge borrowing limits, to avoid popular referendums on bond issues, to give undue stimulus to the flow of construction contracts, and to furnish capital to real estate promoters to develop new subdivisions.

There are two general types of special assessment bonds, those which are contingent obligations of the municipality and those which are secured only by the property against which the improvement is assessed. The latter type, in turn, may have only specific parcels of property as security or may be issued against an entire improvement district. Irrespective of whether special assessment bonds are contingent general obligations or limited obligations, however, their indiscriminate and excessive use is a menace to the financial soundness of any municipality.

It is questionable whether general obligation special assessment bonds should be used at all, the chief point in their favor being the lower interest cost. If used, they should be made to conform to the general features of debt control, such as authorization and inclusion within the borrowing limit, and to fit into a general plan of borrowing within capacity to pay.

The control of special assessment borrowing varies, naturally, for improved and unimproved property. In the case of improved property the owners are likely to have a considerable investment at stake and, therefore, to prove more responsible. Approval of such special assessment financing, however, should be preceded by ample notice and opportunity for public hearing and should be with the consent of a majority of the property owners representing two-thirds of the assessed valuation. Approval should be withheld, furthermore, if tax delinquency in the proposed district is above the average for the city or if the properties are known to be excessively mortgaged. Special care should be taken to relate the improvement properly to the requirements of the area and to avoid the piling up of overlapping assessments.

In the case of unimproved areas the safest procedure is to withhold approval of a plan until such guarantees and arrangements have been made as will obviate the necessity for special assessments. This is easier to state as a principle than to work out in practice as no two subdivisions will pose their problems in quite the same way. The extreme solution is to require the subdivider to install all improvements, with inspection by the city to assure that they are standard. In many communities the city pays for the cost of facilities required of the subdivider and designed to serve areas beyond the subdivision.

Revenue Bonds

A revenue bond is an obligation issued to finance a revenue-producing enterprise and payable, both principal and interest, exclusively from the earnings of that enterprise. Such bonds may be additionally secured by a mortgage on the property — laws and practice vary; but their outstanding characteristic is that they rely exclusively on the earnings of the project which they have paid for, and have no claim on the general credit or taxing power of the governmental unit which issues them.

Appropriate Uses of Revenue Bonds. Laws of the several states vary as to the use of revenue bonds. It should be remembered that the legal availability of such bonds does not justify their indiscriminate use. They should not be employed to evade sound and reasonable debt limits or to engage in speculative ventures. When a municipality has adequate general borrowing power at its disposal, due consideration should be given to which type of bond can be sold at the lower cost. Usually, general obligation bonds sell at a lower interest cost than can be obtained on a revenue bond issue sold by the same municipality. Revenue bonds, however, have certain advantages. They are an aid to municipalities wishing to undertake revenue-producing enterprises which have been held back by unduly restrictive general borrowing provisions; they tend to encourage the businesslike management of such enterprises; and they permit the financing of basically essential utilities by municipalities which are seriously limited as to general credit and taxing power; and they assign the cost of added improvements to those who will benefit from the availability of such new improvements.

In general, the types of undertakings suitable for financing with revenue bonds include those which (1) lend themselves readily to operation on a service charge basis; (2) can be made sufficiently revenue-producing on this basis to cover full operating maintenance, and debt service costs; and (3) can be made to do so without violating any vital economic or social requirements of the community.

In this category would normally fall those types of public service enterprise which experience, either under public or private operation, has demonstrated to have the potentialities for self-support. They include primarily water and sewer systems, light and power systems, gas plants, local transportation systems, off-street parking facilities, toll bridges and traffic tunnels, stadiums, and possibly port facilities, public markets, auditoriums, and airports, as well as certain minor new types of public undertakings which can be shown clearly to have the three qualifications cited.

Revenue Bond Administration. The successful use of revenue bonds requires careful planning of the project to be financed, proper planning of the bonds, and businesslike management of the enterprise. Revenue bonds, on the whole, have a good credit record. Such defaults as have occurred disclose the mistakes to be avoided in planning and management. The technical steps of planning the project, planning the bonds to finance it, and promoting the sale of the bonds call for the consultation and services of specialists. Any new project or extensive improvement of an old one calls for the services of consulting engineers. No matter how experienced a municipality's engineering staff may be, it needs the protection which comes from the independent checking and advice of a competent outside consultant.

The principles to be observed in planning bonds to suit the enterprise may be summarized briefly: Bonds should be scheduled for retirement well within the useful life of the project; but their retirement should be spread out sufficiently to allow a comfortable margin of revenue coverage for debt service without the necessity for charging abnormal rates. The amount of combined annual interest and amortization should follow an even or possibly slightly rising trend in order to coincide with the prospective pattern of revenues. The first payment on principal should be deferred until plant operations have had time to become well established.

Revenues must be sufficient, first, to cover the costs of operations, maintenance, and debt service; second, to provide a comfortable margin of working capital; and third, to create a reserve fund for emergencies and to cover possible dips in income. In addition, the administration of the project must be given such control of revenues that they cannot be diverted recklessly for other purposes. If the enterprise is being operated for profit, the limits of such profit and the conditions under which it may be transferred should be carefully defined and established.

It is absolutely essential, in the light of both favorable and unfavorable experience, that any governmental unit engaged in the financing of its business enterprises by means of revenue bonds establish appropriate and clearly defined fiscal policies along the lines of those outlined, and protect these policies against political tampering. They can be given some degree of permanence by incorporating them in a municipal charter and they can be made even more binding by including them in pledges to bondholders when bonds are authorized and sold. No covenants should be entered into which involve unfair demands or in any way hamper the progress of the project, but there should be no hesitancy in the making of pledges which commit the management to the observance of sound fiscal policies. Not only is this in keeping with revenue bond procedure, but it can be made an invaluable safeguard for the enterprise.

Short-Term Borrowing and the Funding of Floating Debt

Short-term borrowing falls into three general classifications — borrowing in anticipation of taxes, borrowing for operating emergencies not included in the budget, and borrowing for capital purposes in anticipation of issuing bonds.

Tax-Anticipation Borrowing. Borrowing in anticipation of current taxes and other revenues is a routine procedure of the majority of municipalities at all times. It may be by bank loans, by sale of notes or warrants, or by the somewhat casual method of issuance and registration of warrants. In any event it is a form of borrowing which could be and should be rendered unnecessary. Its elimination would result in the saving of interest costs, heavy when short-term money rates are high, and in freedom from dependence on credit which is not always available when needed most. This type of borrowing can be reduced to a minimum if quarterly installment payment of taxes is instituted, if the first payment is placed near the beginning of the fiscal year, and if the tax and budget or fiscal years are so related that taxes become due within the fiscal year. The need for short-term tax anticipation borrowing can also be eliminated by establishing a working capital reserve of sufficient amount to finance the city through its "dry period" when taxes are not due. Adoption of a major nonproperty tax as part of the city's tax structure can also, in addition to better balancing the tax burden, provide a means to avoid tax anticipation borrowing.

Loans should be of no longer duration than the period in which taxes are to be collected, usually marked closely by the delinquency date or by some corresponding date for other revenues. If taxes are collected in installments the loans should be for each period, or for such portion of it as is necessary. The maximum amount of the loan should be dependent upon the amount of revenue antitipated. Sound policy, moreover, dictates a reserve in the budget for delinquency, and the maximum permissible borrowing should be reduced by the amount of the reserve applying to the particular period.

Borrowing against delinquent taxes would be unnecessary if budgetary estimates of revenue receipts were in line with reasonable expectations of amounts that will be collected, or if adequate reserves for delinquency were included in the budget, or if expenditures were kept in line with actual receipts. There is no excuse whatever in normal times and under normal conditions for failure to meet these requirements or for borrowing against delinquent taxes. Even in a period of rising tax delinquency, realistic estimates of receipts and careful execution of the budget can be made to produce "cash basis" operations unless the delinquency is abnormally high.

Emergency Borrowing. Temporary borrowing serves a useful function when contingencies arise which were not foreseen in the making of the budget. These include such emergency expenses as repairs caused by storm or flood, an unusual amount of snow removal, a marked increase in unemployment relief requirements, or the award of a judgment against the city. It should be stressed, however, that such loans are not to be substituted for honest budget making.

Bond-Anticipation Borrowing. Short-term borrowing in anticipation of the issuance of bonds is sometimes a useful type of temporary financing if used with discretion. When a public improvement is undertaken, bond anticipation notes may be issued as needed to finance construction as it progresses. When the improvement is completed, or when, if it is an extensive one, temporary borrowing for it has reached relatively sizeable proportions, permanent bonds are sold and the temporary obligations retired. This procedure has the advantage of avoiding payment of interest on the full amount until it actually is needed, of avoiding the handling of idle funds and of flexibility in choosing the most propitious time to market the bonds. It may avoid bond issues in excess of requirements, and it may even avoid the issuance of bonds for a project which is delayed or abandoned.

Funding of Floating Debt. The exigencies of the depression of the 1930's necessitated, for some cities, an unorthodox type of long-term borrowing — the funding of operating deficits. Needless to say the spreading of a city's normal current operating costs over many years of the future is an unsound practice, but it may be the lesser of two evils. When a city, either because its tax collection and budgetary systems are weak or its economic resources have temporarily declined to abnormally low levels, or both, has accumulated a cash deficiency (represented by delinquent tax borrowings, unpaid bills, and other liabilities) which is so unwieldy as to threaten a breakdown in operations and to defy any prospect of immediate disentanglement, funding is the only recourse.

Two principles, however, should govern such deficiency financing: It should be for as short a term as possible, and it should be a part of a definite plan to restore the city to a firm basis of balanced operations.

There are also two methods of issuing funding bonds. Prevailing conditions, combined with the two general principles stated above, will determine which of the two is the more desirable. Existing statutes, of course, may allow no choice in the matter.

One method is to issue bonds specially secured by a pledge of specific back taxes. When this is done the term of the issue should be no longer than is reasonably necessary for the taxes to be collected, and a special retirement fund should be created for segregation of the pledged taxes as collected.

The second method is to issue funding bonds to be retired exclusively from budget appropriations without any pledging of uncollected revenues. This method, particularly effective when the financial stringency has prospect of continuing for some time, calls for the spreading of maturities over a longer term — perhaps ten or fifteen years — depending on how seriously the current account is involved. It has the outstanding advantage of freeing back taxes from any encumbrance of temporary debt and creating surplus revenue to aid in balancing future budgets, but it has no justification if not accompanied by plans for cash-basis operations in the future.

Marketing Municipal Bonds

The prime objective in marketing bonds is to secure their sale at the most favorable terms possible. This can be done, logically enough, only by shrewd salesmanship of an instrument which is as sound as a community can produce. It calls for a special technique which is a somewhat unusual phase of municipal administration. The requirements, interests, and preferences of investment bankers and investors must be taken into consideration.

Debt Redemption and Interest Payments

It is extremely important that all principal and interest requirements on debt can be paid promptly. This constitutes the most direct evidence of good credit and should never be allowed to lapse through carelessness or poor planning. Even temporary delays rapidly become matters of common knowledge among investment bankers and investors and tend to affect adversely ability to borrow at the best going rates. Thus a well-defined administrative procedure is necessary to assure regularity in redemption and interest payment.

It is usually the part of good management for a municipality to appoint as its fiscal or paying agent a bank or trust company in the financial center in which its bonds are usually marketed. Funds are deposited with the paying agent in advance of due dates, and the agent cares for the payment of coupons and matured bonds as they are submitted. This arrangement is preferred by investors; it saves the city a large amount of routine work; and, since the agent is specially equipped to handle this function, it can be done at low cost.

Municipal Property Management

As a going concern a city must own and manage a large investment in various classes of property including land, buildings, machinery and equipment, and improvements to land other than buildings such as streets, sewer and water mains and other nonstructural improvements that enhance the value of land. Some of these properties, such as parks, sewers, and utility plants, are direct public service facilities which form an integral part of the department responsible for performance of the function in which these properties are used. Other properties such as buildings, office furniture and equipment, automobiles, and so forth, are used by several departments and may be subjected to some sort of centralized control. Management of property that is not a direct part of a department's service function is an auxiliary function which may profitably be centralized to some extent at least. In addition, all property should and can be subject to centralized financial control in the city's centralized accounting system.

Property management requires a complete identification and tabulation of all property owned by the city, utilization of such property to the maximum extent possible and in such a manner as to promote efficient performance of the services for which the property has been acquired and for which the city is responsible, and maintenance of the property in such a manner as to extend the useful life of the property and to keep it at top operating condition.

Basic in property management is the establishment of inventory control procedures. A current inventory of public property establishes fiscal accountability, aids in preventing loss or theft, establishes proof of loss in case of loss by fire or other destruction, and provides accurate information to serve as a guide in future acquisitions or replacements.

Specifically, major purposes of adequate inventory control include the following: (1) Provides an analysis of real property owned by each city department revealing unusually large holdings in excess of present and anticipated departmental needs, and at the same time discloses the lack of certain properties essential for their operation; (2) Assists in the development of the city's master plan by showing a complete and accurate record of land and buildings owned by the city which may then be compared with the long-range needs of the city; (3) Brings together in one place all data related to ownership, use, location, and identification of city-owned property; (4) Facilitates interdepartmental transfers of personal property, brings to light departmental shortages and surpluses of personal property, and helps in planning for future acquisitions of such property; (5) Assists in preventing theft and misuse of personal property and provides an accurate proof of loss of personal property for insurance purposes; and (6) Provides the basis for establishing fixed asset accounts and continuous property control.

Since some phases of property management can be centralized and thus can be administered as an auxiliary function, it need not be a direct responsibility of the chief administrator. It can be delegated to one or more specialized agencies, subject only to the general direction of the chief administrator. However, as pointed out in Chapter 3, the chief administrator may employ the mechanisms of auxiliary services as media of command, coordination, and control. Because these auxiliary services, when administered centrally, provide the chief administrator with channels for the flow of authority and responsibility between himself and his subordinates, they permit the chief administrator to marshal the physical resources of the city and to apply them economically and efficiently toward the achievement of his program.

The Management of Real Property

The total value of real estate holdings of a large city amount to millions of dollars. For both the large and small city the value of such holdings may be several times larger than the city's total annual general revenues. Included among the real estate may be city office buildings, garages, storage yards, comfort stations, off-street parking garages, incinerator plants, police and fire stations, dumps, auditoriums, public housing, and libraries. In addition the city may hold pieces of vacant land that may have been acquired for future developments through purchase or donation, or which may have been added through tax foreclosure procedures. Despite the character and size of its real estate holdings, many cities have assigned a low priority to its management.

Instead of a centralized management over the purchase, use, maintenance and disposal of public land and buildings, management may be dispersed throughout various agencies and departments of the city. As a result of the failure to establish competent machinery for management and maintenance of properties, cities often do not know what property they own, or whether an economical use is being made of it. Under such circumstances one department may purchase or rent new property, while a similar piece of property belonging to another department is unused. Further losses may occur in the purchase rental, and sale of public property since the city lacks sufficient knowledge of its holdings, or through ineffectual management. In the absence of a unified maintenance program, repairs are often neither timely or efficient.

Management of city-owned real estate is closely related to both long-range land-use planning and to municipal revenues and expenditures. A land-use plan of a city, when officially adopted, establishes the use of existing city-owned (as well as privately owned) land, and determines property that must be acquired for future recreation, schools, street widening, park, or other uses. It also indicates city-owned land that will not be used for public purposes and which is, therefore, surplus and available for sale or lease to private interests. A plan for acquisition and use of property materially affects the total cost of land acquisition. Public announcement of intention to acquire property can inflate its price whereas quiet negotiation some time in advance of actual need takes advantage of actual prevailing market values. Such long-range planning can prevent haphazard acquisition of properties that will not be needed and premature disposal of properties that must ultimately be repurchased to complete a project. A complete property record verifies correct uses of public land under zoning restrictions, determines the extent of tax-exempt property, shows the income-producing land and buildings, provides immediate public information on real estate available for purchase or trade, and establishes the asset value of the property for investment and insurance purposes.

Establishment of Plan. The first step to secure economical use of and control over public property is to make a complete inventory of all properties of the city. A property inventory requires the preparation of a complete history of each building and parcel of land possessed by the city. To this end, for each parcel and each improvement a file is provided which contains full descriptive details of the property, of its acquisition, use, disposition, legal title, appraisal, and summary data on annual income and expense.

At least four control records will be required for effective city real estate management: (1) a master map showing the location of all publicly-owned property in the city; (2) an atlas containing detailed plats on all city-owned properties, with improvements indicated thereon; (3) an individual property record card giving all essential data about the property; and (4) a record folder or jacket containing all background data.

A master map can be color coded to show the use and general location of every piece of city-owned real estate. In the case of narrow strips acquired for street widening, this map may not be large enough to show small areas in detail but these should be shown on the atlas.

The atlas shows specific locations of city-owned properties, lot size and shape, and the relative size and location of any buildings thereon. In a large city quarter-section maps are convenient; in a smaller one a larger-scale map may be used. As with the master map, the data in the atlas may be color coded. For example, strips to be acquired for future street widening are shown in one color and then colored over when the land is actually acquired.

The property record or ledger card shows in one place all of the essential summary data about a specific parcel of land. Each parcel has a separate card. Figure 34 illustrates a record appropriate for recording information for each unit of property. Data on

PROPERTY INVENTORY		Atlas Page:	Key:
		½ Section:	
		Assmt. Dist:	Ward:
Description:		DISPOSITION	
Location:			
Resn. No:: Size of Land		Authority:	Date:
		To:	
ACQUISITION: Date Received: Consideration:		Authority:	Date:
		To:	
Method		Authority:	Date:
		To:	
Conveyed to		Authority:	Date:
Annexed by Date		To:	
Deed Recorded Date	Case No.	Authority:	Date:
	Court of	To:	
Plat Recorded Date	Authority	Authority:	Date:
		To:	
TITLE REFERENCE: Date: File: By:		Authority:	Date:
		To:	
Fee simple title rests in:		Authority:	Date:
		To:	
Subject to:		Authority:	Date:
		To:	
		Authority:	Date:
		To:	
INSURANCE (Date)		Authority:	Date:
Fire		To:	
		Authority:	Date:
		To:	

(Front)

ASSESSMENT OR APPRAISAL	19	19	19	19	19	19	19	19
Land								
Improvements								
Total								
By								

YEAR	USE	INCOME	REPAIRS	OTHER EXPENSES	IMPROVEMENTS

(Reverse)

Fig. 34 — Inventory Card for Recording Real Property

income and expenditures, posted annually from the cost records, furnish a convenient reference. Operating records can be geared to the property inventory by the key number of the parcel. In addition to its inventory use, the property record will aid in determining when maintenance and repairs are unduly expensive, and will serve as a basis for computing insurance values, for supporting fire losses, for preparing property valuations, and for calculating depreciation where such expense is distributed to cost accounts or where such estimates are made to determine contributions to capital replacement reserve funds.

In addition to the property record card there should be a folder for each parcel; or, in a mass acquisition, a folder for all parcels in a project. This folder contains copies of all documents leading up to acquisition and possibly additional information maintained after acquisition including pertinent correspondence, options and agreements, resolutions of the council authorizing purchase or condemnation and accepting the deed, legal documents such as titles, leases, and insurance policies, full description of all buildings located on the land, and photographs which show the location and appearance of the buildings.

Financial control over public property requires at least five general ledger control accounts: (1) land, (2) buildings, (3) machinery and equipment, (4) improvements other than buildings such as pavements, sewers, sidewalks, and water mains, and (5) work in progress. Totals in these control accounts will be equal to the sum of the amounts reflected on the individual property cards. As far as possible the value of these assets should be in terms of actual cost; but when these are unknown for any reason appraised values should be used. Asset accounts should be offset by investment accounts showing the sources of revenue from which the property has been acquired and improvements made. Common sources of investment in public property are current revenues, bonds, gifts, special assessments, and grants.[10]

Besides the initial survey, city property should be inspected physically at least once a year to assure that it is in proper use and to determine the condition of land, buildings, and equipment. Land or buildings leased to private individuals for proprietary uses should be inspected more frequently to verify compliance with the lease and other legal requirements.

Suggested Organization. The problem of real property management falls within the technical concern of a number of city agencies. It embraces problems of land titles, contracts, leases, and other agreements in which the city attorney has an interest. The financial phases of property management and the maintenance of property records are of moment to the city's finance officer. The purchasing office frequently plays a part in the acquisition and sale of properties. The planning of the use, disposition, and need for additional properties is a function of the city planning agency. The public works department is responsible for most public improvements requiring land acquisition, easements, and rights-of-way, and this department often possesses facilities for maintenance and repair of properties. Municipal housing authorities are assigned the job of planning, constructing, and managing housing and slum clearance projects. Acquisition of property under urban renewal and redevelopment programs may be the responsibility of a separate board of the housing authority or of regular divisions of the city concerned with property management.

The kind of person best equipped to correlate these various interests is an

---

[10]For details on accounting for public property see Municipal Finance Officers Association, Municipal Accounting and Auditing (Chicago: The Association, 1951), pp. 126-136.

experienced real estate man with knowledge of legal, financial, and managerial phases of property administration. The real estate unit under his direction would be charged with (a) maintenance of the inventory of city-owned real property; (b) appraisal of city-owned property and of property to be acquired for city purposes; (c) title searches to determine ownership and encumbrance of such property; (d) preparation of evidence to support appraisals in condemnation proceedings; (e) formulation, in cooperation with the planning agency, of a program for the acquisition and disposition of property; (f) conduct of the negotiations for acquisition and sale of property; (g) negotiation in right-of-way and easement proceedings; and (h) management of property not used for public purposes. In addition, the unit may sometimes be charged with the maintenance of the city's real property which is used for nonpublic and for public purposes.

The most advantageous location of a property management unit in the departmental structure of a city will depend upon local conditions. Frequently, they are associated with the finance department as in Buffalo, N. Y.; Long Beach, Calif.; Kansas City, Mo.; Concord, N. H.; and Martinsville, Va. In other cities, as in Los Angeles, it may be in a division or bureau of the department of public works. In others, it may be a separate board; for example, in Milwaukee it is under the board of public land commissioners and in Boston it is a separate department consisting of three divisions — property, buildings, and market. A few cities have vested this responsibility in the city attorney's office.

Janitorial Services

The establishment of a properly trained and supervised custodial service as a responsibility of a central property or other central unit will generally result in substantial savings as well as better custodial care. The practice of leaving the custodians to their own devices without competent supervision will often result in a low output of work, mistreatment of the heating plant, and failure to attain clean and attractive buildings. A neat and business-like appearance of city offices will have a direct effect upon the general quality of public service and the *esprit de corps* of employees.

Definite work schedules for custodial activities need to be followed by periodic checks of work and costs. Through study of different techniques and the measurement of results, more efficient methods may be devised for cleaning floors, walls, and windows; for scrubbing, oiling, and dusting, and for boiler operation. Standards can be established for the square foot area to be cleaned by each janitor under different sets of conditions. Many of these operations can be subjected to cost analysis.[11] Careful training of employees in correct work methods will pay ample dividends, and the custodial staff with proper instruction and supervision can be given responsibility for making minor repairs.

Equipment Records and Reports

Inventories. Good equipment management requires an inventory at the beginning of each year of all passenger vehicles, trucks, tractors, power shovels, road rollers, tool wagons, and other rolling equipment larger than a wheelbarrow. (Inventories should also be made, or course, of all tools and materials and of office equipment and other properties). The purpose of this inventory is to account for all equipment and to establish depreciation rates. During the year, the inventory record is adjusted whenever equipment is disposed of, purchased, or transferred to uses which alter its length of life.

---

[11] For detailed cleaning and maintenance schedules and for cleaning workloads see Management of Public Buildings (Washington, D. C.: Buildings Management Division, General Services Administration, 1950).

Two inventory and depreciation schedules have proved advantageous in a number of cities and are recommended for general adoption: see Fig. 35 covering nonpassenger equipment, and Fig. 36 covering passenger cars. Though Fig. 36 provides for depreciation rates either on a mileage or on a monthly basis, the latter is recommended except for passenger cars used in regular inspection or police patrol work. Inasmuch as nonpassenger equipment is charged in the cost accounts on an hourly basis, the "hour" becomes the logical unit for depreciation calculations.

Equipment Numbering. Under any plan of equipment control each piece of city equipment is given a number so that it can be identified on all reports and records. By the grouping of similar types and capacities of equipment (leaving open numbers for additions), equipment rentals for the general and cost accounts can be more easily summarized. If these numbers, together with the name of the city, are painted on all vehicles, misuse of equipment by week-end or after-hour jaunts is less likely to occur.

Any complete system of equipment control must of necessity include a variety of records, forms, and reports. Among them will be individual equipment records, inspection schedules, repair work orders, and requisition for parts and for gas and oil.[12] A statement of equipment costs furnishes a comparison of the operating efficiencies of the various pieces of equipment. This statement will assist equipment supervisors and departmental officials in determining whether a piece of equipment is used often enough to warrant its purchase, whether the mileage or hourly costs are too high, whether it is consuming too much gasoline or lubricants, when the purchase of new equipment will prove more economical than maintenance of the old, and what the most economical types of equipment are. If operating costs on any piece of equipment appear excessive, reference to the individual equipment record may uncover the causes.[13]

Control Over Other Movable Property

In addition to land, buildings, and major pieces of rolling equipment, cities utilize a wide variety of miscellaneous personal property requiring custodial control — office equipment, instruments, and so forth.

An adequate plan of control calls for fixing in some office the responsibility for property inventories and the assignment and disposition of such property. Preferably, the inventory should form a part of the records in the general accounting office. The property ledgers may be employed for this purpose, or a special inventory card record may be maintained. In the latter event, the cards should be controlled by, and periodically reconciled with, the property ledgers. If the chief fiscal officer or central purchasing agent does not operate such an inventory, the public works department and other operating departments will need to do so for their own property. In other cases, the property maintenance division might be charged with this duty for all departments.

Inventory Survey. If a record of such property is not in existence, a survey is necessary to determine the holdings of the city. The information to be gathered by the survey is of course much less detailed than for a land and building inventory. The data to be entered on an inventory card for each item include the name of the item, e.g., "typewriter," "transit," or "microscope"; the inventory item number; a description of the article including make, serial number, model, size, etc.; the seller; the purchase order number, date acquired, and original cost; the department or division to which assigned, including

---

[12] For suggested records and report forms, see Accounting for Municipally-Owned Motor Equipment, op. cit.

[13] See International City Managers' Association, Municipal Public Works Administration (Chicago: The Association, 1957), p. 146 for suggested record form.

Inventory and Depreciation Schedule of Mechanical Equipment (Non-Passenger)

Date _____ 19 ___

Equip. No.	Make	Body or Type	Capacity	Date Pur.	Original Cost	Appraised Value Jan. 1	Estimate Salvage Value	Net Amt. Subject to Depreciation	Remaining Life in Years	Annual Depreciation	Est. Hrs. of Operation This Year	Depreciation Rate per Hour	For What Purpose Used
(1)	(2)	(3)	(4)	(5)	(6)	(7)	(8)	(9)	(10)	(11)	(12)	(13)	(14)

Fig. 35 — Inventory and Depreciation Schedule of Mechanical Equipment (Non-Passenger)

Inventory and Depreciation Schedule of Passenger Equipment

Date _____ 19 ___

Equip. No.	Make	Model	Date Pur.	Orig- Cost	Appraised Value January 1	Estimate Salvage Value	Net. Amt. Subject to Depreciation	Total Operation to Date	Average miles Run per Month Present Use	Remaining Life Un. Present Use	Deprec. Rate Under Pres. Use	Est. Depreciation This Year	For What Purpose Used
(1)	(2)	(3)	(4)	(5)	(6)	(7)	(8)	(9) Miles Mos.	(10) Miles Mos.	(11) Miles Mos.	(12) Miles Mos.	(13)	(14)

Fig. 36 — Inventory and Depreciation Schedule of Passenger Equipment

the room number or other location of the property. Space on the card is needed also for noting transfers of the property and final disposition.

Personal property for purposes of inventory control must be carefully defined to eliminate supplies, parts, and other small and nondurable items and to avoid excessive record keeping. Each city should adopt rules to be observed in determining whether or not certain personal property should be inventoried. Such a statement of what constitutes property to be inventoried might include the following characteristics. (1) They should have an expected normal useful life of one year or more. Personal property should be excluded that has a short life due to (a) one-time use under such conditions that it will be destroyed for futher usefulness; (b) regular replacement because of rapid wear, and (c) frequent unavoidable loss by accident or theft. (2) They must be fixed assets which are more or less of a permanent character necessary to the operation of an enterprise or service. (3) They must not be consumed, unduly altered, or materially reduced in value in their use. (4) They must not be affixed to or form an integral part of another asset or property, since in that instance they would be a part of such asset. (5) They should have a unit cost of not less than a specified amount. This value is arbitrarily selected and so chosen as to fit the needs of a particular municipality and may vary from as low as $5 per unit to as high as $100 per unit.

It may also be desirable to account for some property on a group basis rather than on an individual basis. For example, the finance department may maintain only a single item for library books, but the library card catalog will then serve as a detailed listing of what is included. Tools may be similarly accounted for but the using department may wish to keep a detailed listing of the tools included.

The marking of each item of property with an identifying number is essential. Separate series of numbers may be employed for different classes of property, to which may be added a departmental or divisional code symbol. For example, PW-2035 could mean the thirty-fifth item of office equipment assigned to the public works department. Where proper budget and accounting classifications are employed, the property code should key into them.

Various methods are available for marking property. The best method for most kinds of property is the affixing of decalcomania stamps. Brass tags may easily be fixed to wood items, and self-threading screws may be used to attach the tags to metal articles. Other plans include painting the inventory number with stencils or stamping the number directly on the item with dies. Marking the name of the city on the property makes loss by theft less likely. The identification plan should be submitted to the local police department so that its pawnshop squad and property record clerks will be on the lookout for stolen city property peddled to second-hand dealers or pawnshops.

Pricing of Property

The price assigned to the movable property and miscellaneous equipment covered by this inventory system is the original purchase price. If this price is not ascertainable, an estimated purchase cost should be assigned. This is preferable to an appraised value, since there is no merit in depreciating most types of municipal property.

Only when depreciated values are required to determine profit or loss, as in the case of a municipal utility undertaking, or to fix the true cost of services, is it worth while to set up a depreciation plan or to make periodic appraisals. The motor equipment accounting system outlined above provides for depreciating equipment on the basis of hours or miles used, but no such plan is recommended for the bulk of other equipment and movable property covered here, even though cost accounting is in effect.

Chapter 9

ADMINISTRATIVE RESEARCH AND PLANNING

The Role of Planning and Research in Administration

Nearly every action initiated within an organization requires some foresight and deliberation before a decision can be made to proceed. The application of such administrative planning is an essential element in all municipal activities and is found at all levels in the administrative structure. Some planning may produce a long-range capital improvement program or a comprehensive city plan to guide the growth and development of the directives, administrative regulations, or formal and informal policies governing present or future actions.

Almost every employee of the city does some planning. The fireman studies fire chemistry, building plans, and other technical subjects so that in emergencies he will know what to do. The case work supervisor in the welfare department schedules the work to be done by her group and assigns cases to individual workers. Department heads review the plans of subordinates and weld them into a program of action for departmental plans; translate plans and programs for municipal services into terms of personnel, finance, and organization; and prepare orders, directives, and regulations which set the organization in motion and keep it moving toward getting the mission accomplished. The council reviews the plans of the administrator and sets forth the broad plans and policies which are to guide the administrative organization.

Administrative planning is a continuous process. It includes not only those formal plans which are prepared to outline future actions but also the constant adjustment of plans to conform to changing conditions or to new ideas. The manager cannot set aside two hours on Tuesday for planning and forget about it for the remainder of the week. The planning process, together with organizing, directing, coordinating, and reviewing are tools of the administrator, and must be utilized much as a mechanic uses his tools — when they are needed — selecting the proper one for the task at hand.

It may be convenient in this chapter and in other parts of this volume to call some kinds of study and investigation "research" and other kinds "planning." Actually the terms can almost always be used interchangeably. An important part of every planning process is research. By "research" is meant the collection and analysis of facts and ideas in a more or less systematic manner, and incorporation of the results of this study into policies or programs of action. "Planning" may imply a slightly less formidable or sterile process than "research," but no attempt is made here to draw a sharp distinction between the two words.

Administrative planning and research as used in this chapter should not be confused with the more topographic or physical aspects of the term "planning" which are concerned with the city's physical plan and the program of enforcement of land use and zoning regulations. These are discussed in Chapter 10 under the title "City Planning."

In the field of administrative research and planning there are two distinct areas of endeavor: (1) direct or program planning, which deals with the services the municipality is or should be providing, and (2) procedural planning, which deals with the manner in which the programs are being or should be administered. The one aspect deals with the formulation of basic programs and policies, while the other is concerned with the organizational structure, division of work, and administrative and procedural routines needed for carrying out the work. Since the first of these, program planning, has been covered in some detail in Chapter 5, it will be treated here only in so far as it may become one of the subjects for which research is being conducted. It should be noted, however, that every new substantive plan or policy calls for adjustments in the administrative structure and relationships. If broader problems of public service and improved methods of providing these services are not accompanied by constant adjustments and improvements in management, the whole program becomes unwieldy.

One of the primary objectives of administrative planning and research is to balance substantive improvements with advances in the art and science of management. What changes in organization will be required by the decision of the city council to inaugurate a municipal recreation program? Would the advantages of a central stenographic pool outweigh the disadvantages? Could the welfare department maintain present standards of service with less cost by a change in procedures or organization? What changes in procedure can be made to reduce the "red tape" connected with purchasing? Would a rearrangement of office layout reduce the need for messenger service? What measuring sticks can be devised to appraise the efficiency of the various departments? What information should be contained in departmental reports, and how should this information be presented? These are examples of the problems which require administrative planning and research.

Except for plans which affect only one department or agency, all administrative planning is a managerial responsibility of the chief administrator, subject to guidance and control by the council. Much of the preliminary work of collecting and analyzing evidence, and even of drafting tentative plans or proposals, can be done for him by managerial aides or agencies. Whether these aides and agencies be labeled "Research," "Administrative," or "Management," their essential purpose is the same — to provide information, ideas, and suggestions that will help the administrator to formulate wise plans and policies for the guidance of his administrative organization.

Research Within City Government

There is no consistent pattern in administrative planning and research in United States and Canadian cities. However, a brief review of some of the most common agencies or offices performing such duties will indicate the variety of resources that can be used in the analysis of municipal problems and in the preparation of plans and programs.

Operating Departments

The day-to-day work of all operating departments calls for continuous planning and research. A few illustrations will indicate the scope and importance of departmental contributions of this nature.

The public works department is usually responsible for street construction as well as other physical improvements related to street improvement projects, such as installation of storm drains, sanitary sewers, and water mains. Although the final decision as to whether a street will be improved will be made by the city council upon the recommendation of the chief administrator, it is the public works department's job to furnish information which forms the basis for the decision. All of the engineering and technical aspects of the project must be studied in order to arrive at an estimated cost of the project. The width of the street, right-of-way required, storm drainage, type of paving, the time required, and the best time of the year to do the work are questions to be answered.

It often may be necessary for the public works department to consult with other departments to do a complete planning job. For example, the planning department should be asked to determine how improvement plans for a specific street will fit into the overall master street plan, and the finance department should certify whether funds are available for the project if it is to be financed from general city revenues.

The pre-decision research merely scratches the surface of the total planning job required to see the project through to its conclusion after the council's approval. Construction must be coordinated with other city departments and public utilities to see that all underground improvements are installed before the street is paved. These installations may include storm and sanitary sewers, water and gas mains, and electric and telephone lines. If additional right-of-way is required, plans must be coordinated with the law department and the agency which handles right-of-way acquisition if it is not a responsibility of the public works department itself.

Many of the problems which require decision by the council or the chief administrator may originate with an operating department. For example, the need for repaving certain streets or the impending obsolescence of buildings or other property will first be reported by the public works department to the chief administrator, who may in turn submit the report to the council. In making such reports, operating departments will often include recommendations as to what action should be taken.

The health department is constantly studying problems in its field and making plans which deal primarily with services rather than physical construction. The health department must study mortality and morbidity rates, causes and bearers of communicable diseases, and so forth, so that it can plan and distribute its work to meet the greatest needs.

Other examples of research by operating departments could be cited, but these should illustrate the point that planning and research play an important role in the work of operating departments.

Auxiliary Agencies

Like operating departments, various auxiliary agencies perform a variety of planning and research duties. The purchasing department may conduct technical researches into the qualities of various materials and supplies, and it may also study market trends so that best prices can be obtained. Study of departmental needs for materials and equipment is also essential if these needs are to be anticipated and inventory shortages avoided.

Personnel technicians are constantly studying new testing procedures and methods, service rating systems, and the like, and they must make plans to keep up with the demands of operating departments for personnel of various classes. Legal departments spend much of their time in research and in helping the chief administrator and the department heads to plan their programs so that they will not conflict with constitutions, statutes, and charters.

Managerial Agencies and Aides

Managerial agencies and aides — in addition to special planning and research agencies — may include the budget officer, the finance officer, the personnel officer, and the administrative assistant. Whether all of these positions are found in a city will depend in a large measure upon the size of the city itself and of its organization. Nevertheless, in every case some person or persons will be designated by the chief administrator to carry out the activities normally associated with the positions.

The budget is itself a one-year plan or program covering all municipal activities, and the preparation of the budget is one of the biggest planning jobs of all. The budget officer therefore is involved in administrative research as well as substantive planning. In his task of analyzing estimates and helping the administrator enforce the budget after it has been adopted, he must concern himself with problems of organization, procedures, measurement, and the like.

The chief personnel officer provides research which helps the administrator in many ways. New services or changes in present services usually call for new personnel or for shifting of present personnel, and the personnel officer can advise the administrator on these changes. Recruitment policies also require much study and planning, as do employee relations policies, retirement plans, in-service training, and other phases of personnel management.

Since all substantive plans have financial implications, the finance officer has an important planning role. Long-term capital improvement plans call for long-range financial planning since expansion of existing services requires expansion of revenues. Borrowing policy is another subject for careful research. The finance officer may also be a useful aide in administrative planning and research. Fiscal procedures, accounting controls, and cost accounting may call for his advice and assistance.

The administrative assistant usually serves as the chief administrator's "handy man" although he sometimes may work in specialized areas such as personnel or budgeting. The chief administrator, however, generally relies on him for important research assignments, many of which do not fit into the work of any department or which cross departmental lines. He also helps the administrator coordinate and direct the planning activities of various agencies and officers.

Special Planning Agencies

In addition to the planning activities of operating departments, auxiliary agencies, and managerial agencies and aides, special agencies and personnel devoted almost entirely to planning and research problems are found in many cities.

City Planning Departments. A growing number of cities have established special agencies to deal with the problems of physical planning, which are ordinarily referred to as "city planning." The primary concern of the planning department is to formulate plans to guide the physical growth of the city and the orderly planning of municipal improvements of a material nature. Their importance in community design is evidenced by many of their planning and research activities — economic base studies, land use analysis and zoning, subdivision control, and development of master plans for land use, streets and traffic, and parks and schools. In many cities the planning department is also responsible for the development of a long-range municipal capital improvement program.

Administrative Planning and Research Agencies. Some cities have established special agencies for administrative planning and research. The scope and duties of such agencies may vary greatly. In some cases these agencies are affiliated with the budget agency and deal largely with administrative planning and research. In other cases they combine these duties with publicity or public reporting activities. In still other cities these research agencies are given a miscellany of research and investigative assignments, some dealing with substantive problems and others relating to problems of management. The activities assigned to special research agencies are discussed in greater detail later in this chapter.

Municipal Reference Libraries. A good reference library is an invaluable aid to all city personnel. A few of the larger cities maintain central municipal reference libraries. These libraries may be established as an activity of the municipal library or of the administrative planning and research agency, or as in the largest cities, as a separate activity. Standard reference books, reports on municipal activities in other cities, general and technical bulletins dealing with municipal problems and other materials are kept on file in these libraries, where they are available to all city departments and agencies.

In addition to the mechanical and custodial duties of cataloguing and arranging materials, municipal reference libraries may perform some research activities of a limited nature, regularly circulate bibliographies of reports and materials received, do bibliographical research for city officials, and occasionally send out inquiries to outside libraries and other centers of information.[1]

Organization for Administrative Planning and Research

Need for an Organized Planning and Research Program

The need for an organized administrative planning and research program as an integral part of the municipal operation has been recognized only in very recent years and by a relatively small number of cities. There are at least two factors that will tend to bring about its rapid acceptance in other municipalities. The first is the rapid urbanization of the population, which makes the job of providing essential municipal services larger and more complex, and this in turn calls for the greater application of sound principles of organization and scientific management. The second, although somewhat related to the first, is the recognition by many chief executives that administrative planning and research activities can be delegated in much the same manner as finance, personnel, budgeting, city planning, and other staff functions.

Perhaps at this stage in the development of organizations for administrative planning as much can be learned from analyzing the weaknesses in existing agencies as in enumerating the strong points of some of the more successful agencies. While it is true that organization for administrative planning varies in form and usefulness, three major weaknesses appear in many cities. These are: (1) a limited concept of administrative planning and research, (2) separation of planning from administration, and (3) poor coordination of administrative planning and research activities.

---

[1] For cities which do not have facilities for a central reference library, a bibliographical listing service on public administration materials may be secured from the Joint Reference Library, 1313 East 60 Street, Chicago 37, Illinois. Other bibliographical listings may be found in the Municipal Year Book and most of the periodicals and professional journals concerned with municipal government.

Limited Concept of Administrative Planning and Research. It has already been pointed out that the term "city planning" is commonly used in referring to certain physical planning activities. The value of such planning cannot be questioned, and it is encouraging to note the increasing recognition of the place of this kind of planning in city governments. It is unfortunate, however, that the growth of "city planning" in the narrow sense has not been paralleled by increasing attention to other kinds of planning and research.

Although some progress has been made in securing funds and personnel for studying other city problems, such progress has lagged behind the extension of physical planning facilities. Citizens and officials in many cities seem to think that they have made adequate provision for planning when they have established a "city planning commission" to draw up maps and blueprints for the physical expansion of the community. Important as these physical problems are, they are no more deserving of careful study than welfare policies, public health programs, and technique of management. The weakness is not that there is too much physical planning, but that there is too little systematic study of other problems.

Separation of Planning from Administration. "City planning" agencies, as established in most cities, have not only been concerned with a limited field of planning, namely physical planning, but they have in many cases been set apart from the regular administrative organization. In some cases they have even been given a status semi-independent of the city council itself. The separation of city planning from central administration, an unfortunate fact in the early years is a trend that reversed itself for reasons of practical necessity. This is discussed in Chapter 10.

Poor Coordination. The combination of a narrow concept of planning and of an attempt to separate it from the rest of administration has resulted in poor correlation of plans and incomplete coordination of administrative research and planning activities. Physical plans have often been inadequately supported by administrative plans, and methods of financing. The social and economic implications of physical plans have frequently been neglected or hastily considered. Resources of information, ideas, and critical ability have not been drawn upon as fully as they might have been. In brief, there is an urgent need for a better balanced program of municipal planning and research.

Place of the Administrative Planning Unit in the Organization Structure

Although it is impossible to make specific recommendations that will apply to all municipal governments, the most logical location for an administrative planning and research unit is the agency responsible for preparation of the budget. In smaller cities this function may logically be assigned to the chief executive's administrative assistant, who may in turn find the assistance of an administrative trainee to be of considerable help. In larger cities a department or division of administrative management or budget and research should be established.

"Administrative planning and budgeting are closely interrelated by the unity of their objectives, namely, the provision of a sound plan of administration requiring the least expenditure consistent with effective operation. In both activities it is necessary to determine the volume of work, how it is being performed, whether better plans or methods can be devised for its performance, how many people are necessary to do the job, and how much money will be required under the best plan. The techniques involved in arriving at the answers to these problems are the same for both budgeting and administrative planning, namely, intensive analysis and appraisal of the plan of administration with a view to increasing efficiency and assuring economy of operation.

"Competent administrative planning can be invaluable as a basis for instituting operating economies. A sound organization structure, simplified procedures, and smooth-flowing operations are prerequisites to economical and efficient governmental administration. These ends are the specific objectives of administrative planning, and their achievement demands the close cooperation and coordination of the planning and the budgeting staffs.

"Budget administration adequate for modern needs does not stop at the office review of estimates, but involves firsthand knowledge of operations as well. It is concerned with the scope and adequacy of operations, with long-term as well as immediate work programs, with the quality of administration, with the efficiency of work performed, and with a variety of public policy and fiscal considerations. So, unless the budget staff understands the administrative structure and operating problems of an agency, budgeting tends to become a routine, clerical service. To formulate an intelligent budget plan, the budget officer must have a thorough knowledge of the plan of administration and its operating methods as well as its financial resources. These elements constitute the base upon which budgetary requirements are constructed.

"The administrative planner, on the other hand, cannot formulate a new or revised plan of administration without fully considering its cost in relation to budgetary requirements. For example, in determining the relative merits of centralized or decentralized execution of a particular program, budget considerations must play an important and often dominant role. Problems of organization must be solved in full recognition of their budgetary implications.

"The recommended integration of these two activities does not imply that the same personnel should handle both the budget and administrative planning work. On the contrary, the best effects will usually result if administrative planning and research functions are concentrated in a separate staff which is free from the detailed duties incident to the handling of budget estimates. The close coordination of the two activities should be accomplished, however, through common over-all supervision. Frequent interchange of staff is also desirable." [2]

Regardless of where the administrative planning and research unit is located, it must be recognized as essentially a managerial agency. To a certain extent its services have an auxiliary character; i.e., they are technical or specialized services rendered to operating departments by a central agency. For the most part, however, the problems of administrative planning are broader in scope than a single department, and the outlook of the administrative planner must be broader than that of the technician or specialist.

The recommendation that the administrative planning and research unit be placed in the budget office under the general supervision of the budget officer does not mean that administrative planning is subordinate to budgeting or that it is not of immediate concern to the chief administrator. It means rather that the budget officer should be the principal administrative planning aide of the administrator, coordinating the studies and recommendations of the planning staff with the fiscal aspects of budgeting.

Activities normally assigned to the administrative planning unit include responsibility for making organization and administrative surveys; methods and procedures studies; special factual studies and reports for the chief administrator and city council; review of office layout and design, which might also include making recommendations for assignments of office space; central control over the design and printing of office forms; and the development of policies relating to records management and disposal. The chief

[2] Bernard L. Gladieux, "Administrative Planning in the Federal Government," in Governmental Research and Citizen Control of Government (Detroit: Governmental Research Association, 1940), pp. 69-70.

executive might request the administrative planning unit to review departmental work progress reports and prepare a digest of work accomplishments for the information of the city council and the general public.

The administrative planning unit might also provide advice and assistance to other departments and agencies in their research and planning activities. Its staff might provide a consulting service on planning and research techniques, advising and training personnel of other agencies in research techniques, as well as serving as a clearinghouse for municipal investigations, plans, and information.

In its role as a clearinghouse, such an agency could serve as a central source of reference on all research and planning information. It would be the business of the central agency to keep track of all the research and planning activities of the various departments and agencies of the city. Studies and investigations conducted by private agencies in the community would also come within the scope of the agency's interests and records. In the files of the central agency would be references to past studies and reports, information available from local agencies and also from outside sources, and schedules of studies under way or being planned for the near future.

The advantages of such a clearinghouse would be many. It would help to eliminate duplication and overlapping of research projects. Information collected by one department or agency would be available to others. Studies conducted by private agencies could be more easily related to each other and to official research. The chief administrator and council would be able not only to keep in constant touch with the varied planning and research activities and to secure information and to advise with a minimum of effort, but also could give effective direction and guidance to the study of municipal problems.

Organization and Relationships of the Administrative Planning and Research Agency

There is little point in attempting to prescribe in detail the organization of a central administrative planning and research agency, for the size of the city, the organization of other departments and agencies, and other local conditions will require modifications for each city. A few general suggestions may be offered, however.

The most important suggestion to be made is that the central agency should be not only within the administrative structure of city, but under the direct control and supervision of the chief administrator. The agency that has been proposed in this section is clearly a managerial agency and therefore should operate under the authority of the chief administrator.

The second recommendation is that the central agency should have a single head rather than an administrative board or commission. The principal reason for this recommendation is that the chief administrator needs a planning aide and advisor, and a single official can play the role of advisor and aide more effectively than a board or comission. The many conferences and consultations between the administrator and the planning commission, for example, would be awkward and too formalized if it were necessary to convene a group each time.

The third recommendation is that liberal use be made of advisory committees. Although the managerial character of the central agency calls for a single head responsible to the chief administrator, there are many planning and research problems which require group study and judgment. However, what is needed is not one more or less permanent group or commission, but *ad hoc* committees appointed for specific purposes as the need arises. When the problem has been taken care of, the committee ceases to exist. To select a group of three, or five, or seven laymen to represent various community interests and to provide a variety of background and knowledge does not adequately meet the requirements. The city council is, or should be, better suited to the tasks of representing popular opinion and making broad policy decisions than any specially appointed planning board or commission.

For the consideration of a particular problem, however, several points of view or fields of knowledge may need to be recognized. Special advisory committees might therefore be appointed to assist in certain planning and research projects. In some cases the committee might consist entirely of representatives of different municipal departments. In other cases different citizen groups may be represented, either because they have a particular interest in the problem being studied or because their understanding and support of municipal plans and policies is essential.

Most of these citizen committees should be appointed without definite terms and without any formal status. Their purpose is to assist in the study of particular problems, and when the study has been completed their work is done. The judicious use of such special advisory committees would not only provide and draw upon resources of experience and judgment for the solution of municipal problems, but it would contribute to better municipal public relations.

Departmental Planning and Research. The nature of municipal planning and research and the wide variety of subjects requiring study make it impossible to concentrate all planning activities in any one special agency. Even if it were possible to assign all such activities to some central body, it would not be desirable to do so, for such segregation would further aggravate the already serious problem of promoting unity and continuity between the formulation and the execution of plans and policies. In fact, there is need for more, not less, departmental study and investigation of municipal problems.

Personnel Requirements of the Administrative Planning Unit

"It is not over-emphasis to state that the success of the administrative planning and research unit in forming a vital part of the organization will depend in large measure upon the quality of staff recruited. Success in this type of activity demands imagination, creativeness, analytical insight, good judgment, training in and experience with governmental practices, and knowledge of the principles of public administration. Although some specialization is often desirable for work in such fields as public finance, for example, the successful administrative planner will more often have had broad experience in a number of functional fields.

"In addition to this necessary quality of technical competence, the administrative planner must also be able to work easily and well with people. Administrative planning and research deals not only with figures, organization charts, and reports, but is vitally concerned with personnel and the interplay of personalities. The work of the administrative planner is in large part a 'relationship' job and, on occasion, requires considerable ability in gaining acceptance of a point of view or securing agreement on the solution of a specific problem. The individuals engaged in this activity must, therefore, be personable individuals who are able to deal effectively with people and who can be persuasive and convincing without irritating or seeming to instruct.

"A word might be added about qualifications for the chief of an administrative planning unit. Mere knowledge of the essentials of administration or the theories of governmental practice, important as that is, will not suffice. The person assigned to this job should himself have an aptitude for administration demonstrated, if possible, by actual experience in an administrative capacity. This is necessary not only because the supervision and direction of a planning and research staff is an administrative job in itself but, even more important, because the development of improved administrative practices must be founded on the sound basis of practical knowledge of governmental operation." [3]

It is easier to describe the ideal administrative planning and research aide than it is to find men who fit this description. The need for administrative planning and research has only recently been given general recognition, and there is a very limited supply of men especially trained for this kind of work. Junior members of the administrative planning and research staff may be recruited from colleges and universities having special courses in public administration or city management. But these junior members need to be directed and guided by someone with more practical experience.

Men who have had experience in privately sponsored municipal research bureaus or who have been staff members of private consulting firms in the field of municipal administration are likely prospects, although the supply of such men is limited. Men whose experience includes service as an administrative assistant, administrative analyst, or as a member of a budget office may also be good material. A number of cities also have administrative internship or management trainee programs which provide an excellent background for the post of administrative analyst, and, with proper additional experience, a supervisory position in an administrative planning and research agency.

As to the number of personnel needed in the research agency, there is no set pattern or "rule-of-thumb" that can be used to determine staffing requirements. The number may vary depending on several factors, including the type and number of projects assigned to the research agency by the chief administrator, the amount and quality of planning and research being performed by the operating and auxiliary departments, and the willingness of officials to accept the findings and recommendations of the research agency.

Regular personnel of operating and auxiliary departments must be concerned with administrative problems, and should be encouraged to make criticisms and suggestions with respect to organization, procedures, measurements, and related problems. Police officials, for example, should be expected to give thought to the problems of organization for police services in the various categories. Personnel technicians should be constantly on the alert for opportunities to improve application and certification procedures.

Officials and employees who have other duties to perform, however, seldom have much time to devote to the study of these administrative problems, and their training and experience is usually too limited to qualify them as "experts" in administrative practice. Furthermore, there are many problems of interdepartmental relationships that require a point of view independent of any one department's interests.

The staff assigned to the central administrative planning and research agency will vary considerably according to the size of the city. In the smallest cities it may not be feasible to employ any specially-trained administrative expert other than the chief administrator. In such cases the chief administrator may have to do his own administrative planning and research, and he may find it necessary to devote considerable time to this activity.

In cities of moderate size, administrative planning and research problems may be assigned to an administrative assistant, to the budget officer, or to some other managerial aide who is qualified to do the work. Considerable use is also being made of administrative interns or trainees assigned either to the office of the chief administrator or the

---

[3] Bernard L. Gladieux, op. cit., pp. 75-76.

budget office. In cities of both small and moderate size outside consultants may be employed for major research projects which call for qualifications not possessed by regular personnel.

In the larger cities where administrative problems are both numerous and complex, their study requires a staff of full-time management analysts. The most common nomenclature for positions of this type is "administrative analyst," with levels indicated by such terminology as "junior," "senior," "principal," and "chief." Some large cities have several employees in each of the first three categories. Adequate stenographic and clerical personnel also are required in offices of this type.

Use of Trainees in Administrative Planning and Research

A small number of cities throughout the country have adopted "management trainee" or "administrative intern" programs in conjunction with their administrative planning and research agencies. Under these programs, students graduating from universities with specialized training in municipal management, public administration, and related fields are recruited to serve for periods extending from six months to two years in the capacity of administrative trainee or intern. Ordinarily these trainees are assigned to the agency responsible for administrative planning and research.

Such a program offers several advantages to both the city and the students. To the city it offers a continuous source of trained administrative personnel as well as a flow of the most recent information and techniques being taught by the country's leading colleges and universities. It also offers the city trained personnel to serve as junior staff members in an administrative planning and research agency at a very reasonable salary figure. Trainees usually are willing to work for rather modest salaries for a year or two in exchange for training and experience in solving "top level" municipal problems.

To the trainee a program of this nature provides the opportunity to further his knowledge and gain experience in his chosen field of municipal administration. It gives him an insight into practical management situations, and brings him into intimate contact with operating departments. Through a broadening of his knowledge and experience it also affords him the opportunity to qualify himself for higher administrative positions.

With proper guidance, trainees are qualified to gather information and perform much of the analysis that accompanies organization and administrative studies, development of improved methods and procedures, forms design, budgetary control, office layout and design, and related work. They are also valuable in providing information to the public, answering routine letters, and filling out many of the questionnaires that cities inevitably receive.

Relations With Other Departments and Agencies

Much of the success of an administrative planning and research agency is dependent upon the reception given its staff by the other auxiliary and operating agencies, and the attitude held by these agencies toward the recommendations and other work of the research staff. The working relationships may vary somewhat depending on whether the agency is an operating or auxiliary department.

Operating Agencies. "Since the administrative research and planning unit is necessarily concerned with operations, the relationships of this unit with the operating divisions are especially important. Care must be exercised to insure that the work of the planning unit does not degenerate into a routine review of actions already taken by the operating personnel. On the other hand, if the administrative planning unit is too aggressive and gives the impression of overriding or directing the operating staff, its activities can become a source of friction within the organization. A delicate problem of relationships is involved in placing the administrative planning facilities at the disposition of operating officials and in using them effectively in the organization. This problem of establishing proper working relationships is still unsolved in many organizations.

"Even though the planning unit is directly responsible to the administrator, the degree of its success will depend largely upon the extent to which it engenders confidence on the part of the operating officials within the agency. A spirit of cooperation can be developed only through the respect that emanates from a feeling of confidence in the technical and personal capabilities of the planning and research staff. Furthermore, the operating official will expect this staff to have a fundamental understanding of and sympathy for the program and its objectives. The degree to which the operating official has confidence in and respect for the planning and research unit can usually be measured by the extent to which he solicits its advice and goes to it for aid in solving his administrative problems."[4]

Other Managerial and Auxiliary Agencies. The relationship of administrative planning to budgeting has already been indicated, as has its relationship to substantive planning. There is also a need for close articulation of the administrative planning and research work with the services of the personnel and legal departments or agencies.

There is a particularly close relationship between administrative planning and personnel administration. "All changes in organization, administration, and procedure entail personnel adjustments such as the establishment, abolishment or reclassification of positions. This means transfers, promotions, demotions, new appointments, and sometimes dismissals.

"The personnel agency is in a strategic position to learn of organization and management difficulties and to advise with the administrative planning unit in the job of remedying such difficulties. The classification staff, for example, can bring to bear upon problems of organization, administration, and procedure the wide knowledge of existing practices gained as a part of its regular classification work. Such work requires an examination of the responsibilities and duties of employees at all levels in the organization, analysis of the flow of work, and of the interrelationships of various activities performed. This information is essential to the administrative planning and research unit in the development of any new scheme or organization or in the adjustment of administrative practices. Conversely, the administrative planning unit will encounter cases of improper classification as well as situations where personnel difficulties impede effective management.

"The fact that administrative planning and personnel work require close coordination does not mean that the administrative planning unit should be made a subordinate part of the personnel division unless, by chance, it is not feasible to organize such facilities as a part of the budget unit or directly under the chief administrator. Not only does administrative research call for broader fields of action and more varied techniques than personnel work, but the personnel officer is also likely to be severely handicapped in selling his personnel program to the operating officials if he is charged with formulating and installing organization plans and procedures.

"If personnel facilities have been set up more or less independent of the chief executive, as has been the traditional pattern in most governments up until very recent

---

[4] Bernard L. Gladieux, op. cit., p. 75.

times (usually in the form of independent Civil Service Commission), the location of administrative planning work in such personnel units is most undesirable. Such an arrangement removes from the chief executive command of facilities which are essential to the performance of his job of management.

"Perhaps some further exploration of the proper role of position classification work may help to clarify the relative responsibilities of personnel, budgeting, and administrative planning units. The job of the classification staff is to identify individual positions once the general structure, work distribution, and procedures of the organization have been planned, established, or revised. The study of the personnel unit is to analyze the necessary positions, describe (but not prescribe) the assigned duties and, once positions have been allocated to the proper classes, to secure qualified staff to carry out such duties. To guard against the classification plan freezing a poor organization setup or improper distribution of work, the personnel unit must constantly press for organization and procedural adjustments whenever it discovers that such changes are needed.

"However, this concern which the personnel division, and more specifically the classification unit, has in organization, procedure, and administrative matters does not properly extend to fixing the plan of organization or to determining the number and character of positions allowed. Organization planning falls within the scope of the administrative planner or researcher, while the determination of position requirements, although it cannot be dissociated from administrative planning, is a budget responsibility. As previously described, these planning and budgeting activities are closely interrelated, demand the same over-all approach to administrative problems, require to a considerable extent the same type of staff, and belong either in the same unit or in parallel units under the chief executive."[5]

In many governmental organizations, much of what has been defined in this chapter as administrative planning and research has been traditionally assigned to the law department or to lawyers in other departments and agencies. Because changes in organization and procedures and the preparation of administrative orders have their legal aspects, these matters have been referred to legal counsel for advice, and this advice has often been extended to the nonlegal phases of administrative problems.

"If legal units were staffed with persons skilled in administrative planning work and who have a management rather than formalistic or legalistic approach, the results might be more constructive. However, the assumption of administrative planning duties by a legal staff inevitably leads to a restrictive, functional approach to administration, with a tendency to encumber even the simplest administrative procedure with legal technicalities and to obscure administrative orders and instructions in legal verbiage. The specialized character of legal training and experience in addition to the restricted functions of a legal division usually prevent such a unit from achieving the over-all view of management which administrative planning work requires."[6]

Although the legal staff may not be qualified to deal with the broad problems of administrative planning, it still has an important role to play in supplementing the studies and plans of the administrative planning and research. Not only should the legal department review administrative orders, bulletins, circulars, and other documents to check for conformity with applicable law, but it should be consulted as to the legal implications of organizational changes, delegations of authority and other legal questions.

---

[5] Bernard L. Gladieux, op. cit., pp. 72-74.
[6] Ibid., pp. 72.

Responsibilities of the Administrative Analyst

Knowledge of the purposes and processes of municipal government and administration is a prerequisite for the administrative planning and research staff. Knowledge is not sufficient in itself, however. Principles must be applied systematically and intelligently to all administrative problems. If the administrative planning and research program is to make significant contributions in helping to establish better standards of municipal services, the administrative analyst must approach his assignments with a keen awareness of their importance both to the chief administrator and operating departments.

The analyst's proposals in all likelihood will form the basis for many administrative and policy decisions. This places a great deal of responsibility upon the analyst to make sound recommendations. To carry out his responsibilities to the administrator and operating officials, the analyst should adopt several special approaches to his job and the assignments he receives. These are: (1) the scientific method, (2) objectivity, (3) completed staff work, (4) salesmanship, and (5) the "service" concept.

The Scientific Method

The scientific method or "scientific management" was first suggested by Frederick W. Taylor, an early management specialist in private industry. "Scientific management" as applied to directly productive operations means "the standardization of data of human behavior, and the study and correlation of facts so as to facilitate, coordinate, and simplify work. It means figuring out how to get the most output for the least input."[7]

While scientific management is not a science in the true sense of the word, it does take advantage of scientific methods when it concerns itself with facts and experience and uses them objectively. If factual knowledge is not complete, reliance must be based on creative thinking, use of logic, and deduction of solutions from the factual information available. The analyst then should tackle all problems with a scientific viewpoint with the purpose of discovering facts and relating them to experience and principles of management. He systematically analyzes the factual data and determines if there is a better way of doing the job involved.

As a result of the continued application of scientific methodology in industry, business, and government, a growing body of knowledge and tested techniques of observation and analysis have been developed. In the hands of an analyst with a questioning attitude, they are of practical value in solving administrative problems.

Objectivity

Objectivity on the part of the analyst goes hand-in-hand with the use of the scientific method, although admittedly it may be more difficult to apply in some instances. Biased methodology, however, can result in proposed solutions which are of no more value than subjective decisions. Moreover, the lack of objectivity can disrupt the analyst's relationships with operating departments. Once the analyst has lost the confidence of the operating official, he loses much of his value in administrative planning.

The analyst must realize that the dividing line between objectivity and bias is often quite thin and that through rationalization bias can be made objective. This is a common

---

[7] Comstock Glaser, Administrative Procedure (Washington, D. C.: American Council on Public Affairs, 1941), p. 185.

human failing, but the analyst must strive to rise above it. Through experience, he can learn to discern when his bias is affecting a study and endeavor to compensate for it.

Completed Staff Work

"Completed staff work" is the study of a problem and presentation of a solution in such form that all that remains to be done on the part of the division head or the administrator is to indicate his approval or disapproval of the completed action.

The words "completed action" are emphasized because the more difficult the problem is, the greater is the tendency for the analyst to present the problem to his superior in piecemeal fashion. The analyst should work out the details of the problem without consulting the administrator. When presented to the administrator for approval or disapproval, the product should be worked out in finished form whether it involves the pronouncement of a new policy or affects an established one. The "completed staff work" theory may result in more work for the analyst, but it results in more freedom for the administrator. This is as it should be.

The procedure for completed staff work briefly may be stated as follows: (1) work out all details completely; (2) consult with other staff officers; (3) study, write, restudy, rewrite; (4) present a single, coordinated proposed action and do not equivocate; (5) do not present long memoranda or explanations since correct solutions are usually recognizable; and (6) advise the administrator what to do -- do not ask him.

The final criterion as to whether a report is completed staff work is for the analyst to put himself in the place of the administrator and decide whether he would then sign the paper and stake his professional reputation on being right. If not, the report should be worked over until it meets that criterion.

Use of Salesmanship

Resistance to change is one of the most fundamental human reactions and one which an analyst is likely to encounter in proposing solutions to an administrative problem. This would be a less difficult problem if the analyst possessed the authority to proceed with a recommended change, but usually he does not. The analyst must then sell his recommendations to the department or division head and to the employees who will be affected.

First, the analyst should endeavor to establish a reputation for making only recommendations of real merit. If he is successful in this respect, future recommendations are more likely to meet with attentive hearings. Recommendations should be presented to operating personnel and supervisors in meetings where proposals can be discussed, questioned, and examined by those who are responsible for the activities. The success of the analyst's sales efforts will depend upon four main factors: (1) the soundness of the proposal; (2) the analysis and presentation of the proposal; (3) the analyst's ability to handle and influence people; and (4) the analyst's knowledge of the personal interests and characteristics of the people to be sold.

Several rules of conduct should be observed at all times by the analyst. Always give credit where credit is due and sometimes where it is not due. Never tell anyone directly that he is wrong since this is the easiest way to make an enemy. Refrain from arguments since nothing is to be gained. If a point is important, concede it for the time being and return to it later.

Salesmanship is a special talent in itself and one which is not usually developed overnight. An analyst, however, can become quite adept at selling his ideas if he approaches this part of his work with the same diligence he would display in studying and developing solutions to administrative problems.

The "Service" Concept

An administrative planning and research agency receives many assignments which on the surface may appear to involve a greater or lesser degree of control over other departments and divisions. These assignments usually also require an inquiry into some of the details of operation of other agencies. Because of these peculiar characteristics of planning and research work, it is not unusual to find administrative planning and research agencies stepping beyond the scope of their normal functions. Sometimes they assume some of the chief administrator's authority and make decisions when they should only determine the facts and make recommendations. In other instances the analyst may feel that his research work is more in the nature of an investigation done primarily to "get something on" some of the staff in another department.

Neither the assumption of unauthorized authority nor the "sleuthing" attitude is healthy for the administrative planning and research agency, and if these attitudes persist, they very likely will have the effect of alienating personnel in other agencies and nullifying the effectiveness of the research unit. Administrative and research analysts should not place themselves in a position where they make final decisions that are the responsibility of operating officials. Neither should they place themselves in the position of playing detective and spying on the activities of administrative personnel in other departments and divisions.

The primary function of the analyst is to determine facts, analyze them, discuss these facts and possible alternative solutions with operating personnel, and make recommendations for improvements. The management studies should be undertaken with the full knowledge and support of the operating personnel, and recommendations should be thoroughly discussed with everyone concerned. Officials in other departments should be made to feel that the administrative planning and research agency exists in order to help them solve their problems and improve the efficiency of their departments. They should look upon the planning agency as a "staff" or "service" agency that was established in order to help them and not to stand in their way. Only when this attitude exists in the minds of both the analysts and the operating officials, can the planning and research agency accomplish the mission for which it was created.

Subject Matter of Administrative Planning

It is impossible to list here all of the subjects or problems of municipal administration that call for administrative planning and research, but some of the principal categories may be suggested and illustrated in order to indicate the need for and content of this important phase of municipal government. Assuming that the administrative planning function is assigned to the budget office, major areas of responsibility would include staff assistance to the chief administrator in budget preparation and execution, organization and administrative surveys, work methods and procedure studies, records management, work measurement standards and reporting, preparation of procedure manuals, a variety of office management activities, and special studies designed to provide information to the chief administrator and city council. Consideration also should be given to the assignment of responsibility for coordinating the preparation of the city's long-range capital improvement and financial plan to the administrative planning agency. These major areas of responsibility are discussed in greater detail below.

Budget Preparation and Enforcement

A procedure for preparation of the annual budget is discussed in considerable detail in Chapter 5, and enforcement of the budget is covered in Chapter 8. In these chapters it is pointed out that the responsibility for budget preparation and enforcement lies with the chief administrator. There is, however, a considerable amount of routine clerical work and detailed analysis required in carrying out this responsibility, and a number of minor decisions must be made that can be delegated to subordinate personnel. These duties are normally assigned to a budget staff that works in close coordination with the administrative planning personnel. As a matter of fact, more often than not the same people serve as both budget and administrative planning staff.

The job of ordering an adequate supply of budget forms, inserting historical expenditure information, and otherwise readying the budget estimate forms for transmittal to the various departments and divisions, can be delegated to the budget office. Similarly, the numerous minor research projects and investigations that arise during budget reviews with department heads are appropriate assignments for analysts in the administrative planning agency. Typing of final budget figures and supervision of the final printing of the budget can also be delegated to this agency.

After the budget is adopted by the city council it is referred back to the chief administrator for enforcement, which also requires a considerable amount of routine work that can be delegated. Much of the work connected with establishing allotments, investigating requests for budget transfers, reviewing requests for additional personnel, and making adjustments in the allocations for capital outlay can be assigned to the administrative planning staff. In fact, it is not infrequent that the need for revision in the budget or changes in personnel are brought about by research studies or administrative changes worked out by the administrative planning agency.

Organization and Administrative Surveys

Organization must be dynamic if it is to produce the best results. An organization that is not flexible and responsive to changing needs is an obstacle to progress. Changes in programs, the undertaking of new activities, and the introduction of new and improved methods all demand alterations in the organization structure. An essential corollary of every substantive plan is therefore a study of the necessary changes in organization.

A complete management survey involves a thorough review and analysis of every segment of the organization and how well it is being managed. It requires qualified specialists who have a considerable amount of time to explore the objective of every agency, the organizational structure, the efficiency of methods in use, utilization of the work force, productivity, costs of operation, and many related factors. The value of this type of survey is that it provides a comprehensive review of operations for the purpose of simplifying organizational relationships, improving techniques, and simplifying work processes, all of which helps to improve the efficiency of the operation.

Opportunities to make a complete management survey or to start from scratch and plan a completely new operation are relatively limited, however. Most administrators and analysts run into organizational problems in connection with the reorganization of existing activities, and involving only one or two units or agencies. The decision to reorganize may be brought about because of the inefficient operation of a unit, lack of control, misunderstandings, or other reasons. Whatever the reason, once it is decided to analyze the manner in which the work is performed and the operating relationships of supervisors and workers, the job can best be performed by someone who has had some training and experience in the process of piecing an organization together, and who has sufficient time to give the problems serious study and analysis.

While it is beyond the scope of this chapter to delve into the techniques of making an organizational or administrative survey, it may be helpful to point out some illustrative examples of this type of work.

The Need for Auxiliary Agencies. In Chapter 3 it was pointed out that although the establishment of auxiliary agencies permits increased efficiency and economy due to specialization, this specialization must not be carried so far that the work of operating departments is seriously impaired. It is impossible to make recommendations as to what auxiliary agencies should be established in a particular city without knowing the facts of the local situation. The collection and analysis of these facts are an important part of administrative planning.

If, for example, the desirability of establishing a central purchasing office is being considered, the chief administrator will want to know, among other things, (1) how many departmental officials are now engaged in purchasing activities, (2) how much time these employees are devoting to purchasing, (3) the total volume of municipal purchases per year, (4) how many departments are purchasing identical or similar supplies or equipment, (5) the amounts and prices of these purchases, (6) what savings could be expected as a result of consolidated orders, (7) whether the volume of purchases is sufficient to require a full-time purchasing agent, (8) if not, could purchasing duties be combined with the duties of some other official so as to permit centralization, and (9) what items of equipment or supply, if any, require departmental purchasing.

To find the answers to these and related questions requires not only time, but also familiarity with departmental practice and operation. The chief administrator should not have to spend his own valuable time in making such a survey, even though the final decision must be his. Such a problem, however, does not come within the scope and duties of any of the traditional departments and agencies. It is a managerial problem, and its analysis requires specially trained personnel.

A similar problem is raised in determining the best organization for stenographic and clerical services. Many organizations, both private and public, have experimented with the use of stenographic pools to serve a number of offices and individuals. The use of such pools has been opposed by many executives who believe that the situation in which one man and one stenographer are permanently teamed together is more effective, and by other persons who like the prestige of having a private stenographer. It is a problem of administrative research to determine whether the advantages of such a pool would outweigh its disadvantages under the conditions of a particular city, and how far the "pooling" should go.

Closely related to the stenographers' pool is the question of the value of a central filing system. Some municipalities maintain central files for groups of offices, whereas in other instances individual departments are of sufficient size and are so organized that a central filing unit for that department may be desirable.

Geographic Decentralization. A number of other organization problems are related to the geographic distribution of work and personnel. In the smaller cities there may be no district offices or substations in any of the departments. In most medium and large cities, however, consideration should be given to decentralization of fire and police departments, public health field offices, building inspection substations, conveniently located street maintenance equipment and supply yards, and perhaps other district offices and substations. If this decentralization is to be based on logic rather than tradition or local pressure, careful study of the various problems is needed. In too many cases a geographical distribution which once may have been logical has been allowed to be perpetuated long after the circumstances which justified it originally have been changed. Such problems are particularly appropriate for study by an administrative planning and research unit.

Disaster Preparedness Plans. Good organization planning embraces not only the organizational needs for day-to-day administration but also special circumstances which may require special organization. An outstanding example of this kind of planning is found in the field of preparation for emergencies or disasters. A flood, fire, windstorm, or other emergency puts a terrific strain on municipal personnel and resources. It also may involve a local Civil Defense organization, the Red Cross, and other volunteer agencies or individuals. Emergency situations frequently call for an organization, staff, and working relationships not found in the conventional municipal structure. Moreover, volunteer personnel may not be of any great assistance unless they understand what their assignments are and to whom they are responsible. Many cities have therefore prepared in advance to handle these emergency situations by adopting carefully worked-out disaster preparedness plans.

These illustrative examples of organization problems requiring research and planning have all dealt with organization changes or plans of considerable scope. In addition to such major changes there are countless minor adjustments that need to be made from time to time. There is no point in enumerating all of the problems that may require special investigation, but in every organization there is need for constant study and improvement.

Work Methods and Procedures Studies

Work methods and procedures studies focus attention on *how* the work is being performed, and seek to simplify or otherwise improve the process so that greater productivity will result. There is a normal tendency in most organizations to add controls, checks, and reviews as different problems or situations appear to point out the need for them. There is not the same inclination, however, to review the entire procedure and discard the steps, forms, or processes that have outlived their usefulness. A periodic appraisal of these work methods and procedures is essential if the organization is to continue to operate efficiently and economically.

Procedural studies have been prominent in the application of scientific management to private business. Time and motion studies of every operation have been made in some companies in order to find the one best way to do a job and to eliminate unnecessary routines. Although city officials may not need to go to the extremes that private industrial engineers have in their study of procedures, the basic approach can be very much the same.

One of the most useful techniques for procedural research is to make flow charts of the procedure being studied. Examples of such charts include the Work Distribution Chart, the Process Analysis Chart, and the Forms Distribution Chart. Such charts can be used to show step-by-step the various stages in the procedure, the personnel involved, forms and numbers of carbon copies required, and so forth. When this profile of a procedure is put down in black and white, many of the practices which have been built up by habit can be examined more critically. Some steps in the procedure of copies of certain forms may be revealed as clearly unnecessary, while other steps may well be combined to save the time and effort of the employees doing the work. These savings in time and effort in certain phases of the job should improve efficiency and increase production on other parts of the work.

Among the many procedures that need frequent re-examination are those connected with accounting and cost accounting, payroll preparation, issuance of licenses and permits, purchasing, tax collection, and control over municipal stores and supplies. In addition, there are countless minor procedures or established routines in every office. The easy way is to follow the old established patterns and procedures. The best way is to subject all procedures and routines to frequent re-examination by persons trained to appraise the effects of procedures on administrative efficiency.

Records Management

Nearly every activity of a city government requires a considerable amount of record keeping. An indication of the growth and significance of record keeping is that today there is one office worker to every eight nonoffice employees, while in 1900 there was only one office worker to every 30 nonclerical workers.

Another indication of the importance of records management is the cost of creating and filing office papers. It has been estimated that it costs about $1,000 (including salaries of dictator and stenographer) to create the 1,330 letters of outgoing correspondence for which carbon copies are found in the average file drawer!

The importance of the custody and retention of records is evident from the serious legal penalties attached to "wilfully and unlawfully concealing, removing, mutilating, obliterating, falsifying or destroying" records, to quote from a typical law. Such laws exist because records are the means by which public officials in a democracy render accountings to the people. They also protect legal rights of countless citizens. They are important tools of administration and the sources of many kinds of information. They may be termed the "official memory" of an organization.

A unified records management program insures management that records exist and are used for control of operations, accountability to the public, and protection of legal rights of citizens and the government, without being cluttered by records which have outlived their useful retention periods. Such a program should include a forms control program, a files control program, and a systematic records disposal program. These programs are described briefly below.

Forms Control. Printed and duplicated forms constitute a high percentage of the records requiring control. The records control program is made easier if control is exercised over the creation of forms. Forms control seeks elimination of unnecessary forms, consolidation where possible of related forms, better design of forms for easier use, and selection of paper and ink of a quality in keeping with the retention period determined under the records control program. Study of forms for these purposes cannot be divorced from appraisal of procedures with which forms are used. Process charts, work distribution charts, work counts, and other techniques are often valuable for the study of procedures for use of forms. Such analysis of forms and procedures aims at work simplification, and is a logical function of the administrative planning and research agency.

File Control Program. This is a program of improving office filing systems and methods to facilitate the use of office records, organizing the office filing systems to simplify the removal of office records for disposal or transfer to inactive storage, and controlling the flow of records into and out of office files.

Records Disposal Program. Not all forms placed in a file must be retained indefinitely. Some can be destroyed after a relatively short period; others must be retained for a longer period either because of use or legal requirements, although they may be placed in an inactive file which occupies comparatively inexpensive storage space; and still a third category of records, such as deeds to property, must be retained virtually forever. The goal of a records disposal program is to inventory all existing records and establish schedules for removal to inactive files and ultimately to dispose of all records which the city is not required by law to retain.

Work Measurement Standards and Reporting

One of the most essential steps in establishing management control is to devise methods for measuring and evaluating the work of the various departments and agencies. Not only is some means of reporting productivity essential, but standards or other measuring devices are also needed to give meaning to and serve as the basis for evaluating the reports. These reports provide the superior officer with information as to what his subordinates are doing, how well they are doing their jobs, and what problems they are encountering. If superior officers are to receive the information they need for managerial purposes, the records system must collect sufficient and reliable data and the reporting system must relay this information to the proper officials in the most usable form.

The maintenance of records and the compilation of data in the form of reports may often be assigned to clerical personnel, but the establishment and modification of these records and reporting systems is a job for the administrative research staff. This subject is so important to administrative management that an entire chapter (Chapter 12) is devoted to measurement problems.

Office Management

The term "office management" is used differently in public and private business. In private business, office management usually includes such functions as accounting, building maintenance, collection of statistics, general efficiency studies, the organization and operation of stenographic and clerical services, and other related functions. In governmental organization, office management has no very definite and generally recognized meaning. However, it usually does not include accounting or general research, but is confined to the routine and technical phases of providing clerical and stenographic services.

Regardless of how the term is defined, there are some problems of office management that have broad administrative significance and require careful research and planning. A few of these problems will be suggested and briefly discussed by way of illustration.

Office Design and Layout. Office layout has a vital effect upon efficiency of clerical operations and upon organizational relationships in general. Departments which have frequent interrelations of a routine character should be located in adjoining quarters. For example, the agencies of the treasurer, city clerk, and controller might well be given adjoining offices. Similarly, the budgetary control relationships between the purchasing office, the accounting office, and the budget office warrant assignment of nearby office space. Those departments that have frequent contacts with the public should be given locations within city hall or other public buildings that will facilitate these contacts. The offices of treasurer and city clerk are frequently visited by citizens, and should therefore be located on the first floor so that they are easily accessible from the street.

Internal office design is even more important. In too many cities office arrangements have grown up without any plan or pattern. As a result, many offices are badly crowded, while others are guilty of wasting valuable space. Not only must employees be given sufficient area and adequate fixtures and equipment, but the location of individuals and of office furniture and equipment needs careful study. There are two primary factors to be considered: (1) convenience to the public; and (2) flow of work.

The first factor should be predominant in departments having a large number of public contacts, and it dictates not only the arrangements for public convenience, but also the assigning of the newest furniture to those coming in closest contact with citizens. The second factor involves the movement of papers and materials through and between departments. Work should flow, as nearly as possible, in an unbroken straight line from desk to desk and from department to department. Proper office design and layout require, therefore, careful study of work flows and procedures by the administrative planning and research unit.

Another office management problem that may require considerable research and planning is the question as to which employees shall be entitled to private offices, and where such offices should be located. Use of private offices in the past has probably been too generous, and the trend is toward more critical consideration of their necessity. Now that technical improvements have made it much easier to reduce office noise, one great need for private offices is eliminated. Provision of conference rooms which may be used for talks with visitors and personnel eliminates another need. The actual determination of what private offices are needed will depend upon local circumstances.

The solution of the problem will be found in some cases to lie in the provision of semi-private offices having low partitions of glass construction above the bottom three feet. These will be cheaper than ceiling high partitions and will provide prestige, partial privacy, and freedom from noise without sacrificing ability to supervise the office work.

Selection of Office Machinery and Equipment. The increasing volume and the complexity of municipal business call for modern machinery and equipment in many municipal offices. There are now available many new types of machinery for bookkeeping, accounting, addressing, mailing, record keeping, and other common activities. The need for modernization of office methods by the adoption of new machines is generally recognized, but actual decisions as to what machines are most appropriate and what can be afforded require careful investigation.

Such studies involve complete analyses of present operating methods as to time, total cost, accuracy, and final form, together with analyses as to what machines are available, what their cost is, what savings in time and expense can be effected by machine methods, the adaptability of different machines to various uses, and so forth. Such studies require research personnel who are familiar not only with routines and mechanics but also with the administrative implications of office methods and procedures. Technical advice may have to be secured from outside the agency in many cases, but a competent administrative planning and research staff can be invaluable in the conduct of such surveys.

Standardization of Office Supplies. Unless careful supervision is exercised, there is a natural tendency for individual municipal offices to use too great a variety of office supplies. Personal preferences and habits become crystalized, with the result that the city is purchasing altogether too many different kinds of paper, typewriter ribbons, carbon paper, and other items of supply. To a certain extent this problem is one which the purchasing agent may solve by consultation with different department officials.

In many cases, however, it is more than a problem of standard specifications. For example, studies may be made to determine the most appropriate and economical duplicating methods for various types of reports and inform departmental personnel of the results. The specific duplicating method used will affect the cost of the materials used. If employees are aware of the results that can be attained with the different methods, they will be more likely to choose the method of reproduction involving costs consistent with the results desired. There will be less likelihood then that the most expensive duplicating method will be used when another method would be sufficient.

While a purchasing agent may give technical advice as to sizes of paper or the cost of various kinds of typewriter ribbons, the question of what is best for a particular office extends beyond his normal jurisdiction. The administrative research staff might therefore study the supplies used by the various offices and make suggestions to the chief administrator for adoption of standard specifications to which all offices would be held.

Preparation of Manuals

Development of procedure manuals is one of the best means available to the research unit in accomplishing administrative improvements indicated by organization and methods studies. Whether the development of these manuals provides the motivation for procedural studies or is the culmination of a series of studies, they can be important tools in achieving uniform work within a single unit or throughout the organization as a whole.

Pfiffner and Lane[8] cite five reasons for developing procedure manuals:

a. For use in connection with the development and simplification of standard working procedures and practices.
b. To coordinate and define the various policies, functions, and activities of the organization.
c. To train employees in the details of new procedures.
d. To aid in the development and training of new employees.
e. To encourage improvement in operating methods.

A typical procedure manual for an organizational unit will include or make reference to laws, rules, regulations, and directives which affect all units, and will include descriptions and illustrations of the standard work methods or procedures to be followed. Illustrative materials such as forms used, work flow charts, process charts, and forms distribution charts are helpful in presenting the procedures so that they are both comprehensive and easily understood.

Clarity is the key to a good procedure manual. The manual, to be useful, must be used and referred to by the persons concerned. The best procedures, however, will be of little value unless they are written in such a way as to be clear to every employee — not just to the analyst preparing the manual.

The information presented in the manual will be gathered in much the same fashion

---

[8] John M. Pfiffner and S. Owen Lane, A Manual for Administrative Analysis (Dubuque, Iowa: William C. Brown, 1951), p. 50.

as material for other administrative studies, and many of the analyst's techniques and tools will be used. After the necessary materials have been gathered and analyzed and preliminary drafts have been prepared and edited, the tentative manual should be submitted to key supervisors to obtain their constructive criticism as to the clarity and usefulness of the information. The supervisor also will be able to note and describe any differences between actual procedures and those stated or illustrated in the manual, and can add procedures that may have been omitted from the manual. In addition, the supervisor may be able to clarify the descriptions of new or revised procedures included in the manual.

Special Assignments and Studies

The chief administrator and council members frequently have special questions concerning various activities which may require a considerable amount of investigation or research to answer. Unless there is someone down in the organization to whom these special projects can be assigned, the questions may go unanswered. The administrative research unit is especially well equipped to make these studies and submit reports to those who raise the questions.

A somewhat different task that might also be assigned to the administrative research staff is the drafting of administrative orders, rules, and regulations. On those occasions when such orders or regulations require a formal statement in writing, the job of drafting the documents calls for the very skills which may be expected from the administrative research personnel. The person drafting the order must be thoroughly acquainted with the administrative organization and relationships and with current procedures or practices in the government. He must know what personnel in the organization will be affected and then draft the order so that its meaning will be clearly understood by those for whom it is prepared.

Aside from the need for skilled drafting of orders, it is helpful to have all new orders and regulations cleared through some one office or agency so that they will be correlated with other orders and regulations and with current practice. Central clearance and coordination not only help prevent overlapping and contradiction among different orders, but they also call to the attention of the administrative research staff problems of procedure and relationship that need further analysis.

This list of administrative planning and research assignments and problems is by no means complete, but it may serve to illustrate the kinds of problems the research staff should study.

Long-Range Financial Planning

A long-range financial plan is a plan for the future development of the city for a number of years, including: (1) a program of operating and maintenance expenditures for public services; (2) a capital improvements program based upon the city's master plan; and (3) a comprehensive revenue program. Once formulated, the financial plan is carried out with the aid of three administrative devices: (1) a priority list of proposed capital improvements; (2) a six-year capital budget; and (3) the annual city budget.

Traditionally in many cities responsibility for preparation of the long-range financial plan has been assigned to the planning department or commission. This is probably because of the planning agency's responsibility for the preparation of a comprehensive plan to guide the physical development of the city. Such a plan normally extends to the development of both private and public property. Development of private property is guided through the use of zoning, subdivision control, and building regulations. The acquisition and development of public property and facilities in harmony with the master plan is accomplished by public agencies through a capital improvement program.

Undoubtedly the close relationship that exists between the development of the capital improvement program and the long-range financial plan has, in many instances, resulted in the planning department doing whatever was done in the way of developing a program of operating and maintenance expenditures for public services and a comprehensive revenue program. In many other instances the capital improvement program has been developed with little or no thought being given to a program of public services or the means to finance either the capital improvement or public service programs.

The work of preparing a long-range plan involves the solicitation of recommended capital improvement projects from every department, division, and agency of the city government. It also requires that a system of priorities be established to determine which projects shall be completed first. A considerable amount of planning and research also must be completed by the city's chief fiscal officer in order to determine how many projects can be constructed on a pay-as-you-go basis and how many will require bonds. The chief fiscal officer's advice also should be sought regarding the method of financing, proposed new sources of revenue, and related matters.

Carrying out the plan becomes almost entirely an administrative matter. It involves making provision for an adequate standard of routine municipal services in the annual budget as well as pay-as-you-go financing for as many projects as can be financed. The amount of money that can be allocated to pay principal and interest on bonds must be considered before it is known how much in bonds can be issued. Close correlation between the six-year capital budget and the annual budget also is necessary if long-range plans are to be properly implemented.

All of these activities are the chief administrator's responsibility, and are basically management functions rather than extensions of the physical planning function. While the chief administrator cannot be expected to carry out all of these activities in addition to his multitudinous other duties, he should be held responsible for getting the work done. If the long-range planning function is assigned to an autonomous planning department, over which the chief administrator has no control, he obviously cannot be held responsible for the results.

Even where the planning department is under direct control of the chief administrator, planning personnel sometimes lack the necessary training and administrative orientation to successfully carry out the job of long-range planning. The administrative analysts in the administrative planning and research unit, by virtue of their unique training and experience, may be better qualified to perform the detail work required in the preparation of the long-range plan and to coordinate long-range planning with other aspects of the management process.

Tools for Administrative Planning and Research

A variety of techniques have been developed for doing the job of administrative planning and research. Some are vague and superficial and others are complicated and difficult to use. There are, however, several well-standardized techniques or "tools" in general use by analysts that have proved to be valuable aids in making administrative surveys and work methods studies. These include use of organization charts, a variety of work simplification charts, space layout charts, and related devices for analyzing and presenting information. Several such devices are discussed below.

Organization Charts

Although organization charts have definite limitations (see Chapter 3), they are useful both for making organization and administrative studies and as management tools for use in day-to-day operations. A plan of organization becomes clearer and more useful when it is put on paper so that everyone concerned can see and study it in relation to the organization's problems and objectives. An organization chart helps the analyst to see working relationships more clearly, aids in defining areas of authority and responsibility, defines formal channels of communication, and shows generally where each operation fits into the organization. Charts are helpful in keeping lines of authority straight and in avoiding confusion in giving or receiving instructions. They also aid in orienting and training new employees.

Three variations of the organization chart are commonly used by analysts. These are: (1) the simplified chart, (2) the functional chart, and (3) the staffing chart. The simplified chart is a skeletal outline of the organization, with blocks representing each segment of the organization. Each block contains only the name of the department, division, or other agency. The primary value of this simplified chart is to show lines of authority and responsibility and the relationship of the various units to each other.

The second type, the functional chart, contains blocks representing each segment of the organization connected with lines showing the flow of authority and responsibility, in much the same manner as the simplified chart described above. In addition, however, each block contains not only the name of the unit, but also a carefully worded statement of the functions or activities assigned to each unit. This type of chart, shown in Fig. 37, illustrates the manner in which responsibility is placed and work is divided among the various units.

The third type, the staffing chart, contains blocks representing each segment of the organization, and these blocks are connected with lines showing the flow of authority and responsibility. In addition, each block contains the name of the unit and a listing of each class of employees that the unit is authorized to employ, together with the number of employees authorized for each job class. The principal benefit of this type of chart is the quick reference it provides to the number and classes of employees assigned to the unit.

Work Simplification Charts

Work simplification has been defined as "a method of attacking procedural problems for the purpose of analyzing the division of labor, the flow of work, and the volume of work."[9] Perhaps work simplification can be best summed up, however, as "an organized plan for the application of common sense in finding better and easier ways of doing work." Work simplification sometimes may be referred to as systems and procedures, methods work, operation analysis, or O and M (organization and methods). All of these terms, however, basically have the same meaning.

Work simplification can contribute to better management in the following ways: (1) reduce the number and cost of office procedures by eliminating unnecessary operations and by combining or eliminating forms, records, file copies and so on; (2) utilize personnel more effectively by eliminating unnecessary work; (3) improve service to the public by eliminating or decreasing time-consuming requirements; (4) increase job satisfaction and improve morale by making work easier to perform, clarifying the purpose of the job,

---

[9] John M. Pfiffner and S. Owen Lane, op. cit., p. 26.
[10] Department of State, Guide to Work Simplification (Washington, D. C.: Government Printing Office, 1952), p. 2.

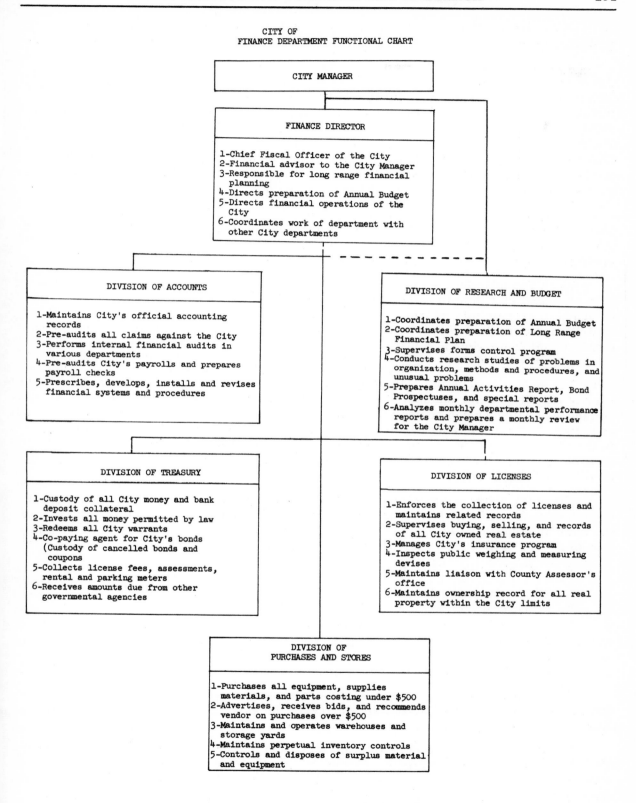

CITY OF
FINANCE DEPARTMENT FUNCTIONAL CHART

CITY MANAGER

FINANCE DIRECTOR

1-Chief Fiscal Officer of the City
2-Financial advisor to the City Manager
3-Responsible for long range financial
  planning
4-Directs preparation of Annual Budget
5-Directs financial operations of the
  City
6-Coordinates work of department with
  other City departments

DIVISION OF ACCOUNTS

1-Maintains City's official accounting
  records
2-Pre-audits all claims against the City
3-Performs internal financial audits in
  various departments
4-Pre-audits City's payrolls and prepares
  payroll checks
5-Prescribes, develops, installs and revises
  financial systems and procedures

DIVISION OF RESEARCH AND BUDGET

1-Coordinates preparation of Annual Budget
2-Coordinates preparation of Long Range
  Financial Plan
3-Supervises forms control program
4-Conducts research studies of problems in
  organization, methods and procedures, and
  unusual problems
5-Prepares Annual Activities Report, Bond
  Prospectuses, and special reports
6-Analyzes monthly departmental performance
  reports and prepares a monthly review
  for the City Manager

DIVISION OF TREASURY

1-Custody of all City money and bank
  deposit collateral
2-Invests all money permitted by law
3-Redeems all City warrants
4-Co-paying agent for City's bonds
  (Custody of cancelled bonds and
  coupons
5-Collects license fees, assessments,
  rental and parking meters
6-Receives amounts due from other
  governmental agencies

DIVISION OF LICENSES

1-Enforces the collection of licenses and
  maintains related records
2-Supervises buying, selling, and records
  of all City owned real estate
3-Manages City's insurance program
4-Inspects public weighing and measuring
  devises
5-Maintains liaison with County Assessor's
  office
6-Maintains ownership record for all real
  property within the City limits

**DIVISION OF
PURCHASES AND STORES**

1-Purchases all equipment, supplies
  materials, and parts costing under $500
2-Advertises, receives bids, and recommends
  vendor on purchases over $500
3-Maintains and operates warehouses and
  storage yards
4-Maintains perpetual inventory controls
5-Controls and disposes of surplus material
  and equipment

Fig. 37 — Functional Organization Chart

and relating the work to other jobs; and (5) bring broader problems of procedure and organization to the attention of department and division heads and the chief administrator.

A considerable variety of formal work simplification tools are at the disposal of the administrative analyst. Their primary purpose is to systematize the gathering of factual data and facilitate the analysis of work processes. In using these tools, the analyst should remember three principles which apply to any work simplification problem. First, all activities should be productive and contribute to the desired end result. Second, an activity should be arranged in an orderly and logical sequence to provide a smooth flow of work and to establish balanced workloads among the employees performing the activity. Finally, activities should be kept as simple as possible by eliminating unnecessary steps and reducing jobs to their barest essentials.

The conduct of work simplification studies is dealt with in considerable detail in several books and manuals listed in the bibliography of this chapter. While it is beyond the scope of this chapter to discuss all of the steps in such studies, the principal work simplification tools are discussed briefly in the following sections.

Work Distribution Chart. The first step in work simplification is to analyze the work distribution within the office being studied. The work distribution chart is a tool designed to provide this information. It shows (1) all of the activities of the unit, (2) the contribution of each employee to each activity, and (3) how much time the unit and each employee takes for each activity.

In preparing the work distribution chart, two types of data are needed: (1) an activity list and (2) a tasks list. An activity list is a general inventory of the principal activities of the office being studied. Listing of detailed activities should be avoided. A "miscellaneous" category can be used to group many secondary activities which do not directly contribute to the main objective of the unit. Tasks lists are prepared by each employee in the office to show jobs or duties performed and the estimated number of hours spent on each one. The form used should show the employee's name and position title as well as the unit being studied.

From the above information the work distribution chart is prepared, showing in a consolidated form the activities performed by both the unit and individual employees and the total time spent on the activity both by the entire unit and by each employee. Examples of a work distribution chart, as well as activity and task lists, are shown in Fig. 38.

An analysis of the chart should be made to determine:

1. What activities take the most time?
2. Is there misdirected effort?
3. Are employee skills being used properly?
4. Are employees doing too many unrelated tasks?
5. Are tasks spread too thinly among employees?
6. Is work directed evenly among employees?

As previously stated, the work distribution chart is only the first step in work simplification. It helps to spot activities which take the most time and indicate areas where other work simplification tools can be used profitably.

Work Flow Charts. A work flow chart is used to study the sequence of major operating steps in an activity and the organization units involved in the performance of the activity. While it is used to trace procedures between units, the work flow chart is in a sense similar to the work distribution chart since it often will indicate specific areas where further investigation should be made.

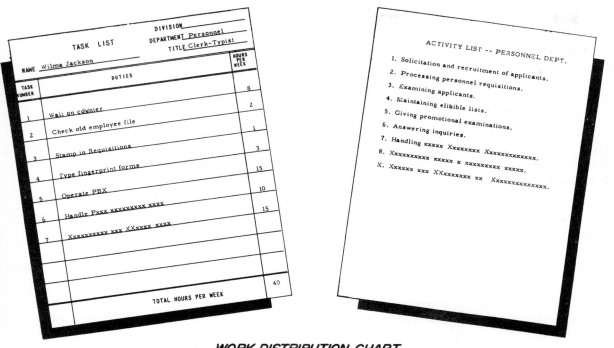

WORK DISTRIBUTION CHART

ACTIVITY	TOTAL MAN-HOURS	Wilma Jackson Clerk-Typist	Man-Hours	Jack Moody Personnel Assistant	Man-Hours	M. Malody Principal Clerk	Man-Hours	M. Dickson Clerk-Typist	Man-Hours	Daisy Hahn Clerk-Typist	Man-Hours	Mrs. Stern (Record Room) Principal Clerk	Man-Hours
Solicitation and Recruitment of Applicants	39	Wait on counter Check old employee file	8 2	Write want ads Wait on counter Check old employee file	1 8 2	Write want ads	2	Type want ads Wait on counter Check old employee files	1 1 3	Wait on counter Check old employee files	7 3		
Processing Requisitions	32	Stamp in Requisition	1	Check Requisition Keep Requisition Register Maintain Suspense File	2 2 2	Check Requisition Allocate Keep Requisition Register Certification	2 10 2 5	Assist Miss Malody	3	Assist Miss Malody	3		
Examining Applicants	1					Make request for needed examination to provide names for certification	1						
Fingerprinting New Employees	16	Type Fingerprint forms	3	Fingerprint new employees Maintain fingerprint files	10 2					Type fingerprint forms	1		
Giving Promotional Examinations	1					Request needed promotional examinations	1						
Maintaining Eligible Lists	21					Supervise maintenance of Eligible and Promotional Lists	8	Maintain Eligible and Promotional Lists	7	Maintain Eligible and Promotional Lists	6		
Answering Inquiries	32	Operate PBX	15	Answer inquiries	5	Answer phone, letter, and personal inquiries	2	Answer inquiries	2	Answer inquiries Relieve on PBX	2		
	240		40		40		40		40		40		40

Fig. 38 — Work Distribution Charting

The chart shows the various units involved in an activity and a general description of the sequences involved. Connecting lines drawn between the different units show the flow of work. Each one of the sequences performed by a unit may require detailed study such as with single-column and multi-column process charts discussed in the next section. The work flow chart, however, is an excellent starting point since it affords an over-all view of the units and sequences involved in a specific activity.

Work Process Charts. Work process charts are used by the analyst to study time-consuming activities involving either a single organizational unit or two or more organizational units. Process charting has been defined as "a graphic representation of the sequence of all operations, inspections, delays, and storages occurring during a process and includes information considered desirable for analysis such as distance moved and time required."[11]

This graphic picture is obtained through the use of symbols which describe the various operations in a sequence of work. These operations are generally illustrated as follows:

1. A large circle indicates an operation or action when something is being created, changed, or added.
2. A small circle indicates transportation or movement when something is moved from one place to another.
3. A triangle indicates storage when something remains in one place awaiting action or is filed.
4. A square indicates inspection when something is checked or verified.

In addition, some process charting systems use the letter "D" to indicate delays when something is idle awaiting action. This additional symbol is used to distinguish planned storage or filing from unplanned delays which may occur. As such, the additional symbol may be useful to the analyst in spotting bottlenecks.

Two types of process charts are commonly used depending either upon the complexity of the procedure or the number of organizational units involved.

Single-column process charts, often drawn on printed forms such as the example shown in Fig. 39, are used to study the detailed steps in a relatively simple procedure within a single organization unit. The work flow is shown by connecting the appropriate symbols with each step described. The time required for storages and the distances in feet for transportation required are recorded on the form. When each step in the procedure has been recorded, the analyst can add the number of different steps performed, the time required for storage, and the distances in feet.

Multi-column process charts, while used in much the same manner as the single-column chart, as needed when the analyst is studying a quite complex flow of work often involving more than one organizational unit. An example of a multi-column process chart is shown in Fig. 40. The same symbols are used, but notes on what is done at each step, time required, and distances are inserted on the chart next to the symbol.

When the analyst has completed charting a work process, he analyzes each step by asking himself several questions designed to eliminate, combine, simplify, or change the sequence of steps in the process. These questions are: (1) What is done? (2) Why is it done? (3) Where should it be done? (4) When should it be done? (5) Who should do the job? and (6) How well is the job being done?

---

[11] Research and Budget Department, Kansas City, Missouri, Municipal Works Simplification (Kansas City, Mo.: The Department), unpaged.

PROCESS ANALYSIS CHART

NO._____
PAGE___OF___

JOB_____

☐ MAN OR ☐ MATERIAL_____
CHART BEGINS_____
CHART ENDS_____
CHARTED BY _____ DATE_____

SUMMARY	PRESENT		PROPOSED		DIFFERENCE	
	NO.	TIME	NO.	TIME	NO.	TIME
◯ OPERATIONS						
⇨ TRANSPORTATIONS						
☐ INSPECTIONS						
D DELAYS						
▽ STORAGES						
DISTANCE TRAVELLED	FT.		FT.		FT.	

DETAILS OF (PRESENT / PROPOSED) METHOD	OPERATION	TRANSPORT	INSPECTION	DELAY	STORAGE	DISTANCE IN FEET	QUANTITY	TIME	WHAT?	WHERE?	WHEN?	WHO?	HOW?	NOTES	ELIMINATE	COMBINE	SEQUE.	PLACE	PERSON	IMPROVE
1	◯	⇨	☐	D	▽															
2	◯	⇨	☐	D	▽															
3	◯	⇨	☐	D	▽															
4	◯	⇨	☐	D	▽															
5	◯	⇨	☐	D	▽															
6	◯	⇨	☐	D	▽															
7	◯	⇨	☐	D	▽															
8	◯	⇨	☐	D	▽															
9	◯	⇨	☐	D	▽															
10	◯	⇨	☐	D	▽															
11	◯	⇨	☐	D	▽															
12	◯	⇨	☐	D	▽															
13	◯	⇨	☐	D	▽															
14	◯	⇨	☐	D	▽															
15	◯	⇨	☐	D	▽															
16	◯	⇨	☐	D	▽															
17	◯	⇨	☐	D	▽															
18	◯	⇨	☐	D	▽															
19	◯	⇨	☐	D	▽															
20	◯	⇨	☐	D	▽															
21	◯	⇨	☐	D	▽															
22	◯	⇨	☐	D	▽															
23	◯	⇨	☐	D	▽															
24	◯	⇨	☐	D	▽															
25	◯	⇨	☐	D	▽															

ANALYSIS WHY?

ACTION CHNGE

Fig. 39 — Process Chart

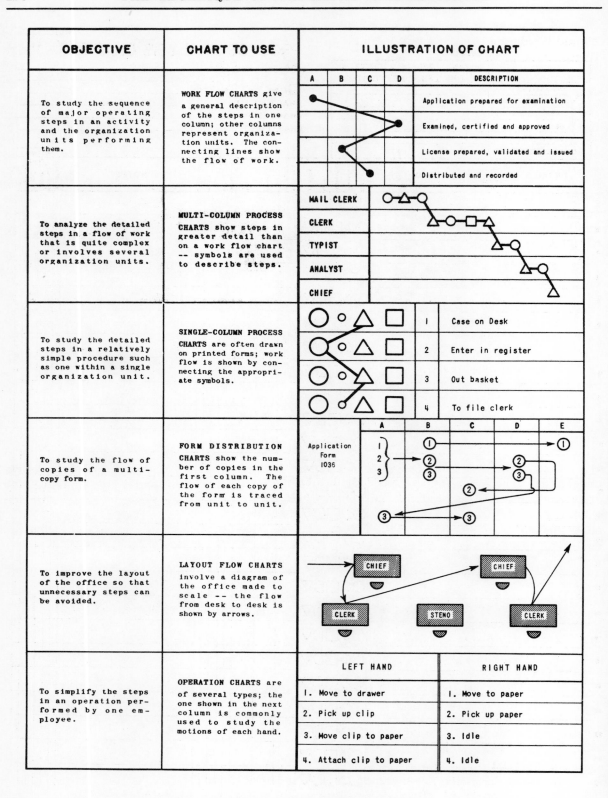

Fig. 40 — Chart Selector

If changes in the process are indicated after the analysis, the proposed procedure should be charted in the same manner as the existing procedure. This affords a comparative picture of what is proposed.

Forms Distribution Chart. The forms distribution chart is another work simplification device. Each form and each copy of a form used in an office requires an employee in the organization to perform a particular task. Forms as such then are one of the starting points in many work simplification studies.

A forms distribution chart is useful in studying the flow of copies of a multiple-copy form since it graphically shows the distribution and use of each copy. It is useful where the handling of forms constitutes a large portion of the time required in a process. Often the information shown on the chart will eliminate the necessity for lengthy, narrative descriptions. As shown in Fig. 40, the forms distribution chart shows the number of copies and traces the flow of each copy from unit to unit with notations on the use and disposition of the copies.

The chart will assist in suggesting answers to several questions which have important implications in simplifying work:

1. Is each copy essential?
2. Does any one department or individual receive any unnecessary duplication of copies?
3. Are too many departments maintaining files of the same form when one would be sufficient?
4. Are all departments who need copies receiving them?
5. Are all departments which need clear copies getting original and early copies?
6. Are other forms created from the original form when additional copies would serve the same purpose?

Layout Flow Chart. Office layout has an important effect on the efficiency of work processes. The layout flow chart is used to study office layout in order that unnecessary steps and time are avoided. It consists of a diagram of the office made to scale with the work flow from desk to desk indicated by arrows. The layout flow chart is intended to show unusually long transportations and back-tracking and is not concerned with what is done with the material. An example of a flow-layout chart is shown in Fig. 41.

Listed below are some of the questions which the analyst should ask in studying the chart:

1. Do the principal work flows follow straight lines without undue back-tracking and crosswise travel?
2. Are persons having most frequent contact located near each other?
3. Are files, cabinets, and other records and materials located near employees who need them?
4. Is there surplus furniture which can be moved to provide space for other purposes?
5. Is the best lighted and ventilated space used for work requiring closest attention and concentration?
6. Do the locations of files or other equipment obstruct proper light and ventilation?
7. Does the office arrangement facilitate supervision?
8. Are employees who use the same equipment grouped together? [12]

---

[12] Department of State, op. cit., p. 47.

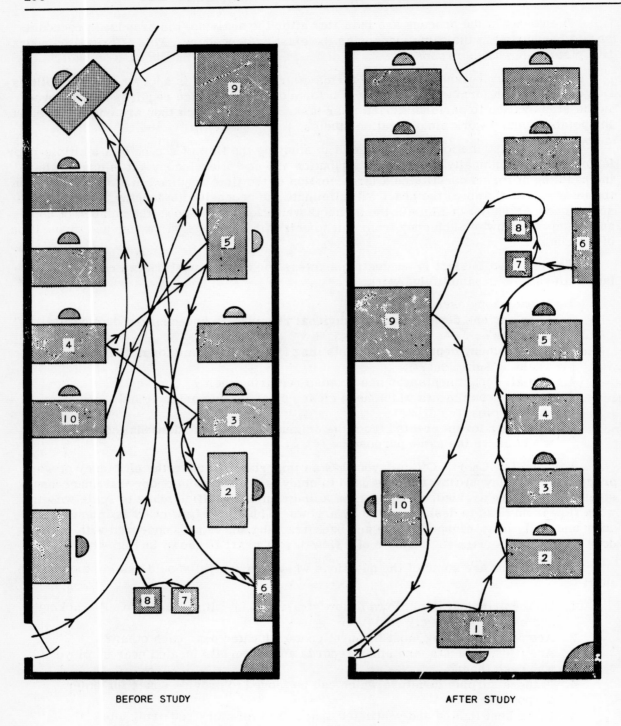

BEFORE STUDY   AFTER STUDY

MANUAL FOR CONTROL OFFICERS
VOLUME III WORK SIMPLIFICATION
CONTROL DIV. HDQTS. ARMY SERVICE FORCES

Fig. 41 — Layout Chart

The Work Count. In many administrative studies the analyst will want to determine the volume of work involved. There are numerous ways to count items and obtain volume data, and the most desirable method will depend on the particular situation as well as the item being counted. In many instances, a representative sampling of the work will adequately serve the purpose of the study and lessen the time and effort involved.

Some of the means of making work counts are: (1) actual count, (2) existing reports, (3) serially numbered forms, (4) weighing, (5) measuring, (6) tally, and (7) recording meters. Typical among things that may be counted are inquiries, checks and vouchers, interviews, postings, letters, phone calls, files pulled, and so forth.

Work counts may be indicated for (1) steps where process charts indicate that work piles up, (2) steps where the flow of work branches off from the main flow, and (3) questionable activities shown on the work distribution chart.

The work count is useful in scheduling work to actual conditions, determining the value of a step, dividing work, spotting bottlenecks, demonstrating personnel needs, and promoting better utilization of personnel. Work counts ordinarily will supplement information the analyst has already obtained through the use of various work simplification tools.

Graphic Presentation. Graphical presentations are quite useful devices in "selling" proposed solutions and in illustrating statistical matter which otherwise might not be clearly understood or might be glossed over in a report if presented in tabular form. While statistics are usually quite significant to an administrative analyst, they may appear unimportant to someone else who is not familiar with all of the details of a problem unless they are presented in a simple, appealing form. The primary purpose of many commonly used charts and graphs is to present various statistical data in a simple, appealing form. Some of these different types of graphs and charts are briefly described below.

Line or curve graphs are useful in showing peaks and valleys or seasonal trends in various activities. If the period that is being charted covers several years, the line graph will in effect present a historical picture of the activity. Often a limited number of different types of related statistical data can be shown on the same graph through the use of lines shown in different colors or with different symbols if only one color is available. This will present the reader not only with a picture of the trends in several activities, but also with a comparison of the different activity trends.

Bar charts are commonly used to compare quantities over a period of time. If a single type of statistical information is being presented, a solid bar will be used for each designated period of time. In some instances, comparison of parts to the whole over a period of time can be effectively shown on a bar chart by using white, black, and shaded areas on each bar. For example, tax rates for overlapping jurisdictions can be shown in this manner. The over-all bar represents the total tax rate for the area with the various shadings or different colors within a bar comparing the rates of individual units of government. Use of several bars to cover a period of years will offer (1) comparisons of the total tax rate and (2) comparisons of rates of the different units and their relative effects on the total rates for these years.

Pie charts or area diagrams are the usual method of presenting statistical information in a manner designed to show the relative importance of parts to the whole. Its most common application by cities has been in showing the importance of different revenue sources in financing city government and in showing what activities are financed with the revenue — "Where the money comes from" and "Where it goes." This common application of the pie chart can be very effective. The principal difficulty with the pie chart however, is the tendency to break the information down into fine segments. When the pie chart is cut into very thin slices, the data can become almost meaningless. Consolidation of closely related data whenever possible helps to make the chart more understandable.

Geographic distribution of data can be shown with statistical maps. Such maps may be used to show police and fire manpower requirements in different sections of the city, determine the adequacy of parks and recreational facilities, or analyze growth and future growth trends.

Work progress can also be shown quite effectively with the use of charts. This type of chart is known as the "Gantt" chart. Estimated time schedule for the completion of certain projects and tasks can be compared on these charts with the actual progress that is being made. The progress chart is basically a production control device and as such is widely used in industry. In municipalities the chart can be applied to many types of public works activities including street improvement projects, construction of water, sanitary sewer, and storm sewer lines, remodeling of buildings, and others. Many variations of these progress charts are available and some are incorporated in patented "control boards" that are for sale. The basic principle involved in all such charts, however, is illustrated in Fig. 42.

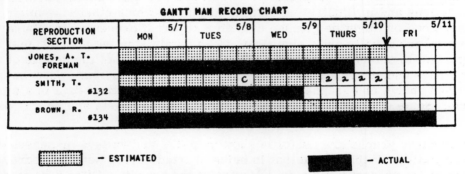

Explanation: The chart is read as of c.o.b. May 10th. The foreman was present but failed to get estimate production completed as scheduled on Thursday night. This was largely because Smith lost two hours in a conference on Tuesday, and took Thursday off. Brown has worked all week, and is 6 hours ahead of schedule.

Fig. 42 – Progress Chart

Research Agencies Outside City Government

In addition to agencies and employees within the city government, a number of outside agencies can and should be used occasionally in the planning and research work of the city. No attempt will be made here to list all such agencies, or to describe in detail the services they are capable of rendering. Some of the most important outside sources of planning and research assistance may be mentioned, however, by way of illustration.

Other Governmental Agencies

Other governmental units — federal, state and local — carry on research programs and planning studies that often have a direct bearing on municipal problems. The recent development of metropolitan and regional planning agencies is particularly notable, for many problems facing municipalities are not confined to the city limits. In some cases, personnel from other governments are available as consultants either on an informal or formal basis. State planning agencies may be able to supply very useful information and advice on local planning problems while state finance and personnel departments may provide assistance in solving problems in their respective fields.

The federal government during the past 25 years has greatly expanded its services to cities. Federal departments and agencies have useful information available in a variety of fields, and much of this information can be obtained without charge or at a nominal cost.

Many federal departments and bureaus collect and publish statistical data from cities on subjects such as population, finance, housing, governmental employment, crime, education, airports, libraries, and public health. This statistical information is often in sufficient detail to provide city officials with data on individual cities. The United States Bureau of the Budget also provides information on sources of data in particular fields to serve as a guide in further gathering of statistical information.

Many federal agencies publish model ordinances on subjects such as airport zoning, building and housing codes, health and sanitation standards, plumbing and electrical codes, traffic and subdivision regulation, and smoke abatement. These ordinances are generally outstanding in technical content even though adaptations may have to be made to comply with state and local legal requirements.

Federal grants and loans are available to cities in a wide variety of fields, including airports, hospitals, public housing, water pollution control, civil defense, slum clearance and urban redevelopment, and planning for various public works projects. Information on these programs can be obtained from the federal agencies concerned. Much information on federal aid programs to cities is also available from the American Municipal Association.

Private Agencies

Study of governmental problems is by no means confined to the activities of governmental agencies and personnel. A variety of private or semi-public agencies are also working in this general field.

Citizen Research Agencies. In many cities privately sponsored municipal research bureaus are important sources of management research. Some of these bureaus play a militant role in municipal policies, taking positive stands on policy questions, while others are content with obtaining and releasing reliable factual information to citizens. In either case they often study and investigate municipal problems and propose possible solutions. Some of their studies deal with physical improvements and municipal services, and others with administrative or managerial subjects. The quality of their research, of course, depends upon the attitude of the sponsoring body and the qualifications of the staff employed, but most of these bureaus are recognized as institutions of creditable standing.

Taxpayers' associations, chambers of commerce, and other special interest groups also conduct researches into municipal problems in many cities. Although such groups are likely to have a biased interest, most of them maintain high standards of accuracy and integrity in their research activities.

University Governmental Research Bureaus. Many state universities have established municipal or governmental research bureaus which provide services to cities. These services tend to vary greatly in degree as do the organization and staffing of the bureaus themselves. Some of the bureaus will work directly with cities while others will work through state leagues of municipalities. Although some of the bureaus have staff members who are assigned full-time to governmental research, most rely primarily on professors of government and public administration supplemented by the part-time services of graduate students. The most active university governmental research bureaus have been developed at those universities which have established graduate programs to prepare students for careers in municipal management or public administration.

The services of these bureaus generally include in-service training programs, correspondence courses, research on governmental problems of state-wide interest, distribution of information and research materials on specific governmental problems, and sponsoring meetings and conferences for governmental officials. Some of the states which have developed university-local relationships to a high degree include California, Colorado, Connecticut, Kansas, Michigan, Minnesota, New Jersey, Oregon, Pennsylvania, Tennessee, Texas, Washington, and Wisconsin.

Field consultation services are provided by some state university research bureaus. Perhaps the most extensive university consulting program for local units is carried on by the Municipal Technical Advisory Service of the University of Tennessee. The large, full-time staff of this organization provides municipalities with consulting services on public works, finance, public relations, planning, general administration, preparation of ordinances, and legal problems.

Technical and Professional Associations. Technical and professional associations of municipal officials have become increasingly important as sources of information in a wide variety of fields. These associations run the gamut of municipal activities since they have been largely organized and supported by officials engaged in different functions of municipal government — city managers, finance officers, personnel officers, public works officials, and others. [13]

A few of these organizations are equipped to provide limited field consulting services, but most confine themselves to a "clearinghouse" type of operation including collecting and disseminating information and materials in their respective fields. These informational or advisory services are generally restricted to the associations' members — either on the basis of a city official's individual membership or an "agency" membership whereby the city itself is a member and any of its personnel may use the service.

Technical and professional agencies are particularly helpful in furnishing information regarding plans and procedures adopted by other municipalities. A city official can use these materials as models or guides and adapt them to the needs of his city. Most of these agencies also publish periodic journals and issue special reports which deal with problems of current interest in their fields. [14]

State leagues of municipalities also should be included in this group. The quantity and quality of services provided by state leagues is quite varied. Several state leagues are staffed to provide extensive field consulting services. Leagues are usually especially good sources of information on problems which are having a state-wide impact on cities or which are peculiar to a specific state because of legal requirements.

Also included in this general grouping are technical organizations, such as the National Board of Fire Underwriters, the National Fire Protection Association, the Urban

---

[13] For a listing of national technical and professional associations and their headquarters' addresses, see The Municipal Year Book (Chicago: International City Managers' Association, published annually).

[14] See David S. Arnold, "Sources of Management Information," Public Management, August, 1956, pp. 173-177.

Land Institute, and others. For example, the National Board of Fire Underwriters not only is a valuable source of information on requirements on fire insurance rating, but will also make local surveys and recommend ways by which a city can improve its fire protection services as well as its fire insurance rating.

Municipal Consultants. There are many private individuals and firms which specialize in surveys and consultation on municipal problems. There are consultants in physical planning, construction and operation, and other special fields. In addition, there are private consulting firms which specialize in surveys and installations of administrative systems and procedures — personnel, finance, record systems, and the like. For a city that does not have an adequate planning and research staff, these consulting firms may provide valuable service. Even those cities that have large and versatile research staffs may occasionally have need for the services of outside consultants. A special study may call for knowledge or skills not possessed by any member of the regular staff, a larger staff than the city normally needs, or an independent appraisal by someone not influenced by local traditions or opinions.

Others. A number of miscellaneous agencies may on occasion contribute information, advice, or active assistance in the study of municipal problems. Privately owned public utilities in the community are interested in plans for physical expansion and for adjusting their physical plants to the changing needs of the community. The local telephone company may have information relating to the rate and direction of extensions of its services that may be useful to city officials in forecasting future city growth. Manufacturers of business machines and equipment are sometimes prepared to offer limited consulting services on some administrative problems, particularly those involving procedures and the flow of paper work.

Use of Outside Consultants

Mention has already been made of the research services that can be provided by municipal consultants. The use of outside professional consultants in specialized and technical fields such as city planning, law, engineering, and utilities has for some years been standard practice in many cities. Employment of consultants who specialize in personnel, finance, and general administration, is a more recent development. That municipal consultants can make significant contributions in these fields is evidenced by the fact that both large and small cities frequently engage consultants for such projects and studies.

Three basic reasons can be listed for employing outside consultants: (1) the urgency or time required for a project and the regular workload of the city's staff indicate that a study can be accomplished more expeditiously by a consultant; (2) the project under consideration is of such a specialized or technical nature that it is felt that a consultant can do the job better; and (3) the final recommendations will be more readily acceptable on a potentially controversial subject because of an outside consultant's professional reputation and because his recommendations are less likely to be subjected to a charge of bias from persons opposed to the program or activity being studied.

Often consultants will be employed by a city for a combination of the above reasons. For example, both large and small cities quite frequently engage consultants to develop position classification and pay plans. This type of study calls for considerable knowledge and experience in the personnel field and is time-consuming. In addition, by obtaining the greatest possible amount of objectivity in the study through the use of a consultant, the city is more likely to have the classification and pay plans accepted by the majority of the employees, thus promoting better employee morale and employee relations.

Types of Consulting Services

Consulting services fall into two general categories: (1) the survey and report project and (2) the installation project.

The "survey and report" project involves a particular subject or problem of municipal administration. This type of study is most useful where basic defects in organization and administration will require legislative action for correction and call for a considerable amount of public information to enlist official and citizen support. An example of this type of project is the general administrative survey of a city to propose a reorganization of functions and departments preparatory to the establishment of a charter commission. In studies of this type the consultant ordinarily departs after submitting a report and recommendations. If the consultant's recommendations are carried out in such cases, it is done by the city officials themselves — the city council, city administrator, or department heads, depending upon the nature of the study, the recommendations and the action required.

The installation project differs considerably. Under this type of project the consultant develops administrative improvements in a prescribed area and assists in putting these improvements into effect without being required to go through elaborate reporting procedures. This type of project is perhaps the more practical when the administrator is aware of the problem and possible remedies, but lacks time or staff to make the indicated improvements. In such cases the consultant may be assigned to develop and install a new system of operation in some field such as in personnel administration, revision of accounting, budgeting, or purchasing practices, or the installation of an equipment and cost record-keeping system.

Selection of a Consultant

The first step in hiring an outside consultant is to define the general nature, type, and scope of the problem, list the technical resources available locally, and decide what technical services are desired. On the basis of such general specifications, inquiry can be made of a number of consulting firms and agencies. These inquiries should invite statements of interest and availability on the part of consultants and suggestions as to possible modifications of the proposed consulting service. [15]

Where a consultant expresses interest in the undertaking, he should be required to indicate at least generally how the project would be staffed, scheduled, and otherwise conducted, and to provide appropriate references in jurisdictions previously served and examples of reports prepared as well as estimates of the probable cost of professional services to be rendered.

After analyzing replies and contacting references, it is usually worthwhile to interview representatives of several firms selected from the list of responses. A municipality should make inquiry particularly of responsible officials who were in office when other

---

[15] Names and addresses of consultants and consulting firms are listed in most magazines and professional journals concerned with municipal government, such as American City, Western City, Public Management, and many others. Another excellent source is the Municipal Index published by the American City Magazine Corporation, 470 Fourth Avenue, New York.

consulting work was done and who have lived with the results of the work. Only in this manner can the municipality assure itself that it is likely to receive technical services of the type and caliber which it desires.

This checking-up process before consulting services are engaged is highly desirable from the point of view both of the municipality and of any reputable consultant. The municipality's interest in such a process is obvious: it is employing personal services and should certainly be as exacting in employing a consultant as it is in putting a top-level professional person on its payroll. Similarly, from the point of view of the consultant, anything which enhances the municipality's confidence in him will contribute to a type of working relationship essential to effective consulting services. Also, possible differences over what is expected should be resolved before, rather than after, consulting services are formally engaged.

Competitive Bids for Consulting Services

While it is desirable for the city to secure statements from several consultants on the extent and kind of work they would perform, and a cost estimate, the city generally is under no obligation to engage the lowest bidder. Even where competitive bidding is required on all contracts, it is generally not necessary or desirable to obtain such bids for the employment of professional people such as accountants, architects, attorneys, engineers and city planners.

This exemption from bidding is based primarily on the fact that professions require special skills or technical training and no useful purpose would be served by requiring competitive bidding. The work performed by such consultants is of a personal nature and if the award is made on a competitive bid basis then the selection may depend on price alone. The quality of the work performed by professional or technical personnel depends very largely upon their training, ability, and integrity. [16]

The Contract or Agreement

Once the consultant has been selected, the city and the consultant should enter into an agreement or contract specifying the type and amount of services to be rendered and their cost and scheduling. This agreement may take the form of an exchange of correspondence between appropriate responsible officials or may be incorporated in a formal contract document.

Formal contracts for consulting services, as well as for other types of professional services, are required by law in many states. Moreover, many cities as a matter of practice will want a formal contract to be executed as a means of protecting the best interests of the city. Reputable professional consultants themselves will have no objections to entering into a formal contract with a city. Among other things, the contract should include the project specifications and cite the services to be provided by the city, the form that the end product will take, and the costs of the consultant's services.

---

[16] This point of view has been quite consistently held by the courts in many states. For example, in McQuillen on Municipal Corporations, Vol. 2, sec. ed. revised, p. 1182, sec. 1292, it is stated with citation of cases: "Provisions as to competitive bidding have been held not to apply to contracts for personal services depending upon the peculiar skill or ability of the individual such as the services of ... an attorney at law, a superintendent or architect ... or a consulting and supervising engineer. And generally the requirement does not apply to the employment of a professional man in which case the authorities have a discretion as to his qualifications."

Services Provided by the City

A city employing a consultant normally is expected to provide the consultant with necessary office space, furniture, and equipment; local telephone service; necessary office supplies; and clerical, stenographic, and related facilities as necessary to assure the effective use of technical staff.

It is also advantageous to the city if one or more of its employees can be assigned to assist the consultant on certain phases of the survey work. Such an arrangement can do much to expedite progress on a consulting project and minimize the cost of the outside services. It also provides employees with useful training and with valuable knowledge of what was done, why it was done, and what future operational requirements will be.

In establishing budgetary and centralized purchasing systems for a small city, for example, a consultant can materially reduce the cost of his services if the city will assign staff members to perform much of the detailed work under the consultant's direction. Staff members could design forms on the basis of verbal instructions or rough copies supplied by the consultant or carry out the detailed work of developing forms and procedures on the basis of a program developed by the consultant. Thus it would be unnecessary for the consultant to remain in the city while this work was being done and the costs of the consulting services would be materially reduced.

Form of End Product

Since results of consulting services may take several forms, an early decision should be made concerning the type of end product to come out of a survey or installation project, with due regard to the audience to which the end product is to be directed.

In many instances, reports must be prepared which will vary depending on the use to which they are to be put. Comprehensive and detailed reports may be prepared to provide detailed guidance for administrative officials; concise reports on the most significant features of the work done may be most appropriate for legislative officials; and popularized summaries may best inform the public. On installation projects the end product is likely to be a series of manuals, circulars, bulletins, and directives to carry out recommendations and help employees charged with the continued operation of the new system.

Cost of Consulting Service

To assure a satisfactory experience in the use of consulting services, the cost of the service should be fixed in the contract or agreement as accurately as possible.

Where the scope of the job and the extent of local participation can be determined accurately, the most satisfactory arrangement is for the consultant to fix a maximum beyond which no charges will be made. The consulting firm should then bill against that amount for transportation costs, staff time, and other items devoted to the project. Where work is done on a cost basis on sizable projects which permit the use of a balanced staff comprised of junior, intermediate, and senior technicians, billing rates averaging up to $100 or more per day worked on the project may be expected.

In addition to the salary of the member of the consulting staff, such rates usually include the expenses he incurs by reason of living away from his headquarters; the cost of providing vacation, sick leave, and retirement privileges; the cost of nonbillable time spent in travel from one project to another; and also a share of the headquarters overhead necessary to provide the field consultant with the direction and reference facilities and other resources which give him a usefulness greater than that of a local employee of perhaps comparable personal competence.

At first glance the daily billing rate for a consultant may appear to be rather high. A careful examination will usually indicate that the discrepancy in the unit cost between an employee of the city and a consultant is not as great as it seems, however. In evaluating the reasonableness of such daily billing rates, it should be remembered that normally they apply only to days actually worked.

As there is little uniformity among state and local governments with respect to length of work week, leave provisions, and the like, the federal service may best be used to illustrate the relationship of days worked to total time. On the basis of federal work schedules, leave provisions, and with only absolute minimum allowances for travel and other unproductive time, the per-day worked cost of an employee approximates 1/200 of his annual salary. This figure does not include subsistence expenses involved in being away from his regular home and headquarters, the cost incurred in recruiting and training him, nor the administrative expense of the headquarters office.

Follow-up on Consultant's Work

The responsibility for following through on work done by a consultant rests primarily with the city. Most of the follow-through aspects of an undertaking lie beyond the authority of the consultant, and even the best of consulting work can be no more effective than the degree of follow-up exercised by local officials. Installation projects, for example, can be ruined through the notion that the completion of the installation has ended the problem for all time. Seldom is this true!

In most instances systems must be continuously revised, at least in detail, to conform to changing circumstances. The consultant will almost always be glad to assist in such follow-up operations and, as his prior work gives him intimate familiarity with the situation, it may be advisable to have him come back occasionally for general review and to assist in working out any new problems that have arisen.

The authority and responsibility for making decisions rests with local officials and not with the consultant. Accordingly, local officials must make decisions on all recommendations, accepting them, rejecting them, modifying them or, in some instances, establishing a specific schedule and procedure for their reconsideration. Also, local officials should make known to the consultant difficulties encountered in the continued operation of systems which the consultant has developed.

Undoubtedly many of the dissatisfactions with consulting work arise from the failure to give the consultant the benefit of specific constructive complaints on the basis of which the consultant can offer either supporting explanation or corrective action. In turn, these complaints strengthen the consultant's ability in solving similar problems in the future.

Chapter 10

CITY PLANNING

Chapter 9 described the role of research and planning in administration, and explained the distinctions and interrelationships of administrative research and planning with the physical planning function. In this chapter special emphasis is placed on how governmental research and planning work is conducted, with special attention to the functions generally grouped under the heading of "City Planning," and how the chief administrator uses these techniques in solving local government problems.

In order to supervise and review the physical plans prepared by the various municipal departments and agencies the chief administrator must be thoroughly familiar with the techniques of "city planning." Among the managerial agencies the planning department is the most important to the discussion in this chapter. Closely related are the departments or agencies charged with public housing and with urban renewal responsibilities.

Scope of Physical Planning

"City Planning" includes consideration of all things that have to do with the physical form and structure of the community and its physical services. A master plan is concerned first with community objectives, then with broad patterns of land use and population distribution, and, finally, in the light of these, with plans for the physical "plant" of the city, including streets, utilities, recreation areas, schools and other public buildings, transit and transportation, standards of neighborhood design, housing, and urban renewal and redevelopment. This is not an exclusive list, and none of the subjects of city planning can be put into a pigeonhole of its own; they are all intimately interrelated since they deal with the city as a functional organism.

City planning is not a somewhat theoretical picture of the future, nor is it a single job that can be done at a given time; rather it is a continuing municipal function. The city is dealing daily with things that fall in the realm of city planning. Many current activities of the city administration and citizens leave some residual effect on the city, such as the improvement of streets and the erection of buildings. All these things affect the physical form and character of the city.

The city of today is the accumulation of the residual effects of these activities during all the years that the city has existed. The city of tomorrow will be these things plus what happens during the years to come, beginning with what is happening today. Planning provides the guidance needed to direct these numerous current activities toward defined objectives.

Organization for Research and Planning

The inclusion of city planning as a part of the official municipal administration has developed in the United States since 1900. After a score of years of experiment and experience, a committee of experts drafted a model planning enabling act which was published by the U. S. Department of Commerce in 1927 and re-issued in a slightly revised form in 1928. Later, in 1935, a further revision was prepared by Alfred Bettman and issued by the Harvard University Press. These models are the basis of the current enabling statutes.

Basically the model laws call for the establishment of a separate, semi-independent plan commission outside the regular municipal administrative family. There is a technical staff on the regular city payroll, with the appointment of the director the prerogative of the plan commission itself, or sometimes with the appointment by the chief executive upon nomination or advice of the commission. The details of organization and selection of personnel vary from state to state and even from city to city within the same state. Nevertheless, the underlying intent has been the same: to set up a commission and staff independent of the central administrative organization.

There were several reasons for establishing planning as an independent function. Although it has not been emphasized in the written discussions, it is quite probable that a prime reason was to divorce planning from "dirty politics." The framers of legislation did not trust the elected officials nor the typical administration of municipal affairs in the early part of the century.

A second reason for the outside planning commission lay in the theory that planning was essentially a legislative process. The "plan" was to be prepared by experts, presented to and adopted by the city council, and from then on it was merely a matter of carrying it out — following the guide lines to a perfect city, enforcing the law. The independent commission and staff could do a much better job if they were removed from the pressures of day-to-day administration.

A third reason for the independent agency was based on the principle that planning is necessarily a long-time process. It must last into the future, beyond the two- or four-year terms of the mayor and council. The independent commission made up of nonpaid citizen members, serving overlapping terms, would outlive several councils and would assure the continuity that is indispensable for successful planning.

There was and still is considerable merit in the reasons given for the independent planning commission. At the same time, city planning has not generally lived up to the potential foreseen by writers of the model laws. While much of this failure can be attributed to the fact that planning was not properly integrated into municipal administration, it is also true that there have been significant changes in the practice of municipal administration. These changes make possible today an integration of planning that would have been impossible in most cities in the 1920's and earlier.

For example, there was every reason to distrust local government in many cities. There was not only venality, but even in the most honest governments scientific management was virtually unheard-of. Both the strong-mayor and the council-manager forms of city government were rare. Today the weak organizational form or the dishonest government is the exception rather than the rule, so that this should be discarded as an argument for an independent commission. In fact it can be stated as a corollary that the quality and accomplishments of city planning can be no better than the quality of the general administration of the city.

It is still true that continuity is necessary for long-range planning, but the contention that continuity is best maintained by an independent board of laymen is not necessarily true. In the first place, continuity of personnel is best maintained through good personnel policies affecting the technical staff. In the second place, while vacillation of a council for petty or improper reasons is bad, changes in plan are absolutely vital to successful planning when they are the result of changed conditions or of changed desires of the citizens. In addition, there are several administrative techniques that have been devised quite specifically to maintain continuity of objectives in municipal development, chief of which is the long-range public works program.

Perhaps the most important reason for the lack of accomplishment in city planning has been the effort to divorce planning from administration. As emphasized throughout this chapter, planning is present in all parts of the administrative structure. "City planning," as the term is understood here, embraces all parts of the city, all aspects of the city — social, economic, and physical — and all parts of the city administration. This does not set it apart and above the city, but merely places it as a staff aid to top administration where the administrative responsibilities likewise embrace all parts and all aspects of the city and all parts of the city government.

It would be unfair to leave the impression that (1) city planning has been a complete failure and accomplished nothing; or that (2) all planning agencies in city government are extra-mural and without contact with administration. City planning has a long list of noteworthy accomplishments and there is wide variation in the place of city planning in the municipal organization chart. However, there are a steadily increasing number of planning "departments" operating within the administrative structure.

Three years after the appearance of the model planning statutes in 1935 there was established in New York a city planning "department." In a reaction to the outside independent board, the pendulum had swung to the other extreme. The charter provision provided an extremely powerful board of paid planning "commissioners" who were very much in the center of municipal government. In fact the theory behind the New York city planning department was that planning must be the fourth branch of government, parallel with the legislative, executive, and judicial branches.

Only one other government adopted an organization structure similar to the New York city planning department, and this was the Commonwealth (then Territory) of Puerto Rico. The record of the Peurto Rico Planning Board has been outstanding, but the early New York city planning department fell short of the hopes of its inventors. Not until some 18 years after its formation was the New York planning department able to overcome some of the unforeseen handicaps that had been unwittingly written into the original charter provisions.

Although the organization details of a planning department will be discussed later, a word is in order concerning the definition of a planning "department" as distinguished from other types of organizations for city planning. By planning "department" is meant a full-fledged staff department under the chief administrative officer, fully integrated into the administrative structure, with or without a lay board or commission that acts primarily in an advisory capacity.

There are many planning departments among American cities. In some cities they carry the name "department." In other cities the charter provisions or the city ordinances would still show independent outside status, but in practice they frequently operate exactly as the integrated staff department.

There is no doubt that it is preferable to have departmental status recognized and legalized. But in many cities this is not easily achieved, because of state statutes or because of the difficulty in getting a charter amendment. In the meantime, perceptive administrators have accomplished the changeover through internal rulings and by agreements with plan commissions. In many cases the change — without benefit of legislation — has been brought about by the planning directors themselves, as they have recognized the need for close ties with on-going municipal administration. In small mayor-council cities where being mayor is only a part-time job, the mayor has sometimes enlisted the planning director as his principal administrative aide, on the theory that planning is one function that cuts across all lines of municipal administration.

Needed Data for City Planning

Before planning as such can be undertaken adequate information must be assembled on the subject of what the city is, physically and functionally. There are well-defined types of surveys covering the various data required: land use surveys, real property surveys, family composition and family income surveys, population studies, surveys of traffic, land values, tax delinquencies, and various other items.

In assembling data of this nature, existing sources of information are first canvassed in order to ascertain what material is already available. Frequently, existing departments or other governmental agencies maintain such data in current form, or if they do not have the information immediately available may be willing to supplement existing data.

It is important that the planning officials know in advance how they will use the collected data. Clearly, there is little reason for getting together data which cannot be tabulated or which when tabulated are so inaccurate as to be unusable. Before any survey is started the tabulation and recapitulation schedules are drafted so that it will be known exactly what data are to be collected and in what form they are to be assembled. Usually other departments will also be interested in the information to be secured in the surveys. These departments and planning agencies should agree on survey schedules that will provide the data needed by all.

Social and Economic Data

History. A brief historical sketch of the community furnishes an interesting background for the surveys of its physical, social, and economic characteristics, and frequently assists in the interpretation of the data which disclose these characteristics.

Land Use, Economic, and Social Surveys. Excellent techniques have been developed for land use surveys, real property surveys, and family composition surveys, and these surveys are frequently made separately. However, since each of them requires sending persons into the field and since two of them require door-to-door canvass, there is considerable advantage in conducting them as one survey. The information collected would include such data as the use of all land not built upon; location and extent of vacant land; location, condition, and use of all buildings; vacancies in occupancy; rent; number of families in each residential building and in each dwelling unit; number of persons in each family, and the age distribution of males and females; number employed in each family, both men and women; the names of employers and location of employment; method of transportation to work; the yearly income; the time of residence in city at the present location and at previous locations; residence before coming to city, and many other matters.

Population. A map is prepared showing population distribution and densities. Data are assembled as to changes in totals, distribution, and densities.

Employment, Trade, and Industry. In this part of the survey data are gathered concerning the respective number of persons gainfully employed in the major categories of occupation; aggregate income of the inhabitants and respective totals for the major categories of occupation; employment and employment capacities in industries; production and production capacities of industries; volumes and values of shipping by major types of transportation broken down as to major classes of goods or products; volumes and values of major classes of goods or products handled through terminal, wholesale, and producer-consumer markets; and bank clearings.

Juvenile Delinquency, Crime, and Disease. The location of cases of juvenile delinquency, major crime, and communicable disease (especially tuberculosis and venereal disease) is plotted on maps.

Taxes and Assessments

Assessed Values. Assessed values of land and buildings are shown separately on a map, indicating front foot values in graded classifications or, in the case of property assessed on an acreage basis, the value per acre by graded classifications.

Tax Delinquency. A map is prepared showing all tax delinquent land in classifications as to the number of years delinquent, and all tax delinquent land for which title has reverted to the public.

Special Assessments and Levies. A map is prepared showing all special assessment and special taxing districts (if any) in a city and indicating the purpose of each, and for each assessment district the type of assessment (ad valorem or direct lien), status and delinquencies.

Traffic, Transit, and Transportation

Thoroughfares. All streets and thoroughfares are shown on a map indicating the width of right-of-way, the type, condition, and width of pavement or other surface, and the grades.

Traffic Flow. The traffic flow on the principal thoroughfares is determined by traffic census, with the counts made at strategically located stations and over a sufficient period to indicate average weekday and Sunday flow. An origin and destination survey is of special value in analyzing the functioning of a traffic thoroughfare system and particularly in determining the need for possible rerouting.

Automobile Parking. Automobile parking surveys are made in all business districts, covering such matters as how many vehicles can be accommodated in available curb space and in off-street parking facilities, how many vehicles are parked daily in each by persons who work in the district and how many by shoppers and others not employed in the district, the daily turnover and what additional areas and structures could be made available for off-street parking. In addition, vehicular loading and unloading requirements and facilities are determined for commercial and industrial establishments.

Transportation Facilities. A map is prepared showing all transportation lines and facilities, including rail lines (other than transit), terminals, and any airports and ports and harbor facilities. Data as to volumes and origin and destination of various classes of traffic are also important.

Transit Facilities. Unless there are no transit facilities whatever, there should be a map showing all existing transit lines, whether motor bus, trolley bus, street car, city rapid transit, or interurban, and indicating areas of effective service on each line. This is done even if there is only one bus route in the city, since it has a bearing on the functioning of the thoroughfare system and the development of residential areas. In a larger city there should be prepared a time-distance map or diagram, indicating transit time to the center of the city and to the principal industrial areas.

Public Property, Schools, and Recreation

Public and Semi-Public Property. All public and semi-public property is shown on a separate map.

Schools. A map is prepared showing all schools and schoolgrounds, distinguishing between public and private, and indicating whether elementary, high school, or collegiate, or whatever intermediate classifications are included in the school system. A map is also prepared showing the home location of all children of school age, distinguished as among the groups to the various classifications of schools. The capacities of the schools, the major facilities provided, and the acreage of the schoolgrounds are indicated. The area served by each school is shown, together with the number of school age children in the respective areas.

Recreation Facilities. All noncommercial recreation facilities in the city and closely adjacent to it are shown on a map, distinguishing between public and quasi-public facilities. Information is obtained as to the extent of use of the various recreation facilities and the home locations of the persons using them. From this can be developed a map showing the areas effectively served by the respective facilities.

Lot Width Map

All lots in the city are shown in each of a series of width groups, beginning with 25 feet or less and in gradations of five-foot intervals greater than 25 feet.

Municipal Income and Costs

This is a study, by census tracts or other districts, of taxes levied and collected and of expenditures for various public purposes. It makes possible the development of "balance sheets" for various neighborhoods and various classes of property.

Utilities

A map is prepared showing the location of sewers, water, light, gas, steam, and power lines; also power plants, pumping stations, sewage disposal facilities, and gas plants. Capacities, overloadings, and reserve capacities are also shown.

Building Construction and Demolition and Fire Hazards

A map is drawn showing new buildings constructed each year for the past ten years; also buildings which have been demolished according to types and uses. Locations of fire department calls are plotted on a separate map.

Subdivisions

The new subdivisions of land laid out each year for recent years (preferably covering a ten-year period) are shown on a map. Shown also are the nature and extent of their development, including public improvements and how provided. Tables are prepared, showing for each year the period covered, the total area of land subdivided, and total number of lots, the areas of land and lots made available for each of the major types of land use, the number of lots of each class sold (if possible), and the number of these lots used and for what purpose. This survey covers both subdivisions within the city and in the suburban areas, distinguishing between the data for each and also giving aggregate totals.

Analysis of Data

The data as to existing conditions provide a photograph of the community as it is, and they make it possible to measure the adequacy of the city's physical plant. More important than this, such data can disclose land-use relationships and trends of development and can indicate potentialities of development. There must therefore be compilations of facts which can be drawn from analyses of the survey data, together with forecasts as to the future. The most important conclusions to be drawn from the basic data include such matters as the adequacy of the physical facilities of the city, nature and function of the city, ratios of land use, rate of utilization of land, housing, trends in development, and population forecasts.

Adequacy of the Physical Facilities

The data as to the physical conditions and capacities of thoroughfares, utilities, recreation areas, schools, and other community facilities, and as to the service being rendered by these facilities (as disclosed by traffic studies, data as to utility studies, studies of the use of recreation areas, and so forth), and the needs for service as disclosed by the land-use and population data make it possible to determine how well these facilities are performing the services which they are called upon to render under existing conditions. Such an analysis indicates deficiencies, as well as reserve capacities, and thus makes it possible to improve present municipal services and to determine the adaptability of existing physical facilities to the servicing of future needs.

Nature and Function of the City

The figures as to employment, trade, and industry; the data from the land use survey, economic and social survey, population and municipal income and cost studies; and facts as to the regional relationships of the city make possible an analysis of the various factors which enter into the economic function of the city. By ascertaining the relationships among these various factors, the relative proportions of the aggregate income of the inhabitants which are derived from the major classes of activity, and the relative proportions of municipal income which are derived from the major classes of property, it is possible to make an appraisal of the relative importance of the various "functions" of the city and of the balance or lack of balance among them. These conclusions are of outstanding importance in influencing the determination of desirable land-use and population density patterns and of desirable physical facilities.

An appraisal of the social and cultural characteristics of the city also serves a useful purpose. In many ways these express its true nature. The economic characteristics of the city will strongly influence and may largely determine its social and cultural nature. Prevailing custom and habits have a large bearing on community character and may be influenced themselves by a historical background. Obviously these things cannot be reduced to figures, as in the case of economic factors, but they must be recognized and evaluated if the nature and function of the city is to be understood.

Ratios of Land Use

These ratios are determined by tabulations of land-use and real property data from the land-use, economic, and social survey, and cover the relative amounts of land (on an area basis) and respective proportions of the total devoted to each of the principal categories of use; and the relation of each of the principal categories of use to population.

Rate of Utilization of Land

A tabulation is made of the amounts of additional property each year devoted to various uses, in relation to the rate of population increase, if any, and to the amount of land subdivided each year, if any, to the total amount of land in vacant subdivided lots. In a city with a stationary population this study may take the form of a determination of changes in the ratio of land use (as discussed under "Trends in Development" below). In the city with a declining population the study may be expressed in reverse terms, that of recession in various types of use in relation to the decreasing population.

Housing

Data from the land-use, economic, and social survey and from the population study will enable a mapping of housing conditions in general and particularly a determination of areas of substandard housing areas. Maps showing the areas occupied by families in the lower-income groups and showing the areas of high ratios of juvenile delinquency, crime, disease, and fire hazard, will indicate the social and economic relationships of the substandard housing in the city.

Trends in Development

A careful analysis of trends of development, both as to ratios of use and as to territorial movements is essential, since these trends will have a bearing on the future needs of the population for various classes of land use and will indicate changes in neighborhood characteristics, with consequent changes in the nature and scale of required public services.

It is important to try to discover why changes in the ratios of land use and territorial movements in land use have been taking place. Some of the movements are normal in the expansion of a growing city; others result from the misuse of land, or conflicts among uses, or from inadequate provision of necessary community facilities. Determination of what these factors are will make it possible to devise plans to encourage tendencies which are beneficial and to counteract those which have resulted in the misuse of property or in the untimely obsolescence of neighborhoods.

Special attention should be given to movements of substandard housing areas and to the spread of areas of blight, since these movements can sap the economic vitality and social stability of neighborhoods and can result in the loss of population from neighborhoods, with consequent inefficiency in the operation of the neighborhood structure of streets, utilities, schools, and other public facilities.

Population Forecasts

These are of special importance. The city cannot plan intelligently for its future needs unless the scale of those needs can be determined by estimates of future population and of rate of population change.

Activities of The Planning Department

The nature of municipal research and planning and the wide variety of subjects requiring study make it impossible to concentrate all research and planning activities in any one special agency. Even if it were possible to assign all research and planning activities to some central body, it would not be desirable to do so, for such segregation would further aggravate the already serious problem of promoting unity and continuity between the formulation and the execution of plans and policies. In fact there is need for more, not less, departmental study and investigation of municipal problems. An important reason for encouraging true coordinated planning in all municipal departments is to introduce the basic philosophy of planning to department heads and employees throughout the municipal administration.

A principal component of the planning process is coordination; and a principal objective of planning is to present a unified course of action for all parts of the municipal operation. For this reason it is necessary to have a centralized planning function to coordinate the planning in the several departments and to assure that there is unity of policy. This central planning function is a responsibility of the chief administrator — subject, of course, to review and confirmation by the legislative body. In the smallest municipal organization it will be not only the responsibility of the chief administrator, but also one of the many jobs he must personally carry out.

The technical details and the volume of work involved in planning coordination, however, quickly exceed the capacity of the administrator if he is to carry on any other duties of his office. It becomes necessary to have technical assistance — to establish a planning department with at least one trained planner on the staff.

Because of the great variation among cities, their geographic situation, their economic base, their demographic composition, and their growth characteristics, it is not possible to say at exactly what point the central planning function should be separately staffed. A number of cities are seeking professional staffing by the time they reach 10,000 population. Certainly, any municipality of 20,000 population or greater can advantageously use a full-time staff planner. There are, of course, a number of cities much larger than 20,000 which still have no staff planner but they are rarely cities that would be singled out as examples of good municipal administration.

Throughout this chapter the central planning agency will be assumed to be a planning department. Earlier discussion in this chapter indicated the reasons for preferring this type of organization. For a number of reasons, clear-cut departmental status may not be possible in a particular city. Nevertheless, it is recommended that the planning staff should operate as a departmental staff, no matter how it appears on the organization chart.

It will also be assumed throughout much of the rest of this chapter that the planning function will be lodged largely in the planning department. However, there are modifications that have been mentioned previously; i.e., responsibility for final planning decisions must rest with the chief administrator and the city council, and much planning should be carried on by individual municipal departments. With these qualifications it is now possible to outline the functions and organization of the planning department itself.

In the abstract, "planning" and "coordination" are reasonably clear concepts in the science of management. At the same time the transition from abstract concepts to workaday directives and operation is not necessarily clear. Over the years there has developed a fairly standard list of duties and operations that has shown up in planning department operation in cities all over the country. These are described briefly.

Advance Planning

In many ways this can be considered the *raison d'etre* for planning and a planning department. Advance planning is the preparation of those guides by which the city develops the general plan and its several parts: land-use plan, transportation plan, park and recreation plan, housing plan, utility plan, public building plan, renewal plan, and so on.

Planning Administration

If advance planning would seem to be the most important function of the planning department in terms of the objective, then planning administration will seem the most important in terms of time and staff efforts devoted to it. It is the tail that very soon wags the dog. The largest part of planning administration is given over to the administration of the subdivision control regulations and the zoning ordinance.

Land subdivision regulation is the guidance of land subdivision development by public authority, preferably the planning agency, enforced through the power to withhold the privilege of public record from plats that do not meet established requirements and standards, together with other means. In its review of the land subdivision layout, the planning agency checks such features as the arrangement and width of streets, particularly as to conformity with the major street plan; the length and depth of blocks; the width and depth of lots; the provision of required public open spaces for parks, playgrounds, and public building sites; the provision of water supply and sewerage systems; the grading and surfacing of streets; and the sufficiency of easements for utility installation. In all these and other matters the subdivider is required to conform to standards prescribed in a published set of land-subdivision regulations prepared and adopted by the city planning agency. This process of land subdivision review and approval is an effective tool for the accomplishment of the master plan of a community.

Regardless of how carefully prepared and sound the zoning ordinance and plan may be, its benefits will not be realized unless it, too, is conscientiously, intelligently, energetically, and fairly administered. Bad or lax zoning administration may, over a period of years, break down and render largely ineffective any zoning ordinance no matter how good it may have been originally. More than that, malpractices in zoning administration are likely to result in adverse judicial decisions, often based on the charge of discrimination, the cumulative effect of which will destroy public respect for zoning, encourage violations, and as a consequence render the effort of better administration and enforcement more difficult.

The task of zoning administration for the ordinary planning agency consists primarily in studying and reporting to the city council its views on every proposed amendment to the text of the zoning ordinance or the map. However, in some communities the planning commission serves as the board of appeals. In such instances it serves as an administrative body with quasi-judicial powers in the application of the zoning ordinance in special and exceptional cases. Sitting as a board of appeals the planning commission must restrict itself to the narrow, though important, field of adjustments falling in its jurisdiction, as defined in the statutes or ordinance under which it was created. Nearly all zoning ordinances provide that if the building commissioner refuses to issue a building permit or certificate of occupancy, because, in his opinion, the structure or use fails to meet the requirements of zoning ordinances, an appeal from his decision may be taken to the board of appeals.

In addition to deciding appeals from the decisions of the building commissioner the board has two other functions: passing upon specified types of special exceptions, and granting variances. The function of passing on certain types of special exceptions arises in those cases in which the zoning ordinance delegates solely to the board of appeals the power to approve the specific location, for example, of telephone exchanges, fire stations, schools, and churches, within residential districts.

The third function of a board of appeals is the authorization, in specific cases, of variances from the strict letter of the law if the literal enforcement of the law would result in unusual and unnecessary hardship in the case of an individual lot. The hardship must be that of an individual lot and not a general hardship which, if it existed, would properly be corrected by an amendment of the zoning ordinance.

Special Studies

Closely related to planning administration are the special studies which always seem to be coming up in the field of municipal administration. These are one-time examinations of particular problems that arise as emergency studies. They may be requested by council members or by the chief administrator or by individual municipal departments, or, in some cases, by powerful and respected citizen groups. Both the chief administrator and the director of planning are apt to overlook these or to consider them as "unusual" demands upon the staff time and the planning department.

Experience throughout the United States, however, shows that there is a steady flow of these special projects in such quantity that they should be taken into consideration in setting up a planning department. In some cases there are studies that may be undertaken by outright consultants — there may even be special financing for them. Nevertheless, there are any number of these special studies that are too small, seemingly, for a special consultant, or there is no fund to provide for employment of such services.

Research

In broadest terms the research function of a planning department will fall in two categories: research specifically aimed at the solution of a particular problem; and continuing record keeping and analysis of statistics. In the first class of research, for example, are such studies as shopper interviews to determine the need for central business district parking. The second class of continuing record keeping and statistical research would include all types of statistics on population size and characteristics, population mobility, construction volume, cost and location, utility installations, and so forth.

Coordination and Effectuation

The simplest example of the method of coordinating municipal activities is illustrated by "mandatory referral." Under such a policy, capital improvement projects of all departments must be referred to the planning department for study and comment. The planning department reviews such projects for (a) determination of whether the project complies with any general plans that are in existence; (b) determination of whether the project is in conflict with any other currently proposed project from another department; and (c) determination of what effects the project will have on all other aspects of city development. Such a review, in addition to assuring coordination of the activities of different departments, can also be said to "effectuate" a general plan. An approved project helps to carry forward the objectives of the general plan.

It is not advisable to give the planning department a veto power over planning projects from other departments. The chief administrator is called upon to give final approval or veto to projects, but he has the benefit of outside review by the planning department. It is up to him and the members of the city council as to whether they will accept an unfavorable opinion by the planning department or whether they will overrule it.

Public Works Program and Capital Budgeting

The most tangible and, in many ways the most important, control of a city's development by the city government is through its program of public works construction. This in turn is carried out in an orderly manner by the device of capital budgeting for five or six or ten years in advance. It is generally agreed that the planning department is the proper organization to prepare a public works program and to try to develop unbiased criteria for arbitrating among competing demands for capital funds. Here again the chief administrator and the legislative body are the final decision makers on capital undertakings. However, experience has shown that the municipal executive and legislative officers are happy to have the advice of the planning department, if for no other reason than to lessen the heat of conflicting claims for a limited amount of capital funds.

Community Relations

Much of the operation of a planning department requires special efforts in community relations. This is particularly true for the zoning ordinance and for subdivision regulations, and to explain large construction expenditures that have been scheduled in a public works program. The ramifications of this function are beyond the scope of this discussion. However, it would include official public hearings and the relations with citizens' advisory committees, with service clubs, and with civic groups. It would include cooperation with other related governmental agencies, such as school boards and the county, state, and federal governments. It would include cooperation with other planning departments if the city is in a metropolitan area. Community relations is also an activity of a planning department frequently underestimated in terms of staff and budget.

Urban Renewal Planning

Later in this chapter is a more complete discussion of the organization for urban renewal. It should be noted at this point that the increasing interest in urban renewal has in the past and will continue to demand more and more of the planning department and the city. As pointed out later, urban renewal is essentially a much speeded-up operation of all the normal activities that take place in a city. A similar situation holds for the activity of the planning department in urban renewal. The planning department will not be called upon to do anything greatly different than it does in a city without urban renewal — but the planning department may have to turn out in six months an amount of research and study that would normally require ten years.

Organization of the Planning Department

Ideally, a planning department will be set up so that each of its several functions is fully staffed and financed. Obviously, the majority of cities will never have large enough staffs so that even one person could be assigned to each separate function. Small cities will be fortunate to have one professional employee and perhaps one stenographer in the planning department. However, experience shows that as soon as any differentiation can be made the technician in charge of advance planning should be exempted as quickly as possible from planning administration. The demands for attention to immediate problems in zoning and subdivision quickly preempt all the available time of all staff members. Because of their immediacy, they seem more important problems than those of next year or of five years in the future.

Some cities are beginning to experiment with the device of a "zoning administrator" to help to solve the problem of planning administration. From the view of quantity of work involved, this seems to be a sensible solution. In any number of cities, requests for zoning variances and zoning amendments occupy 50 per cent to 90 per cent of all of the efforts of the planning staff. Even in those cities in which there is not a formally designated zoning administrator, it is not unusual to find a separate division within the planning department staff whose sole job is servicing the zoning ordinance.

Under the new concept of a zoning administrator, this official is charged with the responsibility of approving or disapproving requests for certain classes of variance from the provisions of the zoning ordinance. The administrator's authority to grant these variances has been assigned to him in an effort to cut down the enormous amount of work that has been, in the past, given to boards of zoning appeals. The administrator's authority must be definitely described and limited. Legitimate requests for variances beyond his authority would still be appealed to a board of zoning appeals.

Planning Tools

The police power is the source of community authority to regulate the activities of its citizens in the interest of the "public health, safety, peace, morals, comfort, convenience, and general welfare," and in the field of planning it is used to give guidance to those activities which affect the physical form of the community. Some, but not all, of the principal types of such regulatory measures are zoning, the regulation of subdivisions, and the protection of land rights-of-way and the areas recommended for public use.

There are a number of specialized instruments and controls used in guiding the development of a city which fall within the operation of a planning department to amend, administer, or maintain. These are mentioned briefly in the following paragraphs.

General Plan

This is the basic document in a city plan and is essentially a guide to the future development of the city. It is sometimes called a "master" or "comprehensive" plan. It usually consists of one or several maps, plus descriptive material, tables, and so on. It is also usually divided into several "functional" plans, chief of which is probably the land-use plan. Other important elements of the general plan include a transportation plan, a park and recreation plan, a public building plan, a public utilities plan, a civic center plan, a school plan, and occasionally other separate plans for minor segments of the municipal operation.

A great many general plans have been prepared in the past by planning consultants. A large percentage of these have never been followed. This only underlines the earlier statement that planning is a *continuing* process and an integral part of municipal administration. Any attempt to freeze irrevocably the future pattern of the city by forcing it into a preconceived mold is foredoomed to failure. Nevertheless, a general plan is a useful tool in guiding city development, provided it is kept alive by constant testing and revision.

Zoning Ordinance

The zoning ordinance is probably the most powerful tool of planning and is the principal legal instrument for carrying out the land-use plan. In a few cities the zoning ordinance is prepared and administered completely apart from the planning department. In such cities there is neither effective planning nor decent land-use zoning control. There are also a few cities without zoning ordinances, but these are rare and in most cases the cities are small and static.

Subdivision Control Regulations

The second principal tool for land-use control is the subdivision control regulation. These are almost as widespread as zoning ordinances, although for special reasons there are no such regulations for either the city of New York or the city of Chicago. In most states, cities are granted the right to regulate subdivisions outside the city limits. The distance of such extra-territorial regulation varies from one-half mile to six miles. A city usually loses extra-territorial subdivision control when the county organizes a planning department and adopts county-wide subdivision regulations.

Official Map

In some states the cities are permitted to map the location of future streets quite accurately (by means of a field survey), to adopt a map of these streets as an official map, and thereafter to prohibit the construction of buildings within the right-of-way of the mapped streets. The state law requires that the city purchase the land from the owner if he insists upon it or surrender its right to prohibit buildings within the future street bed. This type of control is available only in states in which it has been specifically authorized by the legislature.

Capital Improvements

The capital improvement program is in effect a time-table and financing schedule for carrying out improvements in accordance with a general plan of development. This is discussed in considerably more detail in Chapter 5. The responsibility for preparing the program and for keeping it up to date is normally given to the planning department; and it is, without doubt, one of the most valuable tools for carrying out rational municipal development.

Mandatory Referral

The mandatory referral of all capital projects to the plan department has been mentioned earlier. This operation is customarily included in the municipal charter, although in noncharter cities it may be authorized by an ordinance or by an administrative order of the chief executive. It is an extremely valuable method of maintaining coordination of municipal activities.

Urban Renewal

Urban renewal is discussed in other parts of this chapter in enough detail to indicate its importance and its usefulness. It is certainly the most drastic and the most spectacular of tools for carrying out city plans.

Miscellaneous Ordinances

There are a number of miscellaneous ordinances and regulations which, although not properly administered by a planning department, nor in many cases even prepared by the planning department, are, nevertheless, outgrowths of problems studied by the planning department and are the result of suggestions made by the planning department. Among these can be included such ordinances as a housing code, a billboard and sign control ordinance, an air-pollution abatement ordinance, a noise-abatement ordinance, and so on.

Sometimes these controls first appear (probably improperly) as auxiliary controls in a zoning ordinance. It is the duty of the planning department to be alert to all municipal problems, and in particular to those problems which appear as a result of changing technology, changing population characteristics, and city expansion. Many of the problems when they are first recognized are too new to be within the jurisdiction of any existing municipal department.

Relations With Other Departments

There is necessarily a close tie between the planning department and all other municipal departments. The relation is analogous to those between the other major staff departments, legal, budget, and personnel, with the several line departments in the municipal administration. There is also, of course, a close tie between planning and the other staff departments themselves.

The pattern of city development determines and is determined by the construction of sewers, water mains, bridges, tunnels, expressways, streets, and other projects under the control of the public works department. If planning is to contribute to optimum city developments, then this construction must be coordinated with the master plan of the city. The fire department is interested in the reduction of fire hazard and in the elimination of deficiency points in the underwriters' rating schedule. Both of these items are proper considerations for the planning department's research and recommendations. School administrators need all of the help they can get with the problem of locating schools and forecasting pupil loads. This should be a continuing function of the planning department even in those communities in which the schools are completely separate from the municipal administration.

One of the most important functions in city planning is public works programming — scheduling long-term construction programs of the city to best serve the welfare of the city and at the same time stay within the city's ability to finance the program. This in turn calls for close ties with the municipal finance department.

The direct tie of the city planning activities with the traditional operating and staff departments in the city can easily be traced in dozens of ways and there is no need to elaborate on this. However, there is one municipal operation which has come to the front since the end of World War II, and which has an unusually close connection with city planning. This is urban renewal.

Urban Renewal

Urban renewal is a coordinated, planned attack on urban blight and obsolescence by using every method that can be devised, and by enlisting the aid of every municipal tool available. It has evolved from the slum clearance and public housing movement of the 1930's and has been spurred into new heights of activity by the rapid deterioration of central cities which took place after the end of World War II. A federal program of liberal grants-in-aid, included first in the housing act of 1949, and subsequently enlarged, has been particularly important in stimulating local activity.

Urban renewal, as the name indicates, seeks to renew cities and bring them back to health — hopefully in many cases to a better state of health than they originally possessed.

There is no single cause for the decay of cities. But there are many causes which contribute in greater or lesser degree to obsolescence. To name a few: high density residential development, narrow streets, excessive traffic congestion, inter-mixed industries and residences in the same district, heavy truck traffic through residential areas, inadequate schools, fire hazardous structures, conversion of apartments and old dwellings into tiny cubicle apartments, inadequate public services, such as sewerage, water supplies, and refuse collection, and so on.

A list of all the causes of urban obsolescence will include the entire range of urban activities, with improper urban land use as the most dominant single cause. In short, the correction of all of the ills and abuses which cause urban decay are problems that call for a solution by research and planning. Since no city will ever be able to conduct a renewal activity for the entire city all at one time, it is particularly important that the scheme for reconditioning a single renewal area fit into a general plan for the entire city and be coordinated with all municipal activities.

Early in the history of urban renewal, in fact prior to the discovery of the term, when the activity was usually known as "slum clearance and urban redevelopment," the agency which took on the job of arresting decay in the city was, in the majority of instances, the housing authority. The evolution of the housing authority in this role was natural enough. In the 1930's housing authorities had been set up to provide decent low-rent housing for the very poor of the nation. In most cases the people who were to occupy public housing came from slums. It was generally thought that the solution of the housing problem was for a governmental authority to go into slum areas, raze the substandard dwellings, remedy utility and street deficiencies, and erect sanitary, decent housing facilities on the old slum site.

It soon became apparent that frequently a major reason for the growth of slums was the improper location of those buildings as dwellings in the first place. If these sites were not suitable for dwellings under any circumstances, then it was foolish to demolish the substandard housing and erect more dwelling units on the same land.

There was then developed a technique that called for the erection of public housing units on an appropriate site, and the demolition of slum units wherever they might exist on a *quid pro quo* basis.

In the Federal Housing Act of 1949 federal grants-in-aid were set up under a new title for straight "redevelopment" purposes. Under "Title I" the housing aspect of the program was still maintained but soft-pedaled to some extent. Federal grants would be given to assist redevelopment if either (a) the area to be cleared was predominately substandard residential in character, or (b) the construction to take place on the site after it was cleared was predominately residential.

In most cities the housing agencies which had been handling the old slum clearance program moved into the redevelopment program. In some cities, however, the municipality decided to set up a separate and new "redevelopment" or "land clearance" agency. In some cases this function was brought back into the regular city government instead of leaving it under its separate and usually independent housing authority.

Finally the Federal Housing Act of 1955 established a concept of "urban renewal" as the operation for which the federal grants would be paid. Urban renewal differed from urban redevelopment in that it recognized many stages in the process of urban decay. Areas which were in good condition at the moment might be threatened with decay in the forseeable future. Here the remedy was a mild protection or "conservation" program. Areas a little farther along the downward path could be healed by somewhat stronger measures, which were termed "rehabilitation."

Finally, the hopelessly blighted areas could be completely cleared and "redeveloped." The urban renewal program also recognized (in contrast to the earlier slum clearance and redevelopment programs) that it might not be necessary to demolish a large area, but instead individual blocks or even individual structures within a block might be razed, and less radical treatment given to the remainder of the area or the block.

One feature of the federal requirements prerequisite to getting federal aid was extremely significant in the problem of fitting urban renewal into the municipal administrative scheme. This was the insistence by the federal government that the municipality have a "workable program" for fighting blight.

The workable program consists of seven parts:

1. Sound local housing and health codes that are enforced.
2. A general master plan for community development.
3. Basic analysis of the neighborhoods and the kind of treatment necessary to clean up, rehabilitate, or protect them.
4. An effective administrative organization to run the program.
5. Financial capacity to carry out the program.
6. A plan for rehousing families displaced through the operation of slum clearance or any other public program.
7. Full-fledged, community-wide citizen participation, understanding, and support for the program.

It will be immediately apparent that the establishment and continuance of the workable program necessary for renewal inevitably takes the responsibility for renewal away from any single purpose agency, such as the housing authority, and brings it back to general municipal administration with strong emphasis on the planning function in municipal administration. The Urban Renewal Administration, administrator of the urban renewal program, under a "general planning" item, insists on a major thoroughfare plan, a public works program, and a park and recreation plan — thus carrying the urban renewal plan even further beyond the scope of a housing authority, unless that housing authority were to establish itself as a separate and competing total municipal government.

In keeping up with the changing federal requirements, plus related state laws, many cities found themselves with a proliferation of agencies and departments all involved in one program, and not necessarily working toward the same end. The city of Chicago, for example, had two housing authorities (one for low-cost housing and one for middle-income housing), conservation and renewal boards, a land clearance agency, an independent city plan commission (later re-organized as a planning department), a zoning board of appeals, a powerful zoning committee in the board of aldermen, plus at least two important city departments, health and building inspection, all involved in the renewal operation. The mayor established a "housing coordinator" in order to get some sense of unity in the entire program.

The device of "coordinator" was adopted in a number of large cities because of the complex administrative problems involved. In all cases the coordinator is an administrative assistant to the chief executive.

A careful analysis of urban renewal will show that the operations involved are for the most part merely a stepped-up series of normal municipal operations concentrated in a single small area in the city. The city planning department, when it is functioning properly continually gathers data analyzing and appraising the situation with regard to city development for the entire city. But normally this activity cannot be in the detail necessary for specific working plans for urban renewal.

The enforcement of housing, sanitary, health, building, and safety codes is an on-going and customary operation in the several responsible departments. Theoretically, such ordinances should be enforced perfectly and completely at all times. Practically, as every municipal administrator realizes, budgetary limitations and human weakness make perfect enforcement on a city-wide basis impossible. But for proper functioning of the urban renewal program, there must be intensive code enforcement in the urban renewal area, while at the same time the departments must continue inspections and enforcements in the remainder of the city on at least an adequate basis. A public works department attempts to keep its physical plant up to date on a priority system and on a city-wide basis. When a slum area is cleared and scheduled to be redeveloped, the public works department may be suddenly called on to launch an improvement program that it had heretofore not contemplated, and to do so without interrupting the regularly scheduled improvement program for the remainder of the city.

There are other examples of urban renewal calling for merely intensified application of normal municipal functions. In the average city the urban renewal aspect of any operation, building inspection for example, certainly should not dominate the entire operation of the department. At the same time there are few cities that are so liberally staffed that they can handle the demands made by an urban renewal project and at the same time maintain adequate service to the remainder of the city. In the case of building inspection, one city established a new and separate building inspection department merely to handle the inspection and enforcement for urban renewal projects. As a general rule this is ill-advised. It is better to give the existing building commissioner more people to handle the additional work load.

Since urban renewal is primarily concentrated and coordinated municipal administration, the administration of the program should be inside and not outside the regular municipal administrative structure. It cannot very well be concentrated in any single department or person, other than the chief administrator himself. This has been the rationale for the establishment of the position of "urban renewal coordinator" in a number of cities. In a large city the position may require the services of a skilled public administrator at a high salary. The coordinator may require a staff of some size to assist him.

In smaller cities the job may be given to an administrative assistant to the city manager. In some cities it may be an additional duty for the director of planning or for the director of housing, but in the latter case only if housing is handled as an integral department in the regular municipal administration. Urban renewal should not be under the direction of anyone not a part of the official family or not directly responsible to the chief administrator. This would rule out the planning director where the planning staff is responsible to an outside, independent plan commission.

The organization for urban renewal has almost as many different forms as there are cities in which an urban renewal program is being carried out. In some cities it will be found that while most of the urban renewal functions remain with the proper municipal departments, an outside agency will have taken to itself the job of planning for renewal. The only conceivable justification for this arrangement would be that there is no planning agency in the regular city administration.

A basic premise in urban planning is that the city must be planned as a whole, and plans for individual functions or small parts or areas of the city must be related to the plan for the whole. This dictum applies most particularly to all-inclusive planning and development that necessarily accompanies renewal. For this reason the general planning aspects of urban renewal should certainly be retained in the regular municipal planning department, although detailed project planning may need to be lodged elsewhere, or be turned over to a private consultant.

Use of Planning Consultants

The advisability of hiring a city planning consultant frequently faces even those cities with a highly competent professional planning staff. It is a more common and more acute problem, however, in the case of the city with an inadequate or non-existent planning staff. As one professional planner sums it up, "Some towns have followed the device of appropriating a pot of money and hiring a consultant to come in and make a Master Plan. Many towns have thus 'bought' Master Plans all done-up in attractive packages and some of them have pointed the way to real community development."

"We might say that if such a Master Plan is used and modified to fit changing conditions, it is fine. But if there has been little public participation in drawing up one of these attractive packages, there is probably little knowledge regarding its content and little interest in carrying it out. It may turn out to be a high price to pay in order to have something to glance at admiringly and to file away until your successors hire another outside firm to come and make another Master Plan. I should add, however, that consultants are often very important and valuable, particularly where specialists are called in to make special studies or to perform specialized tasks which are beyond the general competence of the resident staff."[1]

Determining Need for Outside Help

Almost any municipality can determine its need for consulting services by deciding first what the nature of the problem is, and second the resources available for its solution. Almost every sizable community has some technical staff with which it can make at least general preliminary studies.

---

[1] Harold V. Miller, Mr. Planning Commissioner (Chicago: Public Administration Service, 1954), p. 27.

Selection of the Consultant

The first step in securing outside aid is to define the general nature, type, and scope of the problem, list the technical resources available locally, and decide what outside technical services are desired. On the basis of these general specifications, inquiry concerning consulting services can be made of a number of consulting firms and agencies. The firms should be invited to state their interest and availability, and to offer suggestions as to possible modifications of the proposed consulting service program.

Where the consultant expresses interest in the undertaking, he should be required to indicate at least generally how the project would be staffed, scheduled, and otherwise conducted, and to provide appropriate references in jurisdictions previously served and examples of reports prepared as well as estimates of the probable cost of professional services to be rendered. After analyzing replies and making inquiry of references it is advisable to hold interviews with representatives of several firms. The prospective consultants might be asked to cite all projects they have performed rather than a few selected undertakings.

Inquiry could then be made of responsible officials who were in office when the consulting work was done and who have lived with the results of the work. Only in this manner, except perhaps in the case of a limited number of nationally known consultants, can the municipality assure itself that it is likely to receive technical services of the type and calibre which it desires. This checking-up process before consulting services are engaged is highly desirable from the point of view both of the municipality and of any reputable consultant.

Since the city is employing personal services it should be as exacting in employing a consultant as it is in putting a top-level professional person on its payroll. Similarly, from the point of view of the consultant, anything which enhances the municipality's confidence in him or his firm will contribute to a type of working relationship essential to effective consulting services. Also, possible differences over what is expected from whom should be resolved before, rather than after consulting services are formally engaged.

In the course of using consulting services, municipal officials will find it profitable to provide full local cooperation and a maximum of competent local technical participation. This can do much to expedite progress and minimize the cost of outside service. In addition, it provides local employees with useful training opportunities and a valuable knowledge of what was done, when it was done, and what the future operational requirements are. Needless to say, this opportunity should not be wasted by assigning to the consultant any other than capable local technicians.

Competitive Bidding

As in the case of the employment of other types of professional consultants, such as accountants, architects, attorneys, and professional engineers, it is not desirable for the city to obtain formal bids and make the award to the lowest bidder. There are real advantages, however, in securing statements from several consultants first as to the extent and kind of work they would perform, and second as to their estimate of the cost of the services.

Follow-Up

The responsibility for following through on work done by a consultant belongs primarily to the local jurisdiction. Most of the follow-through aspects of an undertaking lie beyond the authority of the consultant, and even the best of consulting work can be no more effective than the degree of follow-up exercised by local officials.

The credit for a successful consulting project belongs no more to the consultant than to the public officials who engage him. The objective must be defined clearly, and local officials must recognize project limitations and the capacity of the local staff for work with the consultant, provide the consultant with local facilities that will make for the maximum utilization of the consultant's staff and preferably furnish some local participation of technical grade, make expeditious decisions on those matters which affect project progress, observe the project progress, and make known to the consultant any dissatisfactions.

Above all, the authority and responsibility for making decisions rests with local officials and not with the consultant. Accordingly, local officials must make decisions on all recommendations, accepting them, rejecting them, modifying them, or in some instances establishing a specific schedule and procedure for their reconsideration. Also local officials should make known to the consultant any difficulties encountered in the continued operation of systems which the consultant has developed.

Evaluation

Planning consulting services can be used to advantage on problems which cannot be solved through other readily available resources. If the official selects his consultant carefully he may expect to have brought to the solution of his problem technical resources and experience which offer advantages over local technicians from the point of view of independence, objectivity, a superior analytical approach, and better presentation of findings and recommendations, as well as more highly developed specialized knowledge. The consultant, free from day-to-day operations, has the time to give systematic attention to a problem in a way that harried local operating officials can seldom do.

Chapter 11

LEGAL SERVICES AND REGULATORY PROCEDURES

Law provides the basis for the existence of all cities and sets the framework of rules within which they function. As political subdivisions of the state, municipal corporations are under the absolute control of the legislature. The city receives its grant of powers from the state by general or special action of the legislature. The limitations in the federal constitution, as well as the provisions of the constitution of the state in which the city is located apply to its actions and impose a limit on its powers. These constitutional and legislative grants and limitations apply to the ordinances, administrative rules, and regulations adopted by every municipality.

In a few states the courts have applied the doctrine of inherent right of local self-government as an implied constitutional restriction of the state legislature to control its municipalities.

The inhabitants of some 28 states have adopted amendments to the constitution of their states authorizing home rule either directly under constitutional provisions or by legislative enactments. Constitutional amendments generally fall into two classes: first, those which grant municipalities the privilege of framing their own charters and also providing in detail machinery by which the privilege shall be carried out; and, second, those which do not set forth the detailed machinery, but provide that the state legislature shall, by legislation, provide for the framing, adopting and amending of municipal charters. Where the constitution authorizes municipal corporations to adopt their own charters the powers are derived directly from the constitution, and such charter, and not from the legislature. In those states having constitutional home rule, generally, the grant of power extends the right broadly to control municipal affairs. Constitutional amendments relating to home rule usually provide that a home rule charter may not contravene any provision of the state constitution or general laws, the public policy of the state, or the common law.

The law department of a city is not the only agency concerned with legal questions, for in one sense, every official and employee of the city participates in legal processes. The council is constantly enacting new ordinances or modifying old ones. The chief administrator shares in the law-making process by recommending new legislation to the council, by acting as the chief technical advisor of the council on administrative problems, and by drafting administrative rules and regulations that support the general policies outlined by the council. Similarly, department heads, bureau chiefs, and other subordinate officers participate in the law-making process.

Any realistic account of municipal law-making must recognize that the application or administration of laws is also concerned with law making. The police officer, for example, exercises discretionary powers in deciding what law applies to a particular situation and whether or not a particular violation of law warrants formal action on his part. Other administrative officials and employees in their day-to-day work are constantly making decisions of law that may be described as law making in the practical sense of the term. Finally, of course, the courts play a major role in the processes of law making and administration.

A brief analysis of the way in which legal matters enter into the administration of city government will show that some legal services must be considered operating or line activities, others are of an auxiliary character, while still others are of a managerial nature.

The public official who enforces municipal ordinances through prosecution of ordinance violations, or through licensing and inspectional procedures, is performing an operating function just as is the fireman in extinguishing fires, or the health officer in examining children. Some of these enforcement activities are to be found in the law department — particularly the prosecution of ordinance violations. Others are assigned to building inspection units, the police, fire, and health departments, license bureaus, and other city departments.

When the city attorney or one of his assistants assists the chief administrator and council in the phrasing of a new ordinance, and when he participates in the formulation of plans by suggesting a way to administer an activity without running afoul of a state statute, he is acting as a managerial aide. Most of the managerial functions involving legal advice are assigned to the law department.

In addition, the city attorney and his staff provide auxiliary services to the council, to the chief administrator, and to departmental officers. Attorneys as specialists in legal knowledge, rules, and procedures, are "mechanics" who, because of their special knowledge of the law, are needed in accomplishing the ends of the city government. Just as the engineer is consulted in the building of a bridge because of his knowledge of the laws of physics and best methods of physical construction, the lawyer is consulted in drafting documents because of his knowledge of man-made laws and his familiarity with legal construction. He helps draft legal documents, defends the city and its departments in damage suits, and assists operating departments like the fire prevention bureau to enforce the ordinances which are their responsibility.

Legal services, then, like personnel and finance services, have important managerial and auxiliary aspects which require that the chief administrator have rather closer and more frequent contact with them than with the technical aspects of the work of his operating departments. The remainder of this chapter will discuss the relation between the chief administrator and those officers and employees of the city government who are concerned with legal services. The first section will be concerned with those managerial functions that primarily involve the law department while the final section of the chapter will treat certain problems that are peculiar to the administration of regulatory functions and that have not been adequately treated in Chapter 4.

The Work of the Law Department

Practically all of the legal tasks performed in the city hall, with the exception of the regulatory functions to be discussed later, are generally brought together in a law department under the city attorney. This is a logical and desirable arrangement, since these functions require the direction of a legally-trained administrator, and only the very largest cities can afford to employ attorneys who could supervise these functions in units separate from the law department. The duties of the city attorney and the law department will, of course, be set forth in the city charter but the general scope of these duties is much the same in almost all cities.

The work of the law department includes the following major assignments: (1) representing the city in civil actions (including investigation of claims against the city and collection of fines, taxes and claims in favor of the city); (2) prosecuting violations of city ordinances; (3) giving legal advice to legislative and administrative officials of the city; (4) preparing formal, written opinions; (5) instructing and training city officials in the elements of public law; (6) preparing legal papers and documents; (7) drafting legislative documents — charter and statutory changes, ordinances, and resolutions; (8) aiding in the acquisition of property; (9) assisting in public improvement proceedings; (10) advising and assisting on fiscal procedures; (11) assisting the council and administrative agencies in the conduct of public hearings and investigations; (12) examining all phases of municipal action from its local, county, state, federal and sometimes even its international aspects; (13) participating in local, state and national organizations, committees and groups dedicated to furthering the common interests of municipalities; (14) studying and analyzing legal developments; and (15) administering the city attorney's office.

Civil Actions

The city as a municipal corporation may sue or be sued; consequently it is involved in court actions that run the gamut of civil suits. Although the city council, as the governing body of the municipal corporation, has authority to make the basic policy decisions with respect to the bringing or defending of civil actions (the city attorney stands in the relation of attorney to client with respect to the council), it will of course lean heavily upon the attorney's advice in such matters.

The satisfactory handling of civil actions requires that adequate lines of communication exist between the city attorney's office and other city departments. When suit is initiated against the city, the legal notice will usually be served on the chief administrator, but whoever receives such notice should, of course, immediately transmit it to the attorney.

Civil actions against the city include actions on contracts to which the city is a party, and so-called "tort" actions. The most important examples of tort actions are suits for workmen's compensation instituted by city employees who have been injured, and personal injury or property damage claims by citizens who claim to have suffered injury by the city's negligence.

Tort Liability. A tort may be defined as an injury committed on the person or property of another in violation of his rights as a member of society. The law of torts with respect to the acts of a private corporation or person is relatively well established, but the judicial principles governing the tort liability of municipal corporations are somewhat vague and inconsistent. With respect to private persons, the law holds to the doctrine of *respondeat superior* — the employer is responsible for the torts committed by his employees while in the course of their employment. In the case of municipal corporations, however, the law classifies all functions performed by cities as "governmental" or "proprietary," and generally holds the city liable only for those torts that are committed by its employees while engaged in proprietary functions. In the case of torts classified as nuisances some courts do not recognize the "governmental function" doctrine, and the statutes of some states either expand or lessen the tort liability of cities.

Some municipalities have found at least partial relief from tort claims through modified applications of the sovereign immunity principle in the forms of protective devices such as notice of claim and, more recently, prior notice of defects.

Police and fire protection are considered governmental functions while the maintenance (but not the construction) of streets, and the operation of municipal utilities are usually considered proprietary functions. Thus a city could not, in the absence of a statute imposing liability, be held for damage due to collision with a recklessly driven fire truck, but it might be held if the offending vehicle were a city-owned bus. The line between proprietary and governmental functions differs from state to state, and appears highly arbitrary to the layman (and to many lawyers and judges, as well).

The officer or employee who is himself responsible for the tort is of course personally liable, whether the tort involves a governmental or a proprietary function. When the tort has been committed by an employee in good faith and in the course of his duty (a suit for false arrest against a policeman, for example), the city administration will frequently feel a moral obligation to help defend his case, and to reimburse him for damages even though the city is not legally liable. Although decisions on this point are in conflict, the courts in most states have upheld the right of the municipal corporation to assist in the officer's defense. The policy to be followed on this point, within the limits permitted by law, is of course a matter for the city council to decide.

Liability of the city to pay workmen's compensation for injuries suffered by employees in the course of employment will depend upon the inclusion of municipal corporations in the state workmen's compensation act. In some states, liability will depend on whether the injured person is an "officer" in the eyes of the law, or simply an "employee." A proper procedure rigidly adhered to for handling employee injuries will not only save lives, but will also reduce claims for damages against the city. First, all injuries of city employees should be examined by the city physician or his assistants, even if the employee has gone to a private physician for treatment. All departments should be required to submit a notice and report of accidents suffered by employees, one copy going to the city physician, another copy to the city attorney. The city physician will, in turn, submit a report on his examination to the city attorney. When an employee has been temporarily disabled, his case should be periodically followed up by the city physician, and he should be re-examined at appropriate intervals in order to determine when he is able to return to work and to disallow further compensation after that time.

Claims against the city by private citizens for personal injury and property damage form an even more important class of litigation than workmen's compensation claims. The number of tort liability cases, based on negligence on the city's part has increased to the point where in some sections of the country they present the most important of all the problems affecting government at the local level. The city attorney has the duty of defending tort actions and the municipal financial structure will be affected according to his acumen in handling the rising volume of cases. The taxpayer has a crucial stake in municipal tort cases because, unlike a stockholder in a business corporation, he can be assessed to the point of confiscation for the tortious lapses of his municipal corporation. Especially in the small communities is there the ever-present danger that a municipal employee's negligence might suddenly impose an oppressive burden on the taxpayers.

Another trend, running concurrently with the marked increase in number of tort suits, is the noticeable jump in amounts awarded to successful tort plaintiffs. This fact is especially disturbing when it is remembered that municipalities are extremely vulnerable to suit — more so than individuals in private corporations — because their wide diversity of functions leaves them exposed at so many points. It has been demonstrated that keen, aggressive representation in negligence cases will more than pay for itself. Each tax dollar spent in securing and keeping an able city attorney brings huge dividends in the form of amounts saved in defeating tort claims. Again, success of the law department in handling these claims will depend in large measure upon cooperation from other departments. It is particularly important that early information be obtained concerning accidents that may lead to claims, so that full investigation may be made by the law department while the evidence is still fresh. The police department and other city departments should be required in these cases also to transmit accident reports to the law department.

Although the burden of preliminary investigation of claims against the city rests upon other city departments, the law department will frequently be called upon to complete such investigations, especially in their legal aspects, before the case comes to trial. Particularly in important cases, the attorney and his assistants will find it desirable to make some pertinent pre-trial investigation, interviewing witnesses or inspecting physical evidence such as a defective sidewalk. The exact division of work here between the law department and other departments will depend to a large extent on the size of city. In large cities the law department usually employs one or more claims investigators, while in smaller cities it may rely largely on the cooperation of the police department for investigation.

In cases where the legal liability of the city is clear and the amount demanded is reasonable in relation to the injury or damage suffered, it is often advantageous to make a compromise settlement out of court. Pronounced savings to the city treasury realized by effective settlement demands proper emphasis of this function of the city attorney, so lacking in publicity as to be given but slight recognition. The city attorney has the burden of determining when it would not be to the city's financial or other advantage to press a matter by court action. Court actions in such cases might very well increase the costs of these claims to the city and impose needless work on the city's legal staff and other officers and employees of the city. Authority to make settlements is vested in the city's governing body, which will, of course, rely heavily upon the independent judgment of the city attorney. It should be equally emphasized that a compromise settlement should never be entered into unless the claim is just. Cities that settle claims having no legal basis for a small nuisance value will find over a period of years that this practice results in a much greater cost because of the encouragement it gives to the filing of fraudulent claims.

It is an important question of policy as to what types, if any, of workmen's compensation, or public liability insurance the city should carry. Many cities, both small and large, set up reserve accounts in lieu of insurance and carry their own risks in this manner; others cover direct risks to the municipality by private insurance. Since there is no object in carrying insurance to cover activities where no liability rests on the city, the advice of the attorney will be needed as to the scope of the insurance to be carried. Further, the attorney will be able, in drafting contracts, to impose upon independent contractors with the city all risks that they create.

The charters of some cities provide that when any hazardous conditions are caused by an independent contractor, such contractor and his surety, if any, must be made a party defendant in any action brought against the city to recover damages caused by reason of such defects. The city should therefore require bonds to be posted when issuing permits for street openings, cuts in pavements, street obstructions, overhead signs, and so forth. If the city does not require bonds, permits or contracts should be so written that damages assessed against the city arising out of the work may be recovered by the city in an action against the negligent party.

Contract Liability. Generally speaking, a municipal corporation is liable for faithful performance of its contractual obligations in the same manner as a private person. However, defects in the form of the contract or in the procedure followed in entering into the agreement may bar suit under the contract against the city. That is, municipal corporations do not possess unlimited power to contract, and persons contract with municipalities at their peril and must determine beforehand whether or not the municipal corporation has the power to enter into the particular contract in question. For instance if an agreement is entered into for work on public improvements without observing the requirements of competitive bidding, the contractor cannot recover, even if the work is satisfactorily completed and used by the city. Hence, the legal requirements surrounding municipal contracts must be observed with extreme care, and the procedures that are followed by the city in making contracts need to be periodically reviewed by the city attorney.

Tax Claims. Perhaps the most important and most frequent type of civil suit instituted by the city is the suit to enforce payment of taxes. Policy with respect to tax suits can best be worked out cooperatively by the chief administrative officer, the finance officer, the assessor, and the city attorney. Of course court action against debtors is only a last resort in the collection of fines, penalties, and claims owed the city. The actual work of collection of such claims, prior to court action, occupies a large part of the time of many law departments.

A closely related matter is the defense of taxpayers' actions instituted to reduce the valuation that the assessor has placed on property. The city attorney can be of considerable assistance to the assessor's office in informing assessment officials as to the kind of evidence of valuation that will be most effective in court, and as to assessment procedures that may minimize suits against the city.

Prosecution of Ordinance Violations

The activities of the city attorney relative to criminal or quasi-criminal cases are confined in the main to the prosecution of violations of city ordinances. He may in some instances prosecute certain violations of state laws, but all felonies and major crimes will be prosecuted by the "district" or "state's" attorney in the higher courts. The only obligation resting upon the city attorney in such cases is to see that the complete cooperation of his investigational staff is given to the prosecution.

Under ordinary circumstances the police department, the health department, the fire prevention bureau of the fire department, and the various inspectors operating in other city departments will report violations of city regulations. The city attorney may make an independent investigation of the facts, but in most instances he will have to rely upon the information furnished him by the proper city officers. If the facts warrant prosecution, a criminal complaint should be signed and the prosecution begun immediately.

Under the laws of most states, the city attorney has a legal right to use his own discretion in initiating criminal prosecutions, or in dismissing them. Here again, he has the burden of determining when it would not be to the city's financial or other advantage to press a matter by court action. The city experiences a substantial savings every time the city attorney properly determines that its best interests would not be served by the litigation. In many such instances a proper and beneficial compliance can be secured through arbitration, office consultation or hearings, or by the use of letters. It is possible in these ways to dispose of numerous minor infractions of the zoning, fire, health, licensing and other ordinances without the time, trouble and unnecessary expense of court action being incurred by the local taxpayer.

Neither the city council nor the chief administrative officer has power to force the city attorney to dismiss a case that he believes should be prosecuted. In this particular respect, he is responsible to the people rather than to the council and administrator. It goes without saying that under ordinary circumstances this legal independence does not require the city attorney to maintain any aloofness from other city officials responsible for regulatory administration and that the best results will be obtained only if policies with respect to prosecutions are worked out cooperatively among the city attorney, the council and chief administrative officer, and the regulatory department concerned.

Advisory Functions

Since the city attorney is the legal advisor of the city, one of his most important functions is that of serving as advisor to his council, to administrative officials, to boards and commissions, and to the citizens of the municipality. As a part of this function he has the concurrent, and in many places mandatory, duty of being present at city council meetings and at the meetings of boards and commissions for the purpose of rendering immediate assistance. The importance of this function cannot be overstressed. This advisory function cannot be sharply divided from the auxiliary functions of the city law department, since much of the attorney's advice-giving occurs when he is helping the city officials to draft legal documents or ordinances or to plan legal procedures.

In his advisory capacity, the attorney is and must remain first of all a professional man and must take a professional attitude toward his work. His legal opinions should be free from bias and uncolored by the views of any political group. He may have political views and express them as such, except as may be prohibited by civil service or otherwise, but he should not confuse this privilege with his official obligations. Personal bias should not be permitted to color his advice on administrative or other legal questions.

The city attorney must always remember that he is an attorney to the city, and not a judge of the legality of the city's actions. His job is to assist the city council and chief administrator to discover legal means for carrying out the policies they have decided upon. He may sometimes have to advise them that no legal means exists for carrying out particular wishes, but his real task is to find how it can be done, if this is legally possible in good faith. As one federal administrator has said: "I always keep two lawyers on tap: a hot lawyer to tell me how to do legally what I want to do, and a cold lawyer to tell me why I can't do legally what I don't want to do." If the chief administrative officer participates in the selection of the city attorney, he will want to give considerable weight, in evaluating candidates, to the probability that they will work with other city officials cooperatively and as the members of a team.

Formal Opinions. In addition to rendering advice at meetings and the numerous telephone and personal conversations which sometimes involve opinion, the city attorney has the duty of submitting formal, written opinions — usually on matters of more than routine importance and where the city must proceed with utmost caution. Written opinions may be requested by the city council, any of its commissions or by any city officer. A request for a written opinion, then, constitutes a mandate to the city attorney to exhaust the resources at his command to the end that the city may act with reliance upon his final determination as expressed in the opinion. As a matter of strict demarcation of authority, perhaps, the legal officer should have no voice as to the policy or expediency of the proposed course of action, but legality is often so entwined with policy and expediency that they cannot be considered apart.

It is a responsibility of the chief administrative officer to make certain that department heads are making wise use of the advisory services of the city attorney: that the attorney is consulted early in the process of developing new programs that may have legal implications, and that full use is made of his written opinions. Requests for opinions should always be in writing to insure definiteness and clarity. Since similar legal problems will recur from year to year, and in different departments, the city attorney's office will need to retain a set of written opinions with a complete index. Another set should be found in the office of the chief administrator, and it will usually be well worth the trouble to provide each department with a loose-leaf binder containing copies of all opinions requested by that department or having direct application to the work of that department. As current requests come to the law department, the department head making the inquiry can be referred to former opinions and given any additional information that may be pertinent to the present situation. While departmental officials should be encouraged to make wide use of the opinions already submitted, no attempt should be made to discourage them from requesting legal advice in any current situation.

Studying and Analyzing Legal Developments

In order to render an informed opinion on important legal questions the city attorney must often analyze hundreds of reported and unreported cases. The volume of cases in this extremely complex branch of the law is increasing each month. In addition, the city attorney must give attention to federal and state constitutional provisions, to federal and state statutes, to developments in the Congress and state legislature, to rulings, regulations, orders and decisions by state and federal administrative agencies, to opinions of state and federal attorneys general, to opinions of other city attorneys, to ordinances enacted in his and other cities, and to countless other sources of information. Lately, with the vast increase in international treaties the city attorney must investigate this rapidly growing field of law.

It is not a duty of the city attorney to advise members of the general public as to their rights in relation to the municipal government or the legality of their actions as these relate to municipal ordinances. The city attorney is counsel to the municipal corporation and not to the citizens. Where this principle is expressly stated in the city charter, the law department may be saved some little embarrassment, and often considerable unnecessary work.

Participation in State and National Organizations

The field of municipal law reaches such proportions and is so complex that the enlightened city attorney finds active participation in his state league or association of cities and in national institutes and clearing houses of municipal information, such as the National Institute of Municipal Law Officers, a necessity in order to keep abreast of developments. The monthly and annual publications of these organizations, when supplemented with their valuable research and loan services, annual conferences and scores of other advantages which only united, group action can provide, enable the city attorney to maintain a grasp on the rapidly growing subject of municipal law.

Training Functions

A knowledge of the fundamentals of public law would be of immense value to almost every department head or other city officer who holds a position of responsibility. Of course most public officials acquire a working knowledge of legal rules in the course of their official careers, but there is no reason why this aspect of their training should be left to chance. Cities could make much wider use than they usually do of the facilities of the city attorney's office to conduct in-service training in the principles of constitutional law, municipal corporations, and the law of public officers.

The purpose of such training is, of course, not to make attorneys of all the city's department heads, any more than a course in first aid trains a layman to be his own doctor. Legal first aid is often as necessary as medical first aid, and preventive measures can often save the doctor's — or the attorney's — call. The department head who understands the legal requirements that surround the operation of a city government, and who appreciates the legal implications of his actions will be more likely to consult his attorney before trouble starts, and will be more likely to avoid legal entanglements from which his attorney would otherwise have to extricate him.

Preparation of Legal Papers and Documents

Numerous legal papers must be prepared or reviewed by the municipal law department. Among these papers are contracts, leases, deeds, bills of sale, grants of easement, franchises, notices of improvement proceedings, public notices, and similar documents. In the absence of express charter provisions, the city attorney has no authority to enter into contracts which will be binding on the city — that is a power of the city council.

Department heads need information and advice as to their right to enter into contracts, and as to forms of election notices, special election ballots, advertisements and invitations for bids, and so forth. Some of this information should be prepared by the city attorney for inclusion in the city's administrative manual. Defects of procedure in legal transactions involving public agencies usually have far more serious consequences than similar defects where private parties are involved. Since relatively minor errors may void an entire proceeding, the need for prompt and complete legal advice is correspondingly urgent.

The actual division of labor in drafting legal papers between the law department and other city departments will vary from city to city. In small cities, the law department will generally draft all but the most routine documents. In larger cities, departments like the assessor's office or the finance department may have on their staffs persons sufficiently familiar with the specialized legal work of their particular departments to be competent to draw up routine documents under the functional supervision of the city attorney. The question of whether individual departments should ever have their own legal staffs will be discussed later in the chapter.

Legislative Drafting

From time to time, the city officials will find it desirable to suggest changes in the city's charter or in state legislation affecting the city, and much more frequently it will be necessary to draft or amend city ordinances. In all of these tasks the law department has a central role.

Charter Changes and Statutory Changes. The city charter is the legal basis for the governmental powers that the municipality exercises. The city may have a special charter granted by the legislature, a locally adopted home rule charter, it may operate under one of the optional charter forms specified by the state legislature, or it may operate under a mandatory charter form embodied in state law. Even in home rule states, the city will be governed not only by the provisions of its charter, but also by provisions of the state constitution, and by state legislative acts affecting cities.

The municipality may exercise only those powers which are explicitly granted it by its charter or by state law, or which may be reasonably implied from the powers which are explicitly granted. Hence, before a city undertakes any new activity, it must obtain the advice of the city attorney as to whether the charter or state laws empower it to enter the new field. Where the existing laws do not permit the activity in question, the council and chief administrator may wish to consider legislative changes which will secure the desired permission. This may involve a local referendum, action by the state legislature, or both, depending upon the manner in which the charter may legally be amended. The attorney's advice regarding proposed activities is advice, of course, as to the legality of the action, not as to its desirability. The latter is a question for the city council to decide.

If the city wishes a special law to be adopted by the legislature — a law authorizing it to operate a public utility, for example — the attorney will be called upon to prepare the proposed bill. The city council will then make arrangements with some legislator for the introduction of the bill. But the city attorney should first clear the matter with the secretary of the state league of municipalities in his state, for the proposition may be one that is of interest to other cities in the state, and therefore one that the league may wish to sponsor in the legislature. The city attorney of every city should keep in close touch with all proposals being considered by the state legislature when it is in session in order to keep the chief administrator and the council informed of any possible effect on the city should the legislation be passed.

Preparation of Ordinances and Resolutions. A common function of the city attorney and his staff is the preparation of ordinances and resolutions. It is not necessary at this point to distinguish between these two forms of enactment. The distinction will usually depend upon the city charter or statutory procedure specified in the state law.

Many ordinances and resolutions will be routine in form — for example, the budget ordinance, resolutions for the payment of bills, and formalities in connection with actions on matters before the council. These do not constitute a difficult problem. They should be prepared by the law department, at least in tentative form, in advance of the council or committee meeting and then be referred to the officials to whom the particular matters are delegated. They should be complete in all legal details, ready for action by the proper agency and for the signatures of the designated officers.

The preparation of other ordinances is not so simple. They have their formal parts, to be sure, and for these the attorney must assume responsibility. In addition, ordinances will contain procedural provisions, substantive matter, and penal provisions. In drafting the procedural provisions the attorney will have to draw on his own experiences and the experiences of the administrative officers of the city. Legal methods and principles involved in incorporating such substantive and penal provisions, however, will be the sole responsibility of the legal staff.

In the case of penal provisions to be incorporated in an ordinance where maximum penalties only are imposed by statute or charter, some discretion will be vested in the council to determine within the limits imposed what the penalties should be. The attorney should advise of the limit permitted by law in the particular case. Ordinarily he should not go farther than that, although, as the prosecuting officer of the city, he will have to prosecute violations of the ordinance and will be interested to that extent in their penalties.

Substantive provisions of ordinances and departmental regulations are primarily the responsibility of the governing body or administrative officials. Provisions for amendment of existing ordinances will be requested from time to time. New subjects also will be suggested from time to time upon which ordinances or regulations will be requested, such as new methods of controlling transient vendors, regulations of new types of amusement devices, and the control of various frauds upon the public. The chief administrator will expect the attorney to keep posted on various regulatory devices employed in other cities and to know whether they can or cannot be adopted legally in his city.

Acquisition of Property

In almost all states, cities are to acquire and hold property for what are described as "public" purposes. The first legal question to be settled, then, in acquiring property, is whether the purpose in question is one classified as public in that state. Courts have become increasingly liberal in defining public purpose — but the city attorney's advice is needed in any particular case before steps are taken toward acquisition.

Property may be acquired not only by voluntary lease or purchase, but also by condemnation; and it is the latter mode of acquisition which raises the most difficult legal problems. Condemnation proceedings are in every state a highly complex matter, requiring constant attention from the city attorney's staff.

The law department is not usually vested with the actual management of the city's real estate. For this purpose the city frequently establishes a separate real estate department, or a separate division in the department of finance. Except in large cities, however, the law department will do most of the legal drafting for the real estate department. The examination of title of property to be purchased or sold will also generally be a responsibility of the law department.

Public Improvements

The acquisition of property may be a step in a public improvement program. The same question of public purpose arises in constructing public improvements as in acquiring real estate, and the legality of the purpose may be tested in the courts by a taxpayer's action. In some cases the public improvement will be partly financed by special assessments upon adjoining property owners. Special assessment procedures, like condemnation proceedings, are highly technical matters, requiring careful and painstaking preparation by the law department in cooperation with the assessor's office, the city planning department, the real estate department, and other city departments.

Fiscal Procedures

The levying of taxes, administration of the city's accounts, bond issues, and other fiscal procedures are always governed by a multitude of state laws so that careful attention to legal aspects is necessary.

Bond Issues. Among the legal issues that arise when a city proposes to float a bond issue are the questions of public purpose, the proper procedure for authorization of the bond issue, relation of the city's total debt to statutory debt limits, and the form of the bonds.

It is common practice for municipalities to secure the opinion of recognized "bond attorneys" as to the legality of the bond ordinance and the procedures leading up to the adoption of the ordinance. No matter how competent the city legal staff, where such opinion has not been secured bond buyers will regard the issue as something of a risk and will make allowance for the risk in the terms of their bids.

Public Expenditures. In many states certain mandatory expenditures are imposed on each city by state law. Likewise, state law and the city charter frequently limit the purposes for which particular tax levies or grants-in-aid may be employed. Limitations on the uses of particular levies create for the department of finance the problem of setting up their accounts so as to properly segregate and control these funds. In all of these matters, legal counsel is needed to determine the extent of segregation required, to determine whether proposed expenditures from a particular fund come within the legitimate objects of that fund, and the like.

Hearings and Investigations

There are several city agencies — notably the zoning and assessment appeals boards — whose proceedings have more or less of a judicial character. Likewise, the city council desires occasionally to hold a public hearing or an investigation — the matter of granting or denying a franchise may be before the council, for example. In such cases the assistance of the city attorney may be of the highest value in advising on the legal aspects of the appeal or hearing and in making certain that the procedure followed will satisfy any requirements that the courts may impose as to "due process of law."

Intergovernmental Considerations

Today when the city attorney considers the legal phases of action which his council proposes, he must examine such action from its local, county, state, federal and sometimes even its international aspects. Today we have in excess of 102,000 separate legal entities or units of government in the United States, ranging downward from the federal government to the states, territories, counties, cities, towns, townships, special districts and authorities of many kinds. The relationships embraced in so many units of government are practically unending in number, complexity and variety. Each governmental unit acts and reacts upon the other, for no government can operate in a vacuum.

City-County Relations. Very often a city boundary will not coincide with the economic and social area in which it is located. The city attorney must struggle with a multitude of vexing problems when his city spills over beyond its legal borders into the county and the city attorney must necessarily work with the county authorities for the purpose of discovering new ways to solve health, zoning, traffic, and other problems which arise beyond the city's boundaries but which, nonetheless, have a severe impact on the city. In addition, the council will expect the city attorney to be well-grounded in the pros and cons of annexation.

City-State Relations. The city attorney must be alert to determine whether new statutory powers are required for necessary action at the municipal level. Where the need is seen he must then set himself to the delicate task of preparing suggested legislation. There is a mild but recognizable trend toward increased service by the city attorney as the city's representative before the state legislature in furtherance of municipal objectives.

City-Federal Relations. One of the truly striking developments in American government in the last century is the tremendous increase in federal agencies. Rulings and regulations of these powerful bodies touch every segment of American life. It is extremely important, then, both to the municipal government and to its citizens, that city attorneys understand the workings of these agencies and the legislation under which they function. It is often imperative that a municipality send its lawyer before these agencies to present its views on proposed action or on action already taken which affects the city and its residents.

The city attorney must also keep a watchful eye on the federal aid programs. It has been estimated that these now run to some forty in number, with more than one hundred services rendered by federal agencies directly or indirectly to local government. In the operation of airports, housing, health and other programs, a working knowledge of federal aid programs is now vital to many municipalities.

International Consideration. On the international level, under the aegis of the United Nations, there has grown up a steadily increasing body of law — properly labeled "Treaty Law" — which can sometimes have a tremendous effect on city government. In much of the current litigation over alleged discrimination in the use of school and other government facilities there is injected into the legal arguments the Universal Declaration of Human Rights by the United Nations or the proposed Covenant of Human Rights. There is a vast array of conventions, treaties and covenants with which the city attorney increasingly must be conversant because they may vitally affect the city although, at first blush they may seem to be far afield from the interest of city government.

Administering the City Attorney's Office

The city attorney is a department head in his own right and for that reason a great deal of his time is taken up with matters which are not principally legal, but rather are executive or administrative in nature. The size of the law department varies from that of the small city where the city attorney *is* the department, to the mammoth legal departments of the great metropolitan centers. The larger the legal staff the more the chief legal officer tends to become an administrator rather than a legal technician. But even the one-man staff has need of administrative skill, because the city attorney must very often deal with other officials in his capacity as a department head.

The efficient operation of the law department will depend in great measure on the condition of its records. The city attorney must have the know-how to master the tremendous volume of paper work and recordation in his office in order that he may be free to give the maximum consideration to strictly legal affairs.

Very frequently the city attorney is required to summarize for the city council on an annual or other basis the operations of his department. Customarily, the report will summarize litigation, offer data on the number and kind of contracts and documents prepared, comment on the city attorney's activities with reference to other units of government, and set forth in general the highlights of activity in the law department.

Organization of the Law Department

There is no place in the present volume for a detailed analysis of the activities of the law department, but like other managerial and auxiliary agencies it has numerous relations with operating agencies.

Internal Organization

Internal organization depends, of course, on the size of the agency to be organized, and in all but the largest cities the law department usually employs a relatively small staff. In cities under a quarter million population "organization" of the legal department will mean simply a common-sense division of work among the city attorney and his two or three assistants.

In larger cities, this division of work may be formalized in separate divisions or bureaus of the department. A rather common method of division is the segregation of the law department work into three major parts: (1) Torts Division, in which all personal injury and property damage matters are handled; (2) Prosecuting Division, for the prosecuting of violations of city ordinances; and (3) Special Assignments Division, which embraces the remaining categories of legal work in a municipal law department — writing of formal opinions, drafting of ordinances, statutory and charter changes, preparing legal papers and documents, public utility matters, public improvements, and so forth. In the very large department, additional units may be set up to deal with collections, special assessments, legislation, or particular types of enforcement (zoning, building inspection, and so forth).

A division along the lines suggested will place most, but not all, of the managerial functions of the law department in the special assignments division; while all three divisions will have important auxiliary functions.

Many large cities permit individual departments to employ legal counse. to deal with the legal problems involved in the department's work. However, in few cities under a half million population is there sufficient legal work in any single department to justify an arrangement of this sort. It will usually be desirable to group all attorneys in the single law department, but to permit individual attorneys to specialize, as far as possible, in the work of individual departments or groups of departments. In tort work and the drafting of most routine legal documents, there is very little need for departmental specialization — and very little purpose to be served by it. On the other hand prosecution of zoning ordinances or other particular regulatory measures requires considerable specialized knowledge, as does the management of condemnation and special assessment proceedings, the collection of particular taxes, and the collection of hospital charges or other claims.

It is generally preferable for attorneys who specialize in the work of particular departments to remain under the line direction of the city attorney in order to preserve flexibility in the assignment of the legal staff, and to make certain that these attorneys will receive adequate professional direction. The chief administrator's coordinating skills will frequently be called into play here to make certain that each department receives the cooperation from the law department which it needs to carry out its functions, and that the attorneys accept the basic policy decisions of the departments they are serving.

It is quite common in cities under 25,000 population, and not unknown in larger cities, to employ a part-time city attorney. If it could be done, there would be many advantages to be gained by these cities from the employment of a full-time attorney. Not only would he be more apt to think actively in municipal terms, but he would be more likely to learn the intricacies of public law and to keep abreast of developments affecting municipalities than if he were employed on a fee or part-time basis. Where a properly qualified man could be found it might be possible to utilize his services as assessor or assistant finance director as well as attorney, thus making it possible to attach an adequate salary to the position. An alternate possibility is to combine all the city's regulatory activities under the city attorney's direction, a suggestion that will receive further attention in a subsequent section of this chapter.

Generally speaking, the chief administrator need not give any closer attention to internal procedures in the law department than to those in any other department. He should concern himself, however, to the extent of seeing that the flow of work is organized in an orderly fashion, and that a follow-up system is maintained which fixes responsibility for the handling of each case and which assures that each is carried through to a proper conclusion. If the city attorney has not had previous experience in the management of an organization — and many attorneys have not — the chief administrator must make him aware that his job involves important administrative as well as legal duties.

The Attorney, The Chief Administrator, and The Council

There is little uniformity among cities in the way in which the city attorney is appointed. In about one city out of ten he is elected by popular vote. In the remaining cities he is usually appointed by the council, by the mayor (particularly in strong-mayor cities), by the city manager, or by some combination of these officials. He is probably less often appointed by the chief administrative officer than are most other city department heads. Hence, there may be some question as to whether he is primarily responsible to the chief administrative officer, or directly responsible to the council. Except for his responsibilities for prosecution, in which under certain circumstances at least he must be free from direction, there is no particular reason why his status should be different from that of other department heads. Regardless of charter provisions, therefore, the most satisfactory working relationships is one in which the city attorney considers himself as responsible to the chief administrative officer, and where his contacts with the council are generally carried on through that officer.

This same aloofness from the rest of the city government is often expressed in other charter provisions affecting the city attorney's office. There does not seem to be any very good reason why subordinate personnel in the law department, including the attorneys, should not be appointed in exactly the same manner as subordinates in other city departments, and why civil service provisions should not be applicable to the law department. Where the law department is exempt from civil service, the city attorney or other appointing authorities may want to use the services of the personnel agency to examine candidates before appointment.

It is helpful for the city attorney to attend council meetings so that he may give opinions on legal questions which arise in the course of conducting the business of the meeting. Requests of the city council for formal opinions, or for the drafting of ordinances or resolutions should be transmitted through the chief administrator's office, so that the chief administrator may be kept informed of business that is to come before the council, and so that he may supplement the attorney's opinions and bills with nonlegal information which may assist the council in its deliberations.

Employing Special Counsel

No general rules can be laid down as to when and how often a city is justified in employing special counsel to assist the law department in court proceedings. A number of reasons may be urged in favor of calling in special counsel. The fact that the city's legal staff is highly competent and efficient in handling the regular legal business of the city does not necessarily mean that the regular staff should be asked or expected to carry important cases through the courts without outside assistance. Since trial work is a specialized branch of the law, a good law department administrator may not always be an experienced trial lawyer. During trial, a single important case may take up almost the entire time of the regular legal staff if counsel is not employed, and the regular legal business of the city may meanwhile be neglected. Industrial concerns, except the very largest ones, even though they maintain law departments to handle patent matters, contracts, and other regular legal business, seldom take important cases to trial without retaining outside counsel.

On the other hand, the law of municipal corporations and the law of public officers are highly technical subjects with which the average lawyer does not have frequent contact. Ignorance of these specialties has lost cases for more than one city. It would seem advisable, therefore, that even where special counsel are called in responsibility and final authority for the conduct of the case be left in the hands of the city attorney or one of his assistants. Extremely close cooperation between outside counsel and the law department's staff is absolutely necessary, and if this cannot be secured outside counsel had best be dispensed with.

Enforcement of Regulatory Ordinances

The final section of this chapter is devoted to the special problems that are encountered by city government in enforcing the numerous regulations to which the inhabitants of the city are subjected by city ordinance or state law. The questions with which the chief administrative officer is confronted in this field are quite distinct from his task of directing the members of his own organization.

There is one underlying principle which is common to both fields of administration, however: primary reliance for securing results must not be placed on the use of authority or the threat of punishment. In Chapter 4 it was emphasized that authority, by itself, cannot secure efficiency in the internal management of an organization. The major objective is to see that the regulations are observed, not to see that citizens are punished for failure to observe the regulations.

Regulatory Activities

A large number of city departments, many of which are also responsible for important service functions, are engaged in regulatory administration. Even a partial list of a modern city's regulatory activities would have to include building, electrical, and zoning inspection; subdivision control; elevator, boiler, and other safety inspection; health and food inspection; sealing of weights and measures; regulation of morals, nuisances, and traffic by the police; fire inspection; prosecution of fraudulent welfare claims; regulation of utility franchises, utility connections, and street cuts; and regulation of the disposal of wastes. In addition to these would be a host of miscellaneous regulations generally enforced by the law department and the police. From this list has been omitted suppression of major crimes by the police, for in the case of most of the regulations listed above, the enforcement authorities are dealing with a group of predominately law-abiding citizens, and procedures must be quite different than those used in handling serious crimes and professional criminals.

Some of the regulatory functions — fire inspection and subdivision control, for example — are assigned to the particular city department most concerned with the subject matter that is being regulated. Other regulatory activities which are not closely related to the work of any of the service departments, have commonly been handled by separate regulatory agencies such as building inspection departments.

Regulatory Procedures

Quite as impressive as the array of regulatory activities listed above are the wide variety of techniques available to the regulatory authorities:

Rules and Orders. One method of regulation is simply to pass a city ordinance telling citizens "thou shalt —" or "thou shalt not —." Reliance for enforcement of the ordinance may be placed upon the police and law departments, upon a separate regulatory agency, or upon complaints initiated by the general public.

Licenses and Permits. If more systematic enforcement is desired than is likely to be attained by the first method, persons in the regulated occupation or activity may be required to secure a license. This serves two purposes: first, to identify for the enforcing authorities all persons engaged in the regulated activity; second, to permit the enforcing authorities to determine whether the applicant for the license is complying with the regulations.

Inspection. Rules and orders may be supplemented by a regular process of inspection to determine compliance, and to correct noncompliance.

Noncoercive Methods. When regulations are imposed on citizens, it is usually because the city council believes that an important consideration of public health, safety, or welfare requires the regulation. If there is some good reason, the voluntary compliance of most residents of the city can be secured by explaining that reason to them with sufficient force and persuasion. Education and other methods of securing voluntary compliance will go hand in hand with the more severe enforcement procedures in any well-designed regulatory program.

Developing a Regulatory Program

Although no single pattern will fit the needs of all programs of regulation, it is possible to list some of the questions which should be asked in developing a new regulatory program, or in reviewing periodically the regulatory procedures already being followed in a city.

Is the subject one which, in practice, can be regulated? Everyone, of course, is "against sin," but a city ordinance is not always the best — or even a desirable way — of abolishing "sin." It may displease the eyes of councilmen to see that houses in the city are unpainted, but they would hardly consider a city ordinance requiring biennial repainting as a practical means for correcting the situation.

Just as the administrator, when he issues an order, must weigh the extent to which voluntary compliance can be expected, so a city council, in passing an ordinance, must realize that unless a very large majority of the citizens will comply voluntarily the ordinance cannot be enforced by any means which they are likely to make available to the enforcement officials. If the ordinance cannot meet this test, the city authorities will do well to content themselves by passing a resolution solemnly asserting that they are opposed to the particular activity which displeases them, without attempting to put a new ordinance on the books.

What is the best method, or combination of methods, for the enforcement of this particular regulation? A simple ordinance, to be left to the police and law department for enforcement, is most likely to suffice when citizens can be expected to report on their own initiative violations of the kind in question; and when the indefinite threat of possible detection and punishment will deter most citizens from violating the regulation without one hundred per cent enforcement. A special enforcement staff is likely to be necessary when these conditions are not met, or when specialized knowledge and skill are necessary to detect violations.

Where enforcement must be relatively complete, it is often desirable to require a license. This permits either an inspection at the time the license is requested, or later periodic inspections of all licenses, whichever method is more appropriate for the type of regulation in question. If licenses are required, some additional enforcement procedure must be established to make certain that all persons of whom a license is required actually apply for one; but if licenses are not required, the inspecting authorities have the same problem of determining where inspections need to be made, so the licensing provision really imposes no additional burden in this respect.

Thought should always be given to the possibility of using educational methods to secure voluntary compliance, either in conjunction with enforcement measures, or by themselves. Where the regulation is one which directly affects the public health and safety, enforcement authorities will not generally wish to depend entirely upon voluntary compliance, but will "speak softly and carry a big stick."

To whom is responsibility for enforcement to be delegated? If the subject of regulation is closely related to the work of any existing city department, it will often be most efficient to add the responsibility for enforcement to that department's duties. Some regulations can be enforced by policemen while engaged in their regular patrol duties, but before additional duties are imposed on the patrol force the police chief should certainly be consulted to determine whether the police can realistically be expected to enforce the regulations in question, and what steps need to be taken to train the patrolmen in their new duties and to secure adequate supervision and control of their enforcement activities. Unless these matters are worked out carefully and in detail, a law assigned to the police force for enforcement can easily become just another unenforced ordinance on the books. In deciding whether it is desirable to establish a separate enforcement unit for the regulation in question, the extent to which specialized skill is required in enforcement, and the magnitude of the enforcement job both need to be taken into consideration.

What opportunities for formal hearing or appeal shall be provided? Where regulations affect important personal or property rights, our concept of liberty and democracy demands, and state and federal constitutions require, that "due process" be observed. Every person has a right to a fair and impartial hearing, and if the subject of regulation is an important one, provision should usually be made for formal appeal to an administrative board of some kind. This is generally required by state law for assessments, zoning regulations, and subdivision control, but there may be other types of regulation where the same thing would be desirable — though perhaps on a relatively informal basis — even though not required by law.

How large shall license fees be? Many city licenses are imposed not primarily for regulatory, but for revenue purposes. With those, the present discussion is not concerned. In the case of regulatory measures passed under the city's general police powers, the general legal rule is that cities may only impose license fees sufficient to pay for enforcement of the regulation. This rule is usually sound from the standpoint of public policy as well as law, and when departures are made from this principle they should generally be in the direction of lower, rather than higher fees. A substantial fee attached to the license definitely increases the enforcement problem, as well as the public relations problem of obtaining proper public attitudes toward the regulation.

Securing Compliance

If voluntary compliance is to be the major objective of the regulatory program, then the agency to which the regulation is entrusted must be given sufficient resources to carry on the necessary educational program.

Codification of ordinances. Citizens can be expected to obey regulations only if they have some means of learning what those regulations are. As a bare minimum every city should compile its ordinances in a permanent code, arranged by subject matter, and preferably bound in loose-leaf form so that it can always be kept up-to-date. The initial preparation of the code will give the city council an opportunity to review past legislation, many items of which will be more or less obsolete, and to remove from the books many regulations which have been long deceased and deserve decent burial.

A municipality cannot be operated efficiently today on legal machinery designed and adopted to solve municipal problems ten, twenty, or even fifty years ago. Yet, thousands of cities are trying to do just this in spite of the economic, industrial, educational and other developments in recent years. It is therefore of the utmost importance that the legal machinery be of modern design if our government of laws is to serve the public in an efficient manner. It is generally recognized that in the great majority of cities municipal ordinance records are in a deplorable state causing uncertainty as to what ordinances remain in effect, which of them have been repealed, and as to what extent others have been amended. The chaotic condition of the ordinance material of most cities greatly hampers the work of the law department and makes it difficult to administer the affairs of the city in an efficient manner.

Publicity for new regulations. It is not enough to satisfy the formal legal steps for publication of ordinances. It is essential that every new regulation be brought directly to the attention of the persons being regulated. In the case of license procedures this is fairly well taken care of by the fact that the applicant cannot proceed until he has secured his license, though publicity will be needed to let him know a license is required. In other cases newspaper publicity will help; or direct mailing lists can be secured that will reach most of the persons in the city who will be affected. If the regulation is at all technical, it should be explained and interpreted in simple language, as well as publicized. If the purpose of, or need for, the regulation, is not entirely apparent on its face — and it seldom is to the persons to whom the regulation means inconvenience — publication of the regulation should be accompanied by facts and explanations to show its necessity.

Assistance in compliance. In many cases the persons regulated must be shown how they can comply with a minimum of inconvenience. For example, if an ordinance requires citizens to keep garbage in cans meeting certain minimum standards, a citizen will find it easier to comply if he is told how large a can will be needed for an average family in view of the frequency of collections in that particular city.

Organization for Regulatory Administration[1]

Perhaps no group of municipal functions are carried out with such diverse forms of organization as are the regulatory functions. In recent re-examinations of inspectional services in cities of all sizes, a significant effort has been made to achieve a consolidation of all or most inspectional activities. Where surveys have not suggested full consolidation, the exceptions have related to the most technical inspections in the fields of health and fire. Major opposition to a consolidated organization has been both internal and external. Department heads and personnel often are bound by tradition and are jealous of departmental prerogatives. The consolidation of inspections concerned with building, electrical and plumbing installations is often opposed by building trade unions as well as some interested contractor groups.

---

[1]For more complete coverage of this subject see the International City Managers' Association, Municipal Public Works Administration (Chicago: The Association, 1957), Chapter 15.

There is common agreement that to avoid the harassment of the public by numerous inspectors and the serving of conflicting violation notices, systematic cooperation among the field forces of the several city agencies engaged in this work is necessary. Disagreements, however, arise on the methods of achieving such cooperation. Obviously, a basic consolidated organization can do much to minimize conflicts and duplication of effort. The more the inspectional activities are functionally decentralized, the greater are the opportunities for confusion, conflicts, and duplication.

One goal of consolidation is to train inspectors to perform various types of craft inspections. Los Angeles County, California, since 1933 has had building inspectors perform combined building, electrical, and plumbing inspection work. A typical new dwelling is inspected about 12 times by a general inspector who is capable of performing all three types of inspections. When confronted with a difficult job, he notifies the central office which is staffed with specialists in architecture, structural engineering, plumbing, and electrical work. Such specialists also assist in functional supervision and in the training of the general inspectors. Similar types of inspectional service, with some variations in procedure, have been proposed in other cities such as Detroit, Milwaukee and Philadelphia.

Among the smaller communities where only one or two inspectors are needed to meet service requirements the practice of having a generalized inspector is more common. This is the case in such cities as Antioch and Monterey, California; Boulder and Fort Collins, Colorado; Bluefield, West Virginia; Astoria and Bend, Oregon; Atchison, Kansas; Ashtabula, Ohio; Newport, Kentucky; Jackson, Tennessee; and Ferndale, Michigan. The electrical and plumbing inspections are made by the same inspector in Reno, Nevada. Building and plumbing inspections are performed by the same inspector in University City, Missouri.

An alternative suggestion for the small city would be the following: all regulatory activities involving land use or buildings would be assigned to the agency that is responsible for enforcement of the zoning ordinance and subdivision control. Health and fire regulations would be assigned to those two departments, respectively. All other regulatory activities would be assigned to a section of the law department. This recommendation would work best in a city where the zoning agency and the law department are under the control of the chief administrative officer, and is likely to be less successful if the two agencies in question are independent of the chief administrator. It would have the advantage of permitting a higher salary to obtain a first-class man as head of the law department, or of permitting employment of a full-time city attorney where that might not otherwise be possible.

Role of the Law Department in Regulatory Administration

The law department has two major responsibilities in regulatory administration — even if separate regulatory agencies are established. The first is the prosecution of violations; the second, the training of regulatory personnel in legal requirements and legal procedures.

In certain minor prosecutions — parking tickets, for example — the law department will be concerned only with those rare instances where the defendant demands a jury trial. In most other cases, actual prosecution of the violators of city regulations will be a task for the law department. The attorneys must rely principally upon the regulatory officials for the evidence upon which the prosecution will be based, but the decision to prosecute or not to prosecute, and the actual conduct of proceedings are matters for the attorney.

Best results will be secured if the chief administrator periodically reviews, in conference with the city attorney and the department head responsible for each major regulatory program, the enforcement policy which is to be followed. Both the attorney and the regulatory official will want a voice in the determination of this policy, and should be given such a voice if both are to share responsibility for enforcement. Final responsibility for policy rests, of course, upon the city council, but that body should certainly not proceed until it has had the advice and suggestions of the enforcement officials.

That the same enforcement policy should be followed by the law department as by the regulatory agency is an elementary principle, but one that is not likely to be followed unless the chief administrator brings about a liaison between the two departments concerned. If prosecution is more lax than the policy followed by the regulatory unit, the morale of the staff of that unit will drop sharply when they find that complaints they initiate do not "stick" and are dropped by the law department. On the other hand, if the attorney wishes to follow a sterner policy than does the regulatory unit, he will find that his mill has no grist to grind — that he has no means to secure complaints or evidence upon which to base his prosecutions.

Disagreements on policy are not the only cause for lack of coordination between regulatory agencies and the law department. Equally important may be the failure of regulatory officials to understand the law of evidence and the requirements of "due process" which must be followed in enforcement proceedings. The case that the city attorney pleads before the court can be no better than the evidence on which it is based, and the attorney's office must rely upon the enforcement agency for that evidence.

A major responsibility that the chief administrator should impose upon his law department is to exercise functional supervision, from a technical legal standpoint, over the enforcement practices and the methods of compiling evidence, of the regulatory agencies. This supervision will usually be most successful if it relies principally upon in-service training methods. All city officials engaged in enforcement work should be given periodic training in the rules of evidence. This is commonly done for policemen when they join the department, but less commonly for other regulatory officials, and still less common is any procedure for periodic retraining. The city attorney's office must realize, of course, that prosecution of violations is only a secondary aim of the regulatory agency and that all of its procedures cannot and should not be organized around this particular goal. Nevertheless, there is no excuse for persistent failures to convict violators through careless preparation of prosecutions, and when this occurs the responsibility must be shared by the law department and the regulatory agency.

The educational process carried on by the law department should be a two-way process. In many cases, particularly when the law department is small, there may be experts in particular regulatory agencies who will have a better knowledge of the intricacies of the law which applies to their respective functions than does anyone in the law department. This is often true of the zoning enforcement agency or the building department, where a staff member of the agency is able to follow new court decisions and legislative developments far more closely than can any of the attorneys. Even when the departmental employee, by reason of lack of legal training, cannot properly interpret these new developments he performs a valuable service in calling them to the attorney's attention.

Summary

This chapter has reviewed, from the standpoint of the chief administrator, the work of the law department and those other departments — principally the regulatory agencies — whose work is most closely related to legal matters. It has been seen that the work of the city law department is a composite of every type of activity — operating, auxiliary, and managerial — and that its relation to the chief administrator and to other departments is correspondingly complex.

In many cities, the development of the law department has been hampered, from the administrative standpoint, by the relative independence of the city attorney from the chief administrative officer. Sometimes he is elected, often he is appointed by the city council, and generally his specialized legal training sets him somewhat apart from his colleagues in the city hall — they don't talk his language. This independence may sometimes obscure the fact that legal matters have quite as close a relation to the chief executive's job — from both an auxiliary and a managerial standpoint — as have questions of personnel and finance.

Regulatory procedures have likewise often been ignored, in the general development of the municipal administrative pattern, as compared with the major service functions. In general, the budgets of regulatory agencies are considerably smaller than those of service agencies, and in many ways they tend to be less "glamorous." As a consequence, a real opportunity exists in many cities to improve the administration of regulatory functions, by centralizing regulatory administration to some extent, and by bringing about a closer coordination between the regulatory agencies and the law department.

Regulatory activities generally are administered by a number of departments and in some cities practically every section of the city is visited daily by one, two, or more municipal employees. For example, many inspectors visit homes of citizens, business establishments, or buildings being constructed to see that some ordinance or regulation of the city is complied with. The municipal administrator is interested in determining in his own city how and where inspectional services best fit into the organization, how adequate supervision and control can be provided, and how standards can be developed.

Finally, it has been emphasized that regulatory administration is quite as much a matter of public relations and education as it is a matter of policing. The suggestions which have been offered in this chapter for effective techniques of regulatory administration will be supplemented by further discussion of the topic from the standpoint of public relations in Chapter 13.

Chapter 12

ADMINISTRATIVE MEASUREMENT

Measurement in municipal administration is a more complex subject than some are willing to admit. Still, with study and experimentation, it is a manageable one. An understanding of what can and cannot be done is essential for effective utilization by management of the right tools at the right time and for the solution of the right kinds of problems.

Almost every city administrator would like to be able to answer objectively a self-posed question. "How well are we doing?" Even in the smallest city, or administrative orbit, this is often a difficult question to answer. It is comparatively easy for each member of a baseball team, the manager and the baseball fans to know how each player and the club as a whole rate. Baseball is a precise game, with definite rules, and, more important, it is a one-activity game. All eyes are on one ball. High degrees of skill, coordination, and teamwork are required, but the end-product is measurable in hits, runs and errors. To no less a degree, municipal administration requires skill, coordination, and teamwork, but the rules of the game are not simple, many balls are in motion at one time, the players are numerous, and the end-products, in terms of tangible and intangible services, are multiple. Small wonder that the scoreboard on the team as a whole must necessarily be complicated, and performance of principal, individual players difficult to score.

There is one other major contrast. Measurement in baseball is solely of performance. In municipal administration, measurement includes performance but much more; it is an integral part of many stages of the administrative process. It begins with the measurement of needs and runs almost the whole gamut of the administrative cycle. Questions range from: "What do we really need in this area?" to: "What can we afford to program for this purpose?" "How well are we doing, given our authorizations?" "How adequate are the results compared with the needs?" and "How efficient are we with the money allowed for this activity?" It is understandable that sometimes thinking and terminology about administrative measurement lack clarity.

Despite all difficulties, the science of municipal management has progressed in this area. More reliance than ever before is being placed on facts, tested results, and other products of quantitative measurement, and new experiments with measurement tools and techniques are yielding results.

What in Administration is Measured

It is important to know what aspect of government is being measured by a particular index because administration can be measured in a number of ways. There are really three important questions which the trained administrator recognizes: *what* can be measured; *why* (i.e. for what purpose), and *how* (i.e. by what techniques and procedures). The range of possible measurements is wide. This can be seen from only a brief enumeration:

351

1. Measurement of needs for
   Capital improvements
   New or increased current programs

2. Ability of the tax base to
   support a certain level of
   expenditure

3. Adequacy of program, with
   need as a standard (sometimes
   stated as "potential effectiveness")

4. Performance of
   An individual
   A piece of equipment
   A team or group
   An entire project, or activity

5. Measurement of "input"
   (expressed either as man-hours or
   equipment-hours, or as dollar costs)

6. Measurement of results
   (which are concomitants of
   performance)

7. Effectiveness in
   Performance, as compared with
      standard performance
   Execution of a program, with the
      work program as a standard
   Attainment of goals, with program
      objectives as the standard

8. Efficiency
   "Output" compared with "input,"
   and the resultant laid against a
   standard cost (in dollars or effort)

The terms performance and productivity can often be used interchangeably. Similarly, results and accomplishment usually have the same connotation. To contrast "performance" and "results" the recreation department may be taken as an example. Records on participation in playground sports furnish performance statistics. Results from the playground activity, however, must be measured according to some goal or objective, perhaps in terms of reduction of the number of traffic accidents to children playing in the streets, or according to the effect upon the juvenile delinquency rate.

There are different levels of measurement. The above eight categories are obviously, in importance, not of the same magnitude. Nor do they serve the same purposes. Measurements of need (whether social or economic) become the basis for preparing programs and program changes. Performance of a group may be measured in order to decide the proper combination of labor in executing a given operation or activity. In general, the "products" of measurement are used in planning, programming and budgeting; decision-making; direction and control; communication; and in re-appraisals — in fact, at every stage of the administrative cycle.

Measurement of Needs

Needs can be determined by hit-or-miss methods, or an effort made to measure them more scientifically, even if only reasonable approximations can be attained. Needs for capital improvements are the difference between what the city ought to have and what it actually has, and fall into two broad categories: capital replacements and new capital improvements. A replacement decision may be based primarily on operating records, which may show that the capital item is no longer an efficient unit, and that a replacement will pay.

To determine the need for new capital improvements, other methods are required. For example, the city planner may conduct a traffic pattern and parking survey to measure the need for a new municipal parking lot. An economic base study may indicate that certain types of new industries would give the community a more balanced economic life, but that such industries cannot be attracted until the city expands its water plant or makes

certain other basic public improvements. The need for new school construction, or recreational areas, can be approximated by statistical studies which compare what the city
has with recognized standards, adjusted for the special conditions of the community. Professional, functional standards adjusted to local conditions are in widespread use.

Measurement of needs is usually by planners and the operating heads. Determination of programs is in the final analysis a policy matter for the legislative body, but the
measurements that go into proposals can be classified as administrative measurement.
The responsibility of the legislative body for determining programs (and therefore administrative objectives) must be underscored, but proposals stem often from alert administrators in their advisory and staff roles. To recommend proposed service programs with
measures of probable results, is within the democratic process if the final decision of
programs and objectives remains with the council which expresses the popular will.

Performance

Performance is the most common subject of administrative measurement; and because it is so generally understood, discussion here can be brief. Actual performance
can often be quantified, whether the performance is of an individual, a group (team or
crew), an organizational unit, a piece of equipment, an activity, or an operation. In some
areas of administration, however, it is extremely difficult to develop a work unit, or unit
of measurement. Where performance is in standardized units and can be measured, actual performance can be compared with standard performance. Management can then
center its attention on variances from standard performance, and the cause or causes
of such variance.

Effectiveness

The comparison of actual performance with standard performance gives one measure of effectiveness. Management is also interested in comparing actual performance
(execution) of a program with the budgeted (planned) work program, in order to measure
the effectiveness of an organizational unit in carrying out a program. In addition, management is interested in effectiveness in attaining given goals or objectives, attainment being
expressed in terms of "results" (as opposed to performance units). The question is pertinent to management: "We carried out our work program with 96 per cent effectiveness,
but how well did we come out in achieving the expected *results* from our program?"

Efficiency

Standards for the measurement of effectiveness leave unanswered one very important question: How *efficient* is the administration? For it must not be forgotten that
human efforts are finite. It is not the function of the administrator to establish a Utopia.
It is his function to maximize the attainment of the governmental objectives (assuming
that they have been agreed upon) by the efficient employment of the limited resources
that are available to him. A "good" public library, from the administrative standpoint,
is not one which owns all the books that have ever been published, but one which has used
the limited funds which were allowed it to build up as good a collection as was possible
under the circumstances.

A high degree of efficiency basically means to management getting the most effective program possible for the amount of dollars expended; in other words, achieving the
maximum output for a minimum dollar input. A program can be effective without being

efficient (that is, it costs too much money for the results); or, in turn, it can be highly efficient but not effective (that is, there was not enough to do a good job, but management did the very best possible with the dollar resources which it had). The term "efficiency" is not to be confused with the more general term "economy." Economy is too vague a term, used sometimes as the equivalent of efficiency, but again as something quite different (limited-objective program, or reduction of expenditures).

Relevance of Standards

Measurement requires not only tools (statistics, cost accounting, etc.) but standards. Standards vary, as well as the tools. The administrator not only has to choose the best measurement tools to meet his needs, but also reliable standards pertinent to his problems. Standards might be grouped as:

1. External, professional, and generally, functional standards (e.g. those available from the American Public Health Association, National Recreation Association, and so forth).

2. Internally developed, and generally, functional standards:
   A. Developed scientifically from cost analyses, or from cost accounting or historical records;
   B. Rules of thumb based on the administrator's personal observations and experiences.

Variances of actual performance from standards must be studied for their causes. The "why" of the variances becomes the basis for management action.

The Uses of Administrative Measurement

Decision-Making

Management (whether the chief executive, department head, or middle management) is constantly making decision judgments, and reshaping them as circumstances and changed conditions require. The administrative process is a dynamic one. A decision of day-before-yesterday may not fit today's requirements. Plans and programs (based on decisions), execution thereof, appraisal of results, perhaps new decisions or modification of the original — these constitute important segments of the administrative cycle.

Much of administration rests on hunches and impressions but they are not satisfactory substitutes for careful, objective analyses of governmental services. The administrator's eyes are not all-seeing, his judgments are subject to error. He needs to make use of every available device for increasing the range of his vision and the soundness of his decisions. The difference between good and bad management, or between good management and mediocre management, is often in the quality of the decision-making. Measurement's most important contribution is in supplying the basis for better decision-making. The administrator will not sharpen his decision-making, or in more general terms "will not learn from experience," unless he constantly reappraises objectively.

Applications in the Budget Process

The use of measurement in decision-making comes earliest in the programming and budget formulation period. Each year the administrator must submit estimates of the financial needs of his organization for the ensuing year. Measurement results are embodied in the vast number of decisions that go into budget formulation. This is true whether management is engaged in preparing a capital budget, a current budget on a line-item or lump-sum basis, or a current budget on a performance basis. Measurement enters into projected work programs, current or capital. It is not enough for the chief administrator, his staff, or his operating heads to think solely in terms of dollar input (proposed budgetary expenditures), or of major objects of expenditure, such as labor, supplies, materials and equipment. These must be translated into proposed programs of end-product services. Measurement becomes increasingly important as the budget moves closer to a program or performance basis.

The availability of work program data, unit costs, and statistically established standards will largely determine how scientifically based the budget is. Value-judgments must be made at every step of budget formulation, but administrative measurement data are at hand to improve the quality of these value-judgments. That is all that administrative measurement can do, but that is a lot.

Administrative Research

During the budget execution stage, some types of measurement furnish problem-solving techniques. Only by measuring performance under different conditions, and by alternative approaches, can the administrator scientifically determine which methods and practices are best. Measurement will often help to decide what is the best combination of labor and equipment to carry on a given operation or activity. For example, it may be found that a crew of three with certain equipment is a more effective and efficient team than four with another type of equipment.

Administrative Control

Another important use of measurement is in exercising administrative control over departments and personnel. Measurement techniques furnish the administrator, for the first time, with an operating audit instead of the traditional accounting audit with all of its limitations. The mayor or city manager or department head cannot be everywhere at once. He cannot exercise minute oversight and control over subordinate officials. Even if he could, it would be undesirable for him to do so. Nevertheless, he is responsible for the efficient operation of the city or of his department. Hence arises the necessity for a system of administrative reporting that will allow the administrator to determine the effectiveness and efficiency of operation, locate weak spots, avoid pitfalls, and maintain adequate control over departmental operations.

A system of administrative reports will permit control, not only of the operations of an entire department, but also of individuals within the departments. Departmental reports are ordinarily a composite of reports by individuals, and they should show not only how well the department is functioning as a unit but also how well each of its employees is working. For example, public works records will spot immediately a truck driver or sweeper operator who is covering too few miles, while the police reports will reveal a police officer who is making too few arrests or permitting too much crime in his district.

If labor costs are disproportionately high on a particular construction job, the cost accounts will show this fact immediately, and possible remedies may be applied before the work is completed. Constant study of the various administrative reports of measurements, together with comparison with reports of previous periods, is one of the best methods for the administrator to maintain a current control of the operations of the department and its individual officers and employees.

Representation

Finally, the products of measurement often assist the chief administrator in presenting a full and understandable account of his stewardship, both to the council and to the citizens. Work performance data and unit costs make good reporting material, especially when graphically presented and compared with standards or prior years' performance.

Limitations to the Quantitative Approach

The uses of administrative measurement in municipal administration, however, are not clearly understood until one also understands the limitations upon the applications of yardsticks, ratios, and unit costs. We must not expect the impossible of the quantitative approach. Not all decisions require quantitative facts as a base. Typical are decisions in the realm of human relations and public relations. Even performance sometimes defies quantification. The millions of gallons of water purified monthly at a water filtration plant can be metered, but the end-products of a research worker, or staff member of the city planning department, or of a staff lawyer in the corporation counsel's office cannot accurately be measured. A standard unit end-product which is measurable cannot be found in some cases.

Survey of Measurements Used in Evaluating City Departments

In accordance with the general principles of measurement which have been presented, a rapid survey will be made to show how they are applied in evaluating the various specific municipal functions, and how the measurement techniques may help the administrator on the job.[1] Statistical devices have frequently been misapplied through ignorance or special interest. "You can prove anything with statistics" is a widely current notion. As a result, some administrators are inclined to look with suspicion upon measurement devices and records procedures. They are also likely to view them as so much useless red tape.

Such an attitude would be all right, except for the fact that every day in the week, the administrator must make decisions involving numbers: "How many men will I need for that street repair job?" "How much money shall I allot to the police department in next year's budget?" "How will the establishment of a fire prevention bureau affect insurance rates?" And a sound answer to such questions depends on accurate quantitative information regarding past performance.

The range of problems to which analysis of this kind can profitably be applied is limited only by the ingenuity of the administrator and the adequacy of the records maintained by his organization. The kinds of problems to which measurement techniques may be applied include administrative planning, work programming and budgeting, determining efficiency of personnel; distributing personnel and equipment; measuring efficiency of equipment; and determining relative effectiveness and efficiency of alternative procedures, methods, and commodities.

---

[1] A more detailed discussion and bibliographical references will be found in Clarence E. Ridley and Herbert A. Simon, Measuring Municipal Activities (Chicago: The International City Managers' Association, 1943), 75 pp.

A list of specific fields where measurement techniques have yielded valuable returns in increased effectiveness or efficiency will illustrate their usefulness.

Fire

It is generally agreed that the final objective of fire protection is to minimize fire losses, including indirect losses due to the disruption of business and payment of excess insurance premiums, and to reduce personal injuries and deaths. The fire loss will therefore be the basic measurement of fire department achievement. Three of the criteria in common use can be employed as a means of approximating the general level of fire department effectiveness: the loss per $1,000 valuation probably is the most reliable in comparisons from city to city; the loss per building fire is preferable in comparing results from year to year; and the number of building fires per $1,000 valuation is a check upon fire prevention work.

Before definite and wholly dependable conclusions can be drawn from fire loss comparisons, however, external factors — natural, structural, occupancy, and moral, as well as administrative — must be considered. The Grading Schedule of the National Board of Fire Underwriters used in rating the city's fire defenses for insurance purposes is a recognized measure of fire department physical facilities and potential performance. Though the grading schedule gives inadequate emphasis to intangible factors, such as training and morale, it is perhaps the best measure of the physical aspects of the city's fire protection facilities.

In a number of communities, fire loss data have provided the basis for intelligent attacks on the fire waste problem. In Fort Worth, Texas, arson was materially curbed by analysis of the relation of fire losses to overinsurance. The extent of incendiarism in Boston was determined from a study of fire losses in relation to changes in business conditions. Many cities have used loss records to determine the structures, occupancies, and causes responsible for the bulk of fire loss and have planned fire prevention programs based on the result of these analyses.

In Hartford, New Haven, Providence, Sacramento, and many other cities, the work of fire companies in various parts of the city has been compared to equalize work loads and to raise the effectiveness of individual companies. Cost records have been employed to determine the most efficient types of equipment and the proper time for its renewal. Other cities have made use of purchase records to indicate the proper time for renewal of materials — such as fire truck tires — whose deterioration is a factor of time more than of use.

Police

Although there is no single index which will give a comprehensive picture of police effectiveness, a satisfactory police record system will yield statistics useful in administrative control and research.

Major crimes (Part I classes of the uniform system)[2] are best measured on the basis of "offenses known to the police per 100,000 persons" and "percentage of cases cleared by arrest." The latter indicates police effectiveness in dealing with these crimes. The rate of juvenile delinquency per 1,000 children is an index of some aspects of crime prevention work. Crime rates can be analyzed, and police methods adapted to specific needs as revealed by the records.

---

[2]Uniform Crime Reports, issued by the Federal Bureau of Investigation.

For crimes against property, additional indices are available in "percentage of value of stolen property recovered" and "percentage of stolen automobiles recovered." Effectiveness of traffic regulation can be measured by the accident frequency rate, the accident injury rate, the property or auto damage rate, and the accident fatality rate per 100,000 inhabitants and per 10,000 motor vehicles registered.

One relevant index regarding crimes against the public morals, disturbances of the peace, and similar offenses is: "Number of persons charged by the police." It is in this area of police work that a sound philosophy of administration is still lacking as a basis of measurement, since it is not entirely clear what police are expected to accomplish in this area.

Some additional insight into the investigational activities of the police can be gained by the index of "Percentage of convictions of persons charged." But this index is more a function of the prosecution and the courts than of police administration.

As for measuring police performance, a number of techniques are available. Perhaps the most important are the time studies and statistical analyses which form the basis for scientific determination of police shifts and beats. In the field of traffic regulation, spot maps of accident frequency indicate particular areas that need attention.

Police departments have perhaps made more progress than other municipal departments in the utilization of adequate records and measurement procedures. One reason for this is that records are useful not only for administrative control, but are indispensable to every member of the department in his daily work — for purposes of personal and property identification and in recording the facts of each incident which requires police attention. A number of police departments have found these records a valuable tool of administrative research. Berkeley, Cincinnati, and Wichita, have used crime records as the basis for distributing the available personnel by shifts and by beats. Details and beats have been so arranged in these cities that work loads of all patrolmen are equalized, and all parts of the city are given an equal quality of police services in relation to need. Wichita has used its records to determine the effectiveness of some police procedures. In Wichita, studies of the effectiveness of *modus operandi* identification procedures, and of warnings as compared to traffic tickets and other enforcement measures, were pioneers in police administrative research.

Public Works

Each public works activity must be measured separately (whether for need, effectiveness, adequacy of results, etc.) since each is directed towards its own objective. Measurements of effectiveness and adequacy of results have been used in street cleaning, refuse disposal, sewage disposal, street lighting, and water supply. Such measurements have as yet been less successful in catch-basin cleaning, snow removal, and the construction and maintenance of streets.

Almost all public works activities are well adapted to the measurement of performance. In many cases performance can be related to costs, and the unit costs derived from that relation are highly useful in controlling expenditures and estimating costs. Another promising approach to further refinements of the analysis lies in time studies by means of which performance is related not directly to costs but to the man-hours and equipment-hours of effort which underlie the money expenditure.

Public works activities are somewhat more tangible than most other municipal functions and measurable work units are easier to establish. As a result, it is this field in which cost accounting has found its widest application. Cost accounting procedures for public works were developed originally by the American Public Works Association (and its predecessor) and the International City Managers' Association, and were installed in several cities, including, Flint, Kenosha, and Cincinnati. Additional work has been done by the Municipal Finance Officers Association and Public Administration Service. Many cities have applied cost accounting to some public works areas. Through cost records, close control has been exercised over expenditures for public works activities. Annual budgets have been based on work programs which accurately forecast needs. Special studies have aided in determining the relative frequency of cleaning different streets, the layout of refuse collection and street cleaning routes, and the relative efficiency of different collection and maintenance crews. Cost records have also permitted the application of the principles of engineering economies to the public works field. Through the use of these principles, intelligent capital improvement budgeting and the planning and design of public works structures have become possible.

Public Health

Three types of measurement are possible in the field of health. The first is the measurement of cost and time involved in health services. The second is the appraisal of the health program in terms of performance with the use of the excellent evaluation schedule of the American Public Health Association. The third is the analysis of mortality and morbidity (illness) rates. A very thorough appraisal technique, combining all three types of measurement, has been developed by cooperation between the American Public Health Association and municipalities. For day-to-day administration and control, the same technique can be used by the administrator. Also the National Organization for Public Health Nursing has developed an appraisal form for public health nursing services, and provides a staff for making local appraisals on request.

Public health officers have long used mortality and morbidity statistics as a guide to the effective administration of their departments. Such statistics have enabled officials to appraise the results obtained in lower death rates, through purification of the water and milk supplies, vaccination and inoculation, maternity and child health activities, and other aspects of the public health program.

It is also now recognized that hospitals and public health organizations in the same area must operate as a coordinated community health team. A measure of the effectiveness of this teamwork will have to be developed. The general hospital has come to be regarded as a basic community facility for personal health services as well as for the diagnosis and treatment of disease.

Recreation

The intangible nature of the ultimate objectives of recreation administration makes direct measurement of their attainment very difficult. There are certain symptomatic indices, such as the rates of crime and juvenile delinquency, which give some indication of the effect of the program upon social behavior and human satisfaction, and also data which give a picture of the community's recreational life.

Leadership is the most important single factor in determining the effectiveness of a department. Recreation administrators have used records of attendance as a primary guide, both as a measure of performance and, to a certain extent, of results. Population and attendance statistics help determine the proper distribution of facilities, locate facilities where there is under-use, and indicate the facilities which supply the most popular and economical forms of public recreation. In addition, in the study of certain phases of the recreation program, units of cost, units of effort expended (facilities and personnel provided) can be related to units of performance. Many cities are using the appraisal form of the National Recreation Association as a tool for self-evaluation.[3]

Welfare

Welfare work can, in part, be measured in terms of the needs that it meets and the services that it offers. A problem of central importance is economic dependency. It can be studied from several viewpoints: the direct measure of poverty; the measurement of unemployment and the effects of public employment agencies; the measurement of dependency and relief.

In family welfare work the basis of measurement is the case; the case load, ratio of acceptances to applications, and inactive cases are all useful indices to the administrator. One use of case statistics in some cities has been to determine the efficiency of relief administration under various sized individual case loads.[4] Case load and unemployment statistics have also been used in budgeting welfare expenditures. Institutional care can be measured in terms of inmate days. Quality of care is more difficult to measure, but in institutions for delinquents follow-up studies may be useful.

The tremendous growth of welfare activities during the past 25 years has created a demand, as yet only partly met, for finer measuring devices to rate various degrees of success, and for statistics upon the ultimate results of particular programs and policies. It is one thing to report where a welfare agency is investing its energies and resources; but far more significant is an accounting of results achieved. Periodic re-examination of objectives is also needed. Only as goals are made more explicit is it possible to redirect operations toward more effective goal attainment.[5]

Public Education

The final appraisal of the school system must be in terms of its impact upon the community through the individuals that it trains. The most successful attempts at the measurement of educational results have been made through the survey technique, by testing the intellectual and social attainments of the products of the schools, and by follow-up of school graduates to determine their success in adjustment to life. Some progress has also been made in unit cost measurements in education. In New York state the Regents' Inquiry, for example, developed a "standard enrollment unit" (SEU) to measure the relationship between the service and the recipient of that service, while a standard "use unit" (SUU) was employed to determine the efficiency of operation and maintenance of the plant, land, and buildings. Methods have also been worked out for appraising the adequacies and inadequacies of a school plant, and some beginnings made in evaluating pupil transportation service.[6]

---

[3]National Recreation Association, Schedule for the Appraisal of Community Recreation (New York: The Association, 1951), 45 pp.

[4]Herbert A. Simon et al., Determining Work Loads for Professional Staff in a Public Welfare Agency (Berkeley, California: Bureau of Public Administration, 1941).

[5]A provocative evaluation of measurement and research needs in public welfare appears in David G. French, An Approach to Measuring Results in Social Work (New York: Columbia University Press, New York, 1952), 178 pp.

[6]Ralph D. McLeary, Guide for Evaluating School Buildings (Rev. ed.), New England School Development Council, 1951, 52 pp.; Virgil R. Ruegsegger, Measuring the Quality and the Effectiveness of Pupil Transportation Service, Ph.D. thesis, Cornell University, 1938, 118 pp., typewritten.

Public Libraries

A more precise formulation of objectives is the starting point in a public library which attempts to measure its effectiveness. While services to the community are most crucial in the assessment of library performance, it is exactly this element of service which is least susceptible to measurement except for circulation and registration statistics. These play a measurement role comparable to attendance data in a recreation department, and libraries have been quick to see the need for statistics in planning their programs. There is almost universal awareness, however, that the number of registered readers and the actual count of volumes loaned do not fully record either in quantitative or qualitative terms the total public service performance role of the public library. Through analyses of their borrowers and circulation, however, libraries can attempt to determine the extent to which they are reaching different portions of the population and the kinds of reading matter they are getting into circulation.

In developing performance budgets, libraries have kept abreast of other areas of public administration[7] and some beginnings have been made in measuring the quality of the book stock.

Personnel

The departments thus far considered have been operating agencies, whose function it is to provide services directly to the public. The personnel agency, on the other hand, is largely an auxiliary agency concerned with the internal administration of the city government itself and offering no services directly to the public. Its value must ultimately be found in the increased effectiveness and efficiency it brings about in the operating departments. Measurement of actual results is possible only after the effectiveness and efficiency of the operating departments have been determined, and resort must be made to indirect methods in the construction of a practical measuring device in personnel administration. It is difficult in all of the auxiliary services to separate substantive technique, public policy, and the use of the auxiliary service in management.

In measurements of the work of the personnel agency itself, allowance must be made for the extent of its jurisdiction, the laws under which it performs the duties, and the activities of other agencies which have an effect upon personnel administration. It is necessary first to measure the general public employment situation and then to relate that situation to the factors responsible for it. The personnel agency is just one among those factors.

The public personnel situation can be measured in terms of the quality of personnel, morale, the prestige of the service, and the performance of specific personnel activities. The most useful indices for casting light upon the general situation are: (1) the quality of recruits, as indicated by qualifications and by examinations, (2) the rate of turnover of personnel, (3) absenteeism, and (4) safety records in hazardous phases of municipal administration. Service ratings will be of increasing value in the analysis as they become more objective.

Particular personnel practices must be analyzed with reference to their effect upon

---

[7]The Milwaukee Public Library experience is described in Municipal Finance Officers Association, Performance Budgeting for Libraries (Chicago: The Association, 1954), 12 pp.

Over the years the American Library Association has worked on standards. A substantial revision of its principles and standards appears in American Library Association, Public Library Service: A Guide to Evaluation, with Minimum Standards (Chicago: The Association, 1956), 74 pp. A supplement, with illustrative budgets, is used to translate standard services into changing cost levels. See Cost of Public Library Service for 1956 — A Supplement.

the morale and quality of the service. A fertile field for research would be a study of the relationship of performance units, level of compensation, recruitment procedure, training methods, and so forth, for the achievement of the objectives of personnel administration. Some recent studies indicate that a judicious use of quantitative measures of performance requires awareness of possible side effects and reactions which may outweigh the benefits.[8]

The uses of measurement in increasing the efficiency of personnel administration have not been exploited to anywhere near their full potentialities. In a few jurisdictions, standardized tests have been used to determine trends in the quality of personnel. Turn-over rates have been effectively used in the study of employee morale and the adequacy of compensation rates.[9] Though none of the available rating scales is entirely satisfactory, service ratings are widely used in selecting employees for promotion, transfer, demotion, and salary increases.

Finance

The objectives of finance administration may be characterized as fiscal soundness, economy of resources, and facilitation of administration. Fiscal soundness can be measured by the city's credit rating, the annual audit, and by the effectiveness of its administrative methods. Problems of taxation and debt, on the other hand, involve policy determination as well as administration. The third function is a service activity and must be measured in terms of the information and resources applied to operating departments.

The performance of many specific finance activities can be measured in part or in whole. Tax collections and delinquency, the relation of income to expenditures, and indebtedness are especially good indices of the city's financial status. Budgeting and accounting are somewhat less tangible but can be measured in part. A number of criteria have been developed for the measurement of purchasing.

Cost accounting techniques have already been mentioned. In addition, records have been used to increase the effectiveness of the finance department itself. Tax delinquency data are widely recognized as a necessary basis for intelligent collection activities. Revenues and expenditures are compared with budget estimates in order to improve estimating procedures.

Planning

The measurement of planning is a task of infinite possibilities which have been only slightly explored. Fundamental to measurement is accurate information as a basis for studying community needs and trends. The accuracy of such information must be carefully checked.

As a basis for such information the degree to which community needs are attained can be appraised for each plan. Success of zoning, platting, planning for transportation, planning for recreation, planning for public buildings, and planning for utilities are all measurable to a large extent. The cost side of zoning has not been examined with sufficient thoroughness, and measurement is in a very elementary stage. Studies of community costs and benefits of planning, and the relation of governmental planning to the governmental fiscal status both seem to offer much promise.

[8]V. F. Ridgway, "Dysfunctional Consequences of Performance Measurements," Administrative Science Quarterly, September, 1956, pp. 240-247.
[9]Similar approaches have been applied in business. Robert Saltonstall, "Evaluating Personnel Administration," Harvard Business Review, November-December 1952, pp. 93-104; and Thomas J. Luck, Personnel Audit and Appraisal (New York: McGraw-Hill, 1955), 317 pp.

Measurement techniques form the very core of effective planning work. Budgeting, programming of physical improvements, zoning, transportation, and planning all require basic data on land uses, population distribution and other social, economic, and governmental characteristics of the city.

Some Applications of Measurement Techniques

To illustrate exactly how measurement techniques can be used by the administrator in dealing with problems, a few situations where such techniques have been successfully applied will be presented in some detail. The six problems that will be analyzed are: (1) the development of a police beat layout, (2) the use of cost accounting in administrative control, (3) the use of standards in inspectional activities, (4) performance budgeting in hospitals, (5) the appraisal of library effectiveness, and (6) the analysis of the fire problem.

Layout of Police Beats[10]

The desirability of making an accurate distribution of police personnel is quite evident. The proper distribution of policemen should give each officer his fair share of the load and should give to each part of the city and each group in the city its fair share of police service. It is certainly not conducive to efficiency to have a much greater force on duty during certain hours to perform a given amount of police service than is on duty at other hours to perform an equal or greater volume of police work. The greatest efficiency cannot be reached except by a distribution of manpower that will result in an equal amount of work for each officer and a distribution of police service over the city during the hours of the day and night in proportion to the needs and to the total force available.

How, then, does the police chief distribute his force equitably? The city must be policed during the entire 24 hours, and if patrolmen work on three eight-hour shifts, they are divided into three platoons. The system of having platoons of equal size and beats of about equal size on all platoons is obviously inefficient. Conditions vary in each hour of the day, and varying hazards create varying demands for police service. A police hazard may be created by a poorly lighted area, by the residence of a large number of truants and delinquents in an area, by pool halls or so-called "social clubs" and dance halls where gangs may thrive, by valuable stocks of easily moved merchandise in stores or warehouses, and by many other conditions.

Each store, shop and warehouse presents a different degree of hazard. The hazard of each varies during the different hours of the day and night. The use of any system of distribution of the patrol force which ignores these facts cannot possibly result in a high degree of efficiency. If effective police service is to be rendered, a distribution by rule of thumb or by guess must be replaced by a reasonable distribution based on data which will indicate the actual needs in every section during each tour of duty.

Hazards may seem to be too abstract a device to use as a measure of the police service which must be supplied, but for the most part police hazards are definitely measurable in two ways. First, hazards may be measured by the amount of crime which

---

[10]The basic approach described here was worked out by Chief O. W. Wilson and has been applied, with modifications, in a number of cities: Berkeley, Wichita, San Antonio, Cincinnati, Greensboro (North Carolina) and others. O. W. Wilson, Police Administration (New York: McGraw-Hill, 1950), pp. 500-512; O. W. Wilson, Police Records (Chicago: Public Administration Service, 1942), pp. 240-242.

accompanies them, expressed in terms of Class 1 offenses, miscellaneous complaints, property loss, and arrests. Second, hazards may be measured by the amount of routine duty time required to protect the city properly against them. A good patrolman will off-set the special hazards on his beat by trying the doors and examining the windows more frequently.

It is a relatively simple matter to determine the number of times the doors and windows of the various stores and commercial establishments should be tried during the various tours of duty, and it is likewise a simple matter to determine the average time required for each store tried. When the total number of tries is known, the total time devoted to trying store doors and windows is easily obtained. Similar time tests will determine the average amount of time required in the inspection of pool halls, theaters, rooming houses, garages, and other places which may require regular inspection. Thus it is possible to determine the total routine duty time, and this will be somewhat proportional to the police hazards.

The data from the police department records, then, will indicate the percentage of complaints, Class 1 offenses, arrests, and property loss which fall on each platoon and likewise the relative load of routine duty time falling on each platoon. If it is found that one platoon carries 45 per cent of the load; then that platoon should normally have 45 per cent of the available resources of the force.

The next task is to divide the city into beats for each platoon so that each beat will carry about an equal portion of the load. If there are ten patrolmen available for a given platoon, then the city must be divided into 10 beats in which all of the various factors which go to make up the police service to be performed will average about 1/10 of the total. As before, factors to be considered are complaints, arrests, residence of truants, area, and routine duty time.

While a system of beat distribution based on these methods will not be perfect, it will be far in advance of the system of distribution based entirely upon guess. Further progress toward the goal of a satisfactory beat formula will probably be developed by isolating the above-mentioned factors and adding to them many others, determining the relative value of each as a crime determinant and as a crime deterrent. Then instead of giving an equal weight to a few of the factors, as is done at present, each factor could be weighted in proportion to its value as a crime deterrent or crime determinant.

Cost Accounting

Several brief examples will indicate how cost accounting can be applied as a measurement tool for the analysis and control of departmental operations and in decision-making.

Motorized Equipment. A cost accounting system is used in Meridian, Miss., to support factually a rational replacement policy and to achieve efficiency in vehicle operations. A central garage and supply room are operated as a working capital fund. Purchases of supplies are first charged to the supply room and then by means of an individual charge sheet (in duplicate) directly to the vehicle being serviced or repaired. All charges are broken down into the following accounts: fuel, oil, lubrication and service, tires and tubes, outside repairs, repair parts, labor, and total net cost. The original order is filed at the municipal garage by vehicle number and the duplicate is forwarded to the central bookkeeper for recording.

The monthly totals are tabulated and transferred to an individual equipment record.

The latter form also includes charges for insurance, depreciation, and overhead, thus giving a total operating cost by months for a year's period. Vehicle costs per mile, miles per gallon of gasoline or per hour's run, and cost per hour can readily be obtained from the compiled data, and become the basis for administrative control and planning.[11]

Street Cleaning. In Quincy, Mass., the problem arose of measurement in street cleaning activities. Comments of the City Manager indicate some special aspects of the problem: "In creating the work unit of measurement for street cleaning it would be desirable to select factors which would have some ability to disclose the type of debris generally removed and the source of this material. Management planning must consider alternate methods of eliminating the debris as well as more efficient and economical means of removal.

"Perhaps one of the most costly items in street cleaning for northern cities is the removal in the spring of the sand and cinders used during the winter months for ice control. This material spread by city forces becomes a problem for removal on street surfaces, catch basins and storm sewer mains. Yet this cost can be practically eliminated by the adoption of ice control measures employing soluble ice control chemicals. Cost figures should be able to indicate the relative advantages of one method over the other. There then develops a relationship between street cleaning, snow removal and ice control for which there does not seem to be any justification in the eyes of either the engineer, the public works director of the finance officer but which looms large in the problem of management planning. The selection of the work unit of measurement must be approached with full recognition of these complications."[12]

Office Operations. The City of San Diego, Calif., has applied cost accounting to clerical operations. The measurement units listed below were established for office activities incident to the administration of city licenses and sales tax. The standard unit man-hours were developed after the entire procedure had been subjected to a thorough methods study, advantageous revisions accomplished, and personnel trained in the new methods. The unit man-hour standards were established by the same trained analyst who had made the methods revisions and trained the employees in their application. The standards were developed operation by operation through a combined method of actual on-the-spot observations for repetitive operations and estimates based on past experience for the more elusive elements. Where operations were performed on machines of fixed operating speeds, machine time was computed from the known speed of the machine with observed handling time and normal allowances added to complete the standard.

The work units used were:

1. Number of combined business licenses and sales tax permits issued to licensees for the first time.
2. Number of business license renewal applications prepared and mailed.
3. Number of renewal business licenses issued.
4. Number of business license delinquent notices mailed.
5. Number of sales tax returns prepared and mailed.
6. Number of completed sales tax returns processed.
7. Number of sales tax delinquent notices mailed.
8. Number of dog licenses issued.

---

[11] The American City, March, 1956, p. 164. An installation in University City, Mo. is described in Victor A. Ellman, "Equipment Cost Accounting," Municipal Finance, August, 1956, pp. 14-17.

[12] Wm. J. Deegan, Jr., "Public Works Cost and Work Unit Measurements," Municipal Finance, November, 1952, pp. 73-75.

9. Allowance for the part of the group leader's time actually spent in supervision using the hours worked by employees supervised as the work unit.
10. Allowance for handling telephone or personal requests for information based on the total actual working hours for the group.

Wherever possible, work units were selected which could be accumulated as a by-product of an essential operation. For example, the register on a mailing machine counted the pieces mailed, and an IBM accounting machine (tabulator) furnished a count of business licenses and sales tax permits as a by-product of preparing revenue summaries.

The cost control reports served several purposes. Tabulations of periodic reports furnished excellent supporting data for annual budget requests. The establishment of standards furnished all levels of supervision with yardsticks, and any unfavorable variation in the relationship between actual and standard performance directed attention to unauthorized changes in established methods which might otherwise remain undetected.[13]

Standards in Building and Safety Inspection

In the city of Los Angeles the Building and Safety Department consists of several divisions. Some years ago the Bureau of Budget and Efficiency, after investigating the nature of the inspectional work in four divisions, and after examination of statistics of prior years and consultation with independent contractors and engineers, set up the following standards:

Table 1

STANDARDS FOR INSPECTIONAL WORK

Unit of Measurement	Standard for			
	Building Division	Electrical Division	Plumbing Division	Heating & Ventilating Division
Average number of inspections required per permit	5	2.25	2.6	2.3
Average number of inspections possible per man-day	25	15	22	22
Mileage per inspection	.78	1.50	1.30	1.50
Plans to be checked by a man per day	3.8	--	--	--

The standards are used to determine the personnel requirements of the Department, to prepare and control the department's budget, to adjust personnel requirements during the year, and to increase departmental efficiency. The following are a few examples: On the basis of past records plus forecasts of building trends, it is possible to estimate the number of permits likely to be issued, and thus to arrive at the number of inspections required. Again, a knowledge of the number of inspections to be made and the mileage

---

[13] Abstracted from Orin K. Cope, "Cost Controls for Office Operations," Municipal Finance, February, 1950, pp. 117-122.

per inspection, makes it possible to estimate the number of miles to be traveled and the amount to be allowed for travel expenses in the budget. Finally, the standards can be used as a basis for increasing the efficiency of work performed and reducing costs. If, for example, the mileage per inspection increases over a period, the causes are determined and appropriate action taken.[14]

Performance Budgeting in Hospitals

New York State has made trial performance budget installations in six of its hospitals. The development of standard unit costs for various hospital activities is being built upon basic standards of performance. Where these are absent, the budget examiners have assumed standards, thereby making administrators standard conscious and inviting a re-examination of existing practices to determine their effectiveness and efficiency.

Using a work program as a base, each hospital prepares a "Quarterly Financial Analysis" in which — in addition to consumption and inventory data — it makes the following comparisons:

1. Actual and planned workload
2. Actual and planned expenditures
3. Expenditure requirements based on actual and planned workloads

The quarterly report was selected as the best period for analysis of performance. Monthly reports would probably show variations in one month that might "wash out" in the next, while reports for longer than quarterly intervals might show need for remedial action too late to be useful.

Under performance budgeting, the supervisor of each activity becomes responsible for budgeting, cost control and program operations. Thus the heads of the out-patient service, laboratory, food service, and laundry have dual responsibilities — program content and money — where before their primary concern was program. Cost consciousness is developed at the "firing line," which is the only place where economy of operations can ultimately be achieved.

As for the hospital administrator, he is provided with the same type of information as the supervisor. In addition to appraising performance, the administrator uses the reports as tools for financial planning and for choosing between alternative courses of action.[15]

Measurement in Library Service

Three studies might be abstracted to show the types of progress made by librarians in developing methods of measurement. One study was the result of the cooperation of thirty-seven public libraries.[16] The techniques involved the measurement of time expended in each phase of library operation and determination of the cost of each operation from salaries paid and other expenditures. Each library recorded over a four-month period, April and May in the spring and October and November in the fall of the study year, the time distribution of each professional and nonprofessional worker. Workload statistics were accumulated on certain major areas, such as information and reference

---

[14] Municipal Finance Officers Association, Governmental Cost Accounting In The Los Angeles Area (Chicago: The Association, 1941), pp. 8-9.

[15] Abstracted from Daniel Klepak, "Performance Budgeting for Hospitals and Institutions," Municipal Finance, August, 1956, pp. 17-24.

[16] E. V. Baldwin and W. E. Marcus, Library Costs and Budgets (New York: R. R. Bowker Co., 1941).

questions answered, books purchased, catalogued and circulated, volumes bound or discarded, and so forth.

Seventeen of the cooperating libraries actually used the results of the study in modifying their organizational structure and administrative practices. Unproductive time recorded was analyzed and staff shifts became possible, work space for processing books was rearranged, registration procedures simplified, professional staff was relieved of nonprofessional duties and the duties shifted to clerical workers — these were some of the positive results later reported. The importance of specific job descriptions was established and of training procedures related to actual work done. As to techniques, measurement of reference work and assistance to groups was found to be essential to supplement circulation data as a measure of library effectiveness.

A later time and work unit study broadened its purpose and base.[17] The purpose was not normative standards but a tested approach to the use of time studies and work units which could be applied by any size public library for a self-evaluation of its administrative and management procedures. A Report on Time and Work Units, and detailed instructions for its use, were reproduced. All library activities were broken down into 21 operations and each item classified as professional or nonprofessional, thus indicating whether it required the attention of a professionally trained worker or not. The measurement period extended over only two weeks, but detailed measurements were carried out in three public libraries, and a broad base of sixty cooperating libraries was covered by questionnaire. This study greatly improved the time-cost methodological approach in library surveys.

A third study measured the quality of library book service.[18] A list of books was selected for quality. The standards for selection were that a library should provide up-to-date materials dealing with important personal and social issues; and that such materials should satisfy the criteria of both accuracy and literacy. A total of 350 titles resulted, consisting of 243 nonfiction, 94 substantial fiction, 12 mystery stories, and one light romance.

The survey team then checked against this high-quality list the book collections of libraries in six large cities. For each title it was ascertained from the union catalogue whether the library had it in the main collection and how many of its branches held at least one copy. It was concluded from this study that raw circulation data leave much to be desired as an index of library service. Assuming an educational objective, the library which makes a good showing in supplying socially important books is doing a better job than one lax in this respect. The need was underscored for some way in which this more important job could be evaluated in quantitative terms. A further result of this study was some tangible proof that branches in a large city library system do not fare alike in quality of book service.

Methods of Analyzing the Fire Problem[19]

A final illustration of the use of measurement in administrative research is the statistical analysis of fire department operations. Necessary data would include information on what there is to burn and what is burning and where.

---

[17] Watson O'D. Pierce, Work Measurement in Public Libraries (New York: Social Science Research Council, 1949).

[18] Leon Carnovsky, "Measurement in Library Service," in Current Issues in Library Administration (Chicago: University of Chicago Press, 1939), pp. 240-263.

[19] Abstracted from Municipal Fire Administration (Chicago: International City Managers' Association, 1956), pp. 6-14. This is the textbook for the correspondence course of the same name offered by the Institute for Training in Municipal Administration. For an alternative approach see also Simon, Shepard, and Sharp, Fire Losses and Fire Risks (Berkeley, California: Bureau of Public Administration, 1943).

What There Is To Burn

In order to understand the fire problem in any city it is necessary first of all to know what there is to burn. Certain sections of the city may represent a considerable fire hazard, while the hazard in other sections may not be particularly serious. In most cities there are three principal types of building construction: fire resistive, brick, and frame. The type of construction is important because the character and arrangement of the building affect not only its own fire hazard but that of the contents as well.

A map of the entire city indicating what areas are built up is helpful in showing what there is to burn. Large-scale maps should show fire resistive and brick construction. By comparing the latter maps with one showing the built-up areas, the portions occupied by frame construction can be visualized. In some blocks there is practically no fire break of any importance for a thousand feet or more, which indicates that the possibility of fire is very marked because of the concentration of frame construction.

Another map of the downtown area should show approximate districts according to areas of like building construction and general occupancy. For example, there may be an office building district, a general wholesale district, a manufacturing and warehouse district, a central retail district, and a market district. Such a map, accompanied by a detailed description of building construction in each area, is extremely helpful in studying the fire problem. Superimposed upon it, or on a separate map, should be marked the location of fire resistive and "sprinklered" buildings. These maps, together with other maps and a detailed study of the construction in each district, help to indicate what there is to burn in a city.

When a comprehensive picture of building conditions has been obtained, the question arises as to what is being done about them. For example, what is the effect of the building code on the construction of new buildings and the remodeling of old ones? What are the requirements of the zoning ordinance, and how do these requirements tie in with the building code? A study of the building code may reveal that it has been frequently altered and amended resulting in a disconnected, confused, and conflicting mass of regulations, often with serious omissions. Sometimes the code may operate to discourage the erection of good buildings.

Another step in analyzing fire problems involves the study of the common fire hazards likely to be found in any occupancy: matches — smoking; housekeeping; lockers and cupboards; wiping rags and waste; oily materials; packing materials, combustible fibers, locomotive sparks, sparks on roofs; bearings, power transmission, mechanical ruptures; grinding wheels; blower systems; air conditioning; sun rays; lamps, lanterns, torches; construction operations; fumigation; and fireworks.

A study of the various hazards in relation to occupancy in a given city will give fire department officials a great deal of information as to where fires are likely to occur, the danger of fire when it has started, and how best to attack it. In order to obtain the detailed information about an occupancy it is necessary to make frequent inspections.

An analysis of what there is to burn also should include a detailed study of the different types of property in the city. The picture of a given city's fire experience will be colored by the predominating industry or business. In Grand Rapids, Michigan, the principal industrial fires are in its great furniture factories. Jersey City has its problem of fires in waterfront wharves and piers. In Gloversville, New York, the peculiar susceptibility to smoke and water damage of the fine glove leathers used in its manufacturing plants makes its fire loss record high. Such fire hazards should be charted on a map to show their location.

What Is Burning?

Different means of attack must be used in controlling different kinds of fires, so a study should be made of the fires in which there is a loss. Some alarms, like false alarms are of importance only in causing unnecessary running of apparatus, danger to persons on the street, and lessening of protection while apparatus is out. Fires in buildings, however usually involve some loss. Practically all of the fire losses of a city result from fires which may be classified under the heading of fires in buildings. For practical fire protection purposes, fires in lumber yards, bulk oil storage stations, and fires in raw materials stored in factory yards are considered under this heading.

Building fires should be carefully spotted on a map of the city and studied with a view to evaluating, among other things, such factors as: cause of fire; general type of occupancy; construction of the building; effect of automatic sprinkler protection or lack of this protection; other private fire protection; losses by specific occupancies; exposure protection where a factor; time of day when fire occurred; location of plant with respect to municipal fire protection services; factors responsible for the extent of the loss, and lessons from the fire; and how the fire was fought. An evaluation of such factors, of course, is not possible unless the basic information is available. Fire department reports on fires should be carefully assembled and reported monthly.

In studying the various types of buildings or occupancies in which fires have occurred, an analysis should be made by type of buildings to discover the number of fires and loss for each type. An analysis of loss records may show, as it did in Boston, that one-third of the total loss in building fires was in residence buildings and that of the total loss in such buildings, in a certain year, nearly 80 per cent was in multiple-tenant buildings. The significance of this is that fire departments should inspect all such dwellings thoroughly.

One of the most significant studies of fire losses is by specific occupancy involved. Fire hazards vary more because of occupancy or combinations of occupancy than because of any one other factor. For example, an analysis should be made of the number of fires in each type of occupancy, total loss, and percentage of total fire loss. Such an analysis is especially important in the larger cities with regard to nonresidential buildings. The occupancy data should be sufficiently detailed to be meaningful. For instance, dwelling fires should not be lumped into a single class with no data as to the size of the buildings or whether they are one or two-family private residences or apartments housing numerous facilities. Likewise storehouses and warehouses of all kinds should not be lumped together with no data as to trade or type of manufacture involved.

In order to define those areas of the city with considerable fire hazards a series of spot maps of fires in buildings should be made. These spot maps show that certain sections of the city have more fires with greater losses than others. For this reason they serve the very useful purpose of defining districts where inspections should be made more frequently and intensively.

A special study should be made of the factors causing large losses, with each fire made the subject of a special study. The number of fires causing large losses should be charted according to the time of day of the fire as well as specific cause or causes. Fires in smaller cities involving losses of more than $1,000 should be subjected to a detailed examination from all angles. For all except the very largest cities, the fires for a five-year period should be taken in order to get enough data from which to draw reliable conclusions. In addition, a separate detailed record of the largest fires should be made.

Even if only a few such fires are put on this list there will be enough to assist in drawing conclusions as to the factors which are contributing to the losses in the city. Fire department officers in charge of these fires should furnish supplementary information on how the fire started, what it burned, why it spread, and how it was fought. Such information is of the greatest value to the fire chief and chief administrator in determining the effectiveness of inspections, the use of equipment at the fire, and other factors.

In the largest cities where a sufficient bulk of data are available, it may be helpful to analyze local fire losses and to compare them with local business conditions. Such a comparison may show the extent to which poor business conditions have been reflected in higher fire losses. The extent of correlation between poor business and high fire losses may establish the relative importance of arson as a factor. Monthly fire loss figures can be used to check the correlation between business conditions and fire losses.

Number of Fires

An analysis of the fire problem involves a study of the number of alarms over a period of years. If there has been an increase in total number of alarms, records should be studied to see in what classes of alarms the increase occurred. For example, a perusal of the locations from which alarms were received within a given period may indicate methods to be taken in reducing false alarms.

The number of chimney fires in a given year can be analyzed according to the number of fires and losses per month in residential buildings and other buildings, by fire districts. The frequency of outdoor fires (rubbish fires around buildings, grass and brush fires, dump fires, and fires in vacant lots) should be compared with daily records of rainfall or relative humidity. These fires can be further analyzed as to causes and how they were extinguished. These are only a few of the ways by which the number of fires may be considered in connection with the losses.

Various Approaches to Measurement

We are concerned here primarily with *how* measurement is done, and only to a limited degree with *who* does it and *when*. As to the latter, measurement is often a continuous, routine process; again a periodic operation. Cost accounting is a continuous process. Daily time sheets, equipment mileage records, garbage collection records, *et cetera*, are routine. Cost analyses, on the other hand, are done when needed. An organization-and-methods team may make a performance study, or a performance and unit cost study, in an activity area, or of a particular operation. Both cost accounting reports and the "O & M" study are for management's use.

Who does the measurement? Many employees may be involved: time clerks, supervisors, statistical clerks and cost clerks; or even at higher levels: cost accountants, budget staff, personnel staff, the organization and methods specialists, statisticians, the city engineer, the traffic engineer, the head of the police records bureau, an administrative assistant to the city manager, the research staff, and perhaps others.

The techniques, or the *how* of measurement, may include several major approaches (and this list is by no means all-inclusive):

Simple counting and recording (by hand or mechanically)

Cost accounting (by jobs or projects, or for continuous operations)

Cost analyses (of a particular operation, activity or program, or of the work of a particular employee or group)

Organization and methods surveys or studies (which may include cost analyses)

Statistical analyses and computations (e.g. correlation of two or more sets of data to determine meaningful relationships)

Mapping (and the showing of related data in proper spatial juxtaposition)

The usefulness of the whole measurement process to management depends primarily upon being able to phrase management problems in such a way that quantitative data can shed light. The goal of measurement, record-keeping, and standards development is to bring to bear at the decision-making point the weight of experience, expressed quantitatively. The staff of management, if it is to do its staff job well, must work and experiment in order that the tools of measurement and the standards being used will become ever more adaptable to the task of assisting management. The job of perfecting measurement devices is not an easy one, and never a finished one, but is a fascinating and rewarding activity.

The Statistical Approach

The administrator will need an elementary knowledge of statistical methods and an understanding of the common uses and abuses of statistics. A few suggestions that he may find useful are presented here, but if at all feasible, he should familiarize himself with a textbook on statistics.

Statistical Terms

Many of the available tabulations of urban statistics do not give data for individual cities but are merely summaries for all the cities of a given population group. The correct use of such data involves an understanding of the summarizing devices which have been employed.

In almost all cases an average is shown. The average of measurements for a group of cities is intended to represent the typical value for those cities. In addition to the familiar arithmetic average (which is affected by the extreme values in the figures), the median is often used. The median is a position average. In a group of items it is that item on each side of which one-half of the total number of cities fall, when the items have been arranged in order of size. Thus the median of 21 cities, with respect to per capita library circulation, is the city with the eleventh largest per capita circulation.

An average, whether it be an arithmetic average or a median, is in no sense a standard. The average number of municipal employees in 1949 in cities over 500,000 population was 17.1 per 1,000 population. This does not mean that cities of that size should have that precise number of employees but merely that the average city did have that number. The goal of the administrator is not to provide average service at average cost but to provide the highest possible level of service at the lowest possible cost consistent with sound personnel policies. Averages can indicate only what cities are now accomplishing, not what could be accomplished through intelligent administration. The average is a measure of mediocrity, not of perfection.

Of equal importance are measures of dispersion, which show how closely the individual items adhere to the average, or how widely they are distributed around the average.

The four simplest measures of dispersion are: (1) the lowest item, (2) the first quartile, (3) the third quartile, and (4) the highest item. The lowest and highest items are self-explanatory and indicate the total range covered by the items. The quartiles are similar to the median. When the items are arranged in order of increasing size, the first quartile is that value below which three-quarters of the items lie. Thus one-half of all the items fall in the range between the first and third quartiles. Thus, in a tabulation of salaries in a given department, the lowest salary might be $3000; the first quartile $4000; the median $5000; the third quartile $6000; and the highest figure $9000. In other words, all the employees receive $3000 or more; one fourth between $3000-$4000; a second fourth between $4000-$5000; a third fourth between $5000-$6000; and the upper fourth between $6000-$9000.

Comparison of the statistics of an individual city with the average will indicate only whether it is out of line with usual practices and suggest the need for further analysis of operations. Comparison with quartiles and range will indicate how far the city departs from the typical and will help to determine whether the deviation is of sufficient magnitude to be significant.

Per Capita Data

One additional measure deserves special consideration. This is the measurement index reduced to a per capita basis. It is often assumed that by reducing statistics to a per capita basis valid comparisons between cities can be made. A consideration of why statistics are reduced to per capitas will help to explain both the uses and limitations of such data.

Statistics are reduced to a per capita basis because population is a rough measure of the magnitude of the governmental problem. Therefore an index reduced to a per capita basis will have the same significance as if it were divided by some other measure of problem-magnitude. An index of results reduced to per capita will be a measure of adequacy of service.

The usefulness of such an index is severely limited by the fact that population is only a very crude measure of problem-magnitude. Fire risk, for instance, is related directly to the amount and type of burnable property and only indirectly to population. The per capita fire risk will therefore vary with valuation per capita and with types of property, and per capita fire loss is only a very approximate measure of adequacy of service. And similarly, the street cleaning problem is measured by the length and type of streets, a factor that is only indirectly related to population.

A further limitation on the usefulness of the per capita data is that accurate population statistics are available for only a very limited time after each decennial census. A procedure, however, has been developed whereby the United States Bureau of the Census conducts a special, intercensal population count at the request and expense of the local government.[20]

Measures of performance per capita, effort per capita, and cost per capita are even more severely limited in their usefulness. Since they fail to measure the level of service, they are in no sense indices of efficiency. A high per capita cost may indicate (1) that population does not adequately measure problem-magnitude, that is, that climatic, structural, economic, social, or other extra-governmental factors affect the problem;

---

[20] The International City Managers' Association, The Municipal Year Book, 1957 (Chicago: The Association), pp. 28-32 gives further details.

(2) that the level of service provided is high; (3) that the activity is being inefficiently administered. Thus, a high expenditure for the fire department may result from a high per capita fire risk, from a successful effort to keep losses at a very low level, or from inefficient administration of the fire department.

Without further information about the problem-magnitude and the actual level of service, it is impossible to determine which is the correct answer. However, if care is taken to compare cities which are similar in type and situation, and if allowance is made for unusual conditions, then per capita statistics will be very useful to the administrator in focusing attention on problems and suggesting questions to be answered by further investigation.

Limitations on Statistics

Statistics on urban government should not be used without a full recognition of their limitations. The first of these limitations is accuracy. The original data must usually be compiled from questionnaires returned by individual cities. In many cases there is little or no uniformity in the local records systems from which replies to the questionnaire are compiled. Furthermore, questions may be differently interpreted by the persons answering them. In the case of statistics compiled by reliable agencies, every attempt is usually made, however, to increase the accuracy and validity of the statistics by cross-checking data derived from different sources and by following up questionable returns. The probable margin of error can be determined only by a careful analysis of the kind of data involved and the means by which the data were obtained. Refined analysis of the data beyond the limits of their accuracy is an unjustifiable waste of time and energy.

The problem of comparability has already been raised. Operating statistics cannot be compared between cities unless consideration is given to the relative magnitude of the governmental problem, the level of service provided, and the cost. Cities differ in population, age, sex, and race distribution; in the pattern of land use, the types and distributions of structures and occupancies; in industries and occupations; in economic and social characteristics; in physiography and climate. All of these factors will influence the operation of city government and will invalidate any comparisons in which they are not considered.

Another factor in comparability is the variability in organization and functions of city governments. Services which are normally provided by counties in one part of the country may be provided by cities in other states. This is the case with welfare functions, which are generally administered by cities in New England and by counties elsewhere. The line of demarcation between private and public facilities may also shift from one city to another. The visiting nurse service may be administered by the health department in one city and by private charity in another.

Finally, each unit of measurement must be assigned its true significance. A cost index cannot be used to measure results nor an index of problem intensity to measure performance. Efficiency can be determined only from a consideration of accomplishments in relation to cost.

Proper Use of Statistics

With all these limitations on their use, what good are urban statistics, and what justification is there for publishing them? First of all, summary figures for various population groups are valuable as indicating trends in costs, performance, and accomplishments. Second, it is useful to compare the figures for individual cities with the averages for cities of similar size as a starting point for further analysis. If a city is employing many more employees per 1,000 population than the average, it must find valid justification in unusual climatic or other conditions, superior and more extensive services, or conclude that employment is excessive. The latter conclusion should lead the city to search for the fault.

Third, the information for individual cities can be significantly combined with other data which may be at hand. The annual budget of a personnel agency acquires new significance if related to the number of employees. Information regarding individual departments helps to explain aggregate data for the government as a whole. Fourth, with due care the information for individual cities enables city officials to make comparisons with other cities similarly situated. For example, the official of a wealthy suburb may want to compare salaries with those of other wealthy suburbs. Again, an official of an industrial city of 100,000 population may want to make comparisons with other cities of the industrial type and of similar size.

Adequate Record-Keeping for Measurement

The Importance of Records

The information needed for statistical research can be obtained only if adequate records are maintained. Records, to be adequate, must produce the information needed for administrative purposes, must produce it promptly, must produce it without an excessive amount of "paper work." Records do not exist for their own sake, and they can be justified only in so far as they are necessary and useful for administrative purposes.

Few cities today have records which approach even minimum standards of adequacy and efficiency. This does not mean that the installation of adequate records will be a costly process for those cities which do not now have them. It was found in a large eastern city that careful records of individual fire losses had been kept for a period of 15 years. Not once throughout this whole period had anyone thought to add up these losses or to analyze them by cause or by type of structures involved. With record-keeping of this type the administrator can have no patience. What the administrator needs is not more records but better records if he is to have adequate tools for self-appraisal and effective current control.

Even in small cities which may not have a performance budget or cost accounting records, and will probably lack trained statistical personnel, much can be done. An outside consultant may have to be hired, or technical assistance enlisted from talent in local business firms or a neighboring college or university. How much record-keeping can the city afford? How much can it afford not to do? What is feasible, and what will more than pay for itself, will require very careful study.

Records maintained by cities should conform to national standards, for two reasons. In the first place, a system based upon records which have been developed by agencies of national scope after considerable research and consultation will, if properly adapted, be far superior to a system based on the limited experience of a single city. In the second place, use of nationally accepted records will allow the gradual development of a valuable body of statistical knowledge about American cities, compiled by the individual cities on a somewhat comparable basis. The Uniform Crime Reports, published by the Federal Bureau of Investigation, are illustrative of what can be done through the voluntary cooperation of local officials.

Model Records Systems and Comparative Statistics

Model records systems which can be used with slight adaptation by almost all cities are available in a number of fields. In measuring police service, *Uniform Crime Reporting*, published by the International Association of Chiefs of Police and the Federal Bureau of Investigation, and *Police Records*, by O. W. Wilson, published by Public Administration Service will provide a guide which should be closely followed. In the fire field, the standard records manual is the *Model Records and Reporting System for Fire Departments*, by DeWayne E. Nolting, published jointly by the National Fire Protection Association and Public Administration Service. In public works, there is available a *Manual of Public Works Records and Administration*, based upon an installation made by the research staff of the International City Managers' Association in Flint, Michigan. This manual is based upon the recommendations of the Committee on Uniform Street and Sanitation Records and is also published by Public Administration Service. For public health departments, a standard work by the Commonwealth Fund contains a chapter on record forms and their construction.[21] The Committee on Statistics for Public Recreation, a committee of the National Recreation Association has developed a Manual on Recording Services of Public Recreation Departments. In the welfare field, wide differences in administrative organization in different jurisdictions make standardization difficult. However, some agencies will find useful a little manual entitled, *Substitute Handbook on Statistical Recording and Reporting in Family Service Agencies*, Family Service Association of America, 1956. Satisfactory records are not yet available in the fields of education, libraries, personnel, and planning.

For the city's financial records, the various publications of the National Committee on Governmental Accounting should be consulted. In several states, accounting manuals have been published which reconcile the recommendations of this committee with state law.

Cooperation between the American Water Works Association and the Municipal Finance Officers' Association led to the preparation of a complete system of waterworks accounting based upon the Uniform Classification of Accounts for Water and Electric Utilities of the National Association of Railway and Utilities Commissioners.[22] As the use of this system, which is easily adapted to any type of utility, increases, better comparison between the many municipal utilities will be possible, and comparisons between public and private utilities will be facilitated.

In addition to data obtained from his own records, the administrator will find statistics from other cities useful to him. *The Municipal Year Book*[23] includes each year a list of sources of municipal statistics. This list is a guide to those published compilations of statistics which show comparative data for a number of individual cities. Most of these statistical sources are readily accessible or available at nominal cost. The administrator should be thoroughly familiar with them.

Organization for Record Keeping

What personnel is needed for operating records and what should be its place in the organization? To what extent should records be departmentalized, and to what extent

---

[21] See Frances King and Louis L. Feldman, Office Management for Health Workers (Chicago: Harvard University Press, 1949), 164 pp.

[22] The system is published as Manual of Waterworks Accounting (Chicago: Municipal Finance Officers' Association 1938).

[23] Published annually by the International City Managers' Association.

centralized? What agency or official should be responsible for statistical research? Specific answers cannot be given to all of these questions since they will depend in large measure upon the size and organization of the city, but several considerations must be kept in mind if the records are to reach maximum effectiveness.

Several questions must be asked about each element of the records system: (1) Who will fill out these forms, and (2) who will use the information contained in them? (3) What agency in the city hall has the equipment and trained personnel necessary for the operation of these records? (4) What is the attitude of departmental officials toward the records? If department heads are aware of the usefulness of records procedures and eager to employ them for administrative purposes, a greater measure of departmentalization may be allowed than when the departmental officials are suspicious of records and condemn them as "so much paper work." Conversely, if a managerial or auxiliary agency is able to produce the desired information promptly enough for the administrative needs of the department, the records can usually be operated centrally with more economy than if they are departmentalized. This principle is especially important in the case of cost records, where there is usually wasteful duplication if departmentalization is necessary.

Departmentalization of records should not be permitted to impede cross-fertilization through the interchange of information between departments. The department which is in the best position to obtain information for a particular set of records is not necessarily the department which will make most use of them. Somewhere in a city hall a coordinating agency is needed where situations requiring interchange of information can be recognized and procedures developed to effect the interchange. The agency which will usually be best adapted to the task of coordinating records work in the city hall is the administrative research and planning unit. In the small city, especially, this agency can perform a valuable service, maintaining equipment and trained personnel, and carrying out research projects which would be beyond the resources of individual departments. In the large city, its work will be to a larger degree that of coordinating the records activities of the individual departments.

Personnel Needs. If records and statistics are to be effectively used, there must be somewhere in the city hall at least one man who has more than an elementary knowledge of statistical methods. The task of designing and utilizing records is more than a clerical job and requires a high level of training and imagination. It should not be expected that valuable results will be forthcoming from records if the direction of the system is entrusted to untrained clerks. The statistician should preferably be a college graduate with specialized training in statistics.

In larger cities, similarly trained statisticians should be available in the various departments. The police department in a city over 100,000 population can profitably use a full-time statistician as a part of its records division staff. In a somewhat larger city, the health department should have the services of a statistician with special training in vital statistics. Even if cost records are centrally maintained, a cost accountant should be attached to the public works directors' offices in the larger cities.

Tabulating Equipment. The analysis, classification, and reclassification of records data constitute a long and painstaking job and for all except the simplest analyses may entail considerable clerical expense. Most cities over 50,000 population will find that an installation of special tabulating equipment can be economically used. Cities of 10,000 population or more can make good use of tabulating equipment at a central service bureau which is owned and operated by a tabulating machine company. In such cases a small city can save money by having tax bills run off or other routine tabulating tasks handled in a short time at low cost.

With the rapid developments of recent years in mechanical and electronic data processing machinery even the small city would do well to be alert for the marketing of high-speed data-processing equipment priced for the city's pocketbook. Intermunicipal ownership and operation offers real possibilities for economical compilation and analysis of data.

Statistical Research. As has already been suggested, in the small city the statistical analysis of records data will be part of the work of the statistician attached to the central research agency. In all but the smallest cities the individual departments will wish to make statistical analyses of the data for their own use, and the statistician should be available for advice and consultation in laying out and carrying through such projects.

Census Tracts. Data gathered by the United States Bureau of the Census are ordinarily available only in the form of summary statistics for the entire city. A few simple items such as total population can usually be obtained for individual enumeration districts, but the boundaries of these districts are changed from time to time so that there is no comparability from one census to the next.

In cities over 100,000 population and their adjacent areas the Census Bureau is willing to lay out census tract areas (usually between 3000 to 6000 population) and to make available certain population and other data for these individual tracts.[24] Cities are tracted upon request of local officials or other interested agencies who wish to make use of the data. The value of tracting lies not only in the relative permanence[25] of the areas from census to census and in the data made available by the Census Bureau, but in the fact that all other statistical data which are being gathered in the city may be classified on a tract basis. Thus crime records, fires, cases of communicable diseases, and all other matters upon which the city is gathering data can be allocated to the same set of census tract areas. In this way, the relationships among a host of different but interdependent phenomena can be detected as a basis for cooperation between city departments dealing with different aspects of the same problem and as a clue to the better understanding of the structure and operation of the city. Even in cities too small to be tracted by the Census Bureau, permanent districts of from 3,000 to 6,000 population each should be laid out by agreement among the various city departments as a basis for the uniform compilation of all city data.

Housing reports in which characteristics of dwelling units are shown by blocks are available on each of 209 cities of 50,000 population or more, following the *U.S. Census of Housing - 1950*. The blocks in turn are grouped by census tracts which permits correlation of these valuable social and economic data with other census tract statistics.

Coordination. It is an obvious point, but sometimes overlooked, that someone must be responsible for the "system" of administrative measurement. Cost accountants may keep the cost records and the work performance data, and others may keep additional information. Someone, however, must coordinate and mold the separate segments into a workable system. Equally important, he must be responsible for research and study as to how the system can be improved, and how more and more administrative problems can be resolved by measurement data which the system can develop. Top administrators, if genuinely interested in scientific management, will insist on such continuous effort toward improvement.

---

[24] Not all census tract data are published. Unpublished statistics are available upon request at a small cost. See U. S. Censuses of Population and Housing: 1950, Key to Published and Tabulated Data for Small Areas (Washington, D. C.: United States Government Printing Office, 1951).

[25] The tracts are intended to remain unchanged from census to census, but occasionally special situations require boundary changes.

In few cities have the possibilities for cooperation among the various city departments in securing data necessary for administrative purposes been fully exploited. For instance, data on the land use pattern in a city have been exceedingly difficult to obtain, and usually have been secured, if at all, only on the basis of costly periodic surveys which are soon out of date. Land use data are almost indispensable to planning commissions, to assessment bodies, to housing authorities, to fire and police departments, to public works departments, in planning city services, and in numerous other aspects of city affairs. Much information on land use and occupancy is constantly flowing into the building inspector's office, the fire department records, and the assessor's office. Yet in few cities have cooperative techniques been developed for maintaining current up-to-date files of land utilization data. Here is a striking example of the possibilities which lie in interdepartmental cooperation for statistical and research purposes.[26]

Records Functions of the Finance Department. Another municipal department that will play an important part in the records activities is the finance department. This department will of course maintain all general accounting records. In addition, it is the logical agency for the operation of cost accounting procedures. It must be remembered, however, that it is the individual department heads and the administrator who will be the principal users of cost accounting data, and that the system should be developed to meet their needs. If the finance department is unable to maintain sufficient flexibility to produce promptly and completely the information required by department heads and by the chief administrator, then it will be necessary to consider departmentalizing cost accounts. At any rate, the services of the finance department in suggesting uses and assisting in the interpretation of cost data should be available to department heads.

---

[26]The larger the city the greater may be the need for coordination. See, for example, the guide, Statistical and Research Activities of Municipal Welfare, Health and Education Agencies of New York City, (New York: Welfare and Health Council of New York City, January 1955). 31 pp.

Chapter 13

PUBLIC RELATIONS AND PUBLIC REPORTING

The managerial function of administrative representation includes not only the establishment of satisfactory relations with the council and with external agencies — both public and private — but also the establishment of good relations with the public. The first part of this chapter is largely concerned with those aspects of administrative representation commonly regarded as "public relations" activities. The latter part deals with techniques in the more restricted field of public reporting.

I. Public Relations

Meaning and Scope

What is the meaning of "public relations"? The simplest definition is also the broadest, for public relations as applied to government is no less than the sum total of all the contacts, attitudes, impressions, and opinions that constitute the relationships between the public and its government. For present purposes, however, this definition needs to be refined.

Part of the confusion surrounding the term "public relations" is due to its use to describe both cause and effect. That is, it is applied both to the relationship between the government and the public and to the factors affecting the relationship. To avoid confusion in this chapter, the term "public relations" will be used only to refer to the relationship, and other terms — e.g., public relations program or public relations activities — will be employed to refer to policies and activities which are designed to improve that relationship.

Objectives of a Public Relations Program

The objective of a public relations program is to improve the relationship between the city government and the public and this involves a two-way relationship. The program which seeks to improve that relationship must of necessity concern itself with the attitudes and actions of both parties. No public relations program can be entirely successful if it succeeds in securing favorable public attitudes of confidence, respect and approval toward the government without also fostering among the public officials an attitude of respect and good will toward the public. Such an official attitude is necessary both as a means and as an end. It is a means in that it is itself a strong appeal for public confidence and approval. A government that shows no respect or friendliness toward the public is seldom rewarded with public support. As an end, a favorable official attitude toward the public is essential in any democratic form of government, for a government that is contemptuous of and unresponsive toward the public is by its nature undemocratic.

This analysis of the objectives of a public relations program must also concern itself with methods and means of achieving these objectives. Even if it is agreed that the objective is to secure a relationship based upon mutual respect, confidence, and good will, it does not necessarily follow that every action or device that may produce favorable attitudes may properly be included in a public relations program. This caution applies particularly, of course, to means of securing public good will toward government. It must be admitted that public support and approval can be — and often have been — obtained by trickery and sleight-of-hand methods. Specious arguments, false information, and "glad-hander" tactics have so often achieved popular favor — at least temporarily — that these methods are commonly thought to be the substance of a public relations program. Fortunately this is not true. Good public relations can be fairly earned by practices which are in themselves worthwhile and need no apology. It is with such means that the program to be outlined in this chapter will be concerned.

The Scope of Public Relations

Since public relations has been defined as the sum total of all the relationships between city government and members of the public, and since the principal objective of a public relations program is to improve those relationships, the program must obviously be broad enough in its scope to embrace all of the factors affecting the relationship. What are these factors?

In the first place, the policies of the city government — as expressed in ordinances, resolutions, regulations, and orders — are important. Certainly no city government can expect to have satisfactory public relations if its policies do not meet with public approval. Secondly, the competence and efficiency of the city administration directly affect public relations. The public cannot be expected to react favorably to a city government that does not carry out its policies in an efficient and economical manner. This factor of competence needs, of course, to be broken down into a number of component elements — quality of employees, adequacy of organization, effectiveness of methods, and so forth.

At first glance it might appear that these two factors are so predominantly important as to reduce other considerations to triviality. Surely, it may be argued, any city government that adopts policies that are both wise and in accord with public opinion and that administers these policies efficiently and economically will have good public relations. These factors are basic, and it would be a sad commentary on democratic government if they were not heavily weighted in the public's appraisal of its local government. But they are far from being the only important factors.

Both of these factors of policy and competence need to be supplemented by a third — public knowledge and understanding of city government activities. Even the wisest policies and the most efficient administration will fail to produce good public relations if the citizens do not know about them. Public reporting and publicity are therefore essential elements in the public relations program. Although they are not sufficient in themselves to produce an enlightened public opinion, they are important steps toward that objective.

In addition, there are a number of factors which, although they may seem to be of minor importance individually, have a very important aggregate effect on public relations. It is not necessary to refer to authorities in psychology to prove that such "little things" as courtesy, appearance, and convenience are important factors in any human relationship. Personal contacts between citizens and public servants are a factor of prime importance in public relations. This applies both to face-to-face contacts and to indirect contacts through the media of correspondence and the telephone. Physical appearances are also important, and this includes the appearance of public buildings, property, and equipment as well as the appearance of public employees themselves. Finally, procedures may be listed as a factor affecting public relations — i.e., procedures which directly involve the citizen, such, for example, as those affecting the place, time, and manner of tax collection and the application for and granting of licenses.

Limitations on Program

Although it has been emphasized that the policies and the administrative efficiency of the city government are important elements in the program, neither of these factors will be given any special attention in this chapter.

The program suggested here starts with the assumption that the city deserves good, or at least improved, public relations on the basis of its present policies and operating efficiency. But a government that concerns itself only with basic policies and efficiency falls short of providing the service which the people demand and have a right to expect. Efficiency does not preclude public convenience. Human values are no less real than material values. Competence is not impaired by courtesy. In brief, there need be no conflict between these elements of a public relations program. They supplement each other, and all must be brought into balance if the city is to secure, and deserve, the respect and confidence of the public.

Formulating a Public Relations Program

Now that "public relations" has been defined and the scope of a public relations program has been outlined, it is necessary to analyze briefly the several steps in formulating and establishing a comprehensive program. The following steps are suggested as a logical sequence:

1. Appraisal of present relationship between the city government and the public. This step may in turn be broken down into two principal tasks: first, the identification of the several different groups which constitute the public and, second, the determination of the attitudes of each of these groups toward the city government or any of its component agencies and, in so far as possible, the explanation of these attitudes.

2. Survey and criticism of present administrative policies, contacts, procedures, attitudes, and so forth, in an attempt to explain present public attitudes. This survey, combined with the appraisal described in step (1) above, will largely determine the content and immediate objectives of the public relations program.

3. Revision, adjustment, and improvement of administrative policies, procedures, and attitudes in an attempt to remove causes of friction between officials and citizens and to build "good will" for the city. This step in the process is, of course, the most important one.

4. Preparation and release of publicity to stimulate popular interest in the city government, to correct popular misconceptions, and to acquaint the citizens with the improvements made during step (3).

5. Reappraisal of public attitudes to test effectiveness of public relations activities.

6. Constant revision and improvement of program to keep up with new situations.

It should be added that this is the logical sequence and not necessarily the chronological procedure. In actual practice, several of these steps may be carried on simultaneously. Even so, the logical sequence can be reflected in the emphasis that is placed on the different steps in the program at different times.

Surveying Public Relations

The first two of these logical steps comprise what may be called the public relations survey, for their object is to study the present relationship of the city with the public.

Analysis of the Public

The first step in the survey is to get acquainted with the public, to find out who these people are. For public relations purposes the city may be said to have not one but many "publics," in the sense that there are groups with more or less common interests. A few of the more common publics, selected almost at random, may be mentioned merely by way of illustration: (1) taxpayers — who may be subclassified according to types of taxes; (2) geographical groups or neighborhoods; (3) business and industrial groups; (3) school children; (4) parents of school children; (5) church groups; (6) labor organizations; (7) relief clients; (8) operators of amusement centers; (9) racial groups; (10) city employees; (11) applicants for city jobs; (12) financial houses and creditors; (13) vendors of city purchases; (14) utility consumers; and so on almost without number.

In some cases different departments and agencies of the city government may have their own special publics. The finance department, for example, is responsible for most of the contacts and relationships between the city and financial houses, while the purchasing office deals with the various concerns that supply the city with materials and equipment. In other cases the interests of these special publics may cut across several departments, as in the case of geographical groups or neighborhoods.

The reason for emphasizing the complex composition of the public is that the public relations activities of many cities fail to recognize this diversity of interest. Only those phases of the city's program affecting large numbers of citizens have commonly been regarded as influencing public relations. Municipal reports and publicity have too often been directed at everyone in general and no one in particular. The good will of a few groups has been actively solicited, while the interests of other groups have been slighted or ignored. No public relations program can be truly effective unless it is recognized at the outset that every contact, direct or indirect, with any citizen or group of citizens has a bearing on the city's public relations.

Appraising Public Attitudes Toward the City Government

It is not enough, however, merely to identify the various publics of the city. It is also desirable to appraise as accurately as possible the present relationships between the city and each of its publics. How can public impressions of, and attitudes toward, the city government or any of its agencies be appraised? In small cities and towns this may be a fairly simple task, for officials may be more or less personally acquainted with most of the residents. In larger places, however, the problem is not so simple. Among the appraisal techniques that may be useful are:

1. <u>Informal sampling</u>. If a number of city officials would seek informally to ascertain the attitudes and impressions of such individuals as they may normally encounter in their official or private capacities, considerable information might be collected. No pretense of scientific measurement can be made for such informal research, but it may

reveal some weak points in the city's public relations activities. Regardless of the immediate findings, all city employees should be on the alert in their personal contacts for any attitudes or reactions towards the city or its program.

2. _Advisory bodies._ Administrators in some cities rely on more or less formal advisory bodies composed of representatives of important interest groups within the city. Such bodies may not only reflect current public opinion, but they may also be used as a testing ground for new proposals. More will be said later in this chapter regarding the use of advisory bodies in the public relations program.

3. _Voluntary statements by individuals or groups._ Petitions signed by a number of citizens may bear direct evidence of popular opinion or attitudes. Clubs, associations, labor unions, and other groups of citizens often adopt resolutions or issue public statements revealing their attitudes toward the city administration or certain of its activities. Complaints and requests for information are especially important from a public relations point of view, for they indicate that the citizen is sufficiently interested in some aspect of the city administration to warrant his individual action. Newspapers provide another expression of individual and group opinion. Not only editorials but letters to the editor should be carefully followed for their hints as to which administrative activities meet with popular approval and which with disapproval.

4. _The city council._ As elected representatives of the people, members of the city council may be expected to reflect public opinions and attitudes in some particulars. That is one of their principal functions. In addition to their appraisal of the more general attitudes and opinions of their constituents, council members are frequently approached by individuals or groups that have grievances to be aired or proposals to make.

5. _Elections._ Since elections are as a rule concerned with personalities or with public policies, they seldom provide any direct information as to public attitudes toward administrative personnel, procedures, and the like. Careful analysis of election campaigns and results, however, may provide some useful information. When officials are seeking re-election, the criticisms of their opponents often indicate features of the administrative program that are unpopular or are susceptible to misconstruction. The vote on propositions may also yield hints as to public attitudes. In other words, election results in themselves produce little information for the public relations survey, but the incidents and byplay of elections often reveal broad currents of public opinion that are significant from the public relations point of view.

All of these appraisal techniques are admittedly rather crude, and their results will fall far short of scientific accuracy. They have been suggested, however, because of their simplicity and ease of application and because more scientific techniques are not generally available. Opinion polls, such as those conducted by the American Institute of Public Opinion (Gallup Polls) have made great strides in recent years, however, and offer some promise for use in the field of municipal public relations.

For the present, however, there are several serious obstacles in the way of using this method of opinion measurement in a public relations survey. In the first place, opinion sampling requires special skills. The determination of the sample, the selection and the wording of the questions, and the interpretation of findings are not jobs for novices. To do a thorough job would also require a considerable expenditure of time and effort, if not of actual cash. Furthermore, there may be some indirect difficulties. To circulate a questionnaire asking for opinions and attitudes concerning the city government, city employees, and so forth, might actually do immediate damage to the city's public relations. If the survey showed a very low public regard for the city government, and if the findings were made public, the results might be made a political issue. A hostile press or opposition group could make great capital of such information. There might also be an injurious effect on employee morale. These dangers might be avoided by careful handling of the survey, but they should not be ignored.

Appraising the Administration

In addition to the identification of the city's publics and the appraisal of the publics' attitudes and opinions with regard to the city government, there should be a critical examination of the city's role in current relations with its public, or publics. This examination might be conducted in at least three different ways.

First, city agencies and services might be matched against a list of all of the various publics to see what agencies, personnel, or services may affect each interest group. This would help in accounting for the favorable or unfavorable attitudes found in any group and would also indicate the possible channels or media for improving relations with each group.

Second, the results of the opinion and attitude survey might be used as the starting point for the examination. If they showed definitely favorable or unfavorable attitudes towards any department, service, or procedure, this should call for investigation.

Third, every point of contact, direct or indirect, between the city and a citizen should be carefully checked in an attempt to reduce friction and to make relations with the public more cordial. The details of this examination will be suggested in later sections of this chapter, but a few points may be suggested as illustrations. Every procedure in which citizens are required to participate — registration and voting, tax payment, applications for licenses, and the like — should be critically examined to see if it could not be simplified or made more convenient for the citizen. All employees who have regular contact with members of the public should be appraised on such points as personal appearance, ability to handle complaints or requests for information, courtesy, and so forth. All public buildings should be appraised on the basis of cleanliness, arrangement of offices, lighting, and so on.

The public relations survey, then, consists of three basic questions: What is the composition of the public? How satisfactory are the city's relationships with each of its publics? What is the city doing, or failing to do, that may account for the present status of its public relations?

When the survey has been completed the groundwork has been laid for positive steps towards improving the city's public relations. The remainder of this chapter will be devoted to discussing and illustrating some of the principal steps that may be taken. Neither the choice of steps to be discussed nor the order in which they are presented are intended as specifications for any particular city. A public relations program must be tailor-made to fit local circumstances if it is to be truly effective. The public relations activities suggested in this chapter should, however, be applicable to some degree in most cities.

Contacts With Citizens

The city as an institution or the policies of cities as such may not make a very definite impression upon most citizens. It is not until the citizen has contact with a representative of the city government in the administration of a policy that the government becomes a reality to the citizen. It must be remembered that in every citizen-official contact the city employee is representing his city. In the eyes of the citizen he is, for the time being, the city. What he does and how he does it are therefore of vital importance to the public relations program.

Scope and Variety of Contacts

Even if the importance of personal contacts is accepted, there is a natural tendency to confine one's attention to only a few employees whose public contacts are numerous. As an antidote for this tendency, some of the most important contacts may be briefly reviewed.

Administrative Officials. Most people who have a question to ask or a complaint to make like to see the "head man." Consequently appointments with the city manager, mayor, and department heads are in great demand. Most officials who have been faced with this problem have concluded that an "open door" policy (no formal office hours) is best, even though personal calls make serious inroads upon the official's time. This "open door" policy does not mean that citizens may walk into the administrator's office at any time and for any purpose, but rather that the administrator will arrange to see any citizen whose business cannot be satisfactorily handled by someone else or who insists on seeing the administrator in person. The essence of the "open door" policy is therefore not to see all visitors, but rather to avoid denying an interview to any citizen.

Counter Clerks. The clerks, and cashiers who handle the majority of citizen callers at the city hall have a big public relations load to carry. Although many of these employees are in the lower brackets as far as pay is concerned, their tact, courtesy, and competence in handling citizens are of vital importance to the city's public relations. More will be said about their principal functions — the handling of complaints and requests for information — later in this chapter.

Police Officers. From a public relations point of view, police officers hold a position of peculiar importance. In one sense the police officer may be said to personify the city government, for his work requires him at various times to represent the law and the regulatory and service aspects of city government. Furthermore, his uniform and his presence in all parts of the city make him a particularly conspicuous municipal servant. What the police officer does and how he does it are consequently of vital importance to the public relations program of the city.

The regulatory activities of the police are exceptionally important in the public relations program, for in this field the police are dealing not with criminals but with ordinary citizens who resent any abuse of authority. Traffic regulation is the most important police regulation from a public relations viewpoint, because it brings the police into contact with many citizens.

The police officer should be a walking (or motorized) "information booth" for visitors and local residents. In the training of recruits, special attention should be given to this matter of information. A good knowledge of local geography, the location of important buildings, as well as civic affairs should be part of every officer's equipment. On the material side, his equipment might well include a city map or guide.

Firemen. Although firemen have fewer personal contacts than police officers, their number, their uniforms, and their presence in all sections of the city make them important public relations agents. In their actual fire-fighting activities they are playing dramatic roles that have natural publicity and public relations appeal. One by-product of fire fighting that has frequently caused an unfavorable popular response, however, is the damage to property caused by water, chemicals, and the fireman's ax. A great deal of damage is done as the result of ignorance. Progressive fire departments are now giving special attention to salvage work. Special waterproof covers are put over furniture and other perishable goods, and firemen are especially instructed in the protection of property. One department goes so far as to provide a temporary patch of roofing paper in the case of roof fires when the damage is not too great. Such concern for private property yields big returns in improved public relations.

Fire prevention and inspection activities also provide many personal contacts that can be converted into public relations assets. Special care should be given to the training of officers assigned to inspection duty, not only in the technical aspects of their work but also in the art of dealing with people. It should be a fairly easy task to convince property owners that fire inspection is in their own interests, and these personal contacts provide splendid opportunities for firemen to explain the principles of fire prevention and the activities of the fire department.

Inspectors. In addition to firemen on inspection duty, most cities have a number of other officials to carry on inspectional activities in such fields as health, weights and measures, and building construction. Here again the considerations of appearance, manner of treating the citizen, and the ability to explain the "why" of the service and to answer questions regarding the employee's own department and other city activities have a direct bearing on public relations. Since most inspections are carried on by municipal employees on private premises, it is particularly important that the rights and feelings of the citizens be given particular consideration.

Construction Employees. The engineers and laborers engaged on city construction projects are seldom considered as having any public relations importance, but they can be very useful contact employees. Construction activities hold a peculiar fascination for many people, as is evidenced by the crowd that will always gather to watch a steam shovel at work. Superintendents or foremen in charge of such projects are frequently questioned as to the nature of the project, its purpose, its cost, and so forth. Furthermore, the construction of such projects may often give rise to citizen complaints. Not only the noise and dust which annoy neighboring householders but also any infringement on private property rights may be the cause of complaints. It is certainly in the interest of public relations to see that superintendents and foremen are well-informed and able to answer questions and that they have a clear understanding of their authority and limitations in handling complaints.

Other Employees. The classes of employees that have already been mentioned in particular provide only a sample of the various personal contacts between city employees and citizens. Among the other employees who might have been mentioned are assessors, utility service men, refuse collectors, superintendents of sewage disposal plants or incinerators, health officers, visiting nurses, probation officers, and so on through the whole rank and file of municipal employees. Space limitations prevent special consideration here of the peculiar problems raised in contacts between these employees and members of the public. Careful appraisal should be made of all such contacts, however, to see what special problems of a public relations nature they raise and what formal or informal devices might be utilized to make these contacts advantageous from the public relations point of view.

Inquiries and Complaints

Now that the scope and variety of personal contacts between city employees and members of the public have been indicated, attention may be directed to two special classes of contacts: those arising out of requests for information and those occasioned by the filing of a complaint by a citizen. Such contacts may involve many groups of municipal employees, but, because of space limitations, this discussion will be confined to such contacts as are made at the city hall or in public offices.

Requests for Information. One of the first questions to be asked is: Where can information be obtained? Most citizens are not sufficiently acquainted with public buildings or with departmental functions to know where different kinds of information may be found. Probably the most complete answer to this problem is to be found in the example of those cities that have established central bureaus or offices of information and complaints. If there is no central information desk, the citizen in quest of information may be helped by the use of directories, signs, and arrows. The names of departments and agencies are not always sufficient and signs might well anticipate the citizen's query. For example, signs pointing to the treasurer's office might indicate what bills are payable there. Even after the citizen has reached the proper office, he may not know to whom his question should be addressed. The responsibility for handling citizen contacts should be clearly assigned in each office, and if there is no counter a desk should be clearly marked as the information desk.

These are all precontact considerations. The quality of the contact itself will depend upon the manner of the city employee, his knowledge of city affairs, and his ability to impart that knowledge in terms that the citizen will understand.

The manner of the contact employee will depend in part upon his own personality, and attention should be given to personality factors in the recruitment and assignments of such employees. The employee's manner may be improved, however, if he is given special training. Finally, the general level of employee morale and interest in public relations will affect the employee's manner. It is difficult to impose courtesy and friendliness upon any employee by command.

The ability to answer questions may be acquired through long experience or through special preparation. The first step in providing a well informed information clerk is to collect and prepare material which may be used in answering questions. Such information may be prepared in the form of handbooks, manuals, special announcements, or interoffice memoranda. Any changes in regulations or in important municipal policies should immediately be transmitted to all employees handling informational contacts with the public. It may even be desirable to prepare a special printed or mimeographed announcement or folder for distribution to the public in cases where a number of requests for information are anticipated and where the explanation will be too long or too involved for oral transmission.

Finally, the employee must be able to impart information in clear layman's language. Here again the answer is to be found in special training — presuming of course, that contact employees have been selected for their intelligence and personality.

Handling Complaints. Complaints are the warning signals which call official attention to errors or omissions in the city's service program. If they are ignored, a bad situation may soon become worse. If they are given prompt and careful attention, the city may be able to render even better service to the public. Much of what has just been said concerning the handling of requests for information applies equally to the treatment of complaints, but complaints require some special consideration.

Good complaint procedure may be divided into four principal stages: (1) receiving the complaint; (2) assignment of responsibility for investigation and correction; (3) follow-up of all complaints; and (4) notification of correction.

Receiving Complaints. The attitude and manner of the employee receiving the complaint is of critical importance — even more so than in the case of requests for information. The citizen who files the complaint is seldom in the best of temper. But no matter how trivial or irrational the complaint may seem to the city employee, it must never be forgotten that in the mind of the citizen it is a matter of very great importance. Employees who are quick-tempered or who like to argue with citizens have no place at the complaint counter. If the complaint is based upon a misunderstanding, the employee may try to clarify the situation, but he should never "argue it out."

Clear lines of authority or appeal in complaint matters should be established. Although most complaints may be handled by subordinates, some require a higher decision, and many persons will insist on taking their grievances directly to some high official. Every effort should be made to reduce the number of such cases, but no citizen should ever feel that he has been denied the right to receive satisfaction.

In all except the most trivial cases it is probably wise to prepare a written record of each complaint. A special form containing the name of the complainant, the date of the complaint, the nature of the complaint, the department responsible for correction, the nature and date of correction or investigation, and the notification given to the complainant is used in a number of cities.

Investigation and Correction. If the complaint is important enough to be recorded, it certainly deserves prompt and thorough investigation and adjustment. If a careful investigation reveals that the complaint is unfounded or that the cause cannot be corrected, a report of these findings should be made, preferably in writing. Otherwise action — and prompt action — should be taken. A complaint that is promptly corrected may prove to be a public relations asset, but delay will only further aggravate the citizen's sense of injury.

Follow-up Procedure. In order to make sure that every report is promptly and thoroughly treated, some follow-up system is necessary. In many cities this system covers all municipal services, under the direction of the mayor, manager, or central complaint bureau, while in other cases each department is responsible for its own complaints. A central system is most logical in all except very large cities, for it expedites records and control; furthermore some complaints cut across departmental lines.

The follow-up system is usually built around some standard complaint form, on which is noted the name of the complainant, the date of the complaint, the nature of the complaint, the name of the person receiving the complaint, the official to whom the case is assigned, a report of the investigation made, the disposition of the case, and the nature and date of notification to the complainant. With such a system any complaint that has not been corrected or reported upon within the time specified can readily be detected and proper action taken.

Notification. The final step is to notify the citizen as to what action has been taken on his complaint. In some cases no formal notice will be required, either because a mistake has been admitted in the original interview and specific action promised or because the complaint does not require specific action. In many cases, however, the complaint may be transformed from a liability into an asset simply by calling the citizen's attention to the prompt action taken. In a few cases a letter may be required, but as a rule a post card or a telephone call will suffice. If the complaint calls for action by a service man or other field employee, this employee himself may call the citizen's attention to the action taken. Whatever time and expense may be entailed by these various forms of notification will be amply returned in improved public relations.

Indirect Personal Contacts

So far this discussion has been concerned largely with face-to-face contacts between employees and citizens. But even in local government, where such contacts are frequent, the importance of indirect personal contacts must not be slighted. The two principal media for indirect contacts are correspondence and the telephone, and a few suggestions may be made concerning each.

Contacts by Correspondence. It is a curious fact that many officials who are solic- itous of the citizen's interests in face-to-face contacts, and who overlook no opportunity for making public relations assets out of such meetings, are guilty of some of the worst abuses in their correspondence. They will allow letters to go unanswered for days at a time; they are abrupt or even rude in their phraseology, and they are addicted to the habit of the dull, stilted, "business English." They seem to forget that their letters are simply substitutes for face-to-face contacts.

The tone and appearance of the letter probably have the most direct bearing on pub- lic relations. Those who level the charge of bureaucracy against local governments can find plenty of support for their accusations in the letters that are issued from most city halls. If officials would jar themselves free of the habit of writing letters as if they were drafting legal documents, the city government would be a much more "humanized" institu- tion in the eyes of the public.

Contacts by Telephone. Telephone contacts between citizens and city officials are frequent. How they are handled is an important public relations consideration.

Physical facilities must be considered first. If there is no central switchboard to receive and distribute calls, many confusing and irritating delays and wrong connections will probably be made. If there are insufficient trunk lines, the number of "busy" signals will naturally be large. The equipment of the city should make it possible for a citizen to reach the city hall quickly and easily. A survey by telephone company officials may re- veal possibilities for many improvements along these lines.

The personal factor is even more important. If there is a central switchboard, the central operator is the first point of contact. The salutation and tone of voice of the oper- ator, are very important. "Good morning, this is the city hall" is certainly a better be- ginning than the listless, sing-song "city haw-wull" that many operators reply. There is no standard greeting that can be prescribed, but some local standard should be agreed upon and followed. Voice quality is also an important factor and should be considered in the selection of operators.

Of equal or greater importance is the efficiency of the operator. Calls that are switched from one office to another and then another are very annoying and certainly do not foster the concept of an efficient city government. Very careful instruction, currently revised, should be given to all operators to make sure that they have an accurate knowl- edge of city hall personnel and of the activities and jurisdictions of the several depart- ments.

Persons assigned to respond to telephone calls in each office should be competent to handle at least the most common questions and complaints. Such persons should also be given special training in the proper use of the telephone.

Procedures Involving Citizens

If there is any one popular synonym for governmental procedures, it is "red tape."

Governments are probably no more guilty on this score than large-scale private institutions, but the important point for public relations purposes is that involved procedures and delay are offensive to the public. An important element in the public relations program is the critical review of all procedures directly involving members of the public to see if they cannot be simplified or made less offensive. Public convenience is not the only criterion of municipal procedures, but it certainly must be considered. To discuss all such procedures here is out of the question, but a few examples may be cited.

Tax Collection. No one likes to pay taxes, and there is no magic formula that can make the payment of taxes a joyous experience. Nevertheless much can be done to make tax payments as nearly painless as possible.

The Tax Bill. There is considerable room for improvement in the clarity of the bill presented. In many cases the bills are so complicated and so shrouded with legal and accounting terminology that the ordinary layman has difficulty in determining what he owes and when and where the bill should be paid. There is little excuse for such lack of consideration of the taxpayer.

Collection Procedure. It is unfortunately true that some cities still require the taxpayer to come in person to the city hall and exhaust his patience by standing in a long line before the tax collector's window. Although some taxpayers will always prefer to pay bills in person, it is in the interest of courtesy and good public relations to make it possible to pay tax bills by check through the mail. It is encouraging to note than an increasing number of cities are providing for the installment payment of taxes, a procedure which is designed not only to level out the revenue peaks of the city but also to make the payment of tax bills a less onerous task for the taxpayer.

In some cities special arrangements are provided whereby taxpayers who are sincere in their desire to discharge their delinquent tax obligations are permitted to enter into special contracts for the installment payment of delinquent taxes. It is obviously impossible to make any careful analysis of all the implications of such procedures here; and it is not suggested that the convenience of the taxpayer is the only factor to be considered in the handling of tax collections. Nevertheless, much can be done to reduce the unpleasantness and inconvenience of tax payments without undue hardship to the city or serious inconvenience to its employees.

Traffic Regulation Enforcement. In the discussion of contacts between police officers and the public, the particular importance of contacts with violators of traffic regulations was pointed out. In addition to questions of the attitude and manner of the traffic officers, it is highly important that the procedures involved be subjected to examination from the public relations point of view.

Warning. One procedural device which has been adopted by a number of progressive departments is the warning slip in place of traffic tickets as the first stage in enforcement procedure. In addition to reducing the number of traffic cases in the courts, this procedure presents the traffic officer not in the role of a persecutor, but in the role of a protector and adviser.

Notice to Appear. A somewhat related device that may be mentioned is the use of notices to appear, in place of regular arrests, for citizens of established standing in the community who have committed minor offenses. By this means the onus of arrest is removed, and the offender, while being called to task for his offense, is not humiliated by being subjected to treatment as an ordinary criminal.

Penalties. A third procedural device in connection with traffic violations is the use of traffic violators' schools, where offenders are required to pay for their offenses not by fines or imprisonment but by compulsory attendance at a series of lectures on traffic regulations and the rules of proper driving. Again, the benefits are twofold. Not only does the offender escape the humiliation of criminal punishment, but by this very sentence he is rendered more competent to drive and hence to avoid future violations of traffic regulations.

Other Procedures. These examples should indicate some of the possibilities for procedural improvements. Among the other procedures to which special attention might be given, only a few may be suggested. Procedures governing the securing of permits and licenses affect a large number of citizens and are frequently the cause of popular criticism. Regulations and procedures affecting municipal utilities — service connections, disconnections, repairs, and so forth — also affect many citizens and should be appraised from the consumers' point of view.

Training Employees in Public Relations

In view of the importance of these personal contacts between city employees and members of the public, it is only logical that some special instruction or training be given to employees on this subject. Although no attempt will be made to prescribe a complete training program, several suggestions may be made.

Subject Matter

If employees are to be successful in explaining, interpreting, and possibly defending the objectives, activities, and procedures of a city government, they must themselves first have a full appreciation of these points. This applies both to their contacts on the job and also to the many contacts which they make informally off duty; in answering questions, in handling complaints, and in all their contacts with citizens, public employees should be prepared to answer intelligently all manner of questions concerning the government.

One of the most important phases of public relations training might therefore be a "know-your-government" program embracing as many employees as possible. The organization of the government, the principal activities of the major departments and agencies, some of the major problems and issues confronting these units, and other related subjects might constitute the subject matter for this phase of the training. Some experiments along this line have been made by a few cities, and the response on the part of the employees themselves has been enthusiastic.

It might be added that such a program is more than public relations training. It is also a step toward a good employee relations policy. The better understanding of their government and their jobs should improve the employees' morale and performance as well as their ability to represent the government before the public.

The art of handling citizen complaints, the proper use of the telephone, letter writing, public speaking and the art of dealing with people (courtesy, tact, attentiveness and the like) can all be improved by appropriate training. In addition to these more general subjects, there are a number of special subjects that might be included in the training program for special groups of employees. For example, traffic officers could be given special instruction in the proper approach and manner to be used in arresting or warning violators of traffic regulations. Inspectors need training in calling attention to violations of ordinances in such a manner as to maintain authority and secure enforcement without giving offense. Special attention, especially in larger cities, should also be given to teaching supervisory officials how to train their subordinates in public relations.

Who Shall Be Trained?

All municipal officials and employees should be brought into the training program, although some will of course require more extensive or more specialized training than others. It has been suggested that training in the policies and activities of the city government is an essential part of the training program, and such training should appeal to all employees. As for specialized training, the discussion of subject matter has already suggested a number of classes of employees who need instruction of a particular nature — counter clerks, correspondence clerks, police officers, inspectors, and others. Earlier in this chapter a number of illustrations were cited to show that almost every municipal employee has some public relations responsibilities. The objective of the training program is to see that employees are equipped to handle contacts with citizens in the best possible manner. Just what employees should be brought into special phases of the training program must be decided on the basis of an analysis of the public relations aspects of all municipal positions.

Methods of Training

The variety of subjects recommended for inclusion in the public relations training program obviously requires a variety of training methods. In addition to training through day-to-day supervision there are several training techniques that may be briefly described here.

For some purposes, more or less formal lectures may be useful. In the conduct of a "know-your-government" course for city employees, the lecture may be the only feasible means of instructing a large number of employees. There may also be occasions when an outside authority on some public relations subject can be secured for a single meeting only, and the lecture offers an equal training opportunity to all interested employees.

As a rule, most lectures are more effective for training purposes if they are accompanied by some demonstration. The showing of a film portraying municipal activities may be very useful in educating employees as to the activities of departments other than their own. The Bell Telephone Company has a sound film entitled "Your Company's Voice" that might be shown to a group seeking to improve their use of the telephone. Demonstrations may also accompany an explanation at a police training school of the proper method and manner for issuing a traffic ticket. The demonstration method is also useful apart from lectures. Demonstrations of good and bad answers to questions or of good and bad telephone diction may be more effective than any amount of explanation.

In many cases supervised practice is the most effective teacher. This practice may sometimes be had during the performance of regular duties, or, especially in the case of new employees, in training classes or groups where hypothetical situations are handled by the trainee. The employee may be given a sample complaint to answer or a letter to which a reply may be drafted.

For many kinds of public relations training, the so-called "conference" method seems best designed to secure the desired results. Under this method employees are expected to supply at least a part of the training themselves by self-analysis and by comparing their experience with that of other employees. Take, for example, a conference on the handling of citizen complaints. The first step might be to determine what types of complaints are most common. In some cases this can be determined entirely from the experience of those participating in the conference. In other cases it may be advisable to ask those employees who participate to compile a check-list for a short period of time from which a frequency distribution of complaints made can be determined. Then the participants in the conference might be asked to volunteer what they think is the best way of handling each of the complaints listed. Other members of the conference, if it is properly conducted, are bound to disagree or to offer modifications, and the net result will probably be an answer better than that which has been used by any single employee.

Finally, the results of lectures, demonstrations, and conferences may be summarized and condensed in the form of manuals or guides to good practice. Care should be taken not to make such manuals too complete or too stereotyped. The points to be considered, the best lines of approach, and some illustrative examples might well be covered, but the manual should stop short of any stereotyped phrases or stock answers, for nothing is so deadly to public relations as the employee who is obviously reciting a piece he has memorized.

Who Shall Train?

As has already been suggested, supervisory officials must be relied upon to provide the greater part of all public relations training. It is the supervisor, whatever his title may be, who must observe and correct the faults of the counter clerk in handling complaints, who must make constructive suggestions for improving the manner of the traffic officer in dealing with violators of traffic regulations, who must review and improve the letters written by subordinate employees to citizens. This day-to-day public relations training must of necessity be highly decentralized. In fact, almost all phases of public relations training will be most effective if they are geared into the city's general training activities. This means that, with some exceptions, a decentralized training program will be in order. If, however, the personnel agency or some other central body acts as the coordinator of other training activities, it could well provide central guidance and advice for departmental training in public relations. Outside instructors or advisers will, of course, be useful in some instances.

Making the Training Fit

A word of caution or moderation is needed at the conclusion of these suggestions for public relations training. Training in public relations, like all other training, must be designed and altered to fit local needs. Some of the subjects suggested and some of the methods indicated may not be applicable to all cities. In very small cities, where the few employees are familiar with what the city does, there may be little need for establishing a plan for educating them in the policies and activities of the city government. Formal classes or even conference groups may be too elaborate for some situations. The suggestions that have been made are not intended as specifications for a standard program. What is needed in every city is a careful analysis of the public relations duties of all employees, an appraisal of the present shortcomings in the performance of these duties, and the selection of those subjects and methods of training best fitted to the needs.

Cooperation Between Officials and Citizens

As long as there is a sharp dividing line between citizen and public official groups it will be difficult to overcome the tendency toward suspicion and misunderstanding on the part of each. It would be naive to suggest a return to the "good old days" of the town meeting and of administration by part-time laymen. But some modifications of the practice of complete segregation may be suggested.

Citizen Participation in Municipal Activity

The lay citizen can be made to supplement, rather than to supplant, the technical or professional public servant in a number of ways. Advisory committees are being used in many cities at present, and their possibilities are far from being exhausted. Some such committees are used in the capacity of general advisory bodies on many municipal matters, while in other cases they are confined to a single activity or program. The coordinating council which is found in the fields of welfare and juvenile delinquency suggests another possible method of citizen participation in administration. These councils consist of representatives of the various agencies, both public and private, whose activities are interrelated, and their task is to secure coordination of the community's resources in the solution of problems in their field. It should be emphasized that these coordinating councils are not merely discussion groups, but take an active part in the execution of programs.

Special campaigns in such fields as traffic safety, fire prevention, delinquent tax collection, and so on, offer great possibilities for active citizen participation in achieving the ends of local administration. When citizens have a sense of participation and of responsibility for certain municipal services, their desire for knowledge of what the city is doing is greatly increased, and their habitual attitude of skepticism or hostility may be overcome.

The use of schoolboy patrols to guard traffic crossings during school hours is another excellent example of how nonofficials may participate in administrative activities. These school boys feel greatly honored to be invested with authority and responsibility, and the positive interest that they take in enforcing the traffic regulations is of lasting benefit to them and to the city.

Another illustration of such citizen participation is provided in a number of cities where specially qualified citizens are asked to serve on examining boards for civil service agencies, particularly in the use of oral examinations. This practice has a twofold advantage: (1) the personnel agency acquires a greatly diversified panel of examiners, and (2) this intimate contact and experience with the examining procedure serves to enlighten the citizen participants as to the personnel needs of their city and the progressive techniques which are used in selecting a high caliber of personnel.

Employee Participation in Civic Enterprises

The other side of this program for bringing officials and citizens together in joint enterprises requires that city employees and officials play a normal role in the nongovernmental activities and enterprises of the community. It should be made very clear at the outset that this is not a recommendation for a "boring from within" policy. When it is suggested that city employees should belong to organizations and participate in the civic life of the community, it is simply a recommendation that they be good citizens, as well as good public servants.

Sponsorship or leadership of youth organizations by city officials offers great opportunities for participation in such civic enterprises. In a number of cities, police officers (and in some cases the department itself) act as sponsors for boy scout troops. The primary object of such sponsorship is of course to supplement the crime prevention activities of the police department. At the same time, they are also building up good will on the part of these young citizens and on the part of their parents. Fire department officers and other city employees may also undertake such activities, with resulting benefits for their juvenile charges and the public relations of the city.

Any number of other instances of employee participation in civic enterprises might be enumerated, such as the entering of floats and exhibits in parades or festivals, the entering of athletic teams in interorganization contests, and so forth. These examples should be sufficient, however, to emphasize the point that city employees are also citizens and that the relationship between the city government and the public will be bettered to the extent that public officials and employees take an active part in community life.

Physical Appearances

Looks, as well as actions and attitudes, have an important bearing upon the opinions of others, and the city government must present a pleasing appearance if it seeks the respect of its citizens.

Personal Appearances

The appearance of city employees themselves is of primary importance. This chapter will not assume the role of fashion arbiter for city employees, but a few points may be emphasized.

All employees who have frequent contacts with citizens can be required to be neat and clean. Clerks with soiled linen and dirty hands are poor representatives of the city. Almost as bad is the flashy, overdressed employee. Fashion standards may vary in different communities, but the important point is to set and enforce some standard.

Police and fire officers are conspicuous because of their uniforms, and this conspicuous appearance should be a favorable one. Strict regulations requiring clean, well-pressed uniforms should be enforced. In this connection, it might be advisable to increase the number of employees in uniform. Utility service-men might have some standard dress with a uniform cap, and this applies to refuse collectors as well.

Public Buildings

Exterior Appearance. In most cities the design of the city hall and other public buildings may, for the time being, have to be accepted as they are. But the least that can be done is to see that the building is in good condition. This refers not only to the state of repair, but also to the cleanliness of the building. Civic buildings which are of ramshackle and grimy appearance certainly do not speak well for the government as an institution. The grounds and landscaping surrounding public buildings also deserve consideration.

Interior Appearance. The interior of public buildings is even more important as far as appearances are concerned. Just as the character of housewives is often appraised by the quality of their housekeeping, so are city governments judged by the condition of public offices. The citizen who comes to the city hall and finds long, dingy corridors frequented by loiterers is sure to receive an unfavorable impression of the city government.

Rigorous application of the broom and the mop and frequent application of the paint brush are more than worth their expense in the improved appearance that results. The cleanliness of public rest rooms within such buildings is an important detail that should not be overlooked. Certainly the city government can give as much attention to these matters as gasoline station operators. Even though many of our older public buildings were poorly designed to let in sunlight, this disadvantage can at least be offset by careful attention to artificial lighting.

Other Public Properties

Public streets and alleys are of particular importance, since they are in constant view of all groups within the population of the city. The appearance of a street depends not only upon the condition of the pavement but also upon how clean it is kept and upon the condition of the trees and the median strips. These are primarily questions of public works operating standards, but they also have a very direct bearing upon the city's public relations.

The various utility buildings and structures throughout the city may give good or poor impressions of the city government, depending upon their appearance. Any number of cases might be cited where, with a little attention to landscaping and design, even such structures as sewage disposal plants and incinerators have been made attractive properties.

Machines and Equipment

The many pieces of city-owned equipment, mobile or stationary, need special attention with regard to appearance.

Motor Vehicles. The many automobiles operated by city officials are traveling representatives of the city government, and their appearance is therefore important from a public relations viewpoint. Cars and trucks badly in need of paint and subject to many breakdowns in the line of duty are not likely to win public confidence or approval. Many cities cannot afford to have the newest or best motor equipment, but careful attention to the repair and appearance of old equipment requires very little effort or expense and is "good public relations" as well as good business.

The identification of public vehicles is another public relations consideration. Identification of vehicles by means of easily read letters or insignia is a sound practice. In addition to its other advantages, this identification is a reminder to the citizen of the activity and service of the city government and gives him indirectly some idea of what services his tax money provides.

Other Equipment. In addition to motor vehicles, there are many other pieces of equipment belonging to the city that can be the inanimate causes of public approval or disapproval. Certain street paving tools that are carelessly left on the job after working hours may not only be potential liabilities but are also unsightly. The appearance of municipal yards where equipment is stored can be greatly improved by a little attention to orderly arrangement and by fencing.

Personnel Policies and Practices

A good public relations program begins at home — in the city hall. If the city employees themselves do not respect the city government, it is too much to expect that an "outsider" will. If the employees are not familiar with the policies and activities of the city, they cannot explain them to the public. Furthermore, in city governments particularly, public relations are largely personal relations. Although there are some material and institutional factors involved, the problem is largely one of promoting cordial relationships between one group of persons known as public officials or employees and another group called the public. The public relations program must therefore be very much concerned with matters of personnel. The kind of men and women working for the city, the quality of their performance, and their personal attitudes and manner all have a direct bearing on the city's public relations.

Chapter 6 discussed the elements of a comprehensive personnel program, from recruitment to retirement systems. In one sense that entire chapter might be said to come within the scope of a public relations program, for any policies or procedures affecting the quality, performance, or attitude of employees also affect the city's public relations. For present purposes, however, only a few phases of personnel administration that are of particular importance for public relations purposes can be singled out for special attention.

Recruitment Policy

Active Recruitment. The recruitment programs of most cities are too passive. The general attitude seems to be that the initiative should rest upon the potential employee. In happy contrast with this practice is the progress being made in some jurisdictions towards an active, aggressive recruiting program. Not only are announcements of openings made appealing by attractive typography and clear informal language, but the announcements are supplemented by other practices designed to arouse interest in the service.

There are two primary advantages of such a program from a public relations standpoint. First, it will secure a higher type of public servant, which will in itself enhance the prestige of the municipal service. Second, the effects of an active recruitment program are by no means limited to those who may be interested in employment. It also calls popular attention to the variety of skills required in the administration of a modern city, to the high standards set by the recruiting agency, and to the city's adherence to a policy of recruitment by open competition. No better advertisement can be given to the merit system of the city.

Treatment of Applicants for Employment. If the recruitment program is successful, there may be a rather large number of persons applying for employment with the city. Only a small percentage of this group will survive the examinations and eventually be appointed. This select group will be considered below in the discussion of employee relations.

But how about the others — the hundreds or even thousands who are unsuccessful in their quest for a job? From a strict personnel point of view they may not matter; they have been discarded. From a public relations point of view they are of more direct concern than the successful. Not only are they more numerous, but they comprise one of the city's special "publics," their common interest being an important one, the desire for a job. Here is a group of citizens who are brought into very close contact with their city government. This contact can be either an asset or a liability from a public relations viewpoint.

The application procedure should be made as simple and convenient as possible for the applicant. Many personnel jurisdictions follow the practice of keeping mailing lists of persons who wish to be notified of examinations in certain fields.

The examination itself is bound to make a very definite impression upon the applicant. The form and content of the examination proper were discussed in Chapter 6 but it may be pointed out here that the atmosphere in which the examination is given, the attitude on the part of proctors or examiners, and the facilities which are provided for the examination all need to be considered from the point of view of public relations.

After the examination has been held and the papers have been graded, the next step is the notification of those who were examined. In many jurisdictions the lack of funds and personnel on the part of the recruiting agency cause long delays in the preparation of eligible lists. Such delays are bad not only from the point of view of the personnel agency, but they also have a very bad effect upon those seeking employment. Special care should be given to the form of the notice by which those who have taken the examination are informed of their own standing. A common weakness of such notification forms is the unnecessary abruptness or bluntness with which the results are announced. This applies particularly, of course, to those who have not received satisfactory grades in the examination. No one likes to be told that he is a failure or that he has made a poor showing. A little tact in the wording of such notices will go a long way toward softening the blow.

Employee Relations Policy

Not only does the employee relations policy affect the morale and efficiency of the employees themselves, but it also has a direct bearing upon public approval or disapproval of the employer. Perhaps the most important feature of an effective employee relations policy is the successful attempt to impart a "sense of participation." The goal is participation by all employees, not only in matters directly affecting their working conditions but also in various activities carried on by their own and other city departments. There are several methods for achieving this.

Channels of Communication. A merit system ordinance, personnel rules, labor-management agreements, employee newsletters, and other devices will not succeed in full if management and employees do not have at least some notion of the other's point of view. When a tentative personnel ordinance or set of rules, for example, has been prepared, copies should be distributed to employee groups for comments, criticisms, and counter proposals. Management should encourage full discussion, and both sides may have to compromise on some points. Further, rank and file employees must be convinced that the chief administrator, his immediate staff, and city department heads are sincere in trying to improve working relationships for all city employees.

Communication is a two-way affair. Management must take positive steps to keep employees informed on all phases of the work of the city: city finances, the budget, services, plans for the future, reasons why certain things cannot be done, and so forth. On the other hand, employees need opportunity to ask questions and to discuss matters of personal concern as well as to receive various kinds of information from above. Because first-line supervisors see and deal directly with employees most frequently, the department heads and the chief administrator can use these supervisors as a principal channel for getting information from employees. If the supervisor is kept informed of management's decisions and plans affecting employees, he in turn can keep employees informed, answer questions, and point out the reasons for the decisions.

Classification, Pay, and Conditions of Work. Even with all channels of communication wide open, disagreements still will occur if management is not realistic in providing an equitable basis of employment. There must be internal consistency with respect to duties and responsibilities of various positions and comparability with conditions in outside employment both in private industry and in other governmental agencies.

Conditions of service — vacations, sick leave, hours of work, and physical surroundings — affect both the attractiveness of the municipal service to potential recruits and the morale of the city's employees. An employer who shows little concern for the comfort and welfare of his employees cannot expect high morale in his organization. Furthermore, employees who are overworked or forced to work in dimly lighted, poorly ventilated offices can hardly be blamed if they are sometimes discourteous or grouchy toward the public.

In addition to these indirect effects of the employee relations policy on public relations, there can be some direct advantages. The employees should be brought into the public relations program as the active partners of administrative officials. If there is an employee organization, its own program of activities may include public relations activities that will supplement the city's official activities.

Employee Representation. Where employee groups have been organized, they should be received as normal participants in administration. This generally is all that need be involved in "recognition." Management should not put pressure on individual employees to join a particular organization, and likewise should not try to hinder the formation of unions. A helpful step in union relations is a regularly scheduled meeting of union representatives, department heads, and the mayor or city manager to discuss labor policy matters generally. In this way labor can be kept abreast of management problems and thinking. Difficulties can be met and resolved before they become serious issues.

Even if there is no formal organization of municipal employees, every opportunity should be given to employees, individually or in group meetings, to criticize present practices and make suggestions for improvement. Open forum meetings, suggestion boxes, and questionnaires are among the devices that might be used to secure employee support and suggestions. It is much better to have these suggestions come from the employees themselves than to have the entire program imposed from above. In public relations matters, attitude and spirit are as important as the procedure itself, and the best way to develop the proper spirit is to make the public relations program a joint enterprise of employees and administrators.

Grievance Procedure. Almost all cities that have grievance procedures rely on the traditional method of using administrative channels. The employee appeals first to his foreman and then through successive levels of the administration to the chief administrator. Employees are sometimes at a disadvantage under such a procedure for fear of job reprisals, and an advisory personnel board or employee-management council can help by giving him a measure of protection and assistance outside of the regular organization.

Although no ready-made formula exists for developing an effective grievance plan, some generally recognized principles have developed from experience with grievance plans in both private and public employment. (1) The successive steps in the grievance procedure should be as few and as direct as possible; (2) the grievance should be settled as near as possible to its point of origin; (3) when formal grievance machinery is involved, the grievance should be put in writing; (4) no employee should be penalized for using grievance machinery; (5) grievances should be acted on promptly; (6) employees should be free to present grievances through representatives of their own choosing; and (7) employees should be fully informed about the grievance plan, especially about where and to whom grievances should be presented.

Awards for Distinguished Service. "Man does not live by bread alone" is a maxim that should be remembered by all employers. There are few employees who do not respond to the opinion of their fellows, and to many men the desire for distinction is greater than monetary attraction. Unfortunately, too little attention has been given to this type of recognition in the municipal service. Firemen or policemen who have performed distinguished feats of heroism may be awarded medals, but distinguished service awards for employees in the less spectacular services are a rarity. Many municipal employees have made outstanding records of public service that deserve popular recognition. Without suggesting the exact form which such awards might take or the circumstances under which they might be granted, it may be pointed out that they have a twofold value for public relations purposes. In the first place, they are an incentive to employees whose morale and service will consequently be improved, and, secondly, they offer splendid subject matter for human interest publicity stories.

Relations With the Press

Public reporting and publicity proper are discussed later in the chapter, but special consideration of relations with the press is in order at this point. These are singled out for special treatment because they are more than publicity. The distinction lies primarily in the fact that relations with the press are two-way relations. Not only is the press a medium through which public officials can release publicity material to the public, but newspapers also reflect or express public opinion and convey information from the public to the city government. Relations with the press, therefore, involve a combination of publicity and citizen-official contact considerations.

Municipal policy governing press relationships is something that cannot be laid down arbitrarily and in detail. Local standards, habits, and circumstances will all affect the relationships and there is also the personal element involved. The observations and suggestions of a working newspaper man, however, are quoted here for their essential soundness and their general applicability.

"1. If I were a city official, I would have a clearly defined and systematic policy in all press relations. I would either supervise execution of such policies myself or have a responsible person, preferably with a knowledge of news and reporting techniques, do so under my direction. I would not deny reporters access to department heads but I would consult with the latter from time to time on matters of policy in regard to their own press relations.

"2. I would, after this policy is clearly understood, arrange conferences with the publishers and city editors of each of the local newspapers. I would ask their advice on how to clear the news for their convenience, and how to make that news accurately reflect the best values in public administration. I would discuss the result of these conferences with the reporter on my 'beat' and get his reaction to them. He is my daily contact; I would never make him feel I was 'going over his head.'

"3. I would arrange a convenient, regular 'press conference' time to see all newspapermen, although I would never deny any one of them admittance at any time.

"4. I would develop my own 'nose for news.' If I found it necessary to make 'off-the-record' statements, I would be sure the reporter understood at the outset that I was talking off-the-record. I would be free and helpful to reporters in their news-gathering jobs and answer all questions I thought fair and proper. If I could not answer a question I would, if possible, explain why. If a reporter were after a story which would be detrimental to good government if announced prematurely, I would tell him all the facts on that story, appealing to his sense of fair play in holding it. However, I would promise his paper an equal 'news break' when that story was ready.

"5. I would see that news breaks were distributed as evenly as possible between the morning and evening papers. If I talked to competitive reporters individually I would be careful to give each exactly the same story.

"6. I would not exaggerate the occasional petty criticisms that newspapers print so long as my general press relations were good.

"7. If a 'news leak' occurred and the report, because of inadequate information, was misinterpreted, I would call in newsmen and explain the proper interpretations to them.

"8. I would ask editors to give me a fair chance to answer critical 'letters-to-the-editor' in the same column printing such letters.

"9. I would insist that all municipal and departmental reports designed for public reading be written in terms understandable to the layman, with the qualities of clarity, simplicity, and directness, and with a format that would make people, including newspapermen, want to read them.

"10. On major public reports I would make the matter available to reporters from time to time before the report itself is actually published, if that is possible. These releases would be carefully timed. I would point out to the reporter the significance of more complicated passages in these reports and interpret them so he could write accurate and intelligent stories. I would also point out to him the infinite possibilities in various departments for news features and special Sunday articles. I would help him get pictures for such articles.

"11. I would prepare releases or formal written statements only on those stories of important policy where misconceptions or misquotes might result. Newspapers generally prefer to do their own local stories in their own way, and if I have the right contact with them I can explain any story clearly.

"12. I would look upon newspaper people as intelligent men engaged in a reputable work, and I would instruct all department heads and employees to treat them with respect and courtesy.

"13. Finally, I would make the newspaper an effective instrument in accounting to the public for my stewardship; and I would keep in mind the significant motto of a great newspaper chain: 'Give light and the people will find their way.'"[1]

Need for Coordinated Program

The preceding pages have defined public relations, emphasized the need for a public relations program, and sketched in broad outline the content of such a program. Most of the specific features of such a program will be familiar to many city officials. Any

---

[1] Hal Hazelrigg, "A Newspaper Man Looks at City Hall," in Public Management, March, 1938, pp. 67-70.

novelty or originality in the program that has been outlined probably is to be found in the idea that all of these related activities of service, public contacts, procedures, appearance, and publicity properly belong together. Something needs to be said, therefore, regarding the relationship of these varied activities and techniques to each other, and the importance of welding them together into a coherent and coordinated program.

One of the principal values of having a well-defined public relations program is that the general level of public relations contacts and activities may be enhanced by this unification process. If each department or agency is allowed to have its own way in public relations matters, handling things as best it can and using what ideas occur to departmental officials, many ideas and much talent are wasted. By the pooling of techniques, resources, and ideas, the best that is produced by any individual or office can be applied to the advantage of all, and the interchange of ideas and experiences may lead to a superior standard of performance.

Better balance can also be achieved with respect to the different elements of the public. In most cities, there are many groups that are being almost entirely neglected as far as public relations activities are concerned, and an integrated public relations program under some central direction or coordination offers the logical solution to this weakness.

Organization for Public Relations

If there has been any one theme running throughout this chapter, it is that the public relations program is inseparable from the service program of the city and that every member of the organization is, or should be, a public relations officer. Every employee who has any contact with the public makes his contribution — positive or negative — to the public relations of the city government. To attempt to delegate to any one official or agency the task of improving a city's public relations is therefore to ignore the nature of public relations and the factors which affect them. Planning and administering a public relations program is not a one-man job, or even a one-office job. It is a job for the entire municipal organization.

It does not follow, of course, that responsibility for public relations should be equally shared or that there is no need for special public relations assignments. A rough outline of the distribution of public relations responsibilities, together with some suggestions for special assignments, may be briefly presented.

Division of Responsibility

The Council. Although this chapter has approached municipal public relations from the administrative viewpoint, recognition must be given here to the important role of the council in the public relations program. In the first place, the council determines the basic policies of the city government, and if a government's policies do not generally meet with public approval, its public relations can never be very satisfactory. Beyond its law-making duties the council has other public relations responsibilities. Public relations embrace a two-way relationship, and the public relations program must seek not only to transmit ideas and impressions but also to create receptiveness and responsiveness on the part of public officials.

Council members should always be on the alert to interpret public opinion and attitudes to officials and employees, to see that the citizens' point of view is kept constantly in the foreground in the conduct of public business, and to check any tendencies on the part of professional public servants to adopt official aloofness or indifference toward the public. Council members can also assist in the public relations program by helping to interpret municipal policies and programs to the public through addresses, conferences, interviews, and the like.

The Chief Administrator. The chief administrator — the mayor, city manager, or whatever his title may be — should be the chief public relations officer of the city. As the officer responsible for formulating broad municipal policies and programs for the approval of the council, and as the officer who implements the council's policies with specific programs of action, the chief administrator is the logical person to formulate basic public relations policies, to coordinate and blend the public relations activities of the several departments into a balanced and consistent program. He may assign special public relations duties to his aides and subordinates, but he cannot delegate or escape responsibility for the city's public relations. In every plan or program that he formulates or helps to formulate, in every review of the activities of his subordinates, he must give consideration to the effects of such programs or activities upon the public relations of the city government.

Department Heads. The heads of the various city departments are responsible for seeing that the general public relations policies and standards are applied to the work of their subordinates. Each department head must appraise the principal classes of contacts between employees of his department and members of the public and formulate specific standards governing employee participation in these contacts. The police chief must establish standards of police courtesy and provide instructions for police officers in dealing with the public.

Similarly, the finance director must study the public relations aspects of tax billing and collecting; the public works director must provide standards and instruction for refuse collectors and construction employees in their many public contacts; and the health officer must see that the enforcement of health regulations by members of his department does not unnecessarily offend the rights and feelings of those regulated.

Every department head is also responsible for explaining the work of his department to the public through one or more media of publicity and reporting. He may not make all of the speeches for his department or write all of his department's public reports, but it is his responsibility to decide what information is best suited for publicity purposes and to see that the work of his department is fairly presented to the public.

Supervisors. The council, the chief administrator, and the department heads are responsible for public relations policies and standards, but it remains for supervisory officials — foremen, division heads, sergeants, and the like — to see that the actions and attitudes of individual employees conform to these policies and standards. It is the responsibility of supervisory officials to guide and review the conduct of subordinates and to provide continuous training through criticisms of poor performance and demonstrations of better practice. No public relations program can be effective unless supervisory officials understand and sympathize with the objectives and content of the program.

The Rank and File. The need for bringing every employee into the public relations program has already been stressed. It may also be added, however, that best results can be expected only when individual employees are active and willing participants in the program. Every effort should therefore be made to encourage employees — either individually or as members of employee organizations — to assume initiative and responsibility for improving the city's public relations.

Specialized Public Relations Personnel

A comprehensive public relations program, particularly in the larger cities, may require some specially qualified personnel for specialized tasks.

Contact Employees. Almost every official and employee has some public contacts, but there a few whose work consists chiefly of meeting and dealing with the public. If there is a central information and complaint bureau, employees assigned to this bureau are key public relations personnel. The counter clerks and receptionists in the various departments and offices may also be classed as special public relations employees, as may telephone operators and cashiers in revenue collecting offices. When these employees are selected, special attention should be given to their appearance, tact, disposition, and other qualities that affect their ability to meet the public. After these employees have been selected, they may be given special training for their public relations duties. The nature of this training was suggested earlier in this chapter.

Publicity Staff. If the volume of reports and other publicity material prepared and released by municipal departments is large, it may be wise to employ one or more employees with special publicity or editorial training and experience. The publicity staff could assist the several departments, as well as the chief administrator and the council, in planning, writing, and editing municipal reports. If the city uses the radio or television as publicity media, it may even be feasible to have on the publicity staff some persons experienced in the best use of such media.

Training Instructors. Another group of key public relations officers are the instructors responsible for in-service training. This includes not only those instructors giving training in special public relations techniques — the proper use of the telephone, how to write a letter, handling complaints, preparation of publicity and reports, and so forth — but also the instructors responsible for training employees in the techniques of their day-to-day work. As a matter of fact, the training responsibilities of supervisory officials are so important that they might well be included in this group. In the largest cities it may be possible to have a large number of training instructors in the several departments.

In the smaller cities, where, except for supervisory officers, there are no officials specifically charged with training duties, outside instructors may be brought in from time to time. State boards of vocational education in many states have itinerant instructors available to local governments. Local high schools, colleges, and business schools may have instructors who can give instruction in letter writing, journalism, and other public relations subjects. Arrangements may be made with the local telephone company for instruction in the proper use of the telephone, and local department stores or private utility corporations may have persons qualified to give special instruction in handling customer complaints.

A Public Relations Officer. It is often suggested that a municipal government should employ a special public relations officer or counsel to handle public relations for the city. The implication that public relations responsibilities can be delegated to any one officer or any one office has already been rejected, but there may be a place for a public relations officer, provided that his proper place in the organization is clearly understood and also that the officer selected has the necessary qualifications.

The logical role of a public relations officer in a municipal organization is that of an aide to the chief administrator. It has already been pointed out that the chief administrator should be the chief public relations officer of the city, and the function of a special aide should be to assist the chief administrator in planning, coordinating, and controlling the city's public relations program. Such an aide could help the administrator survey and appraise current public relations and analyze the weak spots in official policies and procedures, and he could help to explain the administrator's policies and standards to department heads. In addition, the public relations officer might also supervise or even perform certain of the specialized public relations services, such as the editing of reports, handling inquiries and complaints, and so forth.

What the public relations assistant should not do or be is equally important. There is a tendency to conceive of the public relations officer as a glorified press agent. Such a public relations officer in a city hall would in most cases do more harm than good. A dynamic press agent, unfamiliar with administrative problems and methods, would be likely to offend the operating officials and employees and to lose their invaluable cooperation in the program. Furthermore the appointment of a municipal press agent might easily prove to be a boomerang as far as the public is concerned. If the public relations program is featured by ballyhoo tactics and is headed by a press agent, the public may interpret the whole program as a propaganda campaign, with the result that the prestige of the city government will be impaired rather than enhanced.

What are the qualifications for a good public relations officer? He should have a talent for appraising and understanding public attitudes and wishes, whether expressed or not. In other words, he needs to be at least a "practical psychologist." He should also understand administrative problems and procedures so that he can suggest improvements that will win public approval and at the same time be feasible from the administrative point of view. He should be able to win the confidence and cooperation of other officials and employees, for alone he can do very little. He should be able to keep himself in the background in order to keep the program from being a one-man program. If, in addition to these general qualifications, he has some special skills in the field of publicity, so much the better, but his primary job is to help the chief administrator plan and coordinate the program.

Unfortunately there is no readily available supply of persons with these qualifications. Most of the public relations counsellors in private business have come from the fields of journalism or publicity. Some of them have done well, but the dangers of entrusting a broad public relations program to a publicity man have been indicated. Some of the young men who are finding places as administrative assistants in the more progressive city halls might be very valuable aides to the chief administrator in public relations matters. The use of a general administrative assistant as a public relations officer has the further merit of emphasizing the interrelationship between public relations problems and other problems of administration.

II. Public Reporting

With the exception of reporting through the press, little has been said as yet about the techniques of reporting. The remainder of this chapter is devoted to a more detailed consideration of some of the principal media of public reporting, together with some specific suggestions as to how these various media can be most effectively employed. Talks before citizen groups, exhibits and demonstrations, motion pictures, radio, television, and printed reports are the principal media of public reporting by municipal governments, and each will be discussed in this chapter.

Under the heading of printed reports, special consideration is given to the annual municipal report and there are several reasons for this. First, the annual report is often the only reporting medium that presents to the citizen a picture of his city government as a whole. As such, it may be considered the special province and responsibility of the chief administrator. Second, the preparation of the annual report is frequently the incentive for the collection of information that can be released through many reporting media. Not only the subject matter but also the exhibits and illustrations prepared for the annual report may be useful in preparing other reporting material. Third, many of the suggestions made relative to the form and content of the annual report can be readily applied to the preparation of other reporting material.

Talks Before Citizen Groups

In the course of a year's time, city officials and employees may be called on for hundreds of public addresses before all kinds of audiences and on any number of subjects. These include after-dinner speeches before civic and social clubs, lectures before groups of school children, lectures before specialized interest groups such as bankers, taxpayers' associations, local improvement associations, and so on. From a public relations point of view, there are three important considerations in any such lecture or speech: the composition of the audience, the material used, and the speaker himself.

The composition of the audience is important for several reasons. First of all, the interests of the audience will determine the subject matter in many cases. City officials who have standardized speeches which they give on all occasions contribute little from the public relations point of view. As in the case of deciding who shall receive printed material, careful attention should be given to the nature and interests of every audience before the speech is prepared. The age and intelligence or education of the audience are also factors. The kind of talk required for school children will differ from that required for the university club or for a labor organization. Finally, the size of the audience is important. Some speakers and some kinds of speeches will be well received by small informal groups but not by large audiences.

The kind of material used is important in all addresses. It is difficult to make any general recommendations on this point, but a suggestion or two may be offered. There seems to be a tendency on the part of officials to rely too heavily upon statistics in one form or another. Illustrative materials accompanying lectures may often help to enliven them or to give them meaning. Displays of charts and large-sized photographs or photographic slides may enliven the subject matter of official speeches.

One answer to the problem raised by the high-ranking official who is a naturally poor speaker is to secure a substitute. This leads to the suggestion that much greater use might be made of subordinate personnel in public speaking engagements required of city officials. Not only will subordinate personnel supply a wider range of talent, but these speaking opportunities will do much to improve the morale of the lower ranking official.

Exhibits and Demonstrations

Open House

One of the most popular reporting devices in some cities has been an annual or special "open house." On such occasions the city hall and sometimes other municipal buildings are thrown open for inspection, and the public is invited to attend at any time during the day or evening. Each department is responsible for preparing special charts, exhibits, working models of equipment and projects, and other features which will attract public interest and help to explain municipal services to the citizens. Municipal employees in attendance at each of these departmental exhibits are available to answer any questions raised by visitors and to explain the exhibits.

Special Exhibits

Although the open house may not be conveniently held more than once or twice a year, it is still possible for some of the exhibits of the kind presented at the city hall to be available for public inspection throughout the year. The foyer of the city hall may provide an excellent space for a series of exhibits representing the different departments of the city government. Most communities do have some local fairs or shows in which municipal exhibits might profitably be entered. For example, the local flower show may provide an excellent opportunity for the park department to enter an attractive and instructive exhibit.

It might also be suggested that public works projects in various parts of the city may well be accompanied by illustrative exhibits or materials. An important new bridge project might be accompanied by an exhibit of a large-scale map, model, or at least a well-prepared architect's sketch. A highway construction project might prove much more interesting and enlightening to the many passers-by if it were accompanied by a cross-section showing the several layers of foundations and pavement material that go into its construction. The principal point is that all of these projects do attract public interest, but few of them are understood by the lay citizen. Given this natural interest, the city should take every opportunity to turn the interest into understanding and appreciation.

Demonstrations

Demonstrations, as the name implies, differ from exhibits in that city employees enact the performance of some service rendered by the city. They may be held in conjunction with or separate from exhibits and may relate to any number of services. The use of drill towers is particularly well adapted to a public demonstration of fire department activities or training. First-aid demonstrations by members of the fire department are often given before local clubs and civic groups. Public demonstrations by the police department in the form of pistol exhibitions or motorcycle drills have aroused considerable interest in a number of cities.

To be effective, the performance of any public demonstration must be carefully planned and thoroughly rehearsed. Impromptu efforts are dangerous and may leave a distasteful as well as inaccurate impression of the organization involved. Since exhibits and demonstrations both offer physical evidence of the services of the city government, it is probable that they will be most effective when used jointly.

Motion Pictures

Another reporting device that has recently grown in popularity with municipal officials is the motion picture. This is a device with universal appeal. All age groups, economic, social and interest groups appear to be attracted by it. In addition, it has the advantage of being presented in a darkened room under conditions which make it all but impossible to ignore the screen. However, in spite of its great potential there has been only a limited effective use of the motion picture. Many have been made but a large proportion suffer from dullness.

The reasons for uninteresting presentations are many. Too much diverse subject matter is covered — often on the theory that the several budget breakdowns should be the basis for the organization of the film. Audiences are interested in a story, not an encyclopedia. Inanimate objects frequently occupy too much footage. Motion is needed. Excessive length is another common weakness. Twenty minutes should normally be considered the limit in length.

If the film prepared by the city is sufficiently attractive, local motion picture houses may be willing to show it as a special educational feature on their general program. In other cases, the film may be used as the basis for private showings to clubs, school children, and other groups.

Radio and Television Reporting and Publicity

In radio and television there is a necessity for instant capture of the audience. The presentation is made at a specific time and no other. In the case of printed materials time has no bearing because these materials are read at a time determined by individual choice. In addition, printed materials may be aimed directly at a specific audience or public, but this is not true of radio and television audiences. Television and radio make much greater demands on time and talent for adequate presentation than do printed materials covering the same subject, but there is a corresponding result. The impact of a good television or radio show is infinitely greater than that of printed materials.

Types of Programs

Cities have used various types of programs: interviews, panel discussions, question-and-answer shows, oral reports, demonstrations, films, dramatic presentations, and broadcasts of city council meetings. Several cities have used and are using the interview type of program. The mayor, city manager, and department heads, are the officials most frequently called upon to participate. In Boulder, Colorado, the city manager acts as interviewer to ask department heads about current happenings and activities in their departments. The program is tape recorded at the convenience of the city officials so that the schedule is flexible.

Although it is better adapted to radio, since the emphasis is on what people are saying rather than what is being done or demonstrated, the interview has been successfully used on television. Philadelphia, Pennsylvania, has presented a television show entitled "Tell It To The Mayor." The program featured citizens in person or by telephone conversation presenting to the mayor and his department heads on a first-hand basis their questions and complaints about the city government. A somewhat similar program has been used in Dayton, Ohio. Eau Claire, Wisconsin, has also had notable success with the television interview. Some of the subjects that have been presented to the citizens of Eau Claire through these programs include disaster planning, clean-up-paint-up week, the necessity for building inspection, polio immunization program, zoning problems, water supply, and summer recreational program for the city.

With proper planning and capable personnel the use of the demonstration-type of program, with visual aids, can be highly effective. Kansas City has made extensive use of charts, models of bridges and models of redevelopment for blighted areas, all of which have helped to interpret the development of expressways, city planning, rehabilitation, and similar subjects.

Greensboro, North Carolina, has made use of documentary-type films produced and edited by the police department and dealing with various activities of the department along with an explanation and narration by a police officer.

Although seldom used by cities but deserving of exploration and experiment is the dramatic presentation. One effort along these lines depicted a selected traffic accident using an entire cast of police officers working from a script written and acted out by members of the department. Events leading up to the accident, the accident itself, and subsequent investigation and findings by the police department's accident investigation division were dramatically presented. Some cities: Minot, North Dakota; West Palm Beach, Florida; Two Rivers, Wisconsin; and Escanaba, Michigan, to name a few, have broadcast council meetings over the radio. Skillful editing of recordings of council meetings, however, is essential to improve the quality and popularity of the broadcast, since many actions of the council are routine and have little general interest for citizens. There are also some powerful arguments, not connected with the matter of public reporting and public relations, for avoiding the broadcast or telecast of regular council meetings.

Scheduling Programs

The sporadic or unscheduled type of program is the least effective. A series of telecasts or broadcasts are best planned to cover a period of six months to a year, even though specific programs may have to be altered or completely changed occasionally. Audiences for programs have to be cultivated and interest must be built up over a period of time. With a series, each program may serve to create interest in succeeding programs. Publicity for a program series is also made more effective. News releases and spot announcements may be made both before and during the series to increase the audience, which at the outset will be very small.

The type of program used as well as the content will determine to a great extent the length of time necessary for the presentation. The average span of attention, however, for a municipal program will normally not exceed 15 minutes. Where a straight oral report is given it is well to limit the program to five or ten minutes.

Various surveys indicate that the best time for getting a potentially large audience is from eight to ten p.m.; next best are the two hours immediately preceding this period. Specifically, the best time is in the evening immediately following a popular network program. The city's program, if properly introduced, will then benefit from the large audience which has received the preceding program. A regular weekly program presented over the same station at the same time is preferable to broadcasting at irregular intervals. In obtaining time from the station, it may be better for the city to accept two 15-minute allotments at a different time than a half-hour or one hour allotment at a less desirable time.

Preparing Programs

Considerable time and work are normally necessary in preparing adequate radio and television programs. The interview and panel discussion programs require the least amount of time for preparation. Rehearsals are not necessary, and the script need not be prepared. Some cities report approximately one hour's preparation for a 15-minute radio program which is presented without script. On the other hand, in Saginaw, Michigan, which has given a 15-minute interview type of program with prepared script, it was estimated that some eight hours were spent in preparation for each program.

Whenever possible, program topics should be timely, and an attempt made to key programs to current problems and activities. A program on budgeting, for example, could be presented when the city council is conducting budget hearings. A program on public improvement could be presented at a time the voters are asked to approve bond issues.

No television program should be presented without the use of visual aids. The basic reason for choosing television rather than radio is that there is something for the audience to see as well as to hear. Charts, graphs, models, actual equipment, photographs, movies, and other visual aids should be carefully selected to illustrate information or activities.

Speakers or participants on municipal TV and radio programs should be selected on the basis of their qualifications for radio broadcasting and telecasting rather than on the basis of their position, although it will be desirable in many instances for top city officials to appear on a program because they are well known and because of their knowledge of municipal activities. Selecting participants from the lower echelons of the administration as well as the upper serves a two-fold purpose: exceptionally qualified personnel may be employed, and additional opportunities for recognition are thus opened to the employees.

It is necessary to arrange for stand-by personnel especially in the case of television programs, where a sudden illness or other circumstance may prevent a participant from appearing or where a program may have to be changed on short notice. Extensive and complete rehearsal are necessary for the demonstration type of television show. All visual aids or props require spotting for predetermined camera angles which must be worked out before the show is presented.

Measuring Public Reaction

A professional survey of public reaction of the city's program will in most cases be too costly. However, the success of the city's program can be measured to some extent by "mail pull" methods. Viewers and listeners may be invited to write or telephone for free pamphlets compiled by the city. Free theater tickets may be offered for the best question submitted concerning the city's organization or activities. In nearly all attempts to get "mail pull," something free is offered to those who respond.

Another method of measuring public reaction is the telephone survey. Wichita, Kansas, ran its own survey on the city's radio program by sampling five hundred homes by telephone during the period of the broadcast. Another measuring technique, used in cooperation with school officials, is that of asking school pupils to fill out a questionnaire to indicate whether or not the city's program has been received in the home, or the questionnaire may be taken home to the parents to fill out.

Printed Reports

The Annual Municipal Report

Of the various media which are used for public reporting, printed reports and pamphlets have come to play a major role, and of these the general annual report has received increasing attention during the past decade. The number of cities issuing annual reports has increased, the physical attractiveness of the reports has improved, and the content of the report has, in many instances, attained high quality.

Content of the Annual Report. What should the annual municipal report contain in order to assume its proper place of importance in the publicity program of the city? The material of the report may be conveniently divided into six parts:

1. Introduction
2. Legislation and general administration
3. Municipal Services
4. The "Managerial" and "Auxiliary" Services
5. The City's Finances
6. Planning Municipal Services

No hard and fast rules can be applied to the method of presenting the content of the report. However, as far as possible, the report should be organized around municipal services and functions rather than individual departments. The citizen on the receiving end of municipal government is far more interested in the service program than in the minutiae of organization. For the same reason the report should include education, libraries, and similar functions, even if they are administered by agencies which are independent of the municipal corporation.

The content and attractiveness of the introductory part of the report will largely determine whether the citizen will read further. The cover is of primary importance. It should be of attractive design, and in addition should make clear that the booklet is the annual report of the city government for a specified period of time. The population and area of the city may also appropriately appear on the cover or on the title page.

A chart of the administrative organization of the city is valuable in the introductory section of the report as a help to the reader in properly orienting himself and in aiding him better to understand the report itself. The chart should indicate, as simply as possible, the main lines of authority and responsibility connecting city departments with the citizens. In order that a complete picture of municipal services may be shown, independent agencies and their relationship to the municipal corporation should be included. Every annual report should also contain a table of contents giving the page on which each municipal function included in the report is covered.

Following the table of contents, most reports include a review of the year, generally in listed form, which gives a bird's-eye view of outstanding events, some results of the year's administrative operations, and the state of municipal affairs. Adherence to the highest standards of public reporting requires that unfavorable as well as favorable results be itemized in this section and that the table actually be a review of the year rather than a list of "outstanding achievements" or "accomplishments." The review might also be accompanied by a list of problems to be faced in the future, with a concise outline of factors relevant to the solution of these problems. Throughout this feature of the report, care must be taken to avoid extensive overlapping of material presented later in the text and detail that is more properly placed in the departmental or functional discussions in the body of the report.

A final desirable feature of the introductory part of the annual report, but one which few cities have included, is a statement of the citizen's part in government, indicating how city services affect the individual in his everyday life. Designed to sell citizenship rather than the city administration to the reader, this statement might mention his opportunities for formal participation in city government through attendance at council meetings and hearings as well as election. It might also instruct the citizen as to how he can obtain information or service and lodge complaints at the city hall. General sources of the city's income and expenditures for major purposes, broken down into the daily or weekly cost of municipal services to the citizen, may also be indicated here (see Fig. 43). The cost of government services can be strikingly presented when compared with costs of familiar items such as a package of cigarettes or a bottle of milk.

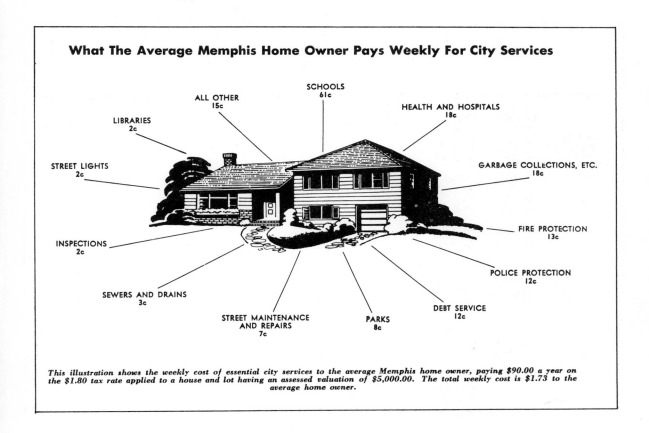

What The Average Memphis Home Owner Pays Weekly For City Services

SCHOOLS
61c

ALL OTHER
15c

HEALTH AND HOSPITALS
18c

LIBRARIES
2c

GARBAGE COLLECTIONS, ETC.
18c

STREET LIGHTS
2c

FIRE PROTECTION
13c

INSPECTIONS
2c

POLICE PROTECTION
12c

SEWERS AND DRAINS
3c

STREET MAINTENANCE
AND REPAIRS
7c

PARKS
8c

DEBT SERVICE
12c

This illustration shows the weekly cost of essential city services to the average Memphis home owner, paying $90.00 a year on the $1.80 tax rate applied to a house and lot having an assessed valuation of $5,000.00. The total weekly cost is $1.73 to the average home owner.

Fig. 43 — Illustration From Annual Report: Use of Tax Dollar (Memphis, Tennessee)

Following the introductory part of the annual report, a second major division of the contents may cover legislation and general administration, indicating briefly the respective roles of the city council and chief administrator in the city government and presenting a review of important legislative action during the year. Special elections, charter changes, and new state laws significantly affecting cities, as well as important ordinances and resolutions passed by the council, might comprise the body of this part of the report. The laws and policies for the execution of which the administrative organization is responsible are of great importance from the viewpoint of public reporting, as they provide a major part of the framework within which municipal services are offered to the citizen.

Next come the four divisions of material that make up the main body of the report: (1) operating services, (2) managerial and auxiliary services, (3) finance, and (4) planning. Finance and planning might be included among the managerial and auxiliary functions of government, but for purposes of reporting they appear to warrant special treatment and

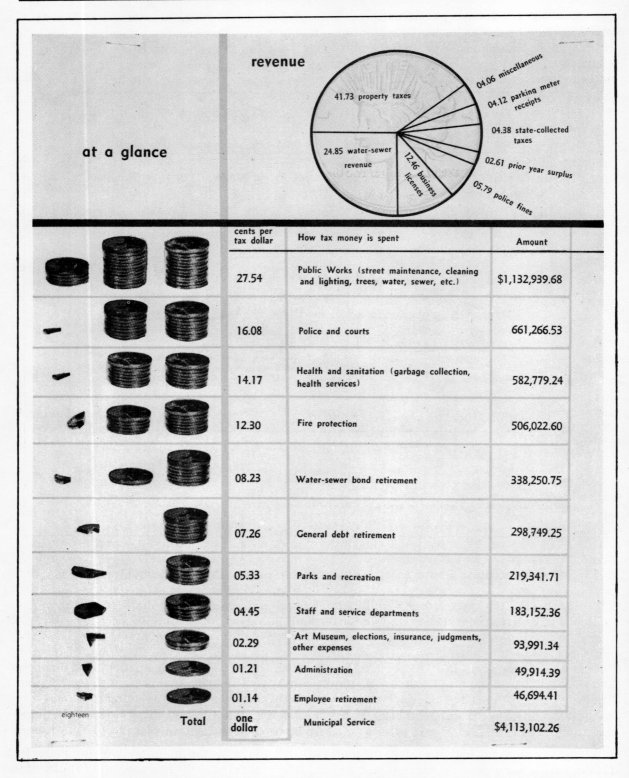

revenue

at a glance

41.73 property taxes

04.06 miscellaneous

04.12 parking meter receipts

04.38 state-collected taxes

02.61 prior year surplus

05.79 police fines

24.85 water-sewer revenue

12.46 business licenses

cents per tax dollar	How tax money is spent	Amount
27.54	Public Works (street maintenance, cleaning and lighting, trees, water, sewer, etc.)	$1,132,939.68
16.08	Police and courts	661,266.53
14.17	Health and sanitation (garbage collection, health services)	582,779.24
12.30	Fire protection	506,022.60
08.23	Water-sewer bond retirement	338,250.75
07.26	General debt retirement	298,749.25
05.33	Parks and recreation	219,341.71
04.45	Staff and service departments	183,152.36
02.29	Art Museum, elections, insurance, judgments, other expenses	93,991.34
01.21	Administration	49,914.39
01.14	Employee retirement	46,694.41
Total one dollar	Municipal Service	$4,113,102.26

eighteen

Fig. 44 — Illustration From Annual Report: Revenue Sources and Expenditures (Columbia, South Carolina)

consequently are classified separately. The reasons for this special treatment will be more fully explained later in the chapter.

The method of presenting the material in these four general divisions is of utmost importance if the report is to be read by those for whom it is intended. Textual material should be generously supplemented by photographs and other illustrative devices. Statistical material can be vividly presented in the form of charts or graphs. To some persons the simplest chart is totally incomprehensible, while to others it conveys the point more readily than words or figures can. Statistical information should therefore be presented both in textual and graphic form. The use of statistics has been greatly overworked in the past, however, and great caution must be exercised in their use. Trends over a period of years should be shown carefully, but comparisons with other cities may often be dangerously misleading.

Although the presentation of material is important, the principal consideration is the kind of material that should be reported. In reporting its activities, the city is striving to provide the citizens with information that will enable them to determine whether their money has been wisely and effectively spent and whether the governmental activities that are being carried on adequately meet civic needs. To answer these demands, a list of suggested specifications for each activity, consisting of topics to be included and measurement units for each topic, has been prepared by the International City Managers' Association.[2] Methods of measuring municipal activities were discussed in Chapter 12, so it is sufficient to summarize here the topics and general information relative to municipal services that should appear in the annual report.

The finance section of the annual report must strive to explain and discuss the soundness of the city's finances, the financial policy, the city's debt policy, and prospects with regard to resources as well as expenditures for services. It should synthesize the viewpoint of the taxpayer who supports city government with that of the citizen who receives services. The central question it should answer is, "Where does the money come from and where does it go?"

The sixth major division in the content of an annual municipal report is concerned with planning, another managerial function that is worthy of special consideration for purposes of public reporting. Like the finance section, the planning section of the report affords an opportunity to present an integrated picture of city services. The nature of planning and the need for planning should be discussed, as well as the present organization for planning. A brief account should be given of each of the major elements of the city plan, of recent planning legislation, and of any research studies completed during the year on land use, population trends, zoning administration, and so forth.

The purpose of zoning and its relation to the present land utilization pattern as well as to land needs should be pointed out, and progress on street, transportation, parking, and public building plans should be indicated. A discussion of subdivision platting activity and subdivision standards should also be included. A final topic for the planning section to discuss is the long-range plan, its objectives, the major improvements contemplated, methods of financing, and the effect of the improvements on the city's budget.

Preparation of the Annual Report. The presentation of topics of special importance should be expanded, and attention should be directed particularly to those activities where major changes in operation or extension of service have taken place and to important

---

[2]Clarence E. Ridley and Herbert A. Simon, Specifications for the Annual Municipal Report (Chicago: International City Managers' Association, 1948). 52 pp.

questions of policy which face the administration and the citizen. For instance, one year a special section of the report may be devoted to sewage disposal: the problem may be pointed out, the adequacy of existing facilities described, and possible courses of action presented. Another year the emphasis might be placed on the zoning needs of the city or the need for reducing traffic congestion. Similarly, in reporting the ordinary operations of municipal services and agencies, considerable ingenuity must be exercised to achieve a variety in presentation that will attract and hold the reader's attention.

The task of cimpiling and preparing the material for the annual report is therefore not a light one and demands trained personnel. Too often, the task is not regularly assigned to a single employee but is entrusted to any official who happens, at the moment, to be available for extra work. Though much of the raw material for the annual report naturally comes from the reports of department heads, the revising and editing of this material and the compilation of other data should devolve upon an individual in the administrative organization who is selected specifically for that purpose. He should have had some training and experience in public relations and public reporting work and should have some familiarity with printing processes.

A staff member of the municipal research bureau, the bureau of public information or public relations, or the municipal reference library may be given the task of editing the annual report in many of the larger cities. In smaller jurisdictions, the city manager, his assistant, or the city clerk may be designated as the report editor. It is important that the job be entrusted to the same individual each year and that he have a clear understanding of his function.

Preparation of the annual report for publication should be carried on throughout the year if the report is to appear within a reasonable time after the close of the period covered. The material should be delivered to the printer within four to six weeks after the close of the period if its content is to be considered as news rather than history.

Among the steps that should be taken during the year in connection with preparation of the manuscript are the improvement of departmental records, from which most of the basic material for the annual report will be obtained; the gathering of information on special projects or changes as they occur; and the interviewing of department heads in order to get advance information on the content and features of their reports. Photographs may be taken, ideas for charts and graphs sketched, and the format and printing details decided during the year.

At the close of the period, the departmental reports should be reorganized on a functional basis, and it is here that the importance of trained reporting personnel becomes apparent. In the process of revising and combining the reports of organization units, care should be taken not to distort facts or confuse statements, and the revised manuscript should be checked by department heads for erroneous statements. When they and the chief executive have approved the manuscript, it is ready for the printer.

It is doubtful whether the report editor should attempt to determine the layout of the annual report unless he or some other official has had considerable experience in composition and typography. Needless expense may be incurred if the layout details are determined without the aid of the printer or of a professional typographer.

Printing Methods and Costs. Recent advances in printing and related techniques have developed several methods of reproduction which may in many circumstances prove to be more flexible and economical than conventional letterpress printing. Four methods which a city should consider for reproducing its annual report, as well as other types of printed publicity, are dittoing or mimeographing, multilithing, typescript lithoprinting, letterpress lithoprinting, and letterpress printing.

Distribution of the Annual Report. The ultimate objective in the distribution of the annual report should be to place a copy in every home in the city. Estimating four persons per home, and allowing for additional copies for other distribution, one copy of the report should normally be printed for every three persons in the city.

Some city officials may feel that they cannot immediately budget a sufficient sum to print this number of reports. If this is the case, the distribution of the annual report should be handled in a manner that will most effectively answer existing demands for the report and create positive interest in it and its content.

In addition to copies of the report distributed according to applications or advance requests, a number of copies should be distributed to certain civic groups and public agencies. These will include the public libraries, municipal councilmen and officials, and the headquarters of all civic organizations that have a manifest interest in the conduct of city affairs. A supply of copies should also be readily available to answer requests during the year from correspondents and from citizens calling at the city hall.

In order to preserve the proper relationship with the public relations program of the city, publicity material should be distributed not only so as to answer existing demand, but also so as to create positive interest in municipal affairs. One of the important values of the annual report is that its secondary audience is, or can be, much greater than its primary audience. When copies of the report are sent to the local newspapers and to the public schools, the information contained in the report and the impression gained from reading it will probably be passed on to a much wider circle of citizens.

Finally, it might be suggested that all municipal employees should receive a copy of the annual report to serve as a basis for a better understanding of the city on their part. Certainly every employee who has official contacts with the public should have a copy and should be expected to know its contents as a basis for answering questions raised by citizens.

The methods to be used for the local distribution of the annual report must be decided by each jurisdiction, although some form of personal delivery is always more impressive, and probably less expensive, than mailing if a large number of copies is to be sent. Employees of the police, fire, or public works department are often utilized for delivering the annual report. Delivery by local Boy Scout troops, a method used by Cincinnati, or by high school groups interested in civic affairs may be feasible. The newspaper supplement, of course, has the advantage of a ready-made method of distribution at no additional cost.

Special Reports

Occasionally circumstances will arise which may require the preparation of a special report dealing with some particular problem or development. Such reports may range from a one-page insert accompanying tax or utility bills to an elaborate, especially prepared report celebrating an anniversary of the city's incorporation. The leaflets or inserts have the advantage of being small and inexpensive; they emphasize single subjects at appropriate times; and they usually may be given wider distribution than the general annual report. They lend themselves to the treatment of a single subject or phase of a subject, such as a breakdown of the city's revenues and expenditures, or questions relative to the water supply, health needs, a clean-up campaign, and so forth.

A special report of another type which is gaining favor is the chief administrator's "newsletter." This is usually a weekly or monthly sheet of information covering city hall events and plans of interest to employees, the city councilmen and, in many cases, to the public.

The usefulness of municipal employees as distribution agents should be re-emphasized. Counter clerks and contact employees will often have occasion, in dealing with citizen requests or complaints, to use special reports or leaflets to illustrate the points they are making. If the citizen seems sufficiently interested in the information contained in the report, he should be given a copy.

The use of police in distributing publicity material is illustrated by a practice in Wichita, Kansas, and in one or two other cities, where a personal greeting is extended to newcomers to the city. The greeting sometimes includes a specially prepared letter from some high-ranking official or from the council, a copy of the annual municipal report, and perhaps some specially prepared lists of instructions and information for new residents. The police officer is suggested for this type of personal contact principally because his uniform and his badge make him an appropriate symbol for the city services and also because the police have a direct interest in becoming acquainted with as many persons as possible and learning something of their background, habits, and special needs for protection. Not to be forgotten are the commercial "welcoming" services, such as the "welcome wagon." These agencies can place helpful leaflets, letters or annual reports about the city in the hands of new city residents.

Summary

In outlining a municipal public relations program it has been suggested in this chapter:

That good municipal service be recognized as the basis for a sound public relations program.

That a careful appraisal and analysis of the public and its attitudes be made to determine what the citizens want their city government to do and how they want it done.

That steps be taken to make it easier for citizens to secure accurate answers to their questions regarding the city services.

That courtesy and respect be accorded to every citizen who has a complaint to make about his city government and that systematic action be taken to satisfy complaints and to prevent their recurrence.

That all procedures involving contacts between citizens and officials be simplified and made as convenient as possible for the citizens.

That citizens be encouraged to take an active part in the administrative affairs of the city and that city employees should assume their responsibilities as citizens as well as public servants.

That careful attention be given to improving the appearance and cleanliness of public buildings, properties, and equipment.

That the city use the best recruiting devices to secure high caliber employees and that it use the most up-to-date personnel administration techniques to keep its employees competent and alert and satisfied with employment by the city.

That public officials be frank and cooperative in their relations with the press; that there be no censorship of information of value or interest to the public.

That the various forms of publicity and reporting be regarded as means for stimulating the interest of citizens in their government and providing them with information that will permit them to understand, properly appraise, and control their local government.

Every one of these recommendations can be justified not only because of its effect on public relations but also because it improves the service of the city government to its citizens. Good public relations must be deserved. Artifice and manipulations may enjoy a temporary success, but in the long run good public relations are based upon giving the public what it wants in a manner that will win the public's respect and friendship.

SELECTED BIBLIOGRAPHY ON MUNICIPAL ADMINISTRATION

GENERAL

Barnard, Chester I. The Functions of the Executive (Cambridge, Massachusetts: Harvard University Press, 1938). 334pp.

--Organization and Management (Cambridge, Massachusetts: Harvard University Press, 1948). 244pp.

Bromage, Arthur W. Introduction to Municipal Government and Administration (New York: Appleton-Century, 1957). 579pp.

Charlesworth, James C. Governmental Administration (New York: Harper & Brothers, 1951). 713pp.

Chatters, Carl H. Inventory of Governmental Activities in the United States (Chicago: Municipal Finance Officers Association, 1947). 15pp.

Follett, Mary Parker. Dynamic Administration. Collected Papers edited by H. C. Metcalf and L. Urwick (New York: Harper and Brothers, 1942). 320pp.

Gaus, John M. Reflections on Public Administration (University, Alabama: University of Alabama, 1947). 153pp.

Gulick, Luther, and L. Urwick, editors. Papers on the Science of Administration (New York: Institute of Public Administration, 1937). 196pp.

International City Managers' Association. The Municipal Year Book (Chicago: The Association). Annual.

Marx, Fritz Morstein, editor. Elements of Public Administration (New York: Prentice-Hall, 1946). 637pp.

Millet, John D. Management in the Public Service (New York: McGraw-Hill, 1954). 417pp.

Simon, Herbert A., Donald W. Smithburg, and V. A. Thompson. Public Administration (New York: Alfred A. Knopf, 1950). 682pp.

White, Leonard D. Introduction to the Study of Public Administration (New York: Macmillan, 1955). 531pp.

Chapter 1

THE ROLE OF THE ADMINISTRATOR

Anderson, William, and Edward W. Weidner. American City Government (New York: Henry Holt, 1953). 625pp.

Barnard, Chester I. The Functions of the Executive (Cambridge, Massachusetts: Harvard University Press, 1938). 334pp.

--Organization and Management (Cambridge, Massachusetts: Harvard University, 1948). 244pp.

Bernays, Edward L., editor. Engineering of Consent (Norman, Oklahoma: University of Oklahoma, 1955).

Biery, John M., and others. Leadership Functions of the Manager. A Symposium. Public Management, March, 1955, pp. 50-54.

Bingham, Walter. Administrative Ability, Its Discovery and Development (Washington, D. C.: Society for Personnel Administration, 1939). 17pp.

Bollens, John C. Appointed Executive Local Government; The California Experience (Los Angeles: Haynes Foundation, 1952). 250pp.

Copeland, Melvin T. The Executive At Work (Cambridge, Massachusetts: Harvard University, 1951). 278pp.

International City Managers' Association. City Management — A Growing Profession (Chicago: The Association, 1957). 84pp.

--Guideposts on Assuming a City Manager Position (Chicago: The Association, 1957). 36pp.

--Selection of a City Manager (Chicago: The Association, 1957). 26pp.

Pfiffner, John M., and R. Vance Presthus. Public Administration (New York: Ronald, 1953). 628pp.

Chapter 2

RELATIONSHIPS WITH COUNCIL AND OTHER AGENCIES

Barnard, Chester I. Organization and Management (Cambridge, Massachusetts: Harvard University Press, 1948). 244pp.

Chase, Stuart. Roads to Agreement (New York: Harper and Brothers, 1951). 250pp.

Drucker, Peter F. The Practice of Management (New York: Harper and Brothers, 1954). 404pp.

International City Managers' Association. Management Practices for Smaller Cities (Chicago: The Association, 1958). Approximately 350pp.

--Monthly Administrative Reports for Cities (Chicago: The Association, 1950). 32pp.

--Supervisory Methods in Municipal Administration (Chicago: The Association, 1958). Approximately 350pp.

Likert, Rensis A., and Samuel P. Hayes Jr., editors. Some Applications of Behavioral Research (Paris, France: United Nations Educational, Scientific and Cultural Organization, 1957). 333pp.

Public Administration Service. The Government of Metropolitan Miami (Chicago: The Service, 1954). 194pp.

Roethlisberger, Fritz J. Management and Morale (Cambridge, Massachusetts: Harvard University, 1941). 194pp.

Schell, Erwin Haskell. Technique of Executive Control (New York: McGraw-Hill, 1957). 357pp.

Simon, Herbert A. Administrative Behavior (New York: Macmillan, 1957). 254pp.

Chapter 3

THE ORGANIZATION PROBLEM

Argyris C. "The Organization and the Individual." Administrative Science Quarterly, June, 1957, pp. 1-24.

Barnard, Chester I. Organization and Management (Cambridge, Massachusetts: Harvard University, 1948). 244pp.

Conway, A. L., John M. Pfiffner, and W. S. High. Factors Influencing Organizational Effectiveness (Los Angeles: University of Southern California, 1945).

Dovey, H. O. Handbook of Organization Methods and Techniques (Chicago: Public Administration Service, 1951). 62pp.

Gulick, Luther and L. Urwick, editors. Papers on the Science of Administration (New York: Institute of Public Administration, 1937). 196pp.

National Municipal League. Model City Charter (New York: The League, 1941). 141pp.
--Model County Charter (New York: The League, 1956). 71pp.

Pfiffner, John M. Organization: A Study of Hierarchy (Los Angeles: University of Southern California, 1957).

Seckler-Hudson, Catheryn. Process of Organization and Management (Washington, D. C.: Public Affairs Press, 1948). 296pp.

Simon, Herbert A. Administrative Behavior (New York: Macmillan, 1947). 259pp.

Chapter 4

THE TECHNIQUES OF DIRECTION

Biery, John M., and others. Leadership Functions of the Manager. A Symposium. Public Management, March, 1955, pp. 50-54.

Bromage, Arthur W. On the City Council (Ann Arbor, Michigan: George Wahr, 1950). 81pp.

Cookingham, L. P. Some Guideposts for City Managers. Public Management, April, 1956, pp. 77-79.

International City Managers' Association. City Management — A Growing Profession (Chicago: The Association, 1957). 84pp.
--Handbook for Councilmen in Council Manager Cities (Chicago: The Association, 1955). 48pp.

Nolting, Orin F. Management Methods in City Government (Chicago: International City Managers' Association, 1942). 60pp.

Riethmayer, Leo C. Relations of the City Manager With Pressure Groups. Public Management, January, 1954, pp. 2-5.

Chapter 5

PROGRAMMING MUNICIPAL SERVICES

Buehler, A. G. Public Finance (New York: McGraw-Hill, 1948). 740pp.

Chatters, Carl H. and A. M. Hillhouse. Local Government Debt Administration (New York: Prentice-Hall, 1939), pp. 431-438.

International City Managers' Association. Monthly Administrative Reports For Cities (Chicago: The Association, 1950), 32pp.

Municipal Finance Officers' Association. Long-Term Financial Planning (Chicago: The Association, 1948). 4pp.

Simon, Herbert A. Fiscal Aspects of Metropolitan Consolidation (Berkeley, California: Bureau of Public Administration, University of California, 1943). 67pp.

Various authors. Financial Planning for Governments. Municipal Finance, February, 1949, entire issue. (Chicago: Municipal Finance Officers Association).

Chapter 6

PERSONNEL ADMINISTRATION

Halsey, George D. Supervising People (New York: Harper and Brothers, 1953). 238pp.

International City Managers' Association. Municipal Personnel Administration (Chicago: The Association, 1958). Approximately 435pp.

--Supervisory Methods in Municipal Administration (Chicago: The Association, 1958). Approximately 350pp.

Likert, Rensis A., and Samuel P. Hayes, Jr., editors. Some Applications of Behavioral Research (Paris, France: United Nations Educational, Scientific and Cultural Organization, 1957). 333pp.

Mosher, William E., and J. Donald Kingsley. Public Personnel Administration (New York: Harper and Brothers, 1950). 671pp.

Pfiffner, John M. The Supervision of Personnel (New York: Prentice-Hall, 1958).

Pigors, Paul J. W., editor. Readings in Personnel Administration (New York: McGraw-Hill, 1952). 483pp.

Public Personnel Association. Placement and Probation in the Public Service (Chicago: The Association, 1946). 201pp.

Stahl, O. Glenn. Public Personnel Administration (New York: Harper and Brothers, 1956). 628pp.

Van Mol, L. J. Effective Procedures For Handling Employee Grievances (Chicago: Public Personnel Association, 1953). 25pp.

Chapter 7

TRAINING

Andrews, Kenneth R. The Case Method of Teaching Human Relations and Administration (Cambridge, Massachusetts: Harvard University, 1953). 271pp.

--Executive Training by the Case Method. Harvard Business Review, September, 1951, pp. 58-70.

Auer, John J. Handbook for Discussion Leaders (New York: Harper and Brothers, 1954). 153pp.

Beckman, R. O. How To Train Supervisors (New York: Harper and Brothers, 1952). 305pp.

Bingham, Walter. Administrative Ability, Its Discovery and Development (Washington, D. C.: Society for Personnel Administration, 1939). 17pp.

Broaded, Charley H. Essentials of Management for Supervisors (New York: Harper and Brothers, 1947). 239pp.

Committee on Employee Training in the Public Service. Employee Training in the Public Service (Chicago: Public Personnel Association, 1941). 172pp.

Goetz, Rachel. Visual Aids for Public Service (Chicago: Public Administration Service, 1954). 89pp.

Halsey, George D. Training Employees (New York: Harper and Brothers, 1949). 263pp.

International City Managers' Association. City Management — A Growing Profession (The Association, 1957). 84pp.

--Supervisory Methods in Municipal Administration (Chicago: The Association, 1958). Approximately 350pp.

Chapter 8

FINANCE ADMINISTRATION

Buehler, A. G. Public Finance (New York: McGraw-Hill, 1948). 740pp.

Forbes, Russell. Purchasing for Small Cities (Chicago: Public Administration Service, 1951). 23pp.

International City Managers' Association. Checklist on How To Improve Municipal Services (Chicago: The Association, 1958). Approximately 60pp.

--Municipal Finance Administration (Chicago: The Association, 1955). 461pp.

Municipal Finance Officers Association. Marketing Municipal Bonds: Some Practical Suggestions (Chicago: The Association, 1946). 12pp.

--Simplified Municipal Accounting (Chicago: The Association, 1950). 162pp.

National Committee on Governmental Accounting. A Standard Classification of Municipal Accounts (Chicago: Municipal Finance Officers Association, 1953). 129pp.

Phillips, Miner E. and Irving Tenner. Financing Municipal Off-Street Parking Facilities (Chicago: Municipal Finance Officers Association, 1948). 65pp.

Sherwood, Frank P., Charles L. Seaman, Richard Gallagher, and Orin K. Cope. Administrative Uses of Performance Budgets (Chicago: Municipal Finance Officers Association, 1954). 16pp.

Sigafoos, Robert A. The Municipal Income Tax: Its History and Problems (Chicago: Public Administration Service, 1956). 176pp.

Tenner, Irving. Financial Administration of Municipal Utilities (Chicago: Public Administration Service, 1947). 152pp.

--Municipal and Governmental Accounting (New York: Prentice-Hall, 1955). 640pp.

Various authors. Municipal Treasury Management. Municipal Finance, February, 1942, entire issue.

Chapter 9

ADMINISTRATIVE RESEARCH AND PLANNING

American Management Association. Office Methods Research and Planning (New York: The Association, 1948). 39pp.

Barnes, Ralph M. Work Measurement Manual (Dubuque, Iowa: W. C. Brown, 1951). 297pp.

Conway, A. L., John M. Pfiffner and W. S. High. Factors Influencing Organizational Effectiveness (Los Angeles: University of Southern California, 1945).

International City Managers' Association. Supervisory Methods in Municipal Administration (Chicago: The Association, 1958). Approximately 350pp.

--Monthly Administrative Reports for Cities (Chicago: The Association, 1950). 33pp.

Pfiffner, John M., and S. Owen Lane. A Manual for Administrative Analysis (Dubuque, Iowa: W. C. Brown, 1951). 81pp.

Sherwood, Frank P., and Marguerite Alstrom. Administrative Analysis Techniques (Los Angeles: University of Southern California, 1956). Mimeo.

United States Air Force. How To Develop a Better Method. Conference Outline 7, AFP 50-2-7 (Washington, D. C.: United States Government Printing Office, 1955). 16pp.

--How To Study the Organization. Conference Outline AFP 50-2-3 (Washington, D. C.: United States Government Printing Office, 1955). 27pp.

--How to Analyze the Distribution of Work. Conference Outline 4 (Washington, D. C.: United States Government Printing Office, 1955). 33pp.

--How to Study Work Methods for Improvement. Conference Outline 6 (Washington, D. C.: United States Government Printing Office, 1955).

United States Navy. Work Simplification for Naval Units (Washington, D. C.: United States Government Printing Office, 1953).

Chapter 10

CITY PLANNING

American Society of Planning Officials. Guideposts for Community Planning—A Bibliography (Chicago: The Society, 1956). 47pp.

Black, Russell Van Nest. Planning for the Small American City (Chicago: Public Administration Service, 1950). 86pp.

Chapin, F. Stuart. Urban Land Use Planning (New York: Harper and Brothers, 1957). 397pp.

Gallion, Arthur B. The Urban Pattern (New York: Van Nostrand, 1950). 445pp.

Housing and Home Finance Agency. Suggested Land Subdivision Regulations (Washington, D. C.: U. S. Government Printing Office, 1952). 65pp.

International City Managers' Association. Local Planning Administration (Chicago: The Association, 1958). Approximately 340pp.

Miller, Harold V. Mr. Planning Commissioner (Chicago: Public Administration Service, 1954). 81pp.

Walker, Robert A. The Planning Function in Urban Government (Chicago: University of Chicago, 1950). 410pp.

Woodbury, Coleman, editor. Urban Redevelopment Problems and Practices (Chicago: University of Chicago Press, 1953). 525pp.

Chapter 11

LEGAL SERVICES AND REGULATORY PROCEDURES

McQuillen, Eugene. The Law of Municipal Corporations (Chicago: Callaghan and Company, 1949-1951). 20 Vols.

Rhyne, Charles S. Codification of Municipal Ordinances (Washington, D. C.: National Institute of Municipal Law Officers, 1950). 93pp.

--Municipal Law (Washington, D. C.: National Institute of Municipal Law Officers, 1957). 1125pp.

Rhyne, Charles S. and Jack M. Merelman. City Attorneys and Their Salaries (Washington, D. C.: National Institute of Municipal Law Officers, 1956). 53pp.

Rhyne, Charles S., Charles H. Burton, and Charlie O. Murphy. Municipal Regulation of Peddlers, Solicitors and Itinerant Merchants (Washington, D. C.: National Institute of Municipal Law Officers, 1947). 165pp.

Siebenschuh, Robert W. The Administration of Municipal Legal Services: The Chicago Law Department (Chicago: Public Administration Service, 1942). 58pp.

Chapter 12

ADMINISTRATIVE MEASUREMENT

Brooks, Phillip C. Public Records Management (Chicago: Public Administration Service, 1949). 19pp.

Croxton, Frederick E. and Dudley J. Cowden. Applied General Statistics (New York: Prentice-Hall, 1939). 944pp.

International City Managers' Association. Monthly Administrative Reports for Cities (Chicago: The Association, 1950). 32pp.

Ridley, C. E., and H. A. Simon. Measuring Municipal Activities (Chicago: The Association, 1943). 75pp.

U. S. Bureau of the Budget. Work Measurement System: Development and Use — A Case Study (Chicago: United States Government Printing Office, 1950). 44pp.

Chapter 13

PUBLIC RELATIONS AND PUBLIC REPORTING

Bernays, Edward L. Public Relations (Norman, Oklahoma: University of Oklahoma, 1952). 374pp.

Bogardus, Emory Stephen. The Making of Public Opinion (New York: Association Press, 1951). 265pp.

City of Beverly Hills. Public Relations Training Manual (Beverly Hills, California: City of Beverly Hills, 1954). 27pp.

Cross, Harold L. The People's Right To Know (New York: Columbia University, 1953). 405pp.

Fitzgerald, Stephen E. Communicating Ideas to the Public (New York: Funk and Wagnalls, 1950). 267pp.

Lundborg, Louis B. Public Relations in the Local Community (New York: Harper and Brothers, 1950). 228pp.

Macdonald, James C. Press Relations for Local Officials (Ann Arbor, Michigan: University of Michigan, 1956). 50pp.

Riethmayer, Leo C. Relations of the City Manager with Pressure Groups. Public Management, January, 1954, pp. 2-5.

Woolpert, Elton D. Municipal Public Relations (Chicago: The International City Managers' Association, 1950). 50pp.

INDEX